MKTG¹³

PRINCIPLES OF MARKETING

CHARLES LAMB
Texas Christian University

JOE HAIR
Louisiana State University

CARL McDANIEL
University of Texas Arlington

∗∴ Cengage

exico • Singapore • United Kingdom • United States

P9-CFG-567

MKTG13
Charles W. Lamb, Joe F. Hair, Carl McDaniel

Senior Vice President, Higher Education & Skills Product: Erin Joyner

Product Manager: Heather Mooney

Content Manager: Kate Begley Reed

Product Assistant: Juleah Morehouse

Marketing Manager: Audrey Wyrick

Marketing Coordinator: Alexis Cortez

Art Director: Bethany Bourgeois

Text Designer: Lou Ann Thesing, Thesing Design

Cover Designer: Michael Stratton, Stratton Design/Bethany Bourgeois

Cover Image: iStockPhoto.com/metamorworks

Back Cover and Special Page Images:

Computer and tablet illustration: © iStockphoto. com/furtaev; Smart Phone illustration: © iStockphoto.com/dashadima; Feedback image: © Rawpixel.com/Shutterstock.com

Intellectual Property Analyst: Diane Garrity

Intellectual Property Project Manager: Nick Barrows

Production Service: MPS Limited

For product information and technology assistance, contact us at
Cengage Customer & Sales Support, 1-800-354-9706 or support.cengage.com.

For permission to use material from this text or product, submit all requests online at **www.copyright.com.**

Library of Congress Control Number: 2020904984

Student Edition ISBN:
978-0-357-12780-3

Cengage
200 Pier 4 Boulevard
Boston, MA 02210
USA

Cengage is a leading provider of customized learning solutions with employees residing in nearly 40 different countries and sales in more than 125 countries around the world. Find your local representative at **www.cengage.com.**

To learn more about Cengage platforms and services, register or access your online learning solution, or purchase materials for your course, visit **www.cengage.com.**

Printed at CLDPC, USA, 10-23

iStockPhoto.com/metamorworks

CONTENTS

Part 1
THE WORLD OF MARKETING

Rawpixel.com/Shutterstock.com

Part 2
ANALYZING MARKET OPPORTUNITIES

Dragon Images/Shutterstock.com

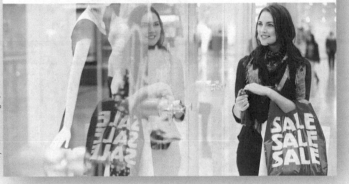

1 | An Overview of Marketing

LEARNING OUTCOMES

After studying this chapter, you will be able to . . .

1-1 Define the term *marketing*

1-2 Describe four marketing management philosophies

1-3 Discuss the differences between sales and market orientations

1-4 Describe several reasons for studying marketing

1-1 WHAT IS MARKETING?

What does the term *marketing* mean to you? Many people think *marketing* means personal selling. Others think it means advertising. Still others believe that marketing has to do with making products available in stores, arranging displays, and maintaining inventories of products for future sales. Actually, marketing includes all of these activities and more.

Marketing has two facets. First, it is a philosophy, an attitude, a perspective, or a management orientation that stresses customer satisfaction. Second, marketing is an organizational function and a set of processes used to implement this philosophy.

The American Marketing Association's (AMA) definition of marketing focuses on the second facet. According to the AMA, **marketing** is the activity, set of institutions, and processes for creating, communicating, delivering, and exchanging offerings that have value for customers, clients, partners, and society at large.[1]

Marketing involves more than just activities performed by a group of people in a defined area or department. In the often-quoted words of David Packard, cofounder of Hewlett-Packard, "Marketing is too important to be left only to the marketing department." Marketing entails processes that focus on delivering value and benefits to customers, not just selling goods, services, and/or ideas. It uses communication, distribution, and pricing strategies to provide customers and other stakeholders with the goods, services, ideas, values, and benefits they desire when and where they want them. It involves building long-term, mutually rewarding relationships when these benefit all parties concerned. Marketing also entails an understanding that organizations have many connected stakeholder "partners," including employees, suppliers, stockholders, distributors, and others.

Research shows that U.S. companies chosen as the top places to work by employees outperformed the stock market by 2.8 to 3.8 points per year, no matter what the broader economic conditions.[2] In 2018, Salesforce, a cloud-computing company in San Francisco, captured the number-one position in *Fortune*'s "100 Best Companies to Work For." The company has fostered an unusual company culture based on trust, growth, innovation, and equality. It offers rich monetary and psychological rewards, and has developed software that looks for strong performers who have gone 18 months without a promotion to help them look for new challenges. Employees also get paid 56 hours a year to do volunteer work in their community.[3]

> "Marketing is too important to be left only to the marketing department."
>
> —DAVID PACKARD, COFOUNDER OF HEWLETT-PACKARD

One desired outcome of marketing is an **exchange**—people giving up something in order to receive something else they would rather have. Normally, we think of money as the medium of exchange. We "give up" money to "get" the goods and services we want. Exchange does not require money, however. Two (or more) people may barter or trade such items as baseball cards or oil paintings.

An exchange can take place only if the following five conditions exist:

1. There must be at least two parties.
2. Each party has something that might be of value to the other party.
3. Each party is capable of communication and delivery.
4. Each party is free to accept or reject the exchange offer.
5. Each party believes it is appropriate or desirable to deal with the other party.[4]

Exchange will not necessarily take place even if all these conditions exist, but they must exist for exchange to be possible. For example, suppose you place an advertisement in your local newspaper stating that your used automobile is for sale at a certain price. Several people may

marketing the activity, set of institutions, and processes for creating, communicating, delivering, and exchanging offerings that have value for customers, clients, partners, and society at large

exchange people giving up something in order to receive something else they would rather have

Salesforce was selected number 1 in Fortune's "100 Best Companies to Work\For" in 2018, partly based on it's unique company culture.

call you to ask about the car; some may test-drive it; and one or more may even make you an offer. All five conditions that are necessary for an exchange to occur exist in this scenario. But unless you reach an agreement with a buyer and actually sell the car, an exchange will not take place.

Notice that marketing can occur even if an exchange does not occur. In the example just discussed, you would have engaged in marketing by advertising in the local newspaper, even if no one bought your used automobile.

1-2 MARKETING MANAGEMENT PHILOSOPHIES

Four competing philosophies strongly influence an organization's marketing processes. These philosophies are commonly referred to as production, sales, market, and societal marketing orientations.

1-2a Production Orientation

A **production orientation** is a philosophy that focuses on the internal capabilities of the firm rather than on the desires and needs of the marketplace. A production orientation means that management assesses its resources and asks these questions: "What can we do best?" "What can our engineers design?" "What is easy to produce, given our equipment?" In the case of

production orientation a philosophy that focuses on the internal capabilities of the firm rather than on the desires and needs of the marketplace

sales orientation the belief that people will buy more goods and services if aggressive sales techniques are used and that high sales result in high profits

a service organization, managers ask, "What services are most convenient for the firm to offer?" and "Where do our talents lie?" The furniture industry is infamous for its disregard of customers and for its slow cycle times. For example, most traditional furniture stores (think Ashley or Haverty's) carry the same styles and varieties of furniture that they have carried for many years. They always produce and stock sofas, coffee tables, arm chairs, and end tables for the living room. Master bedroom suites always include at least a queen- or king-sized bed, two dressers, and two side tables. Regardless of what customers may actually be looking for, this is what they will find at these stores—and they have been so long-lived because what they produce has matched up with customer expectations. This has always been a production-oriented industry.

There is nothing wrong with assessing a firm's capabilities; in fact, such assessments are major considerations in strategic marketing planning (see Chapter 2). A production orientation can fall short if it does not consider whether the goods and services that the firm produces most efficiently also meet the needs of the marketplace. On the other hand, sometimes what a firm can best produce is exactly what the market wants. Apple has a history of production orientation, creating computers, operating systems, and other gadgetry because it can and hoping to sell the result. Some items have found a waiting market (early computers, iPod, iPhone). Other products, like the Newton, one of the first versions of a personal digital assistant (PDA), were simply flops.

In some situations, as when competition is weak or demand exceeds supply, a production-oriented firm can survive and even prosper. More often, however, firms that succeed in competitive markets have a clear understanding that they must first determine what customers want and then produce it, rather than focus on what company management thinks should be produced and hope that the product is something customers want.

1-2b Sales Orientation

A **sales orientation** is based on the belief that people will buy more goods and services if aggressive sales techniques are used and that high sales result in high profits. Not only are sales to the final buyer emphasized, but intermediaries are also encouraged to push manufacturers' products more aggressively. To sales-oriented firms, marketing means selling things and collecting money.

The fundamental problem with a sales orientation, as with a production orientation, is a lack of

Examples of a Sales-Oriented Business

A sales orientation is common for businesses selling products or services in highly competitive markets. This orientation is also used when the consumer is not actively pursuing a company's product. Several examples of industries that tend to use a sales orientation follow.

1. **The insurance industry**

   In the insurance industry, companies create the products and then sell them through representatives, advertising, and other sales techniques. Insurance policies are not influenced by consumer input or demand. Insurance is a product that most consumers feel is necessary, and it requires a sales orientation to educate and drive purchases from consumers. While consumers do shop rates, the business of auto, home, health, and other policies are driven by a sales orientation.

2. **The Automotive Industry**

   While the vehicle itself is often built according to market orientation, vehicle parts and mechanical services are sales oriented. Consumers require sales people to provide information and to understand their needs. Ultimately, the knowledge on the parts and mechanical side primarily drives the sales of parts and services.

3. **Business-to-Business Sales**

   Business-to-business sales also provide an example of a sales-oriented business approach. Companies develop products that may benefit a business and then rely heavily upon aggressive marketing tactics to sell them. Examples of products sold in this type of market can include advertising sales or technologies such as point-of-sale software and machinery that will allow the business to run more efficiently and profitably. Chances are the business owner was not initially looking for the product, but bought it because the salesperson showed him some benefit to buying it.

Zach Lazzari, "Examples of a Sales-Oriented Business, " https://yourbusiness.azcentral.com/examples-salesoriented business 11277.html, May 7, 2018.5; Jared Lewis, "Examples of a Sales-Oriented Business," https://smallbusiness.chron.com/examples-salesoriented-business-25083.html, accessed August 8, 2019.

understanding of the needs and wants of the marketplace. Sales-oriented companies often find that, despite the quality of their sales force, they cannot convince people to buy goods or services that are neither wanted nor needed.

1-2c Market Orientation

The **marketing concept** is a simple and intuitively appealing philosophy that articulates a market orientation. It states that the social and economic justification for an organization's existence is the satisfaction of customer wants and needs while meeting organizational objectives. What a business thinks it produces is not of primary importance to its success. Instead, what customers think they are buying—the perceived value—defines a business. The marketing concept includes the following:

- Focusing on customer wants and needs so that the organization can

> **marketing concept** the idea that the social and economic justification for an organization's existence is the satisfaction of customer wants and needs while meeting organizational objectives

distinguish its product(s) from competitors' offerings

- Integrating all the organization's activities, including production, to satisfy customer wants

- Achieving long-term goals for the organization by satisfying customer wants and needs legally and responsibly

The recipe for success is to develop a thorough understanding of your customers and your competition, your distinctive capabilities that enable your company to execute plans on the basis of this customer understanding, and how to deliver the desired experience using and integrating all of the resources of the firm. For example, Harley-Davidson's current and prospective riders told the company's Customer Insights and Analytics division that they wanted the bikes to be lighter and more powerful and to handle and corner better. The company responded by creating the Softail line of bikes, which offer bigger engines and new frames that are stronger, stiffer, and lighter than on the 2017 models. Some bikes are as much as 35 pounds lighter than previous models. Many of the new bikes also have improved lean angles, which allow for better cornering.[6]

Firms that adopt and implement the marketing concept are said to be **market oriented**, meaning that they assume that a sale does not depend on an aggressive sales force but rather on a customer's decision to purchase a product. Achieving a market orientation involves obtaining information about customers, competitors, and markets; examining the information from a total business perspective; determining how to deliver superior customer value; and implementing actions to provide value to customers.

Some firms are known for delivering superior customer value and satisfaction. For example, in 2018, J.D. Power and Associates ranked Infiniti highest in customer satisfaction with dealer service among luxury automotive brands, while Buick ranked highest among mass-market brands.[7] Rankings such as these, as well as word-of-mouth from satisfied customers, drive additional sales for these automotive companies.

Understanding your competitive arena and competitors' strengths and weaknesses is a critical component of a market orientation. This includes assessing what existing or potential competitors intend to do tomorrow and what they are doing today. For example, specialty-clothing stores such as American Apparel have failed to recognize or successfully respond to their fast-fashion competitors. These competitors—particularly Zara and H&M—offer consumers up-to-date fashions more quickly and at more affordable prices than traditional retailers can. American Apparel has experienced increased debt and decreased sales, resulting in numerous store closings and a bankruptcy filing.[8]

1-2d Societal Marketing Orientation

The **societal marketing orientation** extends the marketing concept by acknowledging that some products that customers want may not really be in their best interests or the best interests of society as a whole. This philosophy states that an organization exists not only to satisfy customer wants and needs and to meet organizational objectives but also to preserve or enhance individuals' and society's long-term best interests. Marketing products and containers that are less toxic than normal, are more durable, contain reusable materials, or are made of recyclable materials is consistent with a societal marketing orientation. The AMA's definition of *marketing* recognizes the importance of a societal marketing orientation by including "society at large" as one of the constituencies for which marketing seeks to provide value.

Although the societal marketing concept has been discussed for more than 30 years, it did not receive widespread support until the early 2000s. Concerns such as climate change, the depleting of the ozone layer, fuel shortages, pollution, and health issues have caused consumers and legislators to become more aware of the need for companies and consumers to adopt measures that conserve resources and cause less damage to the environment.[9]

In the past 10 years, corporate responsibility has evolved from a nice-to-have silo to a fundamental strategic priority. Today, companies of all sorts are spurring change across a broad range of issues, including climate change, education, and poverty. Many have also made a commitment to eliminate waste and reuse valuable materials within their own walls.

For example, CVS has taken several steps to address the health of communities across the United States. To help solve the nation's opioid crisis, it has enhanced opioid utilization management protocols, installed 750 new drug disposal collection units in its pharmacies, and is

market orientation a philosophy that assumes that a sale does not depend on an aggressive sales force but rather on a customer's decision to purchase a product; it is synonymous with the marketing concept

societal marketing orientation the idea that an organization exists not only to satisfy customer wants and needs and to meet organizational objectives but also to preserve or enhance individuals' and society's long-term best interests

CVS Health Corporation proudly provides a link to its social responsibility page on its homepage.

educating its pharmacists on the dangers of prescription drugs. The company is also a strong corporate citizen. During national disasters such hurricanes, floods, and wildfires it has gone above and beyond to make sure patients received the medications they need, and it gave $10 million in relief and recovery support funds to the affected communities. These and other community initiatives have put CVS at the top of Fortune's 2018 "List of World's Most Admired Companies."[10]

1-2e Who Is in Charge?

The Internet and the widespread use of social media have accelerated the shift in power from manufacturers and retailers to consumers and business users. This shift began when customers started using books, electronics, and the Internet to access information, goods, and services. Customers use their widespread knowledge to shop smarter; leading executives such as former Procter & Gamble CEO A. G. Laffey to conclude that "the customer is boss."[11] Founder of Walmart and Sam's Club, Sam Walton, echoed this sentiment when he reportedly once said, "There is only one boss. The customer. And he can fire everybody in the company from the chairman on down, simply by spending his money somewhere else."[12] The following quotation, attributed to everyone, from L.L.Bean founder, Leon Leonwood Bean, to Mahatma Gandhi, has been a guiding business principle for more than 70 years: "A customer is the most important visitor on our premises. He is not dependent on us. We are dependent on him. He is not an interruption in our work. He is the purpose of it. He is not an outsider in our business. He is part of it. We are not doing him a favor by serving him. He is doing us a favor by giving us an opportunity to do so."[13] And as the use of the Internet

and mobile devices becomes increasingly pervasive, that control will continue to grow. This means that companies must create strategy from the outside in by offering distinct and compelling customer value.[14] This can be accomplished only by carefully studying customers and using deep market insights to inform and guide companies' outside-in view.[15]

DIFFERENCES BETWEEN SALES AND MARKET ORIENTATIONS

The differences between sales and market orientations are substantial. The two orientations can be compared in terms of five characteristics: the organization's focus, the firm's business, those to whom the product is directed, the firm's primary goal, and the tools used to achieve the organization's goals.

1-3a The Organization's Focus

Personnel in sales-oriented firms tend to be inward looking, focusing on selling what the organization makes rather than making what the market wants. Many of the historic sources of competitive advantage—technology, innovation, and economies of scale—allowed companies to focus their efforts internally and prosper. Today, many successful firms derive their competitive advantage from an external, market-oriented focus. A market orientation

Shake Shack appeals to higher-income customers, with high-quality products and superior customer service.

has helped companies such as Zappos.com and Bob's Red Mill Natural Foods to outperform their competitors. These companies put customers at the center of their business in ways most companies do poorly or not at all.

CUSTOMER VALUE The relationship between benefits and the sacrifice necessary to obtain those benefits is known as **customer value**. Customer value is not simply a matter of high quality. A high-quality product that is available only at a high price will not be perceived as a good value, nor will bare-bones service or low-quality goods selling for a low price. Price is a component of value (a $4,000 handbag is perceived as being more luxurious and of higher quality than one selling for $100), but low price is not the same as good value. Instead, customers value goods and services that are of the quality they expect and that are sold at prices they are willing to pay.

Value can be used to sell a Mercedes-Benz as well as a Tyson frozen chicken dinner. In other words, value is something that shoppers of all markets and at all income levels look for. Lower-income consumers are price sensitive, so they may respond positively to special offers and generic brands. Low-income consumers who are both paid and shop by the day may respond to reduced packaging sizes that lower the cost per unit while still offering quality and value for the money. Conversely, higher-income customers may value—and be willing to pay for—high-quality products and superior customer service. Shake Shack is a fast-casual burger restaurant that targets people who care about how their food tastes and where it comes from. The company sells its burgers for higher-than-average prices, but it uses humanely raised, antibiotic- and hormone-free meat that is ground fresh from full muscle cuts instead of scraps. This meat is shipped fresh—not frozen—to all of Shake Shack's locations. Further, the company pledges not to use genetically modified organisms (GMOs) in its hamburger buns. Shake Shack's superior service, which founder Danny Meyer calls "enlightened hospitality," places a major emphasis on the happiness of its employees and customers. This service philosophy is based on the belief that white-tablecloth service is not just for expensive restaurants.[16]

CUSTOMER SATISFACTION The customers' evaluation of a good or service in terms of whether

that good or service has met their needs and expectations is called **customer satisfaction**. Failure to meet needs and expectations results in dissatisfaction with the good or service. Some companies, in their passion to drive down costs, have damaged their relationships with customers. Bank of America, Comcast, Dish Network, and AT&T are examples of companies for which executives lost track of the delicate balance between efficiency and service.[17] Firms that have a reputation for delivering high levels of customer satisfaction do things differently from their competitors. Top management is obsessed with customer satisfaction, and employees throughout the organization understand the link between their job and satisfied customers. The culture of the organization is to focus on delighting customers rather than on selling products.

Coming back from customer dissatisfaction can be tough, but there are some key ways that companies begin to improve customer satisfaction. Forrester Research discovered that when companies experience gains in the firm's Customer Experience Index (CxPi), they have implemented one of two major changes. Aetna, a major health insurance provider, executed the first type of change—changing its decentralized, part-time customer service group into a full-time, centralized customer service team. Aetna's CxPi score rose six points in one year. The second type of change involves offering customers what they need. In 2016, the banking industry's American Customer Satisfaction Index scores increased more than 5 percent. Satisfying bank customers involves more personalized service and lower fees.[18]

BUILDING RELATIONSHIPS Attracting new customers to a business is only the beginning. The best companies view new-customer attraction as the launching point for developing and enhancing a long-term relationship. Companies can expand market share in three ways: attracting new customers, increasing business with existing customers, and retaining current customers. Building relationships with existing customers directly addresses two of the three possibilities and indirectly addresses the other.

Relationship marketing is a strategy that focuses on keeping and improving relationships with current customers. It assumes that many consumers and business customers prefer to have an ongoing relationship with one organization rather than switch continually among providers in their search for value. Activision, a leading publisher of the U.S. video game market, engages in relationship marketing by providing continued service to its gamers. For example, Activision monitors social media conversations that are relevant

customer value the relationship between benefits and the sacrifice necessary to obtain those benefits

customer satisfaction customers' evaluation of a good or service in terms of whether it has met their needs and expectations

relationship marketing a strategy that focuses on keeping and improving relationships with current customers

THE ELEMENTS OF VALUE

When customers evaluate the value of a product or service, they weigh its perceived quality against its price. While this process may sound simple, understanding what customers value can be difficult. Academic research can help. A group of scholars has discovered that there are four elements of value that each addresses a basic consumer need. Each element contains multiple attributes. These are:

1. The first, and most basic, need is functional. Consumers look for products that save time, reduce risk, reduce effort, or help them organize. The Container Store and TurboTax are examples of retailers that help consumers organize their things/assets.

2. Emotional. This includes attributes such as meeting needs, including reducing anxiety, good product design and aesthetics, fun and entertainment, and wellness. Apple is an example of good product design that is satisfying to consumers. Television service providers offer fun and entertainment.

3. Life-Changing. Providing hope, motivation, and a feeling of belonging and self-actualization. Fitbit's exercise-tracking programs address the motivation to get healthier. A $10,000 Leica camera offers not only the high quality of the brand, but also self-actualization that arises from the pride of owning a camera that famous photographers have used for a century.

4. Social Impact. Meeting the need for giving back and helping others, which translates into self-transcendence. Giving to nonprofit organizations like United Way or cancer research foundations are examples of social impact.

dennizn/Shutterstock.com

In practice, many companies offer combinations of these elements and attributes. For example, Amazon started by focusing on functional attributes, such as reducing cost and saving time. Then, with Amazon Prime offering services like streaming media and unlimited photo storage, it expanded its value to include fun and entertainment and reducing risk. Restaurants address the attributes of quality, sensory appeal, variety, and design/appeal.

The relevance of the elements varies according to industry. For example, nostalgia or wellness may not mean much to customers buying gas for their cars. Researchers have found that the right combination of elements and attributes results in stronger customer loyalty, greater consumer willingness to try a brand, and sustained revenue growth.[19]

to its products and follows up on those conversations.[20] This long-term focus on customer needs is a hallmark of relationship marketing.

Most successful relationship marketing strategies depend on customer-oriented personnel, effective training programs, employees with the authority to make decisions and solve problems, and teamwork.

Customer-Oriented Personnel For an organization to be focused on building relationships with customers, employees' attitudes and actions must be customer oriented. An employee may be the only contact a particular customer has with the firm. In that customer's eyes, the employee *is* the firm. Any person, department, or division that is not customer oriented weakens the positive image of the entire organization. For example, a potential customer who is greeted discourteously may well assume that the employee's attitude represents that of the whole firm.

Customer-oriented personnel come from an organizational culture that supports its people. Costco believes that treating employees well contributes to good customer service. The company not only pays its employees well at $22 per hour, it also provides them with generous benefits, including full health and dental coverage (even to its part-time employees); a 401(k) with stock options after a year; liberal vacation time; and family leave. Employees are also given a great deal of responsibility, which translates into higher motivation. The company's retention rate for employees who have been there a year is 94 percent—significantly higher than that of its competitors.[21]

Some companies, such as Coca-Cola, Delta Air Lines, Hershey, Kellogg, Nautilus, and Sears, have appointed chief customer officers (CCOs). These customer advocates provide an executive voice for customers and report directly to the CEO. Their responsibilities include ensuring that the company maintains a customer-centric culture and that all company employees remain focused on delivering customer value.

The Role of Training Leading marketers recognize the role of employee training in customer service and relationship building. Atlantic Health System is a company that was voted one of America's Best Companies to Work For in 2017. Employees are offered free courses—many for college credit. There are classes in clinical and non-clinical care, technology, management, leadership, and customer experience, among others. These classes help spark innovation and engagement within the company.[22]

Empowerment In addition to training, many market-oriented firms are giving employees more authority to solve customer problems on the spot. The term used to describe this delegation of authority is *empowerment*. Employees develop ownership attitudes when they are treated like part owners of the business and are expected to act the part. These employees manage themselves, are more likely to work hard, account for their own performance and that of the company, and take prudent risks to build a stronger business and sustain the company's success. In order to empower its workers, the Ritz-Carlton chain of luxury hotels developed a set of 12 "Service Values" guidelines. These brief, easy-to-understand guidelines include statements such as "I am empowered to create unique, memorable and personal experiences for our guests" and "I own and immediately resolve guest problems." The 12 Service Values are printed on cards distributed to employees, and each day a particular value is discussed at length in Ritz-Carlton team meetings. Employees talk about what the value means to them and offer examples of how the value can be put into practice that day.[23]

empowerment delegation of authority to solve customers' problems quickly—usually by the first person the customer notifies regarding a problem

teamwork collaborative efforts of people to accomplish common objectives

Teamwork Many organizations that are frequently noted for delivering superior customer value and providing high levels of customer satisfaction, such as Southwest Airlines and

Thanks to Costco's high pay, generous benefits, and trust in its employees, the company's retention rate is 94 percent—significantly higher than that of its competitors.

Walt Disney World, assign employees to teams and teach them team-building skills. **Teamwork** entails collaborative efforts of people to accomplish common objectives. Job performance, company performance, product value, and customer satisfaction all improve when people in the same department or work group begin supporting and assisting each other and emphasize cooperation instead of competition. Performance is also enhanced when cross-functional teams align their jobs with customer needs. For example, if a team of telecommunications service representatives is working to improve interaction with customers, back-office people such as computer technicians or training personnel can become part of the team, with the ultimate goal of delivering superior customer value and satisfaction. A study of software engineers showed that those who connected with others and helped them with their projects both earned the trust of their peers and were more productive themselves.[24]

1-3b The Firm's Business

A sales-oriented firm defines its business (or mission) in terms of goods and services. A market-oriented firm defines its business in terms of the benefits its customers seek. People who spend their money, time, and energy expect to receive benefits, not just goods and services. This distinction has enormous implications. For example, Microsoft's original mission was "A computer on every desk and in every home," which is product centered. Its current, benefit-oriented mission is "To empower every person and every organization on the planet to achieve more."[25] Answering the question "What is this firm's business?" in terms of the benefits customers seek, instead of goods and services, offers at least three important advantages:

- It ensures that the firm keeps focusing on customers and avoids becoming preoccupied with goods, services, or the organization's internal needs.

- It encourages innovation and creativity by reminding people that there are many ways to satisfy customer wants.

- It stimulates an awareness of changes in customer desires and preferences so that product offerings are more likely to remain relevant.

Market-oriented firms that successfully create a connection with their customers and employees tend to create loyal customers, which can increase overall profitability. These companies shape their mission statements around its core values and in terms of customer benefits. Some examples of good mission statements:

1. Patagonia: "Build the best product, cause no unnecessary harm, use business to inspire and implement solutions to the environmental crisis." Patagonia's mission statement combines both the values that bring them market success (building safe, high-quality products) *and* the values that contribute to a better world (philanthropic efforts to help the environment).

2. American Express: "We work hard every day to make American Express the world's most respected service brand." American Express has a list of core values, many of which emphasize teamwork and supporting employees, so that the people inside the organization can be in the best position to support their customers.

3. IKEA: "To create a better everyday life for the many people." The statement could have been one of beautiful, affordable furniture (product oriented), but instead it's to make *everyday life better* for its customers (market oriented).[26]

Having a market orientation and a focus on customer wants does not mean offering customers everything they want. It is not possible, for example, to profitably manufacture and market automobile tires that will last for 100,000 miles for $25. Furthermore, customers' preferences must be mediated by sound professional judgment as to how to deliver the benefits they seek. Consumers have a limited set of experiences. They are unlikely to request anything beyond those experiences because they are not aware of benefits they may gain from other potential offerings. For example, before the Internet, many people thought that shopping for some

Patagonia offers upscale and outdoor sports clothing for its target market.

products was boring and time-consuming but could not express their need for electronic shopping.

1-3c Those to Whom the Product Is Directed

A sales-oriented organization targets its products at "everybody" or "the average customer." A market-oriented organization aims at specific groups of people. The fallacy of developing products directed at the average user is that relatively few average users actually exist. Typically, populations are characterized by diversity. An average is simply a midpoint in some set of characteristics. Because most potential customers are not "average," they are not likely to be attracted to an average product marketed to the average customer. Consider the market for shampoo as one simple example. There are shampoos for oily hair, dry hair, and dandruff. Some shampoos remove the gray or color hair. Special shampoos are marketed for infants and elderly people. There are even shampoos for people with average or normal hair (whatever that is), but this is a fairly small portion of the total market for shampoo.

A market-oriented organization recognizes that different customer groups want different features or benefits. It may therefore need to develop different goods, services, and promotional appeals. A market-oriented organization carefully analyzes the market and divides it into groups of people who are fairly similar in terms of selected characteristics. Then the organization develops marketing programs that will bring about mutually satisfying exchanges with one or more of those groups. For example, the 116-year-old department store chain Nordstrom has introduced initiatives to attract millennial shoppers, who typically avoid department stores. These include themed pop-up shops, shop-in-shops featuring new fashion designers, and Nike concept shops.[27]

CUSTOMER RELATIONSHIP MANAGEMENT Beyond knowing to whom they are directing their products or services, companies must also develop a deeper understanding of their customers. One way of doing this is through *customer relationship management.* **Customer relationship management (CRM)** is a company-wide business strategy designed to optimize profitability, revenue, and customer satisfaction by focusing on highly defined and precise customer groups. This is accomplished by organizing the company around customer segments, establishing and tracking customer interactions with the company, fostering customer-satisfying behaviors, and linking all processes of the company from its customers through its suppliers. The difference between CRM and traditional mass marketing can be compared to shooting a rifle versus a shotgun. Instead of scattering messages far and wide across the spectrum of mass media (the shotgun approach), CRM marketers now are homing in on ways to effectively communicate with each customer (the rifle approach).

Companies that adopt CRM systems are almost always market oriented, customizing product and service offerings based on data generated through interactions between the customer and the company. This strategy transcends all functional areas of the business, producing an internal system in which all of the company's decisions and actions are a direct result of customer information.

As more customers are moving toward online and social media interactions with companies, the use of **Big Data** is increasingly becoming more important. Big Data is the discovery, interpretation, and communication of meaningful patterns in data. The amount of time that millions of people spend on Google, Facebook, Twitter, and other social media sites generates a large amount of data every day. All the actions people take create digital footprints that companies can tap to find valuable insights into customer behavior. For example, Sweetgreen Inc. is a California-based salad chain that uses a mobile app to gather data on their guests' allergies and tastes. When guests place mobile orders, they are

Sweetgreen's mission is to inspire healthier communities by connecting people to real food. The firm offers apps for ordering using IOS or Android.

asked to select from a list of dietary restrictions that includes soy, nuts, and gluten. Selections cause menu items containing those ingredients to be flagged with a red asterisk so the guests know to avoid them. These selections are saved for future orders and give the company detailed data on what their guests' like and why. These insights can then be used to shape future menus.[28] We will examine specific applications of CRM and Big Data in several chapters throughout this book. Also, see the Appendix to Chapter 9 for more information on Big Data.

The emergence of **on-demand marketing** is taking CRM to a new level. As technology evolves and becomes more sophisticated, consumer expectations of their decision- and buying-related experiences have risen. Consumers (1) want to interact anywhere, anytime; (2) want to do new things with varied kinds of information in ways that create value; (3) expect data stored about them to be targeted specifically to their needs or to personalize their experiences; and (4) expect all interactions with a company to be easy. In response to these expectations, companies are developing new ways to integrate and personalize each stage of a customer's decision journey, which in turn should increase relationship-related behaviors. On-demand marketing delivers relevant experiences throughout the consumer's decision and buying process that are integrated across both physical and virtual environments. Trends such as the growth of mobile connectivity, better-designed websites, inexpensive communication through technology, and advances in handling big data have allowed companies to start designing on-demand marketing programs that appeal to consumers. For on-demand marketing to be successful, companies must deliver high-quality experiences across all touch points with the customer, including sales, service, product use, and marketing.[29]

---

customer relationship management (CRM) a company-wide business strategy designed to optimize profitability, revenue, and customer satisfaction by focusing on highly defined and precise customer groups

Big Data the discovery, interpretation, and communication of meaningful patterns in data

on-demand marketing delivering relevant experiences, integrated across both physical and virtual environments, throughout the consumer's decision and buying process

The marketing mix provides the tools for marketers to bring about mutually satisfying exchanges with target customers.

Many more companies are offering on-demand services. For example, Instacart will deliver groceries to a customer's door, typically within an hour of ordering. Many restaurant chains are now a part of online service GrubHub, which allows customers to type in their zip codes, pick a restaurant, and order items for delivery—all without leaving the GrubHub website. Uber and Lyft provide on-demand transportation by connecting customers to drivers using their own cars—a service that Uber has leveraged into a GrubHub competitor called UberEats.

1-3d The Firm's Primary Goal

A sales-oriented organization seeks to achieve profitability through sales volume and tries to convince potential customers to buy, even if the seller knows that the customer and product are mismatched. Sales-oriented organizations place a higher premium on making a sale than on developing a long-term relationship with a customer. In contrast, the ultimate goal of most market-oriented organizations is to make a profit by creating customer value, providing customer satisfaction, and building long-term relationships with customers. The exception is so-called nonprofit organizations that exist to achieve goals other than profits. Nonprofit organizations can and should adopt a market orientation. Nonprofit organization marketing is explored further in Chapter 12.

1-3e Tools the Organization Uses to Achieve Its Goals

Sales-oriented organizations seek to generate sales volume through intensive promotional activities, mainly personal selling and advertising. In contrast, market-oriented organizations recognize that promotion decisions are only one of four basic marketing mix decisions that must be made: product decisions, place (or distribution) decisions, promotion decisions, and pricing decisions. A market-oriented organization recognizes that each of these four components is important. Furthermore, market-oriented organizations recognize that marketing is not just the responsibility of the marketing department. Interfunctional coordination means that skills and resources throughout the organization are needed to create, communicate, and deliver superior customer service and value.

1-3f A Word of Caution

This comparison of sales and market orientations is not meant to belittle the role of promotion, especially personal selling, in the marketing mix. Promotion is the means by which organizations communicate with present and prospective customers about the merits and characteristics of their organization and products. Effective promotion is an essential part of effective marketing. Salespeople who work for market-oriented organizations are generally perceived by their customers to be problem solvers and important links to supply sources and new products. Chapter 18 examines the nature of personal selling in more detail.

1-4 WHY STUDY MARKETING?

Now that you understand the meaning of the term *marketing*, why it is important to adopt a marketing orientation, and how organizations implement this philosophy, you may be asking, "What's in it for me?" or "Why should I study marketing?" These are important questions whether you are majoring in a business field other than marketing (such as accounting, finance, or management information systems) or a nonbusiness field (such as journalism, education,

or agriculture). There are several important reasons to study marketing: Marketing plays an important role in society, marketing is important to businesses, marketing offers outstanding career opportunities, and marketing affects your life every day.

1-4a Marketing Plays an Important Role in Society

The total population of the United States exceeds 328 million people. Think about how many transactions are needed each day to feed, clothe, and shelter a population of this size. The number is huge. And yet it all works quite well, partly because the well-developed U.S. economic system efficiently distributes the output of farms and factories. The average American eats almost 2,000 pounds of food a year.[30] Marketing makes food available when we want it, in desired quantities, at accessible locations, and in sanitary and convenient packages and forms (such as instant and frozen foods).

1-4b Marketing Is Important to Businesses

The fundamental objectives of most businesses are survival, profits, and growth. Marketing contributes directly to achieving these objectives. Marketing includes the following activities, which are vital to business organizations: assessing the wants and satisfactions of present and potential customers, designing and managing product offerings, determining prices and pricing policies, developing distribution strategies, and communicating with present and potential customers.

All businesspeople, regardless of specialization or area of responsibility, need to be familiar with the terminology and fundamentals of accounting, finance, management, and marketing. People in all business areas need to be able to communicate with specialists in other areas. Furthermore, marketing is not just a job done by people in a marketing department. Marketing is a part of the job of everyone in the organization. Therefore, a basic understanding of marketing is important to all businesspeople.

1-4c Marketing Offers Outstanding Career Opportunities

Between one-fourth and one-third of the entire civilian workforce in the United States performs marketing activities. Marketing offers great career opportunities in such areas as professional selling, marketing research, advertising, retail buying, distribution management, product management, product development, and wholesaling.

Marketing career opportunities also exist in a variety of nonbusiness organizations, including hospitals, museums, universities, the armed forces, and various government and social service agencies.

1-4d Marketing in Everyday Life

Marketing plays a major role in your everyday life. You participate in the marketing process as a consumer of goods and services. About half of every dollar you spend pays for marketing costs, such as marketing research, product development, packaging, transportation, storage, advertising, and sales expenses. By developing a better understanding of marketing, you will become a better-informed consumer. You will better understand the buying process and be able to negotiate more effectively with sellers. Moreover, you will be better prepared to demand satisfaction when the goods and services you buy do not meet the standards promised by the manufacturer or the marketer.

2 | Strategic Planning for Competitive Advantage

LEARNING OUTCOMES

After studying this chapter, you will be able to . . .

2-1 Understand the importance of strategic planning

2-2 Define strategic business units (SBUs)

2-3 Identify strategic alternatives and know a basic outline for a marketing plan

2-4 Develop an appropriate business mission statement

2-5 Describe the components of a situation analysis

2-6 Identify sources of competitive advantage

2-7 Explain the criteria for stating good marketing objectives

2-8 Discuss target market strategies

2-9 Describe the elements of the marketing mix

2-10 Explain why implementation, evaluation, and control of the marketing plan are necessary

2-11 Identify several techniques that help make strategic planning effective

Gajus/Shutterstock.com

2-1 THE NATURE OF STRATEGIC PLANNING

Strategic planning is the managerial process of creating and maintaining a fit between the organization's objectives and resources and the evolving market opportunities. The goal of strategic planning is long-run profitability and growth. Thus, strategic decisions require long-term commitments of resources.

A strategic error can threaten a firm's survival. On the other hand, a good strategic plan can help protect and grow the firm's resources. For instance, if the March of Dimes had decided to focus only on fighting polio, the organization would no longer exist because polio is widely viewed as a conquered disease. The March of Dimes survived by making the strategic decision to switch to fighting birth defects.

Strategic marketing management addresses two questions: (1) What is the organization's main activity at a particular time? (2) How will it reach its goals? Here are some examples of strategic decisions:

- Furniture retailer West Elm wanted to sustain growth without opening too many new stores. Thinking outside the box, the company decided to launch a chain of boutique hotels that it would design, furnish, and market. Partner DDK, a management and development company, would operate the hotels, but the interiors would be all West Elm. Guests, of course, could purchase the room furniture and decor online.[1]

- Ford decided to transform its entire North American lineup of cars by going all-in on hybrids, adding more sports utility vehicles, and using more cutting-edge technology. The company is also scaling back its small cars, phasing out the Fiesta, Taurus, Fusion, and regular Focus passenger cars. Additionally, it will continue to invest in electric and autonomous vehicles and smart mobility solutions that address changes in urban living and transportation.[2]

- Starbucks recently decided to end its "Evenings" program, during which it offers beer and wine at more than 400 Starbucks locations. Launched in 2010, the Evenings program was designed to help increase traffic at night, when demand for coffee typically decreases. However, Starbucks determined that the program simply did not deliver the results it wanted. The company decided to add new menu items to increase sales during lunch instead.[3]

All these decisions have affected or will affect each organization's long-run course, its allocation of resources, and ultimately its financial success. In contrast, an operating decision, such as changing the package design

> "There are a lot of great ideas that have come and gone in [the digital advertising] industry. Implementation many times is more important than the actual idea."
>
> —DAVID MOORE, CEO OF 24/7 REAL MEDIA

for Post Grape-Nuts cereal or altering the sweetness of a Kraft salad dressing, probably will not have a big impact on the long-run profitability of the company.

2-2 STRATEGIC BUSINESS UNITS

Large companies may manage a number of very different businesses, called strategic business units (SBUs). Each SBU has its own rate of return on investment, growth potential, and associated risks and requires its own strategies and funding. When properly created, an SBU has the following characteristics:

- A distinct mission and a specific target market
- Control over its resources
- Its own competitors
- A single business or a collection of related businesses
- Plans independent of the other SBUs in the total organization.

In theory, an SBU should have its own resources for handling basic

strategic planning the managerial process of creating and maintaining a fit between the organization's objectives and resources and the evolving market opportunities

strategic business unit (SBU) a subgroup of a single business or collection of related businesses within the larger organization business functions: accounting, engineering, manufacturing, and marketing. In practice, however, because of company tradition, management philosophy, and production and distribution economies, SBUs sometimes share manufacturing facilities, distribution channels, and even top managers.

2-3 STRATEGIC ALTERNATIVES

Several tools are available that a company, or SBU, can use to manage the strategic direction of its portfolio of businesses. Three of the most commonly used tools are Ansoff's strategic opportunity matrix, the Boston Consulting Group model, and the General Electric model. Selecting which strategic alternative to pursue depends on which of two philosophies a company maintains about when to expect profits—right away or after increasing market share. In the long run, market share and profitability are compatible goals. For example, Amazon lost hundreds of millions of dollars its first few years by offering deep discounts on books and movies. Today, Amazon has a strong and loyal customer base, particularly among its Prime members. The company's current strategy is to charge the lowest online prices for just a selection of products and to charge the same or more than other retailers for the rest. This practice has increased overall profitability for the company.[4]

2-3a Ansoff's Strategic Opportunity Matrix

One method for developing alternatives is Ansoff's strategic opportunity matrix (see Exhibit 2.1), which matches products with markets. Firms can explore these four options:

market penetration
a marketing strategy that tries to increase market share among existing customers

market development
a marketing strategy that entails attracting new customers to existing products

product development
a marketing strategy that entails the creation of new products for present markets

diversification a strategy of increasing sales by introducing new products into new markets

- **Market penetration:** A firm using the market penetration alternative would try to increase market share among existing customers. Retailer JCPenney recently partnered with fashion magazine *InStyle* to offer their customers revamped, updated, and branded Salons by InStyle. The store remodeled their old salons, and expanded its selection

EXHIBIT 2.1 ANSOFF'S OPPORTUNITY MATRIX

	Present Product	New Product
Present Market	*Market Penetration* Starbucks sells more coffee to customers who register their reloadable Starbucks cards.	*Product Development* Starbucks develops powdered instant coffee called Via.
New Market	*Market Development* Starbucks opens stores in Brazil and Chile.	*Diversification* Starbucks launches Hear Music and buys Ethos Water.

of services and salon products. It is counting on the new salons to attract its customers to their stores more often.[5]

- **Market development:** Market development means attracting new customers to existing products. Ideally, new uses for old products stimulate additional sales among existing customers while also bringing in new buyers. McDonald's, for example, has opened restaurants in Russia, China, and Italy and is eagerly expanding into Eastern European countries. In the nonprofit arena, the growing emphasis on continuing education and executive development by colleges and universities is a market development strategy.

- **Product development:** A product development strategy entails the creation of new products for present markets. Yogurt maker Danone (formerly, Dannon) is adding milk-free products to its yogurt line, as well as boosting vegan brands such as Silk. The company has acquired the world's biggest plant-based "milk" producer, WhiteWave Foods, which positions it to better serve the rising interest in vegan products by consumers, especially millennials.[6]

- **Diversification:** Diversification is a strategy of increasing sales by introducing new products into new markets. For example, Lego is teaming up with one of China's biggest technology firms, Tencent, to create online games for Chinese children to take advantage of the technology shifts that are changing how children play. There has been increasing competition in the traditional toy market from growing digital options for children, including mobile games, online videos, and children-targeted social media.[7] A diversification strategy can be risky when a firm is entering unfamiliar markets. However, it can be very profitable when a firm is entering markets with little or no competition.

JCPenney News ✓
@jcpnews

[Follow] ∨

Johnson: We are so excited to be rebranding an additional ~80 salons to The Salon by InStyle this year #jcpGMC

Source: Twitter, Inc.

Struggling JCPenny continues to innovate by hiring 6,000 licensed hair stylists nationwide to staff its rebranded salons named The Salon by InStyle.

2-3b The Innovation Matrix

Critics of Ansoff's matrix mention that the matrix does not reflect the reality of how businesses grow—that modern businesses plan growth in a more fluid manner based on current capabilities rather than the clear-cut sectors outlined by the opportunity matrix. To reflect this, Bansi Nagji and Geoff Tuff, global innovation managers at Monitor Group, developed a system that enables a company to see exactly what types of assets need to be developed and what types of markets are possible to grow into (or create) based on the company's core capabilities, as shown in Exhibit 2.2.

The layout of the innovation matrix demonstrates that as a company moves away from its core capabilities (the lower left) it traverses a range of change and innovation rather than choosing one of the four sectors in Ansoff's matrix. These ranges are broken down into three levels:

1. **Core Innovation:** Represented by the yellow circle in Exhibit 2.2, these decisions implement changes that use existing assets to provide added convenience to existing customers and potentially entice customers from other brands. Blue Apron, the meal kit company, is starting to sell its kits in physical stores, in addition to its subscription online model. This strategy should help the company reach more customers as its growth slows.[8]

2. **Adjacent Innovation:** Represented by the orange arc in Exhibit 2.2, these decisions are designed to take company strengths into new markets. This space uses

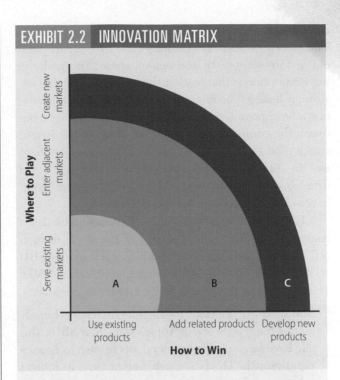

EXHIBIT 2.2   INNOVATION MATRIX

Where to Play (vertical axis): Serve existing markets, Enter adjacent markets, Create new markets

How to Win (horizontal axis): Use existing products, Add related products, Develop new products

A   B   C

Based on Bansi Nagji and Geoff Tuff, "A Simple Tool You Need to Manage Innovation," *Harvard Business Review*, **May 2012, http://hbr.org/2012/05/managing-your-innovation-portfolio/ar/1 (accessed June 1, 2012).**

existing abilities in new ways. For example, Botox, the popular cosmetic drug, was originally developed to treat intestinal problems and to treat crossed eyes. Leveraging the drug into cosmetic medicine has dramatically increased the market for Botox.

3. **Transformational Innovation:** Represented by the red arc in Exhibit 2.2, these decisions result in brand-new markets, products, and often new businesses. The company must rely on new, unfamiliar assets to develop the type of breakthrough decisions that fall in this category. Some notable examples are Apple in technology (including the iPhone, iPad, and Apple Watch), Uber in transportation, and Airbnb in hospitality.

2-3c The Boston Consulting Group Model

Management must find a balance among the SBUs that yields the overall organization's desired growth and profits with an acceptable level of risk. Some SBUs generate large amounts of cash, and others need cash to foster growth. The challenge is to balance the organization's portfolio of SBUs for the best long-term performance.

To determine the future cash contributions and cash requirements expected for each SBU, managers can use the Boston Consulting Group's portfolio matrix. The **portfolio matrix** classifies each SBU by its present or forecast growth and market share. The underlying assumption is that market share and profitability are strongly linked. The measure of market share used in the portfolio approach is *relative market share*, the ratio between the company's share and the share of the largest competitor. For example, if a firm has a 50 percent share and the competitor has 5 percent, the ratio is 10 to 1. If a firm has a 10 percent market share and the largest competitor has 20 percent, the ratio is 0.5 to 1.

Exhibit 2.3 is a hypothetical portfolio matrix for a computer manufacturer. The size of the circle in each cell of the matrix represents dollar sales of the SBU relative to dollar sales of the company's other SBUs. The portfolio matrix breaks SBUs into four categories:

- **Stars:** A **star** is a fast-growing market leader. For example, the iPad is one of Apple's stars. Star SBUs usually have large profits but need lots of cash to finance rapid growth. The best marketing tactic is to protect existing market share by reinvesting earnings in product improvement, better distribution, more promotion, and production efficiency. Management must capture new users as they enter the market.

- **Cash cows:** A **cash cow** is an SBU that generates more cash than it needs to maintain its market share. It is in a low-growth market, but the product has a dominant market share. Personal computers and laptops are categorized as cash cows in Exhibit 2.3. The basic strategy for a cash cow is to maintain market dominance by being the price leader and making technological improvements in the product. Managers should resist pressure to extend the basic line unless they can dramatically increase demand. Instead, they should allocate excess cash to the product categories for which growth prospects are the greatest. For example, Apple's iPhone and Google's search engine are cash cows for their companies.[9]

- **Problem children:** A **problem child**, also called a **question mark**, shows rapid growth but poor profit margins. It has a low

EXHIBIT 2.3 PORTFOLIO MATRIX FOR A LARGE COMPUTER MANUFACTURER

Market growth rate (in constant dollars) — vertical axis (High, 10, Low)

- Netbooks, handheld computers, and tablet PCs (stars)
- Integrated phone/palm device (problem child or question mark)
- Laptop and personal computers (cash cows)
- Mainframe computer (dog)

Market share dominance (share relative to largest competitor): 10x High — 1x — Low — 0.1x

market share in a high-growth industry. Problem children need a great deal of cash. Without cash support, they eventually become dogs. The strategy options are to invest heavily to gain better market share, acquire competitors to get the necessary market share, or drop the SBU. Sometimes a firm can reposition the products of the SBU to move them into the star category. Elixir guitar strings, made by W. L. Gore & Associates, maker of Gore-Tex and Glide floss, were originally tested and marketed to Walt Disney theme parks to control puppets. After trial and failure, Gore repositioned and marketed heavily to musicians, who have loved the strings ever since.

- **Dogs:** A **dog** has low growth potential and a small market share. Most dogs eventually leave the marketplace. In the computer manufacturer example, the mainframe computer has become a dog. Another example is BlackBerry's smartphone line, which started out as a star for its manufacturer in the United States. Over time, the BlackBerry moved into the cash cow category, and then more recently, to a question mark, as the iPhone and Android-based phones captured market share. Even if it never regains its star status in the United States, BlackBerry has moved into other geographic markets to sell its devices. In parts of Africa, Blackberry is seen as a revolutionary company that is connecting people in a way that they have never been before. The company currently owns 48 percent of the mobile market and 70 percent of the smartphone market in South Africa.[10]

While typical strategies for dogs are to harvest or divest, sometimes companies—like BlackBerry—are

portfolio matrix a tool for allocating resources among products or strategic business units on the basis of relative market share and market growth rate

star in the portfolio matrix, a business unit that is a fast-growing market leader

cash cow in the portfolio matrix, a business unit that generates more cash than it needs to maintain its market share

problem child (question mark) in the portfolio matrix, a business unit that shows rapid growth but poor profit margins

dog in the portfolio matrix, a business unit that has low growth potential and a small market share

Grzegorz Czapski/Shutterstock.com

successful with this class of product in other markets. Other companies may revive products that were abandoned as dogs. Surge, a citrus-flavored soft drink developed by Coca-Cola, was launched in the late 1990s to compete with Mountain Dew. After sales died out in 2003, the company took Surge off the market. However, loyal fans organized online and petitioned Coca-Cola to bring the drink back. In 2015, the company reintroduced Surge on Amazon, and eventually brought it back to U.S. convenience stores.[11]

After classifying the company's SBUs in the matrix, the next step is to allocate future resources for each. The four basic strategies are to:

- **Build:** If an organization has an SBU that it believes has the potential to be a star (probably a problem child at present), building would be an appropriate goal. The organization may decide to give up short-term profits and use its financial resources to achieve this goal. Apple postponed further work on the iPad to pursue the iPhone. The wait paid off when Apple was able to repurpose much of the iOS software and the iPhone's App Store for the iPad, making development less expensive and getting the product into the marketplace more quickly.[12]

- **Hold:** If an SBU is a successful cash cow, a key goal would typically be to hold or preserve market share so that the organization can take advantage of the very positive cash flow. Samsung Home Appliances, such as refrigerators, washing machines, and cooking appliances, are the company's cash cows. Over time, Samsung Home Appliances have become a household name and stand for quality and trust. Samsung has been able to attain a good market share across different industry seg-

ments and still holds a good potential to grow in the coming future.[13]

- **Harvest:** This strategy is appropriate for all SBUs except those classified as stars. The basic goal is to increase the short-term cash return without too much concern for the long-run impact. It is especially worthwhile when more cash is needed from a cash cow with long-run prospects that are unfavorable because of a low market growth rate. For instance, Lever Brothers has been harvesting Lifebuoy soap for a number of years with little promotional backing.

- **Divest:** Getting rid of SBUs with low shares of low-growth markets is often appropriate. Problem children and dogs are most suitable for this strategy. Starbucks, for example, is in the process of closing the unprofitable Teavana Tea Bars it acquired in 2012.[14]

2-3d The General Electric Model

The third model for selecting strategic alternatives was originally developed by General Electric (GE). The dimensions used in this model—market attractiveness and company strength—are richer and more complex than those used in the Boston Consulting Group model but are harder to quantify.

Exhibit 2.4 presents the GE model. The horizontal axis, Business Position, refers to how well positioned the organization is to take advantage of market opportunities. Business position answers questions such as: Does the firm have the technology it needs to effectively penetrate the market? Are its financial resources adequate? Can manufacturing costs be held down below those of the competition? Can the firm cope with change? The vertical axis measures the attractiveness of a market, which is expressed

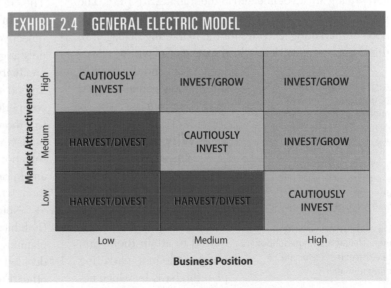

EXHIBIT 2.4   GENERAL ELECTRIC MODEL

	Low	Medium	High
High	CAUTIOUSLY INVEST	INVEST/GROW	INVEST/GROW
Medium	HARVEST/DIVEST	CAUTIOUSLY INVEST	INVEST/GROW
Low	HARVEST/DIVEST	HARVEST/DIVEST	CAUTIOUSLY INVEST

Market Attractiveness (vertical axis)

Business Position (horizontal axis)

both quantitatively and qualitatively. Some attributes of an attractive market are high profitability, rapid growth, a lack of government regulation, consumer insensitivity to a price increase, a lack of competition, and availability of technology. The grid is divided into three overall attractiveness zones for each dimension: high, medium, and low.

Those SBUs (or markets) that have low overall attractiveness (indicated by the red cells in Exhibit 2.4) should be avoided if the organization is not already serving them. If the firm is in these markets, it should either harvest or divest those SBUs. The organization should selectively maintain markets with medium attractiveness (indicated by the yellow cells in Exhibit 2.4). If attractiveness begins to slip, then the organization should withdraw from the market.

Conditions that are highly attractive—a thriving market plus a strong business position (the green cells in Exhibit 2.4)—are the best candidates for investment. For example, Airbus Commercial Aircraft has a solid competitive position, producing the best-selling single-aisle jetliner in the industry. At the same time, there is strong, sustained growth in commercial air travel.[15]

2-3e The Marketing Plan

Based on the company's or SBU's overall strategy, marketing managers can create a marketing plan for individual products, brands, lines, or customer groups. **Planning** is the process of anticipating future events and determining strategies to achieve organizational objectives in the future. **Marketing planning** involves designing activities relating to marketing objectives and the changing marketing environment. Marketing planning is the basis for all marketing strategies and decisions. Issues such as product lines, distribution channels, marketing communications, and pricing are all delineated in the **marketing plan**. The marketing plan is a written document that acts as a guidebook of marketing activities for the marketing manager. In this chapter, you will learn the importance of writing a marketing plan and the types of information contained in a marketing plan.

planning the process of anticipating future events and determining strategies to achieve organizational objectives in the future

marketing planning designing activities relating to marketing objectives and the changing marketing environment

marketing plan a written document that acts as a guidebook of marketing activities for the marketing manager

2-3f Why Write a Marketing Plan?

By specifying objectives and defining the actions required to attain them, you can provide in a marketing plan the basis by which actual and expected performance can be compared. Marketing can be one of the most expensive and complicated business activities, but it is also one of the most important. The written marketing plan provides clearly stated activities that help employees and managers understand and work toward common goals.

Writing a marketing plan allows you to examine the marketing environment in conjunction with the inner workings of the business. Once the marketing plan is written, it serves as a reference point for the success of future activities. Finally, the marketing plan allows the marketing manager to enter the marketplace with an awareness of possibilities and problems. Recent research with entrepreneurs over a six-year period has shown that those who had written marketing plans were 16% more likely to achieve visibility those who had no written plan.[16]

2-3g Marketing Plan Elements

Marketing plans can be presented in many different ways. Most businesses need a written marketing plan because a marketing plan is large and can be complex. The details about tasks and activity assignments may be lost if communicated orally. Regardless of the way a marketing plan is presented, some elements are common to all marketing plans. Exhibit 2.5 shows these elements, which include defining the business mission, performing a situation analysis, defining objectives, delineating a target market, and establishing components of the marketing mix. Other elements that may be included in a plan are budgets, implementation timetables, required marketing research efforts, or elements of advanced strategic planning.

2-3h Writing the Marketing Plan

The creation and implementation of a complete marketing plan will allow the organization to achieve marketing objectives and succeed. However, the marketing plan is only as good as the information it contains and the effort, creativity, and thought that went into its creation. Having a good marketing information system and a wealth of competitive intelligence (covered in Chapter 9) is critical to a thorough and accurate situation analysis. The role of managerial intuition is also important in the creation and selection of marketing strategies. Managers must weigh any information against its accuracy and their own judgment when making a marketing decision.

Note that the overall structure of the marketing plan (Exhibit 2.5) should not be viewed as a series of sequential planning steps. Many of the marketing plan elements are decided simultaneously and in conjunction with one another. Further, every marketing plan has different content,

EXHIBIT 2.5 ELEMENTS OF A MARKETING PLAN

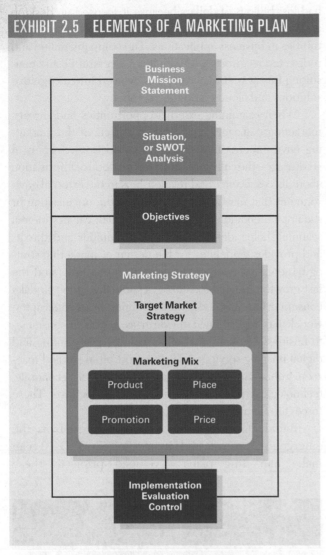

- Business Mission Statement
- Situation, or SWOT, Analysis
- Objectives
- Marketing Strategy
  - Target Market Strategy
  - Marketing Mix
    - Product
    - Place
    - Promotion
    - Price
- Implementation Evaluation Control

A marketing plan is only as good as the information it contains and the effort, creativity, and thought that went into its creation.

depending on the organization and its mission, objectives, targets, and marketing mix components. There is not one single correct format for a marketing plan. Many organizations have their own distinctive format or terminology for creating a marketing plan. Every marketing plan should be unique to the firm for which it was created. Remember, however, that although the format and order of presentation should be flexible, the same types of questions and topic areas should be covered in any marketing plan.

2-4 DEFINING THE BUSINESS MISSION

The foundation of any marketing plan is the firm's **mission statement**, which answers the question **"What business are we in?"** The way a firm defines its business mission profoundly affects the firm's long-run

resource allocation, profitability, and survival. The mission statement is based on a careful analysis of benefits sought by present and potential customers and an analysis of existing and anticipated environmental conditions. The firm's mission statement establishes boundaries for all subsequent decisions, objectives, and strategies.

A mission statement should focus on the market or markets the organization is attempting to serve rather than on the good or service offered. Otherwise, a new technology may quickly make the good or service obsolete and the mission statement irrelevant to company functions. Business mission statements that are stated too narrowly suffer from **marketing myopia** —defining a business in terms of goods and services rather than in terms of the benefits customers seek. In this context, *myopia* means narrow, short-term thinking. For example, Frito-Lay defines its mission as being in the snack-food business rather than in the corn chip business. The mission of sports teams is not just to play games but also to serve the interests of the fans.

Alternatively, business missions may be stated too broadly. "To provide products of superior quality and value that improve the lives of the world's consumers" is probably too broad a mission statement for any firm except Procter & Gamble. Care must be taken when stating what business a firm is in. For example, the mission of Ben & Jerry's centers on three important aspects of its ice cream

mission statement a statement of the firm's business based on a careful analysis of benefits sought by present and potential customers and an analysis of existing and anticipated environmental conditions

marketing myopia defining a business in terms of goods and services rather than in terms of the benefits customers seek business: (1) Product: "To make, distribute and sell the finest quality all natural ice cream and euphoric concoctions with a continued commitment to incorporating wholesome, natural ingredients and promoting business practices that respect the Earth and the Environment"; (2) Economic: "To operate the Company on a sustainable financial basis of profitable growth, increasing value for our stakeholders and expanding opportunities for development and career growth for our employees"; and (3) Social: "To operate the Company in a way that actively recognizes the central role that business plays in society by initiating innovative ways to improve the quality of life locally, nationally, and internationally."[17] By correctly stating the business mission in terms of the benefits that customers seek, the foundation for the marketing plan is set. Many companies are focusing on designing more appropriate mission statements because these statements are frequently displayed on the companies' websites.

2-5 CONDUCTING A SITUATION ANALYSIS

Marketers must understand the current and potential environment in which the product or service will be marketed. A situation analysis is sometimes referred to as a **SWOT analysis**—that is, the firm should identify its internal strengths (**S**) and weaknesses (**W**) and also examine external opportunities (**O**) and threats (**T**).

When examining internal strengths and weaknesses, the marketing manager should focus on organizational resources such as production costs, marketing skills, financial resources, company or brand image, employee capabilities, and available technology. For example, IBM has a history of reinventing itself and adapting to new opportunities and threats. More than 100 years ago, the company started out by manufacturing and selling machinery such as commercial scales and meat and cheese slicers. In 1924, IBM narrowed its focus to business machines, and in the early 1960s, it designed a revolutionary system that made it possible for machines in a product line to work together. IBM introduced its first personal computer in 1981, following market opportunities forged by other computer companies. By the 1990s, however, IBM had lost billions of dollars because it focused on desktop and personal productivity rather than on pursuing opportunities in business applications. The company rallied and redirected its efforts on building a successful IT and consulting business. Today, IBM has evolved into a cognitive solutions and cloud computing company.[18]

When examining external opportunities and threats, marketing managers must analyze aspects of the marketing environment. This process is called **environmental scanning**—the collection and interpretation of information about forces, events, and relationships in the external environment that may affect the future of the organization or the implementation of the marketing plan. Environmental scanning helps identify market opportunities and threats and provides guidelines for the design of marketing strategy. Increasing competition from overseas firms and the fast growth of digital technology essentially ended Kodak's consumer film business. After emerging from bankruptcy, Kodak has repositioned the firm as a smaller, business-to-business company that offers commercial printing and digital imaging services.[19] The six most often studied macroenvironmental forces are social, demographic, economic, technological, political and legal, and competitive. These forces are examined in detail in Chapter 4.

Rapid changes in the environment such as the emergence, spread and impact of COVID-19 can make marketing plans developed prior to these

SWOT analysis identifying internal strengths (S) and weaknesses (W) and also examining external opportunities (O) and threats (T)

environmental scanning collection and interpretation of information about forces, events, and relationships in the external environment that may affect the future of the organization or the implementation of the marketing plan

IBM Watson IoT General Manager Harriet Green delivers an address at the IBM Genius of Things Summit in Munich, Germany, on February 16, 2017. One of the most advanced artificial intelligences in the World, IBM's Watson is currently being used in health care, teaching, tax preparation, and weather forecasting applications.

drserg/Shutterstock.com

environmental changes partially or totally obsolete. In the first quarter of 2020, sales in many product categories plummeted, businesses were forced to close and/or operate at a set proportion of their capacities (e.g., restaurants only allowed to serve 25% of seating capacity and requiring occupants of tables to be seated at least 6 feet from other tables). Consumers were asked or told to self-quarantine except in specific circumstances such as grocery shopping, seeking healthcare or other activities identified by state or local governments.

Creative operators ranging from fast food to exclusive restaurants adapted by offering take-out and drive-through services to produce at least some income during closures and to retain some employees. Some restaurants were able to adapt quickly enough to retain a substantial proportion of the sales that they had experienced prior to the emergence of the pandemic. Other firms, such as spas, hair salons and other "high touch" organizations have been forced to close longer due to the inability to provide required space between individual service providers and customers.

The emergence of COVID-19 was a surprise to most businesses, investors and consumers. Careful environmental scanning and adaptation to new environmental conditions may have major long-term effects on the future of specific organizations.

2-6 COMPETITIVE ADVANTAGE

Performing a SWOT analysis allows firms to identify their competitive advantage. A competitive advantage is a set of unique features of a company and its products that are perceived by the target market as significant and superior to those of the competition. It is the factor or factors that cause customers to patronize a firm and not the competition. There are three types of competitive advantage: cost, product/service differentiation, and niche.

2-6a Cost Competitive Advantage

Cost leadership can result from obtaining inexpensive raw materials, creating an efficient scale of plant operations, designing products for ease of manufacture, controlling overhead costs, and avoiding marginal customers. Southwest Airlines has been successful at bringing down airfares through its short route point-to-point business model, no-frills service, single flight strategy, and highly productive employees.[20] Having a **cost competitive advantage** means being the low-cost competitor in an industry while maintaining satisfactory profit margins. Costs can be reduced in a variety of ways:

- **Experience curves:** Experience curves tell us that costs decline at a predictable rate as experience with a product increases. The experience curve effect encompasses a broad range of manufacturing, marketing, and administrative costs. Experience curves reflect learning by doing, technological advances, and economies of scale. Firms like Boeing use historical experience curves as a basis for predicting and setting prices. Experience curves allow management to forecast costs and set prices based on anticipated costs as opposed to current costs.

- **Efficient labor:** Labor costs can be an important component of total costs in low-skill, labor-intensive industries such as product assembly and apparel manufacturing. Many U.S. publishers and software developers send data entry, design, and formatting tasks to India, where skilled engineers are available at lower overall cost.

- **No-frills goods and services:** Marketers can lower costs by removing frills and options from a product or service. Southwest Airlines, for example, offers low fares, but no seat assignments or meals. Low costs give Southwest a higher load factor and greater economies of scale, which, in turn, mean lower prices.

- **Government subsidies:** Governments can provide grants and interest-free loans to target industries. Such government assistance enabled Japanese semiconductor manufacturers to become global leaders.

- **Product design:** Cutting-edge design technology can help offset high labor costs. BMW is a world leader in designing cars for ease of manufacture and assembly. Reverse engineering—the process of disassembling a product piece by piece to learn its components and obtain clues as to the manufacturing process—can also mean savings. Reverse engineering a low-cost competitor's product can save research and design costs. The car industry often uses reverse engineering.

- **Reengineering:** Reengineering entails fundamental rethinking and redesign of business processes to achieve dramatic improvements in critical measures of performance. It often involves reorganizing functional departments such as sales, engineering, and production into cross-disciplinary teams.

competitive advantage a set of unique features of a company and its products that are perceived by the target market as significant and superior to those of the competition

cost competitive advantage being the low-cost competitor in an industry while maintaining satisfactory profit margins

experience curves curves that show costs declining at a predictable rate as experience with a product increases

- **Production innovations:** Production innovations such as new technology and simplified production techniques help lower the average cost of production. Technologies such as computer-aided design (CAD) and computer-aided manufacturing (CAM) and increasingly sophisticated robots help companies such as Boeing, Ford, and General Electric reduce their manufacturing costs.

- **New methods of service delivery:** Medical expenses have been substantially lowered by the use of outpatient surgery and walk-in clinics. Online-only magazines deliver great savings, and even some print magazines are exploring ways to go online to save material and shipping costs.

2-6b Product/Service Differentiation Competitive Advantage

Because cost competitive advantages are subject to continual erosion, product/service differentiation tends to provide a longer-lasting competitive advantage. The durability of this strategy tends to make it more attractive to many top managers. A **product/service differentiation competitive advantage** exists when a firm provides something that is unique and valuable to buyers beyond simply offering a lower price than that of the competition. Examples include brand names (Lexus), a strong dealer network (Caterpillar for construction work), product reliability (Maytag appliances), image (Neiman Marcus in retailing), or service (Zappos). Google has, from its beginnings, paired sophisticated industrial and software design with strange shapes, novel fabrics and pops of bright color (e.g., the bright power button on its Pixel 2 phone). Comparatively competing products, are angular, black and white, plastic and glass, and completely expressionless. The fun designs Google uses helps its products to stand out.[21]

2-6c Niche Competitive Advantage

A **niche competitive advantage** seeks to target and effectively serve a single segment of the market (see Chapter 8). For small companies with limited resources that potentially face giant competitors, niche targeting may be the only viable option. A market segment that has good growth potential but is not crucial to the success of major competitors is a good candidate for developing a niche strategy.

Many companies using a niche strategy serve only a limited geographic market. Stew Leonard's is an extremely successful but small grocery store chain found only in Connecticut and New York. Blue Bell Ice cream is available in only about 26 percent of the nation's supermarkets, but it ranks as one of the top three best-selling ice creams in the country.[22]

The Chef's Garden, a 225-acre Ohio farm, specializes in growing and shipping rare artisan vegetables directly to its customers. Chefs from all over the world call to order or request a unique item, which is grown and shipped by the Chef's Garden. The farm provides personal services and specialized premium vegetables that aren't available anywhere else and relies on its customers to supply it with ideas for what they would like to be able to offer in their restaurants. The excellent service and feeling of contribution keep chefs coming back.[23]

2-6d Building Sustainable Competitive Advantage

The key to having a competitive advantage is the ability to sustain that advantage. A **sustainable competitive advantage** is one that cannot be copied by the competition. For example, Amazon is the undisputed leader of online retailing. The company has achieved sustainable competitive advantage through its ability to offer the lowest prices, the widest variety of products, and a well-developed, efficient delivery network. In addition, Amazon has a massive number of users with credit cards on file, making the purchase process quick and easy for customers. In contrast, when Datril was introduced into the pain-reliever market, it was touted as being exactly like Tylenol, only cheaper.

matteo_it/Shutterstock.com

Google tries to maintain a competitive advantage by continuous innovation.

product/service differentiation competitive advantage the provision of something that is unique and valuable to buyers beyond simply offering a lower price than that of the competition

niche competitive advantage the advantage achieved when a firm seeks to target and effectively serve a small segment of the market

sustainable competitive advantage an advantage that cannot be copied by the competition

Tylenol responded by lowering its price, thus destroying Datril's competitive advantage and ability to remain on the market. In this case, low price was not a sustainable competitive advantage. Without a competitive advantage, target customers do not perceive any reason to patronize one organization rather than its competitors.

The notion of competitive advantage means that a successful firm will stake out a position unique in some manner from its rivals. Imitation by competitors indicates a lack of competitive advantage and almost ensures mediocre performance. Moreover, competitors rarely stand still, so it is not surprising that imitation causes managers to feel trapped in a seemingly endless game of catchup. They are regularly surprised by the new accomplishments of their rivals.

Rather than copy competitors, companies need to build their own competitive advantages. The sources of tomorrow's competitive advantages are the skills and assets of the organization. Assets include patents, copyrights, locations, equipment, and technology that are superior to those of the competition. Skills are functions such as customer service and promotion that the firm performs better than its competitors. Marketing managers should continually focus the firm's skills and assets on sustaining and creating competitive advantages.

Remember, a sustainable competitive advantage is a function of the speed with which competitors can imitate a leading company's strategy and plans. Imitation requires a competitor to identify the leader's competitive advantage, determine how it is achieved, and then learn how to duplicate it.

2-7 SETTING MARKETING PLAN OBJECTIVES

Before the details of a marketing plan can be developed, objectives for the plan must be stated. Without objectives, there is no basis for measuring the success of marketing plan activities.

A **marketing objective** is a statement of what is to be accomplished through marketing activities.

A strong marketing objective for Purina might be "to increase sales of Purina brand cat food between January 1, 2020, and December 31, 2020, by 15 percent, compared to 2019 sales of $300 million."

Objectives must be consistent with and indicate the priorities of the organization. Specifically, objectives flow from the business mission statement to the rest of the marketing plan.

MARKETING OBJECTIVES SHOULD BE...

▸ **Realistic:** Managers should develop objectives that have a chance of being met. For example, it may be unrealistic for start-up firms or new products to command dominant market share, given other competitors in the marketplace.

▸ **Measurable:** Managers need to be able to quantitatively measure whether or not an objective has been met. For example, it would be difficult to determine success for an objective that states, "To increase sales of cat food." If the company sells 1 percent more cat food, does that mean the objective was met? Instead, a specific number should be stated, "To increase sales of Purina brand cat food from $300 million to $345 million."

▸ **Time specific:** By what time should the objective be met? "To increase sales of Purina brand cat food between January 1, 2020, and December 31, 2020."

▸ **Compared to a benchmark:** If the objective is to increase sales by 15 percent, it is important to know the baseline against which the objective will be measured. Will it be current sales? Last year's sales? For example, "To increase sales of Purina brand cat food by 15 percent over 2019 sales of $300 million."

Carefully specified objectives serve several functions. First, they communicate marketing management philosophies and provide direction for lower-level marketing managers so that marketing efforts are integrated and pointed in a consistent direction. Objectives also serve as motivators by creating something for employees to strive for. When objectives are attainable and challenging, they motivate those charged with achieving the objectives. Additionally, the process of writing specific objectives forces executives to clarify their thinking. Finally, objectives form a basis for control: the effectiveness of a plan can be gauged in light of the stated objectives.

2-8 DESCRIBING THE TARGET MARKET

Marketing strategy involves the activities of selecting and describing one or more target markets and developing and maintaining a

marketing objective
a statement of what is to be accomplished through marketing activities

marketing strategy the activities of selecting and describing one or more target markets and developing and maintaining a marketing mix that will produce mutually satisfying exchanges with target markets marketing mix that will produce mutually satisfying exchanges with target markets.

2-8a Target Market Strategy

A market segment is a group of individuals or organizations who share one or more characteristics. They therefore may have relatively similar product needs. For example, parents of newborn babies need formula, diapers, and special foods.

The target market strategy identifies the market segment or segments on which to focus. This process begins with a **market opportunity analysis (MOA)**—the description and estimation of the size and sales potential of market segments that are of interest to the firm and the assessment of key competitors in these market segments. After the firm describes the market segments, it may target one or more of them. There are three general strategies for selecting target markets.

Target markets can be selected by appealing to the entire market with one marketing mix, concentrating on one segment, or appealing to multiple market segments using multiple marketing mixes. The characteristics, advantages, and disadvantages of each strategic option are examined in Chapter 8. Target markets could be 18- to 25-year-old females who are interested in fashion (*Vogue* magazine), people concerned about sugar and calories in their soft drinks (Diet Pepsi), or parents without the time to potty train their children (Booty Camp classes where kids are potty trained).

Any market segment that is targeted must be fully described. Demographics, psychographics, and buyer behavior should be assessed. Buyer behavior is covered in Chapters 6 and 7. If segments are differentiated by ethnicity, multicultural aspects of the marketing mix should be examined. If the target market is international, it is especially important to describe differences in culture, economic and technological development, and political structure that may affect the marketing plan. Global marketing is covered in more detail in Chapter 5.

market opportunity analysis (MOA) the description and estimation of the size and sales potential of market segments that are of interest to the firm and the assessment of key competitors in these market segments

marketing mix (four Ps) a unique blend of product, place (distribution), promotion, and pricing strategies designed to produce mutually satisfying exchanges with a target market

2-9 THE MARKETING MIX

The term **marketing mix** refers to a unique blend of product, place (distribution), promotion, and pricing strategies (often referred to as the **four Ps**) designed to produce mutually satisfying exchanges with a target market. The marketing manager can control each component of the marketing mix, but the strategies for all four components must be blended to achieve optimal results. Any marketing mix is only as good as its weakest component. For example, the first pump toothpastes were distributed over cosmetics counters and failed. Not until pump toothpastes were distributed the same way as tube toothpastes did the products succeed. The best promotion and the lowest price cannot save a poor product. Similarly, excellent products with poor placing, pricing, or promotion will likely fail.

Successful marketing mixes have been carefully designed to satisfy target markets. At first glance, McDonald's and Wendy's may appear to have roughly identical marketing mixes because they are both in the fast-food hamburger business. However, McDonald's has been most successful at targeting parents with young children for lunchtime meals, whereas Wendy's targets the adult crowd for lunches and dinner. McDonald's has playgrounds, Ronald McDonald the clown, and children's Happy Meals. Wendy's has salad bars, carpeted restaurants, and no playgrounds.

Variations in marketing mixes do not occur by chance. Astute marketing managers devise marketing strategies to gain advantages over competitors and best serve the needs and wants of a particular target market segment. By manipulating elements of the marketing mix, marketing managers can fine-tune the customer offering and achieve competitive success.

2-9a Product Strategies

Of the four Ps, the marketing mix typically starts with the product. The heart of the marketing mix, the starting point, is the product offering and product strategy. It is hard to design a place strategy, decide on a promotion campaign, or set a price without knowing the product to be marketed.

The product includes not only the physical unit but also its package, warranty, after-sale service, brand name, company image, value, and many other factors. A Godiva chocolate has many product elements: the chocolate itself, a fancy gold wrapper, a customer satisfaction guarantee, and the prestige of the Godiva brand name. We buy things not only for what they do (benefits) but also for what they mean to us (status, quality, or reputation).

Products can be tangible goods such as computers, ideas like those offered by a consultant, or services such as medical care. Products should also offer customer

Tesla—a new paradigm for drivers

Few, if any companies have had as fast and profound an impact on the way consumers conceive of a product as common as a car as Tesla. The company is transforming the entire experience of buying and owning a car. Tesla has pushed toward automation and self-driving and has treated the car as software, with system updates beamed out over the air. It has made the electric vehicle cool. The cars are sleek and functional. Getting feedback early in the design process from customers was totally new and different from traditional car companies. And Tesla has transformed the car buying experience and made it pleasurable. Customers can go to a Tesla store in a mall and order their cars online. This experience is very different from the one customers have had with the traditional car dealership model.

Tesla is also designing solar panels and home battery storage units called the Powerwall. The focus of every Tesla product is creating a state-of-the-art, cleaner technology ecosystem. Tesla has a strong differential advantage across a number of markets.[24]

Source: Erika Fry, "Business by Design," Fortune, January 1, 2018, pp. 56–71.

value. Product decisions are covered in Chapters 10 and 11, and services marketing is detailed in Chapter 12.

2-9b Place (Distribution) Strategies

Place, or distribution, strategies are concerned with making products available when and where customers want them. Would you rather buy a kiwi fruit at the 24-hour grocery store within walking distance or fly to Australia to pick your own? A part of this P—place—is physical distribution, which involves all the business activities concerned with storing and transporting raw materials or finished products. The goal is to make sure products arrive in usable condition at designated places when needed. Place strategies are covered in Chapters 13 and 14.

2-9c Promotion Strategies

Promotion includes advertising, public relations, sales promotion, and personal selling. Promotion's role in the marketing mix is to bring about mutually satisfying exchanges with target markets by informing, educating, persuading, and reminding them of the benefits of an organization or a product. A good promotion strategy, like using a beloved cartoon character such as SpongeBob SquarePants to sell gummy snacks, can dramatically increase sales. Each element of this P—promotion—is coordinated and managed with the others to create a promotional blend or mix. These integrated marketing communications activities are

described in Chapters 16, 17, and 18. Technology-driven and social media aspects of promotional marketing are covered in Chapter 19.

2-9d Pricing Strategies

Price is what a buyer must give up in order to obtain a product. It is often the most flexible of the four Ps—the element quickest to change. Marketers can raise or lower prices more frequently and easily than they can change other marketing mix variables. Price is an important competitive weapon and is very important to the organization because price multiplied by the number of units sold equals total revenue for the firm. Pricing decisions are covered in Chapter 19.

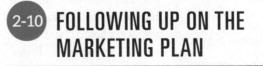 **FOLLOWING UP ON THE MARKETING PLAN**

One of the keys to success overlooked by many businesses is to actively follow up on the marketing plan. The time spent researching, developing, and writing a useful and accurate marketing plan goes to waste if the plan is not used by the organization. One of the best ways to get the most out of a marketing plan is to correctly implement it. Once the first steps to implementation are taken, evaluation and control will help guide the organization to success as laid out by the marketing plan.

Four characteristics of a marketing audit

- **Comprehensive:** The marketing audit covers all the major marketing issues facing an organization—not just trouble spots.

- **Systematic:** The marketing audit takes place in an orderly sequence and covers the organization's marketing environment, internal marketing system, and specific marketing activities. The diagnosis is followed by an action plan with both short-run and long-run proposals for improving overall marketing effectiveness.

- **Independent:** The marketing audit is normally conducted by an inside or outside party that is independent enough to have top management's confidence and has the ability to be objective.

- **Periodic:** The marketing audit should be carried out on a regular schedule instead of only in a crisis. Whether it seems successful or is in deep trouble, any organization can benefit greatly from such an audit.

2-10a Implementation

Implementation is the process that turns a marketing plan into action assignments and ensures that these assignments are executed in a way that accomplishes the plan's objectives. Implementation activities may involve detailed job assignments, activity descriptions, time lines, budgets, and lots of communication. Implementation requires delegating authority and responsibility, determining a time frame for completing tasks, and allocating resources. Sometimes a strategic plan also requires task force management. A *task force* is a tightly organized unit under the direction of a manager who, usually, has broad authority. A task force is established to accomplish a single goal or mission and thus works against a deadline.

Implementing a plan has another dimension: gaining acceptance. New plans mean change, and change creates resistance. One reason people resist change is that they fear they will lose something. For example, when new-product research is taken away from marketing research and given to a new-product department, the director of marketing research will naturally resist this loss of part of his or her domain. Misunderstanding and lack of trust also create opposition to change, but effective communication through open discussion and teamwork can be one way of overcoming resistance to change.

Although implementation is essentially "doing what you said you were going to do," many organizations repeatedly experience failures in strategy implementation. Brilliant marketing plans are doomed to fail if they are not properly implemented. These detailed communications may or may not be part of the written marketing plan. If they are not part of the plan, they should be specified elsewhere as soon as the plan has been communicated. Strong, forward-thinking leadership can overcome resistance to change, even in large, highly integrated companies where change seems very unlikely.

2-10b Evaluation and Control

After a marketing plan is implemented, it should be evaluated. **Evaluation** entails gauging the extent to which marketing objectives have been achieved during the specified time period. Four common reasons for failing to achieve a marketing objective are unrealistic marketing objectives, inappropriate marketing strategies in the plan, poor implementation, and changes in the environment after the objective was specified and the strategy was implemented.

Once a plan is chosen and implemented, its effectiveness must be monitored. **Control** provides the mechanisms for evaluating marketing results in light of the plan's objectives and for correcting actions that do not help the orga-

implementation the process that turns a marketing plan into action assignments and ensures that these assignments are executed in a way that accomplishes the plan's objectives

evaluation gauging the extent to which the marketing objectives have been achieved during the specified time period

control provides the mechanisms for evaluating marketing results in light of the plan's objectives and for correcting actions that do not help the organization reach those objectives within budget guidelines nization reach those objectives within budget guidelines. Firms need to establish formal and informal control programs to make the entire operation more efficient.

Perhaps the broadest control device available to marketing managers is the **marketing audit**—a thorough, systematic, periodic evaluation of the objectives, strategies, structure, and performance of the marketing organization. A marketing audit helps management allocate marketing resources efficiently.

Although the main purpose of the marketing audit is to develop a full profile of the organization's marketing effort and to provide a basis for developing and revising the marketing plan, it is also an excellent way to improve communication and raise the level of marketing consciousness within the organization. It is a useful vehicle for selling the philosophy and techniques of strategic marketing to other members of the organization.

2-10c Postaudit Tasks

After the audit has been completed, three tasks remain. First, the audit should profile existing weaknesses and inhibiting factors, as well as the firm's strengths and the new opportunities available to it. Recommendations have to be judged and prioritized so that those with the potential to contribute most to improved marketing performance can be implemented first. The usefulness of the data also depends on the auditor's skill in interpreting and presenting the data so decision makers can quickly grasp the major points.

The second task is to ensure that the role of the audit has been clearly communicated. It is unlikely that the suggestions will require a radical change in the way the firm operates. The audit's main role is to address the question "Where are we now?" and to suggest ways to improve what the firm already does.

The final postaudit task is to make someone accountable for implementing recommendations. All too often, reports are presented, applauded, and filed away to gather dust. The person made accountable should be someone who is committed to the project and who has the managerial power to make things happen.

2-11 EFFECTIVE STRATEGIC PLANNING

Effective strategic planning requires continual attention, creativity, and management commitment. Strategic planning should not be an annual exercise in which managers go through the motions and forget about strategic planning until the next year. It should be an ongoing process because the environment is continually changing and the firm's resources and capabilities are continually evolving.

Sound strategic planning is based on creativity. Managers should challenge assumptions about the firm and the environment and establish new strategies. For example, major oil companies developed the concept of the gasoline service station in an age when cars needed frequent and rather elaborate servicing. These major companies held on to the full-service approach, but independents were quick to respond to new realities and moved to lower-cost self-service and convenience store operations. Major companies took several decades to catch up.

Perhaps the most critical element in successful strategic planning is top management's support and participation. Google, for example, strongly supports educational and leadership programs for employees, as well as opportunities to address management with ideas and concerns.[25]

marketing audit a thorough, systematic, periodic evaluation of the objectives, strategies, structure, and performance of the marketing organization

3 | Ethics and Social Responsibility

Rawpixel.com/Shutterstock.com

LEARNING OUTCOMES

After studying this chapter, you will be able to…

3-1 Explain the determinants of a civil society

3-2 Explain the concept of ethical behavior

3-3 Describe ethical behavior in business

3-4 Discuss corporate social responsibility

3-5 Describe the arguments for and against society responsibility

3-6 Explain cause-related marketing

3-1 DETERMINANTS OF A CIVIL SOCIETY

Have you ever stopped to think about the social glue that binds society together? That is, what factors keep people and organizations from running amok and doing harm, and what factors create order in a society like ours? The answer lies in **social control**, defined as any means used to maintain behavioral norms and regulate conflict.[1] **Behavioral norms** are standards of proper or acceptable behavior. Social control is part of your life at every level, from your family to your local community, to the nation, to the global civilization. Several modes of social control are important to marketing:

1. **Ethics:** Ethics are the moral principles or values that generally govern the conduct of an individual or a group. Ethical rules and guidelines, along with customs and traditions, provide principles of right action.

2. **Laws:** Often, ethical rules and guidelines are codified into law. Laws created by governments are then enforced by governmental authority. This is how the dictum "Thou shall not steal" has become part of formal law throughout the land. Law, however, is not a perfect mechanism for ensuring good corporate and employee behavior. This is because laws often address the lowest common denominator of socially acceptable behavior. In other words, just because something is legal does not mean that it is ethical. For example, Log Cabin All Natural Table Syrup has no artificial flavors or colors, nor does it contain preservatives or high-fructose corn syrup. It is sold in a traditional jug similar to those used by many Vermont maple sugar makers, complete with a picture of a snow-covered log cabin on the label, evoking the woods of the Green Mountain State. However, while Log Cabin All Natural Table Syrup may indeed be "natural" and "authentic," as the jug suggests, it isn't maple syrup. The top ingredients are brown rice syrup, water, and sugar.[2] Maple Syrup industry groups from Vermont to Michigan recently sent a letter to the Food and Drug Administration protesting food labeled as "maple" that doesn't contain the real thing. These groups say that products such as Quaker Oats Maple & Brown Sugar Instant Oatmeal and Hood's Maple Walnut ice cream are misbranded.[3] Log Cabin does not explicitly state that the product contains real maple syrup, but the packaging certainly suggests it. Is this ethical? What's your opinion? Here's another example: In every state,

koya979/Shutterstock.com

littering is a problem—and has been for many years. Threats of fines and even jail time are shrugged off as people toss food wrappers and everything else imaginable out the car window. Plastic bags are a major source of litter. Also, plastic drinking straws and cups are often tossed out the window far too often. If you want one in a full-service restaurant, you must ask for it. San Francisco previously had passed a law completely banning plastic straws.[4]

3. **Formal and Informal Groups:** Businesses, professional organizations (such as the American Marketing Association and the American Medical Association), and clubs (such as Shriners and

social control any means used to maintain behavioral norms and regulate conflict

behavioral norms standards of proper or acceptable behavior. Several modes of social control are important to marketing

ethics the moral principles or values that generally govern the conduct of an individual or a group

Ducks Unlimited) all have codes of conduct. These codes prescribe acceptable and desired behaviors of their members.

4. **Self-Regulation:** Self-regulation involves the voluntary acceptance of standards established by nongovernmental entities, such as the American Association of Advertising Agencies (AAAA) or the National Association of Manufacturers. The AAAA has a self-regulation arm that deals with deceptive advertising. Other associations have regulations relating to child labor, environmental issues, conservation, and a host of other issues.

5. **The Media:** In an open, democratic society, the media play a key role in informing the public about the actions of individuals and organizations—both good and bad. The Children's Online Privacy Protection Act (COPPA) requires website operators to obtain verifiable consent from parents before collecting personal information about children under age 13. Yelp paid a $450,000 fine for collecting information on children under 13. Also, Hershey Foods has paid an $85,000 fine and Mrs. Fields Cookies $100,000 for the same infraction.[5] It is expected that more than 110 million students will use Google Apps for Education by 2020. This suite of educational apps complies with the U.S. Family Educational Rights and Privacy Act (FERPA)—a fact that Google states explicitly in its contracts with schools. Google also requires that schools using Google Apps for Education obtain parental consent before students can use the apps. This conforms to COPPA requirements.[6]

6. **An Active Civil Society:** An informed and engaged society can help mold individual and corporate ethics as well as socially responsible behavior. Research reveals that 56 percent of U.S. consumers stop buying from companies they believe are unethical. What's more, over one-third (35 percent) of consumers stop buying from brands they perceive as unethical even if there is no substitute available, and 27 percent stop purchasing even if they think the competitor offers lower quality. Overall, 63 percent of consumers feel that ethical issues are becoming more important.[7]

Some 34 percent of consumers tell others when they perceive a brand to be making ethical actions or actions that are honest, fair, and responsible, and another 29 percent take to social media to share their support for ethical companies.[8]

3-2 THE CONCEPT OF ETHICAL BEHAVIOR

It has been said that ethics is something everyone likes to talk about but nobody can define. Others have suggested that defining ethics is like trying to nail Jell-O to a wall. You begin to think that you understand it, but that is when it starts squirting out between your fingers.

Simply put, ethics can be viewed as the standard of behavior by which conduct is judged. Standards that are legal may not always be ethical, and vice versa. Laws are the values and standards enforceable by the courts. Ethics, then, consists of personal moral principles. For example, there is no legal statute that makes it a crime for someone to "cut in line." Yet, if someone does not want to wait in line and cuts to the front, it often makes others very angry.

If you have ever resented a line-cutter, then you understand ethics and have applied ethical standards in life. Waiting your turn in line is a social expectation that exists because lines ensure order and allocate the space and time needed to complete transactions. Waiting your turn is an expected but unwritten behavior that plays a critical role in an orderly society.

So it is with ethics. Ethics consists of those unwritten rules we have developed for our interactions with one another. These unwritten rules govern us when we are sharing resources or honoring contracts. "Waiting your turn" is a higher standard than the laws that are passed to maintain order. Those laws apply when physical force or threats are used to push to the front of the line. Assault, battery, and threats are forms of criminal conduct for which the offender can be prosecuted. But the law does not apply to the stealthy line-cutter who simply sneaks to the front, perhaps using a friend and a conversation as a decoy. No laws are broken, but the notions of fairness and justice are offended by one individual putting himself or herself above others and taking advantage of others' time and position.

Ethical questions range from practical, narrowly defined issues, such as a businessperson's obligation to be honest with customers, to broader social and philosophical questions, such as whether a company is responsible for preserving the environment and protecting employee rights. Many ethical dilemmas develop from conflicts between the differing interests of company owners and their workers, customers, and the surrounding community. Managers must balance the ideal against the practical—that is, they must produce a reasonable profit for the company's shareholders while maintaining honesty in business practices and concern for environmental and social issues.

3-2a Ethical Theories

People usually base their individual choice of ethical theory on their life experiences. The following are some of the ethical theories that apply to marketing.[9]

DEONTOLOGY The **deontological theory** states that people should adhere to their obligations and duties when analyzing an ethical dilemma. This means that a person will follow his or her obligations to another individual or society because upholding one's duty is what is considered ethically correct. For instance, a deontologist will always keep his promises to a friend and will follow the law. A person who follows this theory will produce very consistent decisions because they will be based on the individual's set duties.

Note that deontological theory is not necessarily concerned with the welfare of others. For example, suppose a salesperson has decided that it is her ethical duty (and very practical) to always be on time to meetings with clients. Today she is running late. How is she supposed to drive? Is the deontologist supposed to speed, breaking the law to uphold her duty to society, or is the deontologist supposed to arrive at her meeting late, breaking her duty to be on time? This scenario of conflicting obligations does not lead us to a clear, ethically correct resolution, nor does it protect the welfare of others from the deontologist's decision.

UTILITARIANISM The **utilitarian ethical theory** is founded on the ability to predict the consequences of an action. To a utilitarian, the choice that yields the greatest benefit to the most people is the choice that is ethically correct. One benefit of this ethical theory is that the utilitarian can compare similar predicted solutions and use a point system to determine which choice is more beneficial for more people. This point system provides a logical and rational argument for each decision and allows a person to use it on a case-by-case context.

There are two types of utilitarianism: act utilitarianism and rule utilitarianism. *Act utilitarianism* adheres exactly to the definition of utilitarianism as just described. In act utilitarianism, a person performs the acts that benefit the most people, regardless of personal feelings or societal constraints such as laws. *Rule utilitarianism*, however, takes into account the law and is concerned with fairness. A rule utilitarian seeks to benefit the most people but through the fairest and most just means available. Therefore, added benefits of rule utilitarianism are that it values justice and doing good at the same time.

As is true of all ethical theories, however, both act and rule utilitarianism contain numerous flaws. Inherent in both are the flaws associated with predicting the future. Does President Trump's American Health Care Act help the most people, or does it not? Although people can use their life experiences to attempt to predict outcomes, no human being can be certain that his predictions will come true. This uncertainty can lead to unexpected results, making the utilitarian look unethical as time passes because his choice did not benefit the most people as he predicted.

Another assumption that a utilitarian must make is that she has the ability to compare the various types of consequences against each other on a similar scale. However, comparing material gains such as money against intangible gains such as happiness is impossible because their qualities differ so greatly.

CASUIST The **casuist ethical theory** compares a current ethical dilemma with examples of similar ethical dilemmas and their outcomes. This allows one to determine the severity of the situation and to create the best possible solution according to others' experiences. Usually, one will find examples that represent the extremes of the situation so that a compromise can be reached that will include the wisdom gained from the previous situations.

One drawback to this ethical theory is that there may not be a set of similar examples for a given ethical dilemma. Perhaps that which is controversial and ethically questionable is new and unexpected. Along the same line of thinking, this theory assumes that the results of the current ethical dilemma will be similar to results in the examples. This may not be necessarily true and would greatly hinder the effectiveness of applying this ethical theory.

MORAL RELATIVISM **Moral relativism** is a belief in time-and-place ethics, that is, the truth of a moral judgment is relative to the judging person or group. According to

deontological theory
ethical theory that states that people should adhere to their obligations and duties when analyzing an ethical dilemma

utilitarian ethical theory
ethical theory that is founded on the ability to predict the consequences of an action

casuist ethical theory
ethical theory that compares a current ethical dilemma with examples of similar ethical dilemmas and their outcomes

moral relativism a theory of time-and-place ethics; that is, the belief that ethical truths depend on the individuals and groups holding them a moral relativist, for example, arson is not always wrong—if you live in a neighborhood where drug dealers are operating a crystal meth lab or crack house, committing arson by burning down the meth lab may be ethically justified. If you are a parent and your child is starving, stealing a loaf of bread is ethically correct. The proper resolution to ethical dilemmas is based on weighing the competing factors at the moment and then making a determination to take the lesser of the evils as the resolution. Moral relativists do not believe in absolute rules. Their beliefs center on the pressure of the moment and whether the pressure justifies the action taken.

VIRTUE ETHICS Aristotle and Plato taught that solving ethical dilemmas requires training—that individuals solve ethical dilemmas when they develop and nurture a set of virtues. A **virtue** is a character trait valued as being good. Aristotle taught the importance of cultivating virtue in his students and then having them solve ethical dilemmas using those virtues once they had become an integral part of his students' being through their virtue training.

Some modern philosophers have embraced this notion of virtue and have developed lists of what constitutes a virtuous businessperson. Some common virtues for businesspeople are self-discipline, friendliness, caring, courage, compassion, trust, responsibility, honesty, determination, enthusiasm, and humility. You may see other lists of virtues that are longer or shorter, but here is a good start for core business virtues.

3-3 ETHICAL BEHAVIOR IN BUSINESS

Depending on which, if any, ethical theory a businessperson has accepted and uses in his or her daily conduct, the action taken may vary. For example, faced with bribing a foreign official to get a critically needed contract or shutting down a factory and laying off a thousand workers, a person following a deontology strategy would not pay the bribe. Why? A deontologist always follows the law. However, a moral relativist would probably pay the bribe.

While the boundaries of what is legal and what is not are often fairly clear (e.g., do not run a red light, do not steal money from a bank, and do not kill anyone), the boundaries of

virtue a character trait valued as being good

morals the rules people develop as a result of cultural values and norms

After ethical issues investigated by both the Justice Department and the Securities and Exchange Commission, today Walmart has become an industry leader in the Foreign Corrupt Practices Act compliance best practices.

ethical decision making are predicated on which ethical theory one is following. The law typically relies on juries to determine if an act is legal or illegal. Society determines whether an action is ethical or unethical. Since 2012, the Justice Department and the Securities and Exchange Commission has been investigating allegations that Walmart violated the Foreign Corrupt Practices Act (FCPA) by paying bribes to foreign government officials as it expanded around the world. Walmart has tried and failed to settle the investigation, costing the company more than $877 million. Today, Walmart acknowledges the allegation and says that it is cooperating.

However, discussions surrounding the probe have stalled over several issues, including the size of the potential penalties that Walmart will have to pay if it is found guilty. People familiar with the probe have said that another major sticking point has been Walmart's eligibility to continue accepting food stamps in its 5,300 Walmart and Sam's Club stores across the United States after a settlement is reached. It is now claimed by many knowledgeable people that Walmart has become an industry-leader in FCPA compliance best practices.[10]

Morals are the rules people develop as a result of cultural values and norms. Culture is a socializing force that dictates what is right and wrong. Moral standards may also reflect the laws and regulations that affect social and economic behavior. Thus, morals can be considered a foundation of ethical behavior.

Morals are usually characterized as good or bad. "Good" and "bad" have many different connotations.

One such connotation is "effective" and "ineffective." A good salesperson makes or exceeds the assigned quota. If the salesperson sells a new computer system or HDTV to a disadvantaged consumer—knowing full well that the person cannot keep up the monthly payments—is that still a good salesperson? What if the sale enables the salesperson to exceed his or her quota?

"Good" and "bad" can also refer to "conforming" and "deviant" behaviors. A doctor who runs large ads offering discounts on open-heart surgery would be considered bad, or unprofessional, because he or she is not conforming to the norms of the medical profession. "Good" and "bad" also express the distinction between law-abiding and criminal behavior. And finally, different religions define "good" and "bad" in markedly different ways. A Muslim who eats pork would be considered bad by other Muslims, for example. Religion is just one of the many factors that affect a businessperson's ethics. Academic researchers have examined how consumers react to the trade-offs between highly competent but less moral service providers and less competent but highly moral service providers. In their study, it was found that consumers valued competence more than morality.[11] In other words, purchasers of services want someone who can do the job right . . . even if that person might be a bit shady. For example, a house painting company that does excellent work but has had some legal problems in the past would be preferred over a mediocre painting company that has never had complaints or legal problems.

3-3a Morality and Business Ethics

Today's business ethics actually consist of a subset of major life values learned since birth. The values businesspeople use to make decisions have been acquired through family, educational, and religious institutions.

Ethical values are situation specific and time oriented. Everyone must have an ethical base that applies to conduct in the business world and in personal life. One approach to developing a personal set of ethics is to examine the consequences of a particular act. Who is helped or hurt? How long do the consequences last? What actions produce the greatest good for the greatest number of people? A second approach stresses the importance of rules. Rules come in the form of customs, laws, professional standards, and common sense. "Always treat others as you would like to be treated" is an example of a rule.

3-3b Ethical Decision Making

Ethical questions rarely have cut-and-dried answers. Studies show that the following factors tend to influence ethical decision making and judgments:[12]

- **Extent of ethical problems within the organization:** Marketing professionals who perceive fewer ethical problems in their organizations tend to disapprove more strongly of "unethical" or questionable practices than those who perceive more ethical problems. Apparently, the healthier the ethical environment, the more likely it is that marketers will take a strong stand against questionable practices.

- **Top management's actions on ethics:** Top managers can influence the behavior of marketing professionals by encouraging ethical behavior and discouraging unethical behavior. Researchers found that when top managers develop a strong ethical culture, there is reduced pressure to perform unethical acts, fewer unethical acts are performed, and unethical behavior is reported more frequently.[13]

- **Potential magnitude of the consequences:** The greater the harm done to victims, the more likely that marketing professionals will recognize a problem as unethical.

- **Social consensus:** The greater the degree of agreement among managerial peers that an action is harmful, the more likely that marketers will recognize a problem as unethical. Research has found that a strong ethical culture among coworkers decreases observations of ethical misconduct. In companies with strong ethical cultures, 9 percent of employees observed misconduct, compared with 31 percent in companies with weaker cultures.[14]

- **Probability of a harmful outcome:** The greater the likelihood that an action will result in a harmful outcome, the more likely that marketers will recognize a problem as unethical.

- **Length of time between the decision and the onset of consequences:** The shorter the length of time between the action and the onset of negative consequences, the more likely that marketers will perceive a problem as unethical.

- **Number of people to be affected:** The greater the number of persons affected by a negative outcome, the more likely that marketers will recognize a problem as unethical.

As you can see, many factors determine the nature of an ethical decision. Drugstore chain CVS has ceased all

Mark Wilson/Getty Images News/Getty Images

Former CEO of Turing Pharmaceuticals Martin Shkreli (right) testifies during a House Oversight and Government Reform Committee hearing on unethical practices in the prescription drug market.

sales of cigarettes and other tobacco products, becoming the first national pharmacy to do so.

CVS President and CEO Larry Merlo said that the decision better aligned the company with its purpose of improving customer health, and that it was simply the right thing to do.[15] On the other hand, consider Turing Pharmaceuticals founder Martin Shkreli. In 2015, Shkreli acquired the rights to the drug Daraprim, a decades-old lifesaving medication for parasitic infections, then hiked the price from $13.50 a pill to $750.00 a pill. He vowed to repeat this strategy with other so-called orphan drugs.[16] This is an extreme case, and pharmaceutical manufacturers claim, "He is not one of us."[17] It is true that brand-name drugs are far more expensive in the United States than they are in Canada, Europe, and most of the developed world. In many developed countries, drug prices are controlled by the government.[18] The net result is that American consumers of prescription medicines are paying the research and development costs for new drugs for the entire world. While Shkreli's actions were not illegal at the time, other actions he took were unethical and illegal. In a New York fraud trial, in 2017 Shkreli was found guilty of lying to investors in two failed hedge funds and cheating them out of millions of dollars. He was sentenced to seven years in prison. Fortunately for him, he is in a minimum-security facility with no bars or security towers. Rooms (not cells) have no locks and there are racquet ball courts and volleyball courts, large areas for team sports, pool tables, a music room and facilities for arts and crafts.[19] It is sometimes referred to as "ClubFed."

3-3c Ethical Guidelines and Training

In recent years, many organizations have become more interested in ethical issues. Yet interest and action are not always the same thing. A new global study of 800 executives found that only 44 percent had a chief ethics officer.[20] However, the study *did* find that 82 percent of senior leadership communicates with employees on ethics points. The communication often takes place via email. In addition, many companies of various sizes have developed a **code of ethics** as a guideline to help marketing managers and other employees make better decisions. Creating ethics guidelines has several advantages:

- A code of ethics helps employees identify what their firm recognizes as acceptable business practices.

- A code of ethics can be an effective internal control of behavior, which is more desirable than external controls such as government regulation.

- A written code helps employees avoid confusion when determining whether their decisions are ethical.

- The process of formulating the code of ethics facilitates discussion among employees about what is right and wrong and ultimately leads to better decisions.

Ethics training is an effective way to help employees put good ethics into practice. The Ethics Resource Center's National Business Ethics Survey (NBES) found that 81 percent of companies provide ethics training. Only 33 percent of workers observed misconduct in large companies with effective ethics and compliance programs (E&C). Compare this to a misconduct rate of 51 percent among all large companies and 62 percent among large companies that do not have effective E&C programs. Pressure for workers to compromise standards was just 3 percent among big companies with effective E&C programs, versus 23 percent among those without an effective program.[21] Still, simply giving employees a long list of *dos* and *don'ts* does not really help employees navigate the gray areas or adapt to a changing world market. In Carson City, Nevada, all governmental lobbyists are required to attend a course on ethics and policy before they can meet with lawmakers. The training outlines exactly how and when lobbyists are allowed to interact with lawmakers and how to report any money they spend. A clear understanding of ethical expectations

code of ethics a guideline to help marketing managers and other employees make better decisions is essential to an industry like lobbying, where illicit—often illegal—actions are taken to promote individual causes.

Because artificial intelligence (AI) is becoming so pervasive in marketing interactions with consumers, it must also be taught ethical decision making. Already Microsoft, Adobe, and IBM, along with smaller firms and start-ups, are developing ethical guidelines and best practices for their AI use.

Type *gymnast* into Google's image search, and the vast majority of the top results are female, as are the results for *nurse*. The term *parents* shows almost exclusively heterosexual couples. The results to these searches are driven by AI, which isn't explicitly taught to discriminate. Rather, these prejudices are the result of the data submitted to the AI algorithm.[22] "One of the things that's really endemic to AI and to machine-learning technology is that it has to learn from data, and the data we train it with comes from people," notes Susan Etlinger, an AI industry analyst for Altimer.[23]

THE MOST ETHICAL COMPANIES Each year, *Ethisphere* magazine (targeted toward top management and focused on ethical leadership) examines more than 5,000 companies in 30 separate industries, seeking the world's most ethical companies. It then lists the top 100.

The magazine uses a rigorous format to identify true ethical leadership. A few of the selected winners are shown in Exhibit 3.1.

3-3d Ethics in Other Countries

Ethical beliefs often vary between cultures. Certain practices, such as the use of illegal payments and bribes, are far more acceptable in some places than in others, though enforced laws are increasingly making the practice less accepted. One such law mentioned earlier, the **Foreign Corrupt Practices Act (FCPA)**, was enacted because Congress was concerned about U.S. corporations' use of illegal payments and bribes in international business dealings. This act prohibits U.S. corporations from making illegal payments to public officials of foreign governments to obtain business rights or to enhance their business dealings in those countries. The act has been criticized for putting U.S. businesses at a competitive disadvantage. Many contend that bribery is an unpleasant but necessary part of international business, especially

> **Foreign Corrupt Practices Act (FCPA)** a law that prohibits U.S. corporations from making illegal payments to public officials of foreign governments to obtain business rights or to enhance their business dealings in those countries

EXHIBIT 3.1	SELECTED WINNERS OF THE WORLD'S MOST ETHICAL COMPANIES	
Company	**Industry**	**Country**
3M	Industrial manufacturing	USA
Adobe	Application software	USA
Aflac	Accident and life insurance	USA
Baptist Health South Florida	Nonprofit health care providers	USA
Colgate-Palmolive	Consumer products	USA
Dell	Technology	USA
EDP	Energy and utilities	Portugal
Grupo Bimbo	Food, beverages, and agriculture	Mexico
Illy	Food, beverages, and agriculture	Italy
Kao	Health and beauty	Japan
L'Oreal	Health and beauty	France
Mars	Food, beverages, and agriculture	USA
Natura	Health and beauty	Brazil
Parsons	Engineering and design	USA
Salesforce	Application software	USA
USAA	Insurance	USA
Volvo	Automotive	Sweden

Source: "The 2018 World's Most Ethical Companies Honorees List," http://worldsmostethicalcompanies.ethisphere.com/honorees (accessed October 5, 2018).

in countries such as China, where business gift giving is widely accepted and expected. But, as prosecutions under the FCPA have increased worldwide, some countries are implementing their own antibribery laws. For example, even though China is among the three countries with the most international corruption cases prosecuted under the FCPA, the country is working to develop its own antibribery laws. President Xi Jinping has vigorously attacked corruption and bribery in the Communist party, and has swept tens of thousands out of office. Many have been sent to prison.[24]

corporate social responsibility (CSR) a business's concern for society's welfare

stakeholder theory ethical theory stating that social responsibility is paying attention to the interest of every affected stakeholder in every aspect of a firm's operation

3-4 CORPORATE SOCIAL RESPONSIBILITY

Corporate social responsibility (CSR) is a business's concern for society's welfare. This concern is demonstrated by managers who consider both the long-range best interests of the company and the company's relationship to the society within which it operates.

3-4a Stakeholders and Social Responsibility

An important aspect of social responsibility is **stakeholder theory**. Stakeholder theory says that social responsibility is paying attention to the interest of every affected stakeholder in every aspect of a firm's operation. The stakeholders in a typical corporation are shown in Exhibit 3.2.

EXHIBIT 3.2 STAKEHOLDERS IN A TYPICAL CORPORATION

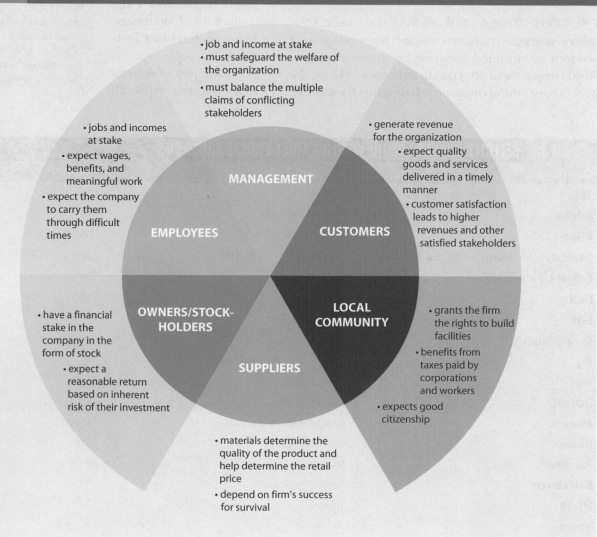

- job and income at stake
- must safeguard the welfare of the organization
- must balance the multiple claims of conflicting stakeholders

- jobs and incomes at stake
- expect wages, benefits, and meaningful work
- expect the company to carry them through difficult times

- generate revenue for the organization
- expect quality goods and services delivered in a timely manner
- customer satisfaction leads to higher revenues and other satisfied stakeholders

MANAGEMENT

EMPLOYEES

CUSTOMERS

OWNERS/STOCK-HOLDERS

LOCAL COMMUNITY

SUPPLIERS

- have a financial stake in the company in the form of stock
- expect a reasonable return based on inherent risk of their investment

- grants the firm the rights to build facilities
- benefits from taxes paid by corporations and workers
- expects good citizenship

- materials determine the quality of the product and help determine the retail price
- depend on firm's success for survival

- *Employees* have their jobs and incomes at stake. If the firm moves or closes, employees often face a severe hardship. In return for their labor, employees expect wages, benefits, and meaningful work. In return for their loyalty, workers expect the company to carry them through difficult times.

- *Management* plays a special role, as they also have a stake in the corporation. Like employees, managers have their jobs and incomes at stake. On the other hand, management must safeguard the welfare of the organization. Sometimes this means balancing the multiple claims of conflicting stakeholders. For example, stockholders want a higher return on investment and perhaps lower costs by moving factories overseas. This naturally conflicts with the interests of employees, the local community, and perhaps suppliers.

- *Customers* generate the revenue for the organization. In exchange, they expect high-quality goods and services delivered in a timely manner. Customer satisfaction leads to higher revenues and the ability to enhance the satisfaction of other stakeholders.

- *The local community*, through its government, grants the firm the right to build facilities. In turn, the community benefits directly from local taxes paid by the corporation and indirectly by property and sales taxes paid by the workers. The firm is expected to be a good citizen by paying a fair wage, not polluting the environment, and so forth.

- *Suppliers* are vital to the success of the firm. For example, if a critical part is not available for an assembly line, then production grinds to a halt. The materials supplied determine the quality of the product produced and create a cost floor, which helps determine the retail price. In turn, the firm is the customer of the supplier and is therefore vital to the success and survival of the supplier. A supplier that fails to deliver quality products can create numerous problems for a firm. Takata is global supplier of vehicle airbags. The National Highway Traffic Safety Administration (NHTSA) has warned that tens of millions of cars with Takata airbags face an increased chance of exploding during a collision after prolonged exposure to hot and humid conditions. NHTSA says that there are 50 million defective Takata airbags in 37 million U.S. vehicles. When the bags explode, they send shrapnel into the passengers. The NHTSA planned to recall more bags bringing the total to 70 million by December 2019. The defective bags have injured 180 people and caused 20 deaths by 2018. Automakers

There may be up to 50 million defective Takata airbags in American vehicles according to the National Highway Traffic Safety Administration.

such as Ford, Nissan, Toyota, and Mazda have paid out hundreds of millions of dollars to settle consumer loss claims.[25]

- *Owners* have a financial stake in the form of stock in a corporation. They expect a reasonable return based on the amount of inherent risk on their investment. Sometimes managers and employees receive a portion of their compensation in company stock. When Facebook went public, it created more than 1,000 employee millionaires. Through stock options, the company has created more billionaires under the age of 40 than any other company.[26]

3-4b Pyramid of Corporate Social Responsibility

One theorist suggests that total corporate social responsibility (CSR) has four components: economic, legal, ethical, and philanthropic. The **pyramid of corporate social responsibility** portrays economic performance as the foundation for the other three responsibilities (see Exhibit 3.3). At the same time that it pursues profits (economic responsibility), however, a business is expected to obey the law (legal responsibility); to do what is right, just, and fair (ethical responsibilities); and to be a good corporate citizen (philanthropic responsibility). These four components are distinct but together constitute the whole. Still, if the company does not make a profit, then the other three responsibilities are moot.

pyramid of corporate social responsibility a model that suggests corporate social responsibility is composed of economic, legal, ethical, and philanthropic responsibilities and that a firm's economic performance supports the entire structure

EXHIBIT 3.3 THE PYRAMID OF CORPORATE SOCIAL RESPONSIBILITY

Philanthropic responsibilities
Be a good corporate citizen.
Contribute resources to the community; improve the quality of life.

Ethical responsibilities
Be ethical.
Do what is right, just, and fair. Avoid harm.

Legal responsibilities
Obey the law.
Law is society's codification of right and wrong. Play by the rules of the game.

Economic responsibilities
Be profitable.
Profit is the foundation on which all other responsibilities rest.

3-5 ARGUMENTS FOR AND AGAINST SOCIAL RESPONSIBILITY

CSR can be a divisive issue. Some analysts believe that a business should focus on making a profit and leave social and environmental problems to nonprofit organizations and government. Economist Milton Friedman believed that the free market, not companies, should decide what is best for the world.[27] Friedman argued that when business executives spend more money than necessary—to purchase delivery vehicles with hybrid engines, pay higher wages in developing countries, or even donate company funds to charity—they are spending shareholders' money to further their own agendas. It would be better to pay dividends and let the shareholders give the money away if they choose.

On the other hand, CSR has an increasing number of supporters based on several compelling factors. One is that it is simply the right thing to do. Some people claim that societal problems, such as pollution and poverty-level wages, have been brought about by corporations' actions; it is the responsibility of business to right these wrongs. Businesses also have the resources, so businesses should be given the chance to solve social problems. For example, businesses can provide a fair work environment, safe products, and informative advertising.

A firm that is socially responsible tends to build trust in that organization. Even the smallest transactions in a free-enterprise society are based upon trust. Trust keeps society running. Just ordering a pizza requires faith that the dough will be well-made, that the pizzeria will not abuse the customer's credit card information, and that the delivery person will not eat the pizza. Trust makes the commitment of resources to an activity where its outcome depends upon the cooperative behavior of others[28]—in this case, the pizza maker, cashier, and delivery person.

Research has found that being socially responsible and training front line employees about social responsibility can have a positive impact on the firm. In a business-to-business environment, researchers found that social responsibility activities can raise customer trust and identification with the firm. These factors, in turn, build customer loyalty, which often leads to higher profits.[29]

Content employees tend to do their jobs better and offer improved customer service. A significant part of that contentment is respecting and admiring their firm, which adds meaning to their lives. Walmart has dozens of programs that target social responsibility. These include using renewable energy, influencing suppliers to make products and packaging more sustainable, and encouraging 2.6 million associates (employees) to directly help communities.[30]

If a customer has a bad experience with a firm, an active social responsibility program can dampen negative word of mouth and social media comments. Even corporations convicted of illegal acts can benefit from being socially responsible. The average fine levied against a firm convicted of bribery under the Foreign Corrupt Practices Act is 40 percent lower if the firm has a comprehensive social responsibility program.[31]

Another, more pragmatic, reason for being socially responsible is that if businesses do not act responsibly, then government will create new regulations and perhaps levy fines against them.

Finally, social responsibility can produce a direct profit. Smart companies can prosper and build value by tackling social problems. GlaxoSmithKline (GSK) is a 300-year-old pharmaceutical company. Its goal is not

PepsiCo's sustainable business philosophy, Performance with Purpose, is deeply engrained into the company's workplace culture. It is even included in PepsiCo's code of conduct, which every employee must sign and pledge to uphold. By 2025, PepsiCo will ask every supplier—down to the individual farm worker—to make that same pledge.

only to serve the wealthier nations of the West, but to serve developing nations around the world as well. The company spent some three decades developing a vaccine for malaria, which has devastated huge swaths of sub-Saharan Africa. (Pilot vaccination programs in the hardest-hit areas began in 2018.) GSK has also partnered with the government of Botswana on an ambitious HIV treatment program and is collaborating with the National Institutes of Health on a vaccine for the Zika virus.[32]

GSK is socially responsible but makes a profit at the same time—the company's operating profit in 2017 was over $10 billion.[33] Corporate leadership is confident that its strategy of slim profit margins on most products sold in the developing world and a huge, growing sales volume is a winning one.[34]

3-5a Growth of Social Responsibility

The social responsibility of businesses is growing around the world. Companies are coming under increasing pressure from governments, advocacy groups, investors, prospective employees, current employees, and consumers to make their organizations more socially responsible. In turn, firms are seeing social responsibility as an opportunity. A recent global study by Cone Communications found that 9 out of 10 consumers expect companies to do more than make a profit. The firms must also operate responsibly to address social and environmental issues. Global consumers echo this in their own

shopping behavior: 84 percent say they seek out socially responsible products. Nearly three quarters (72 percent) believe that their purchases make a moderate to significant impact on social and environmental issues. Four in five global consumers are willing to consume and/or purchase fewer products to preserve natural resources or buy a product from an unknown brand if it has strong corporate social responsibility commitments.[35]

UNITED NATIONS GLOBAL COMPACT One way that U.S. firms can do more is by joining the United Nations Global Compact (UNGC). The UNGC, the world's largest global corporate citizenship initiative, has seen its ranks swell over the past few years. In 2001—the first full year after its launch—just 67 companies joined, agreeing to abide by 10 principles (see "The Ten Principles of the United Nations Global Compact"). Today there are more than 10,000 corporate and 5,000 noncorporate participants.[36]

3-5b Becoming a B Corp

Smaller companies that wish to join the social responsibility and sustainability movement are turning to the B Corp movement. B Corps are for-profit companies certified by the nonprofit B Lab to meet rigorous standards of social and environmental performance, accountability, and transparency. Today, there is a growing community of over 2,650 Certified B Corps from 60 countries representing 150 different industries.[37] To become a B Corp Certified company, a firm must pass a 200-point assessment. Criteria include things like fair compensation for workers, how much waste the company produces, and the company's work with local businesses. Firms such as Patagonia, Ben & Jerry's, online crafts marketplace Etsy, and Danone have qualified. New Seasons Market, a 13-store grocery chain in Oregon, stamps the B Corp logo on all of its grocery bags and gives employees B Corp badges to wear. The logo helps attract socially minded shoppers and helps in recruiting new workers.

Elissa Loughman, Environmental Analyst for Patagonia, says:

> The Assessment incentivized us to quantitatively measure the performance of our programs. We provide several opportunities for employees to participate in environmental or social activism. But we didn't know how many employees participated and to what degree. The Assessment gathers all the information in one place, it allows us to really recognize our strengths as well as see where we have room for improvement.[38]

Ben & Jerry's is a B Corp Certified company.

SUSTAINABILITY A significant part of the B Impact Assessment is measuring a firm's sustainability. Sustainability is the idea that socially responsible companies will outperform their peers by focusing on the world's social, economic, and environmental problems. Sustainable companies view these problems as opportunities to build profits and help the world at the same time. Environmental sustainability is concerned with the physical environment. Environmentally sustainable companies believe that threats to the environment should be minimized or eliminated. For example, developing long-term sources of clean water improves health and preserves local ecosystems while creating a competitive advantage. Social sustainability means developing processes and structures that not only meet the needs of a current community, but benefit future generations as well. Building schools and providing means for children to attend those schools is an example of creating social sustainability. In a business context, economic sustainability is the efficient use of assets so that a company can continue operating profitably over time. A company cannot be socially or environmentally responsible if it goes out of business.

3-5c Green Marketing

An outgrowth of the social responsibility and sustainability movements is green marketing. Green marketing is the development and marketing of products designed to minimize negative effects on the physical environment or to improve the environment. One approach that firms use to indicate that they are part of the green movement is to use third-party eco-logos. Examples include the chasing-arrows recycling logo (the product is either recyclable or contains recycled materials); the Energy Star logo (the product is energy efficient); and Certified Organic (the U.S. Department of Agriculture created standards relative to soil quality, animal raising practices, pest and weed control, and the use of additives). These logos can enhance a product's sales and profitability.

Movement toward green marketing by manufacturers has not always been self-motivated. Powerful retailers including Walmart, Whole Foods, Target, and others have mandated sustainability requirements for their suppliers. Typically, these mandates have not taken place in a collaborative spirit but are implemented on a formal "Here is what we need you to do basis."[39] Even large manufacturers, such as Proctor and Gamble, Heinz Foods, and Colgate Palmolive feel compelled to comply. They can't afford the huge loss of shelf space if they don't.

Proctor and Gamble, whose products include Mr. Clean and Comet, and Reckitt Benckiser Group, the maker of Easy-Off oven cleaner, have been pressured by retailers to disclose—and in some cases remove—ingredients that are harmful to the environment and consumers. Government is getting into the sustainability movement as well. California has passed the Cleaning Product Right to Know Act that takes effect in 2020. Manufacturers of detergents and disinfectants will be required to list online any substances linked to harmful health effects.[40]

Nearly 4 in 10 Americans (about 93 million people) say that they are dedicated to buying green products and services. Green purchasing is driven by young adults (ages 18–34) and Hispanics; about half of the respondents in these groups report that they regularly seek out green products. Young adults are also more likely to be interested in a company's green practices and to avoid companies with poor environmental records.[41]

A European Commission study found that 77 percent of the respondents were willing to pay more for green products.[42] To benefit from consumers' willingness to pay more, some companies are promoting conventional products as green by adding a few green attributes. This is called greenwashing. Aquafina sold water in an "ECO-FINA Bottle" which was a conventional plastic bottle made with 50 percent

sustainability the idea that socially responsible companies will outperform their peers by focusing on the world's social problems and viewing them as opportunities to build profits and help the world at the same time

green marketing the development and marketing of products designed to minimize negative effects on the physical environment or to improve the environment

greenwashing Adding a minimal number of green product attributes in order to promote it as green less plastic. Dasani water was sold in a "Plant Bottle" but it was a plastic bottle made with 30 percent plant ingredients. Herbal Essences shampoo was promoted as "crafted with bio:renew" by adding an ingredient, histidine, that is derived from corn sugar but did not remove other chemicals found in conventional shampoos. Huggies "pure and natural" diapers were claimed to be made from organic cotton but only the outer shells were cotton. The inside was still similar to conventional diapers. Researchers have found that consumers have a negative attitude toward greenwashed products. Consumers also began to question the ethics of the firm's actions.[43]

For a product to be labeled "green," it must meet regulatory guidelines issued by the Federal Trade Commission (FTC).[44] Retailers Bed Bath and Beyond, Nordstrom, JCPenney, and Backcountry.com have been fined $1.3 million by the FTC for misleading environmental claims.[45] These and other companies are now barred from labeling and advertising rayon textiles as being made of bamboo. Jessica Rich, Director of the Bureau of Consumer Protection, says, "It's important for consumers to know that textiles marketed as environmentally friendly alternatives may not be a 'green' as they were led to believe."[46]

3-5d Leaders in Social Responsibility

Two names at the top of many social responsibility lists are Patagonia and Unilever. Patagonia, mentioned earlier in the chapter, is a private outdoor clothing manufacturer founded by Yvon Chouinard, but is now headed by Rose Marcario. Marcario worked in high tech and for a private equity company before landing at Patagonia. After arriving in 2008, one of her first acts was to switch the company's mailing packages to recyclable bags. On Black Friday of that year, the company ran one of its most famous ads, titled, "Don't Buy This Jacket." As part of its Worn Wear program, Patagonia employees 45 full-time repair technicians in Reno, Nevada. The company sends a biodiesel truck around the country to repair Patagonia clothing.

It's not always easy to think about profits and social responsibility at the same time, and Marcario is often tested. Activism is so ingrained in the company culture that it hosts an annual conference, called Tools for

Target is a leader in mandating sustainability requirements for its suppliers.

Unilever has sent employees to over 1,000 villages to encourage people to wash their hands.

Grassroots Activists, that brings together persons of all types, including many who work at Patagonia.[47] Though a noble effort, this initiative met some resistance in Japan, Patagonia's second-largest market after the United States. The problem, Marcario reported, was that what seemed like a gentle nudge in one culture was interpreted as mandatory in another. A number of Japanese stores had recently hosted civil-disobedience and nonviolence training before a protest at a nearby dam, and some employees felt like they were expected to get arrested to prove their loyalty to the company cause.[48]

Unilever is a $176 billion corporation, run by Paul Polman, who strongly believes in "doing well by doing good." That means making more money by acting virtuously. The firm sells environmentally friendly detergent, has installed thousands of water pumps in African villages, and removed gender stereotypes for Unilever's advertising. Since Polman took over in 2009, emissions, water usage, and trash have fallen by 43 percent, 38 percent, and 96 percent, respectively.[49] Unilever staffers have fanned out across India and Africa to install toilets, which will significantly reduce the incidence of infectious diseases. In Vietnam, Unilever employees have gone to over 1,000 villages to encourage people to wash their hands. For children, ages 8 to 10, they teach "the handwashing dance." It goes like this: "Rub your left palm with your right hand, then clap, now right, clap, up, down, thumbs, knuckles, clap. Then repeat, scrubbing vigorously." After the dance, the students are encouraged to pick up free Lifebuoy soap and P/S toothpaste at the school clinic. Naturally, it's all made by Unilever.[50]

cause-related marketing the cooperative marketing efforts between a for-profit firm and a nonprofit organization

3-6 CAUSE-RELATED MARKETING

A sometimes controversial subset of social responsibility is cause-related marketing. Often referred to as simply "cause marketing," it is the cooperative efforts of a for-profit firm and a nonprofit organization for mutual benefit. The for-profit firm hopes to generate extra sales, and the nonprofit in turn hopes to receive money, goods, and/or services. Any marketing effort that targets social or other charitable causes can be referred to as cause-related marketing. Cause marketing differs from corporate giving (philanthropy), as the latter generally involves a specific donation that is tax deductible, whereas cause marketing is a marketing relationship not based on a straight donation.

The popularity of cause-related marketing has grown to over $2.23 billion in 2019.[51] It's no wonder why: cause-related marketing creates good public relations and will often stimulate sales for the brand. One study found that 60 percent of consumers say brands should make it

Walgreens News @WalgreensNews   (Follow)

Atlanta is still holding the top spot in Walgreens #EveryOneCounts Hometown Challenge! Chicago moves into 4th place as residents are encouraged to rally to help end child poverty & boost their city for next week #RedNoseDay bit.ly/2jLoqgW

8:33 AM - 9 May 2018

5 Retweets 13 Likes

♡ 3   ⟲ 5   ♡ 13

Once a year Walgreens encourages customers to buy and wear red noses. The money raised goes to helping raise children out of poverty.

easier to see their values and positions on social issues at the point of sale.[52] Examples of cause-related marketing used by large companies are abundant. Ben & Jerry's ice cream created a "Scoop It Forward" campaign in partnership with Target and Volunteer Match. The program increased ice cream sales and raised funds for charity. For a number of years, it has raised money for the Global Fund to Fight AIDS on World AIDS Day. Starbucks donates 10 cents for every handcrafted beverage sold in their U.S. and Canadian stores. Walmart and Sam's Club have both supported the Children's Miracle Network Hospitals for almost 30 years. For six weeks each year, Walmart employees solicit donations for the cause at checkout. For a dollar or more, customers can put their name on a Miracle Worker balloon or dedicate it to a loved one.

Red Nose Day, which originated in the United Kingdom, is now doing very well in the United States. The six-week campaign is sponsored by Walgreens each year. The idea is for customers to purchase red noses and wear them for group pictures and other Red Nose Day fundraising events to spread awareness. The campaign stands out because of its fun and playful nature. Proceeds from the red nose sales go toward helping lift children out of poverty in the United States. In 2017, the campaign raised $18 million through the sale of over 12 million red noses at Walgreens.[53]

4 | The Marketing Environment

LEARNING OUTCOMES

After studying this chapter, you will be able to…

4-1 Discuss the external environment of marketing and explain how it affects a firm

4-2 Describe the social factors that affect marketing

4-3 Explain the importance to marketing managers of current demographic trends

4-4 Explain the importance to marketing managers of growing ethnic markets

4-5 Identify consumer and marketer reactions to the state of the economy

4-6 Identify the impact of technology on a firm

4-7 Discuss the political and legal environment of marketing

4-8 Explain the basics of foreign and domestic competition

Rawpixel.com/Shutterstock.com

4-1 THE EXTERNAL MARKETING ENVIRONMENT

Perhaps the most important decisions a marketing manager must make relate to the creation of the marketing mix. Recall from Chapters 1 and 2 that a marketing mix is the unique combination of product, place (distribution), promotion, and price strategies. The marketing mix is, of course, under the firm's control and is designed to appeal to a specific group of potential buyers, or target market. A **target market** is a group of people or organizations for which an organization designs, implements, and maintains a marketing mix intended to meet the needs of that group, resulting in mutually satisfying exchanges.

Managers must alter the marketing mix because of changes in the environment in which consumers live, work, and make purchasing decisions. Also, as markets mature, some new consumers become part of the target market; others drop out. Those who remain may have different tastes, needs, incomes, lifestyles, and buying habits than the original target consumers. Technology, and the resulting change in buying habits, meant that consumers no longer have those "Kodak Moments" when taking pictures of a birthday party or an exceptional sunset. Digital photography has sent 35-millimeter film the way of the horse and buggy. Unfortunately, shifting technology ultimately led to the bankruptcy of Eastman Kodak. Smartphones and Amazon have disrupted numerous industries. Artificial intelligence (AI) is on the way to changing our lives and many businesses.

Although managers can control the marketing mix, they cannot control elements in the external environment that continually mold and reshape the target market. Controllable and uncontrollable variables affect the target market, whether it consists of consumers or business purchasers. The uncontrollable elements in the center of the environment continually evolve and create changes in the target market. Think, for example, about how social media have changed your world. In contrast, managers can shape and reshape the marketing mix to influence the target market. That is, managers react to changes in the external environment and attempt to create a more effective marketing mix in order to satisfy customers and remain competitive.

4-1a Understanding the External Environment

Unless marketing managers understand the external environment, the firm cannot intelligently plan for the future. Thus, many organizations assemble a team of specialists to continually collect and evaluate environmental information, a process called *environmental scanning*. The goal in gathering the environmental data is to identify future market opportunities and threats.

UNDERSTAND CURRENT CUSTOMERS AND DESIRES OF POTENTIAL CUSTOMERS Mastercard, Visa, American Express, and others are locked in a battle to maintain existing customers and attract new ones. A credit card is essentially a commodity and card issuers have to continually differentiate their offerings. We have seen card issuers add more and more benefits—airline miles, cash back, club access, concierge service, and even gift products. But does adding more benefits win more customers? And do new benefits have much actual value to cardholders? Interestingly, new research has found that over 80 percent of consumers were not fully aware of all the benefits their card offers.[1] Some basic benefits tend to be important to all cardholders. Beyond these key benefits, each cardholder wants a package of rewards that is relevant to their lifestyle. Value is the dominant feature desired. This means a card's annual fee, the interest rate charged, amount of cash back, and length of the zero-interest rate promotional period. Also, two other must-have basic benefits are identity theft monitoring and 24/7 customer service.[2]

Beyond the critical features of good value, protection, and support, the youngest card holders, ages 18–24, are most focused on technology offerings. They want a great mobile app and tap-to-pay availability. Persons 25–34 are more likely interested in lifestyle benefits such as airline miles and travel rewards.

> **target market** a group of people or organizations for which an organization designs, implements, and maintains a marketing mix intended to meet the needs of that group, resulting in mutually satisfying exchanges

Young adults want a credit card beyond good value, protection, and customer support. They want a great mobile app and tap-to-pay availability.

They tend to have more time and opportunity to take advantage of these benefits. Consumers between 35 and 54 show a strong preference for value above anything else. This group is most likely to be managing responsibilities and expenses for children and perhaps aging parents. Persons 55 years of age or older are the most loyal to their current cards. Features that may push some older cardholders to consider new cards are better travel benefits and "making it easier" such as tap-to-pay and online chat support.[3]

Armed with this type of information, American Express can segment its market and create personalized promotions that offer key desired benefits to each target segment. Knowledge of customer needs and desires, by age segment, saves the credit card company promotional funds, retains existing customers, and helps acquire new ones.

UNDERSTAND HOW CONSUMER DECISIONS ARE MADE IN A RAPIDLY CHANGING ENVIRONMENT

Successful firms realize that creating value for the customer is the key to larger profits and market share. A rapidly changing business environment and continually evolving technology make understanding customer decision-making critical to long run success. Mars Petcare is a pet food company that owns brands such as Pedigree and Whiskas. Although the firm originally sold primarily through retailers, it has made important investments into pet health care solutions, veterinary clinics, and more recently, a Fitbit-like device for dogs. These strategic changes have now enabled the firm to know

more about not only their clients (i.e., pets) but also the pet owners, which translates into more opportunities to precisely design and deliver marketing messages, in addition to offering better products. In other words, Mars Petcare finds itself in a much-changed business environment wherein it can now offer better value proposition to consumers through multiple channels of distribution (online and offline).[4]

Today, companies must operate in an environment that is becoming more demographically diverse, with customer needs and expectations becoming more individualized, and the requirement of ethnic groups more distinct. This means that individual wants and desires such as convenience, personalization, environmental concerns, and social connections have come to the forefront. Companies are reshaping their marketing mix to meet these challenges. Target is teaming with Shipt to offer same-day grocery deliveries, thus providing more convenience. Spotify enables each person to listen to only the music that they want to hear via its personalized playlist recommendations. Many consumers find Tesla's direct-to-consumer sales model preferable to dealing with auto showroom salespeople. Also, Lego is using sugarcane as a sustainable alternative to plastic in its toys, which appeals to consumers who are concerned about our environment.[5]

IDENTIFY THE MOST VALUABLE CUSTOMERS AND UNDERSTAND THEIR NEEDS

Often, 20 percent of a firm's customers produce 80 percent of the firm's revenue. An organization must understand what drives that loyalty and then take steps to ensure that those drivers are maintained and enhanced. Airlines use loyalty programs to satisfy and retain their best customers. For example, persons who fly more than 100,000 miles a year on American Airlines are called Executive Platinum members. They are granted priority boarding and seating, free domestic upgrades, no fees for checked luggage, coupons for international upgrades, and other benefits.

Target has teamed with Shipt to offer same-day grocery delivery.

UNDERSTAND THE COMPETITION Successful firms know their competitors and attempt to forecast those competitors' future moves. Competitors threaten a firm's market share, its profitability, and its very existence. Competitors that crop up because of new technologies can create a challenging competitive environment for traditional old-line firms. Uber and Lyft, for example, have made life difficult for traditional taxi cab companies. Unhappy with the lack of regulation facing these app-driven ride-sharing services, cab drivers in Paris, Delhi, Barcelona, and London went on strike, closing down these major cities' central business districts. The Yellow Cab Company was forced to file for bankruptcy in San Francisco after Uber and Lyft literally drove it out of the market. This story is not uncommon. Increased competition from American Furniture Warehouse, Living Spaces, and Conn's sent The Room Store into bankruptcy. With 463 stores, Sports Authority was one of America's largest sporting goods chains. However, the company filed for bankruptcy because of competition from Dick's Sporting Goods, which offered better in-store merchandise presentation, more modern technology, and shop-in-shops for fast-growing brands like Nike and Under Armour.

 ## 4-2 SOCIAL FACTORS

Social change is perhaps the most difficult external variable for marketing managers to forecast, influence, or integrate into marketing plans. Social factors include our attitudes, values, and lifestyles. Social factors influence the products people buy; the prices paid for products; the effectiveness of specific promotions; and how, where, and when people expect to purchase products.

4-2a American Values

A *value* is a strongly held and enduring belief. America's traditional core values have strongly influenced Americans' attitudes and lifestyles:

- **Self-sufficiency:** Every person should stand on his or her own two feet.

- **Upward mobility:** Success will come to anyone who gets an education, works hard, and plays by the rules.

- **Work ethic:** Hard work, dedication to family, and frugality are moral and right.

- **Equality:** No one should expect to be treated differently from anybody else.

- **Individualism:** Each person is unique and special.

- **Achievement orientation:** People should get things done by setting goals, planning, and measuring results.

- **Helping others:** Those with disabilities who cannot work should be provided with the means to live with dignity. Persons with disabilities who can work and the disadvantaged should be provided with the facilities and training to enable them to become productive members of society.

- **The environment.** The environment must be protected for future generations.

These core values still hold for a majority of Americans today. A person's values are key determinants of what is important and not important, what actions to take or not to take, and how one behaves in social situations.

People typically form values through interaction with family, friends, and other influencers such as teachers, religious leaders, and politicians.

Values influence our buying habits. Today's consumers are demanding, inquisitive, and discriminating. No longer willing to tolerate products that break down, they are insisting on high-quality goods that save time, energy, and often calories. U.S. consumers rank the characteristics of product quality as: (1) reliability, (2) durability, (3) easy maintenance, (4) ease of use, (5) a trusted brand name, and (6) a low price. Shoppers are also concerned about nutrition and want to know what is in their food; many have environmental concerns as well.

4-2b The Growth of Component Lifestyles

People in the United States today are piecing together component lifestyles. A lifestyle is a mode of living; it is the way people decide to live their lives. With component lifestyles, people are choosing products and services that meet diverse needs and interests rather than conforming to traditional stereotypes.

In the past, a person's profession—for instance, banker—defined his or her lifestyle. Today, a person can be a banker and also a gourmet, fitness enthusiast, dedicated single parent, and Internet guru. Each of these lifestyles is associated with different goods and services and represents a different target audience. Component lifestyles increase the complexity of consumers' buying habits. Each consumer's unique lifestyle can require a different marketing mix.

> **component lifestyles** the practice of choosing goods and services that meet one's diverse needs and interests rather than conforming to a single, traditional lifestyle

tommaso lizzul/Shutterstock.com

4-2c How Social Media Have Changed Our Behavior

There are now over 4 billion people around the world using the Internet. Africa has seen the fastest growth rates—almost 20 percent per year.[6] More than 3 billion people use social media each month. More than 9 out of 10 people access social media via their mobile devices.[7] Americans now spend an average of 6 hours a day online.[8] Beyond accessing the Internet via computer, tablet, or smartphone, today many people have embraced the Internet of Things. The number of "things" (clothing, thermostats, washing machines, fitness trackers, and light bulbs, for example) connected to the Internet exceeds the number of people on earth. Dutch start-up Sparked is developing a wireless sensor for cattle. When one is sick or pregnant, the sensor sends a message to the farmer. Similarly, Corventis makes a wireless cardiac monitor that doctors can use to monitor people for health risks in real time. And this is just the beginning—the Internet of Things has the potential to change life as we know it in nearly every area of life.

Social media are making profound changes in the way we obtain and consume information—consumers are interacting; sharing beliefs, values, ideas, and interests; and, of course, making purchases at a dizzying rate. These media have even played a major role in the beginnings of revolutions!

What exactly are social media? They are web-based and mobile technologies that allow the creation and exchange of user-generated content. Social media encompasses a wide variety of content formats—you have most likely used sites such as Facebook, YouTube, Twitter, Tumblr, Instagram, and Pinterest, each of which serves a different function (see Chapter 18). These media have changed the way we communicate, keep track of others, browse for products and services, and make purchases. Social networking is part of regular life for people of all ages. Facebook now has more than 2.2 billion users worldwide. The largest group of Facebook users are ages 25 to 34.[9] Other leading social networks, in order of number of users, are Instagram, Facebook Messenger, Twitter, Pinterest, Snapchat, Reddit, and Tubmlr.[10]

Online reviews play an increasingly important role in consumer behavior, as more Americans opt to purchase items online. Yet when someone rants about a bad experience, it may make the author feel better, but it is actually counterproductive for reviewers seeking to influence potential buyers. A study of 400,000 reviews at Apple's App Store found that when someone writes a flaming, angry review or a gushing, fawning review they are perceived as responding emotionally and not logically, At the same time, reviewers who are overly flat in expressing themselves may be perceived as unhelpful. Readers were much more likely to view a review as helpful when it contained a moderate amount of emotional words and exclamations but not when it was overly emotional.[11]

HOW FIRMS USE SOCIAL MEDIA Social networking has changed the game when it comes to opinion sharing. Now, consumers can reach many people at once with their views—and can respond to brands and events in real time. In turn, marketers can use social media to engage customers in their products and services. Marketers have learned that social media are not like network television, where a message is pushed out to a mass audience. Instead, social media enable firms to create conversations with customers and establish meaningful connections. In other words, social media marketing can humanize brands. Marketers for brands like Absolut Vodka and Hellman's Mayonnaise post custom videos about their products to Facebook and then invite feedback. Marketers will continue to make social media a priority. They plan to boost their social media investments from 10.6 percent to 20.9 percent over the next five years.[12] Not only do firms target customers and potential customers, but they strive for employee involvement as well. Maersk Line, a Denmark-based shipping company, used social media to share the company's rich history. Photos from the company's digital archive were selected to tell the company's story, including video of Clara Maersk and Maersk ships involved in the rescue of more than 3,000 Vietnamese fugitives in 1975. In the first 11 months, Maersk Line attracted more than 400,000 people to its Facebook page—many of whom were its own employees participating in this public forum who not only learned a great deal about the company but shared photos from Maersk ships around the world.[13]

Internal social media networks can improve employee communication across roles, functions, and geographies, especially in large complex organizations. For example, Best Buy created Best Buy Connect, which aggregates tweets, feeds, and blogs from across the Best Buy digital communities and delivers them to a centralized location where employees can learn from one another to solve customer problems.[14]

With 9 out of 10 large and medium-sized U.S. companies now active on social networks, firms are scrambling to build effective social marketing programs. Nearly 80 percent of these companies now have dedicated social media teams to create persuasive marketing campaigns and stay on top of emerging social media trends.

Videos posted on social media are becoming the new normal for marketing a brand. Today, more than 500 million hours of videos are watched on YouTube each day and nearly half of people watch over an hour of video on Facebook or YouTube every week. In fact, more video content has been uploaded to social media over the past 30 days than major U.S. TV networks have created over the past 30 years.[15] This growth in video on social media has ultimately shifted the way we communicate. Marketers know that four times as many consumers would prefer to watch a video about a product than read about it. Branded content can be seen across Facebook, Twitter, Snapchat, and Instagram. Over half of marketers worldwide say that video content, compared to all other types of content, results in the best return on investment (ROI).[16]

One study of videos promoting brands found that 60 percent of the viewers were primarily interested in informative content; 55 percent enjoyed entertaining content, and similarly, 46 percent wanted funny content.[17] Successful branded videos not only entertain but are also informative, thought-provoking, and perhaps inspiring.

Airbnb coined the term "vacation mom" to describe what your mother is like on vacation. They created a heart-warming video of travelers sharing their favorite vacation stories that included their mothers, with each traveler sharing funny things their mom does that qualifies her as a "vacation mom." The result was 2.4 million views and a lot of good feelings for the vacation rental giant.[18]

The cell phone case industry is extremely competitive. Peel sells thin phone cases, with the major selling points being that they are functional and stylish. They use Facebook videos to tell their story of what separates them from everyone else.[19]

When Volvo introduced its new XC60, the company used a three-minute video showing a conversation with a mother and daughter (who tries to imagine her whole life in front of her), on the daughter's first day of school. Traveling. Falling in love. Buying a house. Having her own daughter. Through the video, you watch her imagination come to life. But as soon as she steps out of the house to go to school, another woman in a new XC60 almost runs her down. The automated braking system of this XC60 manages to avert this life-changing collision. The video ends with "One of the safest cars ever made— we celebrate everything that can happen in life, when accidents don't. Because sometimes the moments that never happen, matter the most."[20] The video received wide acclaim and reinforces the image that Volvo builds safe cars.

Like the Volvo video, a number of firms use social media to build goodwill for their products instead of trying to stimulate immediate sales. Travel bag manufacturer eBags knows that its customers are savvy travelers, so its Facebook page keeps customers coming back with tips to make traveling even easier. eBags regularly offers useful content on its page about packing, travel hygiene, and other travel-related tips.

Social media marketing programs are now being used by a vast majority of large and medium size firms.

4-3 DEMOGRAPHIC FACTORS

Another uncontrollable variable in the external environment—also extremely important to marketing managers—is demography, the study of people's vital statistics, such as age, race and ethnicity, and location. Demographics are significant because the basis for

> **demography** the study of people's vital statistics, such as age, race and ethnicity, and location

any market is people. Demographic characteristics are strongly related to consumer buying behavior in the marketplace.

4-3a Population

People are directly or indirectly the basis of all markets, making population the most basic statistic in marketing. There are more than 7.6 billion people alive today. China has the largest population, with 1.4 billion persons; India is second, with 136 billion.[21] The U.S. population is slightly over 327 million. Older Americans have moved to retirement communities like the Villages in Central Florida. This area is one of the nation's fastest-growing metropolitan areas; Frisco, Texas, a 25-minute drive from downtown Dallas. The city of around 180,000 people has award-winning schools and is home to the Dallas Cowboys. Frisco had a population of under 6,000 in 1990. Median household income is $117,000 with is far higher than the national average of $55,352.[22] Other fast-growing areas are McKinney, Texas; Irving, California; Murfreesboro, Tennessee; and Cary, North Carolina.[23]

Rural areas, meanwhile, posted their first-ever net loss of population in 2012. The populations of the U.S. rural regions—from the Great Plains to the Mississippi Delta, to rural New England—are aging. These populations are not receiving many young transplants to replace those who die or migrate to urban areas. In many parts of the country, multigenerational households are increasingly common.

GROWTH OF THE SINGLES POPULATION Singles account for 45 percent of all U.S. adults. Predictions are that a third of Americans now in their 20s will never wed, well above the historical norm of just below 20 percent.[24] Research shows that singles tend to have more friends than married people, are more likely to volunteer their time, and are as healthy as or healthier than their married peers. When it comes to finances, however, the picture isn't as rosy.

Singles make an average of $8,800 less in personal income than their married peers ($52,900 versus $61,700). They're much less likely to own a home than married couples (58 percent versus 90 percent). Four in 10 working singles spend their entire paycheck each month with no money contributed to savings (versus 37 percent of married couples).[25]

Population is a broad statistic that is most useful to marketers when broken into smaller, more specific increments. For example, age groups present opportunities to focus on a section of the population and offer

Generation Z, comprised of 67 million consumers, has never known a world without social media or smartphones.

opportunities for marketers. These groups are called tweens, teens, Millennials (or Generation Y), Generation X, and Baby Boomers. Each cohort has its own needs, values, and consumption patterns.

TWEENS America's tweens (ages 9 to 12) are a population of more than 20 million. With access to information, opinions, and sophistication well beyond their years (and purchasing power to match), these young consumers are directly or indirectly responsible for sales of over $200 billion annually. Tweens themselves spend about $51 billion per year, and the remainder is spent by parents and family members for them.[26]

With such spending power, this age group is very attractive to many markets. In addition, many of the products that they purchase as tweens are products that they will continue to purchase for decades. Mobile devices account for 41 percent of all screen time for tweens.[27] Apps like Snapchat, Kik Messenger, and Instagram have resulted in young appetites for quick, tailored engagement that is also sharable. Many merchants are striving to be more relevant in this capacity of sharing experiences among younger consumers. Macy's One Below concept in Manhattan, for example, offers young female consumers a hair blowout bar, 3D printed accessories, and smartphone charging stations. It targets 13- to 22-year-olds, but these services could easily be extended to aspirational tweens through limited events like parties.[28]

Tweens live in a period of transition. They are bridging being a kid and being a teenager. They still not only look back at the safe world of childhood but also look forward to the unknown but exciting world ahead.

With so many needs, marketers have targeted a broad array of products and services at tweens. These include a tween chef cook-off, Pottery Barn Kids products, nail art kits, a variety of smartphones, a mountaineering club, PBS Kids Digital, Digital Kids Media, 360Kid, and the list goes on. Tweens are also at the age when they begin to establish their own sense of style, which is largely influenced by social media and the Internet. At the same time, they are establishing a young lifestyle and want to make their own looks to reflect it. This means they are likely to be more interested in what is on trend and what is relevant to their idols than in what name is on the label.

GENERATION Z Marketers are talking more and more about **Generation Z** these days—and with good reason. This cohort was born between 1997 and 2012, so some members are in their teenage years while others are children and young adults. This group consists of 67 million consumers, most of whom have never known a world without social media or smartphones. Ninety-five percent of Gen Z have a smartphone or access to one. Forty-five percent say that they are online on a nearly constant basis.[29] Until recently, Facebook was the most popular social media with Gen Zers. The most popular online platform today is YouTube, followed by Instagram, Snapchat, and then Facebook.[30] For the most part, Gen-Zers tend to use similar platforms regardless of their demographic characteristics. However, those living in households earning less than $30,000 a year tend to prefer FaceBook.[31]

With growing biracial and minority populations, Gen Z embraces multiculturalism as a touchstone of who they are. Gen Zers are a more cautious class; they steer away from risky behaviors and toward more sensible careers and choices. Statistics show lower rates of underage drinking and higher seat-belt use by this group, reflecting their cautiousness.

About 17 million members of Generation Z are now adults and starting to enter the U.S. workforce, and employers haven't seen a generation like this since the Great Depression. They came of age during recessions, financial crises, war, terror threats, school shootings, and under the constant glare of technology and social media. The broad result is a hardened generation that has faced economic and social turbulence.[32] They are interested in making good money but less interested in owning their own businesses. Gen Zers entering the workforce tend to be competitive and pragmatic. Almost half are a race other than non-Hispanic white. The oldest Gen Zers are more interested in making work a central part of their lives and are more willing to work overtime than most millennials (discussed next).[33] This is important, as older

generations are now retiring in record numbers and unemployment is at historic lows. Gen Zers will fill large gaps in the workforce.

Gen Zers are expected to account for about 40 percent of all consumers by 2020.[34] Those Gen Zers still in their teen years spend the largest percentage of their income (24 percent) on food. This is followed by beauty products and video games. Female Gen Z teenagers spend around $368 a year on skin care. Traditional retailers continue to lose Gen Z shoppers as more purchases are being made online. Popular brands among teen Gen Zers are Vans, Supreme, and Nike.[35]

Gen Zers rely on social media when shopping. A recent study found that 80 percent of Gen Zers claimed that their purchases were influenced by social media.[36] When shopping in brick and mortar retailers, Gen Zers will usually have their smartphones in hand. They compare prices while in the store, read product reviews, and may end up purchasing online in order to get a cheaper price. More brands are offering apps that give in-store shoppers instant savings while in the store and inviting them to special events. Plus-size retailer Torrid hosts contests featuring special hashtags to promote its products. The firm hosted a contest on Instagram to promote Torrid swimwear. By posting a photo with the hash tag #TheseCurves, customers entered a contest to attend Torrid's Pool Party in Los Angeles.[37]

MILLENNIALS **Millennials**, or Generation Y, are people born between 1981 and 1996. Initially, Millennials were a smaller cohort than Baby Boomers. However, due to immigration and the aging of the Boomer generation, the 81 million Gen Yers in the United States passed the Boomers in total population in 2010.

Millennials are currently in two different stages of the life cycle. The youngest members of Gen Y, born in 1996, have entered young adulthood. By contrast, the oldest Gen Yers, born in 1981, turned 38 years old in 2019. They have started their careers, and many have become parents for the first time, leading to dramatic lifestyle changes. They care for their babies rather than go out, and they spend money on baby products. Although many Millennials have young children, older Gen Yers' kids are entering the teenage years. Interestingly, 59 percent of Millennials are single and have never been married.[38] Millennials in general are delaying marriage longer than any generation before them, in spite of evidence suggesting that many Millennials intend to marry at some point. Domestic partnerships are

Generation Z people born between 1997 and 2012

Millennials people born between 1981 and 1996

P & G found millennials are more likely to do maintenance cleaning.

much more common than among older cohort groups.[39] In 2018, Millennials had more purchasing power than Baby Boomers (discussed later), and by 2020, Millennials will have a collective spending power of $1.4 trillion.[40]

The oldest Millennials have moved up the managerial ranks and have entered their 20 years of peak earning power. Yet both younger and older Millennials tend to look at unemployment a bit differently than do older generations. Gen Yers are more idealistic and eager to please, and they want to do their jobs well. Yet staying at one company for a lifelong career is not high on the list.

Millennials clearly do not view money as the key to happiness, yet they also seem to worry about it quite a bit. One survey of Millennials found that 62 percent described themselves as very "happy" and 65 percent said their life is "meaningful," 69 percent said they want to get over the "anxiety" about money, and only a third said they were "satisfied" with their financial life. At the same time, 98 percent of this generation also said feeling "financially secure" is important to them, along with feeling physically (97 percent) and mentally (97 percent) healthy.[41]

Yet 88 percent said they see success as more about being "happy" and less about "material prosperity" and a quarter of Millennials said, "I don't care about money."

When asked to identify activities they actively engage in to make themselves happier, spending time with family (72 percent) and friends (61 percent) and helping others (59 percent) were highest.[42]

Correspondingly, regarding areas in life that bring satisfaction, the three with the highest levels of satisfaction among Millennials were family relationships (56 percent), intellectual life (52 percent), and recreation and hobbies (50 percent).[43]

Over a third of U.S. home buyers are millennials. But they aren't buying in the cities that they have called home since beginning to work. While millennials still prefer to rent in urban centers, those who want to own a home are mostly moving to the suburbs. The reason is usually not a preferred lifestyle change but simply a matter of cost.[44] A vast majority of those making a transition to the suburbs are first-time homeowners with little knowledge about home maintenance. The Scotts Miracle-Gro Co. has started offering gardening lessons for young homeowners that cover basic tips—really, really basic, like making sure sunlight can reach plants.[45]

P&G, which makes Swiffer, found that Millennials clean their homes differently from older generations. "We find that the younger generation is a bit more crunched for time and less likely to do a big, deep clean," says Kevin Wenzel, an associate brand director for P&G's North America surface care business.[46]

Briggs & Stratton collaborated with Toro Co. to introduce the Mow N'Stow foldable mover, which takes up 70% less room than standard mowers. It is designed to appeal to owners of starter homes, which often have smaller garages. The Mow N'Stow also doesn't require users to know how to prime, choke, or change the oil of its engine.[47]

Millennials have a complex relationship with technology. The constant feedback loop of the Internet is compelling and can be helpful but can also be exhausting. Millennials have a first-generation relationship with technology. They're just old enough to know that the systems they've become adept at are new (Gen Z sees technology as a given—like the weather).

So, while Millennials enthusiastically use technology, they're ambivalent about letting that aspect of life take over. About two-thirds admit they waste time on the Internet often or all the time but roughly the same percentage say they often/all the time spend time with family and have face-to-face conversations.[48]

What Millennials' ambivalence means for brands and businesses that want to connect with them via technology and social channels is that there's an opportunity to do more than just show up in the right social channels. Recognizing Millennials' ambivalence about technology, and their hunger to experience "real" connections as well as digital ones, might encourage offering not just digital content but live events or opportunities for people to touch, talk, and connect in person. It could mean recognizing that the highest-tech solution is not always the one that most millennials will want.[49]

GENERATION X Generation X—people born between 1965 and 1980—consists of 65 million U.S. consumers. It was the first generation of latchkey children—products of dual-career households or, in roughly half the cases, of divorced or separated parents. Gen Xers often spent more time without adult support and guidance than any other age cohort. This experience made them independent, resilient, and adaptable.

Gen Xers are in their primary earning years and have acquired a disproportionate amount of spending power relative to the size of their group. Gen Xers have higher average incomes than their Millennial and Baby Boomer counterparts. Higher incomes have contributed to Gen Xers' optimistic outlook on the future.

Saving money is a major priority for Gen Xers, who tend to be frugal and seek value when making purchases. About half note that providing for their children's college expenses is a major goal. They also want to become financially independent, buy or upgrade a home, and provide an estate for their heirs. Fifty-one percent plan to keep working during their normal retirement years because they haven't yet reached their financial goals.[50] The average retirement savings of Gen X is just $35,000. Also, adults in their mid-40s to mid-50s have higher levels of credit card debt than any other age group.[51]

Many have a parent or family member living with them, and others support aging parents. They place a high value on education and knowledge and tend to do a significant amount of research before making a major purchase. Marketers need to provide a lot of accurate information about their products—particularly about why their goods or services are a great value.

Gen Xers tend not to be overly concerned with fashion. They are core customers at mainstream stores like Old Navy and Kohl's. Because many Gen Xers own homes, practical items like Nest thermostats are popular purchases. When Gen Xers do splurge, it is often at stores like Home Depot and Pottery Barn.

BABY BOOMERS There are approximately 75 million **Baby Boomers** (persons born between 1946 and 1964) in the United States. With average life expectancy at an all-time high of 77.4 years, more and more Americans age 50 consider middle age a new start on life. The size of the Baby Boom cohort group has been decreasing in size since 2012. The pace of this decline will accelerate as the Baby Boomers grow older. When the first Baby Boomers turned 65 in 2011, there were 77 million of them. In 2030, when the Baby Boomers will be between 66 and 84 years old, that number is projected to drop to 60 million.

While Baby Boomers' current incomes are relatively low because many have retired, they accumulated a substantial amount of wealth over their working years. Baby Boomers account for nearly 50 percent of all consumer packaged good sales, 77 percent of prescription drug sales, 80 percent of leisure travel spending, and 41 percent of all new car purchases.[52]

Boomers enjoy going to the movies; they purchase a third of all movie theater tickets. They also spend a disproportionate amount on pets when compared with other cohorts. Gen X and Millennials typically eat at quick-service restaurants, but Boomers have a strong preference for full-service restaurants.

Like other cohort groups, Boomers believe that price and quality are very important when making purchase decisions. Baby Boomers tend to be influenced more by traditional advertising, sales reps, and word-of-mouth recommendations than other groups. Yet they are also very active in seeking product information online. Boomers tend to use laptops and tablets more than smartphones when conducting product research. While Boomers make fewer product purchases online than do some other cohorts, the same is not true for services. Boomers now make most of their travel purchases online.

Baby Boomers spend more time online than watching TV. Eighty-two percent who use the Internet have at least one social media account.[53] Facebook and LinkedIn are the leading platforms. They spend about 1 hour 48 minutes a day on social media networking.[54] Notably, baby boomers are more likely to share content than any other generation.

Marketers targeting Baby Boomers must avoid the perception that Boomers are old. Words such as "senior," "elderly," and "aged" can quickly drive away potential customers. Boomers today are active and feel entitled to enjoy the good life. It is best to target Boomers based on their lifestyles, purchase behaviors, and core values, such as healthy eating, exercise, and family. Simplifying instructions for product assembly and use makes life easier for Boomers. Enlarging font size may enable Boomers to avoid reaching for their reading glasses. Realizing that holding up a heavy paint can and reaching for your glasses at the same time can be tough, Sherwin Williams completely redesigned its can with a clean, crisp look, and large fonts.

4-4 GROWING ETHNIC MARKETS

The American demographic profile is rapidly changing as racial and ethnic groups continue to grow. The minority population today is about

Generation X people born between 1965 and 1980

Baby Boomers people born between 1946 and 1964

180 million. The United States will flip completely to a majority–minority makeup in 2045, meaning that non-Hispanic whites will make up less than 50 percent of the population. During that year, whites will comprise 49.7 percent of the population in contrast to 24.6 percent Hispanics, 13.2 percent for African Americans, 7.9 percent for Asians, and 4.6 percent for multiracial populations. Because minorities as a group are younger than whites, the minority–white tipping point comes earlier for younger age groups. For whites under 18 years old, they will become a minority in 2020; in contrast whites over 60 years old will not reach the tipping point until after 2060.[55] Hawaii, California, New Mexico, and Texas all have minority non-Hispanic white populations today.

4-4a Marketing to Hispanic Americans

With a population of more than 58 million, Hispanics make up the largest U.S. minority. The term *Hispanic* encompasses people from many different Spanish cultures regardless of race. Nearly 60 percent of Hispanic Americans are of Mexican descent. Puerto Ricans, the next largest group, make up just under 10 percent of Hispanics. Other groups, including Central Americans, Dominicans, South Americans, and Cubans, each account for less than 5 percent of all Hispanics. Most Hispanics in the United States today were born here. Still, racial lines are blurring. A quarter of Hispanic marriages now involve a non-Hispanic partner.

Youth is the defining characteristic of the U.S. Hispanic population. The average age is 28 years old.[56] Eighty-one percent of those under 35 were born in America. Intermarriage is high among younger Hispanics. About 28 percent ages 18 to 35 are married to someone who is not Hispanic. English use is on the rise among young Hispanics. Forty-one percent are English dominant and 40 percent claim to be bilingual.[57]

Hispanics spend more than $95 billion a year on consumer-packaged goods. Some of their more popular grocery brands include Chobani yogurt and drinks, Good Thins, Hillshire meats and snacks, Cracker Barrel Macaroni and Cheese, and Birds Eye Steamfresh Veggie Made products.[58]

Hispanics make up the largest group to use mobile devices for any type of transaction, from banking to watching movies. Companies like Metro PCS, Boost Mobile, and Verizon have substantially increased their marketing budgets targeted toward Hispanics. Eighty-two percent of Hispanics use a smartphone and are more habitual social network users than are their non-Hispanic counterparts.[59] Hispanics are heavy social media users. The most popular are Facebook, YouTube, Instagram,

and Snapchat. Hispanics spend nearly 66 percent more of their time watching videos on their smartphones than the rest of the total market. They also share content much more often than non-Hispanics. Additionally, Hispanics are twice as likely as non-Hispanics to purchase the products that they share.[60]

Hispanic Millennials still embrace parts of their original culture, mostly in the areas of family, music, and food. Yet they also look forward to being successful in business and perhaps owning their own company. Hispanic Millennials tend to be more open-minded about relationships than their parents. Yet they willingly accept future family obligations and the difficulties of supporting parents and grandparents.

Hispanic Millennials in the United States are particularly prone to taking a bilingual, bicultural approach to their media consumption. Forty percent of Hispanic Millennials consume an equal amount of Spanish and English media. Spending on Hispanic media now tops $9.2 billion in the United States.[61] The leading advertisers targeting Hispanics are Procter & Gamble, AT&T, and L'Oreal. McDonald's has a history of successfully promoting its products to Hispanics. It even has a separate marketing director for the Hispanic market. One very successful McDonald's campaign, "First Customer," tells the story of a Hispanic teenager's first job through the lens of his parents, who are bursting with pride. The campaign made people laugh, and served as a reminder that McDonald's is the first real work experience for thousands of teenagers.[62]

Toyota's recent campaign for its new Camry made an ad specifically for Spanish-speaking customers. It shows a man driving down a highway in a Camry when

Hispanics are much more likely to watch social media videos and to share content than the general market.

he gets a call from his mother. Instead of answering immediately, he hesitates—eventually declining the call to focus on the joy of driving the car. The goal was to create an ad that reflected the sense of responsibility, especially to family, that many in the Hispanic community feel. The idea was also to note the desire to make some changes—or "soaring with sense" as the ad agency called it.[63]

4-4b Marketing to African Americans

African Americans make up around 13 percent of the U.S. population. They are young—53 percent are under the age of 35—giving them a strong influence on the latest trends, especially with regard to music and pop culture.[64] Higher academic achievement has translated into increases in household income. Today, almost 23 percent of African Americans age 25 or older hold a bachelor's degree or higher.[65]

Anchored by a rich heritage, African Americans believe in strong cultural connections. They expect brands to support social causes, and there is a general expectation that brands reflect their values. As consumers, African Americans' buying patterns focus on family and cooking ingredients tied to cultural traditions. African Americans are voracious radio listeners. African Americans are also heavy users of technology, and 83 percent own a smartphone. Seventy-nine percent of African American women agree that pursuing good health is important. In recent years, there has been a 40 percent increase in the number of African Americans shopping at health food stores (like Whole Foods, Trader Joe's, and Fresh Market). The unemployment rate of African Americans has been steadily declining since 2010. The number of African Americans earning over $100,000 has almost doubled since 2006. This is mainly due to the growth in the number of African Americans in management and professional occupations. Yet, the labor force participation rate remains lower for black workers relative to the overall population. Also, the median household income for a black family is about $20,000 less than all other families in America.[66]

African Americans are more religious than whites by many measures of religious commitment. For instance, three-quarters of black Americans say religion is very important in their lives, compared with smaller shares of whites (49 percent) and Hispanics (59 percent); African Americans also are more likely to attend services at least once a week and to pray regularly. 79 percent of African Americans are self-identified as Christian, compared to 70 percent of the whites and 77 percent of Hispanic Americans.[67]

With $162 billion in buying power, African American Millennials make innovative use of mobile technology and have gained increasing clout across all forms of media. African Americans represent about 14 percent of all Millennials, and African American Millennials represent a quarter of the total black population. The top five markets (by population) for African American Millennials are New York, Atlanta, Chicago, Washington, DC, and Miami/Fort Lauderdale. African American Millennials are 25 percent more likely than other Millennials to say that they are among the first of their friends/colleagues to try new technology products. Fifty-five percent of black Millennials report spending at least an hour each day on social networking sites, while 29 percent spend a minimum of three hours each day. Twenty-eight percent of Twitter users are African American. They also make up a significant percentage of U.S. Gamers. Seventy-three percent of African Americans are gamers, compared with 66 percent of the total population.[68]

African American adults have shown a high degree of brand loyalty to companies like Ford. In turn, Ford has a continuing marketing campaign aimed at maintaining and building loyalty among its black consumers. Ford's "Men of Courage" program has grown rapidly, with the likes of music and tech investor Troy Carter, former Detroit mayor Dave Bing, NFL all-pro DeAndre Levy, and others challenging black men across the country to download #MenOfCourage digital toolkits so they can host gatherings to create positive social change. Through this program, black men across the country unite on Martin Luther King Jr. Day to tell their stories and develop strategies to challenge stereotypes while improving their economic and social status. In 2018, more than 2,000 Men of Courage toolkits had been downloaded.[69]

sirtravelalot/Shutterstock.com

By many measures, African Americans are more committed to religion than whites or Hispanic Americans.

4-4c Marketing to Asian Americans

The Asian American population has reached more than 22 million in 2019. U.S. births have been the primary driving force behind the increase in the Hispanic and African American populations. By contrast, Asian American population growth has been fueled primarily by immigration. Thirty-one percent of Asian Americans were foreign-born.[70] California and Hawaii are home to the largest Asian American populations. Asian Americans, who still represent only 7 percent of the U.S. population, have the highest average family income of all groups. At $110,523, it exceeds the average U.S. household income by roughly $48,000.[71] Fifty-two percent of Asian Americans have a bachelor's degree, compared to 35 percent of the general population.[72] Because Asian Americans are younger (the average age is 34), better educated, and have higher incomes than average, they are sometimes called a "marketer's dream." In 2018, Asian American buying power was over $1 trillion. This group outspent the average consumer in personal insurance, apparel, and housing.[73] Asian American eating habits tend to be healthier than those of the rest of the population. They are less likely to allow junk food into their homes and are more likely to eat organic foods. Many Asian Americans buy fresh seafood more frequently than do the rest of the population. Twenty-eight percent of Asian Americans reside in a multigenerational household, resulting in a diverse spectrum of purchases based on age, health, and dietary habits.[74]

Asian Americans outpace non-Hispanic whites and other groups in ownership of the latest digital devices and are also more likely to use their digital devices to purchase products online, listen to music and radio, watch TV or movies, as well as other daily lifestyle functions.[75]

Although Asian Americans embrace the values of the larger U.S. population, they also hold on to the cultural values of their particular subgroup. Consider language: many Asian Americans, particularly Koreans and Chinese, speak their native tongue at home (though Filipinos are far less likely to do so). Cultural values are also apparent in the ways different groups make big-ticket purchases. In Japanese American homes, husbands alone make large purchase decisions nearly half the time; wives decide only about 6 percent of the time. In Filipino families, however, wives make these decisions a little more often than their husbands do, although, by far, most decisions are made by husbands and wives jointly or with the input of other family members.

Asian Americans like to shop at stores owned and managed by other Asian Americans. Small businesses such as flower shops, grocery stores, and appliance stores are often best equipped to offer the products that Asian Americans want. For example, at first glance, the Hannam Chain supermarket in Los Angeles's Koreatown seems like any other grocery store. But next to the Kraft American singles and the State Fair corn dogs are jars of whole cabbage kimchi. A snack bar in another part of the store cooks up aromatic mung cakes, and an entire aisle is devoted to dried seafood.

4-5 ECONOMIC FACTORS

In addition to social and demographic factors, marketing managers must understand and react to the economic environment. The three economic areas of greatest concern to most marketers are consumers' incomes, inflation, and recession.

4-5a Consumers' Incomes

For four years in a row, through 2019, Americans have seen their household incomes rise. The latest figures show an average annual household income of $61,372.[76] The areas where incomes have grown the most are San Diego; Richmond, Virginia; San Jose; Denver; and Nashville. Cities with the greatest declines were Hartford, Connecticut; Cleveland; Baltimore; San Antonio; and Raleigh, North Carolina.[77] Since 2013, Hispanic household incomes have grown 21 percent. This is followed by African Americans at 8 percent, non-Hispanic whites at 7 percent, and Asian Americans at 6.7 percent.[78]

U.S. employers are boosting benefits faster than wages, which gives them more flexibility to cut back total compensation in case the economy goes into a recession. From June 2009 to June 2018, bonus and supplemental pay rose 59 percent, retirement benefits 42 percent, paid leave 29 percent, and health and other insurance 28 percent.[79] Some of the companies offering bonuses were AT&T, Comcast, American Airlines, and Southwest Airlines. Because of the growth in benefits and wages, the poverty rate in America fell from 14.8 percent in 2014 to 12.3 percent in 2018.[80] The main reasons that poverty fell were that workers had higher take home pay and more people had jobs. The longest expansion since 1854 ended in February 2020 due to the Covid 19 pandemic. The expansion lasted 128 months.

Education is the primary determinant of a person's earning potential. For example, just 1 percent of workers with only a high school education earn over $100,000 annually. By comparison, 13 percent of college-educated workers earn six figures or more. People with a bachelor's degree take home an average of 38 percent more than those with just a high school diploma. Over a lifetime, an individual with a bachelor's degree will earn more than twice as much total income as a non–degree holder.[81]

4-5b Purchasing Power

Even when incomes rise, a higher standard of living does not necessarily result. Increased standards of living are a function of purchasing power. **Purchasing power** is measured by comparing income to the relative cost of a standard set of goods and services in different geographic areas, usually referred to as the *cost of living*. Another way to think of purchasing power is income minus the cost of living (i.e., expenses). In general, a cost-of-living index takes into account housing, food and groceries, transportation, utilities, health care, and miscellaneous expenses such as clothing, services, and entertainment. When examining the average household income by state, and then adjusting it for the cost of living, purchasing power varies substantially from state to state. A high average household income does not necessarily translate into high household purchasing power. California has one of the highest household incomes but the high cost of living erodes buying power, moving it to the midrange of all the states. The states with the greatest household purchasing power are Alaska, Maryland, New Hampshire, North Dakota, Virginia, and Wyoming. The states at the lower end of average household purchasing power are Mississippi, New York, New Mexico, Florida, and West Virginia. Some states, such as Mississippi, have a relatively low cost of living, but a low average household income still places them toward the bottom of the list.[82]

When income is high relative to the cost of living, people have more discretionary income. That means they have more money to spend on nonessential items (in other words, on wants rather than needs). This information is important to marketers for obvious reasons. Consumers with high purchasing power can afford to spend more money without jeopardizing their budget for necessities like food, housing, and utilities. They also have the ability to purchase higher-priced necessities—for example, a more expensive car, a home in a more expensive neighborhood, or a designer handbag versus a purse from a discount store.

4-5c Inflation

Inflation is a measure of the decrease in the value of money, generally expressed as the percentage reduction in value since the previous year, which is the rate of inflation. Thus, in simple terms, an inflation rate of 5 percent means you will need 5 percent more units of money than you would have needed last year to buy the same basket of products. If inflation is 5 percent, you can expect that, on average, prices have risen by about 5 percent since the previous year. Of course, if pay raises are matching the rate of inflation, then employees will be no worse off in terms of the immediate purchasing power of their salaries.

Often, periods of economic growth stimulate inflation. However, America's inflation rate has remained relatively low during the current period. The rate in late 2018 was 2.7 percent.[83] When inflation is ultra-high, it is referred to as "hyperinflation." The International Monetary Fund predicted that inflation would hit 1 million percent in Venezuela at the beginning of 2018.[84] The South American nation's economy has been steadily collapsing since the crash of oil prices in 2014, which left it unable to maintain a socialist system of subsidies and price controls. The world has seen inflation like this only in Germany in 1923 and Zimbabwe in the late 2000s.

In creating marketing strategies to cope with inflation, managers must realize that, regardless of what happens to the seller's cost, the buyer is not going to pay more for a product than the subjective value he or she places on it. No matter how compelling the justification might be for a 10 percent price increase, marketers must always examine its impact on demand. Many marketers try to hold prices level for as long as is practical.

4-5d Recession

A **recession** is a period of economic activity characterized by negative growth. More precisely, a *recession* is defined as occurring when the gross domestic product falls for two consecutive quarters. Gross domestic product (GDP) is the total market value of all final goods and services produced during a period of time. The 2020 pandemic recession resulted in the unemployment rate increasing 10.3 percent from March to April 2020 to a record high of 14.7 percent. This is the highest rate and the largest over-the-month increase in the history of the Bureau of Labor Statistics. The Bureau has been keeping records since January 1948. By the end of April 2020, 23.1 million people had become unemployed. Federal, state, and local restrictions on businesses and quarantines resulted in furloughs and terminations in companies of all sizes. This has forced millions of Americans to turn to food banks, apply for government aid, or to stop paying rent and other bills. Congress approved nearly $3 trillion in funds to help businesses, unemployment

purchasing power a comparison of income versus the relative cost of a standard set of goods and services in different geographic areas

inflation a measure of the decrease in the value of money, expressed as the percentage reduction in value since the previous year

recession a period of economic activity characterized by negative growth, which reduces demand for goods and services aid, and to receive a relief check. By May 2020, unemployment had fallen to 13.3 percent as 2.5 million jobs were added. This was mostly due to states reopening their economies. The profound jolt of the business lockdowns and the quarantines has impacted many areas of marketing. These will be addressed throughout this course.

4-6 TECHNOLOGY AND INNOVATION

Technological success is based on innovation, and innovation requires imagination and risk taking. Bringing new technology to the marketplace requires a corporate structure and management actions that will lead to success. Great corporate leaders must embed innovation into the lifeblood of the company. Managers should hire employees with a tolerance for risk. Then, workers must be told not to fear innovation failure. Not everything works the first time. Some of the greatest innovations in recent years, such as 3-D printing, hydraulic fracturing, quantum computing, autonomous vehicles, and artificial intelligence, all had setbacks before a successful product was created.

Existing businesses often have difficulty adjusting and competing with disruptive (game-changing) technologies. McKinsey and Company, a global consulting firm, recognizes four stages that an existing firm may go through when faced with a disruptive technolody.[85] Stage one occurs when a new technology comes on the market but is yet to be disruptive. This stage is called "Signals Amidst the Noise." Most incumbent firms don't feel much, if any, impact on their core businesses at this stage, so management is simply not motivated to act. Only the most perceptive old-line companies will take action. A company that *does* take action at this stage must disrupt long-standing beliefs about how to make money in the industries where it competes. In order to compete with Amazon and other online retailers, Target recently acquired delivery service Shipt to offer same-day delivery. Best Buy is using its crowdsourcing service DeLiv to also offer the same service.

In stage two, "Change Takes Hold," the core technology and economic factors of the disruptive force are validated. This is the stage at which old-line companies need to establish footholds in the new technology. As the McKinsey authors say, "The idea is to act before one has to."[86] At this point, the disruptive technology still does not have a major impact on the bottom line of the incumbent firms. Even as online classified ads for cars and real estate began to take off, most newspapers simply stood by.

basic research pure research that aims to confirm an existing theory or to learn more about a concept or phenomenon

Stage three is called "The Inevitable Transformation." This is the stage at which the future is pounding at the door. If established companies had the foresight to begin creating small new ventures in stage two, they need to aggressively shift resources to these ventures in stage three. And if they did nothing in stage two but maintain the status quo, now is the time to make a major reallocation of resources to the disruptive technology in order to create a new, and perhaps sole, economic engine for the firm. Faced with the disruptive technology of online retail entering phase three, Best Buy changed its whole philosophy of doing business. One thing the company has that Amazon does not is over 1,000 big-box stores. It saw the benefit of using them as showrooms, which they call "showcases." And they decided to open their showcases to high-tech firms as well. Best Buy was among the first chains to feature Apple boutiques. Next came Samsung showcases and then Microsoft. Amazon and Google received space to display their smart-home technologies. These firms essentially pay rent to Best Buy. The company completely revamped its website and supply chain and began offering price-matching. The Geek Squad is evolving to become in-home advisors. For example, they will come to your home for free and teach you how to ask Alexa questions.[87]

"Adapting to the New Normal" is the last stage. At this stage, the disruption has reached the point at which companies must accept the fact that the industry has fundamentally changed. Firms that were slow to react must either restructure, consolidate, or go bankrupt. Kodak declared bankruptcy in 2012 after failing to capitalize on the market's migration from film to digital cameras. Yellow Cab of San Francisco declared bankruptcy not long after Uber and Lyft came to town. Old-line companies that were too slow or otherwise failed to react to new disruptive technologies are now a footnote in the history books. Old-line banks may find themselves on perilous grounds if they don't adapt to accelerating changes in technology. A financial technology firm in China has developed an app for borrowing money on the fly while shopping. The app senses your voice and passes it to online algorithms for identity recognition; other algorithms fan out and query your bank accounts, credit history, and social-media profile; further intelligent algorithms weigh all these and a suitable credit offer appears on your phone. All within seconds.[88]

4-6a Research

The United States, historically, has excelled at both basic and applied research. **Basic research** (or *pure* *research*) attempts to expand the frontiers of knowledge but is not aimed at a specific, pragmatic problem. Basic research aims to confirm an existing theory or to learn more about a concept or phenomenon. For example, basic research might focus on high-energy physics. **Applied research**, in contrast, attempts to develop new or improved products. The United States has dramatically improved its track record in applied research. For example, the United States leads the world in applying basic research to aircraft design and propulsion systems. Many companies, particularly small and medium-sized firms, cannot afford the luxury of basic research.

The United States became a global leader in research and development (R&D) spending in the 20th century, funding as much as 69 percent of annual global R&D after World War II. Expenditures continue to rise with funding primarily by business, the federal government, and institutions of higher eduction.[89] In 2018, R&D expenditures reached $177 billion, a 13 percent increase over the previous year. The National Institutes of Health, the National Science Foundation, the Department of Energy, and NASA's science programs were all major beneficiaries.[90]

4-6b Stimulating Innovation

Companies attempting to innovate often limit their searches to areas they are already familiar with. This can help lead to incremental progress but rarely leads to a dramatic breakthrough. Disruptive innovation requires firms to invest time, money, and, most importantly, commitment. The cost of basic research has continued to grow. Equipment has generally become more expensive and, relatedly, exclusive—fewer people have access to it. And just as we've moved from single computers to supercomputers, we've moved from a culture of individual researchers making breakthroughs to one of massive teams of highly educated and compensated experts attempting to solve far more complicated problems.[91]

Finding new disruptive innovations has been described as being like prospecting for oil. Within a given field, you get most of the oil out, but then it gets really expensive to get the rest. Researchers have been pumping out oil from information technology for a long time, so perhaps it's time to find a new field. One possibility is genomics, with many new applications, thanks to the gene-editing tool known as Crispr.[92] This new tool allows scientists to snip and edit DNA in order to treat and cure gene disease and mutation in humans, plants, and animals.

> "Adapt or Perish, now as ever, is nature's inexorable imperative."
>
> —H. G. WELLS

4-7 POLITICAL AND LEGAL FACTORS

Business needs government regulation to protect innovators of new technology, the interests of society in general, one business from another, and consumers. In turn, government needs business because the marketplace generates taxes that support public efforts to educate our youth, pave our roads, protect our shores, and the like.

Every aspect of the marketing mix is subject to laws and restrictions. It is the duty of marketing managers or their legal assistants to understand these laws and conform to them, because failure to comply with regulations can have major consequences for a firm. Sometimes just sensing trends and taking corrective action before a government agency acts can help avoid regulation.

4-7a Federal Legislation

Federal laws that affect marketing fall into several categories of regulatory activity: competitive environment, pricing, advertising and promotion, and consumer privacy. The key pieces of legislation in these areas are summarized in Exhibit 4.1. The primary federal laws that protect consumers are shown in Exhibit 4.2. The Patient Protection and Affordable Care Act, commonly called Obamacare, has had a significant impact on marketing since it was signed into law in 2010. A few key provisions of the Act are that:

- Large employers must offer coverage to full-time workers.

- Workers cannot be denied coverage.

- A person cannot be dropped when he or she is sick.

- A worker cannot be denied coverage for a preexisting condition.

- Young adults can stay on their parents' plans until age 26.

In 2018, several important changes were made to the Affordable Care Act (ACA). One new rule adds

applied research research that attempts to develop new or improved products

EXHIBIT 4.1 PRIMARY U.S. LAWS THAT AFFECT MARKETING

Legislation	Impact on Marketing
Sherman Act of 1890	Makes trusts and conspiracies in restraint of trade illegal; makes monopolies and attempts to monopolize illegal.
Clayton Act of 1914	Outlaws discrimination in prices to different buyers; prohibits tying contracts (which require the buyer of one product to also buy another item in the line); makes illegal the combining of two or more competing corporations by pooling ownership of stock.
Federal Trade Commission Act of 1914	Created the Federal Trade Commission to deal with antitrust matters; outlaws unfair methods of competition.
Robinson-Patman Act of 1936	Prohibits charging different prices to different buyers of merchandise of like grade and quantity; requires sellers to make any supplementary services or allowances available to all purchasers on a proportionately equal basis.
Wheeler-Lea Amendments to FTC Act of 1938	Broadens the Federal Trade Commission's power to prohibit practices that might injure the public without affecting competition; outlaws false and deceptive advertising.
Lanham Act of 1946	Establishes protection for trademarks.
Celler-Kefauver Antimerger Act of 1950	Strengthens the Clayton Act to prevent corporate acquisitions that reduce competition.
Hart-Scott-Rodino Act of 1976	Requires large companies to notify the government of their intent to merge.
Foreign Corrupt Practices Act of 1977	Prohibits bribery of foreign officials to obtain business.

exemptions from the requirement that most consumers must be insured. People living in areas where there is only one insurer selling ACA plans can qualify for an exemption. About half of U.S. counties have only one ACA insurer. Also, the government no longer requires that insurers provide a standardized set of benefits. Finally, the federal government is turning over to the 39 states that rely on the federal insurance exchange, HealthCare.gov, responsibility for ensuring that marketplace plans have enough doctors in their networks.[93]

Also in 2010, Congress passed the Dodd–Frank Wall Street Reform and Consumer Protection Act, which brought sweeping changes to bank and financial market regulations. The legislation created the Consumer Financial Protection Bureau (CFPB) to oversee checking accounts, private student loans, mortgages, and other financial products. The agency deals with unfair, abusive, and deceptive practices. Some groups have expressed concerns that the CFPB is assembling massive databases on credit cards, credit monitoring, debt cancellation products, auto loans, and payday loans. CFPB officials claim that they need the information to make effective rules and enforce those policies. One way or another, the CFPB has certainly had a significant impact on several U.S. businesses—the bureau has overhauled mortgage lending rules, stopped abusive debt collectors, prosecuted hundreds of companies, and extracted nearly $12 billion from businesses in the form of canceled debts and consumer refunds. Recently, Wells Fargo bank was fined $1 billion for requiring mandatory insurance for auto loans. The bank was also fined for having student loan practices that increased costs and unfairly penalized borrowers.[94]

4-7b State and Local Laws

Legislation that affects marketing varies state by state. Oregon, for example, limits utility advertising to 0.5 percent of the company's net income. California has forced industry to improve consumer products and has enacted legislation to lower the energy consumption of refrigerators, freezers, and air conditioners. Several states, including California and North Carolina, are considering levying a tax on all in-state commercial advertising.

Many states and cities are attempting to fight obesity by regulating fast-food chains and other restaurants. For example, California and New York have passed a law banning trans fats in restaurants and bakeries, New York City chain restaurants must now display calorie counts on menus, and Boston has banned trans fats in restaurants. New York City enacted a law prohibiting restaurants from selling soft drinks larger than 16 ounces, but the ban was overturned a day before it was to go into effect.

4-7c Regulatory Agencies

Although some state regulatory bodies actively pursue violators of their marketing statutes, federal regulators generally have the greatest clout. The Consumer Product Safety Commission, the Consumer Financial Protection Bureau (discussed in Section 4-7a), the Federal Trade Commission, and the Food and Drug Administration are the four federal agencies most directly and

EXHIBIT 4.2 PRIMARY U.S. LAWS PROTECTING CONSUMERS

Legislation	Impact on Marketing
Federal Food and Drug Act of 1906	Prohibits adulteration and misbranding of foods and drugs involved in interstate commerce; strengthened by the Food, Drug, and Cosmetic Act (1938) and the Kefauver-Harris Drug Amendment (1962).
Federal Hazardous Substances Act of 1960	Requires warning labels on hazardous household chemicals.
Kefauver-Harris Drug Amendment of 1962	Requires that manufacturers conduct tests to prove drug effectiveness and safety.
Consumer Credit Protection Act of 1968	Requires that lenders fully disclose true interest rates and all other charges to credit customers for loans and installment purchases.
Child Protection and Toy Safety Act of 1969	Prevents marketing of products so dangerous that adequate safety warnings cannot be given.
Public Health Smoking Act of 1970	Prohibits cigarette advertising on television and radio and revises the health hazard warning on cigarette packages.
Poison Prevention Labeling Act of 1970	Requires safety packaging for products that may be harmful to children.
National Environmental Policy Act of 1970	Established the Environmental Protection Agency to deal with various types of pollution and organizations that create pollution.
Public Health Cigarette Smoking Act of 1971	Prohibits tobacco advertising on radio and television.
Consumer Product Safety Act of 1972	Created the Consumer Product Safety Commission, which has authority to specify safety standards for most products.
Child Protection Act of 1990	Regulates the number of minutes of advertising on children's television.
Children's Online Privacy Protection Act of 1998	Empowers the FTC to set rules regarding how and when marketers must obtain parental permission before asking children marketing research questions.
Aviation Security Act of 2001	Requires airlines to take extra security measures to protect passengers, including the installation of stronger cockpit doors, improved baggage screening, and increased security training for airport personnel.
Homeland Security Act of 2002	Protects consumers against terrorist acts; created the Department of Homeland Security.
Do Not Call Law of 2003	Protects consumers against unwanted telemarketing calls.
CAN-SPAM Act of 2003	Protects consumers against unwanted email, or spam.
Credit Card Act of 2009	Provides many credit card protections.
Restoring American Financial Stability Act of 2010	Created the Consumer Financial Protection Bureau to protect consumers against unfair, abusive, and deceptive financial practices.
Patient Protection and Affordable Care Act	Overhauled the U.S. health care system; mandated and subsidized health insurance for individuals.

actively involved in marketing affairs. These agencies, plus others, are discussed throughout the book, but a brief introduction is in order at this point.

CONSUMER PRODUCT SAFETY COMMISSION The sole purpose of the **Consumer Product Safety Commission (CPSC)** is to protect the health and safety of consumers in and around their homes. The CPSC has the power to set mandatory safety standards for almost all products consumers use (about 15,000 items) and can fine offending firms up to $500,000 and sentence their officers to up to a year in prison. It can also ban dangerous products from the marketplace. The CPSC oversees about 400 recalls per year. In 2008, Congress passed the Consumer Product Safety Improvement Act. The law is aimed primarily at children's products, which are defined as those used by individuals 12 years old or younger. The law addresses items such as cribs, electronics and video games, school supplies, science kits, toys, and pacifiers. The law requires mandatory testing and labeling and increases fines and prison time for violators.

FOOD AND DRUG ADMINISTRATION The **Food and Drug Administration (FDA)**, another powerful agency, is charged with enforcing regulations against selling and distributing adulterated, misbranded, or hazardous food and drug products. In 2009, the Tobacco Control Act was passed. This act gave the FDA authority to regulate tobacco products, with a special emphasis on preventing their use by children and young people

Consumer Product Safety Commission (CPSC) a federal agency established to protect the health and safety of consumers in and around their homes

Food and Drug Administration (FDA) a federal agency charged with enforcing regulations against selling and distributing adulterated, misbranded, or hazardous food and drug products and reducing the impact of tobacco on public health. Another recent FDA action is the "Bad Ad" program. It is geared toward health care providers to help them recognize misleading prescription drug promotions and gives them an easy way to report the activity to the FDA.

FEDERAL TRADE COMMISSION The **Federal Trade Commission (FTC)** is empowered to prevent persons or corporations from using unfair methods of competition in commerce. The FTC consists of five members, each holding office for seven years. Over the years, Congress has greatly expanded the powers of the FTC. Its responsibilities have grown so large that the FTC has created several bureaus to better organize its operations. One of the most important is the Bureau of Competition, which promotes and protects competition. The Bureau of Competition:

- reviews mergers and acquisitions, and challenges those that would likely lead to higher prices, fewer choices, or less innovation;

- seeks out and challenges anticompetitive conduct in the marketplace, including monopolization and agreements between competitors;

- promotes competition in industries where consumer impact is high, such as health care, real estate, oil and gas, technology, and consumer goods; and

- provides information and holds conferences and workshops for consumers, businesses, and policy makers on competition issues for market analysis.

The FTC's Bureau of Consumer Protection works for the consumer to prevent fraud, deception, and unfair business practices in the marketplace. The Bureau of Consumer Protection claims that it:

- enhances consumer confidence by enforcing federal laws that protect consumers;

- empowers consumers with free information to help them exercise their rights and to spot and avoid fraud and deception; and

- wants to hear from consumers who want to get information or file a complaint about fraud or identity theft.[95]

In 2012, the FTC and the Consumer Financial Protection Bureau signed an agreement to coordinate efforts so they could protect consumers while avoiding duplication of federal law enforcement and regulatory efforts. The objective of the agreement is to avoid overlapping

Federal Trade Commission (FTC) a federal agency empowered to prevent persons or corporations from using unfair methods of competition in commerce

The Dodd–Frank Wall Street Reform and Consumer Protection Act is named for its sponsors, former Senator Chris Dodd (right) and former Representative Barney Frank.

responsibilities and duplications of effort. Another important FTC bureau is the Bureau of Economics. It provides economic analysis and support to antitrust and consumer protection investigations. Many consumer protection issues today involve the Internet.

4-7d Consumer Privacy

The popularity of the Internet for targeted advertising, for collecting consumer data, and as a repository for sensitive consumer data has alarmed privacy-minded consumers. In 2003, the U.S. Congress passed the CAN-SPAM Act in an attempt to regulate unsolicited email advertising. The act prohibits commercial emailers from using false addresses and presenting false or misleading information, among other restrictions.

Internet users who once felt fairly anonymous when using the Web are now disturbed by the amount of information marketers collect about them and their children as they visit various sites in cyberspace. The FTC, with jurisdiction under the Children's Online Privacy Protection Act, requires website operators to post a privacy policy on their home page and a link to the policy on every page where personal information is collected. Despite federal efforts, online tracking has become widespread and pervasive. A vast amount of personal data is collected through apps.

Successful tracking has created a $628 billion global online-advertising business that is now larger than TV advertising. By 2020, digital media's share of total advertising will be near 50 percent.[96] There are more than 300 companies collecting data about users. More than half the time, data collectors piggyback on each other.

Scanrail1/Shutterstock.com

Acxiom's consumer database—the largest in the world—contains data on more than 500 million consumers. This massive database provides companies like E*Trade and Ford with information on more than 1,000 individual consumer traits and 35,000 specific behaviors.

When a user visits a website that has a code for one type of tracking technology, the data collection triggers other tracking technologies that are not embedded on the site. Piggybacking means that websites really do not know how much data are being gathered about their users.

Acxiom uses more than 23,000 computer servers to collect, collate, and analyze consumer data. The firm has created the world's largest consumer database—the servers process more than 50 trillion data transactions a year. The database contains information on over 500 million consumers worldwide, with data on more than 1,000 consumer traits such as location, age, and household income. Acxiom's database provides more than 3,500 specific behavioral insights, such as one's propensity to make a purchase. Acxiom customers include firms like Ford, Macy's, and many other major firms seeking consumer insights. Acxiom integrates online, mobile, and offline data to create in-depth consumer behavior portraits. The firm's proprietary software, PersonicX, assigns consumers to 1 of 70 detailed socioeconomic clusters. For example, the "savvy single" cluster includes mobile, upper-middle-class singles who do their banking online, attend pro sports events, are sensitive to prices, and respond to free-shipping offers. To see to which cluster you are assigned to, go to https://isapps.acxiom.com/personicx/personicx.aspx.

Many consumers don't want to be part of huge databases—they want their privacy back. They are also concerned about major data breaches. In the 2016 presidential campaign, Cambridge Analytica may have misused data from 50 million Facebook users to try to influence elections. Recently, Google exposed the private data of thousands of users of the Google+ social network and then opted not to disclose it. It was reported that Google feared that a disclosure would result in regulatory scrutiny.[97] It has since shut down Google+.

Consumers are not only concerned about data breaches and data collection from laptops and mobile devices but also devices from the "Internet of Things." A recent survey found that 63 percent of the respondents were concerned or very concerned that their personal information was being scrapped via their voice-activated virtual assistant such as Alexa, Google Home and Amazon Echo.[98]

In the United States, there is no single, comprehensive federal law regulating the collection and use of personal data. However, in May 2018, the European Union (discussed in Chapter 5) passed the General Data Protection Regulation (GDPR). It applies to any business that handles personal data of European member residents. The rule covers just about any data point that can be linked to an individual: credit card numbers, addresses, travel records, religion, web search history, biometric data, and more. The world's 500 largest corporations are spending around $7.8 billion to comply with GDPR. Each firm is required to have a "data protection officer." The law applies to all firms using personal data from E.U. citizens even if the firm has no physical presence in the E.U. Firms can collect only data needed immediately and not stockpile it. Data collection policies must be clear and available. Fines can go as high as 4 percent of a company's annual global revenues.[99]

4-8   COMPETITIVE FACTORS

The competitive environment encompasses the number of competitors a firm must face, the relative size of the competitors, and the degree of interdependence within the industry. Management has little control over the competitive environment confronting a firm.

4-8a Competition for Market Share and Profits

As U.S. population growth slows, technology rapidly changes, global competition increases, costs rise, and available resources tighten, firms find that they must work harder to maintain their profits and market share, regardless of the form of the competitive market. Sometimes technology advances can usher in a whole new set of competitors that can change a firm's business model. Bed Bath & Beyond sells towels, bedding, and other home related items to people in the booming U.S. housing market. It outlasted its major competitor, Linens 'n Things. Yet, competition has resulted in declining profits and sales. Bed Bath & Beyond has lagged behind both Wayfair and Home Goods. The firm's most important competitor is, most likely, Amazon. Many people would rather buy the merchandise that Bed Bath & Beyond offers online. Also, even though the company has a 20 percent off loyalty program and sends out coupons analysts say that their prices are too high and the shops look the same as they did decades ago—cluttered.[100] Furthermore, a basket of 50 items sold on Bed Bath & Beyond's website in the summer of 2018 was 16 percent higher than an identical basket sold by Amazon.[101] Will the firm be able to create innovative new strategies to acquire new customers and induce existing ones to buy more? Only time will tell.

There is hope. One study found that only 13 percent of U.S. consumers were fully brand loyal. That is, they remained faithful without considering other choices before purchasing. Categories with the highest loyalty were mobile carriers, auto insurance, and investments. Selected lowest levels of loyalty were for shoes, cosmetics, autos, bath accessories, tablets, and women's clothing.[102]

A vending machine is a perfect example of competition for market share. Several brands are competing for the business of the person who has the munchies.

Lissandra Melo/Shutterstock.com

4-8b Global Competition

Boeing is a very savvy international business competitor. Now Airbus, Boeing's primary competitor, is assembling planes in the United States. Many foreign competitors also consider the United States to be a ripe target market. Thus, a U.S. marketing manager can no longer focus only on domestic competitors. In automobiles, textiles, watches, televisions, steel, digital devices, and many other areas, foreign competition has been strong. In the past, foreign firms penetrated U.S. markets by concentrating on price, but the emphasis has switched to product quality. Nestlé, Volvo, and Rolls-Royce are noted for quality, not cheap prices. Global competition is discussed in much more detail in Chapter 5.

5 | Developing a Global Vision

LEARNING OUTCOMES

After studying this chapter, you will be able to . . .

5-1 Discuss the importance of global marketing

5-2 Discuss the impact of multinational firms on the world economy

5-3 Describe the external environment facing global marketers

5-4 Identify the various ways of entering the global marketplace

5-5 List the basic elements involved in developing a global marketing mix

5-6 Discover how the Internet is affecting global marketing

REWARDS OF GLOBAL MARKETING AND THE SHIFTING GLOBAL BUSINESS LANDSCAPE

Global marketing—marketing that targets markets throughout the world—has become an imperative for most large and many middle-sized businesses. Even smaller firms are beginning to invest in global marketing, often via the Internet.

U.S. managers must develop a global vision not only to recognize and react to international marketing opportunities but also to remain competitive at home. Often a U.S. firm's toughest domestic competition comes from foreign companies. Consider the impact of Toyota and Honda on Ford and General Motors, for example. Moreover, a global vision enables a manager to understand that customer and distribution networks operate worldwide. In summary, having a **global vision** means recognizing and reacting to international marketing opportunities, using effective global marketing strategies, and being aware of threats from foreign competitors in all markets.

Adopting a global vision can be very lucrative for a company. It is no accident that firms like Apple, Nestle, WalMart, and Procter & Gamble are among the largest and most successful multinational firms in the world. Each has a global vision that managers understand and follow.

The foundation of a successful global vision is a corporate structure that provides a continual flow of fresh ideas. One firm that has such a structure is Otis Elevator Company. Otis is the world's largest manufacturer of people-moving products, including elevators, escalators, and moving walkways. The firm employs more than 64,000 people around the world and offers products in more than 200 countries. Manufacturing is done in North America, South America, Europe, and Asia. Engineering and test centers are located in the United States, Austria, Brazil, China, Czech Republic, France, Germany, India, Italy, Japan, Korea, and Spain. Having input from engineers around the world enables Otis to maintain its position as the world leader in people-moving designs. Otis's new Skyrise elevator can move at speeds of up to 5,000 feet per minute!

Of course, global marketing is not a one-way street whereby only U.S. companies sell their wares and services throughout the world. Foreign competition in the domestic market was once relatively rare, but now it is found in almost every industry. In fact, in many industries, U.S. businesses have lost significant market share to imported products. In electronics, cameras, automobiles, fine china, tractors, leather goods, and a host of other consumer and industrial products, U.S. companies have struggled at home to maintain their market shares against foreign competitors.

5-1a Why Nations Trade

One might think that the best way to protect American workers and the domestic economy would be to stop trade with other nations. Then all of the production and consumption would stay within our borders. But then how would we get resources like coffee beans? There are 21 mineral commodities that the U.S. doesn't produce at all, such as manganese, gallium, and vanadium.[1] Manganese is essential in steel making; gallium is used in the manufacture of high-speed semiconductors that are used to make telephones; and vanadium is used for steel alloys.

A country has an **absolute advantage** when it can produce and sell a product or service at a lower cost than any other country or when it is the only country that can provide a product or service. The United States, for example, has an absolute advantage in some genome editing biopharmaceutical technology and other high-tech items. Suppose that the United States has an absolute advantage in air traffic control systems for busy airports and that Brazil has an absolute advantage in coffee. The United States does not have the proper climate for growing coffee, and Brazil lacks the technology to develop air traffic control systems. Both countries would gain by exchanging air traffic control systems for coffee.

Even if the United States had an absolute advantage in both coffee and air traffic control systems, it should still

global marketing marketing that targets markets throughout the world

global vision recognizing and reacting to international marketing opportunities, using effective global marketing strategies, and being aware of threats from foreign competitors in all markets

absolute advantage when a country can produce a product or service at a lower cost than any other country or when it is the only country that can provide the product or service

Brazil has an absolute advantage in growing coffee and the United States has an absolute advantage in creating and producing air traffic control systems. Both countries can gain through trade.

specialize and engage in trade. Why? The reason is the **principle of comparative advantage,** which says that each country should specialize in the products and services that it can produce most readily and cheaply and trade those products and services for goods and services that foreign countries can produce most readily and cheaply. This specialization ensures greater product availability and lower prices.

For example, China has a comparative advantage in assembling smartphones because of lower labor costs, close proximity to component parts manufacturers, and production technology. America has an advantage in more efficient agricultural production in crops such as corn and soybeans, and also jet engines, airplanes, and autos. Both nations are better off with trade. Trade is not a zero-sum game but creates opportunities for mutual gain.

Thus, comparative advantage acts as a stimulus to trade. When nations allow their citizens to trade whatever goods and services they choose without government regulation, free trade exists. **Free trade** is the policy of permitting individuals and businesses in a country to buy and sell in other countries without restrictions. The opposite of free trade is **protectionism,** in which a nation protects its home industries from foreign competition by establishing artificial barriers such as tariffs and quotas (discussed later in the chapter). Global Trade Alert, a Swiss-based trade-monitoring group, counted 642 government actions in one year around the globe that hurt trade with other countries.[2]

5-1b Importance of Global Marketing to the United States

Many countries depend more on international commerce than the United States does. For example, France, the United Kingdom, Canada, and Germany derive 63, 62, 64, and 87 percent of their respective **gross domestic product (GDP)** from world trade—considerably more than the United States' 27 percent.[3] GDP is the total market value of all final goods and services produced in a country for a given time period (usually a year or a quarter of a year). *Final* in this sense refers to final products that are sold, not to intermediate products used in the assembly of a final product. For example, if the value of a brake (an intermediate product) and that of a car (the final product) were both counted, the brake would be counted twice. Therefore, GDP counts only final goods and services in its valuation of a country's production.

Traditionally, only very large multinational companies have seriously attempted to compete worldwide. However, more and more small and medium-sized companies have begun pursuing international markets, and some are even beginning to play a critical role in driving export growth. Today, a record 304,000 small and medium-sized firms export goods from the United States. The U.S. government is working with these firms to expand small business trade. The Export–Import Bank of the United States, for example, helps thousands of small businesses each year. Essentially, the bank

principle of comparative advantage each country should specialize in the products or services that it can produce most readily and cheaply and trade those products or services for goods and services that foreign countries can produce most readily and cheaply

free trade policy of permitting individuals and businesses in a country to buy and sell in other countries without restrictions.

protectionism where a nation protects its home industries from foreign competitors by establishing artificial barriers, such as tariffs and quotas

gross domestic product (GDP) the total market value of all final goods and services produced in a country for a given time period provides two main types of export services. One is accounts receivable insurance, which lets small exporters extend sales terms to their buyers for up to six months. The other is trade financing to foreign buyers, which is primarily used by larger firms. If a foreign purchaser wants to buy planes from Boeing but doesn't have the funds to do so, given the long turnaround time for such expensive orders, the Export–Import Bank will provide the financing.[4]

The Small Business Administration (SBA) provides support for small businesses that export or desire to start exporting. The SBA will provide up to a 90 percent guarantee to lenders that the small business will repay loans up to $5 million. Other SBA support includes participation in foreign trade missions and market sales trips, aid in designing international marketing strategies, export trade show exhibits, and training.[5]

JOB OUTSOURCING AND INSHORING The notion of outsourcing (sending U.S. jobs abroad) has been highly controversial for several decades. Many executives have said that it leads to corporate growth, efficiency, productivity, and revenue growth. Most companies see cost savings as a key driver in outsourcing. But outsourcing also has its negative side. For instance, Detroit has suffered, as many factories in the auto industry have been shut down and relocated around the world. U.S. companies employ about 14 million workers in their overseas affiliates. Kellogg, the maker of cereals, employs 59 percent of its workforce overseas. Fresh Del Monte Produce has 80 percent of its employees in Costa Rica, Guatemala, Kenya, and the Philippines. Other U.S. firms with large overseas workforces include General Electric, United Technologies, Honeywell, Mondelez, Abbott Labs, Philip Morris, Merck, and Hanesbrands.[6]

iStock.com/NoDerog

Fresh Del Monte Produce has around 80 percent of its workforce outside the United States.

Some companies have begun to suspect that outsourcing's negatives outweigh its positives. Improperly designed parts and products have caused production delays, and rising wage in the developing world have rendered American rates more competitive. Increased fuel and transportation costs associated with long-distance shipping, coupled with falling U.S. energy costs, have given impetus to inshoring, or reshoring, returning production jobs to the United States. Rapid consumer product innovation has led to the need to keep product designers, marketing researchers, logistics experts, and manufacturers in close proximity so that they can work quickly as a team. Thus, shrinking development and manufacturing timelines have further contributed to inshoring.

BENEFITS OF GLOBALIZATION Traditional economic theory says that globalization relies on competition to drive down prices and increase product and service quality. Business goes to the countries that operate most efficiently, have lower labor costs, and/or have the technology to produce what is needed. In summary, globalization expands economic freedom, spurs competition, and raises the productivity and living standards of people in countries that open themselves to the global marketplace. For less developed countries, globalization also offers access to foreign capital, global export markets, and advanced technology while breaking the monopoly of inefficient and protected domestic producers. Faster growth, in turn, reduces poverty, encourages democratization, and promotes higher labor and environmental standards. Though government officials in developing countries may face more difficult choices as a result of globalization, their citizens enjoy greater individual freedom. In this sense, globalization acts as a check on governmental power by making it more difficult for governments to abuse the freedom and property of their citizens.

Globalization deserves credit for helping lift many millions out of poverty and for improving standards of living of low-wage families. In developing countries around the world, globalization has created a vibrant middle class that has elevated the standard of living for hundreds of millions of people.

COSTS OF GLOBALIZATION Countries restrict trade and create barriers for a number of reasons (many of which are discussed later in the chapter). In theory, if a country can boost exports and limit imports, then more jobs are created and there is less competition for local businesses. While globalization was a major

outsourcing sending U.S. jobs abroad

inshoring returning production jobs to the United States factor in job losses in the 1980s and 1990s, technology and automation have caused the vast majority of job losses since 2000.[7]

5-2 MULTINATIONAL FIRMS

The United States has a number of large companies that are global marketers. Many of them have been very successful. A company that is heavily engaged in international trade, beyond exporting and importing, is called a **multinational corporation**. A multinational corporation moves resources, goods, services, and skills across national boundaries without regard to the country in which its headquarters is located.

Multinationals often develop their global business in stages. In the first stage, companies operate in one country and sell into others. Second-stage multinationals set up foreign subsidiaries to handle sales in one country. In the third stage, multinationals operate an entire line of business in another country. The fourth stage has evolved primarily owing to the Internet and involves mostly high-tech companies. For these firms, the executive suite is virtual. Their top executives and core corporate functions are in different countries—wherever the firms can gain a competitive edge through the availability of talent or capital, low costs, or proximity to their most important customers.

Many U.S.-based multinationals earn a large percentage of their total revenue abroad. Caterpillar, the construction-equipment company, receives 67 percent of its revenue from overseas markets. Other large American multinationals include Walmart, ExxonMobil, Apple, General Motors, Ford, and Chevron.[8]

5-2a Are Multinationals Beneficial?

Although multinationals comprise far less than 1 percent of U.S. companies, they account for about 20 percent of all private jobs and 25 percent of all private wages. For decades, U.S. multinationals have driven an outsized share of U.S. productivity growth, the foundation of rising standards of living for everyone.

The role of multinational corporations in developing nations is a subject of controversy. The ability of multinationals to tap financial, physical, and human resources from all over the world and combine them economically and profitably can benefit any country. They also often possess and can transfer the most up-to-date technology. Critics, however, claim that often the wrong kind of technology is transferred to developing nations. Usually, it is **capital intensive** (requiring a greater expenditure for equipment than for labor) and thus does not substantially increase employment. A "modern sector" then emerges in the nation, employing a small proportion of the labor force with relatively high productivity and income levels and with increasingly capital-intensive technologies. A supply chain is a group of entities interlinked in the flow of goods and services from the initial suppliers to the ultimate customers (see Chapter 13). Many multinationals have found that the global complexities of worldwide supply chains create more problems than advantages. These problems include partners stealing or copying the firm's technology, complex government regulations and harassment from officials, and lower global profits. For example, Ford and General Motors make more than 80 percent of their profits in North America. Some successful, old-line multinationals such as Coca-Cola, Unilever, and Procter & Gamble have prospered by running a loose federation of national businesses instead of creating complex global supply chains. Others have begun to see the wisdom in this, cutting back on global expansion and returning operations closer to home.

Political pressure has resulted in some U.S. multinationals bringing more production back home. After meeting with President Trump, Amgen announced that it was adding 1,600 manufacturing jobs in the United States by building a new biologics plant. The White House announced that Merck, Pfizer, and Corning have committed to a $4 billion pharmaceutical glass manufacturing facility in the United States. Polaris announced it was reshoring 2,000 jobs to Alabama. And the list goes on.[9] In 2018, Apple announced plans to invest over $30 billion in the United States over the next five years. Apple is also increasing its investment in the Advanced Manufacturing Fund. This money is used to invest in U.S. manufacturing companies and boost domestic manufacturing. Apple is projected to add 20,000 new jobs at its existing campuses and at a new office location.[10]

5-2b Global Marketing Standardization

Traditionally, marketing-oriented multinational corporations have operated somewhat differently in each country. They use a strategy of providing different

multinational corporation a company that is heavily engaged in international trade, beyond exporting and importing

capital intensive using more capital than labor in the production process product features, packaging, advertising, and so on. However, Ted Levitt, a former Harvard professor, has described a trend toward what he refers to as "global marketing," with a slightly different meaning.[11] He contends that communication and technology have made the world smaller so that almost all consumers everywhere want all the things they have heard about, seen, or experienced. Thus, he sees the emergence of global markets for standardized consumer products on a huge scale, as opposed to segmented foreign markets with different products. In this book, *global marketing* is defined as individuals and organizations using a global vision to effectively market goods and services across national boundaries. To make the distinction, we can refer to Levitt's notion as **global marketing standardization**.

Global marketing standardization presumes that the markets throughout the world are becoming more alike. Firms practicing global marketing standardization produce "globally standardized products" to be sold the same way all over the world. Most smartphones and tablets, for example, are standardized globally except for the languages displayed. These devices allow the user to switch easily from one language to another. Uniform production should enable companies to lower production and marketing costs and increase profits. Levitt has cited Coca-Cola, Colgate-Palmolive, and McDonald's as successful global marketers. His critics point out, however, that the success of these three companies is really based on variation, not on offering the same product everywhere. McDonald's, for example, changes its salad dressings and provides self-serve espresso for French tastes. It sells bulgogi burgers in South Korea and falafel burgers in Egypt. Further, the fact that Coca-Cola and Colgate-Palmolive sell some of their products in more than 160 countries does not signify that they have adopted a high degree of standardization for all their products globally. Only three Coca-Cola brands are standardized, and one of them, Sprite, has a different formulation in Japan.

Companies with separate subsidiaries in other countries can be said to operate using a multidomestic strategy. A **multidomestic strategy** occurs when multinational firms enable individual subsidiaries to compete independently in domestic markets. Simply put, multidomestic strategy is how multinational firms use strategic business units (see Chapter 2). Colgate-Palmolive uses both strategies: Axion paste dishwashing detergent, for example, was formulated for developing countries, and La Croix Plus detergent was custom made for the French market.

5-3 EXTERNAL ENVIRONMENT FACED BY GLOBAL MARKETERS

A global marketer or a firm considering global marketing must consider the external environment. Many of the same environmental factors that operate in the domestic market also exist internationally. These factors include culture, economic development, the global economy, political structure and actions, demographic makeup, and natural resources.

5-3a Culture

Central to any society is the common set of values shared by its citizens that determines what is socially acceptable. Culture underlies the family, the educational system, religion, and the social class system. The network of social organizations generates overlapping roles and status positions. These values and roles have a tremendous effect on people's preferences and thus on marketers' options. A company that does not understand a country's culture is doomed to failure in that country. Cultural blunders lead to misunderstandings and often perceptions of rudeness or even incompetence. For example, when people in India shake hands, they sometimes do so rather limply. This is not a sign of weakness or disinterest; instead, a soft handshake conveys respect. Avoiding eye contact is also a sign of deference in India.

When eBay entered China in 2001, it did quite well because it had no competition. But when the Chinese competitor Taobao launched, eBay quickly lost ground. Its market share dropped from 80 percent to 7 percent in just five years. If you looked at eBay's site in China, you would recognize it—it looks very similar to eBay's U.S. site. This failure to adapt to Chinese culture led to eBay's decline: Americans do not want celebrity gossip or social interaction when they shop online, but the Chinese do.

Taobao is more than a one-stop shop for online shoppers—it is a social forum as well. The site features pictures and descriptions—very long descriptions—of products, but shoppers can also chat online about current trends, share shopping tips, and catch up on celebrity news at Taobao. Chinese shoppers are more inclined to follow fashion trends than American shoppers are, so Taobao lists trends in order of popularity, unlike eBay. Finally, when eBay

global marketing standardization production of uniform products that can be sold the same way all over the world

multidomestic strategy when multinational firms enable individual subsidiaries to compete independently in domestic markets

Nopparat Khokthong/Shutterstock.com

Even though eBay had a first mover advantage in the Chinese market, the launch of Taobao soon resulted in a massive loss of market share for eBay. Taobao's website was designed by Chinese for the Chinese market while eBay's website was not fully adapted to the Chinese culture.

entered China, it did not allow direct communication between buyers and sellers. As in the United States, all communication was handled by eBay's messaging system. This system was not well received in China because Chinese are much less likely than Americans to buy from strangers. Chinese Internet users expect websites to be much denser than many Western Internet users are accustomed to. That is, Chinese websites tend to have more links, many more images, and longer page lengths than Western websites do. Eye-grabbing animations and floating images are common on Chinese sites. A page with less text, fewer embedded links, and nice imagery might be called "well-designed" by Western Internet users but "boring" by Chinese ones.

Language is another important aspect of culture that can create problems for marketers. Marketers must take care in translating product names, slogans, instructions, and promotional messages so as not to convey the wrong meaning. Koreans pronounce the name of auto manufacturer Hyundai as "hi-yun-day." In U.S. advertisements, the company name is pronounced "hun-day," like "Sunday." More significantly, the name of baby food manufacturer Gerber is French for vomiting! Free translation software, such as babelfish.com or Google Translate, allow users to input text in one language and output in another language. But marketers must take care using the software, as it can have unintended results—the best being unintelligible, the worst being insulting.

Each country has its own customs and traditions that determine business practices and influence negotiations with foreign customers. In many countries, personal relationships are more important than financial considerations. For instance, skipping social engagements in Mexico may lead to lost sales. Negotiations in Japan often include long evenings of dining, drinking, and entertaining, and only after a close personal relationship has been formed do business negotiations begin.

Making successful sales presentations abroad requires a thorough understanding of the country's culture. Germans, for example, do not like risk and need strong reassurance. A successful presentation to a German client will emphasize three points: the bottom-line benefits of the product or service, that there will be strong service support, and that the product is guaranteed. In southern Europe, it is an insult to show a price list. Without negotiating, you will not close the sale. The English want plenty of documentation for product claims and are less likely to simply accept the word of the sales representative. Scandinavian and Dutch companies are more likely to approach business transactions as Americans do than are companies in any other country.

5-3b Economic Factors

A second major factor in the external environment facing the global marketer is the level of economic development in the countries where it operates. In general, complex and sophisticated industries are found in developed countries, and more basic industries are found in less-developed nations. Average family incomes are higher in the countries that are more developed than in those that are less developed. Larger incomes mean greater purchasing power and demand, not only for consumer goods and services, but also for the machinery and workers required to produce consumer goods.

According to the World Bank, the average *gross national income (GNI)* per capita for the world is $10,366.[12] GNI is a country's GDP (defined earlier) together with its income received from other countries (mainly interest and dividends) less similar payments made to other countries. The U.S. GNI per capita is $58,270, but it is not the world's highest. Switzerland's GNI is $80,560. Of course, there are many very poor countries: Rwanda, $720; Afghanistan, $570; Ethiopia, $740; and Democratic Republic of Congo, $450.[13] GNI per capita is one measure of the ability of a country's citizens to buy various goods and services. A marketer with a global vision can use these data to aid in measuring market potential in countries around the globe.

Not only is per capita income a consideration when doing business abroad, but so is the cost of doing business in a country. Although it is not the same as the cost of doing business, the most expensive places in the world to live are Caracas, Zurich, Geneva, Basel, and Bern. As you can see, four of the top five most expensive cities are in Switzerland.[14]

THE BALANCE OF TRADE AND THE BALANCE OF PAYMENTS The more U.S. firms that export their wares, the better the country's **balance of trade**—the difference between the value of a country's exports and the value of its imports over a given period. A country that exports more goods or services than it imports is said to have a favorable balance of trade; a country that imports more than it exports is said to have an unfavorable balance of trade. In other words, when imports exceed exports, more money flows out of the country than flows into it.

The United States has trade surpluses with the United Kingdom, Hong Kong, Brazil, and Australia, but it has substantial trade deficits with China, Japan, Germany, and Mexico.[15] Indeed, although U.S. exports have been doing well, the country imports more than it exports. The U.S. balance of trade deficit was $621 billion in 2018, marking the 41st straight year of trade deficit. As long as the United States continues to buy more goods than it sells abroad, it will have a deficit and an unfavorable balance of trade.[16]

If Americans consumed less, the deficit would contract along with the broader economy, as happened in 2001 and during the Great Recession. This leaves workers no better off. To increase production, U.S. companies could export more or take market share from imports. Government actions (discussed next) can make this happen, but they often create more problems in the process. The U.S. dollar appreciated in value relative to other currencies in 2018. It was up more than 5 percent against a basket of currencies and over 6 percent against the Euro.[17] This is primarily due to the tax cut and deregulation of business resulting in strong U.S. growth. A strong dollar makes U.S. goods more expensive overseas and imports less expensive in the United States, widening the trade deficit. America's largest trade deficit is with China. America exports around $130 billion to China annually while China exports $506 billion to the United States.[18]

In 2011, the Chinese government picked seven "strategic emerging industries" to support with pubic investment. The plan called for the industries to grow to 15 percent or GDP by 2020, up from 5 percent in 2010. The government gives subsidies in several forms, including loans from state-owned banks with easy terms and low interest rates.

Four years later the initiative grew into the "Made in China 2025" plan, which seeks to make China the global leader in 10 industries, including electric vehicles and biotechnology. Along with subsidies and government help in acquiring foreign companies, the policy explicitly requires foreign companies to transfer intellectual property in return for access to the Chinese market. The goal is to reduce the foreign-supplied value in Chinese manufactured goods to below 30 percent.[19]

Beijing has also stepped up its use of regulations to discriminate against foreign companies. For example, officials use the 2008 Antimonopoly Law to pressure firms to transfer intellectual property that gives them a dominant market position in China.

The difference between a country's total payments to other countries and its total receipts from other countries is its **balance of payments**. This figure includes the balance of imports and exports (the balance of trade), long-term investments in overseas plants and equipment, government loans to and from other countries, gifts and foreign aid, military expenditures made in other countries, and money deposits in and withdrawals from foreign banks.

The United States had a favorable balance of payments from about 1900 until 1971. Since then, the country's overall payments have exceeded its receipts—due largely to the U.S. military presence abroad.

5-3c The Global Economy

A global marketer today must be fully aware of the intertwined nature of the global economy. In the past, the size of the U.S. economy was so large that global markets tended to move up or down depending on its health. It was said, "If America sneezes, then the rest of the world catches a cold." This is still true today, but less so than in the past. Unfortunately, politics is playing an increasingly important role in the development of the BRICS countries (Brazil, Russia, India, China, and South Africa). Brazil has been rife with political scandal, and because of antiquated labor laws, overly generous government pensions, traditional work customs (women retire at age 50 and men at 55), the country is experiencing its worst recession in 25 years. Russia's economy is held back by economic sanctions and the country's over-dependence on energy exports amid plummeting energy prices. Despite China's slowed growth rate, it is now the world's second largest economy behind the United States. By 2030, China will overtake the United States as the world's largest economy.

balance of trade the difference between the value of a country's exports and the value of its imports over a given period

balance of payments the difference between a country's total payments to other countries and its total receipts from other countries

Outside of China, perhaps the brightest light among the BRICS is India, its economy grew around 7.3 percent in 2018. India is less dependent on exports than are the other BRICS countries, making it less vulnerable to slowing economics worldwide. Lower energy prices have helped India as well, as it is a major energy importer. Most importantly, Prime Minister Narendra Modi is opening India up to private investment like never before.[20] This move is poised to spur major economic growth over the next five years.

5-3d Political Structure and Actions

Political structure is a fourth important variable facing global marketers. Government policies run the gamut from no private ownership and minimal individual freedom to little central government and maximum personal freedom. As rights of private property increase, government-owned industries and centralized planning tend to decrease. But a political environment is rarely at one extreme or the other. India, for instance, is a republic with elements of socialism, monopoly capitalism, and competitive capitalism in its political ideology.

Regulation gives businesses the framework they need to grow and prosper. For example, a well-designed land administration system can provide reliable data on the ownership of property and the protection of property rights.

Regulation can also produce fairer outcomes when one business or position is much more powerful than another. In a country with no labor laws, an employer might force employees to work 14 hours a day or longer, for little pay, and under dangerous working conditions.

On the other hand, regulation can overburden businesses and make it virtually impossible for them to operate. The most difficult countries in which to start a new business are Somalia, Eritrea, Venezuela, and South Sudan. (The easiest places to start a new business are New Zealand, Singapore, and Denmark.[21]) It is no surprise, then, that multinationals shy away from the most difficult countries. If resolving a commercial dispute takes too much time (1,402 days in Guatemala), potential clients and suppliers might be hesitant to do business with companies based in that country.

LEGAL CONSIDERATIONS As you can see, legal considerations are often intertwined with the political environment. In France, nationalistic sentiments led to a law that requires pop music stations to play at least 40 percent of their songs in French (even though French teenagers love American and English music).

A major reason that Singapore is thriving is because it is one of the easiest places in the world to start a new business.

Many legal structures are designed to either encourage or limit trade. Recent trends have leaned toward the latter. Nevertheless, the most common legal structures affecting trade are:

- **Tariff:** a tax levied on the goods entering a country. Because a tariff is a tax, it will either reduce the profits of the firms paying the tariff or raise prices to buyers, or both. Normally, a tariff raises prices of the imported goods and makes it easier for domestic firms to compete.

- **Quota:** a limit on the amount of a specific product that can enter a country. Several U.S. companies have sought quotas as a means of protection from foreign competition. The United States, for example, has a quota on raw cane sugar.

- **Boycott:** the exclusion of all products from certain countries or companies. Governments use boycotts to exclude companies from countries with which they have a political dispute. Several Arab nations have boycotted products made in Israel.

- **Exchange control:** a law compelling a company earning foreign exchange (money) from its exports to sell it to a control agency, usually a central bank. A company wishing to buy goods abroad must first obtain a foreign currency exchange from the control agency. For example, if Ford has a plant in Brazil that makes F-150 pickup trucks and then exports them to other South American countries, the money made on those sales is foreign currency and must be sold to a control agency in Brazil. When Ford needs to buy, say, brakes for the F-150 from Mexico, it goes to the control agency to get the funds. Some countries with foreign exchange controls are Argentina,

Brazil, China, Iceland, India, North Korea, Russia, and Venezuela.

- **Market grouping (also known as a common trade alliance):** occurs when several countries agree to work together to form a common trade area that enhances trade opportunities. The best-known market grouping is the EU, which will be discussed later in this chapter.

- **Trade agreement:** an agreement to stimulate international trade. Not all government efforts are meant to stifle imports or investment by foreign corporations. The largest Latin American trade agreement is Mercosur, which has Brazil Paraguay, Uruguay, and Argentina as full members. Venezuela was suspended from membership in 2016. Associate members are French Guiana, Suriname, Guyana, Columbia, Ecuador, Peru, Bolivia, and Chile. Brazil and Argentina account for about 95 percent of Mercosur's GDP.[22] Associate members do not have full voting rights or free access to member markets. Mercosur countries have failed to coordinate their trade policies toward outside countries. Unfortunately, Mercosur members continue to fall back on protectionist policies. As a result, trade among Mercosur countries has fallen since 2011.[23]

THE TRADE WAR President Trump has long been concerned about America's trade deficit. On March 23, 2018, he imposed tariffs on steel and aluminum from many countries, including China. That prompted China to levy $3 billion on American exports to China. Historically, when one country raises tariffs to protect domestic industries, other countries retaliate, which causes the initial country to raise other tariffs—and escalation continues. America quickly announced exemptions to the steel and aluminum tariffs for the European Union (discussed below), Canada, Mexico, South Korea, and other nations. Effectively, those tariffs apply to only three major steel exporters—China, Russia, and Japan. In September 2018, Japan and the United States agreed to launch negotiations on a "Trade Agreement on Goods." America is seeking concessions on the agricultural sector as well as in automobile tariffs. Later discussions would cover insurance, pharmaceuticals, and digital trade.

In September 2018, President Trump announced additional tariffs of 10 percent of goods coming from China. Predictably, China announced retaliatory tariffs on $60 billion in U.S. goods as trade tensions between the world's two largest economies grew.[24] The U.S. had imposed around $260 billion in tariffs on imports from China. During the G20 meeting in June 2019 Presidents Xi and Trump agreed to resume trade negotiations.

A complicating factor in the trade negotiations is the Chinese company Huawei. Huawei is the world's largest manufacturer of telecommunications gear. U.S. officials were worried that certain Huawei products could be used for spying on governments and companies. By early 2019, Huawei was effectively banned for the U.S. market. During June 2019, President Trump agreed to let Huawei buy and sell high tech gear in the U.S. only if it did not impact national security. China, in turn, agreed to increase its purchase of U.S. farm products.

Imposing tariffs can create complicated, and sometimes unintended consequences. Under tariffs that the United States placed on Chinese goods in 2018, Chinese-made finished loudspeakers can enter the United States from China without penalty. However, speaker components (intermediate goods) made in China face a 25 percent tariff. So, a Chinese loudspeaker avoids the tariffs, but one assembled at JL Audio's facility in Florida faces a 25 percent duty on key parts next year. A European loudspeaker also would avoid the tariffs, even if it uses Chinese components.[25]

Enforcing tariffs on goods entering the United States can be very complicated. Every product imported carries a 10-digit designation called an HTS code; there are of these

A wood importer was asked if he wanted to buy some Chinese plywood. The caller just said, "Don't worry we will bring it in under a different code and remove all Chinese markings."

iStock.com/Baloncici

Mercosur the largest Latin American trade agreement; full members include Argentina, Brazil, Paraguay, Uruguay. Associate members are French Guiana, Suriname, Guyana, Chile, Colombia, Ecuador, Peru, and Bolivia.

18,927 in all. One way that firms avoiding the increased tariffs is simply by switching codes. A wood importer in Oregon was asked if he would like to get some Chinese plywood tariff-free. The caller said, "Don't worry about it, we will strip it of its Chinese markings and ship it under another code."[26] After the United States placed a levy of 25 percent on Chinese steel, Chinese steel plates were being imported into the United States as "turbine parts" used in jet engines. In the first six months of 2018, imports of steel plates fell 11 percent, while imports of turbine parts rose 121 percent.[27]

As mentioned at the beginning of the chapter, the law of comparative advantage dictates that trade is beneficial to nations. Trade does not mean that one country wins and the other loses. The notion that "they are stealing our jobs" doesn't hold in today's economy. The imposition of tariffs on steel and aluminum was purportedly taken "to bring steel and aluminum production jobs back to the United States." Yet, the primary reasons for job losses in these industries were due to technology and lower labor costs elsewhere. America imports lower-cost steel and aluminum to make finished goods. This results in lower prices to U.S. consumers. It has been estimated that the steel and aluminum tariffs by themselves will result in net job losses of 70,000 in U.S. manufacturing. That is, 10,000 new jobs in the metals-producing section is being offset by 80,000 jobs lost in metal-consuming sections.[28]

An escalating trade war does not benefit either the United States or China. Both countries, in fact, would benefit from free trade. There are, however, serious Chinese trade abuses that must be addressed. China unfairly subsidizes targeted industries to give them an unfair export advantage. It also has unfairly restricted access to key markets for foreign markets and forced businesses to divulge proprietary technology and trade secrets in order to enter Chinese markets. These matters should be referred to the World Trade Organization (discussed below) if an agreement between the United States and China cannot be reached.

A number of positive signs, in early 2019, gave hope to the possibility of a trade settlement. One Chinese official recently noted that "China's and America's economies are inseparable." China has resumed purchases of American soybeans and announced cuts on auto-import tariffs. China is also examining how state-owned companies can form part of a healthy market economy provided they enjoy no special advantages. After a flurry of approvals, it can argue that China is opening its economy to foreign firms. Tesla is on track to be the first foreign carmaker to have a wholly owned manufacturing facility in China, UBS, a Swiss bank, recently became the first foreign firm to be allowed a majority stake in a Chinese brokerage. Exxon-Mobil will soon start to build a wholly owned petrochemical complex, which until recently foreign firms could not do. China has also published tougher rules for protecting intellectual property, which foreign companies have long demanded.[29]

Yet, the Covid 19 pandemic created an unprecedented decline in global trade in 2020. This has further complicated efforts to reach a trade agreement between the United States and China. While China has agreed to buy some additional agricultural products, a comprehensive agreement seems to be in the distant future.

UNITED STATES–MEXICO–CANADA AGREEMENT

President Trump used the threat of tariffs to push Canada and Mexico into scrapping the North American Free Trade Agreement (NAFTA). The new accord is entitled the "United States–Mexico–Canada Agreement" (USMCA). Key provisions of the new agreement are:

- Country of Origin Rule—Cars and trucks must have 75 percent of their components manufactured in Mexico, United States, or Canada to qualify for zero tariffs. The goal is to boost auto-parts manufacturing in North America.

- Labor Provisions—40 to 45 percent of automobile content must be made by workers who earn at least $16 an hour by 2023. The goal is to drive Mexican wages up and/or shift production to the United States and Canada. The USMCA allows each country to sanction the others for labor violations that impact trade.

- U.S. Farmers Gain More Access to the Canadian Dairy Market—Canada agreed to open its dairy market that has closely regulated how much of each dairy product can be produced and placed strict tariffs and quotas on imports.

- Intellectual Property Protections and Digital Trade Provisions—The agreement extends a copyright from 50 years beyond the life of an author to 70 years. It also extends protection to new biologic drugs from 8 years to 10. This will extend protection for drug manufacturers against generic competition. Also, there will be no duties on products purchased electronically, such as music or e-books. In addition, Internet companies are not held liable for content their users produce.

- Creates a Special Dispute Mechanism—The new agreement sets up an independent mechanism to resolve trade disputes between countries (rather than going to domestic courts).[30]

The agreement also says that if a country makes a free-trade agreement with a "nonmarket economy" then USMCA could be terminated. This is designed primarily to discourage agreements with China.[31] This is an attempt to build a North American alliance when negotiating with China.

Foreign car makers have invested heavily in plants in Canada and Mexico and produce some of their best-selling vehicles there. German manufacturers have built several factories in Mexico and the United States over the past decade. Volkswagen also operates a huge plant in Puebla, Mexico, which exports Beetles and sedans to the United States. Audi AG, VW's luxury unit, opened a plant near Puebla in 2015 to build SUVs. Nearly half the plant's production is exported to the United States.

Toyota Motor Corp. relies on Canadian plants for nearly half its U.S. sales of the RAV4 crossover sport utility vehicle. That dependence is set to increase after Toyota announced plans to spend nearly a billion dollars to double RAV4 production in Canada. Toyota opened a new plant for Tacoma trucks in Mexico in 2019.[32]

USMCA will have to be ratified by all three countries. At press time for this text, that had not yet occurred. Assuming the passage of USMCA, the Trump administration plans to intensify trade negotiations with other countries using the new agreement as a model. The emphasis of new trade pacts will be less on fostering global supply chains for corporations than on prioritizing tougher standards for goods coming into the United States in an attempt to push more manufacturing back to America.[33] The next negotiations will target the European Union, Japan, and the Philippines.

THE WORLD TRADE ORGANIZATION The **World Trade Organization (WTO)** was created in 1994 to foster global trade. There are 164 members (nations) in the WTO. Over the years, the WTO has been very successful in lowering barriers to trade. This has been accomplished through member negotiations called "rounds." The **Uruguay Round**, which created the WTO, reduced tariffs worldwide by one-third.[34] The underlying principle of the WTO is the notion of "most favored nation." This means that, as a WTO member, if a nation reduces a tariff imposed on goods from another country, it will do the same for all other member nations. So, for example, when China entered in 2001, it benefited from reduced tariffs between the European Union and the United States.

At the WTO, disputes between countries are handled by "panels," not courts. There is a dispute-settlement panel and a more powerful appellate body

The World Trade Organization has faced many problems since the failure of the Doha Round of negotiations. The regulations governing world trade need a major update in the complex world of global trade.

Martin Good/Shutterstock.com

consisting of only seven members. The rules and laws of the WTO that enable dispute settlement are created and updated through new "rounds."

The last round of WTO trade talks began in Doha, Qatar, in 2001. For the most part, the periodic meetings of WTO members under the Doha Round were very contentious. One of the most contentious goals of the round was for the major developing countries (BRICS) to lower tariffs on industrial goods in exchange for European and American tariff and subsidy cuts on farm products. Concerned that lowering tariffs would result in an economically damaging influx of foreign cotton, sugar, and rice, China and India demanded a safeguard clause that would allow them to raise tariffs on those crops if imports surged. At a December 2015 meeting of the WTO, trade ministers from more than 160 countries failed to agree that they should keep the negotiations going. After 14 years of talks, members of the WTO effectively ended the Doha Round of negotiations. It became clear in recent years that the talks, which were originally supposed to conclude in 2005, were paralyzed because neither developed economies (like the United States and the European Union) nor developing countries (like China and India) were willing to make fundamental concessions.

World Trade Organization (WTO) a trade organization that replaced the old General Agreement on Tariffs and Trade (GATT)

Uruguay Round a trade agreement to dramatically lower trade barriers worldwide created the World Trade Organization

The failure of the Doha Round has left the WTO seriously out of date in the complex global economy Digital trade remains outside the WTO system. Trade in services is inconsistently covered by existing rules. China's subsidized state-owned enterprises have created overcapacity in the global marketplace overwhelming producers elsewhere. Also, China has pressured American companies wanting to do business in China to transfer their technology to Chinese partners. The Chinese government acknowledges that WTO rules forbid making the transfer of technology a condition for access to a nation's economy. But it argues that the practice is "voluntary" because American firms aren't forced to do business in China—their other option is to stay out of the country. American companies and officials say it's a form of extortion because U.S. firms should have access to the Chinese market, as they do to markets in Europe and elsewhere, without losing their intellectual property.

Although the Chinese practice violates WTO rules, it is difficult to bring a successful technology-transfer case because American companies fear retaliation by Beijing if they complain openly or provide detailed evidence that the U.S. government can be used in pursuing such a case.[35]

The Trump administration claims that the rules under which the WTO operates are outdated and incapable of dealing with China's unfair trade practices. Thus, America has been blocking the appointment of new judges to the WTO appellate panel. As of October 2018, there were only three judges left—the minimum number required to hear a case. This action has resulted in a large backlog of cases and brought the appeals process almost to a standstill.[36] President Trump feels that the WTO is ineffective in addressing today's global trade problems and that bilateral deals suit America's interests better.[37]

THE COMPREHENSIVE AND PROGRESSIVE AGREEMENT FOR TRANS-PACIFIC PARTNERSHIP (CPATPP) This agreement was signed in March 2018 in Santiago, Chile. Originally called simply the "Trans-Pacific Partnership," the name was changed after President Trump withdrew

foreign direct investment a business investment in a foreign country, either by establishing business operations or by acquiring business assets in that country

Dominican Republic-Central America Free Trade Agreement (CAFTA-DR) a trade agreement instituted in 2005 that includes Costa Rica, the Dominican Republic, El Salvador, Guatemala, Honduras, Nicaragua, and the United States

from joining the organization. Interestingly, both Hillary Clinton and President Trump were against joining the agreement. The CPATPP consists of Australia, Brunei, Darussalam, Canada, Chile, Japan, Mexico, Malaysia, New Zealand, Peru, Singapore, and Vietnam. The objective is to cut tariffs and to create common trade laws and regulations. The CPATPP plans to open service sectors, restrict state-owned organization subsidies (like state-owned factories that export at low prices owing to subsidies), protect trade secrets, create higher labor standards, and settle environmental issues through a dispute-settlement panel.[38] The most controversial aspect of CPATPP is its investor-settlement–dispute-settlement mechanism, generally known as ISDS. It means that companies can sue individual governments in the agreement by arguing that they were denied access to that country's market. Countries argue that this means governments cannot make policy without fear of facing a lengthy and costly legal case.[39]

THE PACIFIC ALLIANCE The Pacific Alliance was signed in 2012 by Colombia, Chile, Peru, and Mexico to create a single region for the free movement of goods, services, investment, capital, and people. Implementation of the Pacific Alliance began in 2014 with the goal of abolishing tariffs on 92 percent of merchandise trade as soon as possible, with the remainder being eliminated by 2020. Costa Rica was recently accepted as a fifth member of the Pacific Alliance, but it has not yet formally joined the agreement.

This agreement has gotten the attention of a number of countries around the world. Fifty-five nations from six continents now act as observers at Alliance meetings, and several Asian countries have already asked to be admitted as full members.[40] This interest derives from Alliance members' commitment to free markets, free trade, and democracy—which cannot be said of some South American countries (including Brazil, Argentina, and Venezuela). Observer nations are also attracted to the Pacific Alliance because of market size; the Alliance already accounts for half of all South American exports.[41]

DOMINICAN REPUBLIC CENTRAL AMERICA FREE TRADE AGREEMENT The **Dominican Republic Central America Free Trade Agreement (CAFTA–DR)** was instituted in 2005. Because it joined after the original agreement was signed, the Dominican Republic was amended to the original agreement title (Central America Free Trade Agreement, or CAFTA). In addition to the United States and the Dominican

Republic, the agreement includes Costa Rica, El Salvador, Guatemala, Honduras, and Nicaragua.

As of 2015, all consumer and industrial goods exported to CAFTA-DR countries were no longer subject to tariffs. Tariffs on agricultural goods will be phased out by 2020. The agreement also covers intellectual property rights, transparency, electronic commerce, and telecommunications. The CAFTA-DR is America's third-largest export market in Latin America, right after Mexico and Brazil. CAFTA-DR benefited U.S. exporters of petroleum products plastics, paper, and textiles. It has also aided manufacturers of motor vehicles, machinery, medical equipment, and electronics.[42]

EUROPEAN UNION Encompassing much of Europe, the European Union (EU) is one of the world's most important free trade zones. Actually much more than a free trade zone, it is also a political and economic community comprised of more than 510 million citizens. As a free trade zone, however, the EU guarantees the freedom of movement of people, goods, services, and capital between member states. It also maintains a common trade policy with outside nations and a regional development policy. The EU represents member nations in the WTO. Recently, the EU also began venturing into foreign policy as well, getting involved in issues such as Iran's refining of uranium.

The EU currently has 28 member states: Austria, Belgium, Bulgaria, Croatia, Cyprus, the Czech Republic, Denmark, Estonia, Finland, France, Germany, Greece, Hungary, Ireland, Italy, Latvia, Lithuania, Luxembourg, Malta, the Netherlands, Poland, Portugal, Romania, Slovakia, Slovenia, Spain, Sweden, and the United Kingdom.

The EU's economy is the second largest in the world, behind the United States; China's is the third largest. The EU and the United States have the largest bilateral trade relationship, and the two unions have a highly integrated economic relationship The U.S. total investment in the EU is three times higher than its investment in all of Asia. The EU's total investment in the United States is eight times higher than its investment in India and China combined.[43] Almost every other country in the global economy calls either the EU or the United States its largest trade and investment partner.

AMERICA AND THE EU The United States and the EU together account for nearly half of global economic output—and each is the other's top trading partner. Annual trade in goods and services tops $1 trillion, while

Americas' high-tech firms have faced serious threats and fines regarding data privacy from the European Commission. The Commission is made up of one member from each EU country and is responsible for enforcing the EU's laws.

bilateral foreign-direct investment stands at $5 trillion annually. Average tariffs of 5.2 percent in the EU and 3.5 percent in the United States are among the lowest globally—compared with an average of about 9 percent among the WTO's members.[44]

Despite the overall low tariff rates between the United States and the EU, President Trump has repeatedly criticized EU trade policies. Mr. Trump has focused on specific EU duties—like cars, which at 10 percent are four times the U.S. level for the EU—that the administration blames for altering commerce and worsening the U.S. trade deficit.

Both European and American policy makers have for decades attempted to protect select industries for domestic interests. That has resulted in high tariffs from both sides on certain products, from apparel to agriculture, despite their collective drive toward a tariff-free world.

The United States has safeguarded certain crops for years, with levies of as much as 350 percent on some tobacco products, such as snuff, and up to 32 percent on some cotton apparel. European officials have shielded farmers such as citrus growers with up to 34 percent tariffs on products, including some juices, and still maintain a 10 percent levy on cars despite having 6 of the world's 20 biggest auto makers.[45]

"How you introduce fairness into a system as complex as that is not a simple question, and doing it line-by-line is obviously

European Union (EU) a free trade zone encompassing 28 European countries

UK Prime Minister Theresa May placed a motion before Parliament to withdraw from the European Union on January 15, 2019. It was defeated by the largest margin in U.K. history.

quite a challenge," said Ken Ash, trade and agriculture director for the Organization for Economic Cooperation and Development. "If you look at the EU–U.S. trading relationship, it is remarkably open already."[46]

BREXIT In June 2016, the United Kingdom (UK) voted to leave the EU. Exit polls showed that British citizens wanted their government to control its own political and economic future. The term for the UK for leaving the European Union is called "Brexit." The UK wants a much closer trade and economic relationship after Brexit than the EU says is possible for a country that won't allow free movement of EU citizens and won't follow the rulings on the EU's top court.

The UK left the EU on January 31, 2020. Attention is currently on negotiating the future UK-EU relationship. The most difficult issue is how much access the UK can have to the EU market without being bound by the EU rules. The transition period is scheduled to end on December 31, 2020 which will create abrupt, major changes in trade flows unless there is an agreement. Meeting this tight deadline was a difficult challenge even before the pandemic overwhelmed governments in both the UK and the EU countries. However, Boris Johnson, the UK Prime Minister, has rejected calls to extend the transition.

World Bank an international bank that offers low-interest loans, advice, and information to developing nations

Some politicians on both sides are seeking a compromise via a "bare bones" agreement before the deadline and then leaving the complicated details to be worked out in the future.

EU GOVERNANCE The European Commission is made up of one member from each EU country. The Commission is responsible for proposing legislation, implementing decisions, and managing the day-to-day business of the EU. The European Commission's Directorate General for Competition handles dominant market abuses, collusion, and other anticompetitive practices. The Directorate General, Margrethe Vestager, fined U.S. tech firm Qualcomm $1.2 billion for payments made to Apple for exclusive use of its chips. The Directorate General said that Qualcomm's actions hindered competition in the market for base-band chips, which connect smartphones to cellular networks.[47]

Recall from Chapter 4 that the EU has passed the 260-page General Data Protection Regulations (GDPR). The law requires any firm doing business with EU citizens to explain how their data will be used, allow them to see what is collected, obtain consent, then permit them to withdraw consent at any moment and demand that their data be deleted. It is estimated that companies will spend $78 billion to meet the demands of GDPR.[48] Before passage of GDPR in 2018, France's privacy regulator extended the "right to be forgotten" to all of a company's websites anywhere in the world. In 2015, France fined Google $115,527 for not complying.[49] In 2018, Google appealed this fine to the EU's Court of Justice. The case has not been ruled on at the time of this writing. However, it sets the stage for who will, or should, regulate everything from free speech and privacy to cybercrime and taxes on Internet transactions. Google claims that France's demands will allow the censorship laws of dictators and tyrants to determine what people around the world can see online.[50]

THE WORLD BANK, THE INTERNATIONAL MONETARY FUND, AND THE G-20 Two international financial organizations are instrumental in fostering global trade. The World Bank offers low-interest loans to developing nations. Originally, the purpose of the loans was to help these nations build infrastructure such as roads, power plants, schools, drainage projects, and hospitals. Now the World Bank offers loans to help developing nations relieve their debt burdens. To receive the loans, countries must pledge to lower trade barriers and aid private enterprise. In addition to making loans, the World Bank is a major source of advice and information for developing nations. The **International Monetary Fund (IMF)** was founded in 1945, one year after the creation of the World Bank, to promote trade through financial cooperation and eliminate trade barriers in the process. The IMF makes short-term loans to member nations that are unable to meet their budgetary expenses. It operates as a lender of last resort for troubled nations, such as Greece. In exchange for these emergency loans, IMF lenders frequently extract significant commitments from the borrowing nations to address the problems that led to the crises. These steps may include curtailing imports or even devaluing the currency. Greece, working with both the IMF and the EU, has raised taxes to unprecedented levels, cut government spending (including pensions), and implemented labor reforms such as reducing the minimum wage as part of its austerity measures to receive loans from the IMF and the EU. In 2016, Greece received an additional 86 billion euros and further forgiveness of existing debt. In 2017, 19 finance ministers from EU countries agreed that Greek people needed to see "light at the end of the tunnel of austerity." In August 2018, Greece became the last country to exit financial bailouts extended by the EU and the IMF. The Greek economy is slowly growing again, and unemployment has fallen from record highs. Yet, the economy is still only three-quarters of its size prior to its debt crises and unemployment is still above 20 percent. Greece still has enormous challenges.[51]

The **Group of Twenty (G-20)** finance ministers and central bank governors was established in 1999 to bring together industrialized and developing economies to discuss key issues in the global economy. The G-20 is a forum for international economic development that promotes discussion between industrial and emerging-market countries on key issues related to global economic stability. By contributing to the strengthening of the international financial system and providing opportunities for discussion on national policies, international cooperation, and international financial institutions, the G-20 helps support growth and development across the globe. The members of the G-20 are shown in Exhibit 5.1.

The G-20 sharpened its focus on countries that serve as tax shelters and those that haven't agreed to new international standards on tax transparency and information sharing. The G-20 even declared that it would enforce "punitive sanctions" against uncooperative tax-shelter countries. The G-20 members account for more than 80 percent of the global economic output.[52]

5-3e Demographic Makeup

Two primary determinants of any consumer market are wealth and population. The global urban population has grown by an average of 65 million people every year over the past three decades—the equivalent of adding seven Chicagos a year. In 2018, the world population was 7.7 billion people and it is expected to grow to 10 billion by 2050.[53]

China, India, and Indonesia are three of the most densely populated nations in the world. But that fact alone is not particularly useful to marketers. They also need to know whether the population is mostly urban or rural, because marketers may not have easy access to rural consumers. Belgium, for example, with about 90 percent of its population living in urban settings, may be a more attractive market.

Over the past quarter-century, world economic growth has lifted 1.25 billion people out of poverty. In 1990, 37 percent of the world's population was in extreme poverty, defined by the World Bank as living on less than $1.90 a day. Today, the bank estimates that 10 percent of the world lives in this destitute state—a marked improvement.[54] The increased consumption that helped pull so many people out of poverty was spurred largely by massive population growth. Between 2015 and 2030, however, 75 percent of global consumption growth will be driven by individuals spending more. Three groups will generate about half the world's consumption growth: the retiring and elderly in developed countries, China's working-age population, and North America's working-age population.

Many older adults in developed nations have saved sufficiently for retirement. In the United States, two-thirds of all new cars are sold to consumers over the age of 50. The elderly also spend more per person than younger people do because of their increasing health care needs. By 2030, this group will grow by 20 percent (an additional 100 million

International Monetary Fund (IMF) an international organization that acts as a lender of last resort, providing loans to troubled nations, and also works to promote trade through financial cooperation

Group of Twenty (G-20) a forum for international economic development that promotes discussion between industrial and emerging-market countries on key issues related to global economic stability

EXHIBIT 5.1	MEMBERS OF THE G-20		
Argentina	European Union	Italy	South Africa
Australia	France	Japan	Republic of Korea
Brazil	Germany	Mexico	Turkey
Canada	India	Russia	United Kingdom
China	Indonesia	Saudi Arabia	United States

people) and per capita consumption is expected to more than double.

By 2030, China's working-age population will account for 12 cents of every dollar spent in cities worldwide. This group has the very real potential to reshape global consumption, just as America's Baby Boomers—the richest generation in history—did in their prime years.

In 2018, about 130 million people in America worked full-time. Incomes tend to gradually increase with age among workers in their 20s and 30s. There is, however, a plateau among workers that lasts from their late 30s to their early 60s.[55] The average starting salaries for college graduates in 2018 was slightly above $50,000 a year.[56]

Even though the retiring and elderly are an important part of consumption growth, they present challenges as well. Most notably, the world's population is getting older. While aging has been evident in developed economies for some time—Japan and Russia have seen their populations age for several years running—the demographic deficit is now spreading to China and will soon reach Latin America. The European Commission predicts that by 2060, Germany's population will shrink by one-fifth and the number of working age Germans will fall from 54 million in 2010 to 36 million in 2060. China's labor force peaked in 2012. Thailand's fertility rate has fallen from 5 in the 1970s to 1.4 today.

5-3f Natural Resources

A final factor in the external environment that has become more evident in recent years is the distribution of natural resources.

Due to rapid improvements in shale oil production technology, America produced around 10.8 million barrels of oil per day in 2018. This puts America between Russia and Saudi Arabia as one of the top three oil producers in the world.[57] It marks a remarkable comeback for a country that had seen its oil output steadily decline for more than two decades. America is also the world's leading natural gas producer.[58]

Fresh water makes up just 2.5 percent of the total volume of the world's water. Given that almost 70 percent of this fresh water exists in the form of ice and permanent snow cover, demand for water could soon exceed supply. The United Nations predicts that by 2025, 1.8 billion people will be living in a country with an absolute water scarcity.[59] This will impact agriculture, the location of production facilities, demand for water-conservation products, and many other goods and services.

Some natural resources are already found in just a few select countries. This enables these countries to restrict supply and, therefore, inflate prices. Two rare

The distribution of natural resources has become a major issue in the external environment in the last decade.

Kokhanchikov/Shutterstock.com

earth elements, scandium and terbium, are used in everything from the powerful magnets located in wind turbines to the electronic circuits in smartphones. Although they are not as rare as the name suggests, 97 percent of the world's supply of these materials comes from China. Similarly, plants cannot grow without phosphorus, a key ingredient in fertilizer. Phosphate rock is found in only a handful of countries, including the United States, Morocco, and China.

Natural resources can have a major impact on international marketing. Warm climate and lack of water mean that many of Africa's countries will remain importers of foodstuffs. The United States, on the other hand, must rely on Africa for many precious metals. Vast differences in the locations and quantities available of natural resources create international dependencies, huge shifts of wealth, inflation and recession, export opportunities for countries with abundant resources, and even a stimulus for military intervention.

5-4 GLOBAL MARKETING BY THE INDIVIDUAL FIRM

A company should consider entering the global marketplace only after its management has a solid grasp of the global environment. Companies decide to "go global" for a number of reasons. Perhaps the most important is to earn additional profits. Managers may believe that international sales will result in higher profit margins or more added-on profits. A second stimulus is that a firm may have a unique product or technological advantage not available to other international competitors. Such advantages should result in major business

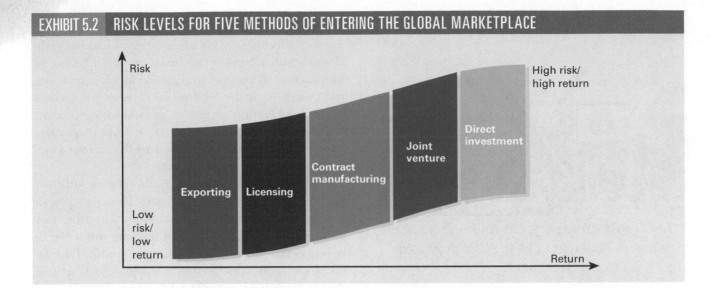

successes abroad. In other situations, management may have exclusive market information about foreign customers, marketplaces, or market situations not known to others. While exclusivity can provide an initial motivation for international marketing, managers must realize that competitors can be expected to catch up with the firm's information advantage. Finally, saturated domestic markets, excess capacity, and potential for economies of scale can also be motivators to go global. Economies of scale mean that average per-unit production costs fall as output is increased.

Many firms form multinational partnerships—called "strategic alliances"—to assist them in penetrating global markets; strategic alliances are examined in Chapter 7. Five other methods of entering the global marketplace are, in order of risk from least to most, exporting, licensing and franchising, contract manufacturing, joint venture, and direct investment (see Exhibit 5.2).

5-4a Exporting

When a company decides to enter the global market, exporting is usually the least complicated and least risky alternative. Exporting is selling domestically produced products to buyers in other countries. A company can sell directly to foreign importers or buyers. China is currently the world's largest exporter, but the United States and Germany are not far behind.

Global trade supports about 36 million U.S. jobs. Exports support over 10 million jobs.[60] Exports from Texas, California, and Washington State support the most jobs, most of them due to the export of goods. America's largest exports are food, beverages, and feed, with soybeans being the largest single item in the category. The fastest-growing form of exports is petroleum products. Boeing is

the nation's largest exporter. Interestingly, BMW's South Carolina plant exports nearly 75 percent of all the SUVs made there making it the biggest car exporter in America![61]

The U.S. Commercial Services, part of the Department of Commerce, helps U.S. businesses export goods and services to markets worldwide. This organization has offices in 14 countries and stations employees in U.S. embassies in nine additional markets. Among its various duties, the Commercial Services holds conferences around the United States to explain the benefits, types, and avenues of exporting. For example, one conference held in Scottsdale, Arizona, focused on helping advanced manufacturers learn about specific global markets. Top managers were invited to meet one on one with U.S. commercial diplomats visiting from abroad. The program also featured panel discussions on the latest industry export trends and how to identify opportunities in new and emerging markets.

The Services also provides marketing research information and conducts trade shows featuring U.S. products and services in countries around the world. Potential exporters can also join trade missions, whereby U.S. companies in specific industries travel together as a delegation, attend market briefings, participate in site visits and networking receptions, and have one-on-one matchmaking appointments with potential buyers. Some recent Services trade missions explored transportation technology and equipment in Turkey and smart technologies in Hong Kong and Taiwan.[62]

Instead of selling directly to foreign buyers, a company may decide to sell to intermediaries located in its domestic market.

exporting selling domestically produced products to buyers in other countries

The biggest car exporter in America is BMW! It exports 75 percent of the SUVs produced in its South Carolina plant.

The most common intermediary is the export merchant, also known as a **buyer for export**, which is usually treated like a domestic customer by the domestic manufacturer. The buyer for export assumes all risks and sells internationally from its own account. The domestic firm is involved only to the extent that its products are bought in foreign markets.

A second type of intermediary is the **export broker**, who plays the traditional broker's role by bringing buyer and seller together. The manufacturer still retains title and assumes all the risks. Export brokers operate primarily in agricultural products and raw materials.

Export agents, a third type of intermediary, are foreign sales agents/distributors who live in the foreign country and perform the same functions as domestic manufacturers' agents, helping with international financing, shipping, and so on. The U.S. Department of Commerce has an agent/distributor service that helps about 5,000 U.S. companies each year find an agent or distributor in virtually any country in the world. A second category of agents resides in the manufacturer's country but represents foreign buyers. This type of agent acts as a hired purchasing agent for foreign customers operating in the exporter's home market.

buyer for export an intermediary in the global market that assumes all ownership risks and sells globally for its own account

export broker an intermediary who plays the traditional broker's role by bringing buyer and seller together

export agent an intermediary who acts like a manufacturer's agent for the exporter; the export agent lives in the foreign market

licensing the legal process whereby a licensor allows another firm to use its manufacturing process, trademarks, patents, trade secrets, or other proprietary knowledge

5-4b Licensing and Franchising

Another effective way for a firm to move into the global arena with relatively little risk is to sell a license to manufacture its product to someone in a foreign country. **Licensing** is the legal process whereby a licensor allows another firm to use its manufacturing process, trademarks, patents, trade secrets, or other proprietary knowledge. The licensee, in turn, pays the licensor a royalty or fee agreed on by both parties.

A licensor must make sure it can exercise sufficient control over the licensee's activities to ensure proper quality, pricing, distribution, and so on. Licensing may also create a new competitor in the long run if the licensee decides to void the license agreement. International law is often ineffective in stopping such actions. Two common ways of maintaining effective control over licensees are shipping one or more critical components from the United States and locally registering patents and trademarks to the U.S. firm, not to the licensee. Garment companies maintain control by delivering only so many labels per day; they also supply their own fabric, collect the scraps, and do accurate unit counts.

Franchising in the global marketplace has grown rapidly in recent years. The world's largest franchisors are McDonald's, KFC, Burger King, Pizza Hut, 7-Eleven, Marriott International, RE/MAX, Dunkin' Donuts, InterContinental Hotels and Resorts, and Subway. InterContinental is based in the UK; the remainder are American.[63] Why are fast-food franchises so popular? They offer consistency. Whether they're in Alabama or Alaska, McDonald's customers can expect the same Big Mac and fries. In international markets, however, chains often have to adapt to local tastes and cultures. In Europe, for example, drinking an espresso is the norm after lunch.

By 2024, Taco Bell expects to be operating in over 40 countries.

In order to avoid standing in line twice or drinking a cold espresso after a burger and fries, McDonald's customers in much of Europe are given a token with their meal. They simply put the token in a self-serve machine, and out comes a steaming espresso.

Sometimes a franchise has to change its recipes to adapt to local cultures. In Japan, one popular Pizza Hut pie is topped with prawn, squid, tuna, mayonnaise, broccoli, onions, and tomato sauce. Another mixes teriyaki chicken with corn, seaweed, and mayonnaise. In South Korea, customers can get their pizza crusts stuffed with sweet potato mousse. In the Middle East, an adventurous customer can order his or her pizza with cheeseburgers embedded into the crust. Both McDonald's and Burger King have introduced all-black burgers in Japan. Americans may mistake them for a meal left on the grill too long—the buns, cheese, and sauce are pitch black—but they've actually been colored by squid ink.

Yum Brands, owner of KFC, Pizza Hut, and Taco Bell, is rapidly moving to an all-franchise model in most of its international markets. In late 2018, Yum spun off its 7,000 company-owned restaurants in the volatile China market as a separate, stand-alone company. At the beginning of 2019, 98 percent of Yum Brands restaurants were owned by franchisees. By 2024, the company expects its Taco Bell brand to be operating in over 40 countries. The firm plans to open a new KFC every five hours somewhere in the world.[64]

5-4c Contract Manufacturing

Firms that do not want to become involved in licensing or to become heavily involved in global marketing may engage in **contract manufacturing**, which is private-label manufacturing by a foreign company. The foreign company produces a certain volume of products to specification, with the domestic firm's brand name on the goods. The domestic company usually handles the marketing. Thus, the domestic firm can broaden its global marketing base without investing in overseas plants and equipment. After establishing a solid base, the domestic firm may switch to a joint venture or direct investment. One industry that uses a lot of contract manufacturing is pharmaceuticals.

5-4d Joint Venture

Joint ventures are somewhat similar to licensing agreements. In an international **joint venture**, the domestic firm buys part of a foreign company or joins with a foreign company to create a new entity. Bayer Crop Science of Germany and Boston start-up Ginkgo Bioworks created a joint venture entitled Joyn Bio. Ginkgo Bioworks genetically engineers microbes for the flavor, fragrance, and food industries. The goal of the joint venture is to design microbes for more sustainable agriculture.[65]

As the example demonstrates, global joint ventures are often made to gain access to a skill, technology, or market that one partner might not otherwise have. Similarly, Chinese heavy machinery maker Yuzhou Construction Machinery Group is discussing entering into a joint venture with Brazilian engineering firm OAS S.A. so it can launch construction projects in Africa and Latin America.

Not all international joint ventures involve a foreign corporation, however. Honda and Hitachi Automotive, both Japanese companies, have formed a joint venture to develop, produce, and sell motors for electric vehicles.

While potentially very lucrative, joint ventures can also be very risky. Many fail. Sometimes joint venture partners simply cannot agree on management strategies and policies. Often, joint ventures are the only way a government will allow a foreign company to enter its country. Joint ventures enable the local firm or government to acquire managerial skills and new technology.

5-4e Direct Investment

Foreign direct investment occurs when a business in one country invests in a business interest in another country. This usually takes the form of active ownership of a foreign company or of overseas manufacturing or marketing facilities. Foreign direct investment by U.S. firms is slightly over $6 trillion. The countries receiving the largest amount of direct foreign investment in 2017 were the Netherlands, the United Kingdom, and Luxembourg.[66] Direct investors have either a controlling interest or a large minority interest in the firm, so they have the greatest potential reward and the greatest potential risk.

A firm may make a foreign direct investment by acquiring an interest in an existing company or by building new facilities. It might do so because it has trouble transferring some resource to a foreign operation or getting that resource locally. One important resource is personnel, especially managers. If the local labor market is tight, the firm may buy an entire foreign firm and retain all its employees instead of paying higher salaries than competitors.

The United States is a popular place for direct investment by international

contract manufacturing private-label manufacturing by a foreign company

joint venture when a domestic firm buys part of a foreign company or joins with a foreign company to create a new entity companies. Foreign direct investment in the United States accounts for approximately $4 trillion.[67] The United States continues to receive more foreign investment flows than any country in the world. The United Kingdom is home to the largest investors in the United States, followed by Canada and Japan. U.S. affiliates of foreign firms employ more than 6 million people in the United States. UK-based BAE Systems recently began construction on a $45 million facility in Huntsville, Alabama. It is expected to create 300 or more new jobs. A leading elevator manufacturer in Germany called Thyssenkrupp announced plans to build a state-of-the-art U.S. headquarters in Atlanta. It will support over 900 new jobs.[68]

While the United States is receptive to foreign direct investment, some countries are not. Countries may block foreign direct investment completely or restrict it to specific industries. In some cases, governments are trying to protect domestic competitors. In others, they are blocking investment for political reasons. India recently opened up foreign investment in several industries, including retail and civil aviation. Apple asked for permission to open retail stores in India, but the country took years to agree. By 2018, there were only nine Apple stores in India despite a population of 1.35 billion.[69]

Facebook has been blocked on China's Internet since 2009. In 2017, China gave Facebook a license to open an office in Beijing—but the license was only good for three months! Even though Facebook has begun developing technology that can block or remove content that the ruling Communist Party of China deems unacceptable, the company still isn't welcome. Now, with native social media competitors WeChat, Weibo, and others in the market, competition will be very strong when and if Facebook ever receives permission to enter. In 2018, Facebook was given permission to open a $30 million subsidiary in Hangzhou called "Facebook Technology." One day later, the government retracted the permission and began to censor mentions of the new planned subsidiary in the news.[70]

5-5 THE GLOBAL MARKETING MIX

To succeed, firms seeking to enter into foreign trade must still adhere to the principles of the marketing mix. Information gathered on foreign markets through research is the basis for the four Ps of global marketing strategy: product, place (distribution), promotion, and price. Marketing managers who understand the advantages and disadvantages of different ways of entering the global market and the effect of the external environment on the firm's marketing mix have a better chance of reaching their goals.

The first step in creating a marketing mix is developing a thorough understanding of the global target market. Often this knowledge can be obtained through the same types of marketing research used in the domestic market (see Chapter 9). However, global marketing research is conducted in vastly different environments. Conducting a survey can be difficult in developing countries, where smartphone ownership is growing but is not always common and mail delivery is slow or sporadic. Drawing samples based on known population parameters is often difficult because of the lack of data. In some cities in Africa, Asia, Mexico, and South America, street maps are unavailable, streets are unidentified, and houses are unnumbered. Moreover, the questions a marketer can ask may differ in other cultures. In some cultures, people tend to be more private than in the United States and will not respond to personal questions on surveys. For instance, in France, questions about one's age and income are considered especially rude.

5-5a Product Decisions

With the proper information, a good marketing mix can be developed. One important decision is whether to alter the product or the promotion for the global marketplace. Other options are to radically change the product or to adjust either the promotional message or the product to suit local conditions.

ONE PRODUCT, ONE MESSAGE The strategy of global marketing standardization, which was discussed earlier, means developing a single product for all markets and promoting it the same way all over the world. For instance, Procter & Gamble (P&G) uses the same product and promotional themes for Head & Shoulders in China as it does in the United States. The advertising draws attention to a person's dandruff problem, which stands out in a nation of black-haired people. Head & Shoulders is now the best-selling shampoo in China, despite costing over 300 percent more than local brands. P&G markets its rich portfolio of personal-care, beauty, grooming, health, and fabric products in more than 180 countries. The firm has 20 brands that sell more than $1 billion annually around the world. Some brands, such as Duracell batteries, are heavily standardized. P&G has moved away from standardization for other brands, however.

Apple is often thought of as leader in global marketing standardization, but even Apple takes local markets into account. For example, although iPhones look and operate the same everywhere, their power cords, pricing, and wireless carrier specifics differ. Apple follows a strict customer service protocol in its stores around the world, but this protocol is always tailored to local cultures. Once a location for a store is selected, Apple executives make certain that the store design is inviting and that it fits into the surrounding architecture. Apple's localized e-commerce websites follow a standardized design, yet the content is always translated into the local language and checked by native speakers to make certain that nothing is lost in translation.

Global marketing standardization has paid well for Tesla in China. Tesla's electric car technology aligned perfectly with the Chinese government's priority to reduce pollution. One way that the government controls the number of new cars on the road is by limiting the number of new license plates issued. Drivers have to wait years to get one through a lottery system. One year, 6.2 million people applied for just 36,757 available Beijing plates.[71] Once they get a plate, they are barred from driving one day a week. But plates for electric cars fall under different rules. Drivers can get a plate without a wait with no one-day driving restrictions or paying a $12,000 plate fee.

When Tesla first entered the Chinese market in 2014, it had too few charging stations. However, the company soon built out a large number of stations, and sales increased. Another factor that helped Tesla gain market share was its direct sales model. New car dealerships in China inflate costs by tens of thousands of dollars through additional fees. Tesla sells direct in China at the same price level that it does in the United States after currency adjustment.

In 2018, Tesla announced plans to build its first Chinese plant in Shanghai. The $2 billion plant will be the first American auto plant without a Chinese partner. Tesla will build 250,000 mass market Model 3 sedans along with battery packs starting in 2021.[72] Due to the recent tariff wars, China has imposed a 40 percent tariff on vehicles manufactured in the United States and exported to China. Producing locally will avoid import tariffs on the Model 3.

Global marketing standardization can sometimes backfire. Unchanged products may fail simply because of cultural factors. Any type of war game tends to do very poorly in Germany, even though Germany is by far the world's biggest game-playing nation. A successful game in Germany is highly detailed and has a thick rulebook. In Russia, Campbell's Soups failed because cooks prefer to make soup from scratch.

PRODUCT INVENTION In the context of global marketing, product invention can be taken to mean either creating a new product for a market or drastically changing an existing product. For example, more than 100 unique Pringles potato chip flavors have been invented for international markets. Prawn Cocktail (the United Kingdom), Seaweed (Japan), Blueberry (China), Cinnamon Sweet Potato (France), and Bangkok Grilled Chicken Wing (Thailand) are some of the many Pringles flavors available outside the United States. Chinese consumers found Oreo cookies "too sweet," while Indian consumers said that they were "too bitter." In response, Kraft changed the recipe in each country and created a new Green Tea Oreo flavor for China.

In the United States, a Kit Kat candy bar is usually just a Kit Kat. But in Japan, where the product comes in 350 flavors, more than 30 of which are on the market at once, the classic candy bar is a trendsetter. The chocolate-covered wafer confection debuted in Japan in 1973 and it enjoys some natural advantages in the country, where Kit Kat fortuitously translates to "You will

Want to buy a car in China? Not so fast there! You may have to wait years to get a license plate!

You can typically find just one flavor of Kit Kat in America. However, in Japan you can choose from over 350 flavors!

surely win."[73] The candy quickly gained status as a good luck charm for school exams. Fueled by Japan's gift-giving culture, Kit Kat continues to grow in popularity. Two best-selling flavors are Mini Rum Raisin (with local Tokyo ingredients) and Purple Sweet Potato (an Okinawa specialty).

PRODUCT ADAPTATION Another alternative for global marketers is to alter a basic product to meet local conditions. In India, Starbucks sells a tandoori paneer roll. KFC makes a "paneer zinger." Burger King sells its classic Whopper hamburger alongside a cheese-based Paneer King burger. This is largely how international food brands court India's 1.25 billion consumers—by playing to local tastes. But Domino's is doing more than simply creating new products in its attempt to woo Indian customers. It has reimagined everything about itself, from changing the flour it uses to maintaining a delicate balance between local tastes and Western influence. This dedication to adaptation has made Domino's India's largest international foreign-food chain.

L'Oréal has realized that small is big in India. Despite 20 years in India's growing beauty and personal care market, the company has had difficulty growing its market share above 4 percent. Taking a new approach, L'Oréal adapted the size of its product offerings to much smaller packages targeted at poorer consumers. Unilever and Procter & Gamble had already moved to smaller packages, or sachets, back in the 1990s. In China and Brazil, sachets account for less than a third of total sales volume. In India, however, more than 4.4 billion small-size personal care products are sold annually. Much of India's retail environment consists of very small stores. With limited shelf space, it is much easier to display a selection of sachet-size products rather than full-size ones. L'Oréal now sells sachets of shampoo, men's face wash, and Garnier hair color in India—with great success. The firm's success in India has inspired the company to try sachet packaging in Kenya and South Africa as well.

About a year after bringing its Echo speakers to foreign markets such as the UK and Germany, Amazon.com Inc. is starting to ship the voice-controlled hardware to India. In that time, teams of linguists, speech scientists, developers, and engineers have given the Echo's virtual assistant, Alexa, a decidedly local makeover.

This Alexa uses Hinglish, a blend of Hindi and English, and speaks with an unmistakably Indian accent. She knows Independence Day is August 15, not July 4, and wishes listeners, "Happy Diwali and a prosperous New Year!" She refers to the living room as the "drawing

Success in India requires Alexa to speak a combination of Hindi and English.

room" and will add *jeera* (cumin), *haldi* (turmeric), and *atta* (flour) to your shopping list. And her cricket jokes are truly, authentically terrible. "We wanted our devices to talk, walk, and feel Indian," says Parag Gupta, head of product management for Amazon Devices in India. "Alexa is not a visiting American. She has a very Indian personality."[74]

5-5b Promotion Adaptation

Another global marketing strategy is to maintain the same basic product but alter the promotional strategy. For example, bicycles are mainly pleasure vehicles in the United States, but in many parts of the world, they are a family's main mode of transportation. Thus, promotion in these countries should stress durability and efficiency. In contrast, U.S. advertising may emphasize escaping and having fun.

Language barriers, translation problems, and cultural differences have generated numerous headaches for international marketing managers. For example, a toothpaste claiming to give users white teeth was especially inappropriate in many areas of Southeast Asia, where the well-to-do chew betel nuts and black teeth are a sign of higher social status.

Coca-Cola sent out a tweet to Russian consumers, featuring a cartoon with a snow-covered map of the country. The map was outdated, omitting several Russian-owned territories such as Kaliningrad, which was annexed by Russia following World War II. Russian patriots were not happy. When Procter & Gamble started selling its Pampers diapers in Japan, it used a stork delivering a baby on the package. This seemed confusing to Japanese moms and dads. After doing some research, Procter & Gamble found that the story of a stork bringing new babies to parents was not part of Japanese folklore. Instead, babies float down a river to their parents inside giant peaches.

Unilever's Lifebuoy hand soap virtually disappeared from the American market 50 years ago, but it is alive and well internationally. Lifebuoy dominates the market in India and is a leading seller in several emerging markets. With its new "Help a Child Reach 5," campaign, Lifebuoy pledged to help save lives by spreading the importance of good handwashing habits around the world. This campaign is driven by two staggering figures. First, 2 million children fail to reach their fifth birthday every year because of illnesses like diarrhea and pneumonia. Second, washing one's hands with soap at key occasions can reduce diarrhea by 45 percent and pneumonia by 23 percent, substantially reducing infant deaths worldwide.

Researchers found that consumer values like hedonism (getting much pleasure out of life as possible) and personal power vary enormously in importance across countries. Thus, promotions that position products on these variables should also vary by country. Attitudes about luxury and status, for example, were more favorable in brand promotions in Russia and China than in Western Europe, the United States, and Australia.[75] Thus, the equality promotion "Campaign for Real Beauty" for Dove soap was much more successful in countries where egalitarianism was very important.

5-5c Place (Distribution)

Solving promotional and product problems does not guarantee global marketing success. The product must still get adequate distribution. For example, Europeans do not play sports as much as Americans do, so they do not visit sporting-goods stores as often. Realizing this, Reebok started selling its shoes in about 800 traditional shoe stores in France. In just one year, the company doubled its French sales.

Taiwanese convenience stores are quite different from what is found in the United States. Beyond the staple snacks, they provide an array of services, including dry cleaning, train and concert ticket reservations, traffic fine and utility payment, hot sit-down meals, mail drop-off, and book pickup. They also deliver everything from refrigerators to multicourse banquets. As you might expect, heavy convenience store patronage is the norm in Taiwan.

Global supply chains and distribution systems will be discussed in detail in Chapter 13.

5-5d Pricing

Once marketing managers have determined a global product, distribution, and promotion strategy, they can select the remainder of the marketing mix. Pricing presents some unique problems in the global sphere. Exporters must not only cover their production costs but must also consider transportation costs, insurance, taxes, and tariffs. When deciding on a final price, marketers need to determine how much customers are willing to spend on a particular product. They also need to ensure that their foreign buyers will pay the price. Because developing nations lack mass purchasing power, selling to them often poses special pricing problems. Sometimes a product can be simplified in order to lower the price. A firm must not assume that low-income countries are willing to accept lower quality, however.

EXCHANGE RATES The **exchange rate** is the price of one country's currency in terms of another country's currency. If a country's currency *appreciates*, less of that country's currency is needed to buy another country's currency. If a country's currency *depreciates*, more of that currency will be needed to buy another country's currency.

How do appreciation and depreciation affect the prices of a country's goods? If, say, the U.S. dollar depreciates relative to the Japanese yen, U.S. residents will need to pay more dollars to buy Japanese goods. As of October 20, 2018, $1.00 was worth ¥112.47. At this exchange rate, a U.S. resident would pay $17,782.52 for a ¥2 million Toyota automobile (¥2 million divided by ¥112.47 = $17,782.52). If the dollar depreciated to being worth ¥98, then the same vehicle would cost the U.S. resident $20,408 (¥2 million divided by ¥98 = $20,408).

As the dollar depreciates, the prices of Japanese goods rise for U.S. residents, so they buy fewer Japanese goods—thus, U.S. imports from Japan may decline. At the same time, as the dollar depreciates relative to the yen, the yen appreciates

exchange rate the price of one country's currency in terms of another country's currency

Currency Exchange Rates

As of May 15, 2017, 1.00 U.S. Dollar (USD) is worth...

- 0.78 British Pound (GBP)
- 0.91 Euro (EUR)
- 1.00 Swiss Franc (CHF)
- 1.36 Canadian Dollar (CAD)
- 3.10 Brazilian Real (BRL)
- 4.33 Malaysian Ringgit (MYR)
- 6.89 Chinese Yuan Renminbi (CNY)
- 18.68 Mexican Peso (MXN)
- 113.67 Japanese Yen (JPY)
- 56.39 Russian Ruble (RUB)
- 64.07 Indian Rupee (INR)
- 1116.36 South Korean Won (KRW)

relative to the dollar. This means prices of U.S. goods fall for the Japanese, so they buy more U.S. goods—and U.S. exports rise.

Although the example above uses depreciation of the U.S. dollar, in reality, the dollar has been appreciating against currencies around the globe in recent years. The U.S. dollar has appreciated over 20 percent from 2014 to 2019.[76] Why? When there is significant chaos in the world, such as the ongoing battle in Syria, and Britain's exit from the EU, investors and businesses look for economic strength, stability, and safety in a currency. Thus, money rushes in to the United States and its currency.

Traditionally, a strong dollar has been a badge of honor for America. However, a strong dollar swells the trade deficit, making imports less expensive and exports more expensive for foreign buyers. The strong dollar has hurt GM and Ford sales in Europe, and John Deere and Caterpillar sales in Asia. Furthermore, when American multinationals make sales outside the United States in foreign currencies such as the yen, euro, and pound, it translates into fewer dollars than before the dollar's rise in value.

Currency markets operate under a system of **floating exchange rates**. Prices of different currencies "float" up and down based on the demand for and the supply of each currency. Global currency traders create the supply of and demand for a particular country's currency based on that country's investment, trade potential, and economic strength. Government actions can also impact exchange rates. Sanctions imposed against Russia for invading Crimea and engaging in the Ukrainian border conflict caused the Russian ruble to plunge in value.

Theoretically, exchange rates should adjust over time so that one dollar buys the same amount everywhere. However, because so many factors can influence exchange rates, currencies sometimes become overvalued or undervalued. Every year, the *Economist* magazine analyzes the cost of a Big Mac around the world to create a somewhat tongue-in-cheek index of currency valuations. In other words, the *Economist* converts the cost of a Big Mac from local currencies to U.S. dollars using current exchange rates and sees how they compare. In 2018, the most undervalued currency was Egypt (undervalued by 68 percent) followed by the Ukraine, Russia, Malaysia, and Indonesia. The most overvalued currency was Switzerland by 19 percent and then Sweden at 6 percent.[77]

floating exchange rates a system in which prices of different currencies move up and down based on the demand for and the supply of each currency

dumping the sale of an exported product at a price lower than that charged for the same or a like product in the "home" market of the exporter

Egypt has the world's most undervalued currency according to the Big Mac currency index.

DUMPING **Dumping** is the sale of an exported product at a price lower than that charged for the same or a like product in the "home" market of the exporter. This practice is regarded as a form of price discrimination that can potentially harm the importing nation's competing industries. Dumping may occur as a result of exporter business strategies that include: (1) trying to increase an overseas market share, (2) temporarily distributing products in overseas markets to offset slack demand in the home market, (3) lowering unit costs by exploiting large-scale production, and (4) attempting to maintain stable prices during periods of exchange-rate fluctuations.

Historically, the dumping of goods has presented serious problems in international trade. As a result, dumping has led to significant disagreements among countries and diverse views about its harmfulness. Some trade economists view dumping as harmful only when it involves the use of "predatory" practices that intentionally try to eliminate competition and gain monopoly power in a market. They believe that predatory dumping rarely occurs and that antidumping rules are a protectionist tool whose cost to consumers and import-using industries exceeds the benefits to the industries receiving protection.

Over the past decade, the U.S. International Trade Commission declared antidumping duties in more than 80 investigations of foreign companies. While most cases were brought against Chinese companies, firms from more than 25 different countries faced antidumping duties. The products being investigated in 2018 ranged from cast-iron pipe, pasta, fresh tomatoes, woven sacks, washing machines, to wind towers and many more. Countries involved include China, Italy, Turkey, Japan, Taiwan, Mexico, Vietnam, Canada, Greece, Korea, Pakistan, Ukraine, Kazakhstan, Belarus, Latvia, Poland, Moldova, Indonesia, France, and India.[78] Thus, dumping problems cover a wide swath of the globe.

In addition to antidumping duties, the U.S. International Trade Commission (ITC) levies countervailing duties on foreign suppliers and manufacturers. A **countervailing duty** is when a foreign government provides subsidies or assistance to a local industry which enables the firms to sell at artificially low prices in the global market. Assistance can be in the form of low-rate loans, tax exemptions, or cash payments. After an investigation by the ITC, a countervailing duty is assessed based on the value of the subsidy.

COUNTERTRADE Global trade does not always involve cash. Countertrade is a fast-growing way to conduct global business. In **countertrade**, all or part of the payment for goods or services is in the form of other goods or services. Countertrade is thus a form of barter (swapping goods for goods), an age-old practice whose origins have been traced back to cave dwellers. The U.S. Department of Commerce says that roughly 30 percent of all global trade is countertrade. In fact, both India and China have made billion-dollar government purchasing lists, with most of the goods to be paid for by countertrade.

One common type of countertrade is straight barter. The Malaysian government purchased 20 diesel-electric locomotives from General Electric in exchange for a supply of 200,000 metric tons of palm oil. Sometimes, countertrades involve both cash and goods. General Motors sold locomotive and diesel engines to Yugoslavia in exchange for $4 million and Yugoslavian cutting tools. Another form of countertrade is the compensation agreement. Typically, a company provides technology and equipment for a plant in a developing nation and agrees to take full or partial payment in goods produced by that plant. For example, General Tire Company supplied equipment and know-how for a Romanian truck tire plant. In turn, General Tire sold the tires it received from the plant in the United States under the Victoria brand name. Both sides benefit even though they do not use cash.

THE IMPACT OF THE INTERNET

In many respects, going global is easier than it has ever been before. Opening an e-commerce site on the Internet immediately puts a company in the international marketplace. Sophisticated language translation software can make any site accessible to people around the world. Global shippers such as UPS, FedEx, and DHL help solve international e-commerce distribution complexities. E4X Inc. offers software to ease currency conversions by allowing customers to pay in the currency of their choice. E4X collects the payment from the customer and then pays the site in U.S. dollars. The Internet has been especially beneficial to global trade in services. An estimated 50 percent of services trade is made possible by digital technology.

Nevertheless, the promise of "borderless commerce" and the global "Internet economy" are still being restrained by the old brick-and-mortar rules, regulations, and habits. For example, Lands' End is not allowed to mention its unconditional refund policy on its e-commerce site in Germany because German retailers, which normally do not allow returns after 14 days, sued and won a court ruling blocking mention of it.

> **countervailing duty** a tax on imported goods to offset a subsidy or other financial assistance given to a foreign exporter by its government that enables the foreign exporter to sell at an artificially low price in the global marketplace
>
> **countertrade** a form of trade in which all or part of the payment for goods or services is in the form of other goods or services

6 | Consumer Decision Making

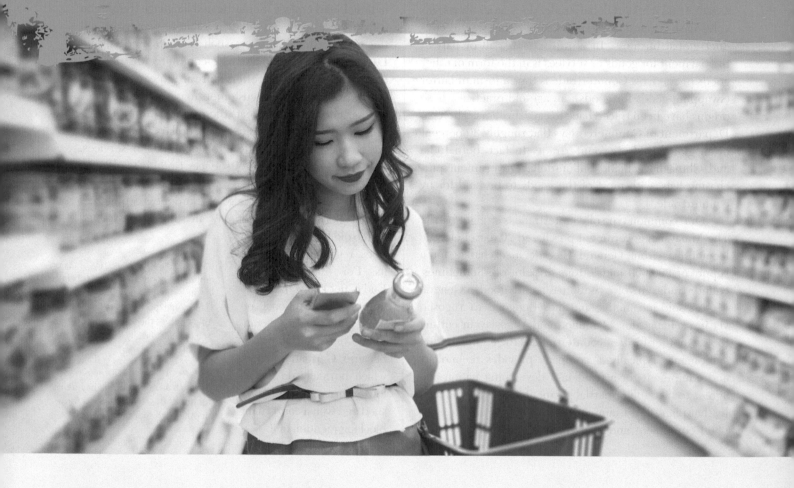

LEARNING OUTCOMES

After studying this chapter, you will be able to . . .

6-1 Explain why marketing managers should understand consumer behavior

6-2 Analyze the components of the consumer decision-making process

6-3 Explain the consumer's postpurchase evaluation process

6-4 Identify the types of consumer buying decisions and discuss the significance of consumer involvement

6-5 Describe how some marketers are reconceptualizing the consumer decision-making process

6-6 Identify and understand the cultural factors that affect consumer buying decisions

6-7 Identify and understand the social factors that affect consumer buying decisions

6-8 Identify and understand the individual factors that affect consumer buying decisions

6-9 Identify and understand the psychological factors that affect consumer buying decisions

Dragon Images/Shutterstock.com

THE IMPORTANCE OF UNDERSTANDING CONSUMER BEHAVIOR

Consumers' product and service preferences are constantly changing. Marketing managers must understand these desires in order to create a proper marketing mix for a well-defined market. So it is critical that marketing managers have a thorough knowledge of consumer behavior. **Consumer behavior** describes how consumers make purchase decisions and how they use and dispose of the purchased goods or services. The study of consumer behavior also includes factors that influence purchase decisions and product use.

Understanding how consumers make purchase decisions can help marketing managers in several ways. For example, if the product development manager for Trek bicycles learns through research that a more comfortable seat is a key attribute for purchasers of mountain bikes, Trek can redesign the seat to meet that criterion. If the firm cannot change the design in the short run, it can use promotion in an effort to change consumers' decision-making criteria. Trek, for example, could promote the ultra-light weight, durability, and performance of its current mountain bikes.

Buying a mountain bike, or anything else, is all about value. **Value** is a personal assessment of the net worth one obtains from making a purchase. To put it another way, value is what you get minus what you give up. When you buy something, you hope to get benefits like durability, convenience, prestige, affection, happiness, a sense of belonging, relief from hunger…the list goes on. In order to receive these benefits, you must give something up. You may sacrifice money, self-image, time, convenience, effort, opportunity, or a combination thereof. *Value* can also mean an enduring belief shared by a society that a specific mode of conduct is personally or socially preferable to another mode of conduct; this definition will be discussed later in the chapter.

Purchases are made based on **perceived value**, which is what you *expect* to get. The actual value may be more or less than you expected. One of your authors bought a well-known brand of coffee maker with a thermal carafe. He likes to drink coffee all morning but found that traditional coffee makers' heating elements tended to turn the coffee bitter and thick-tasting after a few hours. The thermal carafe has no such heating element, so the coffee stays fresh. That is, if the coffee actually makes it into the carafe. The carafe lid has a valve that lets the coffee drip into the carafe basin. However, the valve tends to stick, and after about a week of use, the valve stuck during a fill-up, and coffee went all over the kitchen counter. No value there! (For the curious, the author has moved on to a new capsule-style coffee maker.)

The value received from a purchase can be broken down into two categories. **Utilitarian value** is derived from a product or service that helps the consumer solve problems and accomplish tasks. Buying a washing machine and dryer gives you a convenient means of cleaning your clothes. Buying a new pair of eyeglasses lets you better view the smartphone screen. Utilitarian value, then, is a means to an end. Value is provided because the purchase allows something good to happen.

The second form of value is **hedonic value**. Hedonic value is an end in itself rather than as a means to an end. The purchase tends to give us good feelings, happiness, and satisfaction. The value is provided entirely through the experience and emotions associated with consumption, not because another end is accomplished. Taking a ski vacation or a trip to the beach gives us hedonic value. Spending a day in a spa is a source of hedonic value. A coffee maker provides utilitarian value, but the coffee itself provides hedonic value.

Utilitarian and hedonic values are not mutually exclusive. In some cases, the purchase experience can give you both hedonic and utilitarian value. Morton's The Steakhouse is considered to be one of the top steak restaurant chains in the United States. Going to a Morton's and

consumer behavior processes a consumer uses to make purchase decisions, as well as to use and dispose of purchased goods or services; also includes factors that influence purchase decisions and product use

value a personal assessment of the net worth one obtains from making a purchase, or the enduring belief that a specific mode of conduct is personally or socially preferable to another mode of conduct

perceived value the value a consumer *expects* to obtain from a purchase

utilitarian value a value derived from a product or service that helps the consumer solve problems and accomplish tasks

hedonic value a value that acts as an end in itself rather than as a means to an end enjoying the atmosphere and a fine steak will give you hedonic value. At the same time, it satisfies your hunger pangs and thus provides utilitarian value. Some of the best consumer experiences are high in both utilitarian and hedonic value.

Acquiring value comes from making a purchase. How does one go about making the decision to buy? We explore this topic next.

6-2 THE TRADITIONAL CONSUMER DECISION-MAKING PROCESS

When buying products, particularly new or expensive items, consumers generally follow the consumer decision-making process **shown in Exhibit 6.1: (1) need recognition, (2) information search, (3) evaluation of alternatives, (4) purchase, and (5) postpurchase behavior.** These five steps represent the traditional buying process, which can be used as a guide for studying how consumers make decisions. It is important to note, though, that consumers' decisions do not always proceed in order through all of these steps. In fact, the consumer may end the process at any time or may not even make a purchase. Note, too, that technology is changing how people make decisions. A new conceptualization of the buying process is discussed later in the chapter. We begin, however, by examining the traditional purchase process in greater detail.

6-2a Need Recognition

The first stage in the consumer decision-making process is need recognition. Need recognition is the result of an imbalance between actual and desired states. The imbalance arouses and activates the consumer decision-making process. A want is the recognition of an unfulfilled need and a product that will satisfy it. For example, have you ever gotten blisters from an old running shoe and realized you needed new shoes? Or maybe you have seen a new sports car drive down the street and wanted to buy it. Wants can be viewed in terms of four goals: economizing, sustaining, treating, and rewarding.[1] The specific goal that a consumer is trying to fulfill influences how he or she allocates money, time, and effort. Consider a coffee drinker who has just run out of coffee at home. If she wanted to satisfy an economizing goal, she might purchase one of three brands she uses frequently because it is the one that is currently on sale. If, however, she wanted to satisfy a sustaining goal, she would be more likely to purchase her favorite brand because she prefers the taste over the other two brands she sometimes buys. If she wanted to satisfy a treating goal, she might buy a cup of coffee at Starbucks. Finally, if she wanted to satisfy a rewarding goal, she might opt to order a latte while reading her favorite book at a trendy new cafe.

Need recognition is triggered when a consumer is exposed to either an internal or an external stimulus, which is any unit of input affecting one or more of the five senses: sight, smell, taste, touch, and hearing. *Internal stimuli* are experiences, such as hunger or thirst. For example, you may hear your stomach growl and then realize you are hungry. *External stimuli* are influences from an outside source. In today's digital age, stimuli can come from a multitude of sources. Perhaps it was a YouTube video that created a purchase desire. Perhaps it was a Google search on a smartphone or an interactive advertisement playing on a large touch-enabled screen. Or perhaps it was a friend's video posted on Facebook.

The imbalance between actual and desired states is sometimes referred to as the *want–got gap*. That is, there is a difference between what a customer has and what he or she would like to have. This gap does not always trigger consumer action. The gap must be large enough to drive the consumer to do something. Just because your stomach growls once does not mean that you necessarily will stop what you are doing and go eat.

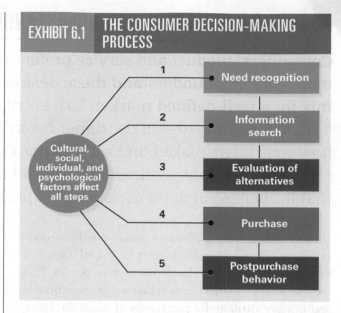

EXHIBIT 6.1 THE CONSUMER DECISION-MAKING PROCESS

1. Need recognition
2. Information search
3. Evaluation of alternatives
4. Purchase
5. Postpurchase behavior

Cultural, social, individual, and psychological factors affect all steps

consumer decision-making process a five-step process used by consumers when buying goods or services

need recognition result of an imbalance between actual and desired states

want recognition of an unfulfilled need and a product that will satisfy it

stimulus any unit of input affecting one or more of the five senses: sight, smell, taste, touch, hearing

A marketing manager's objective is to get consumers to recognize this want–got gap. Advertising, sales promotion, and social media often provide this stimulus. Surveying buyer preferences and data mining provides marketers with information about consumer needs and wants that can be used to tailor products and services. Marketing managers can create wants on the part of the consumer. An ad promoting a healthy, active lifestyle and the fun of fitness tracking may inspire you to purchase a wearable fitness tracker like a Fitbit Alta HR or a Polar M430. A want can be for a specific product or it can be for a certain attribute or feature of a product. Runners may purchase the M430, for example, because they like the heart rate and GPS features as well as the price.

6-2b Information Search

After recognizing a need or want, consumers search for information about the various alternatives available to satisfy it. For example, you know you are interested in seeing a movie, but you are not sure what to see. So you visit the Rotten Tomatoes website to see what is getting great reviews by both critics and your peers on Facebook. This is a type of information search, which can occur internally, externally, or both. In an **internal information search**, the person recalls information stored in the memory. This stored information stems largely from previous experience with a product. For example, while traveling with your family, you may choose to stay at a hotel you have stayed in before because you remember that the hotel had clean rooms and friendly service.

In contrast, an **external information search** seeks information in the outside environment. There are two basic types of external information sources: non–marketing-controlled and marketing-controlled. A **non–marketing-controlled information source** is a product information source that is not associated with marketers promoting a product. These information sources include personal experiences (trying or observing a new product), personal sources (family, friends, acquaintances, and coworkers who may recommend a product or service), public sources (such as Rotten Tomatoes, *Consumer Reports*, and other rating organizations that comment on products and services), and social media. Social media, of course, includes both marketing and non–marketing controlled. Once you have read reviews on Rotten Tomatoes to decide which movie to see (public source), you may search your memory for positive theater experiences to determine where you will go (personal experience). Or you might rely on a friend's recommendation to try out a new theater (personal

source). Marketers gather information on how these information sources work and use it to attract customers. For example, car manufacturers know that younger customers are likely to get information from friends and family, so they try to develop enthusiasm for their products via word of mouth and social media.

Living in the digital age has changed the way consumers get non–marketing-controlled information. It can be from blogs, Amazon, social media, web forums, or consumer opinion sites such as www.consumerreview.com, www.tripadvisor.com, or www.epinions.com. Eighty percent of U.S. consumers research electronics, computers, and media online before making an in-store purchase, and a quarter of shoppers use at least four sources for product information. To give you an idea of the number of searches this implies, Google averages more than 3.5 billion searches a month. This number is only going to expand.

The Internet has changed the quality of information available to make purchase decisions. In the past, consumers used quality proxies to help determine what to buy. A proxy could be a brand name ("it is made by Nike so it must be good"), price ("higher price meant higher quality"), or origin ("made in the USA is better"). Today, consumers can appraise a product based on how it is evaluated by others. If you are looking for a hotel in New York City, for example, you can easily view a ranking of all New York hotels based on thousands of reviews on websites like TripAdvisor. This provides much better information than simply relying on a brand name (such as Hilton) because you have the direct experience of others to guide you. Expedia allows only customers who have purchased a service (such as a flight, car, or hotel room) to write a review. Similarly, Amazon identifies whether a review matches a confirmed transaction. Amazon also bans reviews for which the reviewer received free or discounted items from the company being reviewed.

Social media are playing an ever-increasing role in consumer information search. Eighty-one percent of respondents to a recent survey reported that social media posts made by family and friends directly impacted their purchase decisions. Seventy-eight percent reported that posts made by companies influenced their buying decisions.[2]

Although the use of a smartphones to make

internal information search the process of recalling information stored in the memory

external information search the process of seeking information in the outside environment

non–marketing-controlled information source a product information source that is not associated with advertising or promotion

Smartphones and social media are playing an ever-increasing role in consumer decision making.

purchases is rising, consumers primarily use their smartphones and tablets to research products before buying. Consumers spend more time in stores when using their smartphones. In theory, a smartphone causes consumers to become distracted from their shopping task. Once distracted, they spend more time in the store, examine shelf information more, and divert from their normal shopping path more often. This ultimately increases the purchase total. Researchers have confirmed that in grocery stores, for example, the longer a shopper remains in a store, the more they tend to buy.[3] Therefore, retailers might offer targeted digital coupons while a person shops or reward them for their participation in a simple mobile game or app while shopping. Another option might be placing charging devices on shopping carts and, of course, offering free wi-fi.

Not every information search is about comparing Product or Service Firm A with Product or Service Firm B. Yet, the online search can still influence purchase patterns. For example, a shopper may browse recipe website or watch cooking demonstration videos before deciding on a dinner party menu. This research helps the shopper decide which ingredients to purchase at the supermarket.

A **marketing-controlled information source** is biased toward a specific product because it originates with marketers promoting that product. Marketing-controlled information sources include mass media advertising (radio, newspaper, television, and magazine advertising), sales promotion (contests, displays, premiums, and so

marketing-controlled information source a product information source that originates with marketers promoting the product

forth), salespeople, product labels and packaging, and social media. Research shows that developing a social media community with a dedicated fan base, such as an active Facebook page, significantly strengthens customer relationships with a company and brand. Moreover, it has a positive impact on revenue and profits.[4]

THE EXTENT OF INFORMATION SEARCH The extent to which an individual conducts an external search depends on his or her perceived risk, knowledge, prior experience, and level of interest in the good or service. Generally, as the perceived risk of the purchase increases, the consumer enlarges the search and considers more alternative brands. For example, suppose that you want to purchase a surround-sound system for your home entertainment system. The decision is relatively risky because of the expense and technical nature of the surround-sound system, so you are motivated to search for information about models, prices, options, compatibility with existing entertainment products, and capabilities. You may decide to compare attributes of many speaker systems because the value of the time expended finding the "right" stereo will be less than the cost of buying the wrong system.

A consumer's knowledge about the product or service will also affect the extent of an external information search. A consumer who is knowledgeable and well informed about a potential purchase is less likely to search for additional information. In addition, the more knowledgeable consumers are, the more efficiently they will conduct the search process, thereby requiring less time to search. For example, many consumers know that Spirit Airlines and other discount airlines have much lower fares, so they generally use the discounters and do not even check fares at other carriers.

The extent of a consumer's external search is also affected by confidence in one's decision-making ability. A confident consumer not only has sufficient stored information about the product but also feels self-assured about making the right decision. People lacking this confidence will continue an information search even when they know a great deal about the product. Consumers with prior experience in buying a certain product will have less perceived risk than inexperienced consumers. Therefore, they will spend less time searching and limit the number of products they consider.

A third factor influencing the external information search is product experience. Consumers who have had a positive experience with a product are more likely to limit their search to items related to the positive experience. For example, when flying, consumers are likely to choose airlines with which they have had positive experiences, such as consistent on-time arrivals, and avoid airlines with which they have had a negative experience, such as lost luggage.

Finally, the extent of the search is positively related to the amount of interest a consumer has in a product. A consumer who is more interested in a product will spend more time searching for information and alternatives. For example, suppose you are a dedicated runner who reads jogging and fitness magazines and catalogs. In searching for a new pair of running shoes, you may enjoy reading about the new brands available and spend more time and effort than other buyers in deciding on the right shoe.

The consumer's information search should yield a group of brands, sometimes called the buyer's **evoked set** (or **consideration set**), which are the consumer's most preferred alternatives. From this set, the buyer will further evaluate the alternatives and make a choice. Consumers do not consider all brands available in a product category, but they do seriously consider a much smaller set. For example, from the many brands of pizza available, consumers are likely to consider only the alternatives that fit their price range, location, take-out/ delivery needs, and taste preferences. Having too many choices can, in fact, confuse consumers and cause them to delay the decision to buy, or in some instances, cause them not to buy at all.

6-2c Evaluation of Alternatives and Purchase

After getting information and constructing an evoked set of alternative products, the consumer is ready to make a decision. A consumer will use the information stored in memory and obtained from outside sources to develop a set of criteria. Recent research has shown that exposure to certain cues in your everyday environment can affect decision criteria and purchase. For example, when NASA landed the *Pathfinder* spacecraft on Mars, it captured media attention worldwide. The candy maker Mars also noted a rather unusual increase in sales. Although the Mars bar takes its name from the company's founder and not the planet, consumers apparently responded to news about the planet Mars by purchasing more Mars bars.

The environment, internal information, and external information help consumers evaluate and compare alternatives. One way to begin narrowing the number of choices in the evoked set is to pick a product attribute and then exclude all products in the set that do not have that attribute. For example, assume Jane and Jill, both college sophomores, are looking for their first apartment. They need a two-bedroom apartment, reasonably priced and located near campus. They want the apartment to have a swimming pool, washer and dryer, and covered parking. Jane and Jill begin their search with all 50 apartments in the area and systematically eliminate complexes that lack the features they need. Hence, they may reduce their list to 10 apartments that possess all of the desired attributes. Now, they can use cutoffs to further narrow their choices. Cutoffs are either minimum or maximum levels of an attribute that an alternative must pass to be considered. Suppose Jane and Jill set a maximum of $1,000 per month for rent. Then all apartments with rent higher than $1,000 will be eliminated, further reducing the list of apartments from 10 to 8. A final way to narrow the choices is to rank the attributes under consideration in order of importance and evaluate the products based on how well each performs on the most important attributes. To reach a final decision on one of the remaining eight apartments, Jane and Jill may decide that proximity to campus is the most important attribute. As a result, they will choose to rent the apartment closest to campus.

If new brands are added to an evoked set, the consumer's evaluation of the existing brands in that set changes. As a result, certain brands in the original set may become more desirable. Suppose Jane and Jill find two apartments located an equal distance from campus, one priced at $800 and the other at $750. Faced with this choice, they may decide that the $800 apartment is too expensive given that a comparable apartment is cheaper. If they add a $900 apartment to the list, however, then they may perceive the $800 apartment as more reasonable and decide to rent it.

The purchase decision process described above is a piecemeal process. That is, the evaluation is made by examining alternative advantages and disadvantages along important product attributes. A different way consumers can evaluate a product is according to a categorization process. The evaluation of an alternative depends on the particular category to which it is assigned. Categories can be very general (motorized forms of transportation), or they can be very specific (Harley-Davidson motorcycles). Typically, these categories are associated with some degree of liking or disliking. To the extent that the product can be assigned membership in a particular category, it will receive an evaluation similar to that attached to the category. If you go to the grocery store and see a new organic food on the shelf, you may evaluate it on your liking and opinions of organic food.

> **evoked set (consideration set)** a group of brands resulting from an information search from which a buyer can choose

So, when consumers rely on a categorization process, a product's evaluation depends on the particular category to which it is perceived as belonging. Given this, companies need to understand whether consumers are using categories that evoke the desired evaluations. Indeed, how a product is categorized can strongly influence consumer demand. For example, what products come to mind when you think about the "morning beverages" category? To the soft drink industry's dismay, far too few consumers include sodas in this category. Several attempts have been made to get soft drinks on the breakfast table, but with little success.

Brand extensions, in which a well-known and respected brand name from one product category is extended into other product categories, is one way companies employ categorization to their advantage. Brand extensions are a common business practice. For example, mixed martial arts promotional organization Ultimate Fighting Championship (UFC) has built its brand on pay-per-view events, cable and network television broadcasts, and merchandising. The UFC launched a 24-hour full-service gym in Long Island, New York. In addition to martial arts–themed activities, the UFC Gym features standard fitness equipment, a café, and signature classes like Hot Hula and Hi-Octane Conditioning.

Another factor that can influence the evaluation process is exposure to the price of the product or service. Suppose you walk into a department store and see a display of sweaters that catches your eye. When you walk over to the display, you look at a tag on a sweater to find a price of $49.99. Suppose instead you walk into the store and see a rack of clothes labeled with a large $49.99 sign. With this price in mind, you browse through the options and find a sweater that fits your tastes. Researchers have found that when consumers see the product cue first (scenario one), evaluation is strongly related to the product's attractiveness or desirability. When the first cue is the price (scenario two), evaluation is related more to the product's value.[5]

While the evaluation process sounds completely rational, behavioral economists point out that this is not always the case. The economists ask questions like: Why do people buy a bag of candy instead of a bag of veggies when they are trying to lose weight? Why do people buy a $5 latte when they're trying to save money? Obviously, they are not making economically rational decisions.

In an experiment, researchers sold Lindt Chocolate Truffles for 26 cents each and Hershey's Kisses for 1 cent each. Equal numbers of people bought each. When researchers dropped the price by 1 cent, 90 percent of the people took the free Hershey's Kiss. Behavioral economists say that "the power of free" often makes consumers irrational.[6]

Behavioral economists talk about using a **nudge**. A nudge is a little push; a little intervention that can stimulate changed behavior but is also easy and cheap to avoid and doesn't forbid other options. Nudges are not mandates. A sign reading "$1,000 fine for littering" is not a nudge. However, "Keep America Beautiful" is a nudge. Putting fruit at eye level in a company's restaurant is a nudge. Banning junk food is not.

It was found in Google's cafeteria that people can be nudged toward healthier eating. Researchers found that employees who poured their drinks at a beverage station 6.5 feet from a snack bar were 50% more likely to grab a snack than those who filled their glasses at a beverage station 17.5 feet away from the snack bar. For male Google employees, 11 feet of proximity correlated with gaining one pound of fat each year.[7]

A nudge can be non–price oriented, such as the Google example, or price oriented. If computer analytics identifies your smartphone while you are in an appliance store and knows that you have already gone to a comparison shopping sale online for a certain model LG microwave oven, it can immediately send you a nudge message for 10 percent off if you buy today. Richard Thayler, a behavioral economist who won the 2017 Nobel Prize in Economics, says that one of his favorite examples of a non–price nudge is a small decal of a fly placed in a urinal at Amsterdam's Schiphol Airport. The fly decal improves men's "aim"—the airport reported an 80% reduction in men's room urine spillage after fly decals were installed in all urinals.[8]

TO BUY OR NOT TO BUY Ultimately, the consumer has to decide whether or not to buy. Specifically, consumers must decide:

1. Whether to buy

2. When to buy

3. What to buy (product type and brand)

4. Where to buy (type of retailer, specific retailer, online or in store)

5. How to pay

If a consumer decides to purchase something online, it has been found that people frequently switch from a mobile device (e.g., smartphone or tablet) to a more fixed device such as a desktop as they move through the purchase process. It seems that mobile devices are used

nudge a small intervention that can change a person's behavior more in the information-seeking process. So, shopping for a new washing machine may entail visiting a Lowes store and other retailers to compare models, ratings, prices, and so forth, but the actual purchase is made on a desktop or laptop at home. In fact, consumers are three times more likely to use a more fixed device to close the sale than a mobile device.[9]

PLANNED VERSUS IMPULSE PURCHASE Complex and expensive items are typically purchased only after the consumer has collected a large amount of information. People rarely buy a new home on impulse. Often, consumers will make a *partially planned purchase* when they know the product category they want to buy (shirts, pants, reading lamp, car floor mats) but wait until they get to the store or go online to choose a specific style or brand. Finally, there is the *unplanned purchase*, which people buy on impulse; these are often triggered by a nudge. Researchers have found that 9 out of 10 shoppers have made impulse purchases. Shoppers say that they make impulse purchases because:

- There was a sale or promotion (66 percent).
- They found a coupon (30 percent).
- They simply wanted to pamper themselves (23 percent).[10]

A purchase may be in a planned category (e.g., soup), but decisions regarding the brand (Campbell's), package (can), and type (tomato) may all be made on impulse.

PSYCHOLOGICAL OWNERSHIP Consumers sometimes develop feelings of ownership without even owning the good, service, or brand.[11] For example, think about how you feel when you choose a seat on the first day of class. Then, when you come to class on the second day, where do you usually sit? How do you feel if someone else is sitting in your seat? This feeling of "It's mine!" is called psychological, or perceived, ownership. Psychological ownership is important to marketers because when consumers feel a sense of ownership of a product, they are willing to pay more for it and are more likely to tell other consumers about it.[12] Consumers develop this kind of relationship with a product when they are able to control it, when they invest themselves in it, or when they come to know it intimately. Researchers have found that simply touching a product or imagining owning it enhances feelings of psychological ownership. When customers of Threadless T-Shirts were given the opportunity to vote on upcoming shirt designs, their willingness to pay more for the shirts increased because they felt a greater sense of ownership of them. Even liking a Facebook post can feel like a vote of confidence

The candy, magazines, and small toys that line grocery store checkout lines are there to entice shoppers into making last-minute impulse purchases.

for a product and can enhance customers' feelings of ownership.[13] Clearly, psychological ownership can have a significant influence on consumer behavior. Marketing managers need to be aware of it when developing their marketing strategies.

6-3 POSTPURCHASE BEHAVIOR

When buying products, consumers expect certain outcomes from the purchase. How well these expectations are met determines whether the consumer is satisfied or dissatisfied with the purchase. For example, if a person bids on a used KitchenAid mixer from eBay and wins, she may have fairly low expectations regarding performance. If the mixer's performance turns out to be of superior quality, then the person's satisfaction will be high because her expectations were exceeded. Conversely, if the person bids on a new KitchenAid mixer expecting superior quality and performance, but the mixer breaks within one month, she will be very dissatisfied because her expectations were not met. Price often influences the level of expectations for a product or service.

Have you ever bought a product online or gone to a store to buy a specific item only to find out that it is sold out or not available? This is referred to as the **jilting effect**—that is, the anticipation of receiving a highly desirable option only to have it become inaccessible. One of your authors always buys a bushel of Honeybell oranges

> **jilting effect** anticipation of receiving a highly desirable option only to have it become inaccessible

Apple's Genius Bar eases cognitive dissonance among customers who just made a large purchase, such as an Apple Watch.

every year online for the holidays. They have a wonderful sweet taste that has been described a "out-of-this-world." Unfortunately, they are extremely rare. Last year, when the order was placed online, a little box appeared that simply said "sold out." The author had just experienced the jilting effect! This effect can reduce consumer preferences for the incumbent product or service and increase preferences for alternatives.[14] For a competitor, jilting may represent an opportunity to take market share away from the incumbent brand.

DATA BREACHES Purchasing goods and services online typically results in product preference and financial data capture. Unfortunately, there were 8,069 data breaches between 2005 and 2017.[15] The biggest ever was Yahoo, with 3 billion accounts hacked. Other large breaches were eBay, 145 million; Equifax, 143 million; and J.P. Morgan Chase, 83 million.[16] Breaches result in a significant decrease in consumer spending with the breached company. However, customers who remain will often change to a different channel of distribution for the breached firm. So rather than buying online they may visit the firm's brick-and-mortar store. Researchers also found that heavy users of a retailer are more forgiving of a data breach than those who patronize the firm infrequently.[17]

COGNITIVE DISSONANCE For the marketer, an important element of any postpurchase evaluation is reducing any lingering doubts that the decision was sound. When people recognize inconsistency between their values or opinions and their behavior, they tend

cognitive dissonance
inner tension that a consumer experiences after recognizing an inconsistency between behavior and values or opinions

to feel an inner tension called **cognitive dissonance.** For example, suppose Angelika is looking to purchase an e-reader. After evaluating her options, she has decided to purchase an iPad, even though it is much more expensive than other dedicated e-readers. Prior to choosing the iPad, Angelika may experience inner tension or anxiety because she is worried that the current top-of-the-line technology, which costs much more than the middle-of-the-line technology, will be obsolete in a couple of months. That feeling of dissonance arises as her worries over obsolescence battle her practical nature, which is focused on the lower cost of a Kindle Paperwhite and its adequate—but less fancy—technology.

Consumers try to reduce dissonance by justifying their decision. They may seek new information that reinforces positive ideas about the purchase, avoid information that contradicts their decision, or revoke the original decision by returning the product. In some instances, people deliberately seek contrary information in order to refute it and reduce dissonance. Dissatisfied customers sometimes rely on word of mouth to reduce cognitive dissonance by letting friends and family know they are displeased.

Marketing managers can help reduce dissonance through effective communication with purchasers. For example, a customer service manager may slip a note inside the package congratulating the buyer on making a wise decision. Postpurchase letters sent by manufacturers and dissonance-reducing statements in instruction booklets may help customers feel at ease with their purchase. Advertising that displays the product's superiority over competing brands or guarantees can also help relieve the possible dissonance of someone who has already bought the product. Apple's Genius Bar and superior customer service ease cognitive dissonance among people who buy an Apple Watch because they know that the company is there to support them.

An excellent opportunity for a company to reduce (or if handled poorly, increase) cognitive dissonance is when a customer has a question or complaint and tries to contact the company. Too many firms view their contact centers as cost centers and every contact as a problem to be minimized by making it as hard as possible to speak to a customer representative. Have you ever gone through four or five automated sequences, pushing a series of buttons, only to be told, "We are experiencing a higher than normal call volume and you can expect a lengthy delay." Not only does this raise cognitive dissonance, it can also destroy brand loyalty. Marketing-oriented companies perceive the contact center as an opportunity to engage customers and reinforce the brand promise. At these companies, there is no long menu of buttons to

EXHIBIT 6.2 CONTINUUM OF CONSUMER BUYING DECISIONS

	Routine	Limited	Extensive
Involvement	Low	Low to moderate	High
Time	Short	Short to moderate	Long
Cost	Low	Low to moderate	High
Information Search	Internal only	Mostly internal	Internal and external
Number of Alternatives	One	Few	Many

push. Instead, a service rep answers on the first or second ring and is empowered to solve customer problems. Research has shown that consumers whose customer service questions and complaints are resolved during the first point of contact are nearly twice as likely to remain loyal to the product or company and are four times more likely to spread positive word of mouth.[18] A different survey found that more than 60 percent of companies are not able to handle customer issues in one contact via non–telephone channels (such as self-service, email, live chat, social media, and mobile).[19] These channels involve at least a second contact, during which the customer is sent to a telephone service rep to resolve the problem. This is not only less satisfying for customers, but the more channels that are used prior to resolution, the more expensive it is for the company. Researchers also found that younger customers were most likely to start the process with a non–telephone channel, so this issue remains a point of weakness for many companies.

6-4 TYPES OF CONSUMER BUYING DECISIONS AND CONSUMER INVOLVEMENT

All consumer buying decisions generally fall along a continuum of three broad categories: routine response behavior, limited decision making, and extensive decision making (see Exhibit 6.2). Goods and services in these three categories can best be described in terms of five factors:

- Level of consumer involvement
- Length of time to make a decision
- Cost of the good or service
- Degree of information search
- Number of alternatives considered

The level of consumer involvement is perhaps the most significant determinant in classifying buying decisions. **Involvement** is the amount of time and effort a buyer invests in the search, evaluation, and decision processes of consumer behavior.

Frequently purchased, low-cost goods and services are generally associated with **routine response behavior**. These goods and services can also be called *low-involvement products* because consumers spend little time on search and decision before making the purchase. Usually, buyers are familiar with several different brands in the product category but stick with one brand. For example, a person may routinely buy Tropicana orange juice. Consumers engaged in routine response behavior normally do not experience need recognition until they are nudged by an advertisement or see the product displayed on a store shelf. Consumers buy first and evaluate later, whereas the reverse is true for extensive decision making. A consumer who has previously purchased whitening toothpaste and was satisfied with it will probably walk to the toothpaste aisle and select that same brand without spending 20 minutes examining all other alternatives.

Limited decision making typically occurs when a consumer has previous product experience but is unfamiliar with the current brands available. Limited decision making is also associated with lower levels of involvement (although higher than routine decisions) because consumers expend only moderate effort in searching for information or in considering various alternatives.

involvement the amount of time and effort a buyer invests in the search, evaluation, and decision processes of consumer behavior

routine response behavior the type of decision making exhibited by consumers buying frequently purchased, low-cost goods and services; requires little search and decision time

limited decision making the type of decision making that requires a moderate amount of time for gathering information and deliberating about an unfamiliar brand in a familiar product category

For many consumers, purchasing a new vehicle is a high involvement decision requiring extensive decision making.

For example, what happens if the consumer's usual brand of whitening toothpaste is sold out? Assuming that toothpaste is needed, the consumer will be forced to choose another brand. Before making a final decision, the consumer will likely evaluate several other brands based on their active ingredients, their promotional claims, and the consumer's prior experiences. They may also look online for various brand rankings.

Consumers practice **extensive decision making** when buying an unfamiliar, expensive product, or an infrequently bought item. This process is the most complex type of consumer buying decision and is associated with high involvement on the part of the consumer. This process resembles the model outlined in Exhibit 6.1. These consumers want to make the right decision, so they want to know as much as they can about the product category and available brands. People usually experience the most cognitive dissonance when buying high-involvement products. Buyers use several criteria for evaluating their options and spend much time seeking information. Buying a home or a car, for example, requires extensive decision making.

The type of decision making that consumers use to purchase a product does not necessarily remain constant. For instance, if a routinely purchased product no longer satisfies, consumers may practice limited or extensive decision making to switch to another brand. And people who first use extensive decision making may then use limited or routine decision making for future purchases.

extensive decision making the most complex type of consumer decision making, used when buying an unfamiliar, expensive product or an infrequently bought item; requires use of several criteria for evaluating options and much time for seeking information

For example, when a family gets a new puppy, they will spend a lot of time and energy trying out different toys to determine which one the dog prefers. Once the new owners learn that the dog prefers a bone to a ball, however, the purchase no longer requires extensive evaluation and will become routine.

6-4a Factors Determining the Level of Consumer Involvement

The level of involvement in the purchase depends on the following factors:

- **Previous experience:** When consumers have had previous experience with a good or service, the level of involvement typically decreases. After repeated product trials, consumers learn to make quick choices. Because consumers are familiar with the product and know whether it will satisfy their needs, they become less involved in the purchase. For example, a consumer purchasing cereal has many brands to choose from—just think of any grocery store cereal aisle. If the consumer always buys the same brand because it satisfies his hunger, then he has a low level of involvement. When a consumer purchases a new category of cereal, such as high in fiber, it likely will be a more involved purchase.

- **Interest:** Involvement is directly related to consumer interests, as in cars, music, movies, bicycling, or online games. Naturally, these areas of interest vary from one individual to another. A person highly involved in bike racing will be more interested in the type of bike she owns and will spend quite a bit of time evaluating different bikes. If a person wants a bike only for recreation, however, he may be less uninvolved in the purchase. He may just choose a bike from the most convenient location and in a reasonable price range.

- **Perceived risk of negative consequences:** As the perceived risk in purchasing a product increases, so does a consumer's level of involvement. The types of risks that concern consumers include financial risk, social risk, and psychological risk.

  - Financial risk is exposure to loss of wealth or purchasing power. Because high risk is associated with high-priced purchases, consumers tend to become extremely involved. Therefore, price and involvement are usually directly related: As price increases, so does the level of involvement. For example, someone who is purchasing a new car for the first time (higher perceived risk) will spend a lot of time and effort making this purchase.

- Social risks occur when consumers buy products that can affect people's social opinions of them (e.g., driving an old, beat-up car or wearing unstylish clothes).

- Psychological risks occur if consumers believe that making the wrong decision might cause some concern or anxiety. For example, some consumers feel guilty about eating foods that are not healthy, such as regular ice cream rather than fat-free frozen yogurt.

- **Social visibility:** Involvement also increases as the social visibility of a product increases. Products often on social display include clothing (especially designer labels), jewelry, cars, and furniture. All these items make a statement about the purchaser and, therefore, carry a social risk.

High involvement means that the consumer cares about a product category or a specific good or service. The product or service is relevant and important, and means something to the buyer. High involvement can take a number of different forms. The most important types are discussed below:

- *Product involvement* means that a product category has high personal relevance. Product enthusiasts are consumers with high involvement in a product category. The fashion industry has a large segment of product enthusiasts. These people are seeking the latest fashion trends and want to wear the latest clothes.

- *Situational involvement* means that the circumstances of a purchase may temporarily transform a low-involvement decision into a high-involvement one. High involvement comes into play when the consumer perceives risk in a specific situation. For example, an individual might routinely buy low-priced brands of liquor and wine. When the boss visits, however, the consumer might make a high-involvement decision and buy more prestigious brands.

- *Shopping involvement* represents the personal relevance of the process of shopping. Some people enjoy the process of shopping even if they do not plan to buy anything. For others, shopping is an enjoyable social activity. Many consumers also engage in **showrooming**—examining merchandise in a physical retail location without purchasing it and then shopping online for a better deal on the same item.

- *Enduring involvement* represents an ongoing interest in some product, such as kitchen gadgets, or activity, such as fishing. The consumer is always searching for opportunities to consume the product or participate

Rmnoa357/Shutterstock.com

Tide uses bright, eye-catching packaging to draw customers to what is usually a low-involvement product.

in the activity. Enduring involvement typically gives personal gratification to consumers as they continue to learn about, shop for, and consume these goods and services. Therefore, there is often a link between enduring involvement, shopping, and product involvement.

- *Emotional involvement* represents how emotional a consumer gets during some specific consumption activity. Emotional involvement is closely related to enduring involvement because the things that consumers care most about will eventually create high emotional involvement. Sports fans typify consumers with high emotional involvement.

6-4b Marketing Implications of Involvement

Marketing strategy varies according to the level of involvement associated with the product. For high-involvement product purchases, marketing managers have several objectives. First, promotion to the target market should be extensive and informative. A good ad gives consumers the information they need for making the purchase decision and specifies the benefits and unique advantages of owning the product. For example, Ford has a vehicle with many custom options that is marketed to small business owners. One example of a recent online ad shows how one entrepreneur customized his Ford Transit to help improve the efficiency of his business. Ford highlights the fact that unique businesses need unique and customizable transportation. The Transit comes in three body lengths, each offering a unique volume and

> **showrooming** the practice of examining merchandise in a physical retail location without purchasing it and then shopping online for a better deal on the same item

payload capacity. There are also three different roof heights to choose from, and of course several different engines.

For low-involvement product purchases, consumers may not recognize their wants until they are in the store. Therefore, in-store promotion and targeted mobile ads are important tools when promoting low-involvement products. Marketing managers focus on package design so the product will be eye-catching and easily recognized on the shelf. Examples of products that take this approach are Campbell's soups, Tide detergent, Velveeta cheese, and Heinz ketchup. In-store displays and digital coupons also stimulate sales of low-involvement products. A good display can explain the product's purpose and prompt recognition of a want. Displays of snack foods in supermarkets have been known to increase sales many times above normal. Cents-off deals and two-for-one offers also effectively promote low-involvement items.

Researchers have found that another way to increase involvement is to offer products on a "limited availability" basis. McDonald's, for example, has regularly cycled its McRib sandwich on and off its menu for more than 30 years. Marketers can use several ways to trigger limited availability, including daily specials (e.g., special soup *du jour*), day of the week (e.g., Sunday brunch), promotional periods (e.g., item availability for a limited time only), harvest time (e.g., corn in the summer), and small production runs (e.g., limited edition items). Limited availability creates a "get it now or never" mentality.

6-5 RECONCEPTUALIZING THE CONSUMER DECISION-MAKING PROCESS

Rapid changes in digital technology have given consumers unprecedented power to express likes and dislikes, compare prices, find the best deals, sift through huge numbers of recommendations on sites like TripAdvisor and Yelp, and finally, have items delivered quickly—sometimes on the same day the order was placed. In short, the balance of power has shifted largely from the marketer to the consumer. Because of these remarkable changes, many marketers today are totally reconceptualizing the consumer decision-making process.

6-5a The Consumer Decision Journey

One of the hottest phrases in marketing today is "the consumer decision journey." Exhibit 6.3 depicts this journey and explains how marketers are trying to regain control from consumers by streamlining the decision-making process.

The consumer decision journey begins when an advertisement or other stimulus causes a consumer to research a number of products or services to meet his or her needs. Even at this early stage, the consumer may drop a number of items from the potential purchase set. The second phase of the journey begins when the consumer evaluates the alternatives, using input from peers, reviewers, retailers, the brand itself, and competitors. At

EXHIBIT 6.3 THE CONSUMER DECISION JOURNEY

Classic Journey
In the classic journey, consumers engage in an extended consideration and evaluation phase before either entering into the loyalty loop or proceeding into a new round of consideration and evaluation that may lead to the subsequent purchase of a different brand.

New Journey
The new journey compresses the consider step and shortens or entirely eliminates the evaluate step, delivering customers directly into the loyalty loop and locking them within it.

Source: David Edelman and Mark Singer, "Competing on Customer Journeys," *Harvard Business Review*, November 2015.

this stage, new brands may be added and options from the initial set may be dropped as the selection criteria shift. The consumer then buys (or doesn't buy) the product and, if he or she enjoys the purchase, may advocate and bond with the brand. This feedback loop of ratings, rankings, and referrals pressures brands to deliver a superior experience on an ongoing basis. Researchers have found that 60 percent of consumers of facial skin care products conduct an online search after a purchase is made.[20] This is part of developing a deeper bond with the skin care product while eliminating cognitive dissonance.

Progressive firms armed with new technologies are actively working to exert greater influence over the decision-making journey. In order to minimize (or in some cases eliminate) the "consider and evaluate" phases of the consumer journey, a company must have four distinct but interconnected capabilities:

- *Automation* streamlines journey steps. One example is letting people take a picture of a check and deposit it through an app rather than depositing it in person. While process automation is highly technical, it should always be done with simple, useful, and increasingly engaging consumer-side experiences in mind.

- *Proactive personalization* uses information—either based on past interactions or collected through external sources—to instantaneously customize the customer experience. This capability ranges from a website remembering a customer's log-in preferences to an airline automatically adding a frequent traveler to its upgrade list.

- *Contextual interaction* uses knowledge about where a customer is in the journey to deliver them to the next set of interactions. Consider, for example, a retail website displaying the status of a recent order on its home page. Some hotels are pushing the boundaries of contextual interaction by configuring their apps to operate like keys when guests approach their rooms.

- *Journey innovation* extends customer interactions to new sources of value, such as related products or partnered businesses. Many companies mine their data to figure out what adjacent goods or services a shopper might be interested in, then they put those products in front of the shopper in the middle of his or her journey. The best companies conduct open-ended testing and constantly prototype new services and features to best meet customer needs in the ever-changing, digitally connected market. For example, Delta Airline's app integrates with ride-sharing service Uber so that travelers can book cars to pick them up when they arrive at their destinations.[21]

To understand how a company can influence the consumer decision journey, let's examine California-based solar panel provider Sungevity. This company's "product" is a seamless, personalized customer journey built on innovative data management about the solar potential of each home. Consider the following Sungevity experience:

One of the creators of "The Consumer Decision Journey" model (David) experienced the Sungevity journey firsthand. The process began when he received a mailing with the message "Open this to find out how much the Edelman family can save on energy costs with solar panels." The letter within contained a unique URL that led to a Google Earth image of David's house with solar panels superimposed on the roof. The next click led to a page with custom calculations of energy savings, developed from Sungevity's estimates of the family's energy use, the roof angle, the presence of nearby trees, and the energy-generation potential of the 23 panels the company expected the roof to hold.

Another click connected David through his desktop to a live sales rep looking at the same pages David was. The rep expertly answered his questions and instantly sent him links to videos that explained the installation process and the economics of leasing versus buying. Two days later, Sungevity emailed David with the names and numbers of nearby homeowners who used its system and had agreed to serve as references. After checking these references, David returned to Sungevity's site, where a single click connected him to a rep who knew precisely where he was on the journey and had a tailored lease ready for him. The rep emailed it and walked David through it, and then David e-signed. When he next visited the website, the landing page had changed to track the progress of the permitting and installation, with fresh alerts arriving as the process proceeded. Now, as a Sungevity customer, David receives regular reports on his panels' energy generation and the resulting savings, along with tips on ways to conserve energy, based on his household's characteristics.

Starting with its initial outreach and continuing to the installation and ongoing management of David's panels, Sungevity customized and automated each step of the journey, making it so simple—and so compelling—for him to move from one step to the next that he never actively considered alternative providers. In essence, the company reconfigured the classic model of the consumer decision journey, immediately paring the consideration set to one brand, streamlining the evaluation phase and delivering David directly into the "loyalty loop."[22]

Another way firms are keeping customers in the loyalty loop is by using automated reordering. Express Scripts, the largest pharmacy benefit management organization in the United States, can automatically reorder customer prescriptions when it is time to refill. Customers also receive reminders that they can save money if they transfer their prescriptions to Express Scripts when they fill prescriptions at local pharmacies. Similarly, when a customer orders an e-book on Amazon, the company uses finely tuned algorithms to suggest other books that he or she might want to read. Amazon offers automatic order scheduling on thousands of items from diapers to soft drinks. Customers can customize which items are sent, what day of the month they are sent, and how frequently they are sent. Some coffee makers, printers, and washing machines can even use wi-fi and special sensors to automatically place orders when supplies run low.

While automation can play a key role in keeping a consumer in the loyalty loop, if used incorrectly, it can cause customer loss. For example, when a problem arises and you call customer service you go through a long series of automated prompts. Receiving an automated answer that doesn't fully answer the question can cause customer loyalty to decline quickly. A study of 2000 Swiss and German health-insurance customers found that customers would pay higher premiums when offered more options to interact with the health insurance companies.[23] Clients said that they would pay $16 to $24 more a month to easily be able to speak to an identifiable professional at a service center rather than, for example, receiving only an anonymous response to an online query. A specific advisor for repeated contacts was most preferred. Customers not only want personal interactions by phone or chat but also some automated functions as well. They were happy to do a simple address change, for example, through a digital-only interaction.[24]

Researchers have found two loyalty levels among customers: the satisfied and the committed.[25] The satisfied are those who buy regularly, often out of habit, because they are satisfied with the brand's performance over a long period. With consistently good experiences, they perceive the brand to be familiar, easy to buy, and dependable. The brand has become a comfortable habit, and there is no reason to change. For some low-involvement products, the satisfied are the core loyalty group.

The committed have a more intense and involved relationship with the brand. They are more likely to have an emotional attachment, to receive self-expressive benefits, and to have a use experience that goes beyond the functional. They are also more likely to be brand supporters, even telling others about the brand and its use experience.

The satisfied group can be represented by the phrase "one of my favorite brands," which reflects satisfaction and a lack of motivation to change to another brand. The "committed" group can be represented by the phrase "I can't imagine living without," which suggests that there is a functional or emotional attachment that is so intense that the absence of the brand would be upsetting.

Researchers also identified specific brands that were mentioned most frequently among both the satisfied and the committed. Top brands among the satisfied group include Betty Crocker, Band-Aid, Clorox, KitchenAid, and Folgers. Top among the committed group include Apple, Microsoft, Netflix, and Chick-fil-A.[26]

The objective of companies is to maintain lifetime customers, whether they are satisfied or committed loyal customers. Yet in some industries heavy competition and perhaps customer dissatisfaction results in people switching companies and/or brands. When there is a significant number of customers switching firms or products, it is called **churning**. In the wireless industry, carriers such as T-Mobile and Verizon offer a reimbursement of up to $650 per line to cover early termination fees to customers who are willing to make a switch from another service provider. In 2018, Sprint began a promotion campaign claiming "first to 5G," attempting to entice customers who have slower download speeds. All of this creates churn and destroys loyalty.[27]

Yet, firms have begun to realize that lost customers may not be "dead opportunities." Sometimes exceptional promotional offers can win them back. Sirius, for example, offers "free listening" for a period of time to

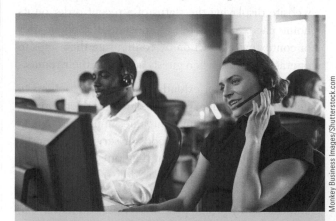

Quickly being able to speak to a live customer service representative instead of receiving automated answers can help a company maintain customer loyalty.

churning when a significant number of customers are switching brands

EXHIBIT 6.4 FACTORS THAT AFFECT THE CONSUMER DECISION JOURNEY

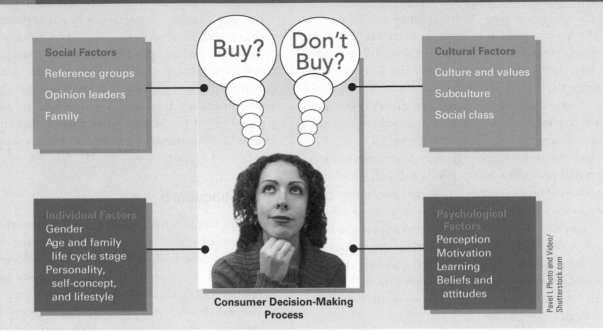

Social Factors
Reference groups
Opinion leaders
Family

Buy?

Don't Buy?

Cultural Factors
Culture and values
Subculture
Social class

Individual Factors
Gender
Age and family life cycle stage
Personality, self-concept, and lifestyle

Psychological Factors
Perception
Motivation
Learning
Beliefs and attitudes

Consumer Decision-Making Process

Pavel L Photo and Video/Shutterstock.com

lost customers in an attempt to regain their business. Once a person has returned, companies should create a proactive strategy of reaching out to these customers to ensure their satisfaction with the product or service. For example, an email stating "we are glad you're back!" followed by a short questionnaire covering reasons for the initial departure and current return and what can be done to improve their satisfaction will provide retention strategies.

6-5b Factors Affecting Consumer Decision Making

Whether framed as the traditional consumer decision-making process or the consumer decision journey, it is important to understand that consumer decision making does not occur in a vacuum. On the contrary, underlying cultural, social, individual, and psychological factors strongly influence the decision process. These factors have an effect from the time a consumer perceives a stimulus and considers the product or service through postpurchase evaluation. Cultural factors, which include culture and values, subculture, and social class, exert a broad influence over consumer decision making. Social factors sum up the social interactions between a consumer and influential groups of people, such as reference groups, opinion leaders, and family members. Individual factors, which include gender, age, family life cycle stage, personality, self-concept, and lifestyle, are unique to each individual and play a major role in the type of products

and services consumers want. Psychological factors determine how consumers perceive and interact with their environments and influence the ultimate decisions they make. These factors include perception, motivation, and learning. Exhibit 6.4 summarizes these influences, and the following sections cover each in more detail.

6-6 CULTURAL INFLUENCES ON CONSUMER BUYING DECISIONS

Of all the factors that affect consumer decision making, cultural factors exert the broadest and deepest influence. Marketers must understand the way people's culture and its accompanying values, as well as their subculture and social class, influence their buying behavior.

6-6a Culture and Values

Culture is the set of values, norms, attitudes, and other meaningful symbols that shape human behavior and the artifacts, or products, of that behavior as they are transmitted from one generation to the next. It is the essential character of a society that distinguishes it from other cultural groups. The underlying elements of every culture are the

> **culture** the set of values, norms, attitudes, and other meaningful symbols that shape human behavior and the artifacts, or products, of that behavior as they are transmitted from one generation to the next

values, language, myths, customs, rituals, and laws that guide the behavior of the people.

Culture is pervasive. Cultural values and influences are the ocean in which individuals swim, and yet most are completely unaware that it is there. What people eat, how they dress, what they think and feel, and what language they speak are all dimensions of culture. Culture encompasses all the things consumers do without conscious choice because their culture's values, customs, and rituals are ingrained in their daily habits.

Culture is functional. Human interaction creates values and prescribes acceptable behavior for each culture. By establishing common expectations, culture gives order to society. Sometimes these expectations are enacted into laws. For example, drivers in our culture must stop at a red light. Other times these expectations are taken for granted: grocery stores and hospitals are open 24 hours, whereas banks are open only during "bankers' hours," typically nine in the morning until five in the afternoon.

Culture is learned. Consumers are not born knowing the values and norms of their society. Instead, they must learn from family and friends what is acceptable. Children learn the values that will govern their behavior from parents, teachers, and peers. As members of our society, they learn to shake hands when they greet someone, to drive on the right-hand side of the road, and to eat pizza and drink Coca-Cola.

Culture is dynamic. It adapts to changing needs and an evolving environment. The rapid growth of technology in today's world has accelerated the rate of cultural change. Our culture is beginning to tell us when it is okay to send a text message and when it is considered impolite. Assume that you are on a first date with someone in a nice, romantic restaurant and your date is talking to you about his or her favorite things to do. Pulling out your smartphone to check a text will probably lead to a very short date. Cultural norms will continue to evolve because of our need for social patterns that solve problems.

The most defining element of a culture is its values. Recall that *value* can refer to an enduring belief shared by a society that a specific mode of conduct is personally or socially preferable to another. People's value systems have a great effect on their consumer behavior. Consumers with similar value systems tend to react alike to prices and other marketing-related inducements. Values also correspond to consumption patterns. For example, Americans place a high value on convenience. This value has created lucrative markets for products such as breakfast bars, energy bars, and nutrition bars that allow consumers to eat on the go. Values can also influence consumers' television viewing habits or the magazines they read. For instance, people who strongly object to violence avoid crime shows and vegetarians avoid cooking magazines that feature numerous meat-based recipes.

6-6b Subculture

A culture can be divided into subcultures on the basis of demographic characteristics, geographic regions, national and ethnic background, political beliefs, and religious beliefs. A subculture is a homogeneous group of people who share elements of the overall culture as well as cultural elements unique to their own group. Within subcultures, people's attitudes, values, and purchase decisions are even more similar than they are within the broader culture. Subcultural differences may result in considerable variation within a culture in what, how, when, and where people buy goods and services.

Once marketers identify subcultures, they can design special marketing to serve their needs. The growing Hispanic population in the United States has made South and Central American subcultures a prime focus for many companies, for example. Recall that marketing to Hispanics was discussed in Chapter 4.

In the United States alone, countless subcultures can be identified. Many are concentrated geographically. People who belong to the Church of Jesus Christ of Latter-Day Saints, for example, are clustered mainly in Utah; Cajuns are located in the bayou regions of southern Louisiana. Many Hispanics live in states bordering Mexico, whereas the majority of Chinese, Japanese, and Korean Americans are found on the West Coast. Other subcultures are geographically dispersed. Computer hackers, people who are hearing or visually impaired, Harley-Davidson bikers, military families, and university professors may be found throughout the country. Yet they have identifiable attitudes, values, and needs that distinguish them from the larger culture.

6-6c Social Class

The United States, like other societies, has a social class system. A social class is a group of people who are considered nearly equal in status or community esteem, who

subculture a homogeneous group of people who share elements of the overall culture as well as unique elements of their own group

social class a group of people in a society who are considered nearly equal in status or community esteem, who regularly socialize among themselves both formally and informally, and who share behavioral norms

The type of products and brands that we buy are influenced by our culture and values.

regularly socialize among themselves both formally and informally, and who share behavioral norms.

A number of techniques have been used to measure social class, and a number of criteria have been used to define it. One view of contemporary U.S. status structure is shown in Exhibit 6.5.

As you can see from Exhibit 6.5, the upper and upper middle classes comprise the small segment of affluent and wealthy Americans. In terms of consumer buying patterns, the affluent are more likely to own their own homes and purchase new cars and trucks and are less likely to smoke. The very rich flex their financial muscles by spending more on vacation homes, jewelry, vacations and cruises, and housekeeping and gardening services. The most affluent consumers are more likely to attend art auctions and galleries, dance performances, operas,

the theater, museums, concerts, and sporting events. What types of things do the wealthiest of the wealthy buy? In 2018, Rolls Royce created a one-of-a-kind car called the "Sweptail." You can't buy one because this car was created for one specific buyer. It seats only two people and has a sunroof that is fully panoramic and tapers down sharply like those of racing yachts (at the customer's request). The price? Only $13 million! The owner is also a collector of super-yachts and private planes.[28]

The majority of Americans today define themselves as middle class, regardless of their actual income or educational attainment. This phenomenon most likely occurs because working-class Americans tend to aspire to the middle-class lifestyle, while some of those who do achieve some affluence call themselves middle class as a matter of principle.

The working class is a distinct subset of the middle class. Interest in organized labor is one of the most common attributes among the working class. This group often rates job security as the most important reason for taking a job. The working-class person depends heavily on relatives and the community for economic and emotional support.

Lifestyle distinctions between the social classes are greater than the distinctions within a given class. The most significant difference between the classes occurs between the middle and lower classes, where there is a major shift in lifestyles. Members of the lower class have annual incomes at or below the poverty level—$12,140 for individuals and $25,100 for families of four (as defined by the federal government).[29]

Social class is typically measured as a combination of occupation, income, education, wealth, and other

EXHIBIT 6.5 U.S. SOCIAL CLASSES

Upper Classes		
Capitalist class	1%	People whose investment decisions shape the national economy; income mostly from assets, earned or inherited; university connections
Upper middle class	14%	Upper-level managers, professionals, owners of medium-sized businesses; well-to-do, stay-at-home homemakers who decline occupational work by choice; college educated; family income well above national average
Middle Classes		
Middle class	33%	Middle-level white-collar, top-level blue-collar; education past high school typical; income somewhat above national average; loss of manufacturing jobs has reduced the population of this class
Working class	32%	Middle-level blue-collar, lower-level white-collar; income below national average; largely working in skilled or semi-skilled service jobs
Lower Classes		
Working poor	11–12%	Low-paid service workers and operatives; some high school education; below mainstream in living standard; crime and hunger are daily threats
Underclass	8–9%	People who are not regularly employed and who depend primarily on the welfare system for sustenance; little schooling; living standard below poverty line

Despite being an accomplished Billboard-charting musician, Canadian indie darling Mac DeMarco projects a distinctly working-class persona.

variables. For instance, affluent upper-class consumers are more likely to be salaried executives or self-employed professionals with at least an undergraduate degree. Working-class or middle-class consumers are more likely to be hourly service workers or blue-collar employees with only a high school education. Educational attainment, however, seems to be the most reliable indicator of a person's social and economic status. Those with college degrees or graduate degrees are more likely to fall into the upper classes, while those with some college experience fall closest to traditional concepts of the middle class.

Marketers are interested in social class for two main reasons. First, social class often indicates which medium to use for promotion. Suppose an insurance company seeks to sell its policies to middle-class families. It might advertise during the local evening news because middle-class families tend to watch more television than other classes do. If the company wanted to sell more policies to upscale individuals, it might place an ad in a business publication like the *Wall Street Journal*. The Internet, long the domain of more educated and affluent families, has become an increasingly important advertising outlet for advertisers hoping to reach blue-collar workers and homemakers.

reference group all of the formal and informal groups in society that influence an individual's purchasing behavior

primary membership group a reference group with which people interact regularly in an informal, face-to-face manner, such as family, friends, and coworkers

secondary membership group a reference group with which people associate less consistently and more formally than a primary membership group, such as a club, professional group, or religious group

Second, knowing which products appeal to which social classes can help marketers determine where to best distribute their products. Affluent Americans, one-fifth of the U.S. population, spend more of their discretionary income on one-of-a-kind items. Many lower-income consumers patronize retailers such as Walmart that sell smaller packages of items because customers do not have enough cash to buy more standard-size products. Walmart, of course, sells large economy sizes at low, competitive prices.

6-7 SOCIAL INFLUENCES ON CONSUMER BUYING DECISIONS

Many consumers seek out the opinions of others to reduce their search and evaluation effort or uncertainty, especially as the perceived risk of the decision increases. Consumers may also seek out others' opinions for guidance on new products or services, products with image-related attributes, or products for which attribute information is lacking or uninformative. Specifically, consumers interact socially with reference groups, opinion leaders, and family members to obtain product information and decision approval.

6-7a Reference Groups

People interact with many reference groups. A reference group consists of all the formal and informal groups that influence the buying behavior of an individual. Consumers may use products or brands to identify with or become a member of a group. They learn from observing how members of their reference groups consume, and they use the same criteria to make their own consumer decisions.

Reference groups can be categorized very broadly as either direct or indirect (see Exhibit 6.6). Direct reference groups are membership groups that touch people's lives directly. They can be either primary or secondary. A primary membership group includes all groups with which people interact regularly in an informal manner, such as family, friends, members of social media, such as Facebook and coworkers. Today, they may also communicate by email, text messages, Facebook, Skype, or other social media as well as face to face. In contrast, people associate with a secondary membership group less consistently and more formally. These groups might include clubs, professional groups, and religious groups.

Consumers also are influenced by many indirect, nonmembership reference groups to which they do not

Christian Bertrand/Shutterstock.com

EXHIBIT 6.6   TYPES OF REFERENCE GROUPS

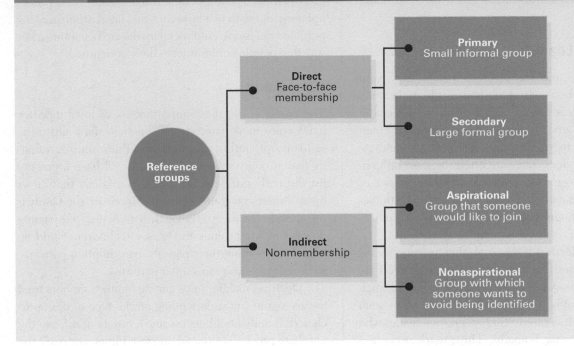

belong. An **aspirational reference group** is a group a person would like to join. To join an aspirational group, a person must at least conform to the norms of that group. (A **norm** consists of the values and attitudes deemed acceptable by the group.) Thus, a person who wants to be elected to public office may begin to dress more conservatively, as other politicians do. He or she may go to many of the restaurants and social engagements that city and business leaders attend and try to play a role that is acceptable to voters and other influential people.

Nonaspirational reference groups, or *dissociative groups*, influence our behavior when we try to

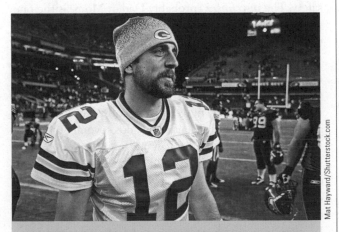

NFL star Aaron Rogers popularity has led to many lucrative endorsement deals.

maintain distance from them. A consumer may avoid buying some types of clothing or cars, going to certain restaurants or stores, or even buying a home in a certain neighborhood to avoid being associated with a particular group. For middle- and upper-middle-class professionals who take an interest in Harley-Davidson motorcycles, biker gangs serve as both an aspirational and a nonaspirational reference group. Though the professionals (derisively called RUBS—rich urban bikers—by hardcore Harley enthusiasts) aspire to the freedom, community, and tough posturing of biker gangs, they do not aspire to the perpetual life on the road, crime, or violence of gangs. Thus, a professional may buy a Harley, but he may intentionally buy a specific model not typically associated with those gangs.

Reference groups are particularly powerful in influencing the clothes people wear, the cars they drive, the electronics they use, the activities they participate in, the foods they eat, and the luxury goods they purchase. In short, the activities, values, and goals of reference groups directly influence consumer behavior. For marketers, reference groups have three important implications: (1) they serve as information sources and influence

aspirational reference group a group that someone would like to join

norm a value or attitude deemed acceptable by a group

nonaspirational reference group a group with which an individual does not want to associate perceptions; (2) they affect an individual's aspiration levels; and (3) their norms either constrain or stimulate consumer behavior.

6-7b Opinion Leaders

Reference groups and social media groups (e.g., your friends on Facebook) frequently include individuals known as group leaders, or **opinion leaders**—persons who influence others. Obviously, it is important for marketing managers to persuade such people to purchase their goods or services. They are often the most influential, informed, plugged-in, and vocal members of society. Technology companies have found that teenagers, because of their willingness to experiment, are key opinion leaders for the success of new technologies.

Opinion leadership is a casual phenomenon and is usually inconspicuous, so locating opinion leaders offline can be a challenge. An opinion leader in one field, such as cooking, may not be an opinion leader in another, such as sports. In fact, it is rare to find an opinion leader who spans multiple diverse domains. Thus, marketers often try to create opinion leaders. They may use high school cheerleaders to model new fall fashions or civic leaders to promote insurance, new cars, and other merchandise. On a national level, companies sometimes use movie stars, sports figures, and other celebrities to promote products, hoping they are appropriate opinion leaders. The effectiveness of celebrity endorsements varies, though, depending largely on how credible and attractive the spokesperson is and how familiar people are with him or her. Endorsements are most likely to succeed if a reasonable association between the spokesperson and the product can be established.

Football star Aaron Rodgers, quarterback of the Green Bay Packers, signed a four-year contract for $134 million in 2018. In addition, he has endorsement deals with Adidas, State Farm, Prevea Healthcare, Bergstrom Automotive, Sharpie, and Izod. Rodgers' multimillion-dollar pact with State Farm is one of the richest endorsement deals in the NFL.[30]

Increasingly, marketers are looking to social media to find opinion leaders, but the sheer volume of posts and platforms makes determining true opinion leaders challenging. So, marketers are focusing their attention on platforms such as Facebook, Pinterest, and Tumblr because those sites better identify the social trends that are shaping consumer behavior. With their unprecedented ability to network and communicate with each other, people often rely on each other's opinions more than marketing messages when making purchase decisions. And social media are becoming a key way that people communicate their opinions.

6-7c Family

The family is the most important social institution for many consumers, strongly influencing values, attitudes, self-concept, and buying behavior. For example, a family that strongly values good health will have a grocery list distinctly different from that of a family that views every dinner as a gourmet event. Moreover, the family is responsible for the **socialization process**, the passing down of cultural values and norms to children. Children learn by observing their parents' consumption patterns, so they tend to shop in similar patterns.

Decision-making roles among family members tend to vary significantly, depending on the type of item purchased. Family members assume a variety of roles in the purchase process. *Initiators* suggest, initiate, or plant the seed for the purchase process. The initiator can be any member of the family. For example, Sister might initiate the product search by asking for a new bicycle as a birthday present. *Influencers* are members of the family whose opinions are valued. In our example, Mom might function as a price-range watchdog, an influencer whose main role is to veto or approve price ranges. Brother may give his opinion on certain makes of bicycles. The *decision maker* is the family member who actually makes the decision to buy or not to buy. For example, Dad or Mom is likely to choose the final brand and model of bicycle to buy after seeking further information from Sister about cosmetic features such as color and then imposing additional criteria of his or her own, such as durability and safety. The *purchaser* (probably Dad or Mom) is the one who actually exchanges money for the product. Finally, the *consumer* is the actual user—in this case, Sister.

Marketers should consider family purchase situations along with the distribution of consumer and decision-maker roles among family members. Ordinarily, marketing views the individual as both decision maker and consumer. Family marketing adds several other possibilities: sometimes more than one family member or all family members are involved in the decision, sometimes only children are involved in the decision, sometimes more than one consumer is involved, and sometimes the decision maker and the consumer are different people. In most households, when parental joint decisions are being made, spouses consider their partner's needs and perceptions to maintain decision fairness and harmony.

opinion leader an individual who influences the opinions of others

socialization process how cultural values and norms are passed down to children

Family decisions can range from one family member making a decision, some members, or all persons in the family involved in the purchase decision.

This tends to minimize family conflict. When couples agree to narrow their options before making a purchase, they are more likely to be satisfied with the eventual outcome and less likely to feel regret.

6-7d Individual Differences in Susceptibility to Social Influences

Social influence plays an important role in consumer behavior, but not all persons are equally influenced in their purchase decisions. Some have a strong need to build the images others have of them by buying products used by other members of their reference groups. Seeking approval of others through the "correct" product ownership is very important to these consumers. This is particularly true for conspicuous items (those that others can easily see) such as clothes, jewelry, cars, and even mobile devices. These individuals have a strong desire to avoid negative impressions in public settings. For example, wearing the wrong bathing suit at the university swimming pool would be very distressing to this type of consumer.

Consumers differ in their feelings of connectedness to other consumers. A consumer with a **separated self-schema** perceives himself or herself as distinct and separate from others. A person with a **connected self-schema** sees himself or herself as an integral part of a group. Research has found that individuals who feel connected respond more favorably to advertisements that promote group belonging and cohesion.

The influence of other people on how a consumer behaves is strongest when that consumer knows or feels that she is being watched. Researchers have found this to be especially true when individuals are consuming

or buying personal products. Some people will not buy memberships to athletic clubs because they don't want to work out with (or even around) a group of people. They fear how they may appear to others.

6-8 INDIVIDUAL INFLUENCES ON CONSUMER BUYING DECISIONS

While individuality impacts a person's susceptibility to social influences, factors such as gender, age, life-cycle stage, personality, self-concept, and lifestyle also play important roles in consumer decision making. Individual characteristics are generally stable over the course of one's life. For instance, the act of changing personality or lifestyle requires a complete reorientation of one's life. In the case of age and life-cycle stage, these changes occur gradually over time.

6-8a Gender

Physiological differences between men and women result in many different needs, such as with health and beauty products. Just as important are the distinct cultural, social, and economic roles played by men and women and the effects that these have on their decision-making processes. Many women have purchased a product based on a marketer's portrayal of women. Messages and videos for companies such as Nike, Always, and Under Armour are perceived as very positive. The Dove "Real Beauty" campaign was named the number-one ad of the 21st century by *Advertising Age*. Under Armour's "I Will What I Want" ad also fared well for its portrayal of women pushing back against the idea of perfection and simply embracing themselves (see an example at www.youtube.com/watch?v=ZY0cdXr_1MA).

Women account for a large percentage of purchase decisions in some key categories, while men are the predominant decision makers in others:

- **Furniture and home accessories:** Women are the sole decision makers 53 percent of the time; men and women are joint decision makers 27 percent of the time.

- **Small appliances:** Women are sole decision makers 51 percent of the time; men and women are joint decision makers 31 percent of the time.

- **Smartphones:** For most electronics, men make the majority of

separated self-schema a perspective whereby a consumer sees himself or herself as distinct and separate from others

connected self-schema a perspective whereby a consumer sees himself or herself as an integral part of a group

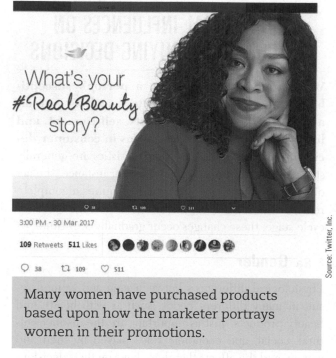

Many women have purchased products based upon how the marketer portrays women in their promotions.

decisions. However, for smartphones, women are sole decision makers 38 percent of the time, and men are sole decision makers 35 percent of the time.

- **Power tools:** Men are sole decision makers 68 percent of the time.

- **Auto tires and batteries:** Men are sole decision makers 61 percent of the time.[31]

6-8b Age and Family Life-Cycle Stage

A consumer's age and family life-cycle stage can have a significant impact on his or her behavior. How old a consumer is generally indicates what products he or she may be interested in purchasing. Consumer tastes in food, clothing, cars, furniture, and recreation are often age related.

Related to a person's age is his or her place in the family life cycle. As Chapter 8 explains in more detail, the *family life cycle* is an orderly series of stages through which consumers' attitudes and behavioral tendencies evolve through maturity, experience, and changing income and status. Marketers often define their target markets in terms of family life cycle, such as "young singles," "young married couples with children," and "middle-aged married couples without children." For instance, young singles spend more than average on alcoholic beverages, education, and

entertainment. New parents typically increase their spending on health care, clothing, housing, and food and decrease their spending on alcohol, education, and transportation. Households with older children spend more on food, entertainment, personal care products, and education, as well as cars and gasoline. After their children leave home, spending by older couples on vehicles, women's clothing, and health care typically increases. For instance, the presence of children in the home is the most significant determinant of the type of vehicle that's driven off the new car lot. Parents are the ultimate need-driven car consumers, requiring larger cars and trucks to haul their children and all their belongings. It comes as no surprise, then, that for all households with children, SUVs rank either first or second among new-vehicle purchases, followed by minivans.

NONTRADITIONAL LIFE CYCLES Marketers should also be aware of the many nontraditional life-cycle paths that are common today and provide insights into the needs and wants of such consumers as divorced parents, lifelong singles, and childless couples. Three decades ago, married couples with children under the age of 18 accounted for about half of U.S. households. Today, such families make up only 39 percent of all households. About one-third of U.S. children are living with an unmarried parent. Most are living with a solo mother.[32] The shift toward more single-parent households is part of a broader societal change that has put more women on the career track.

SINGLE PARENTS Careers often create a *poverty of time* for single parents. To cope with the dual demands of a career and raising children, single parents are always on the lookout for time-saving products like quick-preparation foods and no-iron clothing. Rightly so, more and more marketers are catering to the single-parent market.

LIFE EVENTS Another way to look at the life cycle is to look at major events in one's life over time. Life-changing events can occur at any time. A few examples are death of a spouse, moving, birth or adoption of a child, retirement, job loss, divorce, and marriage. Typically, such events are quite stressful, and consumers will often take steps to minimize that stress. Many times, life-changing events will mean new consumption patterns. For example, a recently divorced person may try to improve his or her appearance by joining a health club and dieting. Someone moving to a different city will need a new dentist, grocery store, auto service center, and doctor, among other things. Marketers realize that life events often mean a chance to gain a new customer. The Welcome Wagon offers free gifts and services for area newcomers. Lowe's sends out a discount coupon to those moving to a new community.

And when you put your home on the market, you will quickly start receiving flyers from moving companies promising a great price on moving your household goods.

6-8c Personality, Self-Concept, and Lifestyle

Each consumer has a unique personality. **Personality** is a broad concept that can be thought of as a way of organizing and grouping how an individual typically reacts to situations. Thus, personality combines psychological makeup and environmental forces. It includes people's underlying dispositions, especially their most dominant characteristics. Although personality is one of the least useful concepts in the study of consumer behavior, some marketers believe personality influences the types and brands of products purchased. For instance, the type of car, clothes, or jewelry a consumer buys may reflect one or more personality traits.

Self-concept, or self-perception, is how consumers perceive themselves. Self-concept includes attitudes, perceptions, beliefs, and self-evaluations. Although self-concept may change, the change is often gradual. Through self-concept, people define their identity, which in turn provides for consistent and coherent behavior.

Self-concept combines the **ideal self-image** (the way an individual would like to be perceived) and the **real self-image** (the way an individual actually perceives himself or herself). Generally, we try to raise our real self-image toward our ideal (or at least narrow the gap). Consumers seldom buy products that jeopardize their self-image. For example, someone who sees herself as a trendsetter would not buy clothing that does not project a contemporary image.

Human behavior depends largely on self-concept. Because consumers want to protect their identity as individuals, the products they buy, the stores they patronize, the social media they use, and the credit cards they carry support their self-image. No other product quite reflects a person's self-image as much as the car he or she drives. For example, many young consumers do not like family sedans like the Honda Accord or Toyota Camry and say they would buy one for their mom but not for themselves. Likewise, younger parents may avoid purchasing minivans because they do not want to sacrifice the youthful image they have of themselves just because they have new responsibilities. To combat decreasing sales, marketers of the Nissan Quest minivan decided to reposition it as something other than a "mom mobile" or "soccer mom car." They chose the ad copy "Passion built it. Passion will fill it up," followed by "What if we made a minivan that changed the way people think of minivans?"

By influencing the degree to which consumers perceive a good or service to be self-relevant, marketers can

Self-concept combines the ideal self-image (the way an individual would like to be perceived) and the real self-image (the way an individual actually perceives himself or herself).

affect consumers' motivation to learn about, shop for, and buy a certain brand. Marketers also consider self-concept important because it helps explain the relationship between individuals' perceptions of themselves and their consumer behavior.

6-9 PSYCHOLOGICAL INFLUENCES ON CONSUMER BUYING DECISIONS

An individual's buying decisions are further influenced by psychological factors: perception, motivation, and learning. These factors are what consumers use to interact with their world. They are the tools consumers use to recognize their feelings, gather and analyze information, formulate thoughts and opinions, and take action. Unlike the other three influences on consumer behavior, psychological influences can be affected by a person's environment because they are applied on specific occasions. For example, you will perceive different stimuli and process these stimuli in different ways depending on whether you are sitting in class concentrating

personality a way of organizing and grouping the consistencies of an individual's reactions to situations

self-concept how consumers perceive themselves in terms of attitudes, perceptions, beliefs, and self-evaluations

ideal self-image the way an individual would like to be perceived

real self-image the way an individual actually perceives himself or herself on the instructor, sitting outside class talking to friends, or sitting in your dorm room streaming a video.

6-9a Perception

The world is full of stimuli. A stimulus is any unit of input affecting one or more of the five senses: sight, smell, taste, touch, and hearing. The process by which we select, organize, and interpret these stimuli into a meaningful and coherent picture is called **perception**. In essence, perception is how we see the world around us. We act based on perceptions that may or may not reflect reality. Suppose you are driving to the grocery and you see a house with smoke pouring from the roof. Your perception is that the house is on fire, so you quickly stop to warn any occupants and to call 911. As you approach the house, you hear laughter coming from the back yard. As you peek around the corner, you see a family burning a big pile of leaves and the wind carrying the smoke over the roof. There is no house fire. When you get to the grocery store, you see a big, beautiful ripe pineapple and immediately put it in your cart. When you get home, you cut into the pineapple—only to find that it has a rotten core and is inedible. In both cases, you acted based on perceptions that did not reflect reality.

People cannot perceive every stimulus in their environment. Therefore, they use **selective exposure** to decide which stimuli to notice and which to ignore. Digital marketing experts estimate that most Americans are exposed to around 4,000 to 10,000 ads per day.[33]

The familiarity of an object, contrast, movement, intensity (such as increased volume), and smell are cues that influence perception. Consumers use these cues to identify and define products and brands. Double Tree hotels always have fresh chocolate chip cookies at the reception desk and the entire area smells like just-baked cookies. For most travelers, this cues feelings of warmth and comfort. Cutting-edge consumer research has found that a cluttered, chaotic environment results in consumers spending more. Why does this occur? The perception of a cluttered environment impairs self-control. Disorganized surroundings threaten one's sense of personal control, which in turn taxes one's self-regulatory abilities.[31] Researchers have found that cluttered and busy websites with too many communication options (such as forums, Q&A sections, chat rooms, and email) actually reduce the average total amount purchased from the retailer. It seems people will spend more time gathering information and less time shopping.[34]

The shape of a product's packaging, such as Coca-Cola's signature contour bottle, can influence perception. Color is another cue, and it plays a key role in consumers' perceptions. Packaged foods manufacturers use color to trigger unconscious associations for grocery shoppers who typically make their shopping decisions in the blink of an eye. Think of the red and white Campbell's soup can and the green and white Green Giant frozen vegetable box, for example.

Two other concepts closely related to selective exposure are selective distortion and selective retention. **Selective distortion** occurs when consumers change or distort information that conflicts with their feelings or beliefs. For example, suppose a college student buys a Dell tablet. After the purchase, if the student gets new information about an alternative brand, such as an Asus ZenPad 10, he or she may distort the information to make it more consistent with the prior view that the Dell is just as good as the ZenPad 10, if not better. Business travelers who are Executive Platinum frequent flyers on American Airlines may distort or discount information about the quality of United Airlines' business class service. The frequent flyer may think to herself, "Yes, the service is okay but the seats are uncomfortable and the planes are always late."

Selective retention is remembering only information that supports personal feelings or beliefs. The consumer forgets all information that may be inconsistent. After reading a pamphlet that contradicts one's political beliefs, for instance, a person may forget many of the points outlined in it. Similarly, consumers may see a news report on suspected illegal practices by their favorite retail store but soon forget the reason the store was featured on the news.

Which stimuli will be perceived often depends on the individual. People can be exposed to the same stimuli under identical conditions but perceive them very differently. For example, two people viewing a television commercial may have different interpretations of the advertising message. One person may be thoroughly engrossed by the message and become highly motivated to buy the product. Thirty seconds after the ad ends, the second person may not be able to recall the content of the message or even the product advertised.

---

perception the process by which people select, organize, and interpret stimuli into a meaningful and coherent picture

selective exposure a process whereby a consumer notices certain stimuli and ignores others

selective distortion a process whereby a consumer changes or distorts information that conflicts with his or her feelings or beliefs

selective retention a process whereby a consumer remembers only that information that supports his or her personal beliefs

MARKETING IMPLICATIONS OF PERCEPTION Marketers must recognize the importance of cues, or signals, in consumers' perception of products. Marketing managers first identify the important attributes, such as price or quality, that the targeted consumers want in a product and then design signals to communicate these attributes. For example, consumers will pay more for candy in expensive-looking foil packages. But shiny labels on wine bottles signify less expensive wines; dull labels indicate more expensive wines. Marketers also often use price as a signal to consumers that the product is of higher quality than competing products. Of course, brand names send signals to consumers. The brand names of Close-Up toothpaste, DieHard batteries, and Caress moisturizing soap, for example, identify important product qualities. Names chosen for search engines and sites on the Internet, such as Yahoo!, Amazon, and Bing, are intended to convey excitement and intensity and vastness.

Consumers also associate quality and reliability with certain brand names. Companies watch their brand identity closely, in large part because a strong link has been established between perceived brand value and customer loyalty. Brand names that consistently enjoy high perceived value from consumers include Disney, National Geographic, Mercedes-Benz, and Fisher-Price. Naming a product after a place can also add perceived value by association. Brand names using the words Santa Fe, Dakota, or Texas convey a sense of openness, freedom, and youth, but products named after other locations might conjure up images of pollution and crime. Marketing managers are also interested in the *threshold level of perception*, the minimum difference in a stimulus that the consumer will notice. This concept is sometimes referred to as the "just-noticeable difference." For example, how much would Apple have to drop the price of its 15-inch MacBook Pro with Retina display before consumers perceived it as a bargain—$100? $300? $500? Alternatively, how much could Hershey shrink its milk chocolate bar before consumers noticed that it was smaller but selling for the same price?

Besides changing such stimuli as price, package size, and volume, marketers can change the product or attempt to reposition its image. But marketers must be careful when adding features. How many new services will discounter Target need to add before consumers perceive it as a full-service department store? How many sporty features will General Motors have to add to a basic two-door sedan before consumers start perceiving it as a sports car?

Marketing managers who intend to do business in global markets should be aware of how foreign consumers perceive their products. For instance, in Japan, product labels are often written in English or French, even though they may not translate into anything meaningful. Many Japanese associate foreign words on product labels with the exotic, the expensive, and high quality.

6-9b Motivation

By studying motivation, marketers can analyze the major forces influencing consumers to buy or not buy products. When you buy a product, you usually do so to fulfill some kind of need. These needs become motives when they are aroused sufficiently. For instance, suppose this morning you were so hungry before class that you needed to eat something. In response to that need, you stopped at Starbucks for a breakfast sandwich and coffee. In other words, you were motivated by hunger to stop at Starbucks. A **motive** is the driving force that causes a person to take action to satisfy specific needs.

Why are people driven by particular needs at particular times? One theory is **Maslow's hierarchy of needs**, illustrated in Exhibit 6.7, which arranges needs in ascending order of importance: physiological, safety, social, esteem, and self-actualization. As a person fulfills one need, a higher-level need becomes more important.

The most basic human needs—that is, the needs for food, water, and shelter—are *physiological*. Because they are essential to survival, these needs must be satisfied first. Ads showing a juicy hamburger or a runner gulping down Gatorade after a marathon are examples of appeals to satisfy the physiological needs of hunger and thirst.

Safety needs include security and freedom from pain and discomfort. Marketers sometimes appeal to consumers' fears and

Coke used its "Name Campaign" to influence the perception of Coke being "local," or simply one of you.

urbanbuzz/Shutterstock.com

> **motive** a driving force that causes a person to take action to satisfy specific needs
>
> **Maslow's hierarchy of needs** a method of classifying human needs and motivations into five categories in ascending order of importance: physiological, safety, social, esteem, and self-actualization

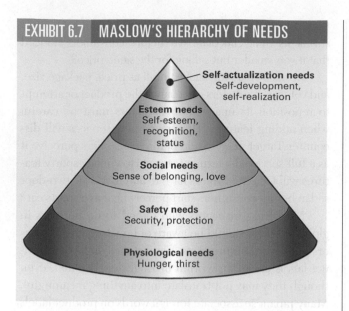

EXHIBIT 6.7 MASLOW'S HIERARCHY OF NEEDS

Self-actualization needs
Self-development,
self-realization

Esteem needs
Self-esteem,
recognition,
status

Social needs
Sense of belonging, love

Safety needs
Security, protection

Physiological needs
Hunger, thirst

anxieties about safety to sell their products. For example, aware of the aging population's health fears, the retail medical imaging centers Heart Check America and HealthScreen America advertise that they offer consumers a full body scan for early detection of health problems such as coronary disease and cancer. Some companies or industries advertise to allay consumer fears. For example, in the wake of the September 11, 2001, terrorist attacks, the airline industry found itself having to conduct an image campaign to reassure consumers about the safety of air travel.

After physiological and safety needs have been fulfilled, *social needs*—especially love and a sense of belonging—become the focus. Love includes acceptance by one's peers, as well as sex and romantic love. Marketing managers probably appeal more to this need than to any other. Ads for clothes, cosmetics, and vacation packages suggest that buying the product can bring love.

Love is acceptance without regard to one's contribution. Esteem is acceptance based on one's contribution to the group. *Self-esteem needs* include self-respect and a sense of accomplishment. Esteem needs also include prestige, fame, and recognition of one's accomplishments. Montblanc pens, Porsche automobiles, and Neiman Marcus stores all appeal to esteem needs.

The highest human need is *self-actualization*. It refers to finding self-fulfillment and self-expression, reaching the point in life at which "people are what they feel they should be." Maslow believed that very few people ever attain this

learning a process that creates changes in behavior, immediate or expected, through experience and practice

level. Even so, advertisements may focus on this type of need. For example, American Express ads convey the message that acquiring an AmEx card is one of the highest attainments in life. The Centurion card, often called simply "the black card," requires a $5,000 initiation fee and carries an annual fee of $2,500.

6-9c Learning

Almost all consumer behavior results from **learning**, which is the process that creates changes in behavior through experience and practice. It is not possible to observe learning directly, but we can infer when it has occurred by a person's actions. For example, suppose you see an advertisement for a new and improved cold medicine. If you go to the store that day and buy that remedy, we infer that you have learned something about the cold medicine.

There are two types of learning: experiential and conceptual. *Experiential learning* occurs when an experience changes your behavior. For example, if the new cold medicine does not relieve your symptoms, you may not buy that brand again. *Conceptual learning*, which is not acquired through direct experience but based on reasoning, is the second type of learning. Assume, for example, that you are standing at a soft drink machine and notice a new diet flavor with an artificial sweetener. Because someone has told you that diet beverages leave an aftertaste, you choose a different drink. You have learned that you would not like this new diet drink without ever trying it.

Reinforcement and repetition boost learning. Reinforcement can be positive or negative. If you see a vendor selling frozen yogurt (stimulus), buy it (response), and find the yogurt to be quite refreshing (reward), your behavior has been positively reinforced. On the other hand, if you buy a new flavor of yogurt and it does not taste good (negative reinforcement), you will not buy that flavor of yogurt again (response). Without positive or negative reinforcement, a person will not be motivated to repeat the behavior pattern or to avoid it. Thus, if a new brand evokes neutral feelings, some marketing activity, such as a price change or an increase in promotion, may be required to induce further consumption. Learning theory is helpful in reminding marketers that concrete and timely strategies are what reinforce desired consumer behavior.

Repetition is a key strategy in promotional campaigns because it can lead to increased learning. Most marketers use repetitious advertising so that consumers will learn what their unique advantage is over the competition. Generally, to heighten learning, advertising messages should be spread out over time rather than clustered together.

A related learning concept useful to marketing managers is **stimulus generalization**. In theory, stimulus generalization occurs when one response is extended to a second stimulus similar to the first. Marketers often use a successful, well-known brand name for a family of products because it gives consumers familiarity with and knowledge about each product in the family. Such brand-name families spur the introduction of new products and facilitate the sale of existing items. OXO relies on consumers' familiarity with its popular kitchen and household products to sell office and medical supplies; Sony's film division relies on name recognition from its home technology, such as the PlayStation. Clorox bathroom cleaner relies on familiarity with Clorox bleach, and Dove shampoo relies on familiarity with Dove soap. Branding is examined in more detail in Chapter 10.

Another form of stimulus generalization occurs when retailers or wholesalers design their packages to resemble well-known manufacturers' brands. Such imitation conveys the notion that the store brand is as good as the national manufacturer's brand.

The opposite of stimulus generalization is **stimulus discrimination**, which means learning to differentiate among similar products. Consumers may perceive one product as more rewarding or stimulating, even if it is virtually indistinguishable from competitors. For example, some consumers prefer Miller Lite and others prefer Bud Light.

With some types of products—such as aspirin, gasoline, bleach, and paper towels—marketers rely on promotion to point out brand differences that consumers would otherwise not recognize. This process, called *product differentiation*, is discussed in more detail in Chapter 8. Usually, product differentiation is based on superficial differences. For example, Bayer tells consumers that it is the aspirin "doctors recommend most."

6-9d The Impact of the COVID 19 Pandemic on Consumer Behavior

For millions of Americans, the COVID-19 pandemic triggered intertwined crises of personal health and personal finance. People were getting fired or furloughed because governments were closing workplaces to prevent the virus from spreading. The Coronavirus Aid, Relief, and Economic Security (CARES) Act put cash in the hands of many consumers but did not eliminate the uncertainty about the future. People dramatically reduced most discretionary spending with grave consequences for restaurants, apparel, and out-of-home entertainment industries such as sporting events. Many big-ticket purchases like cars and major appliances were also postponed. Cancelling vacations meant huge losses for airlines, hotels, attractions such as Disneyworld.

The pandemic brought a rapid rise in online purchasing with groceries being most noteworthy. Part of the rise was due to stockpiling of items such as sanitary wipes, toilet paper, soap, yeast and flour. At home baking became a major past-time for many. Brick and mortar stores and online product outages were common. The lesson for consumers was that certain goods may not always be available to us and we cannot go to the store and get what we want. This may lead to consumers beginning to keep a safety stock of staple and personally preferred items. In addition to a higher rate of online shopping than in the past, related shopping changes may include a growth in BOLPIS-buy online pickup in store, curbside pickup, and subscription services.

Having a lot of time at home during quarantines gave many people time to reflect and perhaps change their behaviors. Many people decide to take up gardening for the first time. They learned a new skill and obtained some needed time in the outdoors. It also meant purchasing seeds and various gardening tools. Other individuals decided that this was a perfect time to get in shape by exercising. Some took classes via Zoom and others bought high-tech equipment such as a Peloton bike. Sales of these machines increase dramatically during the pandemic. Perhaps the biggest decision that some consumers made was to move. As many millions began working from home and found that there was a good chance that this might become a permanent policy, they began looking for cheaper, more spacious surroundings. Many communities see an opportunity to attract educated, well-paid workers and decided to add incentives to attract those seeking a lower cost-of-living. Vermont has started offering newcomers $10,000 over two years to persons working remotely but living full-time in the state. Topeka, Kansas tops that offer with $15,000 for professionals to relocate. Savannah, Georgia is tempting tech workers with $2000 to move.

stimulus generalization
a form of learning that occurs when one response is extended to a second stimulus similar to the first

stimulus discrimination
a learned ability to differentiate among similar products

7 | Business Marketing

LEARNING OUTCOMES

After studying this chapter, you will be able to . . .

7-1 Describe business marketing

7-2 Describe trends in B-to-B Internet marketing

7-3 Discuss the role of relationship marketing and strategic alliances in business marketing

7-4 Identify the four major categories of business market customers

7-5 Explain the North American Industry Classification System

7-6 Explain the major differences between business and consumer markets

7-7 Describe the seven types of business goods and services

7-8 Discuss the unique aspects of business buying behavior

George Rudy/Shutterstock.com

7-1 WHAT IS BUSINESS MARKETING?

Business marketing (also called industrial, business-to-business, B-to-B, or B2B marketing) is the marketing of goods and services to individuals and organizations for purposes other than personal consumption. The sale of a personal computer (PC) to your college or university is an example of business marketing. A **business product**, or **industrial product**, is used to manufacture other goods or services, to facilitate an organization's operations, or to resell to other customers. A **consumer product** is bought to satisfy an individual's personal wants or needs. The key characteristic distinguishing business products from consumer products is intended use, not physical form.

How do you distinguish between a consumer product and a business product? A product that is purchased for personal or family consumption or as a gift is a consumer good. If that same product, such as a PC or a cell phone, is bought for use in a business, it is a business product. Some common items that are sold as both consumer goods and business products are office supplies (e.g., pens, paper, and staple removers). Some items, such as forklifts, are more commonly sold as business products than as consumer goods.

The size of the business market in the United States and most other countries substantially exceeds that of the consumer market. In the business market, a single customer can account for a huge volume of purchases. For example, IBM's purchasing department spends more than $40 billion annually on business products. Procter & Gamble (P&G), Apple, Merck, Dell, and Kimberly-Clark each spend more than half of their annual revenue on business products.[1]

Some large firms that produce goods such as steel, computer memory chips, or production equipment market exclusively to business customers. Other firms market to both businesses and to consumers. Hewlett-Packard marketed exclusively to business customers in the past but now markets laser printers and personal computers to consumers. Sony, traditionally a consumer marketer, now sells office automation products to businesses. Kodak used to sell its cameras exclusively to consumers, but has opted to sell its commercial printing services to businesses since emerging from bankruptcy in 2013. All of these companies have had to make organizational and marketing changes to expand into the new market categories.

> The key characteristic distinguishing business products from consumer products is intended use, not physical form.

7-2 TRENDS IN B-to-B INTERNET MARKETING

Over the past decade, marketers have become more and more sophisticated in their use of the Internet. Companies have had to transition from "We have a website because our customer does" to having a site that attracts, interests, satisfies, informs, and retains customers. B-to-B companies are increasingly leveraging the Internet as an effective sales and promotion platform (much like B-to-C companies have done for decades). B-to-B

business marketing (industrial, business-to-business, B-to-B, or B2B marketing) the marketing of goods and services to individuals and organizations for purposes other than personal consumption

business product (industrial product) a product used to manufacture other goods or services, to facilitate an organization's operations, or to resell to other customers

consumer product a product bought to satisfy an individual's personal wants or needs companies use the Internet in three major ways. First, they use their websites to facilitate communication and orders. Second, they use digital marketing to increase brand awareness. Third, they use digital marketing—primarily in the form of content marketing—to position their businesses as thought leaders and therefore generate sales leads. Companies selling to business buyers face the same challenges as all marketers, including determining the target market and deciding how best to reach it.

Every year, new applications that provide additional information about customers are developed. These applications often also lower costs, increase supply-chain efficiency, or enhance customer retention, loyalty, and trust. Increasingly, business customers expect suppliers to know them personally, monitor people's movement within their company, and offer personal interaction through social media, email, and personal mailers. As such, we have seen B-to-B marketers use technology like smartphones and tablets to facilitate orders and enhance customer experiences.

A few years ago, many people thought the Internet would eliminate the need for distributors. Why would customers pay a distributor's markup when they could buy directly from the manufacturer with a few mouse clicks? This has occurred less frequently than many expected because distributors often perform important functions such as providing credit, aggregating supplies from multiple sources, making deliveries, and processing returns. Many business customers, especially small firms, depend on knowledgeable distributors for information and advice that is not available to them online.

Social media usage has been the most pervasive B-to-B and B-to-C marketing trend of the past five years. Most companies use email marketing, search engine optimization, paid search, and display advertising to pull customers to their websites. This field of marketing requires vigilant adjustment to keep track of new applications and platforms, as well as constant evaluation to determine whether these new avenues are beneficial to (or used by) customers. Generally, B-to-C marketers were faster to adopt social media as part of the promotional mix. B-to-B marketers did not initially see the value in these tools. However, that has changed as social media has become more popular.

Content marketing is a strategic marketing approach focused on creating and distributing valuable, relevant, and consistent content. The goal of this content is to attract and retain a clearly defined

> **content marketing** a strategic marketing approach that focuses on creating and distributing content that is valuable, relevant, and consistent

audience, and ultimately, drive profitable customer action. This strategy has played an important role for B-to-B marketers. Content marketing includes media such as videos, podcasts, webinars, blog posts, white papers, ebooks, slide decks, and more. Sharing valuable insights and interesting content can position a company as a thought leader in an area. A 2018 study by the Content Marketing Institute and MarketingProfs showed that while 91 percent of B-to-B respondents said that they used content marketing, only 24 percent felt as though their organizations were successful with the content marketing strategy. The two most important goals for B-to-B content marketers are lead generation and sales.[2] Most companies use content marketing to increase brand awareness and generate leads. Increasing engagement comes in a close third. Interestingly,

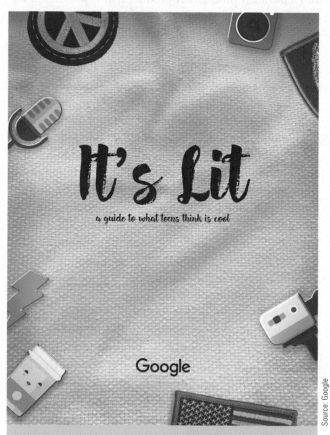

Source: Google

In April 2017, Google released a report called *It's Lit: A Guide to What Teens Think Is Cool*. This B-to-B content marketing piece featured statistics, information, and other insights into reaching this highly sought-after demographic. You can view *It's Lit* at https://storage.googleapis.com /think/docs/its-lit.pdf.

while most B-to-C companies favor Facebook as their primary social media platform, most B-to-B companies see LinkedIn as the most beneficial platform through which to distribute content. Regardless of the platform used, the key to social media–based content marketing for B-to-B marketers is to create compelling and useful content for customers. For example, HubSpot and Marketo develop white papers and e-books on topics such as generating leads through social media for customers and potential customers.

As they build reputations in their business areas, many marketers use social media to increase awareness and build relationships and community. Social media platforms like YouTube, LinkedIn, Twitter, and Facebook provide great conversational platforms for doing just that. While building community is important, B-to-B marketers are also using social media to gather leads (as you may have gathered from the HubSpot and Marketo white paper example). Other goals include product promotion, traffic building, search engine optimization (SEO), competitive intelligence and listening, customer feedback and support, and product development.

As platforms such as mobile and streaming video grow, marketers must develop new ways to measure campaign effectiveness. For example, after using social analytics to determine the most effective hashtag from its "Internet of Everything" campaign, Cisco was able to increase usage of one particularly effective hashtag by 440 percent. Global information and statistical measurement company Nielsen recently launched Nielsen Digital Ad Ratings, which is designed to provide a more holistic view of how consumers engage with digital media.[3] According to data collected through this new platform, less than half of all online advertisement impressions reach their intended audiences. Depending on the medium used, the coverage rate for customer targeting varies between 30 percent and 50 percent. Some metrics that are particularly useful for increasing the success of a social media campaign are awareness, engagement, and conversion. *Awareness* is the attention that social media attracts, such as the number of followers or fans. Awareness is generally used as the first step in the marketing funnel, and social media is often paired with paid digital media like display advertising and text-based ads to increase its effectiveness. *Engagement* refers to the interactions between the brand and the audience, such as comments, retweets, shares, and searches. The purpose of engagement is to get customers to respond to brand-led posts and to start conversations themselves. *Conversions* occur when action is taken and include everything from downloading a piece of content (like a white paper) to actually making a purchase. Each of these metrics affects the return on investment.

7-3 RELATIONSHIP MARKETING AND STRATEGIC ALLIANCES

As explained in Chapter 1, relationship marketing is a strategy that entails seeking and establishing ongoing partnerships with customers. Relationship marketing has become an important business marketing strategy as customers have become more demanding and competition has become more intense. Loyal customers are also more profitable than those who are price sensitive and perceive little or no difference among brands or suppliers.

Relationship marketing is increasingly important, as business suppliers use platforms like Facebook, Twitter, and other social networking sites to advertise themselves

The top social media tools for B-to-B marketers

The Content Marketing Institute, CMI, surveyed hundreds of B-to-B marketers regarding their social media usage, and while LinkedIn, Facebook, and Twitter were used by the majority of respondents, LinkedIn was the most used social media tool overall (chosen by 97 percent of respondents). Runners-up were Twitter (87 percent), Facebook (86 percent), YouTube (60 percent), and Instagram (30 percent). LinkedIn is so popular because it drives more traffic and leads than other platforms for B-to-B marketers. The company has only increased its favor among B-to-B marketers by adding new B-to-B-friendly features like sponsored company updates, groups connected to topics, products and services pages, and a thought leader blogging program.[4]

B-to-B marketers have begun making use of social advertising platforms such as advertisement exchanges on LinkedIn and promoted tweets on Twitter, and many B-to-B marketers are even creating their own blogs. For example, audit and consulting firm Deloitte created an online content hub called Deloitte Insights on which the company utilizes several different content formats, including blog posts, webcasts, and podcasts to provide company and industry information to both current and potential customers.[5]

to businesses. Social networking sites encourage businesses to shop around and research options for all their needs. This means that, for many suppliers, retaining their current customers has become a primary focus, whereas acquiring new customers was the focus in the past. Maintaining a steady dialogue between the supplier and the customer is a proven way to gain repeat business.[6]

7-3a Strategic Alliances

A **strategic alliance**, sometimes called a **strategic partnership**, is a cooperative agreement between business firms. Strategic alliances can take the form of licensing or distribution agreements, joint ventures, research and development consortia, and partnerships. They may be between manufacturers, manufacturers and customers, manufacturers and suppliers, and manufacturers and channel intermediaries.

Business marketers form strategic alliances to strengthen operations and better compete. In order to differentiate it's watch from competitors, Apple formed strategic alliances with high-end fashion brands, such as Hermès, Coach, and Kate Spade, after introducing the Apple Watch to the market. These luxury fashion brands design trendy watch bands that pair with the Apple Watch and allow the product to be sold at high price points. These partnerships have allowed Apple to expand its market to include more fashion-savvy shoppers who might not purchase the product simply for the high-tech benefits. These partnerships led Apple to capture 21 percent of the wearable technology market share in 2017, making the company the biggest shipper of this type of product.[7]

Sometimes alliance partners are fierce competitors. Take, for example, the partnership between Nestlé, parent company of espresso brand Nespresso, and Starbucks. In 2018, Nestlé and Starbucks formed a global coffee alliance to expand the packaged coffee market and to try to make coffee the world's first sustainable agricultural product. This partnership allows Starbucks to expand their global market reach, while Nestlé has the rights to market and distribute Starbucks brand coffee. Additionally, although Starbucks markets its own at-home espresso machines, the partnership allows Starbucks coffee to be manufactured for Nestlé's espresso machines.[8]

Other alliances are formed between companies that operate in completely

Apple Watch Hermès – 44mm Fauve Grained Barenia Leather Single Tour Rallye
$439.00

Case Size
44mm

Designed for Apple Watch Series 4.
Works with all previous versions of Apple Watch.
Learn more about band compatibility ›

Band Size
One Size
Fits 160–195mm wrists.

Add to Bag

Pickup:
Check availability

Delivery:
Currently Unavailable

Need some help? Contact us.
Cases shown are for illustration purposes only.

Source: Apple Inc.

> Sometimes alliance partners are from completely different industries.

different industries. For example, in an effort to become more committed to sustainability, manufacturer of construction equipment Caterpillar recently partnered with SunSelect Produce to construct hydroponic greenhouses.[9] SunSelect is planning to purchase land adjacent to Caterpillar so that it can use the waste products produced by Caterpillar's heat and power cogeneration facilities to power their greenhouses and produce premium vegetables in a sustainable manner.

For an alliance to succeed in the long term, it must be built on commitment and trust. **Relationship commitment** means that a firm believes an ongoing relationship with some other firm is so important that it warrants maximum efforts at maintaining it indefinitely.[10] A perceived breakdown in commitment by one of the parties often leads to a breakdown in the relationship.

Trust exists when one party has confidence in an exchange partner's reliability and integrity.[11] Some alliances fail when participants lack trust in their trading partners. Consider, for example, the recent fallout between American Express and Costco. The two companies had an exclusive partnership for more than 15 years—American Express was the only credit card accepted at Costco stores. But in 2016, the two companies decided to part ways. When the contract between the two companies neared expiration in 2014, Costco decided to solicit bids from other credit card companies. Costco was able to secure a lower bid from Citi and Visa, and therefore chose to end its long-standing partnership with American Express. American Express felt betrayed by Costco because it viewed the retailer as a trusted partner. The move caused American Express to lose tens of thousands of customers and sent its stock price tumbling.[12]

The combined effects of COVID-19 and tax and tariff conflicts have had substantial negative impacts on

strategic alliance (strategic partnership) a cooperative agreement between business firms

relationship commitment a firm's belief that an ongoing relationship with another firm is so important that the relationship warrants maximum efforts at maintaining it indefinitely

trust the condition that exists when one party has confidence in an exchange partner's reliability and integrity relationships between the U.S. and its major trading partners, especially China. There are no signs of these conflicts abating in the near future. Relationship commitments and trust have fallen, leading to shortages and delays in shipping personal protection equipment (PPEs). PPEs such as ventilators, surgical masks, gowns and shields for healthcare professionals have been particularly acute in the first half of 2020. As U.S. businesses suppliers, many alliances are being stressed and the efficacy of these trading relationships are being questioned.

7-3b Relationships in Other Cultures

Although the terms *relationship marketing* and *strategic alliances* are fairly new and popularized mostly by American business executives and educators, the concepts have long been familiar in other cultures. Businesses in China, Japan, Korea, Mexico, and much of Europe rely heavily on personal relationships.

In Japan, for example, exchange between firms is based on personal relationships that are developed through what is called *amae*, or indulgent dependency. *Amae* is the feeling of nurturing concern for, and dependence on, another. Reciprocity and personal relationships contribute to *amae*. Relationships between companies can develop into a *keiretsu*—a network of interlocking corporate affiliates. Within a *keiretsu*, executives may sit on the boards of their customers or their suppliers. Members of a *keiretsu* trade with each other whenever possible and often engage in joint product development, finance, and marketing activity. For example, the Toyota Group *keiretsu* includes 14 core companies and another 170 that receive preferential treatment. Toyota holds an equity position in many of these 170 member firms and is represented on many of their boards of directors.

Many firms have found that the best way to compete in Asian countries is to form relationships with Asian firms. Microsoft recently partnered with several Asian companies in order to expand the availability of its products in China.[13] One such alliance was formed with 21Vianet, a Chinese Internet service provider, and Unisplendour Corporation Limited, a Chinese technology firm. Together, these companies launched a new public cloud service in China. By partnering with local firms, Microsoft became the first U.S. company to launch a public cloud in China.

7-4 MAJOR CATEGORIES OF BUSINESS CUSTOMERS

The business market consists of four major categories of customers: producers, resellers, governments, and institutions.

7-4a Producers

The producer segment of the business market includes profit-oriented individuals and organizations that use purchased goods and services to produce other products, to incorporate into other products, or to facilitate the daily operations of the organization. Examples of producers include construction, manufacturing, transportation, finance, real estate, and foodservice firms. In the United States, there are more than 13 million firms in the producer segment of the business market. Some of these firms are small, and others are among the world's largest businesses.

Producers are often called **original equipment manufacturers**, or **OEMs**. This term includes all individuals and organizations that buy business goods and incorporate them into the products they produce for eventual sale to other producers or to consumers. Companies such as General Motors that buy steel, paint, tires, and batteries are said to be OEMs.

7-4b Resellers

The reseller market includes retail and wholesale businesses that buy finished goods and resell them for a profit. A retailer sells mainly to final consumers; wholesalers sell mostly to retailers and other organizational

After Costco ended its exclusive partnership with American Express, the credit card company lost tens of thousands of customers and saw a significant drop in its stock price.

keiretsu a network of interlocking corporate affiliates

original equipment manufacturers (OEMs) individuals and organizations that buy business goods and incorporate them into the products they produce for eventual sale to other producers or to consumers customers. There are approximately 1.5 million retailers and 500,000 wholesalers operating in the United States. Consumer product firms like P&G, Kraft Foods, and Coca-Cola sell directly to large retailers and retail chains and through wholesalers to smaller retail units. Retailing is explored in detail in Chapter 14.

Business product distributors are wholesalers that buy business products and resell them to business customers. They often carry thousands of items in stock and employ sales forces to call on business customers. Businesses that wish to buy a gross of pencils or a hundred pounds of fertilizer typically purchase these items from local distributors rather than directly from manufacturers such as Empire Pencil or Dow Chemical.

7-4c Governments

A third major segment of the business market is government. Government organizations include thousands of federal, state, and local buying units. Collectively, these government units account for the greatest volume of purchases of any customer category in the United States. The federal government alone spent nearly $4 trillion in the 2017 fiscal year.[14]

Marketing to government agencies can be an overwhelming undertaking, but companies that learn how the system works can position themselves to win lucrative contracts and build lasting, rewarding relationships.[15]

Marketing to government agencies traditionally has not been an activity for companies seeking quick returns. The aphorism "hurry up and wait" is often cited as a characteristic of marketing to government agencies. Contracts for government purchases are often put out for bid. Interested vendors submit bids (usually sealed) to provide specified products during a particular time. Sometimes the lowest bidder is awarded the contract. When the lowest bidder is not awarded the contract, strong evidence must be presented to justify the decision. Grounds for rejecting the lowest bid include lack of experience, inadequate financing, or poor past performance. Bidding allows all potential suppliers a fair chance at winning government contracts and helps ensure that public funds are spent wisely.

FEDERAL GOVERNMENT Name just about any good or service and chances are that someone in the federal government uses it. The U.S. federal government buys goods and services valued at more than $875 billion per year, making it the world's largest customer.[16]

Although much of the federal government's buying is centralized, no single federal agency contracts for all the government's requirements, and no single buyer in

Companies like Kroger are resellers of products offered by P&G and Coca-Cola.

Jonathan Weiss/Shutterstock.com

any agency purchases all that the agency needs. We can view the federal government as a combination of several large companies with overlapping responsibilities and thousands of small independent units. One popular source of information about government procurement is *FedBizOpps*. Until recently, businesses hoping to sell to the federal government found the document (previously called *Commerce Business Daily*) unorganized, and it often arrived too late to be useful. The online version (www.cbd-net.com) is timelier and allows contractors to find leads using keyword searches. Other examples of publications designed to explain how to do business with the federal government include *Doing Business with the General Services Administration*, *Selling to the Military*, and *Selling to the U.S. Air Force*.

STATE, COUNTY, AND CITY GOVERNMENT Selling to states, counties, and cities can be less frustrating for both small and large vendors than selling to the federal government. Paperwork is typically simpler and more manageable than it is at the federal level. But vendors must decide which of the more than 89,000 government units are likely to buy their wares. State and local buying agencies include school districts, highway departments, government-operated hospitals, housing agencies, and many other departments and divisions.

7-4d Institutions

The fourth major segment of the business market consists of institutions that seek to achieve goals other than the standard business goals of profit, market share, and return on investment. This segment includes schools, hospitals, colleges and universities, churches, labor unions, fraternal organizations, civic clubs, foundations, and other so-called nonbusiness organizations. Some institutional purchasers operate similarly to governments in that the purchasing process is influenced, determined, or administered by government units. Other institutional purchasers are organized more like corporations.[17]

7-5 THE NORTH AMERICAN INDUSTRY CLASSIFICATION SYSTEM

The North American Industry Classification System (NAICS) is an industry classification system introduced in 1997 to replace the standard industrial classification system (SIC). NAICS (pronounced *nakes*) is a system for classifying North American business establishments. The system, developed jointly by the United States, Canada, and Mexico, provides a common industry classification system for the North American Free Trade Agreement (NAFTA) partners. Goods- or service-producing firms that use identical or similar production processes are grouped together.

NAICS is an extremely valuable tool for business marketers engaged in analyzing, segmenting, and targeting markets. Each classification group is relatively homogeneous in terms of raw materials required, components used, manufacturing processes employed, and problems faced. Therefore, if a supplier understands the needs and requirements of a few firms within a classification, requirements can be projected for all firms in that category. The number, size, and geographic dispersion of firms can also be identified. This information can be converted to market potential estimates, market share estimates, and sales forecasts. It can also be used for identifying potential new customers. NAICS codes can help identify prospective users of a supplier's goods and services. The more digits in a code, the more homogeneous the group. A sample of how NAICS codes function is shown in Exhibit 7.1. For a complete listing of all NAICS codes, see www.naics.com/search.htm.

7-6 BUSINESS VERSUS CONSUMER MARKETS

The basic philosophy and practice of marketing are the same whether the customer is a business organization or a consumer. Business markets do, however, have characteristics different from those of consumer markets.

EXHIBIT 7.1 HOW NAICS WORKS

The more digits in the NAICS code, the more homogeneous the groups at that level.

NAICS Level	NAICS Code	Description
Sector	51	Information
Subsector	513	Broadcasting and telecommunications
Industry group	5133	Telecommunications
Industry	51332	Wireless telecommunications carriers, except satellite
Industry subdivision	513321	Paging

7-6a Demand

Demand for consumer products is quite different from demand in the business market. Unlike consumer demand, business demand is derived, inelastic, joint, and fluctuating.

DERIVED DEMAND The demand for business products is called **derived demand** because organizations buy products to be used in producing their customers' products. For instance, the demand for timber is derived from, or based on, the demand for new-construction houses. Despite emerging from the Great Recession in the early 2010s, the new U.S. housing market has still not made a strong comeback. A decrease in demand for new-construction houses has resulted in low timber prices, leading many South Carolinian timber producers to delay harvesting their timber.[18] Because demand is derived, business marketers must carefully monitor demand patterns and changing preferences in final consumer markets, even though their customers are not in those markets. Moreover, business marketers must carefully monitor their customers' forecasts, because derived demand is based on expectations of future demand for those customers' products.

Some business marketers not only monitor final consumer demand and customer forecasts but also try to influence final consumer demand. Aluminum producers use television and magazine advertisements to point out the convenience and recycling opportunities that aluminum offers to consumers who

North American Industry Classification System (NAICS) a detailed numbering system developed by the United States, Canada, and Mexico to classify North American business establishments by their main production processes

derived demand the demand for business products

The Unknown Future of Boeing

The success or failure of one bid can make the difference between prosperity and bankruptcy. The Boeing 787 Dreamliner was once called "the most sophisticated aircraft ever made," but Boeing has encountered one problem after another with the ill-fated aircraft. Most recently, a number of 787 operators have reported engine icing problems with a particular engine produced by General Electric. The Federal Aviation Administration Authority has ordered Boeing to carry out an urgent fix on all 176 aircraft equipped with this engine. Boeing has pledged to fix the problem, but incidents such as this can cause irreparable damage to a company's sales and long-term image.[19]

Note: This box feature was written prior to the crashes that took place in 2019 involving the Boeing aircrafts.

can choose to purchase soft drinks in either aluminum or plastic containers.

INELASTIC DEMAND The demand for many business products is inelastic with regard to price. *Inelastic demand* means that an increase or decrease in the price of the product will not significantly affect demand for the product. This will be discussed further in Chapter 19.

The price of a product used in the production of, or as part of, a final product is often a minor portion of the final product's total price. Therefore, demand for the final consumer product is not affected. If the price of automobile paint or spark plugs rises significantly, say, 200 percent in one year, do you think the number of new automobiles sold that year will be affected? Probably not.

JOINT DEMAND Joint demand occurs when two or more items are used together in a final product. For example, a decline in the availability of memory chips will slow production of microcomputers, which will in turn reduce the demand for disk drives. Likewise, the demand for Apple operating systems exists as long as there is a demand for Apple computers. Sales of the two products are directly linked.

FLUCTUATING DEMAND The demand for business products—particularly new plants and equipment—tends to be less stable than the demand for consumer products. A small increase or decrease in consumer demand can produce a much larger change in demand for the facilities and equipment needed to make the consumer product. Economists refer to this phenomenon as the **multiplier effect** (or **accelerator principle**).

Cummins Inc., a producer of heavy-duty diesel engines, uses sophisticated surface grinders to make parts. Suppose Cummins is using 20 surface grinders. Each machine lasts about 10 years. Purchases have been timed so that two machines will wear out and be replaced annually. If the demand for engine parts does not change, two grinders will be bought this year. If the demand for parts declines slightly, only 18 grinders may be needed, and Cummins will not replace the worn-out ones. However, suppose that next year demand returns to previous levels plus a little more. To meet the new level of demand, Cummins will need to replace the two machines that wore out in the previous year, the two that wore out in the current year, plus one or more

joint demand the demand for two or more items used together in a final product

multiplier effect (accelerator principle) phenomenon in which a small increase or decrease in consumer demand can produce a much larger change in demand for the facilities and equipment needed to make the consumer product additional machines. The multiplier effect works this way in many industries, producing highly fluctuating demand for business products.

7-6b Purchase Volume

Business customers tend to buy in large quantities. Just imagine the size of Kellogg's typical order for the wheat bran and raisins used to manufacture Raisin Bran. Or consider that in 2016, the Chicago Transit Authority (CTA) approved a $1.3 billion contract to build 846 new rail cars to replace its aging fleet—quite a bit more than the CTA's $2.25 ride fare.[20]

7-6c Number of Customers

Business marketers usually have far fewer customers than consumer marketers. The advantage is that it is a lot easier to identify prospective buyers, monitor current customers' needs and levels of satisfaction, and personally attend to existing customers. The main disadvantage is that each customer becomes crucial—especially for those manufacturers that have only one customer. In many cases, this customer is the U.S. government.

7-6d Concentration of Customers

Manufacturing operations in the United States tend to be more geographically concentrated than consumer markets. More than half of all U.S. manufacturers concentrate the majority of their operations in the following eight states: California, New York, Ohio, Illinois, Michigan, Texas, Pennsylvania, and New

In 2016, the Chicago Transit Authority approved a $1.3 billion contract to build 846 new rail cars to replace its aging fleet.

Keith Levit/Shutterstock.com

Jersey.[21] Most large metropolitan areas host large numbers of business customers.

7-6e Distribution Structure

Many consumer products pass through a distribution system that includes the producer, one or more wholesalers, and a retailer. In business marketing, however, because of many of the characteristics already mentioned, the channels of distribution are typically shorter. Direct channels, where manufacturers market directly to users, are much more common. The use of direct channels has increased dramatically in the past decade with the introduction of various Internet buying and selling schemes. One such technique is called a **business-to-business online exchange**, which is an electronic trading floor that provides companies with integrated links to their customers and suppliers. The goal of B-to-B exchanges is to simplify business purchasing and to make it more efficient. Alibaba.com is a B-to-B e-commerce portal based in China that allows companies from all over the world to purchase goods and services from Chinese suppliers. The website has begun expanding to include suppliers from countries outside China, including the United States. Alibaba.com serves buyers in more than 190 countries worldwide and has suppliers representing more than 40 major product categories. The mission of Alibaba.com is to allow suppliers to reach a global audience and to help buyers quickly find the products and services they need.[22]

7-6f Nature of Buying

Unlike consumers, business buyers usually approach purchasing rather formally. Businesses use professionally trained purchasing agents, or buyers, who spend their entire career purchasing a limited number of items. They get to know the items and the sellers well. Some professional purchasers earn the designation of Certified Purchasing Manager (CPM) after participating in a rigorous certification program.

7-6g Nature of Buying Influence

Typically, more people are involved in a single business purchase decision than in a consumer purchase. Experts from fields as varied as quality control, marketing, and finance, as well as professional buyers and users, may be grouped in a buying center (discussed later in this chapter).

business-to-business online exchange an electronic trading floor that provides companies with integrated links to their customers and suppliers

In business marketing, buyers and sellers negotiate product specifications, delivery dates, payment terms, and other pricing matters.

Pressmaster/Shutterstock.com

7-6h Type of Negotiations

Consumers are used to negotiating price on automobiles and real estate. In most cases, however, American consumers expect sellers to set the price and other conditions of sale, such as time of delivery and credit terms. In contrast, negotiating is common in business marketing. Buyers and sellers negotiate product specifications, delivery dates, payment terms, and other pricing matters. Sometimes these negotiations occur during many meetings over several months. Final contracts are often very long and detailed.

7-6i Use of Reciprocity

Business purchasers often choose to buy from their own customers, a practice known as **reciprocity**. For example, General Motors buys engines for use in its automobiles and trucks from BorgWarner, which in turn buys many of the automobiles and trucks it needs from General Motors. This practice is neither unethical nor illegal unless one party coerces the other and the result is unfair competition. Reciprocity is generally considered a reasonable business practice. If all possible suppliers sell a similar product for about the same price, does it not make sense to buy from the firms that buy from you?

reciprocity a practice whereby business purchasers choose to buy from their own customers

major equipment (installations) capital goods such as large or expensive machines, mainframe computers, blast furnaces, generators, airplanes, and buildings

accessory equipment goods, such as portable tools and office equipment, that are less expensive and shorter-lived than major equipment

7-6j Use of Leasing

Consumers normally buy products rather than lease them. But businesses commonly lease expensive equipment such as computers, construction equipment and vehicles, and automobiles. Leasing allows firms to reduce capital outflow, acquire a seller's latest products, receive better services, and gain tax advantages.

The leaser, the firm providing the product, may be either the manufacturer or an independent firm. The benefits to the leaser include greater total revenue from leasing as compared to selling and an opportunity to do business with customers who cannot afford to buy.

7-6k Primary Promotional Method

Business marketers tend to emphasize personal selling in their promotion efforts, especially for expensive items, custom-designed products, large-volume purchases, and situations requiring negotiations. The sale of many business products requires a great deal of personal contact. Personal selling is discussed in more detail in Chapter 17.

7-7 TYPES OF BUSINESS PRODUCTS

Business products generally fall into one of the following seven categories, depending on their use: major equipment, accessory equipment, raw materials, component parts, processed materials, supplies, and business services.

7-7a Major Equipment

Major equipment includes capital goods such as large or expensive machines, mainframe computers, blast furnaces, generators, airplanes, and buildings. (These items are also commonly called **installations**.) Major equipment is depreciated over time rather than charged as an expense in the year it is purchased. In addition, major equipment is often custom designed for each customer. Personal selling is an important part of the marketing strategy for major equipment because distribution channels are almost always direct from the producer to the business user.

7-7b Accessory Equipment

Accessory equipment is generally less expensive and shorter-lived than major equipment. Examples include portable drills, power tools, microcomputers, and computer software. Accessory equipment is often charged as an expense in the year it is bought rather than depreciated over its useful life. In contrast to major equipment, accessories are more often standardized and are usually bought by more customers. These customers tend to be widely dispersed. For example, all types of businesses buy microcomputers.

Local industrial distributors (wholesalers) play an important role in the marketing of accessory equipment because business buyers often purchase accessories from them. Regardless of where accessories are bought, advertising is a more vital promotional tool for accessory equipment than for major equipment.

7-7c Raw Materials

Raw materials are unprocessed extractive or agricultural products—for example, mineral ore, timber, wheat, corn, fruits, vegetables, and fish. Raw materials become part of finished products. Extensive users, such as steel or lumber mills and food canners, generally buy huge quantities of raw materials. Because there is often a large number of relatively small sellers of raw materials, none can greatly influence price or supply. Thus, the market tends to set the price of raw materials and individual producers have little pricing flexibility. Promotion is almost always via personal selling, and distribution channels are usually direct from producer to business user.

7-7d Component Parts

Component parts are either finished items ready for assembly or products that need very little processing before becoming part of some other product. Caterpillar diesel engines are component parts used in heavy-duty trucks. Other examples include spark plugs, tires, and electric motors for automobiles. A special feature of component parts is that they can retain their identity after becoming part of the final product. For example, automobile tires are clearly recognizable as part of a car. Moreover, because component parts often wear out, they may need to be replaced several times during the life of the final product. Thus, there are two important markets for many component parts: the OEM market and the replacement market.

The availability of component parts is often a key factor in the ability of OEMs to meet their production deadlines. In 2017, BMW had to stop production of several models, including the 3-series, in Germany, China, and South Africa owing to a shortage of steering gears from their supplier, Bosch. BMW practices "just-in-time" production, so they order parts only when they need them, and Bosch is their only source of steering components. Therefore, the shortage by Bosch caused a major delay in production for and shipments from BMW.[23]

The replacement market is composed of organizations and individuals buying component parts to replace worn-out parts. Because components often retain their identity in final products, users may choose to replace a component part with the same brand used by the manufacturer—for example, the same brand of automobile tires or battery. The replacement market operates differently from the OEM market, however. Whether replacement buyers are organizations or individuals, they tend to demonstrate the characteristics of consumer markets that were discussed in the previous section. Consider, for example, a replacement part for a piece of construction equipment such as a bulldozer or a crane. When a piece of equipment breaks down, it is usually important to acquire a replacement part and have it installed as soon as possible. Purchasers typically buy from local or regional dealers. Negotiations do not occur, and neither reciprocity nor leasing is usually an issue.

7-7e Processed Materials

Processed materials are products used directly in manufacturing other products. Unlike raw materials, they have had some processing. Examples include sheet metal, chemicals, specialty steel, treated lumber, corn syrup, and plastics. Unlike component parts, processed materials do not retain their identity in final products.

Timber, harvested from forests, is a raw material. Fluff pulp, a soft, white absorbent material, is produced from loblolly pine timber by mills such as International Paper Co. The fluff pulp becomes part of a number of different products, including product packaging, paper, disposable diapers, and bandages, among other things.[24]

Most processed materials are marketed to OEMs or to distributors servicing the OEM market. Processed materials are generally bought according to customer specifications or to some industry standard, as is the case with steel and plywood. Price and service are important factors in choosing a vendor.

7-7f Supplies

Supplies are consumable items that do not become part of the final product—for example, lubricants, detergents, paper towels, pencils, and paper. Supplies are normally

raw materials unprocessed extractive or agricultural products, such as mineral ore, lumber, wheat, corn, fruits, vegetables, and fish

component parts either finished items ready for assembly or products that need very little processing before becoming part of some other product

processed materials products used directly in manufacturing other products

supplies consumable items that do not become part of the final product standardized items that purchasing agents routinely buy. Supplies typically have relatively short lives and are inexpensive compared to other business goods. Because supplies generally fall into one of three categories—maintenance, repair, or operating—this category is often referred to as MRO items. Competition in the MRO market is intense. Bic and Paper Mate, for example, battle for business purchases of inexpensive ballpoint pens.

7-7g Business Services

Business services are expense items that do not become part of a final product. Businesses often retain outside providers to perform janitorial, advertising, legal, management consulting, marketing research, maintenance, and other services. Contracting an outside provider makes sense when it costs less than hiring or assigning an employee to perform the task, when an outside provider is needed for particular expertise, or when the need is infrequent.

7-8 BUSINESS BUYING BEHAVIOR

As you probably have already concluded, business buyers behave differently from consumers. Understanding how purchase decisions are made in organizations is a first step in developing a business selling strategy. Business buying behavior has five important aspects: buying centers, evaluative criteria, buying situations, business ethics, and customer service.

7-8a Buying Centers

In many cases, more than one person is involved in a purchase decision. A salesperson must determine the buying situation and the information required from the buying organization's perspective to anticipate the size and composition of the buying center.[25]

A **buying center** includes all the people in an organization who become involved in the purchase decision. Membership and influence vary from company to company. For instance, in engineering-dominated firms like Bell Helicopter, the buying center may consist almost entirely of engineers. In marketing-oriented firms like Toyota and IBM, marketing and engineering have almost equal authority. In consumer goods firms like Clorox Corporation, product managers and other marketing decision makers

business services expense items that do not become part of a final product

buying center all the people in an organization who become involved in the purchase decision

may dominate the buying center. In a small manufacturing company, almost everyone may be a member.

The number of people involved in a buying center varies with the complexity and importance of a purchase decision. The average buying center includes more than one person and up to four per purchase.[26] The composition of the buying group will usually change from one purchase to another and sometimes even during various stages of one buying process. To make matters more complicated, buying centers do not appear on formal organization charts.

For example, even though a formal committee may have been set up to choose a new plant site, that committee is only part of the buying center. Other people, like the company president, often play informal yet powerful roles. In a lengthy decision-making process, such as finding a new plant location, some members may drop out of the buying center when they can no longer play a useful role. Others whose talents are needed then become part of the center. No formal announcement of "who is in" and "who is out" is ever made.

ROLES IN THE BUYING CENTER As in family purchasing decisions, several people may each play a role in the business purchase process:

- The *initiator* is the person who first suggests making a purchase.

- *Influencers/evaluators* are people who influence the buying decision. They often help define specifications and provide information for evaluating options. Technical personnel are especially important as influencers.

- *Gatekeepers* are group members who regulate the flow of information. Frequently, the purchasing agent views the gatekeeping role as a source of his or her power. An assistant may also act as a gatekeeper by determining which vendors get an appointment with a buyer.

- The *decider* is the person who has the formal or informal power to choose or approve the selection of the supplier or brand. In complex situations, it is often difficult to determine who makes the final decision.

- The *purchaser* is the person who actually negotiates the purchase. It could be anyone from the president of the company to the purchasing agent, depending on the importance of the decision.

- *Users* are members of the organization who will actually use the product. Users often initiate the buying process and help define product specifications.

IMPLICATIONS OF BUYING CENTERS FOR THE MARKETING MANAGER Successful vendors realize the importance of identifying who is in the decision-making unit, each member's relative influence in the buying decision, and each member's evaluative criteria. Key influencers are frequently located outside the purchasing department. Successful selling strategies often focus on determining the most important buying influences and tailoring sales presentations to the evaluative criteria most important to these buying center members. An example illustrating the basic buying center roles is shown in Exhibit 7.2.

Marketers are often frustrated by their inability to reach c-level (chief) executives who, in today's economy, play an important role in many buying decisions. Marketers who want to build executive-level contacts must become involved in the buying process early on because this is when most executives get involved.[27] Senior executives are typically not involved in the middle phases of the buying process but often get involved again later in the process to monitor the deal's closing. Executives look for four characteristics in sales representatives:

- The ability to marshal resources
- An understanding of the buyer's business goals
- Responsiveness to requests
- Willingness to be held accountable

Some firms have developed strategies to reach executives throughout the buying process and during nonbuying phases of the relationship. For example, FedEx Corp. has initiated a marketing effort called "access" aimed at c-level executives. It includes direct mail, email, and a custom magazine prepared exclusively for c-level executives.

It also hosts exclusive leadership events for these senior executives. Other firms have developed programs utilizing a combination of print and online products and events to reach the elusive c-level audience.[28]

7-8b Evaluative Criteria

Business buyers evaluate products and suppliers using three important criteria: quality, service, and price.

QUALITY In this case, *quality* refers to technical suitability. A superior tool can do a better job in the production process and superior packaging can increase dealer and consumer acceptance of a brand. Evaluation of quality also applies to the salesperson and the salesperson's firm. Business buyers want to deal with reputable salespeople and companies that are financially responsible. Quality improvement should be part of every organization's marketing strategy.

SERVICE Almost as much as they want satisfactory products, business buyers want satisfactory service. A purchase offers several opportunities for service. Suppose a vendor is selling heavy equipment. Prepurchase service could include a survey of the buyer's needs. After thorough analysis of the survey findings, the vendor could prepare a report and recommendations in the form of a purchasing proposal. If a purchase results, postpurchase service might consist of installing the equipment and training those who will be using it. Postsale services may also include maintenance and repairs.

Another service that business buyers seek is dependability of supply. They must be able to count on delivery of what was ordered when it is scheduled to be delivered. Buyers also welcome services that help them

EXHIBIT 7.2	BUYING CENTER ROLES FOR COMPUTER PURCHASES
Role	**Illustration**
Initiator	Division general manager proposes replacing the company's computer network.
Influencers/ evaluators	Corporate controller's office and vice president of information services have an important say in which system and vendor the company will deal with.
Gatekeepers	Corporate departments for purchasing and information services analyze the company's needs and recommend likely matches with potential vendors.
Decider	Vice president of administration, with advice from others, selects the vendor the company will deal with and the system it will buy.
Purchaser	Purchasing agent negotiates the terms of sale.
Users	All division employees use the computers.

In today's economy, c-level executives play an important role in many buying decisions.

sell their finished products. Services of this sort are especially appropriate when the seller's product is an identifiable part of the buyer's end product.

PRICE Business buyers want to buy at low prices—at the lowest prices, under most circumstances. However, a buyer who pressures a supplier to cut prices to a point at which the supplier loses money on the sale almost forces shortcuts on quality. The buyer also may, in effect, force the supplier to quit selling to him or her. Then a new source of supply will have to be found.

7-8c Buying Situations

Often, business firms, especially manufacturers, must decide whether to make something or buy it from an outside supplier. The decision is essentially one of economics. Can an item of similar quality be bought at a lower price elsewhere? If not, is manufacturing it in-house the best use of limited company resources? For example, Briggs & Stratton Corporation, a major manufacturer of four-cycle engines, might be able to save $150,000 annually on outside purchases by spending $500,000 on the equipment needed to produce gas throttles internally. Yet Briggs & Stratton could also use that $500,000 to upgrade its carburetor assembly line, which would save $225,000 annually. If a firm does decide to buy a product instead of making it, the purchase will be a new buy, a modified rebuy, or a straight rebuy.

NEW BUY A **new buy** is a situation requiring the purchase of a product for the first time. For example, suppose a manufacturing company needs a better way to page its managers while they are working on the shop floor. Currently, each of the several managers has a distinct ring—for example, two short and one long—that sounds over the plant intercom whenever he or she is being paged by anyone in the factory. The company decides to replace its buzzer system of paging with handheld wireless radio technology that will allow managers to communicate immediately with the department initiating the page. This situation represents the greatest opportunity for new vendors. No long-term relationship has been established for this product, specifications may be somewhat fluid, and buyers are generally more open to new vendors.

new buy a situation requiring the purchase of a product for the first time

modified rebuy a situation in which the purchaser wants some change in the original good or service

straight rebuy a situation in which the purchaser reorders the same goods or services without looking for new information or investigating other suppliers

If the new item is a raw material or a critical component part, the buyer cannot afford to run out of it. The seller must be able to convince the buyer that the seller's firm can consistently deliver a high-quality product on time.

MODIFIED REBUY A **modified rebuy** is normally less critical and less time consuming than a new buy. In a modified rebuy situation, the purchaser wants some change in the original good or service. It may be a new color, greater tensile strength in a component part, more respondents in a marketing research study, or additional services in a janitorial contract.

Because the two parties are familiar with each other and credibility has been established, the buyer and seller can concentrate on the specifics of the modification. But in some cases, modified rebuys are open to outside bidders. The purchaser uses this strategy to ensure that the new terms are competitive. An example would be the manufacturing company buying radios with a vibrating feature for managers who have trouble hearing the ring over the factory noise. The firm may open the bidding to examine the price, quality, and service offerings of several suppliers.

STRAIGHT REBUY A **straight rebuy** is a situation vendors prefer. The purchaser is not looking for new information or other suppliers. An order is placed and the product is provided as in previous orders. Usually, a straight rebuy is routine because the terms of the purchase have been agreed to in earlier negotiations. An example would be the previously cited manufacturing company purchasing additional radios for new managers from the same supplier on a regular basis.

One common instrument used in straight rebuy situations is the purchasing contract. Purchasing contracts are used with products that are bought often and in high volume. In essence, the purchasing contract makes the buyer's decision making routine and promises the salesperson a sure sale. The advantage to the buyer is a quick, confident decision; the advantage to the salesperson is reduced or eliminated competition. Nevertheless, suppliers must remember not to take straight rebuy relationships for granted. Retaining existing customers is much easier than attracting new ones.

7-8d Business Ethics

As we noted in Chapter 3, *ethics* refers to the moral principles or values that generally govern the conduct of an individual or a group. Ethics can also be viewed as the standard of behavior by which conduct is judged.

Although we have heard a lot about corporate misbehavior in recent years, most people, and most companies, follow ethical practices. To help achieve this, over half of all major corporations offer ethics training to employees. Many companies also have codes of ethics that help guide buyers and sellers. For example, Home Depot has a clearly written code of ethics available on its corporate website that acts as an ethical guide for all its employees.

7-8e Customer Service

Business marketers are increasingly recognizing the benefits of developing a formal system to monitor customer opinions and perceptions of the quality of customer service. Companies such as FedEx, IBM, and Oracle build their strategies not only around products but also around highly developed service skills.[29] These companies understand that keeping current customers satisfied is just as important as attracting new ones, if not more so. Leading-edge firms are obsessed not only with delivering high-quality customer service but also with measuring satisfaction, loyalty, relationship quality, and other indicators of nonfinancial performance. Delivering consistent, high-quality customer service is an important basis for establishing competitive advantage and differentiating one's company from competitors. Cisco Systems uses a web-based survey to determine the presale and postsale satisfaction of customers.[30]

Most firms find it necessary to develop measures unique to their own strategies, value propositions, and target markets. For example, Andersen Windows and Doors assesses the loyalty of its trade customers by their willingness to continue carrying its windows and doors, recommend its products to colleagues and customers, increase their volume with the company, and put its products in their own homes. Basically, each firm's measures should not only ask "What are your expectations?" and "How are we doing?" but should also reflect what the firm wants its customers to do.

Some customers are more valuable than others. They may have greater value because they spend more, buy

Keeping current customers satisfied is just as important as attracting new ones—if not more so. Delivering consistent, high-quality customer service is an important basis for differentiating one's company from competitors.

higher-margin products, have a well-known name, or have the potential of becoming a bigger customer in the future. Some companies selectively provide different levels of service to customers based on their value to the business. By giving the most valuable customers superior service, a firm is more likely to keep them happy, hopefully increasing retention of these high-value customers and maximizing the total business value they generate over time.

To achieve this goal, the firm must be able to divide customers into two or more groups based on their value. It must also create and apply policies that govern how service will be allocated among groups. Policies might establish which customers' phone calls get "fast tracked" and which customers are directed to use the Web and/or voice self-service, how specific email questions are routed, and who is given access to online chat and who is not.

Providing different customers with different levels of service is a very sensitive matter. It must be handled very carefully and very discreetly to avoid offending lesser-value, but still important, customers.

8 | Segmenting and Targeting Markets

Daniel M Ernst/Shutterstock.com

LEARNING OUTCOMES

After studying this chapter, you will be able to . . .

8-1 Describe the characteristics of markets and market segments

8-2 Explain the importance of market segmentation

8-3 Discuss the criteria for successful market segmentation

8-4 Describe the bases commonly used to segment consumer markets

8-5 Describe the bases for segmenting business markets

8-6 List the steps involved in segmenting markets

8-7 Discuss alternative strategies for selecting target markets

8-8 Explain how CRM can be used as a targeting tool

8-9 Explain how and why firms implement positioning strategies and how product differentiation plays a role

8-1 MARKETS AND MARKET SEGMENTS

The term *market* means different things to different people. We are all familiar with the supermarket, stock market, labor market, fish market, and flea market. All these types of markets share several characteristics. First, they are composed of people (consumer markets) or organizations (business markets). Second, these people or organizations have wants and needs that can be satisfied by particular product categories. Third, they have the ability to buy the products they seek. Fourth, they are willing to exchange their resources, usually money or credit, for desired products. In sum, a **market** is (1) people or organizations with (2) needs or wants and with (3) the ability and (4) the willingness to buy. A group of people or an organization that lacks any one of these characteristics is not a market.

Within a market, a **market segment** is a subgroup of people or organizations sharing one or more characteristics that cause them to have similar product needs. At one extreme, we can define every person and every organization in the world as a market segment because each is unique. At the other extreme, we can define the entire consumer market as one large market segment and the business market as another large segment. All people have some similar characteristics and needs, as do all organizations.

From a marketing perspective, market segments can be described as somewhere between the two extremes. The process of dividing a market into meaningful, relatively similar, and identifiable segments, or groups, is called **market segmentation**. The purpose of market segmentation is to enable the marketer to tailor marketing mixes to meet the needs of one or more specific segments.

8-2 THE IMPORTANCE OF MARKET SEGMENTATION

Until the 1960s, few firms practiced market segmentation. When they did, it was more likely a haphazard effort than a formal marketing strategy. Before 1960, for example, the Coca-Cola Company produced only one beverage and aimed it at the entire soft drink market. Today, Coca-Cola offers dozens of different products to market segments based on diverse consumer preferences for flavors, calories, and caffeine content. Coca-Cola offers traditional soft drinks, energy drinks (including POWERade), flavored teas, fruit drinks (Minute Maid), and water (Dasani).

Market segmentation plays a key role in the marketing strategy of almost all successful organizations and is a powerful marketing tool. Most markets include groups of people or organizations with different product needs and preferences. Market segmentation helps marketers define customer needs and wants more precisely. It leads to a deeper understanding of customer lifestyles, values, jobs to be done, need states, and buying occasions. The increase of the use of real-time big data has provided new ways of reaching that understanding. Research has shown that companies that are the best at putting customer needs at the center of everything they do are more able to identify and execute marketing strategies that drive growth.[1]

Because market segments differ in size and potential, segmentation helps decision makers to more accurately define marketing objectives and better allocate resources. In turn, performance can be better evaluated when objectives are more precise. For example, the successful Swedish furniture company Ikea has stores around the world. For each geographic area, Ikea adjusts the inventory, design, and even food to align with local tastes. In India, because of the way families have impromptu gatherings, the company offers a greater number of stools and folding chairs. Chinese showrooms include a section on balconies, because they are common in Chinese homes. In southern China, the balcony displays show them being used to dry clothes, while in the north, the balconies are shown as another place for food

market people or organizations with needs or wants and the ability and willingness to buy

market segment a subgroup of people or organizations sharing one or more characteristics that cause them to have similar product needs

market segmentation the process of dividing a market into meaningful, relatively similar, and identifiable segments or groups storage—each according to the customs of the area. And in Korea, they sell tiny beds that are designed for the small bedrooms Koreans use.[2]

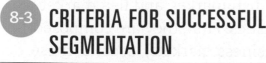

8-3 CRITERIA FOR SUCCESSFUL SEGMENTATION

Marketers segment markets for three important reasons. First, segmentation enables marketers to identify groups of customers with similar needs and to analyze the characteristics and buying behavior of these groups. Second, segmentation provides marketers with information to help them design marketing mixes specifically matched with the characteristics and desires of one or more segments. Third, segmentation is consistent with the marketing concept of satisfying customer wants and needs while meeting the organization's objectives.

To be useful, a segmentation scheme must produce segments that meet four basic criteria:

1. **Substantiality:** A segment must be large enough to warrant developing and maintaining a special marketing mix. This criterion does not necessarily mean that a segment must have many potential customers. For example, marketers of custom-designed homes and business buildings, commercial airplanes, and large computer systems typically develop marketing programs tailored to each potential customer's needs. In most cases, however, a market segment needs many potential customers to make commercial sense. In the 1980s, home banking failed because not enough people owned personal computers. Today, a larger number of people own computers, and home banking is a thriving industry.

2. **Identifiability and measurability:** Segments must be identifiable and their size measurable. Data about the population within geographic boundaries, the number of people in various age categories, and other social and demographic characteristics are often easy to get, and they provide fairly concrete measures of segment size. Suppose that a social service agency wants to identify segments by their readiness to participate in a drug and alcohol program or in prenatal care. Unless the agency can measure how many people are willing, indifferent, or unwilling to participate, it will have trouble gauging whether there are enough people to justify setting up the service.

3. **Accessibility:** The firm must be able to reach members of targeted segments with customized marketing mixes. Some market segments are hard to reach—for example, senior citizens (especially those with reading or hearing disabilities), individuals who do not speak English, and the illiterate.

4. **Responsiveness:** Markets can be segmented using any criteria that seem logical. Unless one market segment responds to a marketing mix differently than other segments, however, that segment need not be treated separately. For instance, if all customers are equally price conscious about a product, there is no need to offer high-, medium-, and low-priced versions to different segments.

8-4 BASES FOR SEGMENTING CONSUMER MARKETS

Marketers use segmentation bases, or variables, which are characteristics of individuals, groups, or organizations, to divide a total market into segments. The choice of segmentation bases is crucial, because an inappropriate segmentation strategy may lead to lost sales and missed profit opportunities. The key is to identify bases that will produce substantial, measurable, and accessible segments that exhibit different response patterns to marketing mixes.

Markets can be segmented using a single variable, such as age group, or several variables, such as age group, gender, and education. Although it is less precise, single-variable segmentation has the advantage of being simpler and easier to use than multiple-variable segmentation. The disadvantages of multiple-variable segmentation are that it is often harder to use than single-variable segmentation, usable secondary data are less likely to be available, and as the number of segmentation bases increases, the size of individual segments decreases. Nevertheless, the current trend is toward using more rather than fewer variables to segment most markets, because multiple-variable segmentation is clearly more precise than single-variable segmentation.

Consumer goods marketers commonly use one or more of the following characteristics to segment markets: geography, demographics, psychographics, benefits sought, and usage rate.

8-4a Geographic Segmentation

Geographic segmentation refers to segmenting markets by region of a country or the world, market size,

segmentation bases (variables) characteristics of individuals, groups, or organizations

geographic segmentation segmenting markets by region of a country or the world, market size, market density, or climate market density, or climate. Market density means the number of people within a unit of land, such as a census tract. Climate is commonly used for geographic segmentation because of its dramatic impact on residents' needs and purchasing behavior. Snowblowers, water and snow skis, clothing, and air-conditioning and heating systems are products with varying appeal, depending on climate.

Consumer goods companies take a geographic approach to marketing for several reasons. First, firms continually need to find ways to grow. Target's growth strategy includes opening smaller stores in urban locations such as San Francisco; Chicago; Washington, DC; and New York City. These stores are designed to provide quick-trip shopping, customized product assortments, and services tailored to customers living in large cities.[3]

8-4b Demographic Segmentation

Marketers often segment markets on the basis of demographic information because it is widely available and often related to consumers' buying and consuming behavior. Some common bases of **demographic segmentation** are age, gender, income, ethnic background, and family life cycle.

AGE SEGMENTATION Marketers use a variety of terms to refer to different age groups. Examples include newborns, infants, young children, tweens, Millennials, Generation X, Baby Boomers, and seniors. Age segmentation can be an important tool, as a brief exploration of the market potential of several age segments illustrates.

Many companies have long targeted parents of babies and young children with products such as disposable diapers, baby food, and toys. Now, other companies that have not traditionally marketed to young children are developing products and services to attract this group. For example, Amazon has created a new service for kids, with the goal of nurturing young readers, called "Amazon Prime Book Box." The company chooses children's books for a monthly subscription that delivers a box of books based on the child's age.[4]

Generation Z, whose members were born from 1997 to 2012, has access to $44 billion in buying power. Gen Zers want to work for their success, believe that brands need to be real, and have their own rules and etiquette for social media.[5] To attract Generation Z, Target has worked with 10 trendsetters among this age group to design an apparel and accessories collection called "Art Class."[6] In the fashion world, stylish preteens have become famous on social media and are called "mini-influencers." Social media makes it easy for this group to see a staggering amount of products and choose exactly

Prime Book Box uses age segmentation to target customers for its subscription program.

what they want to wear, even if their parents are still paying for it.[7]

The Millennial cohort, those born between 1981 and 1996, is comprised of 75.4 million people—more than any other generation.[8] This group is idealistic and pragmatic and is the most technology-proficient generation ever, so social media is an important part of any brand's marketing strategy. The top brand attributes important to Millennials include trustworthiness, creativity, intelligence, authenticity, and confidence.[9] This group loves experiences. Upscale retailer Barneys New York partnered with blog Highsnobbery to host a weekend-long event aimed at Millennials that featured exclusive, limited-edition merchandise and appearances by designers of streetwear. Shoppers could get custom sneakers, tattoos, and piercings. In its first day, the event led to a 25 percent sales increase, with 20 percent of the customers new to Barney's.[10] Millennials love private brands. A typical shopping cart contains 25 percent private label products, while Millennials' baskets contain 32 percent private brands. They shop at stores like Aldi and deep discounters, and they shop online more than other age group.[11]

Generation X, those born between 1965 and 1980, is a smaller group than both the Millennial and the Baby Boomer groups; it makes up only 16 percent of the total population. Members of Generation X are at a life stage where they are often stuck between supporting their aging parents and young children (earning Gen X the nickname "the sandwich generation"). They grew up as *latchkey kids*, meaning that they spent time alone at home while their (often divorced) parents worked long into the night. They are the best-educated generation—29 percent have earned a bachelor's degree or better. They tend to be disloyal to

demographic segmentation
segmenting markets by age, gender, income, ethnic background, and family life cycle

brands and skeptical of big business. Many of them are parents, and they make purchasing decisions with thought for and input from their families.[12] Gen Xers are at their peak earning power, but they don't feel the need to show off their wealth. Instead, they look for products that give them value for the money and good performance. Ford has been successful in targeting this group with its Explorer Sport—nearly 40 percent of the brand's buyers are in Generation X.[13]

Recall from Chapter 4 that people born between 1946 and 1964 are often called Baby Boomers. Boomers make up 24.7 percent of the total population and constitute almost one-third of the adult population. They outspend the average consumer in nearly every product category, including food, household furnishings, entertainment, and personal care.[14] They are living longer, healthier, and more active and connected lives, and they will spend time and money doing whatever is necessary to maintain vitality as they age.[15] This group buys about two-thirds of the cars sold annually, half the computers, and a third of movie theater tickets. Consumer Cellular sells low-priced wireless phones and phone plans that do not require contracts to more than 2 million customers over the age of 50. The company's call center staff receives AARP training to learn how to respond to its older customer base.[16]

Consumers who were born before 1946 are often called the silent generation because of their ability to quietly persevere through great hardships. The smallest generation of the past 100 years, members of this group were taught to play by the rules. They tend to be cautious and are hardworking and disciplined and place significant value on economic resources.[17] As consumers age, they do require some modifications in the way they live and the products they purchase. According to gerontologist Stephen Golant, for example, aging individuals may need to install "well-placed handrails or grab bars, ramps, easy-access bathrooms, easy-access kitchens, stair lifts, widened doors or hallways, and modified sink faucets or cabinets" in their homes.[18]

GENDER SEGMENTATION In the United States, women drive 70 to 80 percent of purchases of consumer goods each year.[19] They are an experienced purchasing group with the responsibility of purchasing the majority of household items. Women have traditionally bought more grocery, personal care, apparel, and cosmetic items than have men. However, a wide variety of companies are beginning to target these typically female products to men. Southern food chain, Lowe's Foods, introduced gourmet sausage stations and "beer dens," where customers can drink while they shop or get a half-gallon jug of craft beer to take home. After they were launched, store management reported that there was an increase in the number of men shopping in the stores.[20] English soccer star David Beckham has launched a grooming brand for men that includes face creams, beard oil, and hair pomades.[21]

On the other hand, companies that traditionally have targeted men are now targeting women. In the past, television sports network ESPN has generally tried to reach male viewers. It is now selling the opportunity to advertise to its female audiences. Financial services company Northwestern Mutual is among advertisers using college football to reach women and families.[22] Harry's—the men's innovative direct-to-consumer shaving company—created Flamingo, which is the same service for women.[23]

INCOME SEGMENTATION Income is a popular demographic variable for segmenting markets because income level influences consumers' wants and determines their buying power. Many markets are segmented by income, including those for housing, clothing, automobiles, and food. Some companies have found success in marketing to the very poor. For example, Clorox makes a wide variety of its popular products available in smaller sizes so they will be more affordable for low-income consumers. These products can be purchased at retailers such as Walmart.[24] In the United States, dollar stores such as Family Dollar Stores and Dollar General have seen rapid growth in recent years. These stores serve not only Americans living below the poverty line, but also higher-income customers and Millennials looking for deals by offering basic groceries and other necessities at deeply discounted prices.[25] Wholesale clubs Costco and Sam's Club also appeal to many income segments. High-income customers looking for luxury want products that

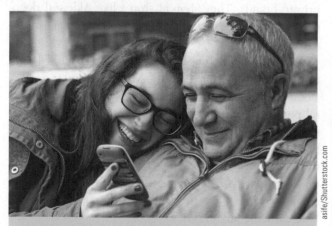

Once known for their grunge music, ratty clothing, and cynical outlook, Gen Xers are now at the peak of their earning power, with teenage children of their own.

Neutrogena creative consultant Kerry Washington discusses new product ideas with General Manager Michelle Freyre and Senior Director of Research & Development Anna Prilutsky (from left).

exhibit careful craftsmanship, timeless design, prestige, and exclusivity. Luxury brands such as Chanel and Louis Vuitton do not focus on mass popularity, but instead try to set long-lasting standards of good taste.[26]

ETHNIC SEGMENTATION In the past, ethnic groups in the United States were expected to conform to a homogenized, Anglo-centric ideal. This was evident in how mass-produced products were marketed as well as in the selective way that films, television, advertisements, and popular music portrayed America's diverse population. Until the 1970s, ethnic foods were rarely sold except in specialty stores. Increasing numbers of ethnic minorities and increased buying power have changed this. Hispanic Americans, African Americans, and Asian Americans are the three largest ethnic groups in the United States. In the American Southwest, Caucasian populations comprise less than half the population and have become the minority to combined population of other ethnic groups. To meet the needs and wants of expanding ethnic populations, some companies, such as McDonald's and Kmart, make products geared toward specific ethnic groups. In an effort to reach the Hispanic population (a group that is beginning to adopt, and in turn, influence national consumption patterns), Stouffer's recently launched a campaign that includes a Spanish-language ad. This ad features a multiethnic working family who value time spent together.[27]

Similarly, a number of companies have begun devoting more resources to developing beauty products for African American women. For example, L'Oreal's Women of Color Lab specializes in products for women with dark skin tones. Neutrogena has been working with Kerry Washington, a popular African American actress, to help expand its range of foundation shades. Head & Shoulders recently introduced hair care products for textured hair.[28]

FAMILY LIFE-CYCLE SEGMENTATION The demographic factors of gender, age, and income often do not sufficiently explain why consumer buying behavior varies. Frequently, consumption patterns among people of the same age and gender differ because they are in different stages of the family life cycle. The **family life cycle (FLC)** is a series of stages determined by a combination of age, marital status, and the presence or absence of children.

The life-cycle stage consisting of the married-couple household used to be considered the traditional family in the United States. Today, however, married couples make up just 48 percent of households, down from 72 percent in the 1960s.[29] Single adults are increasingly in the majority on many fronts. Already, unmarried Americans make up 48 percent of the workforce and 30 percent of home buyers and is one of the most potent consumer groups on record.[30] Exhibit 8.1 illustrates numerous FLC patterns and shows how families' needs, incomes, resources, and expenditures differ at each stage. The horizontal flow shows the traditional FLC. The lower part of the exhibit gives some of the characteristics and purchase patterns of families in each stage of the traditional life cycle. The exhibit also acknowledges that about half of all first marriages end in divorce. If young married couples move into the young divorced stage, their consumption patterns often revert to those of the young single stage of the cycle.

About four out of five divorced persons remarry by middle age and reenter the traditional life cycle, as indicated by the "recycled flow" in the exhibit. Consumers are especially receptive to marketing efforts at certain points in the life cycle. For example, Baby Boomers have increased needs for health care services, while families with babies need diapers, toys, and baby clothes.

During the COVID-19 pandemic, a number of retailers selling necessities, such as grocery stores and pharmacies, set aside specific hours during the day for older consumers (those most at-risk for the virus) to shop.

8-4c Psychographic Segmentation

Age, gender, income, ethnicity, FLC stage, and other demographic variables are usually helpful in developing segmentation strategies, but often, they

> **family life cycle (FLC)** a series of stages determined by a combination of age, marital status, and the presence or absence of children

EXHIBIT 8.1   FAMILY LIFE CYCLE

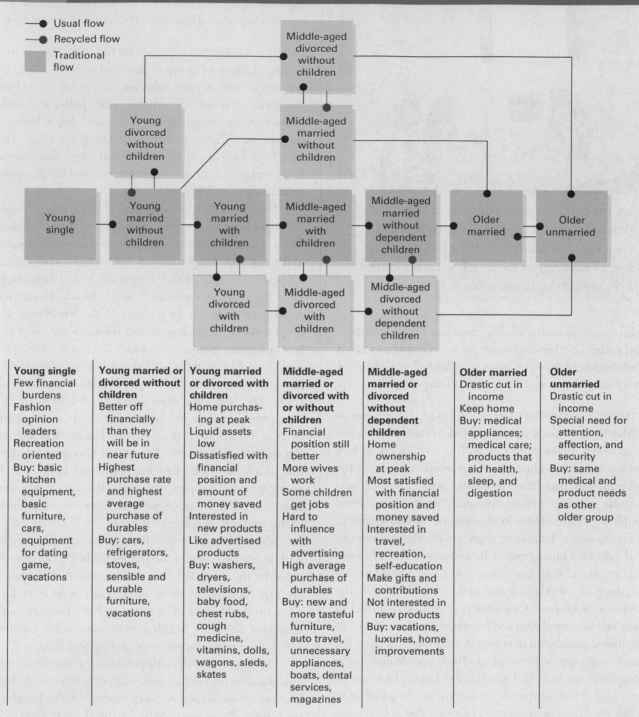

● Usual flow
● Recycled flow
▨ Traditional flow

Middle-aged divorced without children

Young divorced without children

Middle-aged married without children

Young single

Young married without children

Young married with children

Middle-aged married with children

Middle-aged married without dependent children

Older married

Older unmarried

Young divorced with children

Middle-aged divorced with children

Middle-aged divorced without dependent children

Young single	**Young married or divorced without children**	**Young married or divorced with children**	**Middle-aged married or divorced with or without children**	**Middle-aged married or divorced without dependent children**	**Older married**	**Older unmarried**
Few financial burdens	Better off financially than they will be in near future	Home purchasing at peak	Financial position still better	Home ownership at peak	Drastic cut in income	Drastic cut in income
Fashion opinion leaders	Highest purchase rate and highest average purchase of durables	Liquid assets low	More wives work	Most satisfied with financial position and money saved	Keep home	Special need for attention, affection, and security
Recreation oriented	Buy: cars, refrigerators, stoves, sensible and durable furniture, vacations	Dissatisfied with financial position and amount of money saved	Some children get jobs	Interested in travel, recreation, self-education	Buy: medical appliances; medical care; products that aid health, sleep, and digestion	Buy: same medical and product needs as other older group
Buy: basic kitchen equipment, basic furniture, cars, equipment for dating game, vacations		Interested in new products	Hard to influence with advertising	Make gifts and contributions		
		Like advertised products	High average purchase of durables	Not interested in new products		
		Buy: washers, dryers, televisions, baby food, chest rubs, cough medicine, vitamins, dolls, wagons, sleds, skates	Buy: new and more tasteful furniture, auto travel, unnecessary appliances, boats, dental services, magazines	Buy: vacations, luxuries, home improvements		

do not paint the entire picture. Demographics provide the skeleton, but psychographics add meat to the bones. **Psychographic segmentation** is market segmentation on the basis of the following psychographic segmentation variables:

- **Personality:** Personality reflects a person's traits, attitudes, and habits. Clothing is the ultimate

personality descriptor. Fashionistas wear high-end, trendy clothes, and hipsters enjoy jeans and T-shirts with tennis shoes. People buy clothes that they feel represent their personalities and give others an idea of who they are.

- **Motives:** Marketers of baby products and life insurance appeal to consumers' emotional motives—namely, to care for their loved ones. Using appeals to economy, reliability, and dependability, carmakers like Subaru and Suzuki target customers with rational motives. Carmakers like Mercedes-Benz, Jaguar, and Cadillac appeal to customers with status-related motives.

- **Lifestyles:** Lifestyle segmentation divides people into groups according to the way they spend their time, the importance of the things around them, their beliefs, and socioeconomic characteristics such as income and education. For example, record stores specializing in vinyl are targeting young people who are listening to independent labels and often pride themselves on being independent of big business. LEED-certified appliances appeal to environmentally conscious "green" consumers. PepsiCo is promoting its no-calorie, sugar-free, flavored water, Aquafina FlavorSplash, to consumers who are health conscious.

- **Geodemographics:** Geodemographic segmentation clusters potential customers into neighborhood lifestyle categories. It combines geographic, demographic, and lifestyle segmentations. Geodemographic segmentation helps marketers develop marketing programs tailored to prospective buyers who live in small geographic regions, such as neighborhoods, or who have very specific lifestyle and demographic characteristics. College students, for example, often share similar demographics and lifestyles and tend to cluster around campus. Knowing this, marketing teams for start-ups and tech companies often launch ambassador programs at insular college campuses. For example, Pura Vida is a company that provides jobs to struggling local artisans in Costa Rica and donates a percentage of its profits to international environmental organizations. Pure Vida uses college brand ambassadors, or reps, to share the company's mission and products. These ambassadors then receive a commission on every purchase.[31]

Psychographic variables can be used individually to segment markets or can be combined with other variables to provide more detailed descriptions of market segments. Based on data from more than 14,000 people in 22 countries, DuPont Nutrition & Health has identified six core consumer segments in the health and wellness area. The segments are based on demographics, geographics, health concerns, brand influences, attitudes, lifestyle choices, and parenting styles. The six groups are Health Helpers, Weight Strugglers, Health Wise, Taste Driven, Good Life, and Just Food. Insights about these segments will help food and beverage manufacturers to understand the motivations, needs, and behaviors of each group and more clearly define market opportunities.[32]

8-4d Benefit Segmentation

Benefit segmentation is the process of grouping customers into market segments according to the benefits they seek from the product. Most types of market segmentation are based on the assumption that this variable and customers' needs are related. Benefit segmentation is different because it groups potential customers on the basis of their needs or wants rather than on some other characteristic, such as age or gender. The snack-food market, for example, can be divided into six benefit segments: nutritional snackers, weight watchers, guilty snackers, party snackers, indiscriminate snackers, and economical snackers.

Customer profiles can be developed by examining demographic information associated with people seeking certain benefits. This information can be used to match marketing strategies with selected markets. A Tesco grocery store in Scotland is testing what it calls a "relaxed checkout line." It is slower paced than normal lines and is staffed by employees trained by an Alzheimer's group. This checkout line has benefits for anyone who feels they need extra time, such as those with dementia, or perhaps parents with several small children.[33]

8-4e Usage-Rate Segmentation

Usage-rate segmentation divides a market by the amount of product bought or consumed. Categories vary with the product, but they are likely to include some combination of the following: former users, potential users, first-time users, light or irregular users, medium users, and heavy users. Segmenting by usage rate enables marketers to focus their efforts on heavy users or to develop multiple marketing mixes aimed at different segments. Because heavy users often account for a sizable portion of all product sales, some marketers focus on the heavy-user segment.

The **80/20 principle** holds that 20 percent of all customers generate

psychographic segmentation segmenting markets on the basis of personality, motives, lifestyles, and geodemographics

geodemographic segmentation segmenting potential customers into neighborhood lifestyle categories

benefit segmentation the process of grouping customers into market segments according to the benefits they seek from the product

usage-rate segmentation dividing a market by the amount of product bought or consumed

80/20 principle a principle holding that 20 percent of all customers generate 80 percent of the demand

80 percent of the demand. Although the percentages usually are not exact, the general idea often holds true. Research has determined that heavy spenders at department stores are highly likely to own a television with Internet connectivity and to watch streaming video. They are also likely to own a set-top device such as Apple TV. Heavy spenders are likely to give gifts more often than other consumers, and they want to be able to buy in one channel (such as online) and return in another (such as in store). In addition, heavy spenders are more likely to shop on a smartphone.[34]

Developing customers into heavy users is the goal behind many frequency/loyalty programs, such as airlines' frequent flyer programs. Most supermarkets and other retailers have also designed loyalty programs that reward the heavy-user segment with deals available only to them, such as in-store coupon-dispensing systems, loyalty card programs, and special price deals on selected merchandise.

8-5 BASES FOR SEGMENTING BUSINESS MARKETS

The business market consists of four broad segments: producers, resellers, government, and institutions. (For a detailed discussion of the characteristics of these segments, see Chapter 7.) Whether marketers focus on only one or on all four of these segments, they are likely to find diversity among potential customers. Thus, further market segmentation offers just as many benefits to business marketers as it does to consumer product marketers.

8-5a Company Characteristics

Company characteristics, such as geographic location, type of company, company size, and product use, can be important segmentation variables. Some markets tend to be regional because buyers prefer to purchase from local suppliers, and distant suppliers may have difficulty competing in terms of price and service. Therefore, firms that sell to geographically concentrated industries benefit by locating close to their markets.

Segmenting by customer type allows business marketers to tailor their marketing mixes to the unique needs of particular types of organizations or industries. For example, the Amazon Webstore platform allows businesses from single-person operations to multinational corporations to operate Amazon-hosted online shops. Entrepreneurs can easily use the site's templates set up shops featuring products that are warehoused and fulfilled by Amazon, while enterprise-level corporations like Fruit of the Loom, Spalding, and Bacardi can use the platform to manage large-scale, customized web stores. Amazon Webstore's website caters to companies' diverse needs with an array of hosting packages and information pages segmented by both business size and business type.[35]

Volume of purchase (heavy, moderate, light) is a commonly used basis for business segmentation. Another is the buying organization's size, which may affect its purchasing procedures, the types and quantities of products it needs, and its responses to different marketing mixes. Banks frequently offer different services, lines of credit, and overall attention to commercial customers based on their size. Many products, especially raw materials like steel, wood, and petroleum, have diverse applications. How customers use a product may influence the amount they buy, their buying criteria, and their selection of vendors. For example, a producer of springs may have customers who use the product in applications as diverse as making machine tools, bicycles, surgical devices, office equipment, telephones, and missile systems.

8-5b Buying Processes

Many business marketers find it helpful to segment customers and prospective customers on the basis of how they buy. For example, companies can segment some business markets by ranking key purchasing criteria, such as price, quality, technical support, and service. Atlas Overhead Door has developed a commanding position in the industrial door market by providing customized products in just 4 weeks, which is much faster than the industry average of 12 to 15 weeks. Atlas's primary market consists of companies with an immediate need for customized doors.

The purchasing strategies of buyers may provide useful segments. Two purchasing profiles that have been identified are satisficers and optimizers. **Satisficers** contact familiar suppliers and place the order with the first one to satisfy product and delivery requirements. **Optimizers** consider numerous suppliers (both familiar and unfamiliar), solicit bids, and study all proposals carefully before selecting one.

The personal characteristics of the buyers themselves (their demographic characteristics, decision style, tolerance for risk, confidence level, job responsibilities,

satisficers business customers who place an order with the first familiar supplier to satisfy product and delivery requirements

optimizers business customers who consider numerous suppliers (both familiar and unfamiliar), solicit bids, and study all proposals carefully before selecting one and so on) influence their buying behavior and thus offer a viable basis for segmenting some business markets.

8-6 STEPS IN SEGMENTING A MARKET

The purpose of market segmentation, in both consumer and business markets, is to identify marketing opportunities.

a. **Select a market or product category for study:** Define the overall market or product category to be studied. It may be a market in which the firm already competes, a new but related market or product category, or a totally new market.

b. **Choose a basis or bases for segmenting the market:** This step requires managerial insight, creativity, and market knowledge. There are no scientific procedures for selecting segmentation variables. However, a successful segmentation scheme must produce segments that meet the four basic criteria discussed earlier in this chapter.

c. **Select segmentation descriptors:** After choosing one or more bases, the marketer must select the segmentation descriptors. Descriptors identify the specific segmentation variables to use. For example, if a company selects demographics as a basis of segmentation, it may use age, occupation, and income as descriptors. A company that selects usage-rate segmentation needs to decide whether to go after heavy users, nonusers, or light users.

d. **Profile and analyze segments:** The profile should include the segments' size, expected growth, purchase frequency, current brand usage, brand loyalty, and long-term sales and profit potential. This information can then be used to rank potential market segments by profit opportunity, risk, consistency with organizational mission and objectives, and other factors important to the firm.

e. **Select markets:** Selecting markets is not a part of but a natural outcome of the segmentation process. It is a major decision that influences and often directly determines the firm's marketing mix. This topic is examined in greater detail later in this chapter.

f. **Design, implement, and maintain appropriate marketing mixes:** The marketing mix has been described as product, place (distribution), promotion, and pricing strategies intended to bring about a mutually satisfying exchange relationship with a market.

These topics are explored in detail in Chapters 10 through 19.

Markets are dynamic, so it is important that companies proactively monitor their segmentation strategies over time. Often, once customers or prospects have been assigned to a segment, marketers think their task is done. Once customers are assigned to an age segment, for example, they stay there until they reach the next age bracket or category, which could be 10 years in the future. Thus, the segmentation classifications are static, but the customers and prospects are changing. Dynamic segmentation approaches adjust to fit the changes that occur in customers' lives.

SEGMENTATION IS CENTRAL TO NIKE'S SUCCESS

Nike's loyalty program has more than 100 million members. These customers spend almost four times as much on Nike products as do nonmember customers. The company attributes this to correctly targeting customers, which Nike defines by segment. Customers in each segment have different lifestyle-targeted offerings made available to them, many through social media. Three of these segments are:

1. "The Weekend Runner" is a 30-year-old woman who runs half marathons. As an active user of the Nike Run Club app, the company has data on her running and achievements. It recently added an app feature that plays recorded encouragement from coaches and has another that recommends shoes based on her mileage and running habits.

2. "The Style Shopper" is a woman who wants to be on-trend before, during, and after her workouts. The Nike app for this customer features information on athletes and what Nike products they wear. It includes data-based product recommendations, invitations, and a function that automatically reserves select products in the customer's correct size and invites her to buy. The app also lets users message directly with accomplished athletes for product recommendations.

3. "The Dedicated Sneakerhead." For this segment, Nike has taken steps such as gamifying its exclusive product launches with its SNKR Stash experience. With SNKR Stash, customers go on a citywide treasure hunt for virtual "Stash Spots" where they can purchase the products via their mobile phones. The company is planning to enhance this experience by allowing fans in areas remote from a treasure hunt to join a "squad" and watch a live stream of the event and receive the product if their squad wins.[36]

STRATEGIES FOR SELECTING TARGET MARKETS

So far, this chapter has focused on the market segmentation process, which is only the first step in deciding whom to approach about buying a product. The next task is to choose one or more target markets. A target market is a group of people or organizations for which an organization designs, implements, and maintains a marketing mix intended to meet the needs of that group, resulting in mutually satisfying exchanges.

Because most markets will include customers with different characteristics, lifestyles, backgrounds, and income levels, it is unlikely that a single marketing mix will attract all segments of the market. Thus, if a marketer wishes to appeal to more than one segment of the market, it must develop different marketing mixes. The three general strategies for selecting target markets—undifferentiated, concentrated, and multisegment targeting—are illustrated in Exhibit 8.2, which also illustrates the advantages and disadvantages of each targeting strategy.

8-7a Undifferentiated Targeting

A firm using an undifferentiated targeting strategy essentially adopts a mass-market philosophy, viewing the market as one big market with no individual segments. The firm uses one marketing mix for the entire market. A firm that adopts an undifferentiated targeting strategy assumes that individual customers have similar needs that can be met with a common marketing mix.

The first firm in an industry sometimes uses an undifferentiated targeting strategy. With no competition, the firm may not need to tailor marketing mixes to the preferences of market segments. Henry Ford's famous comment about the Model T is a classic example of an undifferentiated targeting strategy: "They can have their car in any color they want, as long as it's black." At one time, Coca-Cola used this strategy with a single product and a single size of its familiar green bottle. Marketers of commodity products, such as flour and sugar, are also likely to use an undifferentiated targeting strategy.

One advantage of undifferentiated marketing is the potential for saving on production and marketing. Because only one item is produced, the firm should be able to achieve economies of mass production. Also, marketing costs may be lower when there is only one product to promote and a single channel of distribution. Too often, however, an undifferentiated strategy emerges by default rather than by design, reflecting a failure to consider the advantages of a segmented approach. The result is often sterile, unimaginative product offerings that have little appeal to anyone.

Another problem associated with undifferentiated targeting is that it makes the company more susceptible to competitive inroads. Hershey lost a big share of the candy market to Mars and other candy companies before it changed to a multisegment targeting strategy. Coca-Cola forfeited its position as the leading seller of cola drinks in supermarkets to PepsiCo in the late 1950s, when Pepsi began offering several sizes of containers.

You might think a firm producing a standard product such as toilet tissue would adopt an undifferentiated strategy. However, this market has industrial segments and consumer segments. Industrial buyers want an economical, single-ply product sold in boxes of a hundred rolls (or jumbo rolls a foot in diameter to use in public restrooms). The consumer market demands a more versatile product in smaller quantities. Within the consumer market, the product is differentiated with designer print or no print, as cushioned or noncushioned, and as economy priced or luxury priced. Undifferentiated marketing can succeed in certain situations, though. A small grocery store in a small, isolated town may define all of the people who live in the town as its target market. It may offer one marketing mix and generally satisfy everyone in town. This strategy is not likely to be as effective if there are three or four grocery stores in town.

8-7b Concentrated Targeting

With a concentrated targeting strategy, a firm selects a market niche (one segment of a market) for targeting its marketing efforts. Because the firm is appealing to a single segment, it can concentrate on understanding the needs, motives, and satisfaction of that segment's members and on developing and maintaining a highly specialized marketing mix. Some firms find that concentrating resources and meeting the needs of a narrowly defined market segment is more profitable than spreading resources over several different segments.

target market a group of people or organizations for which an organization designs, implements, and maintains a marketing mix intended to meet the needs of that group, resulting in mutually satisfying exchanges

undifferentiated targeting strategy a marketing approach that views the market as one big market with no individual segments and thus uses a single marketing mix

concentrated targeting strategy a strategy used to select one segment of a market for targeting marketing efforts

niche one segment of a market

EXHIBIT 8.2   ADVANTAGES AND DISADVANTAGES OF TARGET MARKETING STRATEGIES

Targeting Strategy	Advantages	Disadvantages
Undifferentiated	• Potential savings on production/marketing costs	• Unimaginative product offerings • Company more susceptible to competition
Concentrated	• Concentration of resources • Can better meet the needs of a narrowly defined segment • Allows some small firms to better compete with larger firms • Strong positioning	• Segments too small or changing • Large competitors may more effectively market to niche segment
Multisegment	• Greater financial success • Economies of scale in production/marketing	• High costs • Cannibalization

Intelligentsia Coffee & Tea, a Chicago-based coffee roaster/retailer, targets serious coffee drinkers with hand-roasted, ground, and poured supergourmet coffee or tea served by seriously educated baristas. The company also offers training classes for the at-home or out-of-town coffee aficionado. Starting price—$200 per class.

Small firms often adopt a concentrated targeting strategy to compete effectively with much larger firms. For example, Enterprise Rent-A-Car, number one in the car rental industry, started as a small company catering to people whose cars were in the shop. Some other firms use a concentrated strategy to establish a strong position in a desirable market segment. Porsche, for instance, targets an upscale automobile market through "class appeal, not mass appeal."

Concentrated targeting violates the old adage "Don't put all your eggs in one basket." If the chosen segment is too small or if it shrinks because of environmental changes, the firm may suffer negative consequences. For instance, OshKosh B'gosh was highly successful selling children's wear in the 1980s. It was so successful, however, that the children's line came to define OshKosh's image to the extent that the company could not sell clothes to anyone else. Attempts at marketing older children's clothing, women's casual clothes, and maternity wear were all abandoned. Recognizing it was in the children's wear business, the company expanded into products such as kids' shoes, children's eyewear, and plush toys.

A concentrated strategy can also be disastrous for a firm that is not successful in its narrowly defined target market. Before Procter & Gamble (P&G) introduced Head & Shoulders shampoo, several small firms were already selling antidandruff shampoos. Head & Shoulders was introduced with a large promotional campaign, and

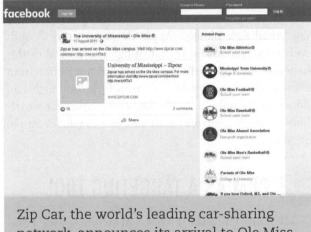

Source: Facebook

Zip Car, the world's leading car-sharing network, announces its arrival to Ole Miss students.

the new brand immediately captured over half the market. Within a year, several of the firms that had been concentrating on this market segment went out of business.

8-7c Multisegment Targeting

A firm that chooses to serve two or more well-defined market segments and develops a distinct marketing mix for each has a **multisegment targeting strategy**. P&G offers 18 different laundry detergents, each targeting a different segment of the market. For example, Tide is a tough, powerful cleaner, and Era is good for stain treatment and removal. Zipcar, a membership-based car-sharing company that rents cars to its members and bills them by the hour or day, shifted its targeting

> **multisegment targeting strategy** a strategy that chooses two or more well-defined market segments and develops a distinct marketing mix for each

strategy from urban centers; it added services for business and universities like the University of Minnesota, which has five Zipcar stations located around its campus. On campuses across the nation, Zipcar targeting is further subdivided into faculty/staff and student markets.[37]

Multisegment targeting offers many potential benefits to firms, including greater sales volume, higher profits, larger market share, and economies of scale in manufacturing and marketing. Yet it may also involve higher costs for product design, production, promotion, inventory, marketing research, and management. Before deciding to use this strategy, firms should compare the benefits and costs of multisegment targeting to those of undifferentiated and concentrated targeting.

Another potential cost of multisegment targeting is **cannibalization**, which occurs when sales of a new product cut into sales of a firm's existing products. For example, consumers are increasingly interested in purchasing second-hand, refurbished smartphones rather than brand new phones. Apple dominates the second-hand market, followed by Samsung. The appeal of this phenomenon comes from a slowdown in innovation from smartphone manufacturers. Thus, refurbished high-end phones are cannibalizing the low-end market for smartphones, which contributes to slower growth for Apple and Samsung.[38]

8-8 CRM AS A TARGETING TOOL

Recall from Chapter 1 that CRM (customer relationship management) entails tracking interactions with customers to optimize customer satisfaction and long-term company profits. Companies that successfully implement CRM tend to customize the goods and services offered to their customers based on data generated through interactions between carefully defined groups of customers and the company. CRM can also allow marketers to target customers with extremely relevant offerings. Etsy is an online marketplace where entrepreneurs can sell products they curate or craft by hand. Understanding that users of all sorts come to Etsy to explore and buy unique items, the company began using CRM to personalize its customer experience. In order to facilitate this, Etsy used data analytics to develop a system that can recommend products based on factors beyond simply what people have looked at. As a result, Etsy shoppers now have an experience that surprises them with unexpected items and engages them to find more.[39]

cannibalization a situation that occurs when sales of a new product cut into sales of a firm's existing products

As many firms have discovered, a detailed and segmented understanding of customers can be advantageous. There are at least four trends that will lead to the continued growth of CRM: personalization, time savings, loyalty, and technology.

- **Personalization:** One-size-fits-all marketing is no longer relevant. Consumers want to be treated as the individuals they are, with their own unique sets of needs and wants. Its personalized nature allows CRM to fulfill this desire.

- **Time savings:** Direct and personal marketing efforts will continue to grow to meet the needs of consumers who no longer have the time to spend shopping and making purchase decisions. With the personal and targeted nature of CRM, consumers can spend less time making purchase decisions and more time doing the things that are important to them.

- **Loyalty:** Consumers will be loyal only to companies and brands that have earned that loyalty and reinforced it at every purchase occasion. CRM techniques focus on finding a firm's best customers, rewarding them for their loyalty, and thanking them for their business.

- **Technology:** Mass-media approaches will decline in importance as advances in market research and database technology allow marketers to collect detailed information on their customers. New technology offers marketers a more cost-effective way to reach customers and enables businesses to personalize their messages. For example, My.Yahoo.com greets each user by name and offers information in which the user has expressed interest. Similarly, RedEnvelope.com helps customers keep track of special occasions and offers personalized gift recommendations. With the help of database technology, CRM can track a business's customers as individuals, even if they number in the millions.

CRM is a huge commitment and often requires a 180-degree turnaround for marketers who spent the last half of the 20th century developing and implementing mass-marketing efforts. Although mass marketing will probably continue to be used, especially to create brand awareness or to remind consumers of a product, the advantages of CRM cannot be ignored.

8-9 POSITIONING

Marketers segment their markets and then choose which segment, or segments, to target with their marketing mix. Then, based on the target market(s), they can develop the product's **positioning**, a process that influences potential customers' overall perception of a brand, product line, or organization in general. **Position** is the place a product, brand, or group of products occupies in consumers' minds relative to competing offerings. Consumer goods marketers are particularly concerned with positioning. Coca-Cola has multiple cola brands, each positioned to target a different market. For example, Coca-Cola Zero is positioned on its bold taste and zero calories, Caffeine Free Coca-Cola is positioned as a no-caffeine alternative, and Tab is positioned as a cola drink for dieters.[40]

Positioning assumes that consumers compare products on the basis of important features. Marketing efforts that emphasize irrelevant features are therefore likely to misfire. For example, Crystal Pepsi and a clear version of Coca-Cola's Tab failed because consumers perceived the "clear" positioning as more of a marketing gimmick than a benefit.

Effective positioning requires assessing the positions occupied by competing products, determining the important dimensions underlying these positions, and choosing a position in the market where the organization's marketing efforts will have the greatest impact. Casual-dining restaurant chain Ruby Tuesday found that what consumers remembered most about eating in a Ruby Tuesday restaurant was the Garden Bar. In response, the company decided to differentiate itself from competitors by focusing on vegetables. Today, Ruby Tuesday is positioned as a place to get a great salad with a full menu on the side. The Garden Bar offers 70 ingredients, customers can make as many trips as they want, and they can customize their salads however they like. This focus addresses a consumer trend toward eating more healthfully and is something most competitors do not offer.[41]

One positioning strategy that many firms use to distinguish their products from competitors is based on **product differentiation**. The distinctions between products can be either real or perceived. For example, Wendy's differentiates itself from other fast-food restaurants by using beef that is fresh, never frozen, as well as offering unique products such as chili and several different flavors of baked potatoes.[42] However, many everyday products, such as bleaches, aspirin, unleaded regular gasoline, and some soaps, are differentiated by such trivial means as brand names, packaging, color, smell, or "secret" additives. The marketer attempts to convince consumers that a particular brand is distinctive and that they should demand it.

Some firms, instead of using product differentiation, position their products as being similar to competing

DON'T SETTLE FOR FROZEN BEEF.

Wendy's 2017 Super Bowl ad featured an "Other Guys" employee defrosting hamburger patties with a hair dryer in a giant meat freezer, highlighting Wendy's use of never-frozen beef.

products or brands. Two examples of this positioning are artificial sweeteners advertised as tasting like sugar and margarine as tasting like butter.

8-9a Perceptual Mapping

Perceptual mapping is a means of displaying or graphing, in two or more dimensions, the location of products, brands, or groups of products in customers' minds. For example, Saks Incorporated, the department store chain, stumbled in sales when it tried to attract a younger core customer. To recover, Saks invested in research to determine its core customers in its 54 stores across the country. The perceptual map in Exhibit 8.3 shows how Saks uses customer demographics such as spending levels and preferred styles to build a matrix that charts the best mix of clothes and accessories to stock in each store.

8-9b Positioning Bases

Firms use a variety of bases for positioning, including the following:

- **Attribute:** A product is associated with an attribute, product feature, or customer benefit. In engineering its products, Seventh Generation focuses on removing common

positioning developing a specific marketing mix to influence potential customers' overall perception of a brand, product line, or organization in general

position the place a product, brand, or group of products occupies in consumers' minds relative to competing offerings

product differentiation a positioning strategy that some firms use to distinguish their products from those of competitors

perceptual mapping a means of displaying or graphing, in two or more dimensions, the location of products, brands, or groups of products in customers' minds

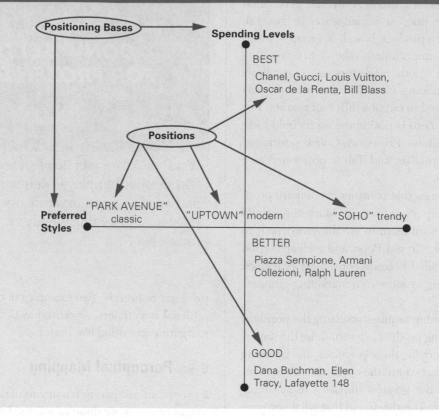

toxins and chemicals from household products to make them safe for everyone in the household.

- **Price and quality:** This positioning base may stress high price as a signal of quality or emphasize low price as an indication of value. Neiman Marcus uses the high-price strategy; Walmart has successfully followed the low-price and value strategy. The mass merchandiser Target has developed an interesting position based on price and quality. It is an "upscale discounter," sticking to low prices but offering higher quality and design than most discount chains.

- **Use or application:** Stressing uses or applications can be an effective means of positioning a product with buyers. Danone introduced its Kahlúa liqueur using advertising to point out 228 ways to consume the product.

- **Product user:** This positioning base focuses on a personality or type of user. Gap Inc. has several different brands: Gap stores offer basic casual pieces, such as jeans and T-shirts, to middle-of-the-road consumers at midlevel prices; Old Navy offers low-priced, trendy casual wear geared to youth and college-age groups; and Banana Republic is a luxury brand offering

fashionable, luxurious business and casual wear to 25- to 35-year-olds.[43]

- **Product class:** The objective here is to position the product as being associated with a particular category of products—for example, positioning a margarine brand with butter. Alternatively, products can be disassociated from a category.

- **Competitor:** Positioning against competitors is part of any positioning strategy. Apple positions the iPhone as cooler and more up-to-date than Windows-based smartphones, and Samsung positions the Galaxy series as cooler and more up-to-date than the iPhone.

- **Emotion:** Positioning using emotion focuses on how the product makes customers feel. A number of companies use this approach. For example, Nike's "Just Do It" campaign did not tell consumers what "it" is, but most got the emotional message of achievement and courage. Researchers have found that after a major apparel retailer implemented a comprehensive emotional-connection strategy, its customer attrition dropped 4 percent while its customer advocacy grew 6 percent and its same-store sales jumped more than 50 percent.[44]

8-9c Repositioning

Sometimes products or companies are repositioned in order to sustain growth in slow markets or to correct positioning mistakes. **Repositioning** is changing consumers' perceptions of a brand in relation to competing brands. For example, Dunkin' Donuts is repositioning the brand to be known for coffee drinks instead of donuts. It has dropped "Donuts" from its name, reduced the number of food items on the menu, and redesigned its stores. Its new stores will include technology-based upgrades, including a dedicated space for mobile order pickups, digital ordering kiosks, and a drive-thru dedicated to customers who have ordered ahead with its smartphone. app.[45]

repositioning changing consumers' perceptions of a brand in relation to competing brands

9 | Marketing Research

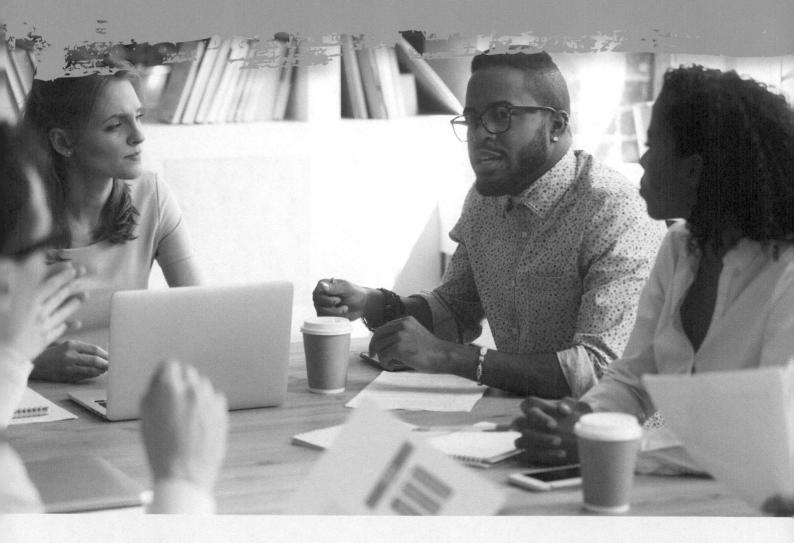

LEARNING OUTCOMES

After studying this chapter, you will be able to . . .

9-1 Define *marketing research* and explain its importance to marketing decision making

9-2 Describe the steps involved in conducting a marketing research project

9-3 Discuss the profound impact of the Internet on marketing research

9-4 Describe the growing importance of mobile research

9-5 Discuss the growing importance of scanner-based research

9-6 Explain when marketing research should be conducted

9-7 Explain the concept of competitive intelligence

THE ROLE OF MARKETING RESEARCH

Marketing research is the process of planning, collecting, and analyzing data relevant to a marketing decision. The results of this analysis are then communicated to management. Thus, marketing research is the function that links the consumer, customer, and public to the marketer through information. Marketing research plays a key role in the marketing system. It provides decision makers with data on the effectiveness of the current marketing mix and with insights for necessary changes. Furthermore, marketing research is a main data source for management information systems. In other words, the findings of a marketing research project become data for decision making by management.

Marketing research has three roles: descriptive, diagnostic, and predictive. Its *descriptive* role includes gathering and presenting factual statements. For example, what are the historical sales trends in the industry? What are consumers' attitudes toward a product and its advertising? Its *diagnostic* role includes explaining data, such as determining the impact on sales of a change in the design of the package. Its *predictive* function is to address "what if" questions. For example, how can the researcher use the descriptive and diagnostic research to predict the results of a planned marketing decision?

9-1a Management Uses of Marketing Research

Marketing research can help managers in several ways. First, it improves the quality of decision making, allowing marketers to explore the desirability of various alternatives before arriving at a path forward. Second, it helps managers trace problems. Was the initial decision incorrect? Did an unforeseen change in the external environment cause the plan to fail? How can the same mistake be avoided in the future? Questions like these can be answered through marketing research. Third, marketing research can help managers understand very detailed and complicated relationships. Most importantly, sound marketing research can help managers serve both current and future customers accurately and efficiently. This in turn can mean greater revenue and profits for the firm.

Firms like Dick's Sporting Goods, Sports Authority, Gander Mountain, Cabelas, and Bass Pro Shops continually tweak their inventory to meet the needs of existing customers and to attract new ones. One such display area in these stores is camping gear and supplies. So, the questions become, "Are more people camping?" "Fewer?" and "Who's camping?" Marketing research determined that the number of campers who camp three or more times a year has increased 64 percent since 2014.[1] That is over 6 million people. Plus, campers want to camp more often; 45 percent planned to increase their number of camping trips in 2019. Researchers found that camping is a very social activity, with campers turning to friends and social media to get information about camping gear. In addition to interacting with fellow campers, they view camping as a time to relax, escape stress, and clear their minds. Ninety-four percent of teens who camp claim that they are enthusiastic about it. New campers are nearly evenly split between non-Hispanic whites and nonwhites. Nearly all millennials (93 percent) and Gen Xers (93 percent) want to try camping in 2019. Millennials lean more toward backcountry camping, while Gen Xers seek unique accommodations, such as an Airstream trailer. Access to technology is getting more people into camping, yet about half say using technology detracts from the overall experience. Tent usage remains high, with 61 percent of campers primarily using tents.[2] About 24 percent use RVs for camping. Others rent accommodations, such as cabins, for their camping experiences. Armed with these and other research data, a sporting goods retailer can then change the camping gear inventory to increase sales. Certainly, one factor would be having a variety of styles and types of tents on hand to meet buyers' needs. Displays

marketing research the process of planning, collecting, and analyzing data relevant to a marketing decision

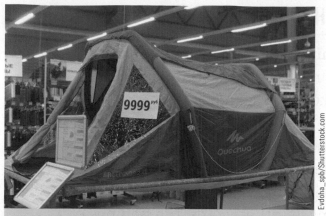

Marketing research can aid retailers in determining the amount and type of camping equipment it should carry in their stores.

should emphasize sociability, relaxation, and a tilt toward younger campers.

Marketing research can also help managers understand whether and when changes should be made to customer service. One large retail apparel chain was considering adding more associates on the floor to improve customer service. Marketing research found that customers were turning away from hands-on, personalized service from store associates and instead turning to friends, family, and social media for advice. Eighty-five percent want to be able to check prices at scanners rather than asking someone. Also, 65 percent want to order online and pick up the items at the store. Technology in apparel store dressing rooms that assist with shopping was deemed important by only 17 percent. And only 6 percent ranked customized lighting as important when shopping for apparel and shoes. Nearly 34 percent felt that receiving promotional and sales information sent directly to their smartphone when entering the store was important. Also, being able to pay a sales associate anywhere in the store was felt to be important by 34 percent.[3] Thus, a number of technological improvements were made by the chain, but the number of associates remained roughly the same.

9-1b Understanding the Ever-Changing Marketplace

Marketing research helps managers to understand what is going on in the marketplace and to take advantage of opportunities. Now, with big data analytics (discussed later in the chapter), we can understand the marketing environment like never before. Historically speaking,

marketing research has been practiced for as long as marketing has existed. The early Phoenicians carried out market demand studies as they traded in the various ports of the Mediterranean Sea. Marco Polo's diary indicates that he performed marketing research as he traveled to China. There is even evidence that the Spanish systematically conducted "market surveys" as they explored the New World, and there are examples of marketing research conducted during the Renaissance.

Returning to the present, one of the hottest trends in technology today is the Internet of Things (IoT). This term refers to everyday devices—such as refrigerators, toys, light bulbs, and hot water heaters—connecting wirelessly to a network to improve their functionality. An early leader in this market was the Nest Thermostat. Nest learns the temperatures you like throughout the week and then turns itself down when you are away. It can be controlled via an app, so you can increase or decrease the temperature while lying in bed. So what does this trend mean to manufacturers of appliances, clothing, fitness devices, and countless other items? At the end of 2015, 13 percent of consumers had an IoT device in their homes. By 2019, 69 percent planned to have at least one IoT device, such as a thermostat or security system. Adoption of wearable IoT technology (such as smart watches and fitness devices) is also expected to increase; nearly half of consumers already own or plan to purchase a device in this category by 2019.

The findings of a nationwide marketing research study indicate that consumers living in the 10 largest U.S. cities are more likely than the national average to identify as early adopters. Findings varied by region, however: 74 percent of consumers living in the Northeast plan to adopt an in-home IoT device by 2019, compared to 68 percent in the Midwest and 66 percent in the Southeast. Consumers living in the Northeast are approximately 50 percent more likely than those living in the Southeast and Midwest to adopt a smart smoke detector in 2016. Fifty-eight percent of consumers living in the Northeast plan to adopt wearable technology by 2019, with the Southeast and Midwest close behind at 57 and 55 percent, respectively. Men are more likely than women to plan to purchase an in-home IoT device by 2019 (70 percent vs. 67 percent). Younger consumers are most likely to adopt connected technologies later on, while older consumers are slightly more likely to already own certain products. The IoT is expected to have sales of $520 trillion by 2020.[4]

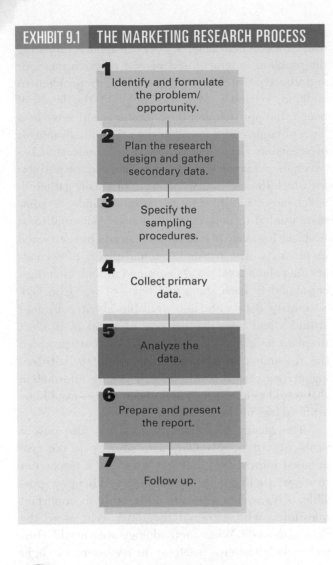

EXHIBIT 9.1 **THE MARKETING RESEARCH PROCESS**

1. Identify and formulate the problem/opportunity.

2. Plan the research design and gather secondary data.

3. Specify the sampling procedures.

4. Collect primary data.

5. Analyze the data.

6. Prepare and present the report.

7. Follow up.

9-2 STEPS IN A MARKETING RESEARCH PROJECT

Virtually all firms that have adopted the marketing concept engage in some marketing research because it offers decision makers many benefits. Some companies spend millions on marketing research; others, particularly smaller firms, conduct informal, limited-scale research studies.

Whether a research project costs $200 or $2 million, the same general process should be followed. The marketing research process is a scientific approach to decision making that maximizes the chance of getting accurate and meaningful results. Exhibit 9.1 traces the seven steps in the research process, which begins with the recognition of a marketing problem or opportunity. As changes occur in the firm's external environment, marketing managers are faced with the questions "Should we change the existing marketing

mix?" and, if so, "How?" Marketing research may be used to evaluate product, promotion, distribution, or pricing alternatives.

A large online retailer felt that there was plenty of room for improvement on its website. The firm decided to examine Amazon, Target, and Walmart to see whether some web page elements were more important than others. The market research found that shoppers that browsed all three companies' product pages were most likely to buy from Walmart. Walmart's pages had a larger product image, a visible and user-friendly "add to cart" section, and visible and user-friendly size and quantity options. The product image area with Walmart was twice as big as the same area with Amazon and 1.5 times bigger than Target's. Also, Walmart's "add to cart" section was large and had sizable buttons. It was positioned close to the product image and highlighted important details such as price, discount, and shipping fees. Ninety-two percent noticed this section on the Walmart page, 86 percent on the Amazon page, and only 34 percent on the Target page. Amazon's strategy of using complementary products, that is, showing products that were frequently bought together, tended to significantly boost sales. Target and Walmart showed alternative products. So, if a page featured women's running shoes, an alternative product strategy would be to show more shoes. A complementary strategy would, perhaps, show socks or a gym bag. The researchers found that a complementary products section holds 30 percent more of viewers' attention than an alternatives product section.[5] Armed with this information, the online retailer was able to significantly improve its website.

This example illustrates an important point about problem/opportunity definition. The **marketing research problem** involves determining what information is needed and how that information can be obtained efficiently and effectively. The **marketing research objective**, then, is the goal statement. The marketing research objective defines the specific information needed to solve the marketing problem and provides insightful decision-making information. This requires specific pieces of information needed to solve the marketing research problem. Managers must combine this information with their own

marketing research problem determining what information is needed and how that information can be obtained efficiently and effectively

marketing research objective the specific information needed to solve a marketing research problem; the objective should be to provide insightful decision-making information experience and other information to make proper decisions. The research problem of the online retailer being discussed was to determine what factors led to greater online views, click-throughs to "add to cart" sales, and add-on sales. The marketing research objective was to increase sales through a rebuilt website.

By contrast, the **management decision problem** is action oriented. Management problems tend to be much broader in scope and far more general than marketing research problems, which must be narrowly defined and specific if the research effort is to be successful. Sometimes several research studies must be conducted to solve a broad management problem. The online retailers' management decision problem was determining whether a rebuilt website would increase the firm's market share and profits.

9-2a Secondary Data

A valuable tool throughout the research process, particularly in the problem/opportunity identification stage, is **secondary data**—data previously collected for any purpose other than the one at hand. Secondary information originating within the company includes the company's websites, annual reports, reports to stockholders, blogs, product testing results perhaps made available to the news media, YouTube videos, social media posts, and house periodicals composed by the company's personnel for communication to employees, customers, or others. Often, this information is incorporated into a company's internal database.

Innumerable outside sources of secondary information also exist, some in the forms of government departments and agencies (federal, state, and local) that compile and post summaries of business data. Trade and industry associations also publish secondary data. Still more data are available in business periodicals and other news media that regularly publish studies and articles on the economy, specific industries, and even individual companies. The unpublished summarized secondary information from these sources corresponds to internal reports, memos, or special-purpose analyses with limited circulation. Competitive considerations in the organization may preclude publication of these summaries.

Secondary data save time and money if they help solve the researcher's

management decision problem a broad-based problem that uses marketing research in order for managers to take proper actions

secondary data data previously collected for any purpose other than the one at hand

problem. Even if the problem is not solved, secondary data have other advantages. They can aid in formulating the problem statement and suggest research methods and other types of data needed for solving the problem. In addition, secondary data can pinpoint the kinds of people to approach and their locations and serve as a basis of comparison for other data. The disadvantages of secondary data stem mainly from a mismatch between the researcher's unique problem and the purpose for which the secondary data were originally gathered, which are typically different. For example, a company wanted to determine the market potential for a fireplace log made of coal rather than compressed wood by-products. The researcher found plenty of secondary data about total wood consumed as fuel, quantities consumed in each state, and types of wood burned. Secondary data were also available about consumer attitudes and purchase patterns of wood by-product fireplace logs. The wealth of secondary data provided the researcher with many insights into the artificial log market. Yet nowhere was there any information that would tell the firm whether consumers would buy artificial logs made of coal.

The quality of secondary data may also pose a problem. Often, secondary data sources do not give detailed information that would enable a researcher to assess their quality or relevance. Whenever possible, a researcher needs to address these important questions: Who gathered the data? Why were the data obtained? What methodology was used? How were classifications (such as heavy users vs. light users) developed and defined? When was the information gathered?

THE GROWING IMPORTANCE OF SOCIAL MEDIA DATA Facebook owns and controls data collected from 1.47 billion daily and 1.79 billion monthly active users.[6] The user databases of social media sites like Twitter, Pinterest, and Facebook tell these companies' marketers a lot about who you are and what you are like, though often on an anonymous basis.

In an effort to expand its information databases even further, Facebook now combines its social data with third-party information from data brokerages like Acxiom, Datalogix, and Alliance Data Systems. Using data collected from loyalty-card programs and other mechanisms, these firms aggregate information about which items and brands consumers buy. Using software that obscures identifying information (such as email addresses and phone numbers), they then combine their databases with those of Facebook and group users on the basis of certain combinations of data. These data include the websites that Facebook members visit, email lists they may have signed up for, and the ways they spend money, both online and offline—among many, many other metrics. General Motors uses this type of data synthesis to target younger buyers who might be interested in its Chevrolet Sonic. Pepsi uses it to show different ads based on whether a user regularly buys Pepsi or Diet Pepsi or is a Pepsi switcher (i.e., a person who tends to switch soda brands and is more price sensitive).

Another new Facebook tool allows advertisers to calculate their *return on investment* (total profit minus expenses divided by the investment made) on Facebook ads by tallying the actions taken by ad viewers. These actions include click-throughs, registrations, shopping cart checkouts, and other metrics. The tool also enables marketers to deliver ads to people who are most likely to make further purchases.

Facebook has shifted much of its focus from tracking cookies (small files stored on users' machines that track online activity) to Facebook log-ins. The goal of this shift is to improve ad targeting by associating views with a person's account instead of a particular device or IP address. (A number of people might use the same computer, but each likely has his or her own Facebook account.) This move has helped Facebook ensure that the 3 million advertisers who buy views from specific age groups and/or genders actually reach the people they want to. According to Facebook, advertisers now reach their intended targets 89 percent of the time. Across Internet ad networks, the average is about 55 percent.[7]

If you see these buttons, Facebook may be tracking your browsing history—whether you click on them or not.

Facebook has also begun using the like and share buttons embedded in non-Facebook websites to track peoples' browsing histories so it can more accurately and narrowly target ads. This tracking ability doesn't even require someone to click the buttons—the embedded code passively watches and records browsing behavior.[9]

THE INCREDIBLE WORLD OF BIG DATA AND MARKET ANALYTICS **Big data** is the exponential growth in the volume, variety, and velocity of information and the development of complex new tools to analyze and create meaning from such data. In the past, the flow of data was slow, steady, and predictable. All data were quantitative (countable)—many firms collected sales numbers by store, by product line, and at most, perhaps by a few other measures. Today, data are constantly streaming in from social media as well as other sources. Advanced databases of big data allow the analysis of unstructured data such as emails, audio files, and YouTube videos.

Market analytics is applying quantitative techniques that enable companies to identify hidden customer shopping patterns and produce actionable insights. These insights enable marketing managers to create the right marketing mix to drive customer satisfaction. Marketing analytics also uncover new opportunities in the marketplace as well as drive efficiency in pricing strategies, supply chain management (discussed in Chapter 13), promotional campaigns, and product development. Market analytics is covered in detail in the Appendix at the end of the book.

9-2b Planning the Research Design and Gathering Primary Data

Good secondary data and big data can help researchers conduct a thorough situation analysis. With that information, researchers can list their unanswered questions and rank them. Researchers must then decide the exact information required to answer the questions. The **research design** specifies which research questions must be answered, how and when the data will be gathered, and how the data will be analyzed. Typically, the project budget is finalized after the research design has been approved.

big data the exponential growth in the volume, variety, and velocity of information and the development of complex, new tools to analyze and create meaning from such data

research design specifies which research questions must be answered, how and when the data will be gathered, and how the data will be analyzed

Sometimes research questions can be answered by gathering more secondary data; otherwise, primary data may be needed. **Primary data**, or information collected for the first time, are used for solving the particular problem under investigation. The main advantage of primary data is that they can answer specific research questions that secondary data cannot answer. Dollar Stores, or deep-discount retailers, have fared quite well in a market dominated by Walmart and Amazon. Contributing to the continual patronage of dollar stores is their image. Customers tend to abandon stores quite rapidly if they develop a negative image. So market research was done to access their image. Marketing research found that 62 percent of U.S. adults said Dollar Tree has a positive effect on its local community, while majorities said the same of Family Dollar (57 percent) and Dollar General (56 percent). Family Dollar is now owned by Dollar Tree.

Each of the dollar stores have localized their community support strategy. The public also has favorable views of Walmart's community offerings. Sixty-five percent said that the company has a positive impact. However, 13 percent said it had a negative impact because they feel that Walmart siphons sales from local retailers. Also, where Walmart donates money to national or global organizations such as the Red Cross, the dollar stores tend to support local causes. For example, Dollar General focuses most of its giving on the Dollar General Literacy Foundation, a program aimed at helping employees and customers within 20 miles of its stores. Family Dollar concentrates on small grants to local community groups that provide "basic necessities," such as local food banks. For persons earning less than $20,000 a year, the dollar stores rank within the top 10 brands on community impact. People living in low-income areas and/or rural areas tend to have the most positive image of the dollar stores.[8] Based on the marketing research, the dollar stores were happy with their images and decided that little change was needed.

Primary data are current, and researchers know the source. Sometimes researchers gather the data themselves rather than assign projects to outside companies. Researchers also specify the methodology of the research. Secrecy can be maintained because the information is

Dollar General has a positive image in the local communities that it serves.

George Sheldon/Shutterstock.com

proprietary. In contrast, much secondary data is available to all interested parties for relatively small fees or for free.

Gathering primary data can be expensive; costs can range from a few thousand dollars for a limited survey to several million for a nationwide study. For instance, a nationwide, 15-minute telephone interview with 1,000 adult males can cost $50,000 or more for everything, including a data analysis and report. Because primary data gathering is so expensive, many firms do not bother to conduct in-person interviews. Instead, they use the Internet. Larger companies that conduct many research projects use another cost-saving technique. They *piggyback studies*, or gather data on two different projects using one questionnaire. Nevertheless, the disadvantages of primary data gathering are usually offset by the advantages. It is often the only way of solving a research problem. And with a variety of techniques available for research—including surveys, observations, and experiments—primary research can address almost any marketing question.

SURVEY RESEARCH The most popular technique for gathering primary data is **survey research**, in which a researcher either interacts with people or posts a questionnaire online to obtain facts, opinions, and attitudes. Exhibit 9.2 summarizes the characteristics of traditional forms of survey research.

In-Home Personal Interviews Although in-home personal interviews often provide high-quality information, they tend to be very expensive because of the interviewers' travel time and mileage costs. Therefore, they are rapidly disappearing from the American and European researchers' survey toolbox. They are, however, still popular in many less-developed countries around the globe.

Mall Intercept Interviews The **mall intercept interview** is conducted in the common area of a

EXHIBIT 9.2 — CHARACTERISTICS OF TRADITIONAL FORMS OF SURVEY RESEARCH

Characteristic	In-Home Personal Interviews	Mall Intercept Interviews	Central-Location Telephone Interviews	Self-Administered and One-Time Mail Surveys	Mail Panel Surveys	Executive Interviews	Focus Groups
Cost	High	Moderate	Moderate	Low	Moderate	High	Low
Time span	Moderate	Moderate	Fast	Slow	Relatively slow	Moderate	Fast
Use of interviewer probes	Yes	Yes	Yes	No	Yes	Yes	Yes
Ability to show concepts to respondent	Yes (also taste tests)	Yes (also taste tests)	No	Yes	Yes	Yes	Yes
Management control over interviewer	Low	Moderate	High	N/A	N/A	Moderate	High
General data quality	High	Moderate	High to moderate	Moderate to low	Moderate	High	Moderate
Ability to collect large amounts of data	High	Moderate	Moderate to low	Low to moderate	Moderate	Moderate	Moderate
Ability to handle complex questionnaires	High	Moderate	High, if computer aided	Low	Low	High	N/A

shopping mall or in a market research office within the mall. To conduct this type of interview, the research firm rents office space in the mall or pays a significant daily fee. One drawback is that it is hard to get a representative sample of the population. One advantage is the ability of the interviewer to probe when necessary—a technique used to clarify a person's response and ask for more detailed information.

Mall intercept interviews must be brief. Only the shortest ones are conducted while respondents are standing. Often, researchers invite respondents into the office for interviews, which are still generally less than 15 minutes long. The overall quality of mall intercept interviews is about the same as telephone interviews. They are often used to conduct taste tests that require respondents to sample several different products.

Marketing researchers have long used laptops and tablets to speed the mall interview process. One technique is **computer-assisted personal interviewing**. The researcher conducts in-person interviews, reads questions to the respondent off a screen, and directly keys the respondent's answers into the mobile device. A second approach is **computer-assisted self-interviewing**. A mall interviewer intercepts and gives willing respondents a mobile device. Each respondent reads questions off the screen and directly keys his or her answers into the device.

Telephone Interviews Telephone interviews cost less than personal interviews, but the cost is rapidly increasing owing to respondent refusals to participate. Most telephone interviewing is conducted from a specially designed phone room called a **central-location telephone (CLT) facility**.

A CLT facility has many phone lines, individual interviewing stations, headsets, and sometimes monitoring equipment. The research firm typically will interview people nationwide from a single location. The federal "Do Not Call" law does not apply to survey research.

Most CLT facilities use computer-assisted interviewing. The interviewer reads the questions from the screen and enters the respondent's data directly into the database, saving time. Hallmark Cards found that an interviewer administered a printed questionnaire for its Shoebox greeting cards in 28 minutes. The same questionnaire administered with computer assistance took only 18 minutes. The researcher can

computer-assisted personal interviewing an interviewing method in which the interviewer reads questions from a computer screen and enters the respondent's data directly into the computer

computer-assisted self-interviewing an interviewing method in which a mall interviewer intercepts; each respondent reads questions off the screen and directly keys his or her answers into the device

central-location telephone (CLT) facility a specially designed phone room used to conduct telephone interviewing stop the survey at any point and immediately print out the survey results, allowing the research design to be refined as necessary.

MAIL SURVEYS Mail surveys have several benefits: relatively low cost, elimination of interviewers and field supervisors, centralized control, and actual or promised anonymity for respondents (which may draw more candid responses). A disadvantage is that mail questionnaires usually produce low response rates. The resulting sample may therefore not represent the surveyed population. Another serious problem with mail surveys is that no one probes respondents to clarify or elaborate on their answers. If a respondent uses the word "convenience," there is no way to clarify exactly what is meant. Convenience could refer to location, store hours, or a host of other factors.

Mail panels offer an alternative to the one-shot mail survey. A mail panel consists of a sample of households recruited to participate by mail for a given period. Panel members often receive gifts in return for their participation. Essentially, the panel is a sample used several times. In contrast to one-time mail surveys, the response rates from mail panels are high. Rates of 70 percent (of those who agree to participate) are not uncommon. One-shot mail surveys and mail panels have rapidly moved online.

Executive Interviews An **executive interview** usually involves interviewing businesspeople at their offices concerning industrial products or services, a process that is very expensive. First, individuals involved in the purchase decision for the product in question must be identified and located, which can itself be expensive and time consuming. Once a qualified person is located, the next step is to get that person to agree to be interviewed and to set a time for the interview. Finally, an interviewer must go to the particular place at the appointed time. Long waits are frequently encountered; cancellations are not uncommon. This type of survey requires the very best interviewers because they are frequently interviewing on topics that they know very little about. Many of these interviews have also moved online.

Focus Groups A **focus group** is a type of personal interviewing. Often recruited by random telephone screening, 7 to 10 people with certain desired characteristics form a focus group. These qualified consumers are usually offered an incentive (typically $40 to $75) to participate in a group discussion. The meeting place (sometimes resembling a living room, sometimes featuring a conference table) has audiotaping and perhaps videotaping equipment. It also likely has a viewing room with a one-way mirror so that clients (manufacturers or retailers) can watch the session. During the session, a moderator, hired by the research company, leads the group discussion. Focus groups can be used to gauge consumer response to a product or promotion and are occasionally used to brainstorm new-product ideas or to screen concepts for new products. Focus groups also represent an efficient way of learning how products are actually used in the home. Lewis Stone, former manager of Colgate-Palmolive's research and development division, says the following about focus groups:

> If it weren't for focus groups, Colgate-Palmolive Co. might never know that some women squeeze their bottles of dishwashing soap, others squeeeeeze them, and still others squeeeeeeeeeeze out the desired amount. Then there are the ones who use the soap "neat"; that is, they put the product directly on a sponge or washcloth and wash the dishes under running water until the suds run out. Then they apply more detergent.

Stone was explaining how body language, exhibited during focus groups, provides insights into a product that are not apparent from reading questionnaires on habits and practices. Panelists' descriptions of how they perform tasks highlight need gaps, which can improve an existing product or demonstrate how a new product might be received.

Questionnaire Design All forms of survey research require a questionnaire. Questionnaires ensure that all respondents will be asked the same series of questions. Questionnaires include three basic types of questions: open-ended, closed-ended, and scaled-response (see Exhibit 9.3). An **open-ended question** encourages an answer phrased in the respondent's own words. Researchers get a rich array of information based on the respondent's frame of reference (What do you think about the new flavor?). In contrast, a **closed-ended question** asks the respondent to

executive interview a type of survey that usually involves interviewing business people at their offices concerning industrial products or services

focus group 7 to 10 people who participate in a group discussion led by a moderator

open-ended question an interview question that encourages an answer phrased in the respondent's own words

closed-ended question an interview question that asks the respondent to make a selection from a limited list of responses

EXHIBIT 9.3 TYPES OF QUESTIONS FOUND ON QUESTIONNAIRES FOR NATIONAL MARKET RESEARCH

Open-Ended Questions	Closed-Ended Questions	Scaled-Response Question

Open-Ended Questions

1. What advantages, if any, do you think ordering online offers compared to shopping at a local retail outlet? (Probe: What else?)

2. Why do you have one or more of your rugs or carpets professionally cleaned rather than cleaning them yourself or having someone else in the household clean them?

3. What is it about the color of the eye shadow that makes you like it the best?

Closed-Ended Questions

Dichotomous

1. Did you heat the Danish product before serving It?

   Yes 1

   No 2

2. The federal government doesn't care what people like me think.

   Agree 1

   Disagree 2

Multiple Choice

1. I'd like you to think back to the last footwear of any kind that you bought. I'll read you a list of descriptions and would like for you to tell me which category they fall into. (Read list and circle proper category.)

   Dress and/or formal 1

   Casual 2

   Canvas/trainer/gym shoes 3

   Specialized athletic shoes 4

   Boots 5

2. In the past three months, have you used Noxzema skin cream .... (Circle all that apply.)

   As a facial wash 1

   For moisturizing the skin 2

   For treating blemishes 3

   For cleansing the skin 4

   For treating dry skin 5

   For softening skin 6

   For sunburn 7

   For making the facial skin smooth 8

Scaled-Response Question

Now that you have used the rug cleaner, would you say that you ... (Circle one.)

Would definitely buy it 1

Would probably buy it 2

Might or might not buy it 3

Probably would not buy it 4

Definitely would not buy it 5

---

make a selection from a limited list of responses. Closed-ended questions can either be what marketing researchers call dichotomous (Do you like the new flavor? Yes or No.) or multiple choice. A **scaled-response question** is a closed-ended question designed to measure the intensity of a respondent's answer.

Closed-ended and scaled-response questions are easier to tabulate than open-ended questions because response choices are fixed. On the other hand, unless the researcher designs the closed-ended question very carefully, an important choice may be omitted. For example, suppose a food study asked this question: "Besides meat, which of the following items do you normally add to tacos that you prepare at home?"

Avocado	1	Olives (black/green)	6	
Cheese (Monterey Jack/cheddar)	2	Onions (red/white)	7	
Guacamole	3	Peppers (red/green)	8	
Lettuce	4	Pimiento	9	
Mexican hot sauce	5	Sour cream	0	

The list seems complete, doesn't it? However, consider the following responses: "I usually add a green, avocado-tasting hot sauce," "I cut up a mixture of lettuce and spinach," "I'm a vegetarian—I don't use meat at all," and "My taco is filled only with guacamole." How would you code these replies? As you can see, the question needs an "other" category.

A good question must be clear and concise and avoid ambiguous language. The answer to the question "Do you live within 10 minutes of here?" depends on the mode of transportation (maybe the person walks), driving speed, perceived time, and other factors. Language should also be clear. Therefore, jargon should be avoided, and wording should be geared to the target audience. A question such as "What is the level of efficacy of your preponderant dishwasher powder?" would probably be greeted by a lot of blank stares. It would be much simpler to say "Are you (1) very satisfied, (2) somewhat satisfied, or (3) not satisfied with your current brand of dishwasher powder?"

scaled-response question a closed-ended question designed to measure the intensity of a respondent's answer

Stating the survey's purpose at the beginning of the interview may improve clarity, but it may also increase the chances of receiving biased responses. Many times, respondents will try to provide answers that they believe are "correct" or that the interviewer wants to hear. To avoid bias at the question level, researchers should avoid leading questions and adjectives that cause respondents to think of the topic in a certain way.

Finally, to ensure clarity, the interviewer should avoid asking two questions in one—for example, "How did you like the taste and texture of the Pepperidge Farm coffee cake?" This should be divided into two questions, one concerning taste and the other texture.

OBSERVATION RESEARCH In contrast to survey research, **observation research** entails watching what people do or using machines to watch what people do. Specifically, it can be defined as the systematic process of recording the behavioral patterns of people, objects, and occurrences without questioning them. A market researcher using the observation technique witnesses and records information as events occur or compiles evidence from records of past events. Carried a step further, observation may involve watching people or phenomena and may be conducted by human observers or machines. Examples of these various observational situations are shown in Exhibit 9.4.

observation research a research method that relies on four types of observation: people watching people, people watching an activity, machines watching people, and machines watching an activity

mystery shoppers researchers posing as customers to gather observational data about a store

behavioral targeting (BT) a form of observation marketing research that combines a consumer's online activity with psychographic and demographic profiles compiled in databases

social media monitoring the use of automated tools to monitor online buzz, chatter, and conversations

ethnographic research the study of human behavior in its natural context; involves observation of behavior and physical setting

Some common forms of people-watching-people research are one-way mirror observations, mystery shoppers, and behavioral targeting. A one-way mirror allows the researchers to see the participants, but the participants cannot see the researchers.

Mystery Shoppers Mystery shoppers are researchers posing as customers to gather observational data about a store (e.g., are the shelves neatly stocked?) and collect data about customer/employee interactions. The interaction is not an interview, and communication occurs only so that the mystery shopper can observe the actions and comments of

EXHIBIT 9.4   OBSERVATIONAL SITUATIONS

Situation	Example
People watching people	Observers stationed in supermarkets watch consumers select frozen Mexican dinners; the purpose is to see how much comparison shopping people do at the point of purchase.
People watching an activity	An observer stationed at an intersection counts traffic moving in various directions.
Machines watching people	Cameras record behavior as in the people-watching-people example above.
Machines watching an activity	Traffic-counting machines monitor traffic flow.

the employee. Mystery shopping is, therefore, classified as an observational marketing research method, even though communication is often involved. Restaurant chains like Subway use mystery shoppers to evaluate store cleanliness and quality of service.

Behavioral Targeting Behavioral targeting (BT), sometimes simply called "tracking," began as a simple process by placing cookies in users' browsers or mobile apps to track which websites they visited, how long they lingered, what they searched for, and what they bought. All of this information can be tracked anonymously—a "fly on the wall" perspective. While survey research is a great way to find out the "why" and the "how," behavioral targeting lets the researcher find out the "how much," the "how often," and the "where." Also, through **social media monitoring**—using automated tools to monitor online buzz, chatter, and conversations—a researcher can learn what is being said about the brand and the competition. Tracking is the basis for input into online databases. Companies like Tapad track customers across multiple devices—personal desktop computers, laptops, smartphones, and tablets, for example. If a customer is using multiple devices at the same time, Tapad knows, and knows what is being done on each.

Ethnographic Research Ethnographic research comes to marketing from the field of anthropology. The technique is becoming increasingly popular in marketing research. **Ethnographic research**, or the study of human behavior in its natural context, involves observation of behavior and physical setting. Ethnographers directly observe the population they are studying. As "participant observers," ethnographers can use their intimacy with the people they are studying to gain richer, deeper insights into culture and behavior—in short, what makes people do what they do?

While conducting research on organic products, marketing consultant Clément Chabert asked participants, "Do you normally purchase organic foods?" One woman, a single mother with limited income, replied, "Are you kidding me? It's too expensive for me. I'll never buy organic products. I can't afford them." Six months later, Chabert was doing ethnographic research and went to the same woman's apartment, where she saw a catalog on the desk for organic products. He asked, "Are you buying those?" and she said, "Yes, definitely." The price of the products was more expensive than the organic products you'd typically see in the supermarket.

After discussing it with her, Chabert discovered that the woman didn't care singularly about the price. She bought the products because they were organic, but most of all, because they were sold through parties like Tupperware parties. The parties, and thus the products, enabled her to meet her new neighbors.

It makes you think—if you're working with an organic brand or a company that sells organic products, you might want to explore new ways of distribution that add relationship and/or socialization benefits. Chabert never would have discovered this if he used only surveys to conduct his research. The woman might have responded "organic never" in one survey and "organic often" in the next. Chabert never would have understood why that change occurred without ethnographic research. This shows the richness of the human being: people might have contradictory behaviors on paper, but they're often driven by emotional motivators that aren't always evident.

Virtual Shopping Advances in computer technology have enabled researchers to simulate an actual retail store environment on a computer screen. Depending on the type of simulation, a shopper can "pick up" a package by touching its image on the monitor and rotate it to examine all sides. Like buying on most online retailers, the shopper touches the shopping cart to add an item to the basket. During the shopping process, the computer unobtrusively records the amount of time the consumer spends shopping in each product category, the time the consumer spends examining each side of a product, the quantity of the product the consumer purchases, and the order in which items are purchased.

A major apparel retailer using a computer-simulated environment recently found that men have trouble putting outfits together. Men also hesitate to pick up clothing items because they can't fold them back the same way. With this knowledge, the apparel chain made two major changes: it began selling items together as complete outfit solutions and folded shirts and other clothes more simply. Sales of men's clothes increased by 40 percent.[9]

Virtual shopping research is growing rapidly. Thousands of new consumer packaged goods are introduced every year. All are vying for very limited retail shelf space. Any process, such as virtual shopping, that can speed product development time and lower costs is always welcomed by manufacturers. Some companies outside of retail have even begun experimenting with virtual shopping and other simulated-environment tools—many telecom, financial, automotive, aviation, and fast-food companies are using such tools to better serve their customers.

EXPERIMENTS An **experiment** is a method a researcher can use to gather primary data. The researcher alters one or more variables—price, package design, shelf space, advertising theme, advertising expenditures—while observing the effects of those alterations on another variable (usually sales). The best experiments are those in which all factors except one are held constant. The researcher can then observe what changes in sales, for example, result from changes in the amount of money spent on advertising.

Holding all other factors constant in the external environment is a monumental and costly, if not impossible, task. Such factors as competitors' actions, weather, and economic conditions are beyond the researcher's control. Yet market researchers have ways to account for the ever-changing external environment. Mars, the candy company, was losing sales to other candy companies. Traditional surveys showed that the shrinking candy bar was not perceived as a good value. Mars wondered whether a bigger bar

Virtual reality has enabled researchers to simulate a retail store environment. Merchandise shelf positioning, store layouts, point-of-purchase displays, and other variables can easily be tested.

g-stockstudio/Shutterstock.com

experiment a method of gathering primary data in which the researcher alters one or more variables while observing the effects of those alterations on another variable

SAMPLE

ANTONIO TRUZZI/Shutterstock.com

UNIVERSE

Anton Starikov/Shutterstock.com

sold at the same price would increase sales enough to off-set the higher ingredient costs. The company designed an experiment in which the marketing mix stayed the same in different markets, but the size of the candy bar varied. The substantial increase in sales of the bigger bar quickly proved that the additional costs would be more than covered by the additional revenue. Mars increased the bar size—along with its market share and profits.

9-2c **Specifying the Sampling Procedures**

sample a subset from a larger population

universe the population from which a sample will be drawn

probability sample a sample in which every element in the population has a known statistical likelihood of being selected

random sample a sample arranged in such a way that every element of the population has an equal chance of being selected as part of the sample

nonprobability sample any sample in which little or no attempt is made to get a representative cross section of the population

convenience sample a form of nonprobability sample using respondents who are convenient or readily accessible to the researcher—for example, employees, friends, or relatives

Once the researchers decide how they will collect primary data, their next step is to select the sampling procedures they will use. A firm can seldom take a census of all possible users of a new product, nor can they all be interviewed. Therefore, a firm must select a sample of the group to be interviewed. A **sample** is a subset from a larger population.

Several questions must be answered before a sampling plan is chosen. First, the population, or **universe**, of interest must be defined. This is the group from which the sample will be drawn. It should include all the people whose opinions, behavior, preferences, attitudes, and so on, are of interest to the marketer. For example, in a study whose purpose is to determine the market for a new canned dog food, the universe might be defined to include all current buyers of canned dog food.

After the universe has been defined, the next question is whether the sample must be representative of the population. If the answer is yes, a probability sample is needed. Otherwise, a nonprobability sample might be considered.

PROBABILITY SAMPLES A **probability sample** is a sample in which every element in the population has a known statistical likelihood of being selected. Its most desirable feature is that scientific rules can be used to ensure that the sample represents the population.

One type of probability sample is a **random sample**—a sample arranged in such a way that every element of the population has an equal chance of being selected as part of the sample. For example, suppose a university is interested in getting opinions from a cross section of students on a proposed sports complex to be built using student activity fees. If the university can acquire an up-to-date list of all the enrolled students, it can draw a random sample by using random numbers from a table (found in most statistics books) to select students from the list. Common forms of probability and nonprobability samples are shown in Exhibit 9.5.

NONPROBABILITY SAMPLES Any sample in which little or no attempt is made to get a representative cross section of the population can be considered a **nonprobability sample**. Therefore, the probability of selection of each sampling unit is not known. A common form of a nonprobability sample is the **convenience sample**, which uses respondents who are convenient or

EXHIBIT 9.5 TYPES OF SAMPLES

Probability Samples	
Simple Random Sample	Every member of the population has a known and equal chance of selection.
Stratified Sample	The population is divided into mutually exclusive groups (such as gender or age); then random samples are drawn from each group.
Cluster Sample	The population is divided into mutually exclusive groups (such as geographic areas); then a random sample of clusters is selected. The researcher then collects data from all the elements in the selected clusters or from a probability sample of elements within each selected cluster.
Systematic Sample	A list of the population is obtained—e.g., all persons with a checking account at XYZ Bank—and a skip interval is obtained by dividing the sample size by the population size. If the sample size is 100 and the bank has 1,000 customers, then the skip interval is 10. The beginning number is randomly chosen within the skip interval. If the beginning number is 8, then the skip pattern would be 8, 18, 28, ...

Nonprobability Samples	
Convenience Sample	The researcher selects the population members from whom it is easiest to obtain information.
Judgment Sample	The researcher's selection criteria are based on personal judgment that the elements (persons) chosen will likely give accurate information.
Quota Sample	The researcher finds a prescribed number of people in several categories—e.g., owners of large dogs versus owners of small dogs. Respondents are not selected on probability sampling criteria.
Snowball Sample	Additional respondents are selected on the basis of referrals from the initial respondents. This method is used when a desired type of respondent is hard to find—e.g., persons who have taken round-the-world cruises in the past three years. This technique employs the old adage "Birds of a feather flock together."

readily accessible to the researcher—for instance, employees, friends, or relatives.

Nonprobability samples are acceptable as long as the researcher understands their nonrepresentative nature. Because of their lower cost, nonprobability samples are sometimes used in marketing research.

Types of Errors Whenever a sample is used in marketing research, two major types of errors may occur: measurement error and sampling error. **Measurement error** occurs when there is a difference between the information desired by the researcher and the information provided by the measurement process. For example, people may tell an interviewer that they purchase Crest toothpaste when they do not. Measurement error generally tends to be larger than sampling error.

Sampling error occurs when a sample somehow does not represent the target population. Sampling error can be one of several types. Nonresponse error occurs when the sample actually interviewed differs from the sample drawn. This error happens because the original people selected to be interviewed either refused to cooperate or were inaccessible.

Frame error, another type of sampling error, arises if the sample drawn from a population differs from the target population. For instance, suppose a telephone survey is conducted to find out Chicago beer drinkers' attitudes toward Coors. If a Chicago telephone directory is used as the *frame* (the device or list from which the respondents are selected), the survey will contain a frame error. Not all Chicago beer drinkers have landline phones, many phone numbers are unlisted, and people may own cell phones with a different area code. An ideal sample (in other words, a sample with no frame error) matches all important characteristics of the target population to be surveyed. Could you find a perfect frame for Chicago beer drinkers?

Random error occurs when the selected sample is an imperfect representation of the overall population. Random error represents how accurately the chosen sample's true average (mean) value reflects the population's true average (mean) value. For example, we might take a random sample of beer drinkers in Chicago and find that 16 percent regularly drink Coors beer. The next day, we might repeat the same sampling procedure and discover that 14 percent regularly drink Coors beer. The

measurement error an error that occurs when there is a difference between the information desired by the researcher and the information provided by the measurement process

sampling error an error that occurs when a sample somehow does not represent the target population

frame error an error that occurs when a sample drawn from a population differs from the target population

random error an error that occurs when the selected sample is an imperfect representation of the overall population

EXHIBIT 9.6   POPCORN CROSS-TABULATION

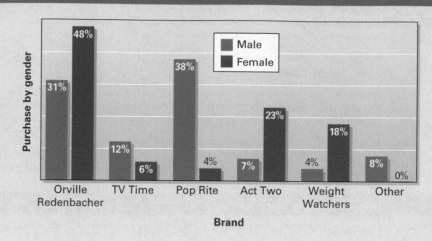

difference is due to random error. Error is common to all surveys, yet it is often not reported or is underreported. Typically, the only error mentioned in a written report is sampling error.

9-2d Collecting the Data

Marketing research field service firms are used to collect some primary data. A **field service firm** specializes in interviewing respondents on a subcontracted basis. Many have offices, often in malls, throughout the country. A typical marketing research study involves data collection in several cities, which may require the marketer to work with a comparable number of field service firms. Besides conducting interviews, field service firms provide focus group facilities, mall intercept locations, test product storage, and kitchen facilities to prepare test food products.

9-2e Analyzing the Data

After collecting the data, the marketing researcher proceeds to the next step in the research process: data analysis. The purpose of this analysis is to interpret and draw conclusions from the mass of collected data. The marketing researcher tries to organize and analyze those data by using one or more techniques common to marketing research: one-way frequency counts, cross-tabulations, and more sophisticated statistical analysis. Of these three

field service firm a firm that specializes in interviewing respondents on a subcontracted basis

cross-tabulation a method of analyzing data that lets the analyst look at the responses to one question in relation to the responses to one or more other questions

techniques, one-way frequency counts are the simplest. One-way frequency tables simply record the responses to a question. For example, the answers to the question "What brand of microwave popcorn do you buy most often?" would provide a one-way frequency distribution. One-way frequency tables are always done in data analysis, at least as a first step, because they provide the researcher with a general picture of the study's results. A **cross-tabulation** lets the analyst look at the responses to one question in relation to the responses to one or more other questions. For example, in Exhibit 9.6, what is the association between gender and the brand of microwave popcorn bought most frequently?

Researchers can use many other more powerful and sophisticated statistical techniques, such as hypothesis testing, measures of association, and regression analysis. A description of these techniques goes beyond the scope of this book but can be found in any good marketing research textbook. The use of sophisticated statistical techniques depends on the researchers' objectives and the nature of the data gathered.

9-2f Preparing and Presenting the Report

After data analysis has been completed, the researcher must prepare the report and communicate the conclusions and recommendations to management. This is a key step in the process. If the marketing researcher wants managers to carry out the recommendations, he or she must convince them that the results are credible and justified by the data collected.

Researchers are usually required to present both written and oral reports on the project. Today, the written report is often no more than a copy of the PowerPoint slides used in the oral presentation. Researchers are slowly moving away from Power Point into digital dashboards. Whatever kind of report is used, it should be tailored to the audience. It should begin with a clear, concise statement of the research objectives, followed by a complete but brief and simple explanation of the research design or methodology employed. A summary of major findings should come next. The conclusion of the report should also present recommendations to management.

Most people who enter marketing will become research users rather than research suppliers. Thus, they must know what to notice in a report. As with many other items we purchase, quality is not always readily apparent. Nor does a high price guarantee superior quality. The basis for measuring the quality of a marketing research report is the research proposal. Did the report meet the objectives established in the proposal? Was the methodology outlined in the proposal followed? Are the conclusions based on logical deductions from the data analysis? Do the recommendations seem prudent, given the conclusions?

9-2g Following Up

The final step in the marketing research process is to follow up. The researcher should determine why management did or did not carry out the recommendations in the report. Was sufficient decision-making information included? What could have been done to make the report more useful to management? A good rapport between the product manager, or whoever authorized the project, and the market researcher is essential. Often, they must work together on many studies throughout the year.

9-3 THE PROFOUND IMPACT OF THE INTERNET AND SMART DEVICES ON MARKETING RESEARCH

More than 90 percent of U.S. marketing research companies conduct some form of online research. Paper questionnaires in marketing research are going the way of the horse and buggy. Online survey research has replaced computer-assisted telephone interviewing as the most popular mode of data collection.

9-3a Advantages of Online Surveys

The huge growth in the popularity of online surveys is the result of the many advantages offered by the Internet.

The specific advantages of Internet surveys, which are often sent to mobile devices, are many:

- **Rapid development, real-time reporting:** Digital surveys can be broadcast to thousands of potential respondents simultaneously. Respondents complete surveys simultaneously; then results are tabulated and posted for corporate clients to view as the returns arrive. The effect: survey results can be in a client's hands in significantly less time than would be required for traditional paper surveys.

- **Dramatically reduced costs:** The Internet can cut costs by 25 to 40 percent and provide results in half the time it takes to do traditional surveys. Traditional survey methods are labor-intensive efforts, incurring training, telecommunications, and management costs. Online methods eliminate these completely. While costs for traditional survey techniques rise proportionally with the number of interviews desired, digital solicitations can grow in volume with little increase in project costs.

- **Personalized questions and data:** Online surveys can be highly personalized for greater relevance to each respondent's own situation, thus speeding the response process.

- **Improved respondent participation:** Smartphone surveys take half as much time to complete as phone interviews, can be accomplished at the respondent's convenience (e.g., after work hours), and are much more stimulating and engaging. As a result, online surveys enjoy much higher response rates.

- **Contact with hard-to-reach groups:** Certain groups—doctors, high-income professionals, top management in Global 2000 firms—are among the most surveyed on the planet and are also the most difficult to reach. Many of these groups are well represented online. Internet surveys provide convenient anytime/anywhere access that makes it easy for busy professionals to participate.

9-3b Uses of the Internet and Smart Devices by Marketing Researchers

Marketing researchers use the Internet to administer surveys, conduct focus groups, and perform a variety of other types of marketing research.

METHODS OF CONDUCTING ONLINE SURVEYS

There are several basic methods for conducting online surveys: web survey systems, survey design and web-hosting sites, and online panel providers.

Web Survey Systems Web survey systems are software systems specifically designed for web questionnaire construction and delivery. They consist of an integrated questionnaire designer, web server, database, and data delivery program designed for use by nonprogrammers.

The web server distributes the questionnaire and files responses in a database. The user can query the server at any time via the Web for completion statistics, descriptive statistics on responses, and graphical displays of data. Some popular online survey research software packages are SurveyMonkey, Typeform, Google Forms, and SurveyPlanet.

There are free versions on all of these tools and paid versions that offer added capabilities such as:

- **Survey logic.** Survey logic uses information from previous answers to determine which questions to go to next. For example, do you own an imported car? If the user answers yes, then the next question might be, "What brand?" If the respondent answers no, then the survey would skip to the next section of questions.

- **Export data**. Many tools won't let you export your data unless you use the paid version.

- **Customer logo.** Paid versions let you get rid of the tools logo and replace it with your own logo.

- **A wider range of question types.** Most free survey creators offer plenty of question options, including multiple choice radio buttons, drop downs, rating scales, and others. Usually paid versions offer more options such as the ability to select multiple options in a drop down menu, star rankings, grids, and others.

Using any of these tools you could create and publish your own survey. Then you are left with the issue of getting people to take your survey. This can be via an email list, where invitations are sent to people on the list, or you could use an online panel like the ones discussed below.

Google Consumer Surveys Google has entered the do-it-yourself web survey arena. It does this in a rather unique manner (see https://marketingplatform.google.com/about/surveys/). Certain websites host premium content that usually requires a subscription or access fee. With Google Consumer Surveys, however, a visitor can gain access to the premium content by answering a couple of questions instead of paying the fee. Surveys are limited to 10 questions. The first is typically a screening question such as, "Have you purchased anything online in the past 90 days?" The remaining questions are more substantive, such as "Which promotion would you be most interested in—free shipping, 15 percent off, free

Get results in three simple steps.

> Web survey systems enable the researcher to query the survey at any time to examine survey results to date.

returns, or saving $25 on your next purchase of $150?" Basic demographic and location information are inferred from Google's database of big data. Google Consumer Surveys are fast and cheap, and the Pew Research Center has found that Google's sample both conforms closely to the overall Internet population and is not biased toward heavy Internet users.[10]

Online Panel Providers Often, researchers use online panel providers for a ready-made sample population. Online panel providers such as Survey Sampling International and e-Rewards pre-recruit people who agree to participate in online market research surveys.

Some online panels are created for specific industries and may have a few thousand panel members, while the large commercial online panels have millions of people waiting to be surveyed. When people join online panels, they answer an extensive profiling questionnaire that enables the panel provider to target research efforts to panel members who meet specific criteria.

In addition to effective panel recruitment, online panel providers must have effective ongoing management of their panel to ensure a high level of quality. Panels must continually see that their participants have positive experiences with every research project. Among other components, good panel management includes frequency controls to see that panel members are not surveyed too little or too much. Panel members should be given enough survey opportunities to stay effectively engaged in the research process, but not surveyed so much as to be burdened with survey invitations. Other keys to guaranteeing a positive experience for panel members is providing respondent privacy, safeguarding personal information, and protecting members from bogus research that attempts to use online surveys as a sales channel (this is the practice of *sugging*—selling under the guise of research).

Panel providers are continually recruiting new members to keep up with the growth in demand for online samples, as well as replacing any panel members who may drop out. Even with exceptional panel member retention, some panel members will become less active in responding to surveys. In addition, panels will often recruit new members to assist in growing certain hard-to-reach segments and/or balancing the panel to have maximum representation of the overall population. Ensuring a growing supply of engaged, active panel members is a constant goal of every panel provider.

Finally, panel management includes ensuring panel freshness. As panel members change, their profiles must be updated. A single, 25-year-old college student with an annual income of $12,000 from last year may now be a married 26-year-old accountant with a new baby and a household income of $45,000. Updating profiles ensures that panel providers are able to consistently target qualified people for surveys.[11] Some panel providers are now using marketing analytics and big data to compose a much more detailed profile of all of their panel members.[12]

ONLINE FOCUS GROUPS A number of research firms are currently conducting focus groups online. The process is fairly simple. The research firm builds a database of respondents via a screening questionnaire on its website. When a client comes to a firm with a need for a particular focus group, the firm goes to its database and identifies individuals who appear to qualify. It sends an email to these individuals, asking them to log on to a particular site at a particular time scheduled for the group. Many times, these groups are joined by respondents on mobile devices. The firm pays them an incentive for their participation.

The firm develops a discussion guide similar to the one used for a conventional focus group, and a moderator runs the group by typing in questions online for all to see. The group operates in an environment similar to that of a chat room so that all participants see all questions and all responses. The firm captures the complete text of the focus group and makes it available for review after the group has finished.

Online focus groups also allow respondents to view things such as a concept statement, a mockup of a print ad, or a short product demonstration video. The moderator simply provides a URL for the respondents to open in another browser window..

More advanced virtual focus group software reserves a frame (section) of the screen for stimuli to be shown. Here, the moderator has control over what is shown in the stimulus area. Many online groups are now conducted with audio and video feeds as well. One advantage of this approach is that the respondent does not have to do any work to see the stimuli. There are many other advantages of online groups:

- **Better participation rates:** Typically, online focus groups can be conducted over the course of days; once participants are recruited, they are less likely to drop out because of time conflicts.

- **Cost-effectiveness:** Face-to-face focus groups incur costs for facility rental, airfare, hotel, and food. None of these costs is incurred with online focus groups.

- **Broad geographic scope:** Time is flexible online; respondents can be gathered from all over the world.

- **Accessibility:** Online focus groups allow access to individuals who otherwise might be difficult to recruit (e.g., business travelers, senior executives, mothers with infants).

ONLINE RESEARCH COMMUNITIES An online research community is a carefully selected group of consumers who agree to participate in an ongoing dialogue with a particular corporation. All community interaction takes place on a custom-designed website. During the life of the community—which may last anywhere from six months to a year or more—community members respond to questions posed by the corporation on a regular basis. In addition to responding to the corporation's questions, community members talk to one another about topics that are of interest to them.

Hyatt used a community of travel enthusiasts from the United States, Britain, France, Australia, Chile, and Mexico to gain insights about various travel-related topics. Hyatt learned, for example, that sampling local cuisine is one of the best parts of business travelers' trips and that women do the majority of packing for family vacations. After several travelers expressed an interest in selecting their rooms online, Hyatt launched an initiative examining what it might take to add that functionality to its system. When Procter & Gamble (P&G) was developing scents for a new product line, it asked members of its online community to record the scents that they encountered over the course of a day that made them feel good. By week's end, P&G had received images, videos, and simple text tributes to cut grass, fresh paint, Play Dough, and other aromas that revealed volumes about how scent triggers not just nostalgia, but also feelings of competence, adventurousness, comfort, and other powerful emotions.

Mobile research is extremely popular among marketers today. In fact, mobile traffic now accounts for about half of all interview responses.

9-4 THE GROWING IMPORTANCE OF MOBILE RESEARCH

Most Americans who have a mobile phone have a smartphone. Because so many people are connected through their phones, mobile phones are a natural vehicle for conducting marketing research surveys. In fact, mobile survey traffic now accounts for about half of all interview responses.[13] Sixty-eight percent of U.S. marketing research firms currently conduct mobile research surveys, and an additional 25 percent are considering doing so.[14]

Mobile surveys are designed to fit into the brief cracks of time that open up when a person waits for a plane, is early for an appointment, commutes to work on a train, or stands in a line. Marketers strive to engage respondents "in the moment" because mobile research provides immediate feedback when a consumer makes a decision to purchase, consumes a product, or experiences some form of promotion. With mobile research, participants can not only send and respond to direct and immediate questions but also share the videos, photos, stories, and moments that are important to them. As new and better apps make the survey experience easier and more intuitive, the use of mobile surveys will continue to rise. New responsive-design technology automatically adjusts the content and navigation of a website to fit the dimensions and resolution of any screen it is viewed on.

scanner-based research a system for gathering information from a single group of respondents by continuously monitoring the advertising, promotion, and pricing they are exposed to and the things they buy

One advertiser wanted to conduct a survey on the televised advertisements that ran during the Super Bowl. The client wanted to measure real-time reactions, but most people do not sit in front of their desktop computers during the big game. They do, however, multitask using their smartphones. Respondents were recruited in advance of game day, and then during the game, surveys were pushed out in real time to collect feedback on commercials as they aired.

Mobile research offers several advantages in addition to real-time reactions:

- *Increased response rates.* Respondents respond at higher rates (and more quickly) on mobile devices.

- *Increased convenience.* Respondents have better experiences when they can provide feedback when and where they want to.

- *Broader reach.* The ability to reach respondents in developing and remote countries creates a huge opportunity to capture insights from those regions.

- *Richer content.* Respondents can easily share media (e.g., photos, videos, voice recordings) via mobile devices.

- *Broader demographic reach.* Respondent cooperation from all demographic groups is higher.

- *Immediate feedback.* Mobile surveys provide immediate feedback on research questions concerning marketing campaigns, ad testing, and more.

- *Cost savings.* Researchers receive faster replies to surveys, shortening project completion time.

- *Additional options.* Can be used as a mobile recruiting tool to direct respondents to online surveys, or connect with hard-to-reach groups. It is another way of reaching people on the go.[15]

9-5 SCANNER-BASED RESEARCH

Scanner-based research is a system for gathering information from respondents by continuously monitoring the advertising, promotion, and pricing they are exposed to and the things they buy. Scanner-based research also entails the aggregation of scanner data from retailers, analysis, and identification of sales trends by industry, company, product line, and individual brand. The variables measured are advertising campaigns, coupons, displays, and product prices. The result is a huge database of marketing efforts and consumer behavior.

The two major scanner-based suppliers are SymphonyIRI Group Inc. and the Nielsen Company. Each has about half the market, but SymphonyIRI is the founder of scanner-based research. SymphonyIRI's **InfoScan** is a scanner-based sales-tracking service for the consumer packaged-goods industry. Retail sales, detailed consumer purchasing information (including measurement of store loyalty and total grocery basket expenditures), and promotional activity by manufacturers and retailers are monitored and evaluated for all bar-coded products. Data are collected weekly from supermarkets, drugstores, and mass merchandisers.

Some companies have begun using neuromarketing to study microscopic changes in skin moisture, heart rate, brain waves, and other biometrics to see how consumers react to things such as package designs and ads. **Neuromarketing** is the process of researching brain patterns and measuring certain physiological responses to marketing stimuli. It is a fresh attempt to better understand consumers' responses to promotion and purchase motivations.

9-6 WHEN SHOULD MARKETING RESEARCH BE CONDUCTED?

When managers have several possible solutions to a problem, they should not instinctively call for marketing research. In fact, the first decision to make is whether to conduct marketing research at all.

Some companies have been conducting research in certain markets for many years. Such firms understand the characteristics of target customers and their likes and dislikes about existing products. Under these circumstances, further research would be repetitive and waste money. P&G, for example, has extensive knowledge of the coffee market. After it conducted initial taste tests with Folgers Instant Coffee, P&G went into national distribution without further research. Sara Lee followed the same strategy with its frozen croissants, as did Quaker Oats with Chewy Granola Bars. This tactic, however, can backfire. Marketers may think they understand a particular market thoroughly and so bypass market research for a product, only to have the product fail and be withdrawn from the market.

If information were available and free, managers would rarely refuse more, but because marketing information can require a great deal of time and expense to accumulate, they might decide to forgo additional information. Ultimately, the willingness to acquire

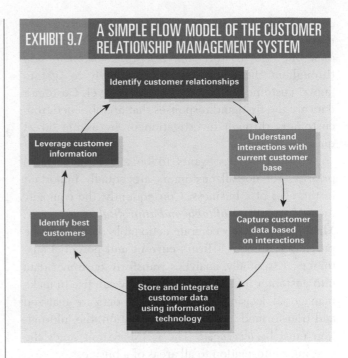

EXHIBIT 9.7 A SIMPLE FLOW MODEL OF THE CUSTOMER RELATIONSHIP MANAGEMENT SYSTEM

additional decision-making information depends on managers' perceptions of its quality, price, and timing. Research should be undertaken only when the expected value of the information is greater than the cost of obtaining it.

9-6a Customer Relationship Management

Recall from the beginning of the chapter that databases and big data play a key role in marketing decision making. A key subset of data management systems is a customer relationship management (CRM) system. CRM was introduced in Chapters 1 and 8. The key to managing relationships with customers is the CRM cycle (Exhibit 9.7).

To initiate the CRM cycle, a company must *identify customer relationships with the organization*. This may simply entail learning who the customers are or where they are located, or it may require more detailed information about the products and services they are using. Next, the company must *understand the interactions with current customers*. Companies accomplish this by collecting data on all types of communications a customer has with the company.

Using this knowledge of its customers and their interactions, the company then *captures relevant*

InfoScan a scanner-based sales-tracking service for the consumer packaged-goods industry

neuromarketing a field of marketing that studies the body's responses to marketing stimuli *customer data on interactions*. Big data analytics are used not only to enhance the collection of customer data but also to *store and integrate customer data* throughout the company, and ultimately to "get to know" customers on a more personal level. Customer data are the firsthand responses that are obtained from customers through investigation or by asking direct questions.

Every customer wants to be a company's main priority. Yet not all customers are equally important in the eyes of a business. Consequently, the company must *identify its profitable and unprofitable customers*. Marketing analytics compile actionable data about the purchase habits of a firm's current and potential customers. Essentially, analytics transform customer data into customer information a company can use to make managerial decisions. Once customer data are analyzed and transformed into usable information, the information must be *leveraged*. The CRM system sends the customer information to all areas of a business because the customer interacts with all aspects of the business. Essentially, the company is trying to enhance customer relationships by getting the right information to the right person in the right place at the right time.

> **competitive intelligence (CI)** an intelligence system that helps managers assess their competition and vendors in order to become more efficient and effective competitors

9-7 COMPETITIVE INTELLIGENCE

Derived from military intelligence, competitive intelligence is an important tool for helping a firm overcome a competitor's advantage. Specifically, competitive intelligence can help identify the advantage and play a major role in determining how it was achieved. It also helps a firm identify areas where it can achieve its own competitive advantages.

Competitive intelligence (CI) helps managers assess their competitors and their vendors in order to become more efficient and effective competitors. *Intelligence* is analyzed information. It becomes decision-making intelligence when it has implications for the organization. For example, a primary competitor may have plans to introduce a product with performance standards equal to those of the company gathering the information, but with a 15 percent cost advantage. The new product will reach the market in eight months. This intelligence has important decision-making and policy consequences for management. CI and environmental scanning (see Chapter 2) combine to create marketing intelligence.

The Internet is an important resource for gathering CI, but noncomputer sources can be equally valuable. Some examples include company salespeople, industry experts, CI consultants, government agencies, Uniform Commercial Code filings, suppliers, periodicals, the Yellow Pages, and industry trade shows.

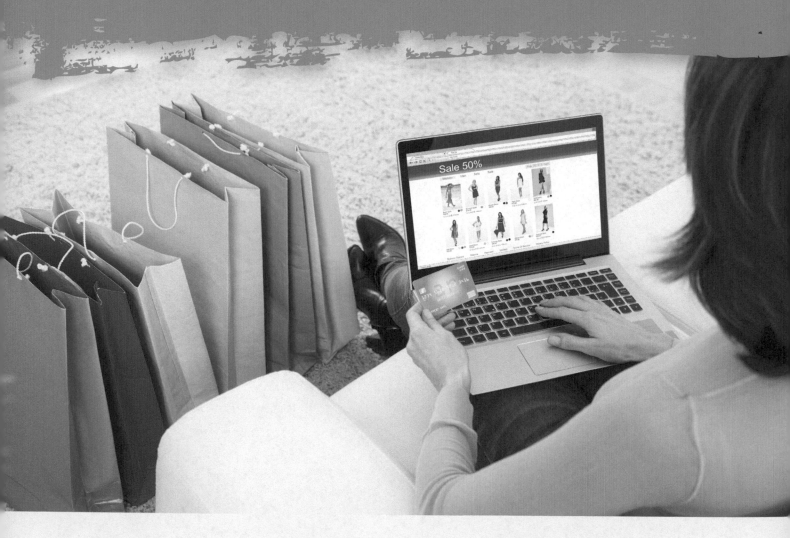

10 | Product Concepts

LEARNING OUTCOMES

After studying this chapter, you will be able to…

10-1 Define the term *product*

10-2 Classify consumer products

10-3 Define the terms *product item, product line,* and *product mix*

10-4 Describe marketing uses of branding

10-5 Describe marketing uses of packaging and labeling

10-6 Discuss global issues in branding and packaging

10-7 Describe how and why product warranties are important marketing tools

10-1 WHAT IS A PRODUCT?

The product offering, the heart of an organization's marketing program, is usually the starting point in creating a marketing mix. A marketing manager cannot determine a price, design a promotion strategy, or create a distribution channel until the firm has a product to sell. Moreover, an excellent distribution channel, a persuasive promotion campaign, and a fair price have no value when the product offering is poor or inadequate.

A **product** may be defined as everything, both favorable and unfavorable, that a person receives in an exchange. A product may be a tangible good like a pair of shoes, a service like a haircut, an idea like "don't litter," or any combination of these three. Packaging, style, color, options, and size are some typical product features. Just as important are intangibles such as service, the seller's image, the manufacturer's reputation, and the way consumers believe others will view the product.

To most people, the term *product* means a tangible good. However, services and ideas are also products. (Chapter 12 focuses specifically on the unique aspects of marketing services.) The marketing process identified in Chapter 1 is the same whether the product marketed is a good, a service, an idea, or some combination of these.

10-2 TYPES OF CONSUMER PRODUCTS

Products can be classified as either business (industrial) or consumer, depending on the buyer's intentions. The key distinction between the two types of products is their intended use. If the intended use is a business purpose, the product is classified as a business or industrial product. As explained in Chapter 7, a business product is used to manufacture other goods or services, to facilitate an organization's operations, or to resell to other customers. A consumer product is bought to satisfy an individual's personal wants or needs. Sometimes the same item can be classified as either a business or a consumer product, depending on its intended use. Examples include light bulbs, pencils and paper, and computers.

We need to know about product classifications because business and consumer products are marketed differently. They are marketed to different target markets and tend to use different distribution, promotion, and pricing strategies.

Chapter 7 examined seven categories of business products: major equipment, accessory equipment, component parts, processed materials, raw materials, supplies, and services. This chapter examines an effective way of categorizing consumer products. Although there are several ways to classify them, the most popular approach includes these four types: convenience products, shopping products, specialty products, and unsought products. This approach classifies products according to how much effort is normally used to shop for them.

10-2a Convenience Products

A **convenience product** is a relatively inexpensive item that merits little shopping effort—that is, a consumer is unwilling to shop extensively for such an item. Candy, soft drinks, aspirin, small hardware items, dry cleaning, and car washes fall into the convenience product category.

Consumers buy convenience products regularly, usually without much planning. Nevertheless, consumers do know the brand names of popular convenience products, such as Coca-Cola, Bayer aspirin, and Old Spice deodorant. Convenience products normally require wide distribution in order to sell sufficient quantities to meet profit goals. For example, the gum brand Extra is available everywhere, including Walmart, Walgreens, gas stations, newsstands, and vending machines.

> A marketing manager cannot determine a price, design a promotion strategy, or create a distribution channel until the firm has a product to sell.

product everything, both favorable and unfavorable, that a person receives in an exchange

convenience product a relatively inexpensive item that merits little shopping effort

CHAPTER 10: Product Concepts

10-2b Shopping Products

A **shopping product** is usually more expensive than a convenience product and is found in fewer stores. Consumers usually buy a shopping product only after comparing several brands or stores on style, practicality, price, and lifestyle compatibility. They are willing to invest some effort into this process to get the desired benefits.

There are two types of shopping products: homogeneous and heterogeneous. Consumers perceive *homogeneous* shopping products as basically similar—for example, washers, dryers, refrigerators, and televisions. With homogeneous shopping products, consumers typically look for the lowest-priced brand that has the desired features. For example, they might compare Kenmore, Whirlpool, and General Electric refrigerators.

In contrast, consumers perceive *heterogeneous* shopping products as essentially different—for example, furniture, clothing, housing, and universities. Consumers often have trouble comparing heterogeneous shopping products because the prices, quality, and features vary so much. The benefit of comparing heterogeneous shopping products is "finding the best product or brand for me"; this decision is often highly individual. For example, it would be difficult to compare a small, private college with a large, public university, or Ikea with La-Z-Boy.

10-2c Specialty Products

When consumers search extensively for a particular item and are very reluctant to accept substitutes, that item is a **specialty product**. Omega watches, Rolls-Royce automobiles, Bose speakers, Ruth's Chris Steak House, and highly specialized forms of medical care are generally considered specialty products.

Marketers of specialty products often use selective, status-conscious advertising to maintain a product's exclusive image. Distribution is often limited to one or a very few outlets in a geographic area. Brand names and quality of service are often very important.

Custom built homes are specialty items.

Reinhardt and Co/Shutterstock.com

10-2d Unsought Products

A product unknown to the potential buyer or a known product that the buyer does not actively seek is referred to as an **unsought product**. New products fall into this category until advertising and distribution increase consumer awareness of them.

Some goods are always marketed as unsought items, especially needed products we do not like to think about or care to spend money on. Insurance, burial plots, and similar items require aggressive personal selling and highly persuasive advertising. Salespeople actively seek leads to potential buyers. Because consumers usually do not seek out this type of product, the company must go directly to them through a salesperson, direct mail, or direct response advertising.

10-3 PRODUCT ITEMS, LINES, AND MIXES

Rarely does a company sell a single product. More often, it sells a variety of things. A **product item** is a specific version of a product that can be designated as a distinct offering among an organization's products. Coca-Cola's Sprite is an example of a product item (see Exhibit 10.1).

A group of closely related product items is called a **product line**. For example, the column in Exhibit 10.1 titled "Soft Drinks" represents one of Coca-Cola's product lines. Different container sizes and shapes also distinguish items in a product line. Coca-Cola, for example, is available in cans and various plastic containers. Each size and each container are separate product items.

shopping product
a product that requires comparison shopping because it is usually more expensive than a convenience product and is found in fewer stores

specialty product
a particular item for which consumers search extensively and are very reluctant to accept substitutes

unsought product a product unknown to the potential buyer or a known product that the buyer does not actively seek

product item a specific version of a product that can be designated as a distinct offering among an organization's products

product line a group of closely related product items

EXHIBIT 10.1 COCA-COLA COMPANY'S PRODUCT LINES AND PRODUCT MIX

	Width of the Product Mix				
	Soft Drinks	**Juice**	**Water**	**Sports Drinks**	**Tea**
	Coca-Cola Coca-Cola Vanilla	Minute Maid Orange Juice	Aquarius	Powerade	Fuze
	Sprite	Simply Orange	Dasani	Powerade Zero	Gold Peak sweetened
	Barq's Root Beer	Odwalla Smoothie	Dasani Sparkling		Gold Peak unsweetened
	Fresca	Honest Kids	Smartwater		Honest Tea Lemon
	Fanta		Vitamin Water		Honest Tea Raspberry

Depth of the Product Lines

Somchai Som/Shutterstock.com

An organization's **product mix** includes all the products it sells. All Coca-Cola's products—soft drinks, juices, waters, sports drinks, teas, and more—constitute its product mix. Each product item in the product mix may require a separate marketing strategy.

In some cases, however, product lines and even entire product mixes share some marketing strategy components. For example, UPS promotes its various services by demonstrating its commitment to helping customers with the tagline "United Problem Solvers." Organizations derive several benefits from organizing related items into product lines:

- **Advertising economies:** Product lines provide economies of scale in advertising. Several products can be advertised under the umbrella of the line. Coca-Cola can use the slogan "Open Happiness" to promote the entire line.

- **Package uniformity:** A product line can benefit from package uniformity. All packages in the line may have a common look and still keep their individual identities. Coca-Cola's soda packaging is again a good example. Coca-Cola Classic, Diet Coke, and Coke Zero all share certain colors and design elements, but each is recognizably unique.

- **Standardized components:** Product lines allow firms to standardize components, thus reducing manufacturing and inventory costs. For example, General Motors uses the same parts on many automobile makes and models.

- **Efficient sales and distribution:** A product line enables sales personnel for companies like Procter &

Gamble to provide a full range of choices to customers. Distributors and retailers are often more inclined to stock the company's products if it offers a full line. Transportation and warehousing costs are likely to be lower for a product line than for a collection of individual items.

- **Equivalent quality:** Purchasers usually expect and believe that all products in a line are about equal in quality. Consumers expect that all Campbell's soups and all Gillette razors will be of similar quality.

Product mix width (or breadth) refers to the number of product lines an organization offers. In Exhibit 10.1, for example, the width of Coca-Cola's product mix is five product lines. **Product line depth** is the number of product items in a product line. As shown in Exhibit 10.1, the sports drink product line consists of two product items; the water product line includes five product items.

Firms increase the *width* of their product mix to diversify risk. To generate sales and boost profits, firms spread risk across many product lines rather than depending on only one or two. Firms also widen their product mix to capitalize on established reputations. For example, leading fitness wear manufacturer Under Armour recently added a wearable activity tracker to its product mix. Called the Health-Box, this device analyzes sleep, daily activity, workout intensity, and weight.

product mix all products that an organization sells

product mix width the number of product lines an organization offers

product line depth the number of product items in a product line

The Galaxy TAB Nook 9 is a product item.

The company is working to widen its product mix across the industry of health and fitness.[1]

Firms increase the *depth* of their product lines to attract buyers with different preferences, to increase sales and profits by further segmenting the market, to capitalize on economies of scale in production and marketing, and to even out seasonal sales patterns.

10-3a Adjustments to Product Items, Lines, and Mixes

Over time, firms change product items, lines, and mixes to take advantage of new technical or product developments or to respond to changes in the environment. They may adjust by modifying products, repositioning products, or extending or contracting product lines.

product modification
changing one or more of a product's characteristics

PRODUCT MODIFICATION Marketing managers must decide if and when to modify existing products. **Product modification** is a change in one or more of a product's characteristics:

- **Quality modification:** a change in a product's dependability or durability. Reducing a product's quality may let the manufacturer lower the price and appeal to target markets unable to afford the original product. Conversely, increasing quality can help the firm compete with rival firms. For example, Barnes & Noble offers a color version of its Nook that runs Android apps, allowing it to compete with tablet and laptop makers such as Microsoft and Apple. Increasing quality can also result in increased brand loyalty, greater ability to raise prices, or new opportunities for market segmentation.

- **Functional modification:** a change in a product's versatility, effectiveness, convenience, or safety.

Within the product image area (as shown): Samsung Galaxy Tab E NOOK 9.6 by Barnes & Noble, ★★★½☆ 33 Reviews | Read Reviews, $199.99, bullet list (Just right in size, versatility, and price; Best for movies and magazines; Spacious 9.6" display for landscape or portrait reading; Personalize your experience with Profiles; Members save 10% off all NOOK tablets, eReaders, and accessories), Ship This Item — Qualifies for Free Shipping, PROTECT YOUR NOOK - $49.99, ADD TO CART. Source: Barnes & Noble, Inc.

Oil-Dri Corporation of America, a leading manufacturer of quality cat litter, recently introduced Cat's Pride Fresh & Light Ultimate Care litter. This product has a unique formula that is 50 percent lighter than other litters and features 10-day odor control, ultra-strong clumping, and dust-free scooping.[2]

- **Style modification:** an aesthetic (how the product looks) product change rather than a quality or functional change. Clothing and auto manufacturers commonly use style modifications to motivate customers to replace products before they are worn out.

Planned obsolescence is a term commonly used to describe the practice of modifying products so that those that have already been sold become obsolete before they actually need replacement. For example, products such as printers and cell phones become obsolete because technology changes so quickly.

Some argue that planned obsolescence is wasteful; some claim it is unethical. Marketers respond that consumers favor style modifications because they like changes in the appearance of goods such as clothing and cars. Marketers also contend that consumers, not manufacturers and marketers, decide when styles are obsolete.

REPOSITIONING Repositioning, as Chapter 8 explained, involves changing consumers' perceptions of a brand. SeaWorld, one of America's leading tourist attractions, received negative publicity from the documentary film *Blackfish*, which exposed how the company trained and treated orcas. As a result, the company decided to phase out orca breeding and end the stunt-based shows featuring these animals. SeaWorld repositioned its brand toward preserving and protecting sea creatures and made animal care and sensitivity to wildlife central to its mission. Now, orcas at SeaWorld are presented in naturalistic settings rather than in theatrical shows.[3]

Changing demographics, declining sales, changes in the social environment, and competition often motivate a firm to reposition an established brand. In order to better compete in the health and wellness category, Weight Watchers has rebranded itself as WW, and overhauled its products and services to focus more on healthy living than on weight loss alone. This repositioning includes a new logo, color palette, corporate images, and the slogan "Wellness that works." A new program was created called "WellnessWins," which rewards members for tracking their meals, physical activity, weight, and workshop attendance. These actions qualify for "wins" that can be exchanged for exclusive products, services, and experiences designed to inspire members on their wellness journey."[4]

PRODUCT LINE EXTENSIONS A product line extension occurs when a company's management decides to add products to an existing product line in order to compete more broadly in the industry. Yogurt maker Chobani recently introduced a dessert-style product called Flip, which includes flavors such as Peppermint Perfection and Cinnabun Fun. The company also recently rolled out new yogurt-based drinks.[5]

A company can add too many products, or over time demand can change for the type of products that were introduced. When this happens, a product line is overextended. Product lines can be overextended when:

- Some products in the line do not contribute to profits because of low sales or they cannibalize sales of other items in the line.

- Manufacturing or marketing resources are disproportionately allocated to slow-moving products.

- Some items in the line are obsolete because of new-product entries in the line or new products offered by competitors.

PRODUCT LINE CONTRACTION Sometimes marketers can get carried away with product extensions. (Does the world really need 31 varieties of Head & Shoulders shampoo?) Contracting product lines is a strategic way to deal with overextension. In early 2016, Toyota axed Scion, which the company had positioned as a "youth" brand. Scion helped Toyota attract younger buyers (with an average age of 36), but the company failed to clearly differentiate Scion from its other small cars. Toyota did not provide enough marketing support to generate a critical sales mass, and what marketing there was focused on fuel economy and price—not enough to give Scion a competitive differentiation, particularly as gas prices plummeted.[6]

Indeed, three major benefits are likely when a firm contracts an overextended product line. First, resources become concentrated on the most important products. Second, managers no longer waste resources trying to improve the sales and profits of poorly performing products. Third, new-product items have a greater chance of being successful because more financial and human resources are available to manage them.

planned obsolescence the practice of modifying products so those that have already been sold become obsolete before they actually need replacement

product line extension adding additional products to an existing product line in order to compete more broadly in the industry

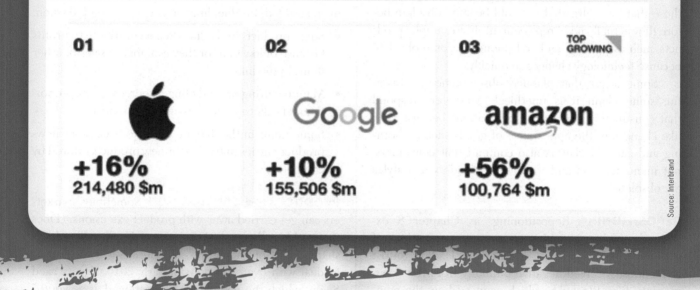

Interbrand's Best Global Brands

In 2018, Interbrand announced that Apple, Google, and Amazon were the top three most valuable brands in the world. For six consecutive years, Apple and Google have held the top positions. Apple's brand value grew by $215 billion and Google's brand value grew by $155 billion. Other brands in the Top 10 were Microsoft, Coca-Cola, Samsung, Toyota, Mercedes-Benz, Facebook, and McDonald's. More than half of the 100 Best Global Brands came from five industry sectors: Automotive, Financial Services, Luxury, and Fast-Moving Consumer Goods. Luxury was the Top Growing Sector in percentage terms, followed by Retail. The combined total value of the Top 100 crossed the $2 billion mark—an increase of almost 8% from 2017.[7]

01

+16%
214,480 $m

02

Google

+10%
155,506 $m

03 TOP GROWING

amazon

+56%
100,764 $m

Source: Interbrand

10-4 BRANDING

The success of any business or consumer product depends in part on the target market's ability to distinguish one product from another. Branding is the main tool marketers use to distinguish their products from those of the competition.

A **brand** is a name, term, symbol, design, or combination thereof that identifies a seller's products and differentiates them from competitors' products. A **brand name** is that part of a brand that can be spoken, including letters (GM, YMCA), words (Chevrolet), and numbers (WD-40, 7-Eleven). The elements of a brand that cannot be spoken are called the **brand mark**—for example, the well-known Mercedes-Benz and Nike symbols.

10-4a Benefits of Branding

Branding has three main purposes: product identification, repeat sales, and new-product sales. The most important purpose is *product identification*. Branding allows marketers to distinguish their products from all others. Many brand names are familiar to consumers and indicate quality.

The term **brand equity** refers to the value of a company or brand name. A brand that has high awareness, perceived quality, and brand loyalty among customers has high brand equity—a valuable asset indeed. See Exhibit 10.2 for some classic examples of companies that leverage their brand equity to the fullest.

brand a name, term, symbol, design, or combination thereof that identifies a seller's products and differentiates them from competitors' products

brand name that part of a brand that can be spoken, including letters, words, and numbers

brand mark the elements of a brand that cannot be spoken

brand equity the value of a company or brand name

The term **global brand** refers to a brand that obtains at least one-third of its earnings from outside its home country, is recognizable outside its home base of customers, and has publicly available marketing and financial data. Yum! Brands, which owns Pizza Hut, KFC, and Taco Bell, is a good example of a company that has developed strong global brands. Yum! management believes that it must adapt its restaurants to local tastes and different cultural and political climates. In Japan, for instance, KFC sells tempura crispy strips. In northern England, KFC focuses on gravy and potatoes, and in Thailand, it offers rice with soy or sweet chili sauce.

The best generator of *repeat sales* is satisfied customers. Branding helps consumers identify products they wish to buy again and avoid those they do not. **Brand loyalty**, a consistent preference for one brand over all others, is quite high in some product categories. More than half the consumers in product categories such as cigarettes, mayonnaise, toothpaste, coffee, headache remedies, bath soap, and ketchup are loyal to one brand. Many students go to college and purchase the same brands they used at home rather than choosing by price. Brand identity is essential to developing brand loyalty.

The third main purpose of branding is to *facilitate new-product sales*. Having a well-known and respected company and brand name is extremely useful when introducing new products.

10-4b Branding Strategies

Firms face complex branding decisions. They may choose to follow a policy of using manufacturers' brands, private (distributor) brands, or both. In either case, they must then decide among a policy of individual branding (different brands for different products), family branding (common names for different products), or a combination of individual branding and family branding.

Taco Bell is a global brand.

EXHIBIT 10.2	THE POWER OF BRAND EQUITY
Product Category	**Dominant Brand Name**
Children's Entertainment	Disney
Laundry Detergent	Tide
Tablet Computer	Apple
Toothpaste	Crest
Microprocessor	Intel
Soup	Campbell's
Bologna	Oscar Mayer
Ketchup	Heinz
Bleach	Clorox
Greeting Cards	Hallmark
Overnight Mail	FedEx
Copiers	Xerox
Gelatin	Jell-O
Hamburgers	McDonald's
Baby Lotion	Johnson & Johnson
Tissues	Kleenex
Acetaminophen	Tylenol
Coffee	Starbucks
Information Search	Google

MANUFACTURERS' BRANDS VERSUS PRIVATE BRANDS The brand name of a manufacturer—such as Coca-Cola, La-Z-Boy, and Fruit of the Loom—is called a **manufacturer's brand**. Sometimes "national brand" is used as a synonym for "manufacturer's brand," but this term is not always accurate because many manufacturers serve only regional markets. Using "manufacturer's brand" precisely defines the brand's owner.

A **private brand**, also known as a private label or store brand, is a brand name owned by a wholesaler or a retailer. Private labels tend to be more successful in markets where product differentiation is low. Many food and beverage products are privately branded, for example. In this market, consumers no longer see private brands as low-cost, low-quality products. Research by the Food Marketing

global brand a brand that obtains at least a one-third of its earnings from outside its home country, is recognizable outside its home base of customers, and has publicly available marketing and financial data

brand loyalty consistent preference for one brand over all others

manufacturer's brand the brand name of a manufacturer

private brand a brand name owned by a wholesaler or a retailer

EXHIBIT 10.3 COMPARISON OF MANUFACTURER'S AND PRIVATE BRANDS FROM THE RESELLER'S PERSPECTIVE

Key Advantages of Carrying Manufacturers' Brands	Key Advantages of Carrying Private Brands
• Heavy advertising to the consumer by manufacturers such as Procter & Gamble helps develop strong consumer loyalties.	• A wholesaler or retailer can usually earn higher profits on its own brand. In addition, because the private brand is exclusive, there is less pressure to mark down the price to meet competition.
• Well-known manufacturers' brands, such as Kodak and Fisher-Price, can attract new customers and enhance the dealer's (wholesaler's or retailer's) prestige.	• A manufacturer can decide to drop a brand or a reseller at any time or even become a direct competitor to its dealers.
• Many manufacturers offer rapid delivery, enabling the dealer to carry less inventory.	• A private brand ties the customer to the wholesaler or retailer. A person who wants a DieHard battery must go to Sears.
• If a dealer happens to sell a manufacturer's brand of poor quality, the customer may simply switch brands and remain loyal to the dealer.	• Wholesalers and retailers have no control over the intensity of distribution of manufacturers' brands. Walmart store managers don't have to worry about competing with other sellers of Sam's American Choice products or Ol' Roy dog food. They know that these brands are sold only in Walmart and Sam's Club stores.

Institute found that 69 percent of consumers said it's important for retailers to have a good assortment of private brands in food and beverage. In fact, 53 percent of consumers were found to use store brands to determine where they shop.[8] Sensing these trends, Amazon has created over 125 private-brands, including apparel, batteries, lighting, computer cables, paper shredders, and pet products to name a few.[9]

Retailers love consumers' greater acceptance of private brands. Because overhead is low and there are no marketing costs, private-label products bring 10 percent higher profit margins, on average, than manufacturers' brands. More than that, a trusted store brand can differentiate a chain from its competitors. Exhibit 10.3 illustrates key issues that wholesalers and retailers should consider in deciding whether to sell manufacturers' brands or private brands. Many firms offer a combination of both.

Instead of marketing private brands as cheaper and inferior to manufacturers' brands, many retailers are creating and promoting their own **captive brands**. These brands carry no evidence of the store's affiliation, are manufactured by a third party, and are sold exclusively at the chains. This strategy allows the retailer to ask a price similar or equal to manufacturers' brands, and the captive brands are typically displayed alongside mainstream products. This strategy is particularly important as Millennials come to dominate the grocery shopping arena. One study found that members of this group are more loyal to their stores of choice than their parents were. They are well informed about where specific brands and foods come from, read labels, are equally aware of national brands and store brands, and look for good value. Millennials also desire products that are clean, natural, and organic. H-E-B, a large grocery chain in Texas, has introduced the Select Ingredients line, which eliminates more than 200 synthetic ingredients from its products. The company hopes this new line will be a hit among Millennials.[10] Similarly, Kroger has seen continuing growth of its Simple Truth and Simple Truth Organic lines of private label products.[11]

INDIVIDUAL BRANDS VERSUS FAMILY BRANDS

Many companies use different brand names for different products, a practice referred to as **individual branding**. Companies use individual brands when their products vary greatly in use or performance. For instance, it would not make sense to use the same brand name for a pair of dress socks and a baseball bat. Procter & Gamble targets different segments of the laundry detergent market with Bold, Cheer, Dash, Dreft, Era, Gain, and Tide.

By contrast, a company that markets several different products under the same brand name is practicing **family branding**. Jack Daniel's family brand includes whiskey, coffee, barbeque sauce, heat-and-serve meat products like brisket and pulled pork, mustard, playing cards, and clothing lines.

CO-BRANDING Co-branding entails placing two or more brand names on a product or its package. Three common types of co-branding are ingredient branding, cooperative branding, and complementary branding. *Ingredient branding* identifies the brand of a part that makes up the product. For example, in 1975, Bonne Bell launched a Dr. Pepper-flavored Lip Smacker lip balm—a product

captive brand a brand manufactured by a third party for an exclusive retailer, without evidence of that retailer's affiliation

individual branding using different brand names for different products

family branding marketing several different products under the same brand name

co-branding placing two or more brand names on a product or its package

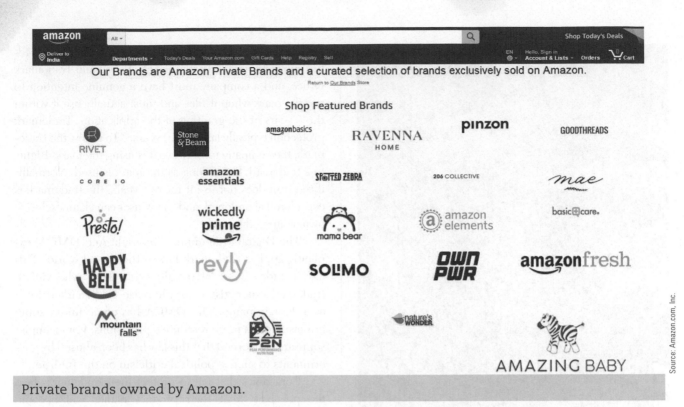

Our Brands are Amazon Private Brands and a curated selection of brands exclusively sold on Amazon.

Return to Our Brands Store

Shop Featured Brands

Private brands owned by Amazon.

that has been popular with teenage girls for decades.[12] *Cooperative branding* occurs when two brands receiving equal treatment (in the context of an advertisement) borrow from each other's brand equity. A promotional contest jointly sponsored by Ramada Inn, American Express, and United Airlines used cooperative branding. Guests at Ramada who paid with an American Express card were automatically entered in a contest and were eligible to win more than 100 getaways for two at any Ramada in the continental United States and round-trip airfare from United. Bruegger's Bagels and Jamba Juice have opened co-branded and co-operated locations across the country. "Pairing Bruegger's Bagels with [Jamba Juice parent company] Great Service Restaurants is a fantastic match," said Paul Carolan, chief development officer for Le Duff America, which owns Bruegger's Bagels. "Great Service Restaurants shares our passion for community, quality, and providing exceptional guest experiences."[13] Finally, with complementary branding, products are advertised or

Manufacturer's brands and private brands often compete for retail shelf space.

marketed together to suggest usage, such as a spirits brand (Seagram's) and a compatible mixer (7Up).

Co-branding is a useful strategy when a combination of brand names enhances the prestige or perceived value of a product or when it benefits brand owners and users. Co-branding may also be used to increase a company's presence in markets where it has little room to differentiate itself or has limited market share. For example, New York–based skater-punk brand Supreme and French luxury brand Louis Vuitton are teaming up to form a new menswear line called FW17. The collaboration will give Louis Vuitton some street cred among a new, younger customer base.[14]

The killing of George Floyd, an unarmed black man, by Minneapolis police in early 2020 sparked nationwide riots. As a result, some companies whose brands have origins in racist imagery of black people are rethinking these brands and marketing. PepsiCo will retire its Aunt Jemima brand, Mars will change its Uncle Ben's brand, and Conagra Brands plans to review its Mrs. Butterworth's bottle. NASCAR has banned the Confederate battle flag from its events.

10-4c Trademarks

A **trademark** is the exclusive right to use a brand or part of a brand. Others are prohibited from using the brand without permission. A **service mark** performs

> **trademark** the exclusive right to use a brand or part of a brand
>
> **service mark** a trademark for a service

Source: Amazon.com, Inc.

HodagMedia/Shutterstock.com

Empire star Terrance Howard at premier event.

the same function for services, such as H&R Block and Weight Watchers. Parts of a brand or other product identification may qualify for trademark protection. Some examples are:

- Sounds, such as the MGM lion's roar.

- Shapes, such as the Jeep front grille and the Coca-Cola bottle.

- Ornamental colors or designs, such as the decoration on Nike tennis shoes, the black-and-copper color combination of a Duracell battery, Levi's small tag on the left side of the rear pocket of its jeans, or the cutoff black cone on the top of Cross pens.

- Catchy phrases, such as BMW's "The Ultimate Driving Machine," McDonald's "I'm Lovin' It," and Nike's "Just Do It!"

- Abbreviations, such as Bud, Coke, or the Met.

It is important to understand that trademark

rights come from use rather than registration. An intent-to-use application is filed with the U.S. Patent and Trademark Office, and a company must have a genuine intention to use the mark when it files and must actually use it within three years of the granting of the application. Trademark protection typically lasts for 10 years.[15] To renew the trademark, the company must prove it is using the mark. Rights to a trademark last as long as the mark is used. Normally, if the firm does not use it for two years, the trademark is considered abandoned, and a new user can claim exclusive ownership of the mark.

The Digital Millennium Copyright Act (DMCA) explicitly applies trademark law to the digital world. This law includes financial penalties for those who violate trademarks or register an otherwise trademarked term as a domain name. The DMCA has come under some criticism for its more restrictive provisions. For example, some are concerned that this law has been abused by governments to silence political criticism on the Internet.[16]

Companies that fail to protect their trademarks face the possibility that their product names will become generic. A **generic product name** identifies a product by class or type and cannot be trademarked. Former brand names that were not sufficiently protected by their owners and were subsequently declared to be generic product names by U.S. courts include aspirin, cellophane, linoleum, thermos, kerosene, monopoly, cola, and shredded wheat.

Companies such as Rolls-Royce, Cross, Xerox, Levi Strauss, Frigidaire, and McDonald's aggressively enforce their trademarks. Rolls-Royce, Coca-Cola, and Xerox even run newspaper and magazine ads stating that their names are trademarks and should not be used as descriptive or generic terms. Television network Fox recently won a trademark victory for the name of hit show *Empire* against San Francisco–based hip-hop music company Empire. The

Knockoff retail outlets can be found in many parts of the world.

music company offered to recall the claim—that its brand was being tarnished by the show's portrayal of a music label run by a drug dealer who liked to murder his friends—for $8 million or for guest spots for their artists and $5 million. The judge who decided the case wrote that "'Empire' has genuine relevance to the *Empire* Series and it was not arbitrarily chosen to exploit Empire Distribution's fame."[17]

To try to stem the number of trademark infringements, violations carry steep penalties. But despite the risk of incurring a penalty, infringement lawsuits are still common. Serious conflict can occur when brand names resemble one another too closely. Tiffany & Co. recently sued Costco for trademark infringement after the warehouse club created display signage and other in-store marketing that used terms such as "Tiffany Setting" to describe non–Tiffany-brand diamond rings. Costco unsuccessfully argued that Tiffany has become a generic term, and had to pay Tiffany & Co. over $13 million in damages.[18]

Companies must also contend with fake or unauthorized brands. Knockoffs of trademarked clothing lines are easy to find in cheap shops all over the world, and loose imitations are found in some reputable department stores as well. Today, whole stores are faked in China. These stores are selling copied versions of brands such as Louis Vuitton, Prada, Apple, and New Balance. The offerings of these stores are unauthorized and their brands are fake. Above the door on one fake Louis Vuitton store, the "Louis" is spelled "Loius." In Beijing, a fake Apple store complete with automated iPhone check-ins and a faux Genius bar was shut down by local authorities.[19] In Europe, you can sue counterfeiters only if your brand, logo, or trademark is formally registered. Formal registration used to be required in each country in which a company sought protection. However, today a company can register its trademark in all European Union member countries with one application.

(10-5) PACKAGING

Packages have always served a practical function—that is, they hold contents together and protect goods as they move through the distribution channel. Today, however, packaging is also a container for promoting the product and making it easier and safer to use.

10-5a Packaging Functions

The three most important functions of packaging are to contain and protect products; promote products; and facilitate the storage, use, and convenience of products. A fourth function of packaging that is becoming increasingly important is to facilitate recycling and reduce environmental damage.

CONTAINING AND PROTECTING PRODUCTS The most obvious function of packaging is to contain products that are liquid, granular, or otherwise divisible. Packaging also enables manufacturers, wholesalers, and retailers to market products in specific quantities, such as ounces.

Physical protection is another obvious function of packaging. Most products are handled several times between the time they are manufactured, harvested, or otherwise produced and the time they are consumed or used. Many products are also shipped, stored, and inspected several times between production and consumption. Some, like milk, need to be refrigerated. Others, like beer, are sensitive to light. Still others, like medicines and bandages, need to be kept sterile. Packages protect products from breakage, evaporation, spillage, spoilage, light, heat, cold, infestation, and many other conditions.

PROMOTING PRODUCTS Packaging does more than identify the brand, list the ingredients, specify features, and give directions. A package differentiates a product from competing products and may associate a new product with a family of other products from the same manufacturer. However, some products' packaging lacks useful information. The Food and Drug Administration (FDA) is looking to remedy inconsistent and incomplete food packaging information by adding more facts to nutrition labels. These changes include listing the number of servings in each container and printing the calorie count for each serving in larger, bolder type. The FDA hopes that these changes will catch consumers' eyes and help them better manage their health.[20] Similarly, the Canadian government is proposing mandatory front-of-package labeling for foods high in ingredients that are a public health concern, such as sugars, sodium, and saturated fat.[21]

Packages use designs, colors, shapes, and materials to try to influence consumers' perceptions and buying behavior. For example, marketing research shows that health-conscious consumers are likely to think that any food is probably good for them as long as it comes in green packaging. Packaging can influence other consumer perceptions of a brand as well. For example, Coca-Cola introduced the Diet Coke It's Mine program, which featured millions of unique package designs for the brand. The company partnered with HP Inc. to use the innovative HP Indigo digital printing technology to design the labels. "IT'S MINE is about the pursuit of a Diet Coke fan's ultimate object of desire—Diet Coke," said Kate Santore, senior manager of integrated marketing communications, Coca-Cola North America. "These bottles make your favorite beverage even more special—every bottle is completely unique, which means a fan can now own a piece of the brand no one else in the world owns."[22]

FACILITATING STORAGE, USE, AND CONVENIENCE

Wholesalers and retailers prefer packages that are easy to ship, store, and stock on shelves. They also like packages that protect products, prevent spoilage or breakage, and extend the product's shelf life.

Consumers' requirements for storage, use, and convenience cover many dimensions. Consumers are constantly seeking items that are easy to handle, open, and reclose, although some consumers want packages that are tamperproof or childproof. Research indicates that hard-to-open packages are among consumers' top complaints—especially when it comes to clamshell electronics packaging. There is even a Wikipedia page devoted to "wrap rage," the anger associated with trying to open clamshells and other poorly designed packages.[23] As oil prices force the cost of plastics used in packaging skyward, companies such as Amazon, Target, and Walmart are pushing suppliers to do away with excessive and infuriating packaging. Such packaging innovations as zipper tear strips, hinged lids, tab slots, screw-on tops, simple cardboard boxes, and pour spouts were introduced to solve these and other problems. Easy openings are especially important for kids and aging Baby Boomers.

Some firms use packaging to segment markets. For example, a C&H sugar carton with an easy-to-pour, reclosable top is targeted to consumers who do not do a lot of baking and are willing to pay at least 20 cents more for the package. Different-sized packages appeal to heavy, moderate, and light users. Campbell's soup is packaged in single-serving cans aimed at the elderly and singles market segments. Packaging convenience can increase a product's utility and therefore its market share and profits.

FACILITATING RECYCLING AND REDUCING ENVIRONMENTAL DAMAGE

One of the most important packaging issues today is eco-consciousness, a trend that has recently been in and out of consumer and media attention. Studies conflict as to whether consumers will pay more for eco-friendly packaging, though consumers repeatedly iterate the desire to purchase such products. One study showed that 63 percent of U.S. consumers believe that reusable and repurposable packaging is important when choosing products. Companies have responded by looking for alternative packaging materials that are more ecologically friendly.[24] For example, for its brand seed Phytonutrients, L'Oréal designed a paper bottle that is easy on the earth, but stands up to water in the shower. The water resistance is achieved by mixing proprietary minerals with paper fibers and using heat and pressure to bind the fibers during production. A number of recycled materials are also used in making the bottles.[25]

10-5b Labeling

An integral part of any package is its label. Labeling generally takes one of two forms: persuasive or informational. **Persuasive labeling** focuses on a promotional theme or logo, and consumer information is secondary. Note that the standard promotional claims—such as "new," "improved," and "super"—are no longer very persuasive. Consumers have been saturated with "newness" and thus discount these claims.

Informational labeling, by contrast, is designed to help consumers make proper product selections and lower their cognitive dissonance after the purchase. Most major furniture manufacturers affix labels to their wares that explain the products' construction features, such as type of frame, number of coils, and fabric characteristics. The Nutritional Labeling and Education Act of 1990 mandated that detailed nutritional information appear on most food packages, as well as standards for health claims on food packaging. An important outcome of this legislation has been guidelines from the Food and Drug Administration for using terms such as *low fat, light, reduced cholesterol, low sodium, low calorie, low carb,* and *fresh*. Getting the right information is very important to consumers, so some corporations are working on new technologies to help consumers shop smart. For example, microsensor technology is being developed to sense the freshness of food. On-package sensors indicate a food's shelf life and alert customers when it is safe to consume, in order to avoid early disposal or excessive purchasing.[27]

GREENWASHING There are numerous products in every product category that use *greenwashing* to try to sell products. Greenwashing is when a product or company attempts to give the impression of environmental friendliness whether or not it is environmentally friendly.

As consumer demand for green products appeared to escalate, green certifications proliferated. Companies could create their own certifications and logos, resulting in more than 300 possible certification labels, ranging in price from free to thousands of dollars. Consumer distrust and confusion caused the Federal Trade Commission to issue new rules. Starting in late 2011,

persuasive labeling
a type of package labeling that focuses on a promotional theme or logo; consumer information is secondary

informational labeling
a type of package labeling designed to help consumers make proper product selections and lower their cognitive dissonance after the purchase

Creative Packaging Design Trends

Product package design can have a large influence on what consumers choose. As human needs are changing, package design must evolve to remain relevant and address those needs. Some of the top packaging design trends include:

artdee2554/Shutterstock.com

1. **Simplicity.** Minimalist package design has been around for a long time, and feedback from buyers shows it to be a continuing trend. Simple designs involve presenting signs and symbols that everybody can relate to, so this can be a challenging thing for designers.

2. **Pastels.** Pastel colors have fragile and feminine characteristics that bring out a calming effect that bright colors cannot. Many people see pastels as a message that welcomes them to the products.

3. **Outstanding Shapes and Materials.** Unusual shapes and packaging materials can attract children and those who love art. A resin package that is designed to look like a sheltering tree trunk or a juice can is designed to look like a bamboo segment can stand out from other packages and speak to the emotional side of customers.

4. **Doodles.** This design element speaks to consumers' kid side. When a package design incorporates doodles into its design, it brings out the fun side of a product, and can attract a wide range of target markets.

5. **Vintage Design.** With vintage designs, consumers are reminded of the past. In many cases this design type represents important aspects of our history and culture.[27]

new regulations apply to labeling products with green-certification logos. If the same company that produced the product performed the certification, that relationship must be clearly marked. This benefits organizations such as Green Seal, which uses unbiased, third-party scientists and experts to verify claims about emissions or biodegradability and hopes to increase consumer confidence in green products.[28]

10-5c Universal Product Codes

The **universal product codes (UPCs)** that appear on most items in supermarkets and other high-volume outlets were first introduced in 1974. Because the numerical codes appear as a series of thick and thin vertical lines, they are often called *bar codes*. The lines are read by computerized optical scanners that match codes with brand names, package sizes, and prices. They also print information on cash register tapes and help retailers rapidly and accurately prepare records of customer purchases, control inventories, and track sales. The UPC system and scanners are also used in scanner-based research (see Chapter 9).

universal product codes (UPCs) a series of thick and thin vertical lines (bar codes) readable by computerized optical scanners that represent numbers used to track products

The Nutrition Facts label has been a mandatory part of most foods' packaging since 1990. The informational label has been revised several times since its introduction, including a major overhaul in 2014.

10-6 GLOBAL ISSUES IN BRANDING AND PACKAGING

When planning to enter a foreign market with an existing product, a firm has three options for handling the brand name.

- **One brand name everywhere:** This strategy is useful when the company markets mainly one product and the brand name does not have negative connotations in any local market. The Coca-Cola Company uses a one-brand-name strategy in more than 195 countries around the world. The advantages of a one-brand-name strategy are greater identification of the product from market to market and ease of coordinating promotion from market to market. For example, Coca-Cola has adopted a one-brand global strategy for its cola products. The company's new packaging, developed to support this strategy, has a unified visual identity. Now, all of Coca-Cola's trademarked package designs feature the company's signature shade of red.[29]

- **Adaptations and modifications:** A one-brand-name strategy is not possible when the name cannot be pronounced in the local language, when the brand name is owned by someone else, or when the brand name has a negative or vulgar connotation in the local language. The Iranian detergent Barf, for example, might encounter some problems in the U.S. market.

- **Different brand names in different markets:** Local brand names are often used when translation

or pronunciation problems occur, when the marketer wants the brand to appear to be a local brand, or when regulations require localization. Unilever's Axe line of male grooming products is called Lynx in England, Ireland, Australia, and New Zealand. PepsiCo changed the name of its eponymous cola to Pecsi in Argentina to reflect the way the word is pronounced with an Argentinian accent.

In addition to global branding decisions, companies must consider global packaging needs. Three aspects of packaging that are especially important in international marketing are labeling, aesthetics, and climate considerations. The major *labeling* concern is properly translating ingredient, promotional, and instructional information on labels. Care must also be employed in meeting all local labeling requirements. Several years ago, an Italian judge ordered that all bottles of Coca-Cola be removed from retail shelves because the ingredients were not properly labeled. Labeling is also harder in countries like Belgium and Finland, which require packaging to be bilingual.

Package *aesthetics* may also require some attention. Even though simple visual elements of the brand, such as a symbol or logo, can be a standardizing element across products and countries; marketers must stay attuned to cultural traits in host countries. For example, colors may have different connotations. Red is associated with witchcraft in some countries; green may be a sign of danger; and white may be symbolic of death. Such cultural differences could necessitate a

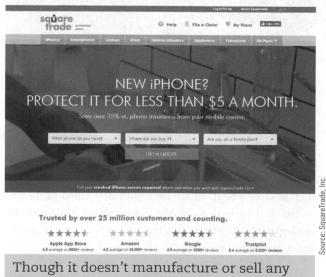

Though it doesn't manufacture or sell any goods itself, SquareTrade Inc. provides extended warranties for all sorts of consumer electronics and appliances.

packaging change if colors are chosen for another country's interpretation. In the United States, green typically symbolizes an eco-friendly product, but that packaging could keep customers away in a country where green indicates danger. Aesthetics also influence package size. Soft drinks are not sold in six-packs in countries that lack refrigeration. In some countries, products such as detergent may be bought only in small quantities because of a lack of storage space. Other products, such as cigarettes, may be bought in small quantities, and even single units, because of the low purchasing power of buyers.

Extreme climates and long-distance shipping necessitate sturdier and more durable packages for goods sold overseas. Spillage, spoilage, and breakage are all more important concerns when products are shipped long distances or frequently handled during shipping and storage. Packages may also need to ensure a longer product life if the time between production and consumption lengthens significantly.

 10-7 PRODUCT WARRANTIES

Just as a package is designed to protect the product, a warranty protects the buyer and gives essential information about the product. A warranty confirms the quality or performance of a good or service. An **express warranty** is a written guarantee. Express warranties range from simple statements—such as "100 percent cotton" (a guarantee of quality) and "complete satisfaction guaranteed" (a statement of performance)—to extensive documents written in technical language. In contrast, an **implied warranty** is an unwritten guarantee that the good or service is fit for the purpose for which it was sold. All sales have an implied warranty under the Uniform Commercial Code.

Congress passed the Magnuson–Moss Warranty–Federal Trade Commission Improvement Act in 1975 to help consumers understand warranties and get action from manufacturers and dealers. A manufacturer that promises a full warranty must meet certain minimum standards, including repair "within a reasonable time and without charge" of any defects and replacement of the merchandise or a full refund if the product does not work "after a reasonable number of attempts" at repair. Any warranty that does not live up to this tough prescription must be "conspicuously" promoted as a limited warranty.

warranty a confirmation of the quality or performance of a good or service

express warranty a written guarantee

implied warranty an unwritten guarantee that the good or service is fit for the purpose for which it was sold

11 | Developing and Managing Products

LEARNING OUTCOMES

After studying this chapter, you will be able to . . .

11-1 Explain the importance of developing new products and describe the six categories of new products

11-2 Explain the steps in the new-product development process

11-3 Understand why some products succeed and others fail

11-4 Discuss global issues in new-product development

11-5 Explain the diffusion process through which new products are adopted

11-6 Explain the concept of product life cycles

THE IMPORTANCE OF NEW PRODUCTS

New products are important to sustain growth, increase revenues and profits, and replace obsolete items. Each year *Fast Company* rates and ranks its most innovative companies, based on the ability to buck tradition in the interest of reaching more people, building a better business, and spurring mass-market appeal for unusual or highly technical products or services. In 2018, the top five companies were Apple, Netflix, Square, Tencent, and Amazon.[1] All of these firms have reputations for relying heavily on technology.

11-1a Introduction of New Products

Some companies spend a considerable amount of money each year developing new products. At Pfizer, the world's largest research-based pharmaceutical company, approximately $1.2 billion is spent on research and development for every new product released.[2] Other companies with high research and development (R&D) spending include Amazon ($22.6 billion per year), Volkswagen ($15.8 billion per year), and Samsung ($15.3 billion per year).[3]

Sometimes it is difficult to decide when to replace a successful product. Gillette Co. has a history of introducing new shaving systems (razors and accompanying blades) before the previous generation of products begins experiencing a sales decline. In fact, Gillette *expects* to cannibalize the sales of older models with its newer introductions. In early 2018, Apple released the newest edition of its MacBook Air laptops, one of the company's most popular laptop lines. Apple executives agreed that the MacBook Air needed to be replaced to keep customers satisfied, but the design of the new laptop required complex decisions, tradeoffs, and risks. The new version features a larger screen, more lightweight design, and a Touch ID sensor.[4] Clearly, the introduction of a new product is a monumental undertaking with a lot of open-ended questions—even for an established, multibillion-dollar company like Apple.

11-1b Categories of New Products

The term **new product** is somewhat confusing because its meaning varies widely. Actually, the term has several "correct" definitions. A product can be new to the world, the market, the producer, the seller, or some combination of these. There are six categories of new products:

- **New-to-the-world products** (also called discontinuous innovations): These products create an entirely new market. For example, Gatorade recently

> The average fast-moving consumer goods company introduces 70 to 80 new products per year.

announced that it is developing a microchip-fitted "smart cap" water bottle that will inform users how much they need to drink to stay properly hydrated during workouts. The bottle will communicate digitally with a sweat patch worn by the user to provide the updates.[5] New-to-the-world products represent the smallest category of new products.

- **New-product lines:** These products, which the firm has not previously offered, allow it to enter an established market. For example, Moleskine's first products were simple black-covered journals. Since then, the company has expanded into pens, travel bags, and even digital creative tools available on the iPhone and iPad.[6]

- **Additions to existing product lines:** This category includes new products that supplement a firm's established line. Fast-food restaurant chain Taco Bell recently added the "quesalupa"—a combination of a quesadilla and a chalupa—to its menu. Leading up to the quesalupa's unveiling, Taco Bell launched an advertising campaign in early 2016 to encourage customers to preorder a mysterious new menu item to be unveiled in a Super Bowl commercial. Customers who preordered the quesalupa, without knowing exactly what they were ordering, were able to try it a day earlier than the

> **new product** a product new to the world, the market, the producer, the seller, or some combination of these

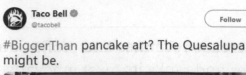

Taco Bell ✓
@tacobell

(Follow ⌄)

#BiggerThan pancake art? The Quesalupa
might be.

6:56 PM - 9 Feb 2016

325 Retweets **1,001** Likes

Introducing Taco Bell's "quesalupa," a
combination of a quesadilla and a chalupa.

masses. According to Taco Bell's chief marketing officer, Marisa Thalberg, the campaign was a success, resulting in tens of thousands of preorders for the new line-extension item.[7]

- **Improvements or revisions of existing products:** The "new and improved" product may be significantly or only slightly changed. For example, every year Apple introduces a new version of the iPhone. Some new versions are vastly different from earlier versions, while others focus on more minimal updates. In late 2017, Apple introduced the iPhone X, which featured Face ID, a TrueDepth Camera system, and a super retina display. 2018's iPhone XS and XR, by contrast, added only incremental improvements over the iPhone X, such as a dual-SIM card system and a few new camera features.[8]

- **Repositioned products:** These are existing products targeted at new markets or market segments or products that are repositioned to change the current market's perception of the product or company, which may be done to boost declining sales. Historically, 90 percent of LEGO sets were purchased by boys. In recent years, however, LEGO has been working to reposition its products so they appeal to more girls. For example, the company recently updated the packaging of its LEGO Friends line of toys to be more girl-friendly. LEGO

new-product strategy a plan that links the new-product development process with the objectives of the marketing department, the business unit, and the corporation

has also started to include bricks that can be used to make structures such as a pop star's house and a cupcake café.[9]

- **Lower-priced products:** This category refers to products that provide performance similar to competing brands at a lower price. The HP LaserJet Color MFP is a scanner, copier, printer, and fax machine combined. This new product is priced lower than many conventional color copiers and much lower than the combined price of the four items purchased separately.

11-2 THE NEW-PRODUCT DEVELOPMENT PROCESS

The management consulting firm Booz Allen Hamilton has studied the new-product development process for more than 30 years. Analyzing five major studies undertaken during this period, the firm has concluded that the companies most likely to succeed in developing and introducing new products are those that take the following actions:

- Make the long-term commitment needed to support innovation and new-product development.

- Use a company-specific approach, driven by corporate objectives and strategies, with a well-defined new-product strategy at its core.

- Capitalize on experience to achieve and maintain competitive advantage.

- Establish an environment—a management style, organizational structure, and degree of top management support—conducive to achieving company-specific new-product and corporate objectives.

Most companies follow a formal new-product development process, usually starting with a new-product strategy. Exhibit 11.1 illustrates the seven-step process, which is discussed in detail in this section. The exhibit is funnel-shaped to highlight the fact that each stage acts as a screen to filter out unworkable ideas.

11-2a New-Product Strategy

A **new-product strategy** links the new-product development process with the objectives of the marketing department, the business unit, and the corporation. A new-product strategy must be compatible with these objectives, and in turn all three of the objectives must be consistent with one another.

A new-product strategy is part of the organization's overall marketing strategy. It sharpens the focus and provides general guidelines for generating, screening, and evaluating new-product ideas. The new-product strategy specifies the roles that new products must play in the organization's overall plan and describes the characteristics of products the organization wants to offer and the markets it wants to serve.

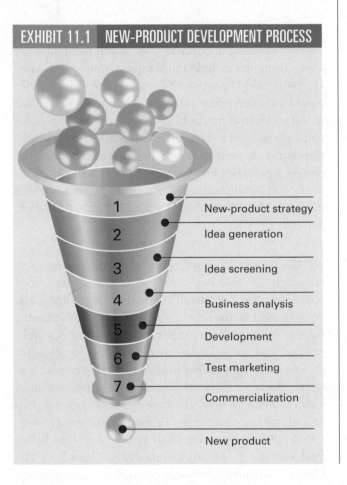

EXHIBIT 11.1 NEW-PRODUCT DEVELOPMENT PROCESS

1 New-product strategy
2 Idea generation
3 Idea screening
4 Business analysis
5 Development
6 Test marketing
7 Commercialization

New product

11-2b Idea Generation

New-product ideas come from many sources, including customers, employees, distributors, competitors, R&D, consultants, and other experts.

CUSTOMERS The marketing concept suggests that customers' wants and needs should be the springboard for developing new products. Companies can derive insight from listening to Internet chatter or reading blogs, which often indicate early trends or areas consumers are interested in seeing develop or change. Another approach for generating new-product ideas is using what some companies are calling "customer innovation centers." The idea is to provide a forum for meeting with customers and directly involving them in the innovation process.

EMPLOYEES Sometimes employees know a company's products and processes better than anyone else. Many firms have formal and informal processes in place for employees to propose new-product ideas. To encourage participation, some companies run contests, hold votes, and set up idea kiosks.

Some companies even allow their employees time at work to try to come up with new ideas. Google encourages its engineers to spend 20 percent of their time working on innovative independent projects. This policy has led to several successful innovations, such as Gmail and Google News.[10]

Some firms reward employees for coming up with creative new ideas. In an effort to encourage risk-taking through new ideas, companies like Google have begun implementing rewards for employees who fail after taking a big risk. Some of the most innovative Google ideas (such as driverless cars and Google glass) were developed through the Google X program. In order to

Customization is key in the luxury handbag market

High-end accessories designer Edie Parker uses customization as a way to stand out in the saturated handbag market. Creative designer Brett Heyman founded Edie Parker in 2010 after being disappointed by the evening bag selection at her favorite store. A few years later, Heyman introduced a line of customizable bags. Clients can choose the shape and color of their bag and even add a word or phrase of their choosing to it. Edie Parker's line of customized bags has not only helped the company stand out in a crowded market, but also garnered many celebrity fans, including Mindy Kaling, Emma Roberts, and Kate Hudson.[11]

promote innovative thinking and eliminate the fear of coming up with bad ideas among Google X employees, the company rewards failure. According to Google X employee Astro Teller, "We work hard at X to make it safe to fail. Teams kill their ideas as soon as the evidence is on the table because they're rewarded for it. They get applause from their peers. Hugs and high fives from their managers—me in particular. They get promoted for it."[12]

DISTRIBUTORS A well-trained sales force routinely asks distributors about needs that are not being met. Because they are closer to end users, distributors are often more aware of customer needs than are manufacturers. The inspiration for Rubbermaid's Sidekick, a litter-free lunch box, came from a distributor who suggested that the company place some of its plastic containers inside a lunch box and sell the box as an alternative to plastic wrap and paper bags.

COMPETITORS No firms rely solely on internally generated ideas for new products. As discussed in Chapter 9, a big part of any organization's marketing intelligence system should be monitoring the performance of competitors' products. One purpose of competitive monitoring is to determine which, if any, of the competitors' products should be copied. There is plenty of information about competitors on the Internet. Fuld & Company is a preeminent research and consulting firm in the field of competitive intelligence. Its clients include more than half of the U.S. *Fortune* 500 list and numerous international firms.[13]

RESEARCH AND DEVELOPMENT R&D is carried out in four distinct ways. You learned about basic research and applied research in Chapter 4. The other two ways are product development and product modification. **Product development** goes beyond applied research by converting applications into marketable products. Product modification makes cosmetic or functional changes to existing products. Many new-product breakthroughs come from R&D activities.

Winterstick Snowboards recently opened a new R&D Lab at Sugarloaf Mountain in Maine. According to the president of Winterstick, Tom Fremont-Smith, "The R&D Lab provides [employees] with the unique capabilities to turn [their] riders' dream boards into a

product development
a marketing strategy that entails the creation of marketable new products; the process of converting applications for new technologies into marketable products

brainstorming the process of getting a group to think of unlimited ways to vary a product or solve a problem

reality."[14] While the United States is the global leader in research and development, this lead is beginning to slip. The United States spent more than $500 billion on R&D in 2015, but China recently took a commanding lead in terms of late-stage R&D spending. By 2018, China will invest up to $658 billion on late-stage research—twice as much as the United States spends in this stage. Investing at the later stages of R&D is of critical importance because this stage is when ideas turn into actual commercial products.[15]

CONSULTANTS Outside consultants are always available to examine a business and recommend product ideas. Examples include the Weston Group, Booz Allen Hamilton, and Management Decisions Inc. Traditionally, consultants determine whether a company has a balanced portfolio of products and, if not, what new product ideas are needed to offset the imbalance. For example, Continuum is an award-winning consultancy firm that designs new goods and services, works on brand makeovers, and conducts consumer research. Clients include PepsiCo, Moen, American Express, Samsung, Reebok, and Sprint.[16]

OTHER EXPERTS A technique that is being used increasingly to generate new-product ideas is called "crowdsourcing." General information regarding ideas being sought is provided to a wide range of potential sources such as industry experts, independent researchers, and academics. These experts then develop ideas for the company. In addition to field experts, firms such as Quirky Inc. and General Electric Company have used crowdsourcing to generate ideas from the general public and freelance inventors. Tupperware is using crowdsourcing to develop new ideas to help it create better food containers. In 2018, Tupperware launched The Clever Container Challenge to explore ways through which it could create a more technologically advanced, but still reusable, and affordable, food container. The contest ran for a month and gave away $10,000 in prizes to the top three entries.[17] For a more thorough discussion of crowdsourcing, see Chapter 18.

Creativity is the wellspring of new-product ideas, regardless of who comes up with them. A variety of approaches and techniques have been developed to stimulate creative thinking. The two considered most useful for generating new-product ideas are brainstorming and focus group exercises. The goal of **brainstorming** is to get a group to think of unlimited ways to vary a product or solve a problem. Group members avoid criticism of an idea, no matter how ridiculous it may seem. Objective

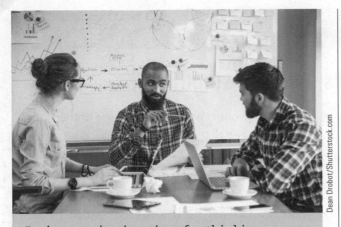

Brainstorming is a time for thinking outside the box and exploring every avenue. When brainstorming, group members should avoid criticizing ideas no matter how ridiculous they may seem.

evaluation is postponed. The sheer quantity of ideas is what matters. As noted in Chapter 9, an objective of focus group interviews is to stimulate insightful comments through group interaction. In the industrial market, machine tools, keyboard designs, aircraft interiors, and backhoe accessories have evolved from focus groups.

11-2c Idea Screening

After new ideas have been generated, they pass through the first filter in the product development process. This stage, called screening, eliminates ideas that are inconsistent with the organization's new-product strategy or are obviously inappropriate for some other reason. The new-product committee, the new-product department, or some other formally appointed group performs the screening review.

Concept tests are often used at the screening stage to rate concept (or product) alternatives. A concept test evaluates a new-product idea, usually before any prototype has been created. Typically, researchers get consumer reactions to descriptions and visual representations of a proposed product. Concept tests are considered fairly good predictors of success for line extensions. They have also been relatively precise predictors of success for new products that are not copycat items, are not easily classified into existing product categories, and do not require major changes in consumer behavior—such as Betty Crocker Tuna Helper. However, concept tests are usually inaccurate in predicting the success of new products that create new consumption patterns and require

major changes in consumer behavior—such as microwave ovens, digital music players, and computers.

11-2d Business Analysis

New-product ideas that survive the initial screening process move to the business analysis stage, where preliminary figures for demand, cost, sales, and profitability are calculated. For the first time, costs and revenues are estimated and compared. Depending on the nature of the product and the company, this process may be simple or complex.

The newness of the product, the size of the market, and the nature of the competition all affect the accuracy of revenue projections. In an established market like soft drinks, industry estimates of total market size are available. Forecasting market share for a new entry in a new, fragmented, or relatively small niche is a bigger challenge.

Analyzing overall economic trends and their impact on estimated sales is especially important in product categories that are sensitive to fluctuations in the business cycle. If consumers view the economy as uncertain and risky, they will put off buying durable goods such as major home appliances, automobiles, and homes. Likewise, business buyers postpone major equipment purchases if they expect a recession. Understanding the market potential is important because costs increase dramatically once a product idea enters the development stage.

11-2e Development

In the early stage of development, the R&D or engineering department may develop a prototype of the product. A process called 3D printing, or additive manufacturing, is sometimes used to create three-dimensional prototypes quickly and at a relatively low cost. During this stage, the firm should start sketching a marketing strategy. The marketing department should decide on the product's packaging, branding, labeling, and so forth. In addition, it should map out preliminary

screening the first filter in the product development process, which eliminates ideas that are inconsistent with the organization's new-product strategy or are obviously inappropriate for some other reason

concept test a test to evaluate a new-product idea, usually before any prototype has been created

business analysis the second stage of the screening process, where preliminary figures for demand, cost, sales, and profitability are calculated

development the stage in the product development process in which a prototype is developed and a marketing strategy is outlined

Common questions in the business analysis stage

These questions are commonly asked during the business analysis stage:

- What is the likely demand for the product?

- What impact would the new product probably have on total sales, profits, market share, and return on investment?

- How would the introduction of the product affect existing products? Would the new product cannibalize existing products?

- Would current customers benefit from the product?

- Would the product enhance the image of the company's overall product mix?

- Would the new product affect current employees in any way? Would it lead to increasing or reducing the size of the workforce?

- What new facilities, if any, would be needed?

- How might competitors respond?

- What is the risk of failure? Is the company willing to take the risk?

---

promotion, price, and distribution strategies. The feasibility of manufacturing the product at an acceptable cost should be thoroughly examined. The development stage can last a long time and thus be very expensive. It took 10 years to develop Crest toothpaste, 15 years to develop the Polaroid Colorpack camera and the Xerox copy machine, 18 years to develop Minute Rice, and 51 years to develop the television. Video games typically take years to develop. Games that are rushed to market are often buggy, and some are even unplayable. Recently, Marvel—the entertainment group behind iconic comic books such as Spider Man and the X-Men—announced plans to bring more Marvel characters to video games. Jay Ong, vice president of games for Marvel, stresses the importance of giving the new video games an adequate amount of development time. According to Ong, "Things like [games] you cannot under-resource. You can't not give the development time . . . to do justice to the game."[18]

The development process works best when all the involved areas (R&D, marketing, engineering, production, and even suppliers) work together rather than sequentially, a process called **simultaneous product development**.

simultaneous product development a team-oriented approach to new-product development

This approach allows firms to shorten the development process and reduce costs. With simultaneous product development, all relevant functional areas and outside suppliers participate in all stages of the development process. Rather than proceeding through highly structured stages, the cross-functional team operates in unison. Involving key suppliers early in the process capitalizes on their knowledge and enables them to develop critical component parts.

The Internet is a useful tool for implementing simultaneous product development. On the Web, multiple partners from a variety of locations can meet regularly to assess new-product ideas, analyze markets and demographics, and review cost information. Ideas judged to be feasible can quickly be converted into new products. The best-managed global firms leverage their global networks by sharing best practices, knowledge, and technology.[19] Without the Internet, it would be impossible to conduct simultaneous product development from different parts of the world. Some firms use online brain trusts to solve technical problems. InnoCentive Inc. is a network of 80,000 self-selected science problem solvers in 173 countries. Its clients include NASA, *Popular Science*, and the *Economist*. When one of InnoCentive's partners selects an idea for development, it no longer tries to develop the idea from the ground up with its own resources and time. Instead, it issues a brief to its network of thinkers, researchers, technology entrepreneurs, and inventors around the world, hoping to generate dialogue, suggestions, and solutions.

Innovative firms are also gathering a variety of R&D input from customers online. For example, leading manufacturer of power tools DeWALT recently created an online community called the DeWALT Insights Forum. Customers can use this forum both to provide feedback about current products and to submit ideas for new products. Twelve thousand members participate in DeWALT's Insights Forum community.[20]

Laboratory tests are often conducted on prototype models during the development stage. User safety is an important aspect of laboratory testing, which actually subjects products to much more severe treatment than that expected by end users. The Consumer Product Safety Act of 1972 requires manufacturers to conduct a "reasonable testing program" to ensure that their products conform to established safety standards.

Many products that test well in the laboratory are also tried out in homes or businesses. Examples of product categories well suited for such use tests include human and pet food products, household cleaning products, and industrial chemicals and supplies. These products are all relatively inexpensive, and their performance characteristics are apparent to users. For example, P&G tests a variety of personal and home-care products in the community around its Cincinnati, Ohio, headquarters.

Customers use DeWALT's Insights Forum to provide feedback about current products and to submit ideas for new products.

digitalreflections/Shutterstock.com

11-2f Test Marketing

After products and marketing programs have been developed, they are usually tested in the marketplace. Test marketing is the limited introduction of a product and a marketing program to determine the reactions of potential customers in a market situation. Test marketing allows management to evaluate alternative strategies and to assess how well the various aspects of the marketing mix fit together. Even established products are test marketed to assess new marketing strategies.

The cities chosen as test sites should reflect market conditions in the new product's projected market area. However, no "magic city" exists that can universally represent market conditions, and a product's success in one city does not guarantee that it will be a nationwide hit. When selecting test market cities, researchers should therefore find locations where the demographics and purchasing habits mirror the overall market. The company should also have good distribution in test cities. Wendy's uses Columbus, Ohio, as a test market for new burgers. Because the city has a nearly perfect cross section of America's demographic breakdown, it is the perfect testing ground for new products. Most recently, Wendy's tested the reception of its vegan-friendly Black Bean Burger.[21] Moreover, test locations should be isolated from the media. If the television stations in a particular market reach a very large area outside that market, the advertising used for the test product may pull in many consumers from outside the market. The product may then appear more successful than it really is.

THE HIGH COSTS OF TEST MARKETING Test marketing frequently takes one year or longer, and costs can exceed $1 million. Some products remain in test markets even longer than a year. In an effort to expand its product offerings, Starbucks launched an "affogato" drink combining ice cream and espresso in 100 Orange County, California, stores at the beginning of 2017. If the test market responds positively to the new offering, the drink will be rolled out nationwide.[22]

Despite the cost, many firms believe it is better to fail in a test market than in a national introduction. Because test marketing is so expensive, some companies do not test line extensions of well-known brands.

The high cost of test marketing is not just financial. One unavoidable problem is that test marketing exposes the new product and its marketing mix to

test marketing the limited introduction of a product and a marketing program to determine the reactions of potential customers in a market situation

Wendy's test markets new burgers such as its Black Bean Burger in Columbus, Ohio.

competitors before its introduction. Thus, the element of surprise is lost. Competitors can also sabotage or "jam" a testing program by introducing their own sales promotion, pricing, or advertising campaign. The purpose is to hide or distort the normal conditions that the testing firm might expect in the market.

ALTERNATIVES TO TEST MARKETING Many firms are looking for cheaper, faster, safer alternatives to traditional test marketing. In the early 1980s, Information Resources Inc. pioneered one alternative: scanner-based research (discussed in Chapter 9); a typical supermarket scanner test costs about $300,000. Another alternative to traditional test marketing is **simulated (laboratory) market testing**. Advertising and other promotional materials for several products, including the test product, are shown to members of the product's target market. These people are then taken to shop at a mock or real store, where their purchases are recorded. Shopper behavior, including repeat purchasing, is monitored to assess the product's likely performance under true market conditions. Research firms offer simulated market tests from $25,000 to $100,000; compare this with the $1 million or more for full-scale test marketing.

The Internet offers a fast, cost-effective way to conduct test marketing. P&G uses the Internet to assess customer demand for potential new products. Many products that are not available in grocery stores or drugstores can be sampled from P&G's website devoted to samples and coupons.[23]

Despite these alternatives, most firms still consider test marketing essential for most new products. The high price of failure simply prohibits the more-expensive widespread introduction of most new products without testing.

11-2g Commercialization

The final stage in the new-product development process is **commercialization**, the decision to market a product. The decision to commercialize the product sets several tasks in motion: ordering production materials and equipment, starting production, building inventories, shipping the product to field distribution points, training the sales force, announcing the new product to the trade, and advertising to potential customers.

The time from the initial commercialization decision to the product's actual introduction varies. The time for simple products that use existing equipment may be only a few weeks. Technical products that require custom manufacturing equipment could take several years until introduction, and the total cost of development and initial introduction can be staggering.

11-3 WHY SOME PRODUCTS SUCCEED AND OTHERS FAIL

Despite the amount of time and money spent on developing and testing new products, a large proportion of new-product introductions fail. Products fail for a number of reasons. One common reason is that they simply do not offer any discernible benefit as compared with existing products. Another commonly cited factor in new-product failures is a poor match between product features and customer desires. For example, there are telephone systems on the market with more than 700 different functions, although the average user is happy with just 10 functions. Other reasons for failure include overestimation of market size, incorrect targeting or positioning, a price too high or too low, inadequate distribution, poor promotion, or simply an inferior product.

Estimates of the percentages of new products that fail vary. Many estimates range as high as 80 to 90 percent.[24] Failure can be a matter of degree, however. Absolute failure occurs when a company cannot recoup its development, marketing, and production costs—the product actually loses money for the company. A relative

simulated (laboratory) market testing the presentation of advertising and other promotional materials for several products, including a test product, to members of the product's target market

commercialization the decision to market a product

product failure results when the product returns a profit but fails to achieve sales, profit, or market share goals. Some of the biggest product failures of all time include New Coke, Facebook Phone, Crystal Pepsi, Google Glass, and Burger King's Satisfries, a healthier alternative to regular fries.[25]

High costs and other risks of developing and testing new products do not stop many companies, such as Newell Rubbermaid, Colgate-Palmolive, Campbell Soup Company, and 3M, from aggressively developing and introducing new products. These companies depend on new products to increase revenues and profits. The most important factor in successful new-product introduction is a good match between the product and market needs—as the marketing concept would predict. Successful new products deliver a meaningful and perceivable benefit to a sizable number of people or organizations and are different in some meaningful way from their intended substitutes.

11-4 GLOBAL ISSUES IN NEW-PRODUCT DEVELOPMENT

Increasing globalization of markets and competition provides a reason for multinational firms to consider new-product development from a worldwide perspective. A firm that starts with a global strategy is better able to develop products that are marketable worldwide. In many multinational corporations, every product is developed for potential worldwide distribution, and unique market requirements are satisfied during development whenever possible.

One of the most successful new products of 2017 was the fidget spinner—a bearing-based spinning toy used to relieve stress and do tricks.

Some global marketers design their products to meet regulations in their major markets and then, if necessary, meet smaller markets' requirements country by country. Nissan develops car models for these lead countries that, with minor changes, can be sold in most markets. With this approach, Nissan has been able to reduce the number of its basic models from 48 to 18. Some products, however, have little potential for global market penetration without modification. Succeeding in some countries (such as China) often requires companies to develop products that meet the unique needs of these populations. In other cases, companies cannot sell their products at affordable prices and still make a profit in many countries.

11-5 THE SPREAD OF NEW PRODUCTS

Managers have a better chance of successfully marketing products if they understand how consumers learn about and adopt products.

11-5a Diffusion of Innovation

An **innovation** is a product perceived as new by a potential adopter. It really does not matter whether the product is "new to the world" or some other category of new. If it is new to a potential adopter, it is an innovation in this context. **Diffusion** is the process by which the adoption of an innovation spreads. Five categories of adopters participate in the diffusion process.

INNOVATORS Innovators are the first 2.5 percent of all those who adopt the product. Innovators are eager to try new ideas and products; it is almost an obsession. In addition to having higher incomes, they are more worldly and more active outside their community than noninnovators. They rely less on group norms and are more self-confident. Because they are well educated, they are more likely to get their information from scientific sources and experts. Innovators are characterized as being venturesome.

EARLY ADOPTERS Early adopters are the next 13.5 percent to adopt the product. Although early adopters are not the very first, they do adopt early in the product's life cycle.

innovation a product perceived as new by a potential adopter

diffusion the process by which the adoption of an innovation spreads

As compared with innovators, they rely much more on group norms and values. They are also more oriented to the local community, in contrast to the innovators' worldly outlook. Early adopters are more likely than innovators to be opinion leaders because of their closer affiliation with groups. Early adopters are a new product's best friends. Because viral, buzz, and word-of-mouth advertising is on the rise, marketers focus a lot of attention identifying the group that begins the viral marketing chain—the influencers. Part of the challenge is that this group of customers is distinguished not by demographics, but by behavior. Influencers come from all age, gender, and income groups, and they do not use media any differently than do the users who are considered followers. The characteristic influencers share is their desire to talk to others about their experiences with goods and services. A desire to earn the respect of others is a dominant characteristic among early adopters.

EARLY MAJORITY The next 34 percent to adopt are called the "early majority." Members of this group weigh the pros and cons before adopting a new product. They are likely to collect more information and evaluate more brands than early adopters, thereby extending the adoption process. They rely on the group for information but are unlikely to be opinion leaders themselves. Instead, they tend to be opinion leaders' friends and neighbors. Consumers trust positive word-of-mouth reviews from friends, family, and peers.[26] According to Nielsen research, 92 percent of consumers believe that recommendations from friends and family are the most trustworthy source of product information. Additionally, 84 percent of consumers trust online reviews.[27] Product discussions often drive Millennial conversations, so word-of-mouth marketing is particularly powerful among this demographic. In an effort to appeal to Millennials and encourage them to discuss its products on social media, Coca-Cola recently launched a campaign that featured the hashtag #ShareaCoke on its cans. The campaign was a huge success for the brand, and the hashtag was used more than 600,000 times on Instagram.[28]

While word-of-mouth marketing is important to Millennials, actually getting them to discuss products concretely can be difficult. According to Eric Pakurar, executive director and head of strategy at G2 USA, "They kind of ping-pong back and forth. They do a little research, then talk to their friends, and then do a little more research and check back with their friends and family."[29]

Seven characteristics of successful product introductions

Firms that routinely experience success in new-product introductions tend to share the following seven characteristics:

- A history of listening carefully to customers
- An obsession with producing the best product possible
- A vision of what the market will be like in the future
- Strong leadership
- A commitment to new-product development
- A project-based team approach to new-product development
- Getting every aspect of the product development process right

All word of mouth is not positive. Four out of five U.S. consumers report telling people around them about negative customer service experiences. Thirty-nine percent of consumers share customer service experiences on social media, roughly half of which is negative.[30] The early majority is an important link in the process of diffusing new ideas because its members are positioned between earlier and later adopters. A dominant characteristic of the early majority is deliberateness.

LATE MAJORITY The late majority is the next 34 percent to adopt. The late majority adopts a new product because most of their friends have already adopted it. Because they also rely on group norms, their adoption stems from pressure to conform. This group tends to be older and below average in income and education. They depend mainly on word-of-mouth communication rather than on the mass media. The dominant characteristic of the late majority is skepticism.

LAGGARDS The final 16 percent to adopt are called laggards. Like innovators, laggards do not rely on group norms. Their independence is rooted in their ties to tradition. Thus, the past heavily influences their decisions. By the time laggards adopt an innovation, it is probably outmoded and has been replaced by something else. For example, they may have bought their first color television set after flat screen televisions were already widely diffused. Laggards have the longest adoption time and the lowest socioeconomic status. They tend to be suspicious of new products and alienated from a rapidly advancing society. The dominant value of laggards is tradition. Marketers typically ignore laggards, who do not seem to be motivated by advertising or personal selling and are virtually impossible to reach online.

Note that some product categories may never be adopted by 100 percent of the population. The adopter categories refer to all of those who will eventually adopt a product, not the entire population.

11-5b Product Characteristics and the Rate of Adoption

Five product characteristics can be used to predict and explain the rate of acceptance and diffusion of a new product:

- **Complexity:** the degree of difficulty involved in understanding and using a new product. The more complex the product, the slower is its diffusion.

- **Compatibility:** the degree to which the new product is consistent with existing values and product knowledge, past experiences, and current needs. Incompatible products diffuse more slowly than compatible products.

- **Relative advantage:** the degree to which a product is perceived as superior to existing substitutes. Because it can store and play back thousands of songs, the iPod and its many variants have a clear relative advantage over the portable CD player.

- **Observability:** the degree to which the benefits or other results of using the product can be observed by others and communicated to target customers. For instance, fashion items and automobiles are highly visible and more observable than personal-care items.

- **"Trialability":** the degree to which a product can be tried on a limited basis. It is much easier to try a new toothpaste or breakfast cereal, for example, than a new personal computer.

11-5c Marketing Implications of the Adoption Process

Two types of communication aid the diffusion process: *word-of-mouth communication* among consumers and communication from marketers to consumers. Word-of-mouth communication within and across groups, including social media and viral communication, speeds diffusion. Opinion leaders discuss new products with their followers and with other opinion leaders. Marketers must therefore ensure that the types of information they want to convey is available to opinion leaders in the media that they use. Suppliers of some products, such as professional and health care services, rely almost solely on word-of-mouth communication for new business.

Many large-scale companies like Procter & Gamble, Cisco Systems, and Salesforce.com seek out opinion leaders among their employees. Some companies conduct surveys to identify opinion leaders while others use technology to map connections between individuals and postings. Once identified, these influential employees are provided with specially tailored communication training and are invited to attend senior management briefings. The hope is that these opinion leaders will field coworkers' questions and build positive buzz. Influencers are frequently rewarded for their skills with promotions and other forms of recognition.[31]

The second type of communication aiding the diffusion process is *communication directly from the marketer to potential adopters*. Messages directed toward early adopters should normally use different appeals from messages directed toward the early majority, the late majority, or the laggards. Early adopters are more important than innovators because they make up a larger group, are more socially active, and are usually opinion leaders.

As the focus of a promotional campaign shifts from the early adopters to the early majority and the late majority, marketers should study the dominant characteristics, buying behavior, and media characteristics of these target markets. Then they should revise messages and the media strategy to fit. The diffusion model helps guide marketers in developing and implementing promotional strategy.

11-6 PRODUCT LIFE CYCLES

The product life cycle (PLC) is one of the most familiar concepts in marketing. Few other general concepts have been so widely discussed.

product life cycle (PLC) a concept that provides a way to trace the stages of a product's acceptance, from its introduction (birth) to its decline (death)

EXHIBIT 11.2   FOUR STAGES OF THE PRODUCT LIFE CYCLE

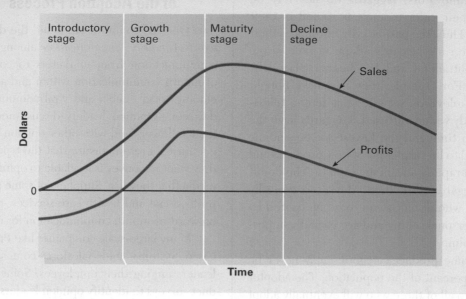

Although some researchers and consultants have challenged the theoretical basis and managerial value of the PLC, many believe it is a useful marketing management diagnostic tool and a general guide for marketing planning in various life-cycle stages.

The PLC is a biological metaphor that traces the stages of a product's acceptance, from its introduction (birth) to its decline (death). As Exhibit 11.2 shows, a product progresses through four major stages: introduction, growth, maturity, and decline.

The PLC concept can be used to analyze a brand, a product form, or a product category. The PLC for a product form is usually longer than the PLC for any one brand. The exception would be a brand that was the first and last competitor in a market for the product form. In that situation, the brand and product-form life cycles would be equal in length. Product categories have the longest life cycles. A **product category** includes all brands that satisfy a particular type of need, such as shaving products, passenger automobiles, or soft drinks.

The time a product spends in any one stage of the life cycle may vary dramatically. Some products, such as fad items, move through the entire cycle in weeks. Fads are typically characterized by a sudden and unpredictable spike in sales followed by a rather abrupt decline. Examples of fad items are Silly Bandz, Beanie Babies, and Crocs. Other products, such as electric clothes washers

and dryers, stay in the maturity stage for decades. Exhibit 11.2 illustrates the typical life cycle for a consumer durable good, such as a washer or dryer. In contrast, Exhibit 11.3 illustrates typical life cycles for styles (such as formal, business, or casual clothing), fashions (such as miniskirts or baggy jeans), and fads (such as leopard-print clothing). Changes in a product, its uses, its image, or its positioning can extend that product's life cycle.

The PLC concept does not tell managers the length of a product's life cycle or its duration in any stage. It does not dictate marketing strategy. It is simply a tool to help marketers forecast future events and suggest appropriate strategies.

11-6a Introductory Stage

The **introductory stage** of the PLC represents the full-scale launch of a new product into the marketplace. Computer databases for personal use, room-deodorizing air-conditioning filters, and wind-powered home electric generators are all product categories that have recently entered the PLC. A high failure rate, little competition, frequent product modification, and limited distribution typify the introductory stage of the PLC.

Marketing costs in the introductory stage are normally high for several reasons. High dealer margins are often needed to obtain adequate distribution, and incentives are needed to get consumers to try the new product. Advertising expenses are high because of the need to educate consumers about the new product's benefits.

product category all brands that satisfy a particular type of need

introductory stage the full-scale launch of a new product into the marketplace

EXHIBIT 11.3 PRODUCT LIFE CYCLES FOR STYLES, FASHIONS, AND FADS

Production costs are also often high in this stage, as product and manufacturing flaws are identified and corrected and efforts are undertaken to develop mass production economies.

Sales normally increase slowly during the introductory stage. Moreover, profits are usually negative because of R&D costs, factory tooling, and high introduction costs. The length of the introductory phase is largely determined by product characteristics, such as the product's advantages over substitute products, the educational effort required to make the product known, and management's commitment of resources to the new item. A short introductory period is usually preferred to help reduce the impact of negative earnings and cash flows. As soon as the product gets off the ground, the financial burden should begin to diminish. Also, a short introductory period helps dispel some of the uncertainty as to whether the new product will be successful.

Promotional strategy in the introductory stage focuses on developing product awareness and informing consumers about the product category's potential benefits. At this stage, the communication challenge is to stimulate primary demand—demand for the product in general rather than for a specific brand. Intensive personal selling is often required to gain acceptance for the product among wholesalers and retailers. Promotion of convenience products often requires heavy consumer sampling and couponing. Shopping and specialty products demand educational advertising and personal selling to the final consumer.

11-6b Growth Stage

If a product category survives the introductory stage, it then advances to the **growth stage** of the life cycle. In this stage, sales typically grow at an increasing rate, many

competitors enter the market, and large companies may start to acquire small pioneering firms. Profits rise rapidly in the growth stage, reach their peak, and begin declining as competition intensifies. Emphasis switches from primary demand promotion (e.g., promoting e-readers) to aggressive brand advertising and communication of the differences between brands (e.g., promoting Kindle vs. promoting Nook).

Distribution becomes a major key to success during the growth stage as well as in later stages. Manufacturers scramble to sign up dealers and distributors and to build long-term relationships. Others are able to market directly to consumers using electronic media. Without adequate distribution, it is impossible to establish a strong market position.

As the economy recovers, more companies are entering the growth stage and more workers are being hired. Because of this employment boom, staffing agencies are seeing a huge increase in revenues. On Assignment, a company that places temporary and permanent workers in several different industries, ranked third on *Fortune*'s list of the fastest growing companies for 2014. In 2012, On Assignment acquired IT staffing agency ApexSystems, becoming the second largest infotech staffing agency in the United States. The company's stock rose 26.6 percent the day after the acquisition.[32]

11-6c Maturity Stage

A period during which sales increase at a decreasing rate signals the beginning of the **maturity stage** of the life cycle. New users cannot be

growth stage the second stage of the product life cycle, when sales typically grow at an increasing rate; many competitors enter the market; large companies may start to acquire small pioneering firms; and profits are healthy

maturity stage a period during which sales increase at a slower rate

Starbucks targets its gourmet line at new, young drinkers—the only segment that is growing.

added indefinitely, and sooner or later the market approaches saturation. Normally, this is the longest stage of the PLC. Many major household appliances are in the maturity stage of their life cycles.

For shopping products such as durable goods and electronics, and many specialty products, annual models begin to appear during the maturity stage. Product lines are lengthened to appeal to additional market segments. Service and repair assume more important roles as manufacturers strive to distinguish their products from others. Product design changes tend to become stylistic (How can the product be made different?) rather than functional (How can the product be made better?).

As prices and profits continue to fall, marginal competitors start dropping out of the market. Dealer margins also shrink, resulting in less shelf space for mature items, lower dealer inventories, and a general reluctance to promote the product. Thus, promotion to dealers often intensifies during this stage in order to retain loyalty.

Heavy consumer promotion by the manufacturer is also required to maintain market share. Cutthroat competition during this stage can lead to price wars. Another characteristic of the maturity stage is the emergence of "niche marketers" that target narrow, well-defined, underserved segments of a market. Starbucks Coffee targets its gourmet line at new, young, affluent coffee drinkers, the only segment of the coffee market that is growing.

11-6d Decline Stage

decline stage a long-run drop in sales

A long-run drop in sales signals the beginning of the **decline stage**. The rate of decline is governed by how rapidly consumer tastes change or substitute products are adopted. Many convenience products and fad items lose their market overnight, leaving large inventories of unsold items, such as designer jeans. Others die more slowly. Landline telephone service is an example of a product in the decline stage of the product life cycle. Nearly 60 percent of American homes do not have a landline, which represents a continued steady increase since 2009—and a steady drop in the use of landlines.[33] People abandoning landlines to go wireless and households replacing landlines with Internet phones have both contributed to this long-term decline.

Some firms have developed successful strategies for marketing products in the decline stage of the PLC. They eliminate all nonessential marketing expenses and let sales decline as more and more customers discontinue purchasing the products. Eventually, the product is withdrawn from the market.

11-6e Implications for Marketing Management

The new-product development process, the diffusion process, and the PLC concept all have implications for marketing managers. The funnel shape of Exhibit 11.1 indicates that many new-product ideas are necessary to produce one successful new product. The new-product development process is sometimes illustrated as a decay curve, with roughly half of the ideas approved at one stage and rejected at the next. While the actual numbers vary widely among firms and industries, the relationship between the stages can be generalized. This reinforces the notion that an organized effort to generate many ideas from various sources is important for any firm that wishes to produce a continuing flow of new products.

The major implication of the diffusion process for marketing managers is that the message may need to change over time. The targeted adopter and media may need to shift based on how various categories of adopters gather product information. A message developed for and targeted toward early adopters will not be perceived similarly by late majority adopters.

Exhibit 11.4 shows the relationship between the adopter categories and stages of the PLC. Note that the various categories of adopters buy products in different stages of the life cycle. Almost all sales in the maturity and decline stages represent repeat purchases.

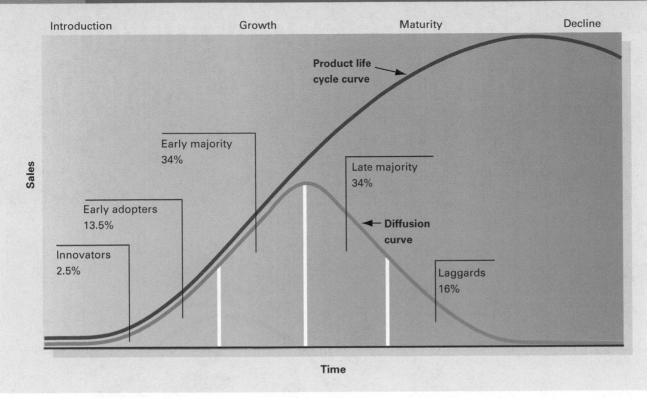

12 | Services and Nonprofit Organization Marketing

LEARNING OUTCOMES

After studying this chapter, you will be able to…

- 12-1 Discuss the importance of services to the economy
- 12-2 Discuss the differences between services and goods
- 12-3 Describe the components of service quality and the gap model of service quality
- 12-4 Develop marketing mixes for services

- 12-5 Discuss relationship marketing in services
- 12-6 Explain internal marketing in services
- 12-7 Describe nonprofit organization marketing
- 12-8 Discuss global issues in services marketing

12-1 THE IMPORTANCE OF SERVICES

A service is the result of applying human or mechanical efforts to people or objects. Services involve a deed, a performance, or an effort that cannot be physically possessed. The service sector substantially influences the U.S. economy, accounting for approximately 80 percent of the country's economic output. The service-oriented industries contributing to much of this output include technology, financial services, health care, and retail.[1]

The marketing process described in Chapter 1 is the same for all types of products, whether they are goods or services. In addition, although a comparison of goods and services marketing can be beneficial, in reality it is hard to distinguish clearly between manufacturing and service firms. Indeed, many manufacturing firms can point to service as a major factor in their success. For example, maintenance and repair services offered by the manufacturer are important to buyers of copy machines. Nevertheless, services have some unique characteristics that distinguish them from goods, and marketing strategies need to be adjusted for these characteristics.

12-2 HOW SERVICES DIFFER FROM GOODS

Services have four unique characteristics that distinguish them from goods. Services are intangible, inseparable, heterogeneous, and perishable.

12-2a Intangibility

The basic difference between services and goods is that services are intangible performances. Because of their intangibility, they cannot be touched, seen, tasted, heard, or felt in the same manner that goods can be sensed.

Evaluating the quality of services before or even after making a purchase is harder than evaluating the quality of goods because, compared to goods, services tend to exhibit fewer search qualities. A search quality is a characteristic that can be easily assessed before purchase—for instance, the color of an appliance or automobile. At the same time, services tend to exhibit more experience and credence qualities. An experience quality is a characteristic that can be assessed only after use, such as the quality of a meal in a restaurant. A credence quality is a characteristic that consumers may have difficulty assessing even after purchase because they do not have

the necessary knowledge or experience. Medical and consulting services are examples of services that exhibit credence qualities.

These characteristics also make it harder for marketers to communicate the benefits of an intangible service than to communicate the benefits of tangible goods. Thus, marketers often rely on tangible cues to communicate a service's nature and quality. For example, Travelers Insurance Company uses an umbrella symbol as a tangible reminder of the protection that insurance provides.

The facilities that customers visit, or from which services are delivered, are a critical tangible part of the total service offering. Messages about the organization are communicated to customers through such elements as the décor, the clutter or neatness of service areas, and the staff's manners and dress. Hotels know that guests form opinions quickly and are more willing than ever before to tweet them within the first 15 minutes of their stay. Some hotels go to great lengths to make their guests feel at home. For example, Four Seasons makes sure that no plumbing is touching concrete at its hotels to create the quietest possible rooms. The company also gives all of its employees—from parking attendants to managers—the authority to act instantly when a guest makes a request. This allows Four Seasons to offer excellent personalized service from check-in to check-out.[2]

12-2b Inseparability

Goods are produced, sold, and then consumed. In contrast, services are often sold, produced, and consumed at the same time. In other words, their

---

service the result of applying human or mechanical efforts to people or objects

intangibility the inability of services to be touched, seen, tasted, heard, or felt in the same manner that goods can be sensed

search quality a characteristic that can be easily assessed before purchase

experience quality a characteristic that can be assessed only after use

credence quality a characteristic that consumers may have difficulty assessing even after purchase because they do not have the necessary knowledge or experience production and consumption are inseparable activities. This **inseparability** means that, because consumers must be present during the production of services like haircuts or surgery, they are actually involved in the production of the services they buy. That type of consumer involvement is rare in goods manufacturing.

Simultaneous production and consumption also means that services normally cannot be produced in a centralized location and consumed in decentralized locations, as goods typically are. Services are also inseparable from the perspective of the service provider. Thus, the quality of service that firms are able to deliver depends on the quality of their employees.

12-2c Heterogeneity

One great strength of McDonald's is consistency. Whether customers order a Big Mac in Chicago or Seattle, they know exactly what they are going to get. This is not the case with many service providers. Because services have greater **heterogeneity**, or variability of inputs and outputs, they tend to be less standardized and uniform than goods. For example, physicians in a group practice or barbers in a barbershop differ within each group in their technical and interpersonal skills. Because services tend to be labor intensive and production and consumption are inseparable, consistency and quality control can be hard to achieve.

Standardization and training help increase consistency and reliability. In the information technology sector, a number of certification programs are available to ensure that technicians are capable of working on (and within) complex enterprise software systems. For example, professional certifications for big data engineers such as those at Microsoft, Oracle, SAS, and INFORMS ensure a consistency of knowledge and ability among those who can pass these programs' rigorous exams.[3]

12-2d Perishability

Perishability is the fourth characteristic of services. Perishability refers to the inability of services to be stored, warehoused, or inventoried. An empty hotel room or airplane seat produces no revenue that day. The revenue is lost. Yet service organizations are often forced to turn away full-price customers during peak periods.

One of the most important challenges in many service industries is finding ways to synchronize supply and demand. The philosophy that some revenue is better than none has prompted many hotels to offer deep discounts on weekends and during the off-season.

12-3 SERVICE QUALITY

Because of the four unique characteristics of services, service quality is more difficult to define and measure than is the quality of tangible goods. Business executives rank the improvement of service quality as one of the most critical challenges facing them today.

12-3a Evaluating Service Quality

Research has shown that customers evaluate service quality by the following five components:

- **Reliability:** the ability to perform the service dependably, accurately, and consistently. Reliability is performing the service right the first time. This component has been found to be the one most important to consumers.

- **Responsiveness:** the ability to provide prompt service. Examples of responsiveness include calling the customer back quickly, serving lunch fast to someone who is in a hurry, or mailing a transaction slip immediately. The ultimate in responsiveness is offering service 24 hours a day, seven days a week. Priceline Group's global business, which operates in more than 220 countries and territories, shows responsiveness to its customers by hiring people who can answer calls in dozens of languages.[4]

Friendly hardware store worker showing customer a sander.

michaeljung/Shutterstock.com

---

inseparability the inability of the production and consumption of a service to be separated; consumers must be present during the production

heterogeneity the variability of the inputs and outputs of services, which causes services to tend to be less standardized and uniform than goods

perishability the inability of services to be stored, warehoused, or inventoried

reliability the ability to perform a service dependably, accurately, and consistently

responsiveness the ability to provide prompt service

Wells fargo fallen into gap 4?

In 2016, Wells Fargo & Company's employees were found to have opened more than 2 million bank accounts and 565,000 credit cards without the permission of their customers. Adding insult to injury, the company also charged fees on these fake accounts. As a result of this scandal, Wells Fargo was fined $185 million, 5,300 employees were fired, and CEO John Stumpf was forced to resign. In 2017, the company found itself in trouble once again for modifying mortgages without customers' knowledge and charging over half a million customers for auto insurance they did not need. These scandals caused Wells Fargo's service reputation score to drop almost 21 points in 2017. Indeed, the bank fell into gap 4 because it failed to properly communicate with its customers—to put it mildly.[5]

- **Assurance:** the knowledge and courtesy of employees and their ability to convey trust. Skilled employees, who treat customers with respect and make customers feel that they can trust the firm, exemplify assurance.

- **Empathy:** caring, individualized attention to customers. Firms whose employees recognize customers and learn their specific requirements are providing empathy. LUX Resorts, a hospitality company based in Mauritius, recently initiated a company-wide plan to offer creative personalized service. Understanding that highly scripted employees are often less able to empathize with customer needs, LUX's CEO started an educational program focused on getting employees to anticipate and understand guests' priorities. Knowing more about customers' wants and needs maximized employees' opportunities for providing great service, and two years after the program began, half of TripAdvisor's Top 10 list for Mauritius was filled with LUX properties.[6]

- **Tangibles:** the physical evidence of the service. The tangible parts of a service include the physical facilities, tools, and equipment used to provide the service, as well as the appearance of personnel.[7]

Overall service quality is measured by combining customers' evaluations for all five components.

12-3b The Gap Model of Service Quality

A model of service quality called the **gap model** identifies five gaps that can cause problems in service delivery and influence customer evaluations of service quality.[8] These gaps are illustrated in Exhibit 12.1.

- **Gap 1:** the gap between what customers want and what management thinks customers want. This gap results from a lack of understanding or a misinterpretation of the customers' needs, wants, or desires. A firm that does little or no customer satisfaction research is likely to experience this gap. To close gap 1, firms must stay attuned to customer wishes by researching customer needs and satisfaction.

- **Gap 2:** the gap between what management thinks customers want and the quality specifications that management develops to provide the service. Essentially, this gap is the result of management's inability to translate customers' needs into delivery systems within the firm. For example, KFC used to rate its managers according to "chicken efficiency," or how much chicken they threw away at closing; customers who came in late would either have to wait for chicken to be cooked or settle for chicken several hours old.

- **Gap 3:** the gap between the service quality specifications and the service that is actually provided. If both gaps 1 and 2 have been closed, then gap 3 is due to the inability of management and employees to do what should be done. Management needs to ensure that employees have the skills and the proper tools to perform their jobs. Other techniques that help to close gap 3 are training employees so they know what management expects and encouraging teamwork.

assurance the knowledge and courtesy of employees and their ability to convey trust

empathy caring, individualized attention to customers

tangibles the physical evidence of a service, including the physical facilities, tools, and equipment used to provide the service

gap model a model identifying five gaps that can cause problems in service delivery and influence customer evaluations of service quality

EXHIBIT 12.1   GAP MODEL OF SERVICE QUALITY

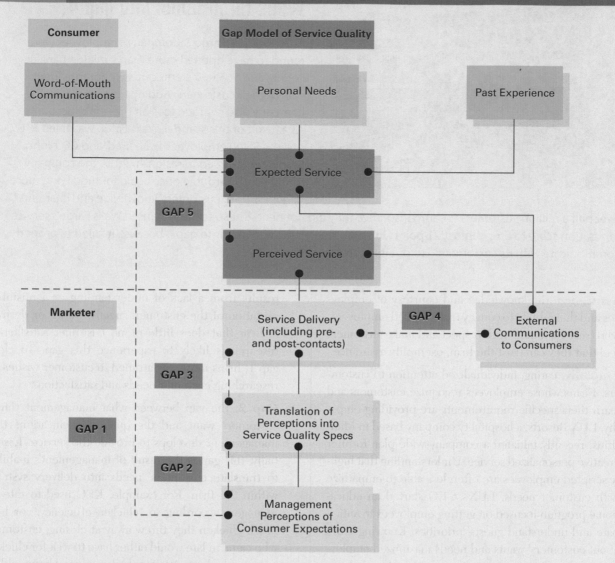

The gap analysts model measures consumer perceptions of service quality. Managers use the model to analyze sources of quality problems and to understand how service quality can be improved.

Source: Based on Valarie A. Zeithaml, Mary J. Bitner, and Dwayne Gremler, *Services Marketing*, 4/e, © 2006 (New York: McGraw-Hill, 2006).

- **Gap 4:** the gap between what the company provides and what the customer is told it provides. This is clearly a communication gap. It may include misleading or deceptive advertising campaigns promising more than the firm can deliver or doing "whatever it takes" to get the business. To close this gap, companies need to create realistic customer expectations through honest, accurate communication about what the firms can provide.

- **Gap 5:** the gap between the service that customers receive and the service they want. This gap can be positive or negative. For example, if a patient expects to wait 20 minutes in the physician's office before

seeing the physician but actually waits only 10 minutes, the patient's evaluation of service quality will be high. However, a 40-minute wait would result in a lower evaluation. Nordstrom, a company whose service quality is legendary, consistently performs at a level above and beyond what customers expect, resulting in few to no signs of gap 5.[9]

When one or more of these gaps is large, service quality is perceived as low. As the gaps shrink, perceptions of service quality improve. Bank of America has joined a growing number of financial institutions working to close a persistent and wide gap 1—customers' desire for full-featured mobile banking. To meet the needs of highly mobile, technologically tuned-in customers, Bank of America has invested heavily in its banking app. Among other things, the app allows users to securely send and receive money using a mobile number or email address, pay eBills, schedule payments, and edit pay-to accounts. For assistance, customers can use the app to reach a representative for help with their accounts.[10]

Several other companies consistently get their service quality right. According to a survey done by 24/7 Wall St. in collaboration with research survey group Zogby Analytics, the top five companies offering exceptional customer service in 2017 were

1. Amazon

2. Apple

3. Costco

4. Netflix

5. YouTube[11]

These companies have three core beliefs in common: good service starts at the top; service is seen as a continual challenge; and companies work best when people want to work for them.

12-4 MARKETING MIXES FOR SERVICES

Services' unique characteristics—intangibility, inseparability of production and consumption, heterogeneity, and perishability—make marketing more challenging. Elements of the marketing mix (product, place, promotion, and pricing) need to be adjusted to meet the special needs created by these characteristics.

12-4a Product (Service) Strategy

A product, as defined in Chapter 10, is everything a person receives in an exchange. In the case of a service organization, the product offering is intangible and consists in large part of a process or a series of processes. Product strategies for service offerings include decisions on the type of process involved, core and supplementary services, standardization or customization of the service product, and the service mix.

SERVICE AS A PROCESS Two broad categories of things are processed in service organizations: people and objects. In some cases, the process is physical, or tangible, while in others the process is intangible. Based on these characteristics, service processes can be placed into one of four categories:

Theater performances like Broadway's *Hamilton* are considered mental stimulus processing services.

Joseph M. Arseneau/Shutterstock.com

- *People processing* takes place when the service is directed at a customer. Examples are transportation services and health care.

- *Possession processing* occurs when the service is directed at customers' physical possessions. Examples are lawn care, dry cleaning, and veterinary services.

- *Mental-stimulus processing* refers to services directed at people's minds. Examples are theater performances and education.

- *Information processing* describes services that use technology or brainpower directed at a customer's assets. Examples are insurance and consulting.[12]

Because customers' experiences and involvement differ for each of these types of services, marketing strategies may also differ. For example, people-processing services require customers to enter the *service factory*, which is a physical location, such as an aircraft, a physician's office, or a hair salon. In contrast, possession-processing services typically do not require the presence of the customer in the service factory. Marketing strategies for the former would therefore focus more on an attractive, comfortable physical environment and employee training on employee–customer interaction issues than would strategies for the latter.

CORE AND SUPPLEMENTARY SERVICE PRODUCTS
The service offering can be viewed as a bundle of activities that includes the **core service**, which is the most basic benefit the customer is buying, and a group of **supplementary services** that support or enhance the core service. Exhibit 12.2 illustrates these concepts for a luxury hotel. The core service is providing bedrooms

core service the most basic benefit the consumer is buying

supplementary services a group of services that support or enhance the core service

EXHIBIT 12.2 CORE AND SUPPLEMENTARY SERVICES FOR A LUXURY HOTEL

Source: Christopher H. Lovelock and Jochen Wirtz, *Services Marketing*, 7/e, ©2011. Electronically reproduced by permission of Pearson Education, Inc., Upper Saddle River, New Jersey.

for rent, which involves people processing. The supplementary services, some of which involve information processing, include food services and reservation, parking, phone, and television services.

In many service industries, the core service becomes a commodity as competition increases. Thus, firms usually emphasize supplementary services to create a competitive advantage. On the other hand, some firms are positioning themselves in the marketplace by greatly reducing supplementary services.

CUSTOMIZATION/STANDARDIZATION An important issue in developing the service offering is whether to customize or standardize it. Customized services are more flexible and respond to individual customers' needs. They also usually command a higher price. Standardized services are more efficient and cost less.

Instead of choosing to either standardize or customize a service, a firm may incorporate elements of both by adopting an emerging strategy called **mass customization**. Mass customization uses technology to deliver customized services on a mass basis, which results in giving each customer whatever she or he asks for. To mass-customize coffee drinks, Starbucks uses different kinds of coffee, dairy, flavor shots, and temperature levels, resulting in a diverse array of options for customers. Aiding the mass customization process, Starbucks uses a machine called a Clover,

mass customization a strategy that uses technology to deliver customized services on a mass basis

which allows baristas to customize brew times down to the second, specifies how much exposure the water has to the coffee grounds, and dials in a precise temperature.[13]

THE SERVICE MIX Most service organizations market more than one service. For example, TruGreen offers lawn care, shrub care, carpet cleaning, and industrial lawn services. Each organization's service mix represents a set of opportunities, risks, and challenges. Each part of the service mix should make a different contribution to achieving the firm's goals. To succeed, each service may also need a different level of financial support. Designing a service strategy, therefore, means deciding which new services to introduce to which target market, which existing services to maintain, and which services to eliminate.

12-4b Place (Distribution) Strategy

Distribution strategies for service organizations must focus on such issues as convenience, number of outlets, direct versus indirect distribution, location, and scheduling. A key factor influencing the selection of a service provider is *convenience*. An interesting example of this is an e-commerce solution to shopping that offers customers the convenience of an online marketplace and the reassurance of the in-person experience is the "try before you buy" option now offered by several companies. Customers order the items they select (or the items a personal stylist selects), return what they don't like for free, and are get charged only for what they keep. For example, customers can visit Warby Parker's site and select five glasses frames to test out for five days, and the company will ship them for free. If one or two of the selections are chosen, they can be purchased at any time online and Warby Parker will send the customer a fresh new pair. Trunk Club pairs customers with a personal stylist who will ask questions about fit, style, and budget to get a sense of their personal style. When the customer's personalized "trunk" is ready, they get a digital preview of the items in it and they have 48 hours to approve or amend the contents. Once the customer gives the go-ahead, UPS will deliver the trunk within four to six business days with free shipping. Five days are given for customers to try things on and then return what they don't want to keep. Returns are free with an included shipping label. There is a $25 styling fee, but because Trunk Club is owned by Nordstrom, that fee is waived for any Nordstrom card holder.[14]

An important distribution objective for many service firms is the number of outlets to use or the number of outlets to open during a certain time. Generally, the intensity of distribution should meet, but not exceed, the target market's needs and preferences. Having too few outlets may

Nordstrom's Trunk Club lets customers shop using personal stylists that select clothes and mail them directly to the customer.

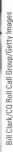

Celebrity is a powerful tool for services and nonprofits alike. Here, Ashton Kutcher co-founder of THORN, preparing to testify during the Senate Foreign Relations Committee hearing on ending modern slavery.

inconvenience customers; having too many outlets may boost costs unnecessarily. Intensity of distribution may also depend on the image desired. Having only a few outlets may make the service seem more exclusive or selective.

The next service distribution decision is whether to distribute services to end users *directly* or *indirectly* through other firms. Because of the intangible nature of services, many service firms have to use direct distribution or franchising. Examples include legal, medical, accounting, and personal-care services. The most-used form of direct distribution is the Internet. Most major airlines are now using online services to sell tickets directly to consumers, resulting in lower distribution costs for the airlines. Other firms with standardized service packages have developed indirect channels using independent intermediaries. Partnerships with technology firms also allow service firms more options for distribution. For example, Domino's Pizza has partnered with Starship Technologies, a robot delivery start-up, to begin delivering pizza in Germany. The robots are just under two feet tall and travel at about four miles an hour.[15]

The *location* of a service most clearly reveals the relationship between its target market strategy and distribution strategy. For time-dependent service providers such as airlines, physicians, and dentists, *scheduling* is often a more important factor.

How and where consumers interact with service organizations has been impacted by the COVID-19 pandemic. Shoppers want and expect social distancing services such as curbside pickup, local delivery and contactless payments. A large majority of consumers, 84%, have used these types of services and 86% expect to continue using them once the pandemic subsides.

12-4c Promotion Strategy

Consumers and business users have more trouble evaluating services than goods because services are less tangible. In turn, marketers have more trouble promoting intangible services than tangible goods. Here are four promotion strategies they can try:

- **Stressing tangible cues:** A tangible cue is a concrete symbol of the service offering. To make their intangible services more tangible, hotels turn down the bedcovers and put mints on the pillows.

- **Using personal information sources:** A personal information source is someone consumers are familiar with (such as a celebrity) or someone they admire or can relate to personally. Service firms may seek to simulate positive word-of-mouth communication among present and prospective customers by using real customers in their ads.

- **Creating a strong organizational image:** One way to create an image is to manage the evidence, including the physical environment of the service facility, the appearance of the service employees, and the tangible items associated with a service (such as stationery, bills, and business cards). For example, McDonald's golden arches are instantly recognizable. Another way to create an image is through branding.

- **Engaging in postpurchase communication:** Postpurchase communication refers to the follow-up activities that a service firm might engage in after a customer transaction. Postcard surveys, telephone calls, and other types of follow-up show customers that their feedback matters.

12-4d Price Strategy

Considerations in pricing a service are similar to the pricing considerations to be discussed in Chapter 19. However, the unique characteristics of services present two special pricing challenges.

First, in order to price a service, it is important to define the unit of service consumption. For example, should pricing be based on completing a specific service task (cutting a customer's hair), or should it be time based (how long it takes to cut a customer's hair)? Some services include the consumption of goods, such as food and beverages. Restaurants charge customers for food and drink rather than the use of a table and chairs.

Second, for services that are composed of multiple elements, the issue is whether pricing should be based on a "bundle" of elements or whether each element should be priced separately. A bundled price may be preferable when consumers dislike having to pay "extra" for every part of the service (e.g., paying extra for baggage or food on an airplane), and it is simpler for the firm to administer. Alternatively, customers may not want to pay for service elements they do not use. Many furniture stores now have "unbundled" delivery charges from the price of the furniture. Customers who wish to can pick up the furniture at the store, saving on the delivery fee.

Marketers should set performance objectives when pricing each service. Three categories of pricing objectives have been suggested:

- Revenue-oriented pricing focuses on maximizing the surplus of income over costs. This is the same approach that many manufacturing companies use. A limitation of this approach is that determining costs can be difficult for many services.

- Operations-oriented pricing seeks to match supply and demand by varying prices. For example, matching hotel demand to the number of available rooms can be achieved by raising prices at peak times and decreasing them during slow times.

- Patronage-oriented pricing tries to maximize the number of customers using the service. Thus, prices vary with different market segments' ability to pay and methods of payment (such as credit) are offered that increase the likelihood of a purchase. Senior citizen and student discounts at movie theaters and restaurants are examples of patronage-oriented pricing.[16]

A firm may need to use more than one type of pricing objective. In fact, all three objectives probably need to be included to some degree in a pricing strategy, although the importance of each type may vary depending on the type of service provided, the prices that competitors are charging, the differing ability of various customer segments to pay, or the opportunity to negotiate price. For customized services (such as construction services), customers may also have the ability to negotiate a price.

12-5 RELATIONSHIP MARKETING IN SERVICES

Many services involve ongoing interaction between the service organization and the customer. Thus, these services can benefit from relationship marketing, the strategy described in Chapter 1, as a means of attracting, developing, and retaining customer relationships. The idea is to develop strong loyalty by creating satisfied customers who will buy additional services from the firm and are unlikely to switch to a competitor. Satisfied customers are also likely to engage in positive word-of-mouth communication, thereby helping to bring in new customers.

Many businesses have found that it is more cost-effective to hang on to the customers they have than to focus only on attracting new ones. It has been estimated that companies spend $7 to market to an existing customer, but $34 to market to a new one.[17]

Services that purchasers receive on a continuing basis (e.g., cable television, banking, insurance) can be considered membership services. This type of service naturally lends itself to relationship marketing. When services involve discrete transactions (e.g., in a movie theater, at a restaurant, or on public transportation), it may be more difficult to build membership-type relationships with customers. Nevertheless, services involving discrete transactions may be transformed into membership relationships using marketing tools. For example, the service could be sold in bulk (e.g., a theater series subscription or a commuter pass on public transportation). Or a service firm could offer special benefits to customers who choose to register with the firm (e.g., loyalty programs for hotels and airlines). The service firm that has a more formalized relationship with its customers has an advantage because it knows who its customers are and how and when they use the services offered.[18]

Relationship marketing can be practiced at four levels:

- **Level 1: Financial.** The firm uses pricing incentives to encourage customers to continue doing business with it. Frequent-flyer programs are an example of level 1 relationship marketing. This level of relationship marketing is the least effective in the long term

Salesforce was the top ranked "Best Companies to Work For" by *Fortune Magazine* in 2018.

because its price-based advantage is easily imitated by other firms.

- **Level 2: Social.** This level of relationship marketing also uses pricing incentives but seeks to build social bonds with customers. The firm stays in touch with customers, learns about their needs, and designs services to meet those needs. One example of this is when a company sends its customers birthday cards. Level 2 relationship marketing is often more effective than level 1 relationship marketing.

- **Level 3: Customization.** A customization approach encourages customer loyalty through intimate knowledge of individual customers (often referred to as *customer intimacy*) and the development of one-to-one solutions to fit customers' needs.

- **Level 4: Structural.** At this level, the firm again uses financial and social bonds but adds structural bonds to the formula. Structural bonds are developed by offering value-added services that are not readily available from other firms.[19] Travelers are both more health conscious and interested in special local experiences rather than experiences that are standardized across a hotel brand. Most hotels with spas have created signature treatments and products based on their locations. For example, the Ritz-Carlton in New Orleans, Louisiana, has a signature VooDoo Ritual spa treatment.[20]

12-6 INTERNAL MARKETING IN SERVICE FIRMS

Services are performances, so the quality of a firm's employees is an important part of building long-term relationships with customers. Employees who like their jobs and are satisfied with the firm they work for are more likely to deliver superior service to customers. In other words, a firm that makes its employees happy has a better chance of retaining customers. Thus, it is critical that service firms practice **internal marketing**, which means treating employees as customers and developing systems and benefits that satisfy their needs. While this strategy may also apply to goods manufacturers, it is even more critical in service firms. This is because in service industries, employees deliver the brand promise—their performance as a brand representative—directly to customers. To satisfy employees, companies have designed and instituted a wide variety of programs such as flextime, on-site day care, and concierge services. Salesforce was the number-one ranked "Best Company to Work For" by *Fortune Magazine* in 2018. The company encourages employees' philanthropy by paying them 56 hours a year to volunteer in their communities. There are dedicated "mindfulness" rooms and entire floors celebrating the company *Ohana* (Hawaiian for "family"). Many companies pay employees who refer new hires; Salesforce has paid out $5.5 million worth. The company also looks for strong performers who have gone 18 months without a promotion to help them find new challenges.[21]

12-7 NONPROFIT ORGANIZATION MARKETING

A nonprofit organization is an organization that exists to achieve some goal other than the usual business goals of profit, market share, or return on investment. Both nonprofit organizations and private-sector service firms market intangible products, and both often require the customer to be present during the production process. Both for-profit and nonprofit services vary greatly from producer to producer and from day to day from the same producer.

Few people realize that nonprofit organizations account for more than 20 percent of the economic activity in the United States. The cost of government (i.e., taxes), the predominant form of nonprofit organization, has become the biggest single item in the American family budget—more than housing, food, or health care. Together, federal, state, and local governments collect tax revenues that amount to

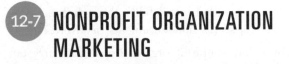

internal marketing treating employees as customers and developing systems and benefits that satisfy their needs

nonprofit organization an organization that exists to achieve some goal other than the usual business goals of profit, market share, or return on investment more than one-third of the U.S. gross domestic product (GDP). In addition to government entities, nonprofit organizations include hundreds of thousands of private museums, theaters, schools, and churches.

12-7a What Is Nonprofit Organization Marketing?

Nonprofit organization marketing is the effort by nonprofit organizations to bring about mutually satisfying exchanges with target markets. Although these organizations vary substantially in size and purpose and operate in different environments, most perform the following marketing activities:

- Identify the customers they wish to serve or attract (although they usually use other terms, such as clients, patients, members, or sponsors)

- Explicitly or implicitly specify objectives

- Develop, manage, and eliminate programs and services

- Decide on prices to charge (although they use other terms, such as *fees, donations, tuition, fares, fines,* or *rates*)

- Schedule events or programs, and determine where they will be held or where services will be offered

- Communicate their availability through brochures, signs, public service announcements, or advertisements

Often, the nonprofit organizations that carry out these functions do not realize they are engaged in marketing.

12-7b Unique Aspects of Nonprofit Organization Marketing Strategies

Like their counterparts in business organizations, nonprofit managers develop marketing strategies to bring about mutually satisfying exchanges with target markets. However, marketing in nonprofit organizations is unique in many ways—including the setting of marketing objectives, the selection of target markets, and the development of appropriate marketing mixes.

OBJECTIVES In the private sector, profit motives are both objectives for guiding decisions and criteria for evaluating results. Nonprofit organizations do not seek to make a profit for redistribution to owners or shareholders. Rather, their focus is often on generating enough funds to cover expenses.

nonprofit organization marketing the effort by nonprofit organizations to bring about mutually satisfying exchanges with target markets

PBS, the Public Broadcasting Service, receives its funding from donations.

Andy Borysowski/Shutterstock.com

Most nonprofit organizations are expected to provide equitable, effective, and efficient services that respond to the wants and preferences of multiple constituencies. These include users, payers, donors, politicians, appointed officials, the media, and the general public. Nonprofit organizations cannot measure their success or failure in strictly financial terms.

The lack of a financial "bottom line" and the existence of multiple, diverse, intangible, and sometimes vague or conflicting objectives make prioritizing objectives, making decisions, and evaluating performance hard for nonprofit managers. They must often use approaches different from the ones commonly used in the private sector.

TARGET MARKETS Three issues relating to target markets are unique to nonprofit organizations:

- **Apathetic or strongly opposed targets:** Private-sector organizations usually give priority to developing those market segments that are most likely to respond to particular offerings. In contrast, nonprofit organizations must often target those who are apathetic about or strongly opposed to receiving their services, such as vaccinations and psychological counseling.

- **Pressure to adopt undifferentiated segmentation strategies:** Nonprofit organizations often adopt undifferentiated strategies (see Chapter 8) by default. Sometimes they fail to recognize the advantages of targeting, or an undifferentiated approach may appear to offer economies of scale and low per capita costs. In other instances, nonprofit organizations are pressured or required to serve the maximum number of people by targeting the average user.

- **Complementary positioning:** The main role of many nonprofit organizations is to provide services, with available resources, to those who are not adequately served by private-sector organizations. As a result, the nonprofit organization must often complement, rather than compete with, the efforts of others. The positioning task is to identify underserved market segments and to develop marketing programs that match their needs rather than target the niches that may be most profitable. For example, a university library may see itself as complementing the services of the public library rather than as competing with it.

PRODUCT DECISIONS There are three product-related distinctions between business and nonprofit organizations:

- **Benefit complexity:** Nonprofit organizations often market complex behaviors or ideas. Examples include the need to exercise or eat right and the need to quit smoking. The benefits that a person receives are complex, long term, and intangible, and therefore, they are more difficult to communicate to consumers.

- **Benefit strength:** The benefit strength of many nonprofit offerings is quite weak or indirect. What are the direct, personal benefits to you of driving 55 miles per hour or donating blood? In contrast, most private-sector service organizations can offer customers direct, personal benefits in an exchange relationship.

- **Involvement:** Many nonprofit organizations market products that elicit very low involvement ("Prevent forest fires") or very high involvement ("Stop smoking"). The typical range for private-sector goods is much narrower. Traditional promotional tools may be inadequate to motivate adoption of either low- or high-involvement products.

PLACE (DISTRIBUTION) DECISIONS A nonprofit organization's capacity for distributing its service offerings to potential customer groups when and where they want them is typically a key variable in determining the success of those service offerings. For example, many large universities have one or more satellite campus locations to provide easier access for students in other areas. Some educational institutions also offer classes to students at off-campus locations through the use of interactive video technology or at home via the Internet.

The extent to which a service depends on fixed facilities has important implications for distribution decisions. Services like rail transit and lake fishing can be delivered only at specific points. Many nonprofit services, however, do not depend on special facilities.

PROMOTION DECISIONS Many nonprofit organizations are explicitly or implicitly prohibited from advertising, thus limiting their promotion options. Most federal agencies fall into this category. Other nonprofit organizations simply do not have the resources to retain advertising agencies, promotion consultants, or marketing staff. Nonprofit organizations have a few special promotion resources to call on, however:

- **Professional volunteers:** Nonprofit organizations often seek out marketing, sales, and advertising professionals to help them develop and implement promotion strategies. In some instances, an advertising agency donates its services in exchange for potential long-term benefits. Donated services create goodwill; personal contacts; and general awareness of the donor's organization, reputation, and competency.

- **Sales promotion activities:** Sales promotion activities that use existing services or other resources are increasingly being used to draw attention to the offerings of nonprofit organizations. Sometimes nonprofit charities even team up with other companies for promotional activities. The city of Glasgow, Scotland developed a branding strategy for very little money when it staged a competition among its residents to choose a city tag line. At the end of the competition, the city selected a tag line that has a story behind it: "People Make Glasgow." This phrase expresses the Glaswegian quality of working with one another with a common sense of purpose. Glasgow's successful story-telling strategy has since expanded to include "Food Makes

GlassesUSA donates $5 to Alex's Lemonade Stand Foundation for every pair of Lemonade glasses it sells.

Glasgow" and "Music Makes Glasgow."[22] In another example, GlassesUSA.com launched two new pairs of glasses inspired by and in support of Alex's Lemonade Stand Foundation (ALSF). The lemonade-colored frames are available only online and will "add a fresh twist to the brand's frame variety for anyone who wants to look good, while doing good." The glasses are named Alex—after Alexandra Scott who was only eight years old when she passed away from cancer—and Lemonade after her Foundation that was founded to help cure childhood cancer. For each pair sold, GlassesUSA.com donates $5 to the Foundation. GlassesUSA.com has also developed products and donated to organizations such as FREE THE GIRLS, amfAR, Hanalei-Haena Flooding Fund, and Breast Cancer Prevention Partners.[23]

- **Public service advertising:** A public service advertisement (PSA) is an announcement that promotes a program of a federal, state, or local government or of a nonprofit organization. Unlike a commercial advertiser, the sponsor of the PSA does not pay for the time or space. Instead, it is donated by the medium. During the midterm elections in 2018, the nonprofit organization Acronym was trying to get young people—who historically have posted lower voter turnout rates than their older peers—to register to vote. To achieve its mission the group released a series of tongue-in-cheek, if not dark, films that mainly aimed to scare Millennials into casting a ballot. The campaign, featured senior citizens talking straight into the camera as they explained why they'd prefer it if young people didn't vote this year. The one-minute ad portrays elderly voters as out-of-touch with current issues. The point of the effort was to remind young people that Baby Boomers are essentially calling the shots when it comes to who is elected to office: according to the U.S. Census Bureau, 70.9 percent of citizens 65 years or older voted in the last election, while only 46.1 percent of those ages 18 to 29 did. The campaign, which also included three 15-second spots, ran on Facebook, Instagram, Snapchat, Hulu, and YouTube.[24]

PRICING DECISIONS Five key characteristics distinguish the pricing decisions of nonprofit organizations from those of the for-profit sector:

- **Pricing objectives:** The main pricing objective in the profit sector is revenue or, more specifically, profit maximization, sales maximization, or target return on sales or investment. Many nonprofit organizations must also be concerned about revenue. Often, however, nonprofit organizations seek to either partially or fully defray costs rather than to achieve a profit for distribution to stockholders. Nonprofit organizations also seek to redistribute income—for instance, through taxation and sliding-scale fees. Moreover, they strive to allocate resources fairly among individuals or households or across geographic or political boundaries.

- **Nonfinancial prices:** In many nonprofit situations, consumers are not charged a monetary price but instead must absorb nonmonetary costs. The importance of those costs is illustrated by the large number of eligible citizens who do not take advantage of so-called free services for the poor. In many public assistance programs, about half the people who are eligible do not participate. Nonmonetary costs include time, embarrassment, and effort.

- **Indirect payment:** Indirect payment through taxes is common to marketers of "free" services, such as libraries, fire protection, and police protection. Indirect payment is not a common practice in the profit sector.

- **Separation between payers and users:** By design, the services of many charitable organizations are provided for those who are relatively poor and are largely paid for by those who are better off financially. Although examples of separation between payers and users can be found in the profit sector (such as insurance claims), the practice is much less prevalent.

Indirect payment through taxes is common to marketers of "free" services such as libraries, fire protection, and police protection.

- **Below-cost pricing:** An example of below-cost pricing is university tuition. Virtually all private and public colleges and universities price their services below full cost.

12-8 GLOBAL ISSUES IN SERVICES MARKETING

The international marketing of services is a major part of global business, and the United States has become the world's largest exporter of services. Competition in international services is increasing rapidly, but many U.S. service industries have been able to enter the global marketplace because of their competitive advantages. U.S. banks, for example, have advantages in customer service and collections management.

For both for-profit and nonprofit service firms, the first step toward success in the global marketplace is determining the nature of the company's core products. Then the marketing-mix elements (additional services, place, promotion, pricing, and distribution) should be designed to take into account each country's cultural, technological, and political environment. Pizza Hut creates pizza flavors that reflect its varying global locations. For example, customers can get Prawn Pizza in Australia, Cheesy Poutine (beef gravy, French fries, and cheese curds) Pizza in Canada, and Tuna Sweet Corn Melt Pizza in the United Kingdom.[25]

13 | Supply Chain Management and Marketing Channels

LEARNING OUTCOMES

After studying this chapter, you will be able to . . .

13-1 Define the terms *supply chain* and *supply chain management*, and discuss the benefits of supply chain management

13-2 Discuss the concepts of internal and external supply chain integration and explain why each of these types of integration is important

13-3 Identify the eight key processes of excellent supply chain management, and discuss how each of these processes affects the end customer

13-4 Understand the importance of sustainable supply chain management to modern business operations

13-5 Discuss how new technology and emerging trends are impacting the practice of supply chain management

13-6 Explain what marketing channels and channel intermediaries are, and describe their functions and activities

13-7 Describe common channel structures and strategies and the factors that influence their choice

13-8 Discuss omnichannel and multichannel marketing in both B-to-B and B-to-C structures, and explain why these concepts are important

Zapp2Photo/Shutterstock.com

13-1 SUPPLY CHAINS AND SUPPLY CHAIN MANAGEMENT

Many modern companies are turning to supply chain management for competitive advantage. A company's **supply chain** includes all of the companies involved in the upstream and downstream flow of products, services, finances, and information, extending from initial suppliers (the point of origin) to the ultimate customer (the point of consumption). The goal of **supply chain management** (SCM) is to coordinate and integrate all of the activities performed by supply chain members into a seamless process, from the source to the point of consumption, ultimately giving supply chain managers "total visibility and control" of the materials, processes, money, and finished products both inside and outside the company they work for. The underlying philosophy is that by visualizing and exerting control over the entire supply chain, companies can balance demand for their products and services as perfectly as possible with available supply. This approach maximizes customer outcomes while also creating efficiency at each level of the chain. Understanding and integrating supply-and-demand–related information at every level enables supply chain managers to optimize their decisions, reduce waste, and respond quickly to sudden changes in supply or demand or other factors in the supply chain.

When performed well, SCM reflects a completely customer-driven management philosophy. In the mass production era, manufacturers produced standardized products that were "pushed" down through marketing channels to consumers, who were then convinced by salespeople to buy whatever was produced. In today's marketplace, this logic is completely inverted—customers expect to receive product configurations and services matched to their unique needs and are therefore seen as catalysts that are increasingly driving demand. The focus of businesses has shifted to determining how products and services are being "pulled" into the marketplace by customers and on partnering with members of the supply chain to enhance customer value. For example, online retailer Fresh Gab offers customized clothing, watches, phone cases, and other fashion products. Customers design the products themselves, based on a wide array of materials, color palettes, and styles.[1] This differs dramatically from the mass-manufacturing approach apparel companies have historically taken, whereby a focus on efficiency led to a narrower range of selections and few opportunities for customization.

The reversal of the flow of demand from "push" to "pull" has resulted in a radical reformulation of traditional marketing, production, and distribution functions toward a philosophy of **supply chain agility**. Agile companies synchronize their activities through the sharing of supply-and-demand market information, spend more time than their competitors focusing on activities that create direct customer benefits, partner closely with suppliers and service providers to reduce customer wait times for products, and constantly seek to reduce supply chain complexity through the evaluation and reduction (or elimination) of stock-keeping units (SKUs) that customers aren't buying, among other strategies.

> In today's marketplace, products are being driven by customer demand, and businesses need to balance demand with supply in order to ensure economic profits.

supply chain the connected chain of all of the business entities, both internal and external to the company, that perform or support the logistics function

supply chain management a management system that coordinates and integrates all of the activities performed by supply chain members into a seamless process, from the source to the point of consumption, resulting in enhanced customer and economic value

supply chain agility an operational strategy focused on creating inventory velocity and operational flexibility simultaneously in the supply chain

For example, in the fashion industry, trends are constantly changing. Each season's demand is influenced by weather and pop culture events, announcements in the media, and even politics. If customers behave unpredictably in response to these situations, businesses can react by postponing their own purchasing and manufacturing processes until just before sales occur in order to minimize the costs of making and holding incorrect inventory. "Fast fashion" industry leaders like Zara manage to integrate agility into their supply chains despite producing roughly 450 million items per year. To remain efficient while maximizing customer satisfaction, Zara employs regular, small-batch deliveries to all of its stores twice a week and harnesses the power of real-time data related to transactions and consumer preferences to better understand current and future demand, so that the supply chain can react accordingly.[2] Shoppers want, and companies therefore promise, that items will be available faster, cheaper, and with greater convenience and choice than ever before. It is up to the supply chain managers of their favorite companies to deliver on those promises!

Unfortunately, most companies do not manage their supply chains alone or in isolation. Effective SCM requires a team effort between the firm and its partners. **Outsourcing**, or **contract logistics**, is a rapidly growing initiative in which a manufacturer or supplier turns over an entire logistical function (often buying and managing transportation, warehousing, and/or postponed manufacturing) to an independent **third-party logistics company (3PL)** that helps manage warehouse space, provides transportation solutions, assists with information sharing, or provides enhanced technological innovations. For example, when a major manufacturer in the health care industry outsourced its distribution operations to Kenco, a prominent leader in the 3PL industry, the company's waste dropped by nearly 60 percent, leading to both substantial cost savings and a greener and more sustainable supply chain.[3]

Outsourcing enables companies to cut inventories, and locate stock at fewer plants and distribution centers, while still providing the same level of service (or sometimes, performing even better). While in the past, firms often looked around the world for partners to help with customer service needs or manufacturing in order to secure lower costs, many companies are now seeking solutions within (**reshoring**) or close to (**nearshoring**) their primary base of operations, in order to reduce supply chain risk and maintain tighter control over operations. This is not to say, however, that supply chains are becoming more domestic. Strategically, there are many reasons why a company might wish to globalize its supply chain. The allure of foreign markets is strong, due to increasing demand for imported products worldwide. Furthermore, cheap labor advantages and trade barriers/tariffs have encouraged firms to expand their global manufacturing operations. Unfortunately, globalization has brought about great uncertainty as well. Moving operations offshore exposes companies to risks associated with geopolitical conflict, foreign nationalization of assets, unintended knowledge leakage to foreign competitors, and highly variable quality standards.

As the world continues to globalize, supply chain management will undoubtedly continue to take on a multinational flavor. Worldwide, the resources needed to manufacture and sell goods that are increasingly in demand are becoming scarcer, and market boundaries are melting together. Free trade is expanding globally, and consumers in nations where demand has traditionally been low are viewing goods and placing orders via the Internet. The effort to achieve world-class global supply chain management means that the balancing of supply and demand—and the satisfaction of more and more customers worldwide—are becoming a reality for many companies. Though the United States and Great Britain have recently signaled that they may revert to a less global and more protectionist stance, possibly with fewer imports being allowed, it is uncertain whether these changes will be sustainable in the long term. In the meantime, nations such as China and India are signaling that, now more than ever, they are "open for business," as they extend the global reach of their supply chains into Africa and other less-developed parts of the planet.

13-1a Benefits of Effective Supply Chain Management

SCM is a key means of differentiation for a company, and therefore represents a critical component in marketing and corporate strategy. Organizations that focus on supply chain management commonly report lower inventory, transportation, warehousing, and packaging costs; greater

---

outsourcing (contract logistics) a manufacturer's or supplier's use of an independent third party to manage an entire function of the logistics system, such as transportation, warehousing, or order processing

third-party logistics company (3PL) a firm that provides functional logistics services to others

reshoring the reinstitutionalization of a business process from an outsource location/country back to the original location for the purpose of gaining economic advantage

nearshoring the transfer of an outsourced activity from a distant to a nearby country logical flexibility; improved customer service; and higher revenues. Research has shown a clear relationship between supply chain performance and both profitability and company value. Additionally, because well-managed supply chains are able to provide better value to customers with only marginal incremental expenditure on company assets, best-in-class supply chain companies such as Walmart can use SCM as a means of demonstrating a competitive differential. The retail giant uses strategic partnerships with suppliers, advanced inventory technologies, and state-of-the-art network design processes to stay competitive—all while providing consumers with thousands of their basic needs at very low prices. Walmart openly shares point-of-sale demand data and forecasts, as well as inventory replenishment data, with its supplier and manufacturing partners using a central database that enables all parties to coordinate efforts. Additionally, Walmart uses technologies such as **RFID** (radio-frequency identification) and smart tags to keep track of inventory locations and restocking needs in real time.[4]

Lean supply chains have become widespread in recent years, but a dark side to these lean systems emerged during the pandemic. A lean strategy requires balancing the inventory needs of a business while minimizing the possibility of overstocking goods and maximizing the company's cash flow. The Covid-19 virus exposed how fragile lean supply chains can be and taught supply chain managers the hard way to always be prepared for the unexpected. In fact, some managers are learning their supply chains are just too lean and are making adjustments. What the managers are learning is adopting an agile strategy also carries risks, such as lost or incorrectly allocated inventories. A primary example was the toilet paper shortages for the residential market in the early stages of the pandemic. The manufacturing and distribution systems were optimized for two separate markets—commercial (office buildings, hotels, restaurants, etc.) and residential, but when the market immediately switched to residential only, since almost everyone was working from home, shortages were widespread. Later in the pandemic, similar shortages emerged for aluminum can beverages, particularly aluminum packaging for soft drink and beer cans. In response to these supply chain problems, many businesses have begun rethinking what it means to be agile.

Redesigning a supply chain can do more than just improve the bottom line. Hewlett-Packard helped its suppliers avoid 800,000 metric tons of CO_2 emissions, in the process saving them over $65 million, by working with them to simplify the supply chain and reduce the number of overall shipments needed to ensure the supply of materials.[5]

13-2 SUPPLY CHAIN INTEGRATION

A key principle of supply chain management is that multiple entities (firms and/or their functional areas) should work together to perform tasks as a single, unified system, rather than as multiple individual units acting in isolation. Companies in a world-class supply chain combine their resources, capabilities, and innovations across multiple business boundaries so that they are used for the best interest of the supply chain as a whole. The goal is that the overall performance of the supply chain will be greater than the sum of its parts.

As companies become increasingly focused on supply chain management, they develop a **supply chain orientation**. This means they implement management practices that are consistent with a "systems thinking" approach. Leading supply chain–oriented firms like Amazon, McDonald's, and Unilever possess five characteristics that, in combination, set them apart from their competitors:

1. *They are credible.* They have the capability to deliver on the promises they make.

2. *They are benevolent.* They are willing to accept short-term risks on behalf of others, are committed to others, and invest in others' success.

3. *They are cooperative.* They work with rather than against their partners when seeking to achieve goals.

4. *They have the support of top managers.* These managers possess the vision required to do things that benefit the entire supply chain in the short run so they can enjoy greater company successes in the long run.

5. *They are effective at conducting and directing supply chain activity.* As a result, they are better off in the long run financially than those who are not as effective.

Management practices that reflect a highly coordinated effort between supply chain firms or across business functions within the same or different firms are "integrated." In other words, **supply chain integration** occurs when multiple firms or their functional areas in a supply chain coordinate business processes so they are seamlessly linked to one another. In a world-class supply chain, the customer may not know where the

RFID radio-frequency identification; a device that uses radio waves as a means of locating a piece of inventory within a confined geographic space

supply chain orientation a system of management practices that are consistent with a "systems thinking" approach

supply chain integration when multiple firms or business functions in a supply chain coordinate, their activities and processes so that they are seamlessly linked to one another in an effort to satisfy the customer

Airbus has co-located its engineering, logistics and procurement divisions in order to build synergies between them. The newest Airbus 350-1000 is on display at Suvarnabhumi Airport, Bangkok.

business activities of one company or business unit end and where those of another begin—each actor keeps his or her own interests in mind, but all appear to be reading from the same script, and from time to time, each makes sacrifices that benefit the performance of the system as a whole.

In modern supply chain systems, integration can be either internal or external to a specific company or, ideally, both. From an internal perspective, the very best companies develop a managerial orientation toward **demand–supply integration (DSI)**. Under the DSI philosophy, the functional areas in a company charged with creating customer demand (such as marketing, sales, or research and development) communicate frequently and are synchronized with the parts of the business charged with fulfilling the created demand (purchasing, manufacturing, and logistics). Some companies, like Airbus, are beginning to co-locate their engineering, logistics, and procurement divisions in order to build synergies between them.[6] This type of alignment enhances customer satisfaction by ensuring that, for example, salespeople make promises to customers that can actually be delivered on by the company's logistics arm or that raw materials being purchased actually meet customer specifications before they are placed into production. Simultaneously, the company gains efficiencies from ordering and using only materials that lead directly to sales. In short, companies operating under a DSI philosophy are better at their business because all of the divisions within the company "play from the same sheet of music."[7]

> **demand–supply integration (DSI)** a supply chain operational philosophy focused on integrating the supply-management and demand-generating functions of an organization

In addition to being internally integrated, the group of connected organizations in a world-class supply chain behave as though they have a common mission and leadership. To accomplish this task across companies that have different ownership and interests, five types of external integration are sought by firms interested in providing top-level service to customers[8]:

- *Relationship integration* is the ability of two or more companies to develop social connections that serve to guide their interactions when working together. More specifically, relationship integration is the capability to develop and maintain a shared mental framework across companies that describes how they will depend on one another when working together. This includes the ways in which they will collaborate on activities or projects so that the customer gains the maximum amount of total value possible from the supply chain.

- *Measurement integration* reflects the idea that performance assessments should be transparent and measurable across the borders of different firms; it should also assess the performance of the supply chain as a whole while holding each individual firm or business unit accountable for meeting its own goals.

- *Technology and planning integration* refers to the creation and maintenance of information technology systems that connect managers across the firms in the supply chain. It requires information hardware and software systems that can exchange information when needed between customers, suppliers, and internal operational areas of each of the supply chain partners.

- *Material and service supplier integration* requires firms to link seamlessly to those outsiders that provide goods and services to them so that they can streamline work processes and thereby provide smooth, high-quality customer experiences. Both sides need to have a common vision of the total value-creation process and be willing to share the responsibility for satisfying customer requirements to make supplier integration successful.

- *Customer integration* is a competency that enables firms to offer long-lasting, distinctive, value-added offerings to the customers who represent the greatest value to the firm or supply chain. Highly customer-integrated firms assess their own capabilities and then match them to customers whose desires they can meet and who offer large enough sales potential for the linkage to be profitable over the long term.

Success in achieving both the internal and external types of integration is very important. Highly integrated supply chains (those that are successful in achieving many

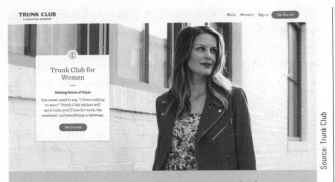

Source: Trunk Club

Trunk Club, a web-based personal shopper service, uses a customer-integrated supply chain to offer its customers high-quality, customized product offerings.

or all of these types of integration) have been shown to be better at satisfying customers, managing costs, delivering high-quality products, enhancing productivity, and utilizing company or business unit assets, all of which translate into greater profitability for the firms and their partners working together in the supply chain.

Integration involves a balance between barriers and enablers. Companies that work closely with their suppliers encounter problems such as corporate culture, information hoarding, and trust issues. For example, Häagen-Dazs and General Mills share information with their vanilla suppliers to increase yields and improve sustainability practices, but at the same time, there is a danger. Giving supply chain partners this information enables those partners to share it with competitors. On the other hand, integration can be improved through long-term agreements, cross-organizational integrated product teams, and improved communication between partners. These factors all aid in integrating supply chain operations.[9]

An unanticipated dark side to agile supply chain systems emerged during the pandemic. In addition to hand towels and toilet paper, consumers began to hoard products like hand sanitizers and Clorox wipes. In response, governments enacted restrictions on selected exports like medical supplies, ventilators, and personal protective equipment (PPE). These shortages affected some industries more than others, but almost all sectors were affected in some way. These disruptions on the supply side and the emphasis on customer and worker health and safety, as well as the need for continued distribution efficiency, slowed down supply chain responsiveness and increased costs. The primary lesson was to be better prepared in the future to ensure supply chains continue to perform at a high level in the future. Moreover, to do so middle and upper management, often including the CEO, must be involved in developing solutions. Most companies had allocated insufficient resources to drive supply chain innovations, and yet innovations are among the most resilient forces to deal with a disaster or pandemic.

13-3 THE KEY PROCESSES OF SUPPLY CHAIN MANAGEMENT

When firms practice good supply chain management, their functional departments or areas, such as marketing, research and development, and/or production, are integrated both within and across the linked firms. Integration, then, is "how" excellent supply chain management works. The business processes on which the linked firms work together represent the "what" of supply chain management—they are what firms, departments, areas, and people focus on when working together to reduce supply chain costs or to generate additional revenues. **Business processes** are composed of bundles of interconnected activities that stretch across firms in the supply chain. They represent key areas that some or all of the involved firms are constantly working on to reduce costs and/or generate revenues for everyone throughout supply chain management. There are eight critical business processes on which supply chain managers must focus:

1. Customer relationship management
2. Customer service management
3. Demand management
4. Order fulfillment
5. Manufacturing flow management
6. Supplier relationship management
7. Product development and commercialization
8. Returns management[10]

13-3a Customer Relationship Management

The **customer relationship management (CRM) process** enables companies to prioritize their marketing focus on different customer groups according to each group's long-term value to the company or supply chain. Once higher-value customers are identified, firms should focus more on

business processes bundles of interconnected activities that stretch across firms in the supply chain

customer relationship management (CRM) process allows companies to prioritize their marketing focus on different customer groups according to each group's long-term value to the company or supply chain providing customized products and better service to this group than to others. The CRM process includes customer segmentation by value and subsequent generation of customer loyalty for the most attractive segments. This process provides a set of comprehensive principles for the initiation and maintenance of customer relationships and is often carried out with the assistance of specialized CRM computer software. For example, national pet supplies retailer Petco leverages CRM by zeroing in on new pet owners and capturing their loyalty early in the pet–owner relationship. They do this by providing the new owners with customized pet guides, shopping lists, coupons, and merchandise information that stimulates demand at just the moment when the enthusiasm about their new pet is highest. In addition to attracting new pet owners, Petco utilizes CRM to retain existing customers by offering convenience features such as two-hour delivery for online purchases, subscription delivery services for foods and medicines, and a loyalty program that provides uniquely low prices for the most frequent customers.[11]

13-3b Customer Service Management

While the CRM process is designed to identify and build relationships with good customers, the customer service management process is designed to ensure that those customer relationships remain strong. The **customer service management process** presents a multicompany, unified response system to the customer whenever complaints, concerns, questions, or comments are voiced. When the process is well executed, it can have a strong positive impact on revenues, often as a result of a quick positive response to negative customer feedback and sometimes even in the form of additional sales gained through the additional customer contact. Customers expect service from the moment a product is purchased until it is disposed of, and the customer service management process facilitates touch points between the buyer and seller throughout this life cycle. The use of customer care software enables companies to enhance their customer service management process. Consider that leading video game producer Activision prides itself on providing consistent and continuous service to its gamers. Via a cloud-based CRM application, Activision can monitor social media sites for conversations that relate to the company's products, and then respond to the conversations with customer service solutions right away. Using CRM to monitor social media and identify customer service opportunities has reduced the company's annual customer service operating expenses by 25 percent, while at the same time increasing gamer satisfaction.[12]

13-3c Demand Management

The **demand management process** seeks to align supply and demand throughout the supply chain by anticipating customer requirements at each level and creating customer-focused plans of action prior to actual purchases being made. At the same time, demand management seeks to minimize the costs of serving multiple types of customers who have variable wants and needs. In other words, the demand management process allows companies in the supply chain to satisfy customers in the most efficient and effective ways possible. Activities such as collecting customer data, forecasting future demand, and developing activities that smooth out demand help bring available inventory into alignment with customer desires.

Though it is very difficult to predict exactly what items and quantities customers will buy prior to purchase, demand management can ease pressure on the production process and allow companies to satisfy most of their customers through greater flexibility in manufacturing, marketing, and sales programs. One key way this occurs is through the sharing of customer demand forecasts and data during **sales and operations planning (S&OP)** meetings. During these meetings, the demand-generating functions of the business (marketing and sales) work together with the production side of the business (procurement, production, and logistics) in a collaborative arrangement designed to both satisfy customers and minimize waste. After implementing S&OP, one U.S.-based supplier of steel products saved almost $9 million in transportation costs, increased delivery performance by more than 30 percent, and reduced inventory levels by 12 percent, leading to significant cost savings that were passed along to customers.[13]

13-3d Order Fulfillment

One of the most fundamental processes in supply chain management is the order fulfillment process, which

customer service management process presents a multicompany, unified response system to the customer whenever complaints, concerns, questions, or comments are voiced

demand management process seeks to align supply and demand throughout the supply chain by anticipating customer requirements at each level and creating demand-related plans of action prior to actual customer purchases

sales and operations planning (S&OP) a method companies use to align production with demand by merging tactical and strategic planning methods across functional areas of the business involves generating, filling, delivering, and providing on-the-spot service for customer orders. The order fulfillment process is a highly integrated one, often requiring persons from multiple companies and multiple functions to come together and coordinate to create customer satisfaction at a given place and time. The best order fulfillment processes reduce order cycle time—the time between order and customer receipt—as much as possible, while ensuring that the customer receives exactly what he or she wants. The shorter lead times are beneficial in that they allow firms to carry reduced inventory levels and free up cash that can be used on other projects. Overall, the order fulfillment process involves understanding and integrating the company's internal capabilities with customer needs, and matching these together so that the supply chain maximizes profits while minimizing costs and waste. FedEx Fulfillment, a subsidiary of FedEx Corporation, was created to help small and medium-sized companies fulfill orders from multiple channels with streamlined efficiency while maximizing effectiveness. This service provider offers an integrated supply chain system with a user-friendly platform that provides users access to timely information about FedEx's transportation networks, warehouses, packaging, and even reverse logistics options for managing returns. With FedEx's infrastructure backing them, smaller companies can enhance their otherwise limited order fulfillment potential, and can achieve better financial performance through faster and more accurate shipments.[14]

13-3e Manufacturing Flow Management

The manufacturing flow management process is concerned with ensuring that firms in the supply chain have the needed resources to manufacture with flexibility and to move products through a multistage production process. Firms with flexible manufacturing have the ability to create a wide variety of goods and/or services with minimal costs associated with changing production techniques. The manufacturing flow process includes much more than simple production of goods and services—it means creating flexible agreements with suppliers and shippers so that unexpected demand bursts can be accommodated without disruptions to customer service or satisfaction.

The goals of the manufacturing flow management process are centered on leveraging the capabilities held by multiple members of the supply chain to improve overall manufacturing output in terms of quality, delivery speed, and flexibility, all of which tie directly to profitability. Depending on the product, supply chain managers may choose between a lean or agile supply chain strategy. In a lean supply chain, products are built before demand occurs, but managers attempt to reduce as much waste as possible. Lean supply chains first appeared within the Toyota Production System (TPS) as early as the 1950s. Agile strategies lie on the other end of the continuum—they prioritize customer responsiveness more so than waste reduction. Instead of trying to forecast demand and reduce waste, agile supply chains wait for demand to occur and use communication and flexibility to fill that demand quickly.[15] One way U.S. aircraft manufacturer Boeing has created manufacturing agility is by building its aircraft subsystems to be modular, such that a cockpit instrument panel or software platform can be used in (for instance) both the 737 airliner and the KC-46 tanker. By using redundant parts and systems across different models, the company can quickly switch from producing one type of aircraft to another, thereby reducing production machine downtime and producing substantial cost savings.[16]

13-3f Supplier Relationship Management

The supplier relationship management process is closely related to the manufacturing flow management process and contains several characteristics that parallel the customer relationship management process. The manufacturing flow management process is highly dependent on supplier relationships for flexibility. Furthermore, as in the customer relationship management process, supplier relationship management provides structural support for developing and maintaining relationships with suppliers. Thus, by integrating these two ideas, supplier relationship management supports manufacturing flow by identifying and maintaining relationships with highly valued suppliers.

Just as firms benefit from developing close-knit, integrated relationships with customers, close-knit, integrated relationships with suppliers provide a means through which performance advantages can be gained. For example, careful management of supplier relationships is

order fulfillment process a highly integrated process, often requiring persons from multiple companies and multiple functions to come together and coordinate to create customer satisfaction at a given place and time

order cycle time the time delay between the placement of a customer's order and the customer's receipt of that order

manufacturing flow management process process concerned with ensuring that firms in the supply chain have the needed resources to manufacture with flexibility and to move products through a multistage production process

modular a standardized form of component parts manufacturing designed so the parts are easily replaced or interchanged

supplier relationship management process supports manufacturing flow by identifying and maintaining relationships with highly valued suppliers a key step toward ensuring that firms' manufacturing resources are utilized to their maximum potential. It is clear, then, that the supplier relationship management process has a direct impact on each supply chain member's bottom-line financial performance. In certain instances, it can be advantageous for the supply chain to integrate via a formal merger. AT&T recently purchased Time Warner Inc., a choice that will enable the company to vertically integrate with their supplier of media content. Through AT&T's decision to acquire a key supplier, the company can leverage synergies of controlling global media and entertainment products with its own highly developed capabilities in high-speed–network technology, premium content delivery, and customer relationship management across video, mobile, and broadband services. By merging the two companies, AT&T anticipates $1.5 billion in cost savings and $1 billion in revenue earned by 2021.[17]

13-3g Product Development and Commercialization

The **product development and commercialization process** (discussed in detail in Chapter 11) includes the group of activities that facilitate the joint development and marketing of new offerings among a group of supply chain partner firms. In many cases, more than one supply chain entity is responsible for ensuring the success of a new product. Commonly, a multicompany collaboration is used to execute new-product development, testing, and launch, among other activities. The capability for developing and introducing new offerings quickly is key for competitive success versus rival firms, so it is often advantageous to involve many supply chain partners in the effort. The process requires the close cooperation of suppliers and customers, who provide input throughout the process and serve as advisers and co-producers for the new offering(s).

Designing a new product with the help of suppliers and customers can enable a company to introduce features and cost-cutting measures into final products. Customers provide information about what they want from the product, while suppliers can help design for quality and manufacturability. Research has shown that when each supply chain partner shares responsibility for the design and manufacture of a new product, more obstacles can be identified early and opportunities for

product development and commercialization process includes the group of activities that facilitates the joint development and marketing of new offerings among a group of supply chain partner firms

returns management process enables firms to manage volumes of returned product efficiently while minimizing returns-related costs and maximizing the value of the returned assets to the firms in the supply chain

Jarretera/Shutterstock.com

The AT&T and Time Warner merger enables the new combined company to more efficiently serve global markets with a consistent message, as illustrated here by the Official websites of the two companies in Amsterdam, the Netherlands.

cost reduction are made possible. For example, Boeing involved a team of suppliers early in the development phase of its 787 Dreamliner aircraft, leading to a shift to a lighter composite material for the fuselage's outer shell. The lighter material is expected to make the aircraft substantially cheaper to operate on long-haul flights.[18]

13-3h Returns Management

The final supply chain management process deals with situations in which customers choose to return a product to the retailer or supplier, thereby creating a reverse flow of goods within the supply chain. The **returns management process** enables firms to manage volumes of returned product efficiently while minimizing returns-related costs and maximizing the value of the returned assets to the firms in the supply chain. Returns have the potential to affect a firm's financial position in a major and negative way if mishandled. In certain industries, such as apparel e-retailing, returns can amount to as much as 40 percent of sales volume.

In addition to the value of managing returns from a pure asset-recovery perspective, many firms are discovering that returns management also creates additional marketing and customer service touch points that can be leveraged for added customer value above and beyond normal sales and promotion-driven encounters. Handling returns quickly creates a positive image and gives the company an additional opportunity to please the customer, and customers who have positive experiences with the returns management process can become very confident buyers who are willing to reorder, since they know any problems they encounter with purchases will be quickly and fairly corrected. In addition, the returns management process allows the firm to recognize weaknesses in product design and/or areas for potential improvement through the direct customer feedback that initiates the process.

Many retailers, such as Nordstrom and Trader Joe's, have implemented generous return policies to develop loyalty within their customer base and serve their needs. For example, Nordstrom, a large department store, has no time limit on when a customer must return a product. It assesses each return on a case-by-case basis to find a solution that benefits the customer and company. Additionally, grocery retailer Trader Joe's offers shoppers a full refund on any private-label products and explicitly encourages the customer to return the product to the store if he or she is dissatisfied. Although Trader Joe's is unable to resell used grocery items after recovery, their liberal returns policy builds stronger relationships with their customers without creating too much inefficiency.[19]

Some major retailers are limiting generous product return policies while others, such as Trader Joe's, continue with flexible return policies as a means of encouraging store loyalty.

13-4 SUSTAINABLE SUPPLY CHAIN MANAGEMENT

In response to the need for firms to both reduce costs and act as leaders in protecting the natural environment, many are adopting sustainable supply chain management principles as a key part of their supply chain strategy. **Sustainable supply chain management** involves the integration and balancing of environmental, social, and economic thinking into all phases of the supply chain management process. In doing so, the organization both better addresses current business needs and develops long-term initiatives that allow it to mitigate risks and avail itself of future opportunities in ways that preserve resources for future generations and ensure long-term viability. Success at supply chain sustainability is measured using a concept known as the **triple bottom line**, which includes measures of economic success, environmental impact, and social well-being. The general logic is companies that fail to balance these performance objectives appropriately are susceptible to risks that, in the long-term, can endanger the continuity of the business.

Sustainability activities within the supply chain include environmentally friendly materials sourcing; the design of products with consideration given to their social and environmental impact; and end-of-life product management that includes easy recycling and/or clean disposal. By effectively enacting sustainable supply chain management

principles, companies can simultaneously generate cost savings, protect the Earth's natural resources, and ensure that socially responsible business practices are enacted. Research has demonstrated a strong business case supporting many sustainability initiatives. For example, the recycling of used pallets is both an environmentally sustainable practice and cheaper than purchasing new ones.[20]

Companies such as UPS work continuously to develop a more sustainable supply chain. By integrating new transportation technologies into its fulfillment networks, UPS mechanics and employees are able to facilitate package delivery in ways that are more fuel- and emissions-efficient. For example, UPS has replaced about 12 percent of the diesel and gasoline it uses with alternative fuels, leading to a 14.5 percent reduction in the company's carbon footprint over the past decade. Today, UPS has logged more than 200 million miles on alternative-fuel vehicles and offers carbon-neutral delivery in 36 countries.[21]

In addition to environmental sustainability, modern businesses are also balancing economic success with social sustainability practices like human rights, labor rights, employee-diversity initiatives, and quality-of-life concerns. The benefits of social sustainability efforts have been demonstrated by retailers such as Lowe's and Walgreens, where the hiring and training of disabled workers has increased productivity in the host facilities by up to 20 percent. These

sustainable supply chain management a supply chain management philosophy that embraces the need for optimizing social and environmental costs in addition to financial costs

triple bottom line the financial, social, and environmental effects of a firm's policies and actions that determine its viability as a sustainable organization companies have found that disabled workers are far less likely to miss work and are often as effective at performing job tasks as their able-bodied counterparts—while frequently exceeding them in terms of process execution and safety standards.[22]

A common misconception surrounding both the environmental and social aspects of sustainability is that their practice increases costs disproportionately, and therefore should be enacted only when business leaders are willing to act altruistically or for the purposes of good public relations. In other words, some businesses believe investment in these aspects necessarily trades off against corporate profitability. Companies that have been unable to successfully capture economic value from environmental or social initiatives sometimes practice **greenwashing**, whereby they use marketing techniques to portray that their operations are environmentally or socially friendly, when in reality they are not. However, emerging research has begun to conclusively demonstrate that positive long-term financial returns accrue as a result of environmentally and socially sustainable practices if firms are willing to commit sufficient resources to the sustainability effort.[23]

New transportation technologies, such as drone delivery, are increasingly impacting digitalized distribution and ultimately fulfillment networks.

manufacturing), and digitalized product and supply chain integrity/verification (blockchain). These clusters of technologies are working together to improve the speed and accuracy with which supply chains can serve end users with desired products and services, but their best-case uses are only beginning to be fully understood.

13-5a Digitalized Demand Sensing and Decision Making

The first frontier on which the digital supply chain is impacting business pertains to the heightened ability to acquire and process data to support decision making. First, a rapidly increasing prevalence of sensory equipment that connects physical objects to the Internet is allowing for the collection of massive data sets that can be used to make better decisions about the best time, place, and form of products. This phenomenon is referred to as the **Internet of Things (IoT)**, which enables physical objects to relay chunks of information about themselves and their surroundings to people or computers over the Internet in real time, without overt human interaction. There are currently more devices on Earth connected to the Internet than people, and the number of devices is expected to grow exponentially faster than the human connections in the future. The potential impact of the IoT is tantalizing. For example, connections between containers, cargo vessels or trucks, and transportation infrastructures is leading to the development of smart transportation modes that reroute vehicles in real time based on local traffic patterns, weather events, and accidents. Alternatively, the traffic grid can react to a need for emergency supplies by enabling a sequence of green stoplights along a critical emergency route. The

13-5 THE DIGITALIZATION OF THE SUPPLY CHAIN

Several technological advances and business trends are affecting the job of the supply chain manager today. The most impactful of these is the increasing digitalization of the supply chain. **Digitalization** refers to the use of digital technologies to change ways of doing business, and to provide new revenue and value-producing opportunities. This is occurring throughout the sequence of events that make up modern SCM, including demand sensing and decision making (via the Internet of Things, big data, supply chain analytics, and AI/machine learning), digitalized process management (via advanced robotics and cloud computing), digitalized distribution (via automated vehicles/drones and three-dimensional printing/additive

greenwashing when a firm publicly feigns support for environmental or social sustainability but fails to live up to these standards in practice

digitalization the use of digital technologies to change a business model and provide new revenue or value

Internet of Things (IoT) a system of interrelated computing devices, mechanical and digital machines, objects, animals, or people that are connected and able to transfer data over a network without overt human effort possibilities are essentially endless for the IoT to positively impact the supply chain, and many companies have already launched projects related to the development of IoT-enabled supply chain management strategies.

The increasing prevalence of sensors on products, their containers, and the transportation and storage modes that carry them has allowed for powerful data-capturing capabilities to develop in some companies, with the output taking the form of huge databases of customer, supplier, and company information. Over the past few years, the appearance of **big data** has presented both great opportunities and significant problems for supply chain managers. There is indeed more information available about supply chain operations than ever before, but the challenge of extracting usable data from this information is very expensive. When processed by humans, a key aspect to dealing with big data is the ability to "make it small again," by developing a capability for extracting only the elements that are critical for making a desired decision. This capability, as well as many others related to the linkage of data elements for SCM decision making, falls under the umbrella of **supply chain analytics**. Supply chain analytics programs that can interpret big data have great potential for improving supply chain operations. For example, the use of bigger (and better) data should allow supply chain forecasting to become more accurate; shipments to be rerouted in the event of traffic or bad weather; and warehouses to be stocked with exactly the products customers want (and none they don't want). Each of these ambitions, if realized, would offer lower prices for customers and lead to greater customer satisfaction.

However, not all of the decisions required for the efficient and effective operation of a modern, global supply chain are made by humans anymore. In many cases, the data are so complex or unwieldy that it makes more sense for businesses to let computers not only calculate the answers to complicated problems, but sometimes also to ask the questions. **Artificial intelligence (AI)** refers to the field of computer science that creates machines capable of solving problems more quickly and accurately than humans can. Traditionally, AI applications work by analyzing a set of inputs and coming up with the correct output more reliably than humans can. In the supply chain context, AI enables decisions related to procurement, manufacturing, logistics, and planning by assessing many different data sets (often housed within different businesses) simultaneously and coming up with a solution that is as close to optimal as possible for all the parties involved. However, sometimes, supply chain managers are better off letting the application do more of the decision-making. **Machine learning** is a subset of artificial intelligence that reverses the traditional AI

processing method. Rather than teaching the computer the required logic to solve a problem (by inputting data), machine learning gives the computer a set of known answers to the problem. Then the computer is responsible for generating, or learning, the logic it needs to solve similar problems. It then can begin to not only answer, but also to ask questions about supply chain processes. For example, if the objective is to deliver a shipment to a retail store within a predefined time window, the application can look at patterns of inputs and outputs from similar usages in prior data and suggest several different route/mode combinations, and then ask the user which is most preferred. By engaging with AI and machine learning, supply chain managers take some of the heavy lifting out of the big data analysis process, and can improve firm and supply chain performance as a result.

13-5b Digitalized Supply Chain Processes

In addition to digitalized demand sensing and decision making, other applications and tools are useful for executing supply process tasks. In order to leverage useful information across organizational interfaces for better joint decision making, many companies are using **cloud computing** as a means to collaborate on big data projects and analyze findings in a quick and cost-effective manner.

Advanced logistical technologies enabled by big data and analytics or AI is also improving supply chain operations at the tactical level. Increasingly, modern companies are automating many of their supply chain processes, substituting mechanized labor for human labor. Many tasks that are done repetitively and require significant precision can be accomplished more cheaply and accurately via **advanced robotics**. For example, scientists at the University of California have developed robots—powered by cloud-based data about surgical

big data the rapidly collected and difficult-to-process large-scale data sets that have recently emerged and push the limits of current analytical capability

supply chain analytics data analyses that support the improved design and management of the supply chain

artificial intelligence (AI) the computer science area focused on making machines that can simulate human intelligence processes

machine learning (ML) an application of artificial intelligence that provides systems the ability to automatically learn and improve from experience without being explicitly programmed

cloud computing the practice of using remote network servers to store, manage, and process data

advanced robotics devices that act largely or partially autonomously, that interact physically with people or their environment, and that are capable of modifying their behavior based on sensor data patients—that are capable of performing basic hip and knee replacement surgery. Cloud-based robots are already being used for large-scale production tasks like automobile and airplane manufacturing. However, robotics is not the only form of automation that has emerged to assist with supply chain tasks. **Automated vehicles** and **drones** are in use for the purpose of making complicated or costly deliveries of goods or information easier. Drones—unmanned aerial vehicles—are already being used in many nations to complete "final mile" deliveries to customers, including delivery of vital medicines and blood supplies to disease-stricken customers in Africa, as well as prepared meals for lunch in China.[24] Some companies are also experimenting with unmanned surface transportation, often in the form of delivery trucks. AB InBev completed its first experimental beer delivery route in Colorado during late 2016, and since then many other companies have been rushing to get into the driverless vehicle game. Ford Motor Company, Walmart, and delivery service Postmates have announced a strategic alliance to design a service for delivering groceries and other goods to Walmart customers at their homes or businesses beginning in 2019.[25]

And finally, sometimes it's not even necessary for transportation to be involved for automation to have value. In some cases, even services can be automated. A San Francisco–based company, Atrium, aims to be a full-service corporate law firm that leverages AI technology and analytics to streamline routinized legal tasks such as start-up paperwork, employee hiring, and commercial contract writing. The company's software uses machine learning to understand legal documents and to automate repetitive tasks. By automating these tasks, Atrium's clients get reduced hourly fees and more focused legal advice.[26]

13-5c **Digital Distribution**

Digital distribution is the most recent development in the logistics arena. Broadly defined, **digital distribution** includes any kind of product or service that can be distributed electronically, whether over traditional forms such as fiber-optic cable or through satellite transmission of electronic signals. Companies like E°TRADE, Apple (iTunes), and Movies.com have built their business models around electronic distribution.

In the near future, however, digital distribution will not be limited only to products and services that are mostly composed of electronic bits and bytes of information that are easily transferred via electronic connections. Experiments with **three-dimensional printing (3DP)** have been successful in industries such as auto parts, biomedical, and even fast food. Using 3DP technology, objects are built to precise specifications using raw materials at or near the location where they will be consumed. Lowe's hopes to alleviate the need to carry vast quantities of rarely purchased inventory by installing kiosks where customers can design and print their own doorknobs, lamps, and replacement parts.[27] Shipping raw materials such as powdered brass or ceramic composite is cheaper than shipping finished products because these materials can be packaged in perfectly cubic containers, making transportation much more efficient and cost-effective. Raw materials are used only when they are needed, so virtually no waste is produced during printing.

The potential uses for 3DP are virtually endless. Reebok is teaming up with its materials supplier BASF to open a Rhode Island facility where 3D printed shoes will be first custom-made and later, as unit costs fall, mass-manufactured. This strategy will eventually enable the company to leverage its 3D printing operations to offer shoes with a high-rebound outsole, which conserves more energy for the wearer with each step. Additionally, by 3D printing instead of using a traditional mold,

asharkyu/Shutterstock.com

Using 3DP technology, objects as diverse as shoes and aircraft engines will be built to precise specifications at or near the location where they will be consumed, thereby disrupting supply chains.

automated vehicles cars, trucks, or other ground transportation modes for which human drivers are not required to take control to safely operate the vehicle

drones unmanned aerial vehicles that can be controlled remotely or can fly autonomously when executing a task

digital distribution includes any kind of product or service that can be distributed electronically, whether over traditional forms such as fiber-optic cable or through satellite transmission of electronic signals

three-dimensional printing (3DP) the creation of three-dimensional objects via an additive manufacturing (printing) technology that layers raw material into desired shapes

Reebok will avoid having to buy costly new molds each time a design change is desired.[28]

Many industry experts project that 3DP (also referred to as *additive manufacturing*) will radically transform the ways global supply chains work by changing the basic platforms of business. With 3DP, smaller, localized supply chains will become the norm and small manufacturers will produce many more custom products than ever before with very short lead times. And because such platforms will remove much of the need for transportation of finished goods to distribution centers and retailers, 3DP is expected to have a very positive impact on businesses' carbon footprints and the environment at large. Research shows that additive manufacturing will significantly decrease wasted materials, since parts can be printed on demand, reducing component-part waste and providing large savings in energy and materials costs. Furthermore, it's been estimated that by 2025, 3D printing could reduce global costs by over $500 billion and reduce CO_2 emissions by over 500 megatons.[29]

13-5d Digitalizing Supply Chain Integrity

In closing our discussion of supply chain digitalization, it is worth noting that as supply chains globalize, they get longer and more complex, often stretching around the world and including dozens of suppliers, intermediate customers, and service providers. And yet, end users of goods and services expect that the final output of the chain will be a perfect order, and there is little tolerance for error. But, because mistakes will inevitably be made, **supply chain traceability**—the ability to map the paths of raw materials, component parts, subassemblies, and finished goods throughout the global network—has become a primary challenge for many businesses.

Until recently, achieving traceability has been a nearly impossible exercise that required extensive manual reporting and personal one-to-one communications. However, the digital era has brought with it a very important new reporting mechanism, **blockchain**, that has not only transformed traceability from a pipedream to a reality, but has also ensured that any transactions between supply chain partners are impartially recorded and therefore beyond dispute. A blockchain is a digital ledger of transactions that can be accessed by all parties in real time; it allows products or components to be traced from origin to final destination including all stops in between. Because it is constantly visible and can be audited by any supply chain partner at any time, the blockchain eliminates fraud, lowers the cost of administration for shipments, increases accuracy, and reduces delays and disputes pertaining to the content of shipments. When

Blockchain technology makes traceability of all global supply chain product movements and transactions.

combined with IoT, it can also be used to detect and record inventory locations and initiate automatic payments upon delivery. In one shipping partnership between global ocean freight carrier Maersk and IBM, blockchain has already recorded over 150 million shipping events, which enabled shippers to cut out intermediaries doing inspections and manual tracing, leading to massive savings for customers worldwide.[30] Though blockchain is relatively new to supply chain management applications, it is already proving to be a very effective tool for ensuring the integrity of global commercial trade, and supply chain professionals are optimistic about the many new types of value it will create in the near future.

13-6 MARKETING CHANNELS AND CHANNEL INTERMEDIARIES

A marketing channel can be viewed as a canal or pipeline through which products, their ownership, communication, financing and payment, and accompanying risk flow to the consumer. A **marketing channel** (also called a **channel of distribution**) is a business structure of interdependent organizations that reaches from the point of production to the consumer and facilitates the downstream physical movement of goods through the supply chain. Channels represent the "place" or "distribution" element of the marketing mix (product, price,

---

supply chain traceability the degree to which a business is able to track a product's development through stages beginning with a raw material state and ending with delivery to the final consumer

blockchain a digital ledger in which transactions are made and recorded chronologically and publicly

marketing channel (channel of distribution) a set of interdependent organizations that eases the transfer of ownership as products move from producer to business user or consumer

Igor Strukov/Shutterstock.com

Sheila Fitzgerald/Shutterstock.com

Vitali Michkou/Shutterstock.com

promotion, and place), in that they provide a route for company products and services to flow to the customer. In essence, the marketing channel is the "downstream" portion of the supply chain that connects a producer with the customer. While "upstream" supply chain members are charged with moving component parts or raw materials to the producer, members of the marketing channel propel finished goods toward the customer, and/or provide services that facilitate additional customer value.

Many different types of organizations participate in marketing channels. **Channel members** (also called *intermediaries*, *resellers*, and *middlemen*) negotiate with one another, buy and sell products, and facilitate the change of ownership between buyer and seller in the course of moving finished goods from the manufacturer into the hands of the final consumer. As products move toward the final consumer, channel members facilitate the distribution process by providing specialization and division of labor, overcoming discrepancies, and providing contact efficiency.

13-6a How Marketing Channels Work

According to the concepts of *specialization* and *division of labor*, breaking down a complex task into smaller, simpler ones and assigning these tasks to specialists create greater efficiency and lower average production costs via economies of scale. Marketing channels attain economies of scale through specialization and division of labor by aiding upstream producers

(who often lack the motivation, financing, or expertise) in marketing to end users or consumers. In most cases, such as for consumer goods like soft drinks, the cost of marketing directly to millions of consumers—taking and shipping individual orders—is prohibitive. For this reason, producers engage other channel members such as wholesalers and retailers to do what the producers are not well suited to do. Some channel members can accomplish certain tasks more efficiently than others because they have built strategic relationships with key suppliers or customers or have unique capabilities. Their specialized expertise enhances the overall performance of the channel.

Because customers, like businesses, are specialized, they also rely on other entities for the fulfillment of most of their needs. Imagine what your life would be like if you had to grow your own food, make your own clothes, produce your own television shows, and assemble your own automobile! Luckily, members of marketing channels are available to undertake these tasks for us. However, not all goods and services produced by channel members exist in the form we'd most prefer, at least at first. Marketing channels are valuable because they aid producers in creating time, place, and exchange utility for customers, such that products become aligned with their needs. Producers, who sit at the top of the supply chain, provide **form utility** when they transform oats grown on a distant farm into the Cheerios that we like to eat for breakfast. **Time utility** and **place utility** are created by channel members, when, for example, a transport company hired by the producer physically moves boxes of cereal to a store near our homes in time for our next scheduled shopping trip. And the retailer, who is often the closest channel member to the customer, provides a desired product for some reasonable amount of money that we are willing to give, creates **exchange utility** in doing so.

13-6b Functions and Activities of Channel Intermediaries

Intermediaries in a channel negotiate with one another, facilitate transfer of ownership for finished goods between buyers and sellers, and physically move products from the producer toward the final consumer. The most prominent difference separating intermediaries is whether they take title to the product. *Taking title* means they actually own the merchandise and control the terms of the sale—for example, price and delivery date. Retailers and merchant wholesalers are examples of intermediaries that take title to products in the marketing channel and resell them. **Merchant wholesalers** are organizations that facilitate the movement of products and services from the manufacturer to producers, resellers, governments, institutions, and retailers. All merchant wholesalers take title to the goods they sell, and most of them operate one or more warehouses where they receive finished goods, store them, and later reship them to retailers, manufacturers, and institutional clients. Since wholesalers do not dramatically alter the form of a good or sell it directly to the consumer, their value hinges on their providing time and place utility and contact efficiency to retailers.

Other intermediaries do not take title to goods and services they market, but do facilitate exchanges of ownership between sellers and buyers. **Agents and brokers** facilitate the sales of products downstream by representing the interests of retailers, wholesalers, and manufacturers to potential customers. Unlike merchant wholesalers, agents or brokers only facilitate sales and generally have little input into the terms of the sale. They do, however, get a fee or commission based on sales volume. For example, grocery chains often employ the services of food brokers, who provide expertise for a range of products within a category. The broker facilitates the sale of many different manufacturers' products to the grocery chain by marketing the producers' stocks, but the broker never actually takes ownership of any of the products.

Many different variations in channel structures are possible, with choices made based in large part on the numbers and types of wholesaling intermediaries that are most desirable. Generally, product characteristics, buyer considerations, and market conditions determine the types and number of intermediaries the producer should use, as follows:

- Customized or highly complex products such as computers, specialty foods, or custom uniforms are usually sold through an agent or broker, who may represent one company or multiple companies. In contrast, standardized products such as soda or toothpaste are often sold through a merchant wholesaler and retailer channel.

- Buyer considerations such as purchase frequency or customer wait time influence channel choice. When there is no time pressure, customers may save money

on books by ordering online and taking direct distribution from a wholesaler. However, if a book is needed immediately, it will have to be purchased at retail—for example, at the school bookstore—and will include a markup.

- Market characteristics such as how many buyers are in the market and whether they are concentrated in a general location also influence channel design. In a home sale, the buyer and seller are localized in one area, which facilitates the use of a simple agent–broker relationship, whereas mass-manufactured goods such as automobiles may require parts from all over the world and therefore many intermediaries.

Retailers are the firms in the channel whose primary function is to sell directly to consumers. A critical role fulfilled by retailers within the marketing channel is that they provide contact efficiency for consumers. Suppose you had to buy your milk at a dairy, your meat at a stockyard, and so forth. You would spend a great deal of time, money, and energy just shopping for just a few groceries. Retailers simplify distribution by reducing the number of transactions required by consumers and by making an assortment of goods available in one location. Consider the example illustrated in Exhibit 13.1. Four consumers each want to buy a tablet computer. Without a retail intermediary like Best Buy, tablet manufacturers Samsung, Microsoft, Apple, and Lenovo would each have to make four contacts to reach the four consumers who are in the target market, for a total of 20 transactions. But when Best Buy acts as an intermediary between the producer and consumers, each producer needs to make only one contact, reducing the number to nine transactions. This benefit to customers accrues whether the retailer operates in a physical store location or online.

13-6c Channel Functions Performed by Intermediaries

Intermediaries in marketing channels perform three essential functions that enable goods to flow between producer and consumer. *Transactional* functions involve contacting and communicating with prospective buyers to make them aware of existing

merchant wholesaler an institution that buys goods from manufacturers and resells them to businesses, government agencies, and other wholesalers or retailers and that receives and takes title to goods, stores them in its own warehouses, and later ships them

agents and brokers wholesaling intermediaries who do not take title to a product, but facilitate its sale from producer to end user by representing retailers, wholesalers, or manufacturers

retailer a channel intermediary that sells mainly to consumers

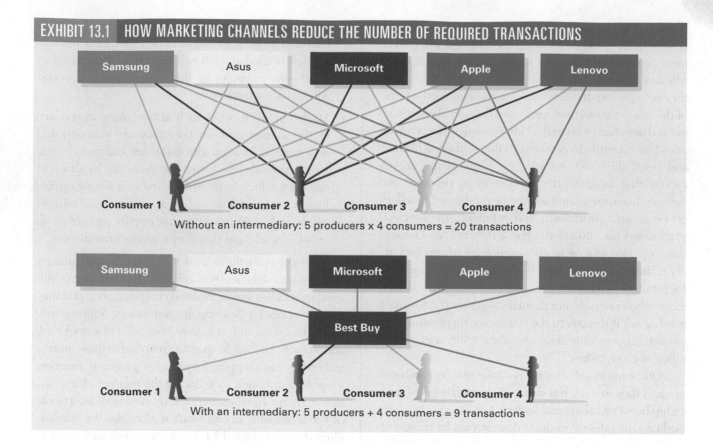

EXHIBIT 13.1 HOW MARKETING CHANNELS REDUCE THE NUMBER OF REQUIRED TRANSACTIONS

Samsung   Asus   Microsoft   Apple   Lenovo

Consumer 1   Consumer 2   Consumer 3   Consumer 4

Without an intermediary: 5 producers x 4 consumers = 20 transactions

Samsung   Asus   Microsoft   Apple   Lenovo

Best Buy

Consumer 1   Consumer 2   Consumer 3   Consumer 4

With an intermediary: 5 producers + 4 consumers = 9 transactions

products and to explain their features, advantages, and benefits. Intermediaries in the channel also provide *logistical* functions. *Logistical* functions typically include transportation and storage of assets, as well as their sorting, accumulation, consolidation, and/or allocation for the purpose of conforming to customer requirements. *Facilitating* includes research and financing. Research provides information about channel members and consumers by getting answers to the key questions: Who are the buyers? Where are they located? Why do they buy? Financing ensures that channel members have the money to keep products moving through the channel to the ultimate consumer. Although individual members can be added to or deleted from a channel, someone in the channel must perform these essential functions. Producers, wholesalers, retailers, or consumers can perform them, and sometimes nonmember channel participants such as service providers elect to perform them for a fee.

13-7 CHANNEL STRUCTURES

direct channel a distribution channel in which producers sell directly to consumers

A product can take any of several possible routes to reach the final consumer. Marketers and

consumers each search for the most efficient channel among many available alternatives. Constructing channels for a consumer convenience good such as candy differs from doing so for a specialty good like a Prada handbag. Exhibit 13.2 illustrates four ways manufacturers can route products to consumers. When possible, producers use a **direct channel** to sell directly to consumers in order to keep purchase prices low. Direct marketing activities—including telemarketing, mail order and catalog shopping, and forms of electronic retailing such as online shopping and shop-at-home television networks—are good examples of this type of channel structure. There are no intermediaries. Producer-owned stores and factory outlet stores—like Sherwin-Williams, Polo Ralph Lauren, Oneida, and WestPoint Home—are also examples of direct channels.

By contrast, when one or more channel members are small companies that lack marketing power, an *agent–broker channel* may be the best solution. Agents or brokers bring manufacturers and wholesalers together for negotiations, but they do not take title to the merchandise. Ownership passes directly from the producer to one or more wholesalers and/or retailers, who sell to the ultimate consumer.

Most consumer products are sold through distribution channels similar to the other two alternatives: the

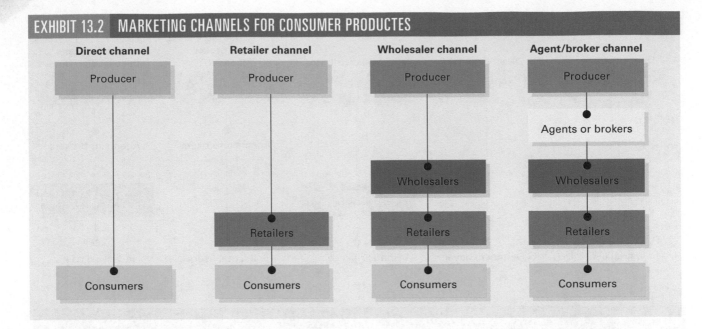

EXHIBIT 13.2 MARKETING CHANNELS FOR CONSUMER PRODUCTES

retailer channel and the wholesaler channel. A *retailer channel* is most common when the retailer is large and can buy in large quantities directly from the manufacturer. Walmart, Target, and car dealers are examples of retailers that often bypass a wholesaler. A *wholesaler channel* is commonly used for low-cost items that are frequently purchased, such as candy, cigarettes, and magazines.

Regardless of the number of channels used, managers must decide whether it is better to organize channels around *customers* or *tasks*. Organizing channels around customers—for example, by creating a special distribution system for larger and more important customers—increases customer satisfaction at the expense of internal coordination and operating costs for the seller. On the other hand, organizing channels around tasks—for example, by using the company website to generate sales leads and the call center to handle after-sales service—enables the company to perform those tasks more efficiently across the customer base as a whole and to cut costs. Customer perceptions of the company's service quality may decrease, however, since there is not a single, one-stop point of contact.[31]

13-7a Channels for Business and Industrial Products

As Exhibit 13.3 illustrates, five channel structures are common in business and industrial markets. First, *direct channels* are typical in business and industrial markets. For example, manufacturers buy large quantities of raw materials, major equipment, processed materials, and supplies directly from other producers. Manufacturers

that require suppliers to meet detailed technical specifications often prefer direct channels. For instance, Apple uses a direct channel to purchase high-resolution retina displays for its innovative iPad tablet line. To ensure sufficient supply for iPad manufacturing, Apple takes direct shipments of screens from Sharp, LG, and Samsung.[32]

Alternatively, companies selling standardized items of moderate or low value often rely on *industrial distributors*. In many ways, an industrial distributor is like a supermarket for organizations. Industrial distributors are wholesalers and channel members that buy and take title to products. Moreover, they usually keep inventories of their products and sell and service them. Often small manufacturers cannot afford to employ their own sales forces. Instead, they rely on manufacturers' representatives or selling agents to sell to either industrial distributors or users. Additionally, the Internet has enabled virtual distributors to emerge and has forced traditional industrial distributors to expand their business models. Many manufacturers and consumers are bypassing distributors and going directly to customers, often via the Internet.

13-7b Alternative Channel Arrangements

Rarely does a producer use just one type of channel to move its product. It usually employs several different strategies, which include the use of multiple distribution, nontraditional channels, and strategic channel alliances. When a producer selects two or more channels to distribute the same product to target

EXHIBIT 13.3 CHANNELS FOR BUSINESS AND INDUSTRIAL PRODUCTS

Direct channel	Direct channel	Industrial distributor	Agent/broker channel	Agent/broker–industrial distributor
Producer	Producer	Producer	Producer	Producer
			Agents or brokers	Agents or brokers
		Industrial distributors		Industrial distributors
Industrial users	Government buyers	Industrial users	Industrial users	Industrial users

You can now test a Casper mattress at West Elm before you buy it online.

Source: Twitter, Inc

markets, this arrangement is called **dual or multiple distribution**. Dual or multiple distribution systems differ from single channel systems, and managers should recognize the differences. Multiple distribution channels must be organized and managed as a group, and managers must orchestrate their use in synchronization if whole system is to work well. As consumers increasingly embrace online shopping, more retailers are employing a multiple distribution strategy. This arrangement allows retailers to reach a wider customer base, but may also lead to competition between distribution channels through cannibalization (whereby one channel takes sales away from another). When multiple separate channels are used, they must all complement each other. Some customers use "showrooming" as a way of learning about products but may then also shop as a way of making price comparisons. Regardless of which channel customers choose when making the final purchase, they should receive the same messages and "image" of the products.

The use of **nontraditional channels** may help differentiate a firm's product from the competition by providing additional information about products. Nontraditional channels include approaches such as mail-order television or video channels and infomercials. Although nontraditional channels may limit a brand's coverage, they can give a producer serving a niche market a way to gain market access and customer attention without having to establish physical channel intermediaries; they can also provide another sales avenue for larger firms.

Furthermore, companies often form **strategic channel alliances** that enable them to use another manufacturer's already-established channel. Alliances are used most often when the creation of marketing channel relationships may be too expensive and time consuming. For example, popular bedding and mattress e-tailer Casper partnered with West Elm, a high-end furniture company, to increase consumer confidence in purchasing their products. By harnessing West Elm's preestablished brick-and-mortar stores as a shared channel, Casper customers could try out mattresses before purchase and West Elm could more effectively advertise its chic bedroom furniture. The synergies created through the partnership benefitted both companies by creating more buying confidence in their shared consumer-base.[33]

In addition to using primary traditional and nontraditional channels to flow products toward customer markets, many businesses also employ secondary channels, using either an active or passive approach. For example, though most automobile manufacturers sell their finished products to end users through networks of owned or franchised dealers, they also sell cars to rental agencies such as Enterprise or Hertz, that then rent them to potential customers. Similarly, fashion apparel companies might distribute their premium products, such as silk ties or branded watches, through primary channels such as department stores or specialty stores while using an off-brand or discount outlet for distribution of low-end products. In each case, the goal of the company is the same: to engage a segment of customers who might otherwise never experience the product by offering it at a more easily affordable price or under trial conditions.

Marketers must also be aware, however, that some unintended secondary channels also exist. In some countries, **gray marketing channels** may be used to sell stolen or counterfeit products, which could detract from the profitability of the primary and secondary channels controlled by the business. Counterfeit products such as North Face outerwear, Rolex watches, and Prada handbags can be very difficult to distinguish from the real thing, and their presence provides unintended competition for the producer when such products are distributed through unauthorized intermediaries.

Along with marketing channels that move products downstream to end customers, retailers and manufacturers also manage channels that move products upstream, in the direction of the producer. These **reverse channels** enable consumers to return products to the retailer or manufacturer in the event of a product defect or at the end of the product's useful life to the consumer. The retailers or manufacturers can then recycle the product and use components to manufacture new products or refurbish and resell the same product in a secondary market. Several large companies, including Apple, Best Buy, and Walmart, offer opportunities to recycle items ranging from plastic bags and batteries to televisions and Christmas trees. Consumers and companies alike view reverse channels not just as a way to reduce the firm's environmental impact but also as a means to gain some financial benefits. For example, Intel offers its customers a completely free mail-back recycling program in which the consumer can send back certain products to the company via a reverse logistics organization as a sustainable alternative to throwing away a valuable item. The company was cited by Forbes as a leader in recycling initiatives for 2018; it recycles more than 75 percent of the total waste generated by its operations and aims to achieve "zero hazardous waste to landfill" by 2020.[34] To incentivize customer cooperation in such initiatives, retailers are using **drop and shop** programs to get consumers to recycle products like batteries or cell phones during a regular trip to the store.

13-7c Digital Channels

With technology changing rapidly, many companies are turning to digital channels to facilitate product distribution. **Digital channels** are pathways for moving products and information toward customers so they can be sent and/or received with electronic devices, such as computers, smartphones, tablets, or video game consoles. Digital channels allow either push- or pull-based information and product flows—sometimes simultaneously. For example, a downloaded video game or music file purchased by a customer can also include a digital ad for more games or a new music player.

strategic channel alliance a cooperative agreement between business firms to use the other's already established distribution channel

gray marketing channels secondary channels that are unintended to be used by the producer, and which often flow illegally obtained or counterfeit product toward customers

reverse channels channels that enable customers to return products or components for reuse or remanufacturing

drop and shop a system used by several retailers that allows customers to bring used products for return or donation at the entrance of the store

digital channels electronic pathways that allow products and related information to flow from producer to consumer

In response to the growth of digital channels, customers are turning in droves to **M-commerce**, whereby a mobile device is used to assess, compare, and/or buy products. For example, suppose you need a ride from one point in Chicago to another. Instead of having to hail a cab or walk to the nearest elevated train station, you can use Uber's smartphone app to contact a local driver who will take you directly to your destination. A key advantage of Uber and similar apps is their frictionless payment interface. When you are done with your ride, you just get out of the car and walk away while the app charges your credit or debit card to pay the driver. M-commerce is currently experiencing the largest growth in both retail and channel decision making, compared to other types of digital channels, in part because of its more than $20 billion annual revenue.[35]

M-commerce also enables consumers using wireless mobile devices to connect and shop online. Essentially, M-commerce goes beyond text message advertisements to allow consumers to purchase goods and services using wireless mobile devices. M-commerce users adopt the new technology because it saves time and offers more convenience in a greater number of locations. The use of M-commerce has become increasingly important as users grow in both number and purchasing power. Consumers have become more reliant on digital technologies, as shown in the world's first fully digital generation, the Millennials, and firms that fail to react to this trend risk losing a rapidly growing group of M-commerce customers.

Many major companies, ranging from Polo Ralph Lauren to Apple, already offer shopping on mobile phones, and the growth potential is huge. The amount of mobile shopping consumers do with tablets and smartphones is about equal, with each channel contributing a little over $70 billion annually around the globe. M-commerce reached $459.38 billion annual revenue in 2018 and is anticipated to surpass $693.[36] billion in 2019.[36] Smartphones contributed roughly $150 billion annually in 2018 and represented 71.5 percent of M-commerce. However, while 77 percent of American own smartphones today, in recent years, tablets' portion of M-commerce has continued to decline, and in 2018 tablet sales represented only 27.7 percent of sales, or about $58 billion annually.[37] Globally, more than 2 billion people engage in some form of M-commerce transaction every year, and 95 percent use their devices to prepare for calling or visiting a business.[38] A 2018 RetailMeNot survey found that, of their sample group, 47

M-commerce the ability to conduct commerce using a mobile device for the purpose of buying or selling goods or services

percent said that they use a mobile device to look up a retailer's offers and discounts and 46 percent use their device in the brick-and-mortar store to comparison shop. Importantly for marketers, the average M-commerce purchase costs is about twice as much as the average purchase made through traditional brick-and-mortar channels.[39]

Along with smartphone technology, companies are starting to look into other digital channels with which to connect with their customers. Social shopping allows multiple retailers to sell products to customers through social media sites. Aaramshop brings hundreds of neighborhood grocery stores to customers through Facebook. Customers make their purchases online, and their specific neighborhood stores take care of delivering the items directly to customers' homes.[40] Home delivery extends beyond groceries in many heavily populated areas. In China and India, McDonald's has started delivering directly to its customers instead of making consumers come to them.

Firms are also using social media websites as digital channels—even in some cases without offering a purchasing opportunity. Companies create profiles on websites like Pinterest or Facebook and use them not only to give customers information about their products but also to collect customer information. According to one study, 38 percent of all online customers follow at least one retailer on a social networking site, and almost 40 percent of users are following their favorite brands on social media. Additionally, 95 percent of the people who follow brands via social media sites are in the age range of 18–34. Many customers use these websites to find product information or get information on special deals, and those who follow a company's blog or profile on a social media site often end up clicking through to the firm's website.[41]

While some services group retailers together in order to bring products to customers, others allow consumers to combine and order larger amounts. Websites like Groupon and LivingSocial give customers the opportunity to fulfill their individual needs at group prices. Many of these sites are organized and managed by intermediaries between manufacturers and customers, but others may be customer initiated or even created by firms to better promote their own products and manage demand.[42]

13-7d Factors Affecting Channel Choice

Marketing managers must answer many questions before choosing a marketing channel. A book manufacturer must decide, for example, what roles physical and electronic distribution will play in the overall marketing strategy and how these two paths will fare against each

Smartphone and tablet device payment capabilities are on the verge of replacing cash from the traditional leather wallet.

other. In addition, managers must decide what level of distribution intensity is appropriate and must ensure that the channel strategy they choose is consistent with product, promotion, and pricing strategies. The choice of channels depends on a holistic analysis of market factors, product factors, and producer factors.

MARKET FACTORS Among the most important market factors affecting distribution channel choices are market considerations. Specifically, managers should answer the following questions: Who are the potential customers? What do they buy? Where do they buy? When do they buy? How do they buy? Additionally, the choice of channel depends on whether the producer is selling to consumers directly or through other industrial buyers because of differences in the buying routines of these groups. The geographic location and size of the market are also important factors guiding channel selection. As a rule, if the target market is concentrated in one or more specific areas, then direct selling through a sales force is appropriate, whereas intermediaries would be less expensive in broader markets.

PRODUCT FACTORS Complex, customized, and expensive products tend to benefit from shorter and more direct marketing channels. These types of products sell better through a direct sales force. Examples include pharmaceuticals, scientific instruments, airplanes, and mainframe computer systems. On the other hand, the more standardized a product is, the longer its distribution channel can be and the greater the number of intermediaries that can be involved without driving up costs. For example, with the exception of flavor and shape, the formula for chewing gum is fairly standard from producer to producer. As a result, the distribution channel for gum tends to involve many wholesalers and retailers.

The product stage in the life cycle is also an important factor in choosing a marketing channel. In fact, the choice of channel may change over the life of the product. As products become more common and less intimidating to potential users, producers tend to look for alternative channels. Similarly, perishable products such as vegetables and milk have a relatively short life span, and fragile products like china and crystal require a minimum of handling. Therefore, both require fairly short marketing channels. Online retailers such as eBay facilitate the sale of unusual or difficult-to-find products that benefit from a direct channel.

PRODUCER FACTORS Several factors pertaining to the producer itself are important to the selection of a

Perishable products spoil if they don't reach customers in time, so they tend to benefit from shorter, more direct marketing channels.

marketing channel. In general, producers with large financial, managerial, and marketing resources are better able to perform their own marketing, and thus will use more direct channels. These producers have the ability to hire and train their own sales forces, warehouse their own goods, and extend credit to their customers. Smaller or weaker firms, on the other hand, must rely on intermediaries to provide these services for them. Compared to producers with only one or two product lines, producers that sell several products in a related area are able to choose channels that are more direct. Therefore, sales expenses can be spread over more products.

A producer's desire to control pricing, positioning, brand image, and customer support also tends to influence channel selection. For instance, firms that sell products with exclusive brand images, such as designer perfumes and clothing, usually avoid channels in which discount retailers are present. Manufacturers of upscale products, such as Gucci (handbags) and Godiva (chocolates), may sell their wares only in expensive stores in order to maintain an image of exclusivity. Many producers have opted to risk their image, however, and test sales in discount channels. For example, Levi Strauss expanded its distribution network to include JCPenney, Target and Walmart.

TIMING FACTORS A final consideration driving channel choice is the elapsed time between the introduction of a

product into one channel and the secondary introduction of the same or a very similar product into another channel. Timing decisions such as when to release a product in different channels, how long to keep a product on the market, and when to launch new products are critical. For example, companies that offer products in multiple channels (such as online and in-store) must decide whether to launch in both channels simultaneously or to launch them sequentially—and if sequentially, in what order. They must also decide when to withdraw a product from a particular channel if that channel is no longer providing the expected value. Research shows companies that introduce movies into the primary channel (theater box office) often introduce the same movies into alternate channels (Blu-ray disc, download, and streaming) as much as eight weeks too early, thereby suppressing aggregate revenues by up to 2.5 percent. Similarly, aggregate revenues can decrease by as much as 2.5 percent if movies are released from theaters to a secondary channel too soon. One study found that 99 percent of the theater revenues are captured within the first four months, and 80 to 90 percent is captured in the first month, but the exact percentage depends on the success of the film.[43]

13-7e Levels of Distribution Intensity

Organizations have three options for intensity of distribution: intensive, selective, and exclusive. **Intensive distribution** is a form of distribution aimed at maximum market coverage. Here, the manufacturer tries to have the product available in every outlet where potential customers might want to buy it. If buyers are unwilling to search for a product, it must be made very accessible to them. The next level of distribution, **selective distribution**, is achieved by screening dealers and retailers to eliminate all but a few in any single area. Because only a few are chosen, the consumer must seek out the product. For example, HBO selectively distributes its popular television shows through a series of its own subscription-based channels (HBO, HBO on Demand, and HBO Go for mobile devices) and sells subscriptions or single episodes through Apple, Amazon.com, and Sony's online stores but does not stream them through Netflix or Hulu Plus. The most restrictive form of market coverage is **exclusive distribution**, which entails only one or a few dealers within a given area. Because buyers may have to search or travel extensively to buy the product, exclusive distribution is usually confined to consumer specialty goods, a few shopping goods, and major industrial equipment. Products such as Rolls-Royce automobiles, Chris-Craft powerboats, and Pettibone tower cranes are distributed under exclusive arrangements.

EMERGING DISTRIBUTION STRUCTURES In recent years, rapid changes in technology and communication have led to the emergence of new, experimental distribution methods and channel structures. For example, fashion flash sale sites like Gilt and Rue La La have recently boomed in popularity. On these sites, new designer clothing items are made available every day—often at a discount from 15 to 80 percent, and always for an extremely limited time. The average fashion flash sale shopper is between 25 and 40 years of age and makes $100,000 a year—an ideal demographic for many marketers.

Another emerging channel structure involves renting items that are usually sold only to end consumers. For example, some websites allow customers to rent and return high fashion products (renttherunway.com), handbags and accessories (bagborroworsteal.com), and even

intensive distribution a form of distribution aimed at having a product available in every outlet where target customers might want to buy it

selective distribution a form of distribution achieved by screening dealers to eliminate all but a few in any single area

exclusive distribution distribution to only one or a few dealers within a given area

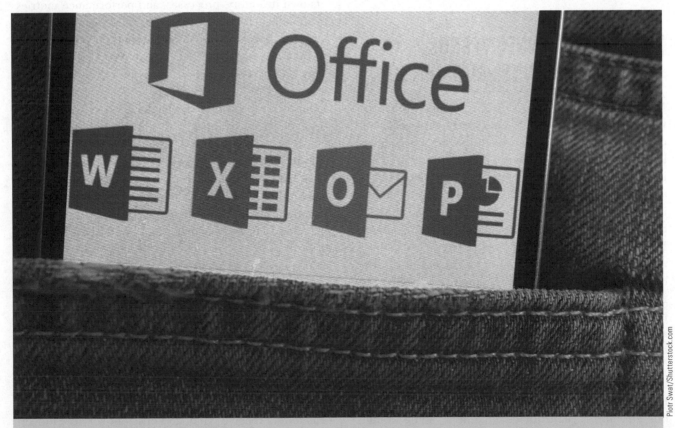

Microsoft Office logo displayed on smartphone in jeans pocket expands opportunities to increase product awareness of its new subscription service.

furniture (fashionfurniture.com). Rental versus retail channels open up an entirely new customer base for certain products that were once reserved for a much smaller group.

For many years, subscription services such as book-of-the-month clubs have provided customers products periodically over time. More recently, subscription services have expanded far beyond books and magazines to include clothing (bombfell.com), shoes (shoedazzle.com), crafting kits (craftaholicsanonymous.net), and wine (wine.com). Many websites require subscriptions to view premium content, and streaming media services like Spotify, Netflix, and OnLive offer a wholly new type of subscription service.

Digital marketplaces like Steam and the Google Play Store constitute another recent trend in marketing channels. Digital licensing adds an interesting facet to customer sales; instead of selling a tangible product, digital marketplaces sell the rights to songs, movies, and television shows through their websites and applications. Instead of leaving home to purchase a physical album, game, or movie, consumers can select specific media and download them directly to their computers or mobile devices.

13-8 OMNICHANNEL VERSUS MULTICHANNEL MARKETING

Marketing channels are valuable because they provide a route for products and services to reach the customer. Customers have different preferences, however, as to which channels to use when browsing, seeking information, comparing products to one another, and making a purchase. A single customer may use different channels for each of these activities, including both traditional and digital channels! For example, a customer might first learn about a new smartwatch when browsing a catalog, then conduct research about it on the company's website. She might later go to a physical retail location to try out the product before finally purchasing the device using a mobile app. Because of these varying preferences through different stages of the shopping cycle, many companies have begun to employ a multichannel marketing strategy, whereby customers are offered information, goods, services, and/or support through one or more synchronized channels. Some studies have demonstrated that customers who use multiple channels when shopping become more engaged during the purchase process and tend to spend more than customers who shop one channel only. The exception is when customers are buying simple, utilitarian products that are well known and intended for frequent use. Since customers are already familiar with these product types, single-channel designs are just as effective.[44]

Because consumers use multiple channels during the shopping experience, it has become important for channel members to create a seamless shopping experience across all physical and digital channels. Facilitating such customer activities as checking a store's inventory online, purchasing an item through an app for in-store pickup, allowing online purchases to be returned in-store, and enabling mobile payment while shopping in a store are only a few strategies that producers and retailers are using to create customer perceptions that multiple channels are behaving as one.

However, it is important to understand that the multichannel design does create redundancy and complexity in the firm's distribution system. Selling through multiple channels is typically accompanied by the construction of multiple, parallel supply chains, each with its own inventory, processes, and performance metrics. Multichannel systems typically have meant that each channel would operate different transportation and distribution systems, hold and account for its own inventory, and otherwise act as independent sales and profit centers, with little knowledge of the operations of the other. This proved problematic for one retailer who was selling its products both in physical stores and on its website. The company had a distribution center in Kentucky for its Internet retailing business and another near Chicago for its physical stores located there. When a customer in Chicago visited the local store looking for a certain product, the shelves were empty, and he was directed to order products from the company's website if he wanted one in time for the holidays. He did so, and the product was shipped to his home—at significant expense—from the Kentucky distribution center while unused product sat only miles from his home in the Chicago distribution center, waiting to be stocked on local store shelves.

Because of situations like these, many companies are transitioning to an omnichannel distribution operation that supports their multichannel retail operations and unifies their retail interfaces so that all customers receive equal and efficient service. For example, retailers such as The Gap and Burberry allow customers to reserve items online for pickup in nearby stores; have employed a find-in-store feature on their websites that displays real-time stock information so customers can avoid unnecessary trips to the mall; and are beginning to provide in-store computer terminals or iPads for customers to search their websites for offerings that the customer's local store may not carry.

By making their inventory data available to customers in real time, these retailers have effectively merged their multiple distribution channels in such a way that creates greater customer control over the shopping experience, leading to greater satisfaction and loyalty. We discuss further implications of this strategy in Chapter 15.

14 | Retailing

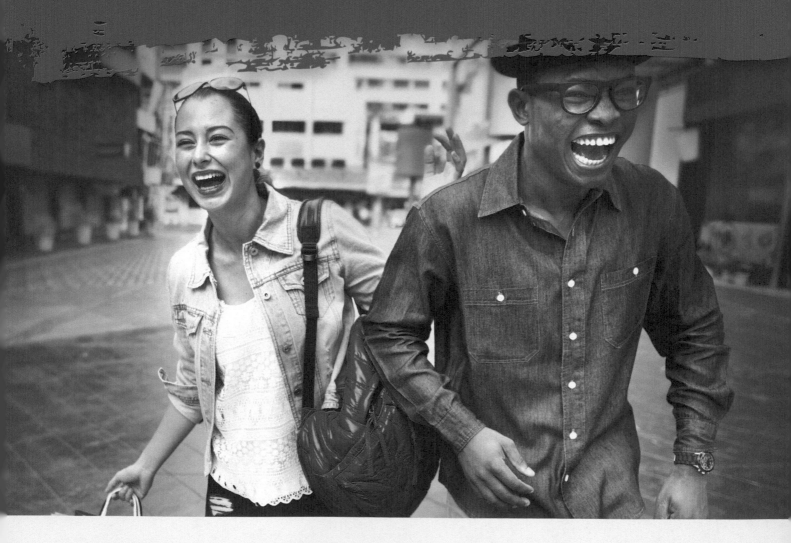

Rawpixel.com/Shutterstock.com

LEARNING OUTCOMES

After studying this chapter, you will be able to …

14-1 Explain the importance of the retailer within the channel and the U.S. economy

14-2 List and understand the different types of retailers

14-3 Explain why nonstore retailing is on the rise, and list the advantages of its different forms

14-4 Discuss the different retail operations models, and understand why they vary in strategy and format

14-5 Explain how retail marketing strategies are developed and executed

14-6 Discuss how services retailing differs from goods retailing

14-7 Understand how retailers address product/service failures, and discuss the opportunities that service failures provide

14-8 Summarize current trends related to customer data, analytics, and technology

THE IMPORTANCE OF RETAILING

Retailing represents all the activities directly related to the sale of goods and services to the ultimate consumer for personal, nonbusiness use. Retailing has enhanced the quality of our daily lives in countless ways. When we shop for groceries, hair care, clothes, books, or other products and services, we are doing business with retailers. The millions of goods and services provided by retailers mirror the diverse needs, wants, and trends of modern society. The U.S. economy depends heavily on the retail sector. On its own, the U.S. retail industry is responsible for generating 5.9 percent of gross domestic product (GDP), which equates to $1.14 trillion in value added. Retail sales currently amount to around 26 percent of nominal GDP and the industry accounts for 10.8 percent of total non–farm workers in the economy.[1]

Retailing affects everyone, both directly and indirectly. The retail industry consists of more than 3.7 million retail establishments and supports 42 million jobs, equal to about one in every four American jobs. According to the U.S. Small Business Administration, 99.9 percent of all businesses in the United States employ fewer than 500 people, signifying that small businesses should comprise most of the retailing industry. However, the retail industry is dominated by a small number of large companies. Walmart, for example, employs 2.2 million people around the world, 1.5 million of them in the United States alone; the company's global employment exceeds the total population of Iceland by 6.5 times.[2] If its employees were an army, it would be the second largest army in the world—just behind China's.[3] As the retail environment changes, so do retailers. Trends and innovations relating to customer data, social media, and alternative forms of shopping are constantly developing, and retailers have no choice but to react. The *best* retailers actually lead the way by anticipating change and developing new and exciting ways to interact with customers. We discuss each of these issues and more in this chapter.

14-2 TYPES OF RETAILERS AND RETAIL OPERATIONS

Retail establishments can be classified in several ways, such as type of ownership, level of service, product assortment, and price. These variables can be combined in several ways to create numerous unique retail operating models. Exhibit 14.1 lists the major types of retailers and classifies them by their key differentiating characteristics.

14-2a Ownership Arrangement

Depending on its ownership arrangement, a retailer can gain advantages from having a broad brand identity or from having the freedom to take risks and innovate. Retail ownership takes one of three forms—independently owned, part of a chain, or a franchise outlet.

- An **independent retailer** is owned by a person or group and is not operated as part of a larger network. Around the world, most retailers are independent, with each owner operating a single store in a local community.

- A **chain store** is a group of retailers (of one or more brand names) owned and operated by a single organization. Under this form of ownership, a home office for the entire chain handles retail buying; creates unified operating, marketing, and other administrative policies; and works to ensure consistency across different locations. Target and Starbucks are retail chains.

- A **franchise** is a retail business for which the operator is granted a license to operate and sell a product under the brand name of a larger supporting organizational structure, such as Subway or Supercuts.

retailing all the activities directly related to the sale of goods and services to the ultimate consumer for personal, nonbusiness use

retailer a channel intermediary that sells mainly to consumers

independent retailer a retailer owned by a single person or partnership and not operated as part of a larger retail institution

chain store a store that is part of a group of the same stores owned and operated by a single organization

franchise a relationship in which the business rights to operate and sell a product are granted by the franchisor to the franchisee

EXHIBIT 14.1 TYPES OF STORES AND THEIR CHARACTERISTICS

Type of Retailer	Level of Service	Product Assortment	Price	Gross Margin
Department store	Moderately high to high	Broad	Moderate to high	Moderately high
Specialty store	High	Narrow	Moderate to high	High
Supermarket	Low	Broad	Moderate	Low
Drugstore	Low to moderate	Medium	Moderate	Low
Convenience store	Low	Medium to narrow	Moderately high	Moderately high
Full-line discount store	Moderate to low	Medium to broad	Moderately low	Moderately low
Specialty discount store	Moderate to low	Medium to broad	Moderately low to low	Moderately low
Warehouse club	Low	Broad	Low to very low	Low
Off-price retailer	Low	Medium to narrow	Low	Low
Restaurant	Low to high	Narrow	Low to high	Low to high

Under this arrangement, a **franchisor** originates the trade name, product, methods of operation, and so on. A **franchisee**, in return, pays the franchisor for the right to use its name, product, and business methods and takes advantage of the franchisor's brand equity and operational expertise. Franchises can provide both goods and services, but increasingly, the most successful franchises are services retailers. Three of the top five franchises recognized by Entrepreneur Magazine are fast-food restaurants.[4]

14-2b Level of Service

The service levels that retailers provide range from full service to self-service. Some retailers, such as exclusive clothing stores, offer very high or even customized service levels. They provide alterations, credit, delivery, consulting, liberal return policies, layaway, gift wrapping, and personal shopping. By contrast, retailers such as factory outlets and warehouse clubs offer virtually no service. After stock is set out for sale, the customer is responsible for any information gathering, acquisition, handling, use, and product assembly. At the extreme low end of the service continuum, a retailer may take the form of a product kiosk or vending machine.

franchisor the originator of a trade name, product, methods of operation, and the like that grants operating rights to another party to sell its product

franchisee an individual or business that is granted the right to sell another party's product

14-2c Product Assortment

Retailers can also be categorized by the width and depth of their product lines. *Width* refers to the assortment of products offered; *depth* refers to the number of different brands offered within each assortment. Specialty stores such as Best Buy, Staples, and GameStop have the thinnest product assortments, usually carrying single or narrow product lines that are considerably deep. For example, a specialty home improvement store like Home Depot is limited to home-related products, but may carry as many as 90 brands of refrigerators in a variety of colors and finishes with unique capacities and features. On the width end of the spectrum, full-line discounters typically carry very wide assortments of merchandise that are fairly shallow.

Stores often modify their product assortments in order to accommodate factors in the external environment. For example, a recent shift in customer preference toward bold and exotic flavors, snacking, and health and wellness has led to the inclusion of on-the-go, conveniently packaged healthy meals on store shelves. Some of these options include bowl-based choices featuring kale, quinoa, and other nutritious ingredients. Large packaged food companies that haven't stayed on-trend with healthy options have suffered declining sales in recent years, demonstrating the importance of recognizing shifting customer lifestyles and offering new products to accommodate them.[5] Similarly, food products ranging from milk to vitamins to dog treats have been excluded from retail product lines in order to better ensure customer safety. However, the type of product can influence customers' expectations about product assortments. Researchers have found that customers expect less variety among items that are of higher quality.[6]

14-2d Price

Price is the fourth way to position retail stores. Traditional department stores and specialty stores typically charge the

A shift in customer preferences toward healthier food options has led gas stations and quick markets to offer salads and other healthier food products.

full "suggested retail price." In contrast, discounters, factory outlets, and off-price retailers use low prices and discounts to lure shoppers. The last column in Exhibit 14.1 shows the typical **gross margin**—how much the retailer makes as a percentage of sales after the cost of the goods sold is subtracted. (Margins are covered in more detail in Chapter 19.) Today, prices in any store format might vary not just from day to day, but from minute to minute! Online retailers and traditional brick-and-mortar stores that have invested in electronic tagging systems are increasingly adopting dynamic pricing strategies that enable them to adjust to an item's surging popularity or slow movement in real time.[7] The rise in the number of smartphones and other mobile devices has added a new layer of complexity to pricing decisions. Customers have more information than ever before and can compare prices from dozens of retailers at once. Consequently, many are not willing to pay full price anymore. Recognizing this trend, some retailers have begun using pricing techniques to make customers believe that they are getting a bargain—even if they aren't. Some online retailers use customer information such as income, location, and browsing history to adjust their prices. That is, depending on the information that Amazon has about you, the price you see for a book on Amazon might be different from the price your instructor sees and the prices that your fellow classmates see. This practice can lead to negative reactions from consumers if they realize that they are not receiving equal prices or if they feel that their privacy has been invaded.[8]

14-2e Types of In-Store Retailers

Traditionally, retailers fall into one of several distinct types of retail stores, each of which features a product assortment, types of services, and price levels that align with the intended customers' shopping preferences. In recent years, however, retailers began experimenting with alternative formats that blend the features and benefits of the traditional types. For instance, supermarkets are expanding their nonfood items and services; discounters are adding groceries; drugstores are becoming more like convenience stores; and department stores are experimenting with smaller stores. Nevertheless, many stores still fall into the traditional archetypes:

- **Department stores** such as Nordstrom and Macy's carry a wide range of products and specialty goods, including apparel, cosmetics, housewares, electronics, and sometimes furniture. Each department acts as a separate profit center, but central management sets policies about pricing and the types of merchandise carried.

- **Specialty stores** typically carry a deeper but narrower assortment of merchandise within a single category of interest. The specialized knowledge of their salesclerks allows for more attentive customer service. Office Depot, Ulta Beauty, and Foot Locker are well-known specialty retailers.

- **Supermarkets** are large, departmentalized, self-service retailers that specialize in food and some nonfood items. Some conventional supermarkets are being replaced by much larger *superstores*. Superstores offer one-stop shopping for food and nonfood needs, as well as services such as pharmacists, florists, salad bars, photo-processing kiosks, and banking centers.

- **Drugstores** primarily provide pharmacy-related products and services, but many also carry an extensive selection of cosmetics, health and beauty aids, seasonal merchandise, greeting cards, toys, and some refrigerated, nonrefrigerated, and frozen convenience foods. As other retailer types have begun to add pharmacies and direct-mail prescription services have become more popular, drugstores have competed by adding more services such as 24-hour drive-through windows and low-cost health clinics staffed by nurse practitioners.

gross margin the amount of money the retailer makes as a percentage of sales after the cost of goods sold is subtracted

department store a store housing several departments under one roof

specialty store a retail store specializing in a given type of merchandise

supermarket a large, departmentalized, self-service retailer that specializes in food and some nonfood items

drugstore a retail store that stocks pharmacy-related products and services as its main draw

- A **convenience store** resembles a miniature supermarket but carries a much more limited line of high-turnover convenience goods. These self-service stores are typically located near residential areas and offer exactly what their name implies: convenient locations, long hours, and fast service in exchange for premium prices. In exchange for higher prices, however, customers are beginning to demand more from convenience store management, such as higher-quality food and lower prices on staple items such as gasoline and milk.

- **Discount stores** compete on the basis of low prices, high turnover, and high volume. Discounters can be classified into several major categories:

- **Full-line discount stores** such as Walmart offer consumers very limited service and carry a vast assortment of well-known, nationally branded goods such as housewares, toys, automotive parts, hardware, sporting goods, garden items, and clothing.

- **Supercenters** extend the full-line concept to include groceries and a variety of services, such as pharmacies, dry cleaning, portrait studios, photo finishing, hair salons, optical shops, and restaurants. For supercenter operators such as Target, customers are drawn in by food but end up purchasing other items from the full-line discount stock.

- Single-line **specialty discount stores** such as Foot Locker offer a nearly complete selection of merchandise within a single category and use self-service, discount prices, high volume, and high turnover to their advantage. A **category killer** such as Best Buy is a specialty discount store that heavily dominates its narrow merchandise segment.

- A **warehouse club** sells a limited selection of brand name appliances, household items, and groceries. These are sold in bulk from warehouse outlets on a cash-and-carry basis to members only. Currently, the leading stores in this category are Sam's Club, Costco, and BJ's Wholesale Club.

- **Off-price retailers** such as TJ Maxx, Burlington Coat Factory, and Nordstrom Rack sell at prices 25 percent or more below traditional department store prices because they buy inventory with cash and they don't require return privileges. These stores often sell manufacturers' overruns, irregular merchandise, and/or overstocks that they purchase at or below cost. A **factory outlet** is an off-price retailer that is owned and operated by a single manufacturer and carries one line of merchandise—its own. Manufacturers can realize higher profit margins using factory outlets than they would by disposing of the goods through independent wholesalers and retailers. **Used goods retailers** turn customers into suppliers: preowned items bought back from customers are resold to different customers. Used goods retailers can be either brick-and-mortar locations (such as Goodwill stores) or electronic marketplaces (such as Poshmark).

- **Restaurants** provide both tangible products—food and drink—and valuable services—food preparation and presentation, table service, and sometimes delivery. Most restaurants are also specialty retailers in that they concentrate their menu offerings on a distinctive type of cuisine—for example, Olive Garden Italian restaurants and Starbucks coffeehouses.

14-3 THE RISE OF NONSTORE RETAILING

The retailing formats discussed so far entail physical stores where merchandise is displayed and to which customers must travel in order to shop. In contrast, **nonstore retailing** enables customers to shop without visiting a physical store location. Nonstore retailing adds a level of convenience for customers who wish to shop from their current locations. Broad changes in culture and society have led nonstore retailing currently

---

convenience store a miniature supermarket, carrying only a limited line of high-turnover convenience goods

discount store a retailer that competes on the basis of low prices, high turnover, and high volume

full-line discount store a discount store that carries a vast depth and breadth of product within a single product category

supercenter a large retailer that stocks and sells a wide variety of merchandise including groceries, clothing, household goods, and other general merchandise

specialty discount store a retail store that offers a nearly complete selection of single-line merchandise and uses self-service, discount prices, high volume, and high turnover

category killer a large discount store that specializes in a single line of merchandise and becomes the dominant retailer in its category

warehouse club a large, no-frills retailer that sells bulk quantities of merchandise to customers at volume discount prices in exchange for a periodic membership fee

off-price retailer a retailer that sells at prices 25 percent or more below traditional department store prices because it pays cash for its stock and usually doesn't ask for return privileges

factory outlet an off-price retailer that is owned and operated by a manufacturer

used goods retailer a retailer whereby items purchased from one of the other types of retailers are resold to different customers

restaurant a retailer that provides both tangible products—food and drink—and valuable services—food preparation and presentation

nonstore retailing shopping without visiting a store

Marla Aaron

We have a vending machine...

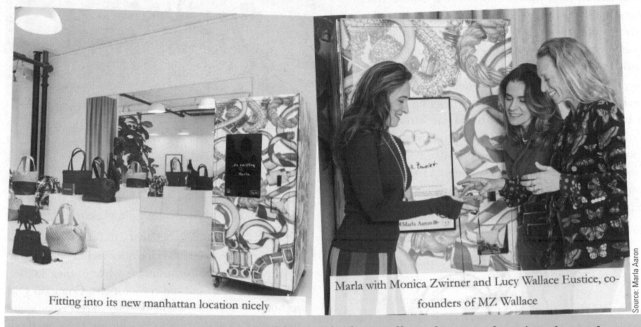

Fitting into its new manhattan location nicely

Marla with Monica Zwirner and Lucy Wallace Eustice, co-founders of MZ Wallace

Source: Marla Aaron

Self-service technologies are being used increasingly to sell products such as jewelry and purses that previously were sold mostly by salespersons.

growing faster than in-store retailing. The major forms of nonstore retailing are automatic vending, direct retailing, direct marketing, and Internet retailing (or *e-tailing*). In response to the successes seen by nonstore retailers, many grocery stores have started offering curbside pick-up services. These services, such as Instacart Pickup and Walmart Grocery Pickup, offer consumers the ease of online shopping without the inconvenience of waiting days for a delivery. In addition to pickup services, Walmart is competing with Amazon and other e-commerce players with their recent launch of an app that enables in-store shoppers to order and pay online for items that are sold out in stores. If a shopper finds that the item they want to purchase is sold out, they simply find a Walmart employee who has a device with the app and have them take the order, set up shipping details, and provide a ticket that enables the customer to pay for the item at checkout.[9] For its part, Target is trying to compete by integrating the in-store experience with mobile technology. The company now offers exclusive in-store savings and rewards through its Cartwheel app.[10]

- **Automatic vending** entails the use of machines to offer goods for sale—for example, the soft drink, candy, and snack vending machines commonly found in public places and office buildings. Retailers are continually seeking new opportunities to sell via vending. As a result, vending machines today sell merchandise such as DVDs, digital cameras, perfumes, and even ice cream. A key aspect of their continuing success is the proliferation of cashless payment systems in response to consumers' diminishing preference for carrying cash. Automatic vending has allowed marketers to tap into a new, unlikely audience: customers seeking luxury items on the go. Upscale Brooklyn hotel, The William Vale, recently acquired a vending machine that dispenses fine jewelry designed by New York's own Marla Aaron. Guests wanting a high-quality accessory can now choose between 12 items with prices ranging from $165 to $1,500.[11]

automatic vending the use of machines to offer goods for sale

- **Self-service technologies (SST)** comprise a form of automatic vending where services are the primary focus. Automatic teller machines, pay-at-the-pump gas stations, and movie ticket kiosks allow customers to make purchases that once required assistance from a company employee. However, as with any sort of self-service technology, automatic vending comes with failure risks due to human or technological error. Unless customers expect that they can easily recover from such errors, they may end up shopping elsewhere. Naturally, some customers are frustrated with the growing trend toward self-service technology. Many can recall an incident of a self-service technology failure that left them begging to speak to a live human being. Some banks are attempting to avoid service failures at ATMs by reintroducing live interactions between customers and service employees. In the most advanced systems, ATM customers can video chat with a live teller at any hour, including customized service based on customer preferences.[12]

- **Direct retailing** representatives sell products door to door, in offices, or at in-home sales parties. Companies like Avon, Mary Kay, and The Pampered Chef have used this approach for years. Social media selling has flourished among direct sellers seeking to increase the number of products and services sold. Many direct sellers now host digital parties on social media, where people can shop from the comfort of their own homes for items ranging from do-it-yourself manicures to weight loss body wraps. Traveling Vineyard, a Massachusetts-based wine company, uses direct sales representatives, otherwise known as "Wine Guides," to connect with hosts of wine-tasting events to arrange free, in-home wine tastings. Wine Guides complete online training modules, attend annual conferences, and participate in regional meetings in addition to their direct selling. Traveling Vineyard requires each Wine Guide to order an

Herbalife's nutritional supplements are one of the most popular products being sold on social media websites like Facebook.

initial starter kit of wine samples and marketing materials, but offers flexibility in working hours, enabling each Wine Guide to earn a commission-based income best suited to his or her own needs.[13]

- **Direct marketing (DM)** includes techniques used to elicit purchases from consumers while in their homes, offices, and other convenient locations. Common DM techniques include telemarketing, direct mail, and mail-order catalogs. Shoppers who use these methods are less bound by traditional shopping situations. Time-strapped consumers and those who live in rural or suburban areas are most likely to be DM shoppers because they value the convenience and flexibility it provides. DM occurs in several forms, as described below.

- **Telemarketing** is a form of DM that employs outbound and inbound telephone contacts to sell directly to consumers. Telemarketing is a highly effective marketing technique; one survey indicates that 12 percent of sales and marketing leads come from telemarketing activity alone, surpassing the impact of public relations, print advertising, direct mail, and media buying activity.[14]

- Alternatively, **direct mail** can be a highly efficient or highly inefficient retailing method, depending on the quality of the mailing list and the effectiveness of the mailing piece. With direct mail, marketers can precisely target their customers according to demographic, geographic, and/or psychographic characteristics. Direct mailers are becoming more sophisticated in targeting the right customers. **Microtargeting** based on data analytics of census data, lifestyle patterns, financial information, and past purchase and credit history allows direct mailers to pick out those most likely to buy their products.[15] According to one report, U.S. companies

self-service technologies (SST) technological interfaces that allow customers to provide themselves with products and/or services without the intervention of a service employee

direct retailing the selling of products by representatives who work door to door, office to office, or at home sales parties

direct marketing (DM) techniques used to get consumers to make a purchase from their home, office, or other nonretail setting

telemarketing the use of the telephone to sell directly to consumers

direct mail the delivery of advertising or marketing material to recipients of postal or electronic mail

microtargeting the use of direct marketing techniques that employ highly detailed data analytics in order to identify potential customers with great precision

Back stock ready for future sales.

Floor stock displayed for immediate sale.

spend over $42 billion each year on direct mail, and thanks to microtargeting initiatives, the customer response rates to direct mail have increased 37 percent in the past few years, despite companies sending fewer pieces of direct mail each year.[16] Microtargeting is also an effective tool for online retailing. Many companies have purchased access to online search engine data, making it easier than ever to pinpoint customer preferences. A customer's online search history enables retailers to match his or her specific customer wants through targeted digital advertisements.

- **Shop-at-home television networks** such as HSN and QVC produce television shows that display merchandise to home viewers. Viewers can phone in their orders directly on toll-free lines and shop with their credit cards. The shop-at-home industry has quickly grown into a multibillion-dollar business with a loyal customer following and high customer penetration.

- **Online retailing**, or **e-tailing**, enables customers to shop over the Internet and have items delivered directly to their door. Global online shopping accounts for about $2.3 trillion annually and is projected to grow to around $4.48 trillion by 2021. Additionally, 1.66 billion people worldwide purchase goods online in a single year. Online retailer Amazon earns $54.5 billion in revenue annually and sells over 564 million products to consumers in the United States.[17] Online, interactive shopping tools and live chats substitute for the in-store interactions with salespeople and product trials that customers traditionally used to make purchase decisions. Shoppers can use a variety of devices to look at a much wider variety of products online, because physical space restrictions do not exist. While shopping, customers can take their time deciding what to buy. Research has demonstrated that as shoppers begin to engage multiple devices in a single shopping task, the likelihood of an eventual purchase increases—especially when the consumer progresses from more mobile devices, such as a phone or tablet, to more fixed devices such as a desktop computer.[18]

- As consumers have become more connected, the **sharing economy** has emerged as a more efficient exchange of resources. *Sharing economy* refers to the way connected consumers exchange goods and services with one another through a digital marketplace. This phenomenon has given rise to online exchange communities such as Craigslist, a system of local message boards where users can buy, sell, and trade almost any product or service. Other companies match people looking for specific services, such as ride sharing (Uber), vacation rentals (Airbnb), crowd funding (Kickstarter), peer-to-peer loans (SoFi), and freelance work (Upwork). These companies provide a platform—not just to match buyers and sellers but also to track ratings and reviews for service providers and clients alike.

In addition to retailer websites, consumers are increasingly using social media applications as shopping platforms. Social networking sites such as Facebook, Instagram, and Twitter enable users to immediately purchase items recommended by their social connections, a phenomenon known as *social shopping*. Companies are eager to establish direct linkages between social networking

shop-at-home television network a specialized form of direct response marketing whereby television shows display merchandise, with the retail price, to home viewers

online retailing (e-tailing) a type of shopping available to consumers with personal computers and access to the Internet

sharing economy the way connected consumers exchange goods and services with each other through a digital marketplace platforms and their own websites owing to the belief that a product or service recommended by a friend will receive higher consideration from the potential customer.

14-4 RETAIL OPERATIONS MODELS

The retail formats covered so far are co-aligned with unique operating models that guide the decisions made by their managers. Each operating model can be summarized as a set of guiding principles. For example, off-price retailers deemphasize customer service and product selection in favor of lower prices, which are achieved through a greater focus on lean inventory management.

Alternatively, specialty shops generally adopt a high-service approach that is supported by an agile approach to inventory. By keeping a greater amount of **floor stock** (inventory displayed for sale to customers) and **back stock** (inventory held in reserve for potential future sale in a retailer's storeroom or stockroom) on hand, a broader range of customer demands can be accommodated. This operating model also implies higher prices for customers, however, so retail managers must make sure that they deliver on the promises their firms make to customers in order to secure their loyalty. At the same time, these retail managers must control demand via promotions and other sales events in order to sell off slow-moving and perishable items, thereby making more room for items that are more popular.

Regardless of the type of stocking strategy a retailer chooses, there is always a chance that a wanted item will be out of stock. This is obviously bad for the retailer, but research suggests that there may be a bright side to stock-outs. One study found that customers view stockouts as an indication of how desirable a product is, and in turn will buy an item that is similar to the out-of-stock item, regardless of whether they even wanted the original item.[19]

These sorts of trade-offs have been partially responsible for the recent emergence of hybrid retail operating models. As an example of a hybrid strategy, the Spanish women's fashion retailer Zara employs a specialty retail format with a twist: it uses a mass-merchandising inventory strategy. Zara offers high-quality products and excellent customer service to draw customers into its stores but never replenishes specific inventory items that are sold. Rather, its designers and buyers are continually introducing new products in small or medium quantities. Once a product sells out, a new one replaces it, allowing for a very lean operation. This strategy not only lowers inventory costs (and thereby increases profitability) but

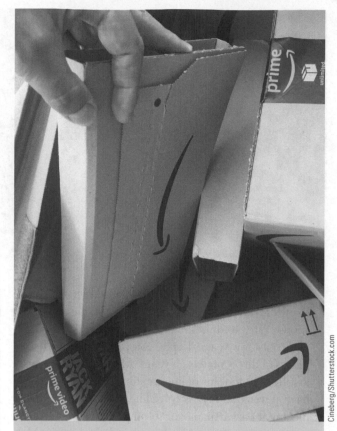

Amazon's Prime membership expedited delivery options have extended their market reach into new products, including household items and food.

also creates an aura of exclusivity around each piece that the retailer sells: each skirt, blouse, and accessory is effectively a limited-edition item. This strategy also has the ancillary benefit of driving customers back to the store in order to see what new products have arrived, and thus has the potential to increase the number of additional purchases.[20]

Likewise, with the growing trend of experiential shopping, some retailers carry no inventory at all. For instance, Nordstrom unveiled a new concept store in West Hollywood called Nordstrom Local in which shoppers can try on sample clothes, get manicures, and enjoy beer, wine or coffee while working with personal stylists on site to craft their desired look. Once the customer chooses an item to buy, the personal stylist will retrieve the good from one of the nine Nordstrom department store locations in Los Angeles or through its website.[21]

The trade-offs inherent in retail operating models have both spurred the recent success of online-only retailers and led to a surge in online storefront development among retailers who have traditionally operated in physical formats only. A key advantage of online retail is that no physical retail store space is needed for displaying and selling

floor stock inventory displayed for sale to customers

back stock inventory held in reserve for potential future sale in a retailer's storeroom or stockroom merchandise. Lower-cost remote distribution centers can be used, since all of the showcasing occurs on the company's website. By moving online, a specialty store can gain the operational benefits of a mass merchandiser. It can showcase exclusive or trendy items in an almost-free space to potential customers located around the world and can then fulfill demand from one of several localized distribution centers in a very short time. Fulfillment times are specified by the customer (according to their willingness to pay for greater shipping and delivery speed), and even this trade-off is becoming less of a sticking point every year. Amazon's Prime subscription program, for example, includes free two-day shipping. The company has even introduced its own fleet of airplanes to decrease shipping times and minimize reliance on other shippers. Considering that there are about 63 million Prime members worldwide, shipping speed is at the heart of what the Amazon customer values.

The Chicago-based software as a service (SaaS) company Bringg is currently the leading delivery logistics solution for some of the world's best-known brands in more than 50 countries. Bringg helps its customers, including retail giant Walmart, to compete with Amazon and manage their challenging last-mile and delivery operations through its powerful retail delivery technology platform designed to enhance control, speed, visibility, and cost containment.[22] It will be exciting to see how these advances continue to change retail strategies and operations in the years to come.

During the pandemic online shopping increased substantially. Customers were avoiding instore shopping at many retailers where they previously purchased clothing, shoes, paper towels and toilet paper. But at some major online operations, like Walmart and particularly Amazon, workers began complaining about safety procedures, including the lack of protective equipment. The increases in online demand and employee complaints about working conditions put additional pressure on these large retail online operations. Amazon in particular encountered difficulty in maintaining its promise of one or two-day delivery, and many purchases were not able to be delivered on time. In fact, Amazon delayed its annual Prime Day sale, one of the most popular shopping events along with Black Friday.

Today, most retail stores remain operationally and tactically similar to those that have been in business for hundreds of years, with one or more physical locations that the customer must visit in order to purchase a stocked product and with strategies in place to attract customers to visit. The sorts of differences we have described among retail operating models imply that managing one type of store instead of another can involve very different experiences. But most of the decisions that retail managers make can be distilled down to six categories of activity, referred to as the retailing mix. These categories, described in the next section, are relatively universal to all forms of retailing but are applied in different ways based on the retail format.

14-5 EXECUTING A RETAIL MARKETING STRATEGY

Retail managers develop marketing strategies based on the goals established by stakeholders and the overall strategic plans developed by company leadership. Strategic retailing goals typically focus on increasing total sales, reducing costs of goods sold, and improving financial ratios such as return on assets or equity. At the store level, more tactical retailing goals include increased store traffic, higher sales of a specific item, developing a more upscale image, and creating heightened public awareness of the retail operation and its products or services. The tactical strategies that retailers use to obtain their goals include having a sale, updating décor, and launching a new advertising campaign. The key strategic tasks that precede these tactical decisions are defining and selecting a target market and developing the retailing mix to successfully meet the needs of the chosen target market.

14-5a Defining a Target Market

The first and foremost task in developing a retail strategy is to define the target market. This process begins with market segmentation, the topic of Chapter 8. Successful retailing has always been based on knowing the customer. Sometimes retailing chains flounder when management loses sight of the customers the stores should be serving. Customers' desires and preferences change over their personal and professional life spans, and it is important for retailers to be sensitive to these changes by migrating their customers to new and different products as their buying patterns evolve.

Target markets in retailing are often defined by demographics, geographic boundaries, and psychographics. For example, supermarket chain Publix recently introduced an app that makes shopping easier and more convenient for its customers. App users can even request that their groceries be delivered directly to their homes to reduce shopping time. This app is targeted squarely at Millennials, who often have busy schedules and are technology savvy. In contrast, Amazon's recent acquisition of Whole Foods was largely a strategic move to gain access to this highly coveted consumer demographic, as

EXHIBIT 14.2 THE RETAILING MIX

Product
Width and depth of
product assortment

Personnel
Customer service
and personal
selling

Place (distribution)
Location and
hours

**Target
market**

Presentation
Layout and
atmosphere

Promotion
Advertising,
publicity, and
public relations

Price

well as achieve a foothold in the brick-and-mortar world to create a true omnichannel experience for customers. Though Amazon has traditionally prided itself on offering affordable options for a diverse group of consumers, by purchasing Whole Foods, Amazon increased its access to a new class of consumers who are often affluent and educated and who value cultural knowledge above many other luxury items. By purchasing the preferred grocery store of Millennials, Amazon can now easily become an integral part of their daily lives and shopping habits.[23]

14-5b Choosing the Retailing Mix

As previously noted, defining a retail operation entails combining the elements of the retailing mix to come up with a single retailing method to attract the target market. The **retailing mix** consists of six Ps: the four Ps of the marketing mix (*product, promotion, place,* and *price*) plus *presentation* and *personnel* (see Exhibit 14.2). The combination of the six Ps projects a store's (or website's) image and influences customers' perceptions. Using these impressions, shoppers can position one store or website against another. Managers must make sure that the positioning is aligned with target customers' expectations.

PRODUCT The first element in the retailing mix

> **retailing mix** a combination of the six Ps—product, promotion, place, price, presentation, and personnel—to sell goods and services to the ultimate consumer

is the product offering, also called the "product assortment" or "merchandise mix." Developing a product offering is essentially a question of the width and depth of the product assortment. Price, store/website design, displays, and service are important to customers in determining where to shop, but the most critical factor is merchandise selection. This reasoning also holds true for online retailers. Amazon.com, for instance, offers enormous width in its product assortment with millions of different items, including books, music, toys, videos, tools and hardware, health and beauty aids, electronics, and software. Conversely, online specialty retailers such as Mouse to Minx and Beg Bicycles focus on a single category of merchandise, hoping to attract loyal customers with a larger depth of products at lower prices and excellent customer service. Many online retailers purposely focus on single product-line niches that could never attract enough foot traffic to support a traditional brick-and-mortar store. For instance, websites such as bugbitingplants.com and petflytrap.com sell and ship live carnivorous plants in the United States. After determining what products will satisfy target customers' desires, retailers must find sources of supply and evaluate the products. When the right products are found, the retail buyer negotiates a purchase contract.

PROMOTION Retail promotion strategies includes advertising, public relations and publicity, and sales promotions. The goal is to help position the store or website in customers' minds. Retailers design intriguing ads, stage special events, and develop promotions aimed at their target markets. Today's grand openings are a carefully orchestrated blend of advertising, merchandising, goodwill, and glitter. All the elements of an opening—press coverage, special events, media advertising, and store displays—are carefully planned. Other promotions that are often used successfully include sales events, coupons, and discounts for certain products or customer groups.

One risk associated with store promotions, however, is **brand cannibalization**, a situation whereby the promotion intended to draw in new customers simply shifts current customers from buying one brand to another brand. For example, discount apparel and home decor store TJ Maxx recently added an online retail option. TJ Maxx has promoted this online shopping outlet cautiously, however, because the company is concerned that online shopping will decrease in-store sales. Cannibalization, in this case, is dangerous to the retailer for two reasons. First, the retailer has incurred a significant expense by setting up and promoting the new online store. Second, promoting the online outlet reduces the accuracy of sales forecasts, which leads to higher costs.[24] Brand cannibalization is dangerous to the retailer for two reasons. First, the retailer incurs significant expense in executing the promotion itself. Second, the promotion creates inaccurate sales forecasts for both the promoted and cannibalized products, leading to stockouts of the promoted brand and financial losses from discounting surplus inventory of the cannibalized brand. The latter types of losses can sometimes be significantly greater than the cost of the promotion itself. Therefore, retail managers should design their promotional activities carefully, with gaining new customers being the primary objective.

Much retail advertising is focused on the local level. Local advertising by retailers usually provides specific information about their stores, such as location, merchandise, hours, prices, and special sales. In contrast, national retail advertising generally focuses on image. For example, Target uses advertisements similar to designer fashion advertisements to depict high-quality goods. Paired with the ubiquitous red target and tag line "Expect more. Pay less," Target is demonstrating that it sells products that consumers normally aspire to own at prices they can afford.

Target's advertising campaigns also take advantage of cooperative advertising, another popular retail advertising practice. Traditionally, marketers would pay retailers to feature their products in store mailers, or a marketer would develop a television campaign for the product and simply tack on several retailers' names at the end. But Target's advertising uses a more collaborative trend by integrating products such as Tide laundry detergent or Coca-Cola into the actual campaign. Another common form of cooperative advertising involves promotion of exclusive products. For example, retailer JC Penney recently collaborated with the American television series "Project Runway" in a cooperative advertising campaign. For the partnership, JCPenney brought exclusive "Project Runway" merchandise into its stores to strategically enhance their assortment of apparel, and to better fit the desires of women assembling a stylish wardrobe. In return, JC Penney was named the exclusive retailer for seasons 16 and 17 of the "Project Runway" series.[25]

PLACE The retailing axiom "location, location, location" has long emphasized the importance of place to the retail mix. The physical *location* decision is important first because the retailer is making a large, semipermanent commitment of resources that can reduce its future flexibility. Second, the physical location will almost inevitably affect the store's future growth and profitability. Many retailers work with consultants and/or city planners to determine the best sites for current sales as well as potential future growth.

Physical site location begins by choosing a community. Important factors to consider are the area's economic growth potential, the amount of competition, and geography. For instance, retailers like TJ Maxx and Walmart often build stores in new communities that are still under development. Convenience stores, such as Walgreens or CVS, often locate on the path of their customers' daily commutes, which regularly means choosing a space situated in or near a transit hub or along heavily trafficked routes. Specialty stores, like Sephora or Foot Locker, can benefit from locating themselves close to other shopping locations, since their products, and the product offerings of other stores in the area, can complement one another. Furniture, automobile, or upscale clothing retailers often gain an advantage by locating their stores as far away from their rivals as possible so their customers will not be able to assess competing prices or easily comparison shop.[26] Even after careful research, however, the perfect location can be elusive in the face of changing markets. Mobile food trucks circumvent this problem by being able to relocate at will. By moving from spot to spot over the course of a day and parking outside events and heavily trafficked areas, mobile food trucks can maximize their exposure and adapt to changing markets.

After identifying a geographic region or community, retailers must choose a specific site. In addition to growth potential, the important

brand cannibalization
the reduction of sales for one brand as the result of the introduction of a new product or promotion of a current product by another brand

With its own in-store stylists, makeup and perfume retailer Sephora is a popular destination store for shoppers who want to try out a new look.

factors to consider are neighborhood socioeconomic characteristics, traffic flows, land costs, zoning regulations, and public transportation. A particular site's visibility, parking, entrance and exit locations, accessibility, and safety and security issues are also important considerations.

A retailer should consider how its store fits into the surrounding environment. Retail decision makers probably would not locate a Dollar General store next door to a Neiman Marcus department store. Furthermore, brick-and-mortar retailers have to decide whether to have a freestanding unit or to become a tenant in a shopping center or mall. Large retailers like Target and sellers of shopping goods like furniture and cars often use an isolated, freestanding location. A freestanding store location may have the advantages of low site cost or rent and no nearby competitors. On the other hand, it may be hard to attract customers to a freestanding location, and no other retailers are around to share costs. To be successful, stores in isolated locations must become "destination stores." A **destination store** is one that consumers seek out and purposely plan to visit. Websites can also be destinations for shoppers. Amazon is a destination website for a wide variety of products, and Google is a destination website for search information.

Freestanding units are increasing in popularity as brick-and-mortar retailers strive to make their stores more convenient to access, more enticing to shop, and more profitable. Freestanding sites now account for more than half of all retail store construction starts in the United States as more and more retailers are deciding not to locate in pedestrian malls. Perhaps the greatest reason for developing a freestanding site is greater visibility. Retailers often feel they get lost in huge shopping centers and malls, but freestanding units can help stores develop an identity with shoppers. Also, an aggressive expansion plan may not allow time to wait for shopping centers to be built. Drugstore chains like Walgreens have been purposefully relocating their existing shopping center stores to freestanding sites, especially street corner sites for drive-through accessibility.

Shopping centers first appeared in the 1950s when the U.S. population started migrating to the suburbs. The first shopping centers were *strip centers*, typically located along busy streets. They usually included a supermarket, a variety store, and perhaps a few specialty stores. Then *community shopping centers* emerged, with one or two small department stores, more specialty stores, a couple of restaurants, and several apparel stores. These community shopping centers provided off-street parking and a broader variety of merchandise. *Regional malls* offering a much wider variety of merchandise started appearing in the mid-1970s. Regional malls are either entirely enclosed or roofed to allow shopping in any weather. Most are landscaped with trees, fountains, sculptures, and the like to enhance the shopping environment. They have acres of free parking. The *anchor stores* or *generator stores* (often major department stores) are usually located at opposite ends of the mall to create heavy foot traffic.

According to shopping center developers, *lifestyle centers* are emerging as the newest generation of shopping centers. Lifestyle centers typically combine outdoor shopping areas composed of upscale retailers and restaurants, with plazas, fountains, and pedestrian streets. They appeal to retail developers looking for an alternative to the traditional shopping mall, a concept rapidly losing favor among shoppers. Though shopping malls bring multiple retail locations together, location is often not the most important motivator for a customer to choose a specific store. Instead, most shoppers look for stores that guarantee product availability, more service employees, and timesaving opportunities. Research indicates, for example, that to succeed, malls need to focus on transforming into *Consumer Engagement Spaces* based upon the rising demand for things to do, rather than things to buy and own. Consumer Engagement

destination store a store that consumers purposely plan to visit prior to shopping

Spaces focus heavily on experiential retail store formats complete with virtual reality, augmented reality, or mixed reality for the consumer to enjoy a personalized brand experience. Additionally, pop-up shops are an important component, as they give the shopper an unexpected treasure-hunting experience while simultaneously providing an experimental space for new retail concepts. Finally, these spaces need to include plenty of creative ways for visitors to spend their time, since time is the consumers' ultimate luxury, including options like restaurants, theaters, museums, and other engaging attractions. Four types of Consumer Engagement Spaces are likely to emerge: destination centers, values centers, innovation centers and "retaildential centers," and each type of Consumer Engagement Space tailored to fit a different segment of consumers.[27]

Yet, despite the popularity of shopping malls in recent decades, there is reason to believe that they are slowly being replaced by online retail. In fact, many traditional brick-and-mortar malls are struggling to survive. Anchor stores such as Sears and Macy's have closed hundreds of stores in recent years because of increased competition. Moreover, mall traffic is concentrating at fewer locations in affluent areas and tourist locations, and is eroding in most other places.[28]

PRICE Another important element in the retailing mix is price. Retailing's ultimate goal is to sell products to consumers, and the right price is critical to ensure sales. Because retail prices are usually based on the cost of the merchandise, an essential part of pricing is efficient and timely buying. Another pricing strategy is "value-based pricing," which focuses on the value of the product to the customer more than the cost of the product to the supplier. Price is also a key element in a retail store's positioning strategy. Higher prices often indicate a level of quality and help reinforce the prestigious image of retailers, as they do for Lord & Taylor and Neiman Marcus. On the other hand, discounters and off-price retailers, such as Target and TJ Maxx, offer a good value for the money.

PRESENTATION The presentation of a retail store helps determine the store's image and positions the retail store in consumers' minds. For instance, a retailer that wants to position itself as an upscale store would use a lavish or sophisticated presentation. The main element of a store's presentation is its **atmosphere**, the overall impression conveyed by a store's physical layout, decor, and surroundings. The atmosphere might create a relaxed or busy feeling, a sense of luxury or efficiency, a friendly or cold attitude, a sense of organization or clutter, or a fun or serious mood. Urban Outfitters stores,

targeted to Generation Y consumers, use raw concrete, original brick, rusted steel, and unfinished wood to convey an urban feel. The following are the most influential factors in creating a store's atmosphere:

- *Employee type and density: Employee type* refers to an employee's general characteristics—for instance, neat, friendly, knowledgeable, or service oriented. Density is the number of employees per thousand square feet of selling space. While low employee density creates a do-it-yourself, casual atmosphere, high employee density denotes readiness to serve the customer's every whim. Retailers must take care, therefore, to ensure that high employee density does not feel like "stalking" behavior to the customer. Research suggests that if shoppers feel as though they are being watched too closely by store staff, they can become uncomfortable and leave without completing their purchase.[29]

- *Merchandise type and density:* A prestigious retailer like Nordstrom or Neiman Marcus carries the best brand names and displays them in a neat, uncluttered arrangement. Discounters and off-price retailers often carry seconds or out-of-season goods crowded into small spaces and hung on long racks by category—tops, pants, skirts, and so on—creating the impression that "We've got so much stuff, we're practically giving it away."

- *Fixture type and density:* Fixtures can be elegant (rich woods) or trendy (chrome and smoked glass); they can even consist of old, beat-up tables, as in an antiques store. The fixtures should be consistent with the general atmosphere the store is trying to create.

> **atmosphere** the overall impression conveyed by a store's physical layout, decor, and surroundings

Mohd Syis Zulkipli/Shutterstock.com

Studies show sounds and odors may influence which products customers purchase. Do you think sounds and odors affect your choice of which product to purchase?

- *Sound:* Sound can be pleasant or unpleasant for a customer. Music can entice some customers to stay in the store longer and buy more or to eat quickly and leave a table for others. It can also control the pace of the store traffic, create an image, and attract or direct the shopper's attention. Studies show the type of music played can even influence a customer's choice of product. Ethnic music increases the likelihood of a customer choosing a menu item from the same country, and country western music increases customers' willingness to pay for functional, everyday products.[30] Additionally, the presence of fast-tempo music has recently been demonstrated to entice customers to remain longer in crowded stores, which can increase the size of their purchases.[31]

- *Odors:* Smell can either stimulate or detract from sales. Research suggests that people evaluate merchandise more positively, spend more time shopping, and are generally in a better mood when an agreeable odor is present. Other research shows that certain scents empower consumers and lead to more premium purchases.[32] Retailers use fragrances as an extension of their retail strategy.

- *Visual factors:* Colors can create a mood or focus attention and therefore are an important factor in atmosphere. Red, yellow, and orange are considered warm colors and are used when a feeling of warmth and closeness is desired. Cool colors like blue, green, and violet are used to open up closed-in places and create an air of elegance and cleanliness. Many retailers have found that natural lighting, either from windows or skylights, can lead to increased sales. Outdoor lighting can also affect a customer's choice of retailer.

The **layout** of retail stores is also a key factor in their success. The goal is to use all of the store's space effectively, including aisles, fixtures, merchandise displays, and non-selling areas. In addition to making shopping easy and convenient for the customer, an effective layout has a powerful influence on traffic patterns and purchasing behavior. Layout also includes where products are placed in the store. Many technologically advanced retailers are using a technique called *market-basket analysis* to sift through the data collected by their point-of-purchase scanning equipment. The analysis looks for products that are commonly purchased together to help retailers find ideal locations for each product. Walmart uses market-basket analysis to determine where in the store to stock products for customer convenience. Tissues, for example, are in the paper-goods aisle and also beside the cold medicines.

layout the internal design and configuration of a store's fixtures and products

Retailers can better acquire and use assets when they customize store layouts and merchandise mixes to the tastes of local consumer bases. For example, O'Reilly Auto Parts designs each of its retail outlets with the wants and needs of local auto drivers in mind, creating a neighborhood-specific strategy for each location. By customizing layout and product mix to the vehicles owned and operated in a particular area, the company can simultaneously provide greater levels of availability and reduce inventory, creating savings that the company passes along to customers.[33]

Retailers have had to adapt physical operations to a new normal that includes health and safety for both workers and customers, and experts expect many of these changes will be permanent. Retailers have also had to make the in-store experience more intriguing to draw customers out of the safety of their homes and into the physical space. A primary example has been the emergence of luxury cinemas. This redesign for delivery of luxury offerings is also evident in retailer electronic platforms. As an example, Artificial Intelligence enabled personal robot stylists are being used to assist in clothing selections. Moreover, in response to customer requests for social distancing by many customers, Walmart and Target have introduced payment systems entirely based on self-checkout. Touchless payment systems can be enabled with barcode scanning and RFID, as facilitated by mobile phones carried by almost all customers, so the technological cost of these updates has been relatively low. If touchless checkout approaches become the new standard, other retail formats such as specialty stores and restaurants will follow.

PERSONNEL People are a unique aspect of retailing. Most retail sales involve a customer–salesperson relationship, if only briefly. Sales personnel provide their customers with the amount of service prescribed by the retail strategy of the store.

Retail salespeople serve another important selling function: They persuade shoppers to buy. They must therefore be able to persuade customers that what they are selling is what the customer needs. Salespeople are trained in two common selling techniques: trading up and suggestion selling. *Trading up* means persuading customers to buy an item with a higher price than the one they originally intended to purchase. To avoid selling customers something they do not need or want, however, salespeople should take care when practicing trading-up techniques. *Suggestion selling*, a common practice among most retailers, seeks to broaden customers' original purchases with related items. For example, if you buy a new printer at Office Depot, the sales representative will ask if you would like to purchase paper, a USB cable, and/or extra ink cartridges. Suggestion selling by sales or service associates should always help shoppers recognize true needs rather than sell them unwanted merchandise.

Providing great customer service is one of the most challenging elements in the retail mix because customer expectations for service vary greatly. What customers expect in a department store is very different from what they expect in a discount store. Customer expectations also change. Ten years ago, shoppers wanted personal, one-on-one attention. Today, many customers are happy to help themselves as long as they can easily find what they need.

14-5c Enacting Shopper Marketing

Shopper marketing is an emerging retailing strategy that employs market data to best serve customers as they prepare to make a purchase. Shopper marketing focuses first on understanding how a brand's target consumers behave as shoppers in different channels and formats and then using this information in business-based strategies and initiatives that are carefully designed to deliver balanced benefits to all stakeholders—brands, channel members, and customers. It may sound simple, but it is anything but. While brand manufacturers used to advertise widely and tried to ensure that their products were available wherever consumers shopped, now they are placing far more emphasis on partnering with specific retailers or websites. Brand manufacturers work with retailers on everything from in-store initiatives to customized retailer-specific products. Shopper marketing brings brand managers and account managers together to connect with consumers along the entire path to purchase, whether it be at home, on the go via mobile marketing, or in the store. Both manufacturers and retailers now think about consumers specifically while they are in shopping mode. They use **shopper analytics** to dig deeply into customers' shopping attitudes, perceptions, emotions, and behaviors—and are thereby able to learn how the shopping experience shapes differences in these traits.

Shopper marketing is becoming increasingly popular as businesses see the implications of this new method of customer research. One implication is the strategic alignment of customer segments. Brands' core target consumers are compared to retailers' most loyal shoppers in an effort to find intersecting areas where brands and retailers can pool their resources. The ideal outcome is a more focused marketing effort and a three-way win for brands, channel members, *and* customers.

14-6 RETAILING DECISIONS FOR SERVICES

The fastest-growing part of our economy is the service sector. Although distribution in the service sector is difficult to visualize, the same skills, techniques, and strategies used to manage inventory can also be used to manage service inventory, such as hospital beds, bank accounts, or airline seats. The quality of the planning and execution of distribution can have a major impact on costs and customer satisfaction.

Because service industries are so customer oriented, service quality is a priority. To manage customer relationships, many service providers, such as insurance carriers, physicians, hair salons, and financial services, use technology to schedule appointments, manage accounts, and disburse information. Service distribution focuses on four main areas:

- *Minimizing wait times:* Minimizing the amount of time customers wait in line is a key factor in maintaining the quality of service.

- *Managing service capacity:* If service firms don't have the capacity to meet demand, they must either turn down some prospective customers, let service levels slip, or expand capacity.

- *Improving service delivery:* Service firms are now experimenting with different distribution channels for their services. Choosing the right distribution channel can increase the times that services are available or add to customer convenience.

- *Establishing channel-wide network coherence:* Because services are to some degree intangible, service firms also find it necessary to standardize their service quality across different geographic regions to maintain their brand image.

14-7 ADDRESSING RETAIL PRODUCT/ SERVICE FAILURES

In spite of retailers' best intentions and efforts to satisfy each and every customer, all retailers inevitably disappoint a subset of their customers. In some cases, customer disappointment

shopper marketing understanding how one's target consumers behave as shoppers, in different channels and formats, and leveraging this intelligence to generate sales or other positive outcomes

shopper analytics searching for and discovering meaningful patterns in shopper data for the purpose of fine-tuning, developing, or changing market offerings occurs by design. No retailer can be everything to every customer, and by making strategic decisions related to targeting, segmentation, and the retailing mix, retailers implicitly decide which customers will be delighted and which will probably leave the store unsatisfied. In other cases, service failures are unintentional. A product may be located where customers cannot easily find it (or it may remain in the stockroom, entirely out of customer view), or an employee may provide mistaken information about a product's features or benefits. Customers are generally indifferent to the reasons for retailer errors, and their reactions to mistakes such as product stockouts and unexpectedly poor-quality products can range widely. Some may simply leave the store, while others will respond with anger or even revenge behaviors intended to prevent other customers from visiting the store.[34]

The best retailers have plans in place to not only recover from inevitable lapses in service but perhaps even to benefit from them. For these top-performing stores, service recovery is handled proactively as part of an overarching plan to maximize the customer experience. Actions that might be taken include:

- Notifying customers in advance of stockouts and explaining the reasons why certain products are not available

- Implementing liberal return policies designed to ensure that the customer can bring back any item for any reason (if the product fails to work as planned or even if the customer simply doesn't like it)

- Issuing product recalls in conjunction with promotional offers that provide future incentives to repurchase

In short, the best retailers treat customer disappointments as opportunities to interact with and improve relations with their customers. Evidence indicates that successful handling of such failures can sometimes yield even higher levels of customer loyalty than if the failure had never occurred at all.

14-8 RETAILER AND RETAIL CUSTOMER TRENDS AND ADVANCEMENTS

Though retailing has been around for thousands of years, it continues to change every day. Retailers are constantly innovating. They are always looking for new products and services (or ways to offer them) that will attract new customers or inspire current ones to buy in greater quantities or more frequently. Many of the most interesting and effective retail innovations that have recently taken hold are related to the use of purchase and shopping data to better understand customer wants and needs. Finding new and better ways to entice customers into a store—and then to spend more money once there—is another hotbed of innovation. This chapter concludes with an examination of emerging trends and recent advancements in retailing.

It is important to recognize that, fundamentally, retailers decide what to sell on the basis of what their target market wants to buy. They base these decisions on market research, past sales, fashion trends, customer requests, and other sources. Recently, the need for more and better information has led many retailers to use **big data analytics**, a process whereby retailers use complex mathematical models to make better product mix decisions. Dillard's, Target, and Walmart use big data analytics to determine which products to stock and at what prices, how to manage markdowns, and how to advertise to draw their intended customers. The data that these and other companies collect at the point of sale and throughout their stores enable retailers and suppliers alike to gain better customer insights. For example, instead of simply unloading products into the distribution channel and leaving marketing, sales. and relationship building to local dealers, auto manufacturers use websites to keep in touch with customers and prospects. They inquire about lifestyles, hobbies, and vehicle needs in an effort to develop long-lasting relationships in the hopes that these consumers will reward them with brand loyalty in the future.

For many years retail customers had become used to liberal return policies, for both instore and online purchases. This liberal policy on returns was made possible by retail data analytics systems. Retailers had no choice but to pause product returns at brick-and-mortar locations during state-mandated COVID-19 shutdowns. But after those closed businesses were opened up, many encountered obstacles in setting up safe and effective returns management systems. As a result, companies are increasingly focusing on becoming more data driven in terms of forecasting returns. Some retailers are adjusting their traditional retail timelines to accommodate shopping patterns, including returns management, and allowing time for products that have been in warehouses or returned to continue selling. A major pandemic issue for retailers, therefore, has been the need to focus on the safety of returns-handling employees. This challenge will continue until a vaccine is widely available.

big data analytics the process of discovering patterns in large data sets for the purposes of extracting knowledge and understanding human behavior

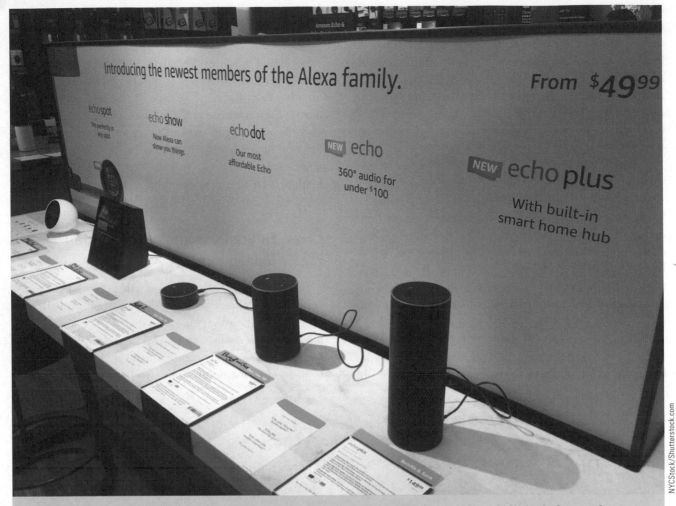

Voice-assisted commerce is being used increasingly in both physical and digital channels.

Retailers are increasingly using **beacons**—devices that send out connecting signals to customers' smartphones and tablets. These devices recognize when a customer is in or near the store and indicate to an automated system that the customer is ripe to receive a marketing message via email or text. Beacons can also notify sales associates to offer (or not offer) a coupon at the point of sale. Some retailers are using an app called Swarm to map customer foot traffic data, which they use to make better decisions about product placement within the floor grid. Carefully designed beacons can even have an aesthetic appeal. At some retailers, cameras and beacons are built into mannequins located inside the store and in window displays. These beacons act not as only data-collection devices but also as primary displays for the clothing and jewelry that appeal to customers' eyes.[35]

RFID (radio-frequency identification) is not a new technology, but its use has diversified greatly over the past few years. Traditionally used for inventory management purposes prior to items reaching the sales floor, retailers have begun using RFID to track items that customers pick up while shopping. This enables a retailer to instantly create a promotion for the specific item in a customer's hand. For example, if a customer picks up a set of sheets, the retailer can use RFID and digital advertising to suggest related items, such as pillowcases, blankets, and even paint colors that match the sheets. The advertisement can provide guidance as to where to find the promoted items in the store. Additionally, RFID has the potential to make the checkout process much faster by enabling an entire cart of products to be scanned in seconds.[36]

Retailers have begun using another emerging technology: facial recognition. Suppose a retailer scans a customer to determine the customer's gender and age group. The retailer can then cross-reference these

> **beacon** a device that sends out connecting signals to customers' smartphones and tablets in order to bring them into a retail store or improve their shopping experience

data with the customer's location in the store, providing promotions and information with pinpoint accuracy. Facial recognition even allows retailers to identify customers, call them by their names, and target them with advertising as they walk through the retail space. Similarly, biometric sensors can be used to measure how long a customer views an ad or product in the store. These data can be used as a measure of interest and/or ad effectiveness.[37]

By the end of 2021, more than 1.6 billion people will use voice assistants, like Alexa, Siri, or Google Home, on a regular basis. Conversational artificial intelligence (AI) powers these voice technology systems and is quickly revolutionizing retail. Retailers use this emerging technology to develop highly personalized relationships with customers and to become their first and only choice, especially when reordering simple items. As conversational artificial intelligence continues to improve, retailers aspire to use its capabilities to provide a world-class customer service experience for shoppers, complete with AI-driven personalized recommendations and on-demand customer support. Additionally,

by engaging in voice-assisted commerce, the consumer enjoys a dialogue throughout their product search process, which capitalizes on the recent trend toward experiential retailing. Retailers will find the most success from this emerging technology, however, if they are able to quickly and seamlessly integrate the **voice-assisted commerce** activity into their existing physical and digital channels to create an effective omnichannel experience for the user.[38] In fact, the emergence of voice-assisted commerce is motivating retailers to seek guidance on the most effective voice strategy to serve their customers.

14-8a Future Developments in Retail Management

A retailing trend with great growth potential is the leveraging of technology to increase touchpoints with customers and thereby generate greater profitability. The use of mobile devices and social media while browsing, comparison shopping, and actually making a purchase is becoming extremely pervasive, leading retailers to

Beyond Time/Shutterstock.com

Though it's not quite virtual reality, home furnishing companies like IKEA and Home Depot allow customers to design 3D renders of their rooms to help pick out features like cabinets, countertops, appliances, and more.

rethink how they should appeal to shoppers in the decision-making mode. Recall that customers who "showroom" visit a physical retail store to examine product features or quality firsthand, but then eventually make the purchase online. This practice has motivated a showrooming response from retailers themselves, who reduce the amount of stock kept on hand, rent or lease smaller spaces, and ramp up their fulfillment capabilities at distribution centers. Showrooming and data analytics have even led to the development of virtual reality apps that enable customers to see themselves wearing articles of desired clothing without physically putting them on! These approaches have led some retailers to pursue a strategy of **retail channel omnification** (recall the discussion of omnichannel distribution operations in Chapter 13). Retailers like Nordstrom used to treat their physical stores as entirely different businesses from their online stores, with each channel having a unique distribution system and a dedicated inventory. Now, retailers are combining these ventures into a single system that is responsible for delivering on customer demand regardless of whether it originated in a physical store or in cyberspace.[39] This single system avoids redundancies in inventory and transportation, saving costs and enabling retailers to offer competitive prices across their various outlets. Customers of Nordstrom, Nordstrom Rack, Nordstrom.com, hautelook.com, and nordstromrack.com can seamlessly transition between each of these channels when shopping, returning purchased goods or scheduling services such as alterations.

However, not all retailers are embracing omnification as the way of the future. The alternative strategy, **click-and-collect**, also enables customers to make their purchases online. Rather than waiting for orders to arrive at their homes, customers drive to physical stores to pick their orders up.[40] When retailers use this strategy, customers benefit from greater speed of delivery (in fact, they become the delivery vehicle), while retailers themselves benefit from the fact that customers must enter their stores in order to claim their purchases. Once inside, customers can be marketed to, increasing the likelihood that they will purchase add-on items or otherwise engage in impulse buying. It remains to be seen whether one or both of these strategies will stand the test of time, but it is certain that retailers are preparing for the inevitability of the Internet as an important shopping and purchasing medium for the foreseeable future.

Another fascinating trend is the use of artificial intelligence as a touch point for customers. Robots are replacing or augmenting retail employees at restaurants, supermarkets, and airports across the globe. As technology progresses, customers will begin to see virtual reality used in many retail contexts. Virtual reality enables customers to try items before they buy—even if those items don't actually exist yet. Currently, customers shopping online can use virtual technology to see how outfits might look on their own bodies or how furniture might look in their own homes.[41] Imagine if customers could do the same for furniture or kitchen appliances! The integration of these new technologies will bring customers a shopping experience like they have never had before—both highly interactive and customized.

Shopper marketing faced a number of challenges when the COVID-19 pandemic increased the demand for online shopping, one of which was the need to add omnichannel options. As a result, omnichannel was no longer a "nice to have" approach for retailers—it increasingly was a strategy retailers had invest in to survive. At the same time, integration of inventory for brick and click operations motivated companies to rethink inventory strategies, and some found out cost savings were possible. The increase in online shopping produced higher demand for warehouse space, resulting in some price increases unless a better balance could be achieved between demand and manufacturing. Retailers have already begun thinking about whether better inventory balancing is possible and also evaluating whether to focus on improved forecasting accuracy or increasing warehousing space. In short, more storage space will likely be needed unless retailers can more effectively integrate their inventory for brick and click operations as a single, coordinated system.

As retailers became accustomed to constrained supply during the pandemic, they recognized that narrower customer choice had become an unexpected benefit, thereby increasing profitability through cost savings that offset sales price reductions. At the same time, the long-held mantra that more choice results in more revenue was adjusted by the realization that incremental variety can lead to incremental costs that outstrip the revenue gained from merchandise variety. Finally, as omnichannel distribution accelerated retail analytics has been increasingly applied to create real time automated/flexible pricing changes. This technology tool has enabled many retailers to better track, monitor and compare their product and pricing offers, and facilitated real-time reactions that have increased online competitiveness.

retail channel omnification the reduction of multiple retail channel systems into a single, unified system for the purpose of creating efficiencies or saving costs

click-and-collect the practice of buying something online and then traveling to a physical store location to take delivery of the merchandise

15 | Marketing Communications

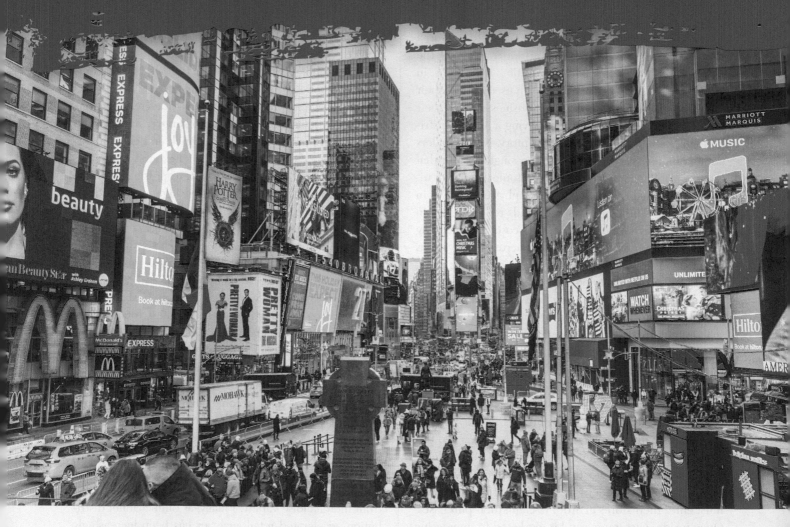

Manu Padilla/Shutterstock.com

LEARNING OUTCOMES

After studying this chapter, you will be able to...

15-1 Discuss the role of promotion in the marketing mix

15-2 Describe the communication process

15-3 Explain the goals and tasks of promotion

15-4 Discuss the elements of the promotional mix

15-5 Discuss the AIDA concept and its relationship to the promotional mix

15-6 Discuss the concept of integrated marketing communications

15-7 Describe the factors that affect the promotional mix

THE ROLE OF PROMOTION IN THE MARKETING MIX

Few goods or services, no matter how well developed, priced, or distributed, can survive in the marketplace without effective promotion—communication by marketers that informs, persuades, and reminds potential buyers of a product in order to influence an opinion or elicit a response.

Promotional strategy is a plan for the optimal use of the elements of promotion: advertising, public relations, personal selling, sales promotion, and digital and social media. Promotion is a vital part of the marketing mix, informing consumers of a product's benefits and thereby positioning the product in the marketplace. As Exhibit 15.1 shows, the marketing manager determines the goals of the company's promotional strategy in light of the firm's overall goals for the marketing mix—product, place (distribution), promotion, and price. Using these overall goals, marketers combine the elements of the promotional strategy (the promotional mix) into a coordinated plan. The promotion plan then becomes an integral part of the marketing strategy for reaching the target market.

The main function of a marketer's promotional strategy is to convince target customers that the goods and services offer provide a competitive advantage over the competition. A **competitive advantage** is the set of unique features of a company and its products that are perceived by the target market as significant and superior to those of the competition. Such features can include high product quality, rapid delivery, low prices, excellent service, or some feature not offered by the competition. Promotional strategies have changed a great deal over the years as many targeted customer segments have become more difficult to reach. Informative television advertisements are no longer enough, forcing marketers to think more creatively. Most campaigns utilize a variety of tactics—such as digital paid media, social media, and influencer marketing—in addition to more traditional media like television and print. Spotify is an example of a company that uses data analytics to develop campaigns and also to connect campaigns to pop culture. For example, consider Spotify's "Thanks, It's Been Weird" campaign, which was inspired by major events going on in the world, such as the Brexit vote. Throughout the campaign, a data-driven approach was used to highlight interesting music streaming trends in 14 global markets. A U.K. advertisement reads: "Dear 3,749 people who streamed 'It's The End Of The World As We Know It' the day of the Brexit Vote. Hang in There." Other ads are

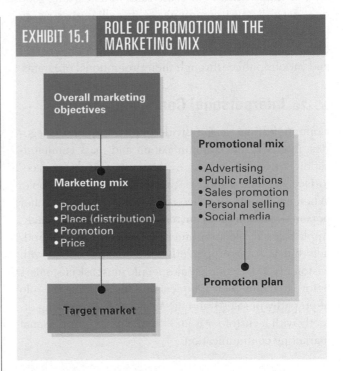

EXHIBIT 15.1 ROLE OF PROMOTION IN THE MARKETING MIX

Overall marketing objectives

Marketing mix
- Product
- Place (distribution)
- Promotion
- Price

Promotional mix
- Advertising
- Public relations
- Sales promotion
- Personal selling
- Social media

Promotion plan

Target market

even more localized, such as, "Dear person in the Theater District who listened to the Hamilton soundtrack 5,376 times this year. Can you get us tickets?" Spotify's Chief Marketing Officer Seth Farbman said about the campaign: "For us, data inspires and gives insights into the emotions people are expressing."[1] Spotify followed this campaign with a global out-of-home advertising campaign that crunched user data and transformed it to develop headlines on billboards, much of which was based on personal listening habits. For example, one billboard read "Goals: Be as humble as the person who got an entire billboard for listening to HUMBLE 1,251 times."

promotion communication by marketers that informs, persuades, and reminds potential buyers of a product in order to influence an opinion or elicit a response

promotional strategy a plan for the optimal use of the elements of promotion: advertising, public relations, personal selling, sales promotion, and social media

competitive advantage one or more unique aspects of an organization that cause target consumers to patronize that firm rather than competitors

15-2 MARKETING COMMUNICATION

Promotional strategy is closely related to the process of communication. As humans, we assign meaning to feelings, ideas, facts, attitudes, and emotions. Communication is the process by which meanings are exchanged or shared through a common set of symbols. When a company develops a new product, changes an old one, or simply tries to increase sales of an existing good or service, it must communicate its selling message to potential customers. Marketers communicate information about the firm and its products to the target market and various publics through their promotional programs.

15-2a Interpersonal Communication

Communication can be divided into two major categories: interpersonal communication and mass communication. Interpersonal communication is direct, face-to-face communication between two or more people. When communicating face-to-face, people see the other person's reaction and can respond almost immediately. Apple salespeople are trained not only on Apple's products but also on proper etiquette for interacting with customers. For example, salespeople must ask customers before touching their iPhones, thus highlighting the role of empathy in sales training. A salesperson speaking directly with a customer is an example of an interpersonal marketing communication.

15-2b Mass Communication

Mass communication involves communicating a concept or message to large audiences. A great number of marketing communications are directed to consumers as a group, usually through a mass medium such as television or newspapers. When a company advertises, it generally does not personally know the people with whom it is trying to communicate. Moreover, the company often cannot respond immediately to consumers' reactions to its messages unless they are using social media or digital-based tools. Clutter from competitors' messages or other distractions in the environment can reduce the effectiveness of mass-communications efforts.

Mass communication involves communicating a concept or message to large audiences. If you've ever seen a commercial on television, you've been a target of mass communication.

Apple, for example, uses many different mass media vehicles (including magazines and digital media) to reach its target audience.

15-2c The Communication Process

Marketers are both senders and receivers of messages. As *senders*, marketers attempt to inform, persuade, and remind the target market to take actions compatible with the need to promote the purchase of goods and services. As *receivers*, marketers listen to the target market in order to develop the appropriate messages, adapt existing messages, and spot new communication opportunities. In this way, most marketing communication is a two-way, rather than one-way, process. The two-way nature of the communication process is shown in Exhibit 15.2.

THE SENDER AND ENCODING The sender is the originator of the message in the communication process. In an interpersonal conversation, the sender may be a parent, a friend, or a salesperson. For an advertisement, press release, or social media campaign, the sender is the company or organization itself. Social media influencers are people who promote products and services on social media platforms like Instagram and YouTube; they are also considered senders on behalf of marketers. In fact, it sometimes is difficult to tell who the sender of a promotional message is, especially in the case of bold, avant-garde advertisements. For example, when Always wanted to take advantage of a growing "femvertising" trend, it launched the campaign #likeagirl. The campaign was based on research showing that 7 out of 10 girls felt

communication the process by which we exchange or share meaning through a common set of symbols

interpersonal communication direct, face-to-face communication between two or more people

mass communication the communication of a concept or message to large audiences

sender the originator of the message in the communication process

EXHIBIT 15.2 COMMUNICATION PROCESS

Noise
- Other advertisements
- News articles
- Other store displays

Sender
- Marketing manager
- Advertising manager
- Advertising agency
- Other consumers

Encoding the message
- Advertisement
- Sales presentation
- Store display
- Coupon
- Press release
- Social media

Message channel
- Media
- Salesperson
- Retail store
- Local news show

Decoding the message
- Receiver interpretation of message

Receiver
- Customers
- Viewers/ listeners
- News media
- Clients

Feedback channel
- Market research
- Sales results
- Change in market share
- Social media

like they did not belong in sports and that many girls quit when they reached puberty. The campaign used the hashtag #likeagirl to combat the negative connotation of doing things like a girl (you've likely heard the expression "He hits like a girl"). A video advertisement served as the centerpiece of the campaign, showing girls being active, engaged, and passionate about a variety of sports. The campaign also relied heavily on social media and had educational components to reach additional audiences. The campaign was a hit for Always, winning several awards.[2]

Encoding is the conversion of the sender's ideas and thoughts into a message, usually in the form of words, signs, images, or videos. A basic principle of encoding is that what the source says is not what matters, it is what the receiver hears. In the case of the Always #likeagirl campaign, videos used emotionally resonant stereotypes that girls have heard for years to get the message across.[3] One way of conveying a message the receiver will hear properly is to use concrete words and pictures.

MESSAGE TRANSMISSION Transmission of a message requires a **channel**—a voice, radio, newspaper, computer, smartphone, social media platform, or other communication medium. A facial expression or gesture can also serve as a channel. For Always, the centerpiece of the campaign

was a video, and eventually a Super Bowl ad. The video was seeded on social media platforms.[4] The response to these viral activities clearly created a lot of free publicity.

Reception occurs when the message is detected by the receiver and enters his or her frame of reference. In a two-way conversation such as a sales pitch given by a sales representative to a potential client, reception is normally high. Similarly, when the message is a recommendation from a friend, the reception is high. Even in social media, if the social media influencer responds to likes and comments, the reception is high. By contrast, the desired receivers may or may not detect the message when it is mass communicated because most media are cluttered by **noise**—anything that interferes with, distorts, or slows down the transmission of information. In some media overcrowded with advertisers, such as newspapers and television, the noise level is high and the reception level is low.

THE RECEIVER AND DECODING Marketers communicate their

encoding the conversion of a sender's ideas and thoughts into a message, usually in the form of words or signs

channel a medium of communication—such as a voice, radio, or newspaper—for transmitting a message

noise anything that interferes with, distorts, or slows down the transmission of information message through a channel to customers, or **receivers**, who will decode the message. It is important to note that there can be multiple receivers, as consumers share their experiences and their recommendations online through social networks and other types of social media. Online conversations are an influential way to promote products and services. Indeed, this empowerment of the receiver has transformed marketing and advertising. Receivers can easily share new information with their friends and followers on social media, and those new receivers can then also share that information. In fact, reviews and online comments have become important information for other receivers. This leads to a more diverse inter-relationship between senders and receivers of social media messages. **Decoding** is the interpretation of the language and symbols sent by the source through a channel. Common understanding between two communicators, or a common frame of reference, is required for effective communication. Therefore, marketing managers must ensure a proper match between the message to be conveyed and the target market's attitudes and ideas.

Even though a message has been received, it may not necessarily be properly decoded because of selective exposure, distortion, and retention. When people receive a message, they tend to manipulate it to reflect their own biases, needs, experiences, and knowledge. Therefore, differences in age, social class, education, culture, and ethnicity can lead to miscommunication. Further, because people do not always listen or read carefully, they can easily misinterpret what is said or written. In fact, researchers have found that consumers misunderstand a large proportion of both printed and televised communications. Bright colors and bold graphics increase consumers' comprehension of marketing communications. But these techniques are not foolproof. The Always #likeagirl campaign was easily decoded by its target audience, and it resonated with them. For example, research following the campaign showed improvements in girls' views of the phrase "like a girl."[5]

Marketers targeting consumers in foreign countries must also worry about the translation and possible miscommunication of their promotional messages by other cultures. Global marketers must decide whether to standardize or customize the message for each global market in which they sell.

FEEDBACK In interpersonal communication, the receiver's response to a message is direct **feedback** to the source. Feedback may be verbal, as in saying "I agree" or "I do not like this new product." But it can also be nonverbal, as in nodding, smiling, frowning, or gesturing. Feedback can also occur digitally, as in a like or comment on social media platforms, a comment on a blog post, or a message sent through a website contact form. In fact, social media influencers do all they can to encourage engagement on social media platforms through comments and responses. Mass communicators are often cut off from some direct feedback, so they must rely on market research, social media, or analysis of viewer responses for indirect feedback. They may use such measurements as the percentage of television viewers who recognized, recalled, or stated that they were exposed to the company's messages. Indirect feedback enables mass communicators to decide whether to continue, modify, or drop a message.

With online advertising, marketers are able to get more feedback than before digital platforms became such a driving social force. Using web analytics, marketers can see how long customers stay on a website and which pages they view. Moreover, social media enable companies such as Southwest Airlines, Nike, American Airlines, and Comcast to provide instant feedback by responding to consumers' posts on Facebook and to complaints on social network platforms such as Twitter.

Digital platforms and social media have had an impact on the communication model in two major ways. First, consumers are now able to become senders (as opposed to only brands being senders). For example, a professional blogger or Instagram influencer who recommends a product, and thus influences a consumer's decision to buy it, is a sender. Similarly, everyday consumers who make casual recommendations on Facebook and Yelp are essentially senders as well. Clearly, the communication model is much more complicated today than it was just a few years ago. Second, the communication model displays the feedback channel as primarily impersonal and numbers driven. In the traditional communication process, marketers can see the results of customer behavior (e.g., a drop or rise in sales) but are able to explain those changes only by using their judgment. Today, customers use social media platforms like Facebook, Twitter, and Instagram to comment publicly on marketing efforts. These platforms enable marketers to personalize the feedback channel by opening the door for direct conversations with customers. But because social media conversations occur in real time and are public, any negative posts or complaints are highly visible. Thus, many companies have crisis communication strategies to deal with negative information and to promote good brand reputations.

receiver the person who decodes a message

decoding interpretation of the language and symbols sent by the source through a channel

feedback the receiver's response to a message

GPS-enabled tracking sticker manufacturer TrackerPad uses video and social media to make potential customers aware of the product's features and benefits.

Source: TrackerPad

15-3 THE GOALS OF PROMOTION

People communicate with one another for many reasons. They seek amusement, ask for help, give assistance or instructions, provide information, and express ideas and thoughts. Promotion, on the other hand, seeks to modify behavior and thoughts in some way. For example, promoters may try to persuade consumers to buy a Samsung Galaxy phone rather than an Apple iPhone. Promotion also strives to reinforce existing behavior—for instance, getting consumers to continue buying Samsung once they have switched. The source (the seller) hopes to project a favorable image or to motivate purchase of the company's goods and services.

Promotion can perform one or more of four tasks: *inform* the target audience, *persuade* the target audience, *remind* the target audience, or *connect* with the audience. The ability to *connect* to consumers is one task that can be facilitated through social media. Often a marketer will try to accomplish two or more of these tasks at the same time.

15-3a Informing

Informative promotion seeks to convert an existing need into a want, or to stimulate interest in a new product. It is generally more prevalent during the early stages of the product life cycle. People typically will not buy a product or service or support a nonprofit organization until they know its purpose and its benefits. Informative messages are important for promoting complex and technical products such as automobiles, computers, and investment services. For example, shortly after announcing a revised model of the Apple Watch, Apple released a video on YouTube showing updates and new uses for the smartwatch. The video focused on new features but did not overtly explain the watch's functions. Instead, the company allowed users to discover those on their own.[6] Informative promotion is also important for a "new" brand being introduced into an "old" product class. For example. Apple is using additional technology to make its Apple Watch even more attractive. The Apple Watch Series 4 includes technology for a personal electrocardiogram thanks to a new sensor. This will enable people to monitor their heart health and is Apple's biggest bet yet that personal technology will transform personal health. Magazine articles, videos and the website have been used to promote this new feature.[7] New products cannot establish themselves against more mature products unless potential buyers are aware of them, value their benefits, and understand their positioning in the marketplace.

15-3b Persuading

Persuasive promotion is designed to stimulate a purchase or an action. Persuasion typically becomes the main promotion goal when the product enters the growth stage of its life cycle. By the growth stage, the target market should have general product awareness and some knowledge of how the product can fulfill its wants. Therefore, the promotional task switches from informing consumers about the product category to persuading them to buy the company's brand rather than that of the competitor. The promotional message therefore emphasizes the product's real and perceived competitive advantages, often appealing to emotional needs such as love, belonging, self-esteem, and ego satisfaction. For example, SoulCycle, a popular fitness brand, is focusing on persuading consumers to try their classes over other fitness brands. Advertising messages, therefore, highlight the unique benefits of a SoulCycle class like the quality of instructors, the upbeat music selections and the meditative experience of the class.

Persuasion is important when the goal is to inspire direct action. Levi Strauss & Co is a 165-year-old "lifestyle brand" known traditionally for its denim jeans. It has seen its ups and downs and sits squarely in the hypercompetitive denim market worth more than $95 billion worldwide. Levi's has been squeezed on both sides—from discounters to designers. In the past 20 years, it has executed a merchandising overhaul including T-shirts and other apparel offerings. A large part of the recent resurgence is the result of the "Live in Levi's" marketing platform that positions the brand for all activities (from cliff diving to weddings). Tactics include a new flagship store in Times Square, one of the most watched ads on YouTube, and a strong voice on social issues in order to appeal to younger audiences. Also included was a campaign during the midterm elections encouraging young

ALS ICE BUCKET CHALLENGE

TAKE THE CHALLENGE, DONATE AND HELP CREATE A WORLD WITHOUT ALS!

#ICEBUCKETCHALLENGE

Dashikka/Shutterstock.com

The ALS Ice Bucket Challenge was very successful in creating awareness and understanding of a little known disease.

people to vote. The company is also continuing its sustainability efforts along with growing its digital platforms and e-commerce capabilities, and utilizing technology facilitating more customization.[8] Persuasion can therefore be an important goal for very competitive mature product categories, such as household items and soft drinks. In a marketplace characterized by many competitors, the promotional message often encourages brand switching and aims to convert some buyers into loyal users. But some critics believe promotional messages and techniques can be too persuasive, causing consumers to buy products and services they don't really need.

15-3c Reminding

Reminder promotion is used to keep the product and brand name in the public's mind. This type of promotion prevails during the maturity stage of the life cycle. It assumes that the target market has already been persuaded of the merits of the good or service. Its purpose is to trigger a memory that leads to a purchase. Colgate toothpaste and other consumer products often use reminder promotion. Reminder advertising is often used for consumer services as well. Companies that produce products like automobiles and appliances advertise throughout the year to remind people about the brands when they are looking to purchase. Recently IHOP, known for its pancakes,

decided to remind people that it had other menu items as well. With a Tweet, it launched a name change, which turned out to be fake, from IHOP to IHOb to focus on its burgers. The company is not as popular for lunch and dinner and wanted to change perceptions and remind potential customers that they have food other than pancakes. The campaign produced 30 billion media impressions and was the topic of more than 20,000 news stories.[9]

15-3d Connecting

The focus of social media is to form relationships with customers and potential customers through technological ties such as Facebook, Twitter, YouTube, or other social media platforms. In forming these relationships, the goal is for them to lead to customer engagement with the products or services, and ultimately to purchases. Indeed, some companies, such as Starbucks, have their own social networks that enable customers to share ideas, information, and feedback. By facilitating this exchange of information through a transparent process, brands are increasingly connecting with their customers in hopes that they become brand advocates who promote the brand through their own social networks. Tools for connection include social networks, social games, and social publishing tools as well as social commerce. For example, Adidas created personalized videos for 30,000 runners in the Boston Marathon in 24 hours. Each video has the runner's name and times at various checkpoints. By the next day, 15 percent of the videos were shared on Facebook with 8,000 comments and 36,000 reactions. Within the next few days after the race, there were 12,000 unique views on the videos with a 95 percent completion rate. "We flipped the script on how to bring content to life, and celebrated the runners' stories, which was a perfect alignment," said Scott Frost, digital marketing manager for Adidas Running in the United States. "The Boston Marathon is no easy feat in either qualifying or meeting the charity parameters, and those who made it had to be creative in their own lives to make it there."[10]

When the COVID-19 global pandemic spread globally, millions of Americans were suddenly sequestered in their homes, working and learning online, and trying to adapt to the "new normal". Consumers were anxious about family and health, finances, and availability of some essential products, to name a few. Suddenly, brands were faced with a challenge as well—how to be sensitive to the needs of customers while continuing to generate revenue. For the first few weeks, most brands were silent—simply assessing the situation. But brands soon realized they needed to be sensitive to these new realities, deliver value to consumers and foster connectivity.

15-4 THE PROMOTIONAL MIX

Most promotional strategies use several ingredients—which may include advertising, public relations, sales promotion, personal selling, and social media—to reach a target market. That combination is called the **promotional mix**. The proper promotional mix is the one that management believes will meet the needs of the target market and fulfill the organization's overall goals. Data and data analytics play a very important role in how marketers distribute funding among their promotional mix tactics. Netflix, for example, uses data analytics to identify what people are organically interested in, to determine the content they invest in, and how to promote that content. The more funds allocated to each promotional ingredient and the more managerial emphasis placed on each technique, the more important that element is thought to be in the overall mix.

15-4a Advertising

Almost all companies selling a good or a service use advertising, whether in the form of a multimillion-dollar campaign or a simple classified ad in a newspaper. **Advertising** is any form of impersonal paid communication in which the sponsor or company is identified. Media—such as television, radio, newspapers, magazines, pay-per-click search advertising, digital display advertising, social media advertising, direct mail, billboards, and transit advertising (such as on buses and taxis and at bus stops), websites, email marketing, blog, video and interactive games—are often used to transmit advertisements to consumers. But recently, marketing budgets are shifting away from traditional communication media and more toward digital options (such as social media). In fact, spending on digital advertising now exceeds spending on advertising through traditional media. And as digital marketing becomes a more vital component of many companies' promotion and marketing mixes, consumers and lawmakers are increasingly concerned about possible violations of consumers' privacy. Social media sites like Facebook and Instagram are having to reexamine their privacy policies, especially in light of recent privacy breaches through Cambridge Analytica and others as well as the new General Data Protection Regulation (GDPR) in the EU, which forces companies to notify consumers how they collect data.

One of the primary benefits of advertising is its ability to communicate to a large number of people at one time. Cost per contact, therefore, is typically very low. Advertising has the advantage of being able to reach the masses (e.g., through national television networks), but it can also

Advertising can show up in many ways, shapes and forms. Television personality Ashley Iaconetti attends the premier of *Spider-Man: Homecoming* in front of a backdrop that displays advertising for Audi, Dell, and Synchrony Bank.

be microtargeted to small groups of potential customers, such as through television ads on a targeted cable network or shows on digital streaming services, such as Hulu or ESPN. Although the *cost per contact* in advertising is very low, the *total cost* to advertise, particularly for traditional media, is typically very high. This hurdle tends to restrict advertising on a national basis for many brands. Chapter 16 examines advertising in greater detail.

15-4b Public Relations

Concerned about how they are perceived by their target markets, organizations often spend large sums to build a positive public image. **Public relations** is the marketing function that evaluates public attitudes, identifies areas within the organization the public may

> **promotional mix** the combination of promotional tools—including advertising, public relations, personal selling, sales promotion, and social media—used to reach the target market and fulfill the organization's overall goals
>
> **advertising** impersonal, one-way mass communication about a product or organization that is paid for by a marketer

be interested in, and executes a program of action to earn public understanding and acceptance. Public relations helps an organization communicate with its stakeholders, including customers, suppliers, stockholders, government officials, employees, and the community in which it operates. The Internet has expanded the role of public relations, as crisis communication and online stakeholder management becomes more important. Marketers use public relations not only to maintain a positive image, but also to educate the public about the company's goals and objectives, introduce new products, support the sales effort, and increasingly to respond to customer-generated communications.

A public relations program can generate favorable publicity—public information about a company, product, service, or issue appearing in the mass media as a news item. Social media sites like Twitter can provide large amounts of publicity quickly. Organizations generally do not pay for the publicity and are not identified as the source of the information, but they can benefit tremendously from it. However, while organizations do not directly pay for publicity, it should not be viewed as free. Preparing news releases, staging special events, and persuading media personnel to broadcast or print publicity messages costs money. Public relations and publicity are examined further in Chapter 16.

15-4c Sales Promotion

Sales promotion consists of all marketing activities—other than personal selling, advertising, and public relations—that stimulate consumer purchasing and dealer effectiveness. Sales promotion is generally a short-run tool used to stimulate immediate increases in demand. Sales promotion can be aimed at end consumers, trade customers, or a company's employees. Sales promotions include free samples, contests, premiums, trade shows, vacation giveaways, and coupons. They also include experiential marketing whereby marketers create or participate in events that enable customers to connect with brands. For example, many brands participate in the annual Macy's Thanksgiving Day parade to gain exposure, since more than 24.1 million viewers watch this traditional event.[11] Companies like Groupon have combined social networks and sales promotions, and social media sites like Facebook are expanding their promotion platforms through built-in contest and sweepstakes tools. National grocer Whole Foods was struggling to attract new customers; new owner Amazon began using data analytics to optimize Whole Foods product assortments at the store level and to understand combinations that lead to higher consumer purchases. To further increase sales, a loyalty program was created in combination with Amazon Prime customers, and their analytics showed that rewards program members spend more, resulting in 50 percent higher sales. In short, Whole Foods new strategy is using sales promotion to engage and keep its most loyal customers.[12]

Marketers often use sales promotion to improve the effectiveness of other ingredients in the promotional mix, especially advertising and personal selling. Research shows that sales promotion complements advertising by yielding faster sales responses. In many instances, more marketing money is spent on sales promotion than on advertising.

15-4d Personal Selling

Personal selling is a purchase situation involving a personal, paid-for communication between two people in an attempt to influence each other. In this dyad, both the buyer and the seller have specific objectives they wish to accomplish. The objective for the buyer, for example, may be to minimize cost or facilitate the selection of a quality product, while the seller often wants to maximize sales and profits.

Traditional methods of personal selling include a planned presentation to one or more prospective buyers for the purpose of making a sale. Whether it takes place face to face or over the phone, personal selling attempts to persuade the buyer to accept a point of view. For example, a car salesperson may try to persuade a car buyer that a particular model is superior to a competing model in certain features, such as gas mileage, or available in-car technology. Once the buyer is somewhat convinced, the salesperson may attempt to elicit some action from the buyer, such as a test drive or a purchase. Frequently, in this traditional view of personal selling, the objectives of the salesperson are at the expense of the buyer, creating a win–lose outcome.

More current notions on personal selling emphasize the relationship that develops between a salesperson and a buyer. Initially, this concept was more typical in business-to-business selling situations, involving the sale of products like heavy machinery or computer systems.

public relations the marketing function that evaluates public attitudes, identifies areas within the organization the public may be interested in, and executes a program of action to earn public understanding and acceptance

publicity public information about a company, product, service, or issue appearing in the mass media as a news item

sales promotion marketing activities—other than personal selling, advertising, and public relations—that stimulate consumer buying and dealer effectiveness

personal selling a purchase situation involving a personal, paid-for communication between two people in an attempt to influence each other

More recently, both business-to-business and business-to-consumer selling focus on building long-term relationships rather than on making a one-time sale.

Relationship selling emphasizes a win–win outcome and the accomplishment of mutual objectives that benefit both buyer and salesperson in the long term. Rather than focusing on a quick sale, relationship selling attempts to create a long-term, committed relationship based on trust, increased customer loyalty, and a continuation of the relationship between the salesperson and the customer. Personal selling, like other promotional mix elements, is increasingly dependent on digital communications. Most companies use their websites to attract potential buyers seeking information on products and services and to drive customers to their physical locations, where personal selling can close the sale. Personal selling is discussed further in Chapter 17.

15-4e Content Marketing and Social Media

As promotional strategies change, and since brands now have the ability to become publishers, content marketing is an increasingly crucial part of promotion. Recall from Chapter 7 that content marketing entails developing valuable content for interested audience members, and then using digital marketing, search engine optimization, paid search, and display advertising to pull customers to the company's website or social media channel so that the audiences can learn about the brand or make a purchase. Content created by brands is typically distributed through social media and other digital channels.

Recall that social media are promotion tools used to facilitate conversations and create engagement and other interactions among people online. When used by marketers, these tools facilitate consumer empowerment. For the first time, consumers are able to speak directly to other consumers, the company, and web communities. Social media include blogs, microblogs (such as Twitter), video platforms (such as YouTube), podcasting (online audio and video broadcasts), and social networks (such as LinkedIn, Pinterest, Instagram, and Snapchat).

Initially, individuals used social media tools primarily for self-expression. For example, a lawyer might develop a blog to talk about politics because that is her hobby. Or a college freshman might develop a profile on Facebook to stay in touch with high school friends. But soon, businesses realized that these tools could be used to engage with consumers. Today, social media are ubiquitous. The rise of streaming video, for example, has created a completely new way for marketers to manage their image, connect with consumers, and generate interest in, engagement with, and desire for their companies' products.

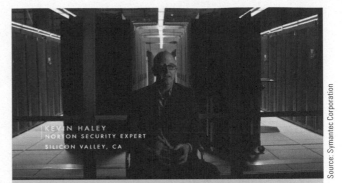

Norton Antivirus software company won a Gold Lion Award at the Cannes Lions Festival for *The Most Dangerous Town on the Internet*, a 20-minute documentary about a Romanian town known for being the hacker capital of the world. Watch this at the following social media website: https://www.youtube.com/watch?v=un_XI4MM6QI.

Blogging has also led to a new type of influencer marketing, whereby social media celebrities create their own digital channels (on YouTube, Instagram, and other social media platforms) to promote brands and products and to earn income. Marketers are now using social media as integral components of their campaigns and as a way to extend the benefits of their use of traditional media. Social media are discussed in more detail in Chapter 18.

15-4f The Communication Process and the Promotional Mix

The Internet and digital communications have changed how businesses promote their brands. Traditionally, marketing managers have been in charge of defining the essence of the brand. This included complete brand control and mostly one-way communication between the brand and customers. All of the content and messages were focused on defining and communicating the brand value. The focus for many campaigns was pure entertainment, and the brand created all of the content for promotional campaigns—from the website to television spots to print ads.

That approach has now changed. The consumer has much more control (which makes some brands quite nervous!), as the communication space and the brand message are increasingly controlled by the consumer. Perception is reality, as consumers have more control to adapt the brand message to fit their ideas. Instead of repetition, social media rely on the idea of customization and adaption of the message. Information is positioned as more valuable rather than being strictly entertaining.

EXHIBIT 15.3 DIGITAL MEDIA TYPES

Owned Media
- Websites
- Blogs
- Social media presence

Social media is concentrated here, between owned and earned media, with some (but not much) paid media depending on the strategy.

Paid Media
- Banner ads
- Sponsored posts

Earned Media
- Media coverage
- SEO
- Publicity activities

Adapted from Dave Fleet, "Why Paying Bloggers for Posts Changes the Game," December 12, 2010, http://davefleet.com/2010/12/bloggers-money-postsgame (accessed January 2019).

Probably the most important aspect is the idea of consumer-generated content, whereby consumers are able to both take existing content and modify it, or to create completely new content for a brand. For example, Doritos has the "Crash the Super Bowl" promotion, where ordinary people are invited to create television commercials for Doritos that are then uploaded to www.crashthe superbowl.com and voted on by millions of Doritos fans. The winning spots then run during the Super Bowl.

As a result of the impact of social media as well as the proliferation of new platforms, tools, and ideas, promotional tactics can also be categorized according to media type—paid, earned, or owned, as shown in Exhibit 15.3. **Paid media** is based on the traditional advertising model, whereby a brand pays for media space. Traditionally, paid media has included television, magazine, outdoor, radio, or newspaper advertising. Paid media also includes display advertising on websites, pay-per-click advertising on search engines, paid ads on Facebook and Instagram, and even ads on Instagram Stories. Paid media is quite important, especially as it migrates to the Web. Paid media is used with other media types to develop an integrated message strategy.

Earned media is based on a public relations or publicity model. The idea is to start people talking about the brand—whether through media coverage (as in traditional public relations) or through word of mouth (WOM). Word of mouth traditionally occurred face-to-face. But electronic word of mouth (EWOM)—for example, sharing a movie review on a social media site—has grown rapidly in recent years. Earned media is often created when people talk and share content on social media. Additionally, search engine optimization (SEO), whereby companies embed key words into content to increase their positioning on search engine results pages (SERPs), can also be considered earned media. **Owned media** is a new promotional tactic in which brands are becoming publishers of their own content in order to maximize the brand's value to customers as well as increase their search rank in Google. Owned media includes the company's websites as well as its official presence on Facebook, Twitter, YouTube channels, blogs, and other digital platforms. These media are controlled by the brand but continuously keeps customers' needs in mind as videos, blog posts, contests, photos, and other types of content are created. Owned media, also called "content marketing," is important for both B-to-B and B-to-C companies. The most effective campaigns typically employ all three types of media: owned media is created to increase WOM, while earned media and paid media are used to get the message out to target audiences.

The elements of the promotional mix differ in their ability to affect the target audience. For instance, promotional mix elements may communicate with the consumer directly or indirectly. The message flow may be one-way or two-way. Feedback may be fast or slow, a little or a lot. Likewise, the communicator may have varying degrees of control over message delivery, content, and flexibility. Exhibit 15.4 outlines characteristics among the promotional mix elements with respect to mode of communication, marketer's control over the communication process, amount and speed of feedback, direction of message flow, marketer's control over the message, identification of the sender, speed in reaching large audiences, and message flexibility.

From Exhibit 15.4, you can see that many elements of the promotional mix are indirect and impersonal when used to communicate with a target market, providing only one direction of message flow. For example, advertising, public relations, and sales promotion are generally impersonal, one-way means of mass communication. Because they provide little opportunity for direct feedback, it is more difficult to adapt these promotional elements to changing consumer preferences, individual differences, and personal goals.

Personal selling, on the other hand, facilitates direct two-way communication. The salesperson receives

paid media a category of promotional tactics based on the traditional advertising model, whereby a brand pays for media space

earned media a category of promotional tactics based on a public relations or publicity model that gets customers talking about products or services

owned media a new category of promotional tactics based on brands becoming publishers of their own content in order to maximize the brands' value to customers

EXHIBIT 15.4 CHARACTERISTICS OF THE ELEMENTS IN THE PROMOTIONAL MIX

	Advertising	Public Relations	Sales Promotion	Personal Selling	Social Media
Mode of Communication	Indirect and impersonal	Usually indirect and impersonal	Usually indirect and impersonal	Direct and face-to-face	Indirect but instant
Communicator Control over Situation	Low	Moderate to low	Moderate to low	High	Moderate
Amount of Feedback	Little	Little	Little to moderate	Much	Much
Speed of Feedback	Delayed	Delayed	Varies	Immediate	Intermediate
Direction of Message	One-way	One-way	Mostly one-way	Two-way	Two-way, multiple ways
Control over Message Content	Yes	No	Yes	Yes	Varies, generally no
Identification of Sponsor	Yes	No	Yes	Yes	Yes
Speed in Reaching Large Audience	Fast	Usually fast	Fast	Slow	Fast
Message Flexibility	Same message to all audiences	Usually no direct control over message to audiences	Same message to varied targets	Tailored to prospective buyer	Some of the most targeted opportunities

immediate feedback from the consumer and can adjust the message in response. Unlike other promotional tools, personal selling is very slow in dispersing the marketer's message to large audiences. Because a salesperson can communicate to only one person or a small group at one time, it is a poor choice if the marketer wants to send a message to many potential buyers. Social media are also considered two-way communications, though not quite as immediate as personal selling. Social media can disperse messages to a wide audience and allow for engagement and feedback from customers through Twitter, Facebook, and blog posts.

15-5 PROMOTIONAL GOALS AND THE AIDA CONCEPT

The ultimate goal of any promotion is to get someone to buy a good or service or, in the case of nonprofit organizations, to take some action (e.g., donate to a cause organization like the ASPCA). A classic model for reaching promotional goals is called the AIDA concept.[13] The acronym AIDA stands for *attention, interest, desire*, and *action*—the stages of consumer involvement with a promotional message. It mimics many "funnel-like" models that require audiences to move through a set of steps or stages.

15-5a The AIDA Model

This model proposes that consumers respond to marketing messages in a cognitive (thinking), affective (feeling), and conative (doing) sequence. First, a promotion manager may focus on attracting a consumer's *attention* by training a salesperson to use a friendly greeting and approach or by using loud volume, bold headlines, movement, bright colors, and the like in an advertisement. This could also include search ads that pop up on SERPS when a search occurs or a message from a social media influencer. The goal is to gain attention, which in a crowded marketplace is often quite difficult. Next, a good sales presentation, demonstration, or advertisement creates *interest* in the product and then, by illustrating how the product's features will satisfy the consumer's needs, arouses *desire*. Finally, a special offer or a strong closing sales pitch may be used to motivate purchase *action*.

The AIDA concept assumes that promotion propels consumers along the following four steps in the purchase–decision process:

1. **Attention:** The advertiser must first gain the attention of the target market. A firm cannot sell something if the market does not know the good or service exists. When Apple introduced the iPad, it quickly became one of the largest electronics product launches in history. To create awareness and gain attention for its revolutionary tablet computer, Apple not only used traditional media advertising but also contacted influential bloggers and journalists so they would

> **AIDA concept** a model that outlines the process for achieving promotional goals in terms of stages of consumer involvement with the message; the acronym stands for attention, interest, desire, and action

write about the product in blogs, newspapers, and magazines. Because the iPad was a brand extension of the Apple computer, it required less effort than an entirely new product or brand would have. At the same time, because the iPad was an innovative new product line, the promotion had to get customers' attention and create awareness of a new idea from an established company.

2. **Interest:** Simple awareness of a brand seldom leads to a sale. The next step is to create interest in the product. A print ad cannot tell potential customers all the features of the iPad. Therefore, Apple had to arrange iPad demonstrations and target messages to innovators and early adopters to create interest in the new tablet computer. To do this, Apple used both online videos on YouTube and personal demonstrations in Apple Stores. The iPad also received extensive media coverage from both online and traditional media outlets.

3. **Desire:** Potential customers for the Apple iPad may like the concept of a portable tablet computer, but they may not necessarily think that it is better than a laptop or smartphone. Therefore, Apple had to create brand preference with the iTunes music store, specialty apps, multiple functionality, and features such as better power management, a lighter-weight unit, and synchronization with the Apple ecosystem. Specifically, Apple had to convince potential customers that the iPad was the best solution to their desire for a combination tablet computer and smartphone.

4. **Action:** Some potential target market customers may have been persuaded to buy an iPad but had not yet made the actual purchase. To motivate them to take action, Apple continued advertising to communicate the features and benefits more effectively. And the strategy worked—more than 250 million people now own an iPad.[14]

Most buyers involved in high-involvement purchase situations pass through the four stages of the AIDA model on the way to making a purchase. The promoter's task is to determine where on the purchase ladder most of the target consumers are located and design a promotion plan to meet their needs. For example, if Apple learned from its market research and data analytics that many potential customers were in the desire stage but had not yet bought an iPad for some reason, it could place advertising on Facebook and Google, and perhaps in video games, to target younger individuals and professionals with messages motivating them to buy an iPad.

The four steps of the AIDA process describe how consumers make purchases. These steps are:

1. **ATTENTION:** First, Apple uses a number of media outlets to gain the attention of the target market.

2. **INTEREST:** Next, it arranges iPad demonstrations and develops target messages to create interest among innovators and early adopters.

3. **DESIRE:** Then, Apple creates brand preference and convinces potential customers that they want the new iPad.

4. **ACTION:** Finally, having been attracted to the new iPad and convinced that they need it, customers purchase the iPad.

The AIDA concept does not explain how all promotions influence purchase decisions. The model suggests that promotional effectiveness can be measured in terms of consumers progressing from one stage to the next. However, the order of stages in the model, as well as whether consumers go through all steps, has been much debated. A purchase can occur without interest or desire, perhaps when a low-involvement product is bought on impulse. Regardless of the order of the stages or consumers' progression through these stages, the AIDA concept helps marketers by suggesting which promotional strategy will be most effective.[15]

15-5b AIDA and the Promotional Mix

Exhibit 15.5 depicts the relationship between the promotional mix and the AIDA model. It shows that although advertising does have an impact in the later stages, it is most useful in gaining attention for goods or services. By contrast, personal selling reaches fewer people at first. Salespeople are more effective at developing customer interest for products and services and at creating desire. For example, advertising may help a potential computer purchaser gain knowledge about competing brands, but the salesperson may be the one who actually encourages the buyer to decide that a particular brand is the best choice. The salesperson also has the advantage of having the computer physically there to demonstrate its capabilities to the buyer.

The greatest impact of public relations is as a method of gaining attention for a company, good, or service. Many companies can attract attention and build goodwill

EXHIBIT 15.5 THE PROMOTIONAL MIX AND AIDA

	Attention	Interest	Desire	Action
Advertising	●	●	○	●
Public Relations	●	●	○	●
Sales Promotion	○	○	●	●
Personal Selling	○	●	●	●
Social Media	●	●	○	○

● Very effective ○ Somewhat effective ● Not effective

by sponsoring community events that benefit worthy causes such as an anti-bullying campaign or a global poverty program. Such sponsorships project a positive image of the firm and its products in the minds of consumers and potential consumers. Book publishers, for instance, push to get their titles on the best-seller lists of major publications, such as *Publishers Weekly* or the *New York Times*. Book authors make appearances on talk shows and at bookstores to personally sign books and speak to fans. They also frequently engage with fans on social media like Facebook and Twitter.

Sales promotion's greatest strength is in creating strong desire and purchase intent. Coupons and other price-off promotions are techniques used to persuade customers to buy new products. Frequent-buyer sales promotion programs, popular among retailers, enable consumers to accumulate points or dollars that can be redeemed for goods, or to obtain discounts. The Amazon Prime program, for example, offers reduced costs for shipping, benefits such as discounts at Whole Foods, and access to online movies and video series. Frequent-buyer programs tend to increase purchase intent and loyalty and encourage repeat purchases.

Social media are a strong way to gain attention and interest in a brand. It is particularly effective if content goes viral and reaches large audiences. Social media are also effective at engaging with customers and enabling companies to maintain interest in the brand if properly managed.

15-6 INTEGRATED MARKETING COMMUNICATIONS

Ideally, marketing communications from each promotional mix element (personal selling, advertising, sales promotion, social media, and public relations) should be integrated. That is, the message reaching the consumer should be the same regardless of whether it is from an advertisement, a salesperson in the field, a magazine article, a Facebook fan page, or a coupon in a newspaper insert.

From the consumer's standpoint, a company's communications are already integrated. Consumers do not think in terms of the five elements of promotion: personal selling, advertising, sales promotion, public relations, and social media. Instead, everything is an "ad." The only people who recognize the distinctions among these communications elements are the marketers themselves. Unfortunately, too many marketers overlook this when planning promotional messages, and they fail to integrate their communication efforts across all elements of the promotional mix. The most common lack of integration is between personal selling and the other elements of the promotional mix.

The need for a common approach for all elements of the promotion mix has led many companies to adopt the concept of **integrated marketing communications (IMC)**. IMC is the careful coordination of all promotional messages—traditional advertising, direct marketing, social media, public relations, sales promotion, personal selling, event marketing, and other communications—for a product or service to ensure the consistency of messages at every point at which a company has contact with the consumer. Following the concept of IMC, marketing managers carefully work out the roles that various promotional elements will play in the marketing mix. Timing of promotional activities is coordinated, and the results of each campaign are carefully monitored to improve future use of the promotional mix tools. A marketing communications director is often appointed; this person has overall responsibility for integrating the company's marketing communications.

The IMC concept has been growing in popularity for several reasons. First, the proliferation of thousands of media choices beyond traditional television has made promotion a more complicated task. Instead of promoting a product just through mass-media options, like television and magazines, promotional messages today can appear in many varied sources.

Further, the mass market has also fragmented into more selectively segmented markets. The result has been an increase in niche marketing that has replaced the traditional broad market groups marketers promoted to in the past. Marketers have also slashed their advertising

integrated marketing communications (IMC) the careful coordination of all promotional messages for a product or a service to ensure the consistency of messages at every point at which a company has contact with the consumer spending to focus on promotional techniques that generate immediate sales responses and are more easily measured, such as direct marketing. Online advertising has been allocated a bigger share of the budget as well because of its measurability. Thus, the interest in IMC is largely a reaction to the scrutiny that marketing communications has come under and, particularly, to suggestions that uncoordinated promotional activity leads to a strategy that is wasteful, inefficient, and ineffective.

15-7 FACTORS AFFECTING THE PROMOTIONAL MIX

Promotional mixes vary a great deal from one product and one industry to the next. Advertising and personal selling typically are used to promote goods and services. These primary tools are often supported and supplemented by sales promotion. Public relations help develop a positive image for the organization and the product line. Social media have been used more for consumer goods, but business-to-business marketers are increasingly using social media. A firm may not use all five promotional elements in its promotional mix, or it may choose to use them in varying degrees. The particular promotional mix chosen by a firm for a product or service depends on several factors: the nature of the product, the stage in the product life cycle, target market characteristics, the type of buying decision, funds available for promotion, and whether a push or a pull strategy will be used.

15-7a Nature of the Product

The characteristics of the product itself can influence the promotional mix. For instance, a product can be classified as either a business product or a consumer product. (Refer to Chapters 7 and 10.) Business products are often custom-tailored to the buyer's exact specifications, so they generally are not well suited to mass promotion. As a result, most business goods rely more heavily on personal selling than on advertising, but advertising still serves a purpose in the promotional mix. Advertising in trade media can also help the sales force locate potential customers. For example, print media advertising often includes coupons soliciting the potential customer to "fill this out for more detailed information."

In contrast, since consumer products are seldom custom-made, they do not require the selling efforts of a company representative who can tailor them to the user's needs. Thus, consumer goods are promoted mainly through advertising or social media to create brand familiarity. Television and radio advertising, consumer-oriented

v.s.anandhakrishna/Shutterstock.com

The clothes and jewelry a person chooses to wear can send a nonverbal message about that person's social class, culture, life stage, and overall aesthetic. Therefore, clothing and jewelry often carry a large degree of social risk.

magazines, and increasingly the Internet and other highly targeted media are used to promote consumer goods, especially nondurables. Sales promotion, the brand name, and the product's packaging are about twice as important for consumer goods as for business products. But persuasive personal selling is important at the retail level for goods such as automobiles and appliances.

The costs and risks associated with a product also influence the promotional mix. As a general rule, as the costs or risks of buying and using a product or service increase, personal selling becomes more important. Inexpensive items cannot support the cost of a salesperson's time and effort unless the potential volume is high. On the other hand, expensive and complex machinery, cars, and new homes represent a considerable investment. A salesperson must assure buyers that they are spending their money wisely and not taking an undue financial risk.

Social risk is an issue as well. Many consumer goods do not have great social importance because they do not reflect social position. For example, people do not experience much social risk in buying a loaf of bread or a candy bar. However, buying many specialty products such as jewelry and clothing involves a social risk. When social risk is involved, therefore, many consumers depend on sales personnel for guidance in making the "proper" choice.

15-7b Stages in the Product Life Cycle

The product's stage in its life cycle is a big factor in designing a promotional mix (see Exhibit 15.6). During the *introduction stage*, the basic goal of promotion is to inform the target audience that the product is available.

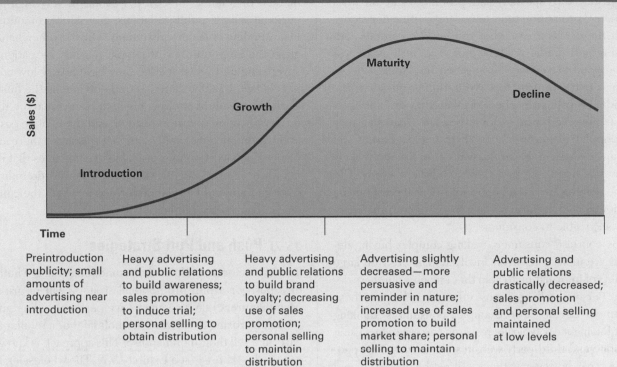

EXHIBIT 15.6 PRODUCT LIFE CYCLE AND THE PROMOTIONAL MIX

| Preintroduction publicity; small amounts of advertising near introduction | Heavy advertising and public relations to build awareness; sales promotion to induce trial; personal selling to obtain distribution | Heavy advertising and public relations to build brand loyalty; decreasing use of sales promotion; personal selling to maintain distribution | Advertising slightly decreased—more persuasive and reminder in nature; increased use of sales promotion to build market share; personal selling to maintain distribution | Advertising and public relations drastically decreased; sales promotion and personal selling maintained at low levels |

Initially, the emphasis is on the general product class—for example, fitness trackers. This emphasis gradually changes to gaining attention for a particular brand, such as Fitbit, Jawbone, Garmin, or Apple. Typically, both extensive advertising and public relations inform the target audience about the product class or brand and heighten awareness levels. Sales promotion encourages early trial of the product, and personal selling gets retailers to carry the product.

When the product reaches the *growth stage* of the life cycle, the promotion blend will often shift. Change is necessary because different types of potential buyers are targeted. Although advertising and public relations continue to be major elements of the promotional mix, sales promotion can be reduced because consumers need fewer incentives to purchase. The promotional strategy is to emphasize the product's differential advantage over the competition. Thus, persuasive promotion is used to build and maintain brand loyalty during the growth stage. By this stage, personal selling has usually succeeded in getting adequate distribution for the product.

As the product reaches the *maturity stage* of its life cycle, competition becomes fiercer, and persuasive and reminder advertising are therefore emphasized more strongly. Sales promotion also comes back into focus as sellers try to increase their market share.

All promotion, especially advertising, is reduced as the product enters the *decline stage*. Nevertheless, personal selling and sales promotion efforts may be maintained, particularly at the retail level.

15-7c Target Market Characteristics

A target market characterized by widely scattered potential customers, highly informed buyers, and brand-loyal repeat purchasers generally requires a promotional mix with more advertising and sales promotion and less personal selling. Sometimes, however, personal selling is required even when buyers are well informed and geographically dispersed. Although industrial installations may be sold to well-educated people with extensive work experience, salespeople must be present to explain the product and work out the details of the purchase agreement.

Often firms sell goods and services in markets where potential customers are hard to locate. Print advertising can be used to find them. The reader is invited to go online, call, or mail in a reply card for more information. As the online queries, calls, or cards are received, salespeople are sent to visit the potential customers.

15-7d Type of Buying Decision

The promotional mix also depends on the type of buying decision—for example, a routine decision or a complex decision. For routine consumer decisions like buying toothpaste, the most effective promotion calls attention to the brand or reminds the consumer about the brand. Advertising, and especially sales promotion, are the most productive promotion tools to use for routine decisions.

If the decision is neither routine nor complex, advertising and public relations help establish awareness for the good or service. Suppose an individual is looking for a bottle of wine to serve to dinner guests. If the individual is primarily a beer drinker, they are not likely to be familiar with wines. But if they have read an article in a popular magazine about Silver Oak Cabernet and seen an advertisement for the wine, they are more likely to buy this brand because they are already aware of it. Online reviews are often important in this type of buying decision as well because reviews by other consumers are easily accessible to consumers.

By contrast, consumers making complex buying decisions are more extensively involved. They rely on large amounts of information to help them reach a purchase decision. Personal selling is most effective in helping these consumers decide. For example, consumers thinking about buying a car typically research the car online using corporate and third-party websites like Carfax. Few people buy a car, however, without visiting the dealership and driving the car. They depend on a salesperson to provide the information they need to reach a decision. In addition to online resources, print advertising may also be used for high-involvement purchase decisions because it often provides a large amount of information to the consumer.

15-7e Available Funds

Money, or the lack of it, may easily be the most important factor in determining the promotional mix. A small, undercapitalized manufacturer may rely heavily on free publicity if its product is unique. If the situation warrants a sales force, a financially strained firm may turn to manufacturers' agents, who work on a commission basis with no advances or expense accounts. Even well-capitalized organizations may not be able to afford the advertising rates of publications like *Time*, *Sports Illustrated*, and the *Wall Street Journal*, or the cost of running television commercials during *This is Us*, *Thursday Night Football*, or the Super Bowl. The price of a high-profile advertisement in these media could support several salespeople for an entire year.

When funds are available to permit a mix of promotional elements, a firm will generally try to optimize its return on promotion dollars while minimizing the *cost per*

push strategy a marketing strategy that uses aggressive personal selling and trade advertising to convince a wholesaler or a retailer to carry and sell particular merchandise

contact, or the cost of reaching one member of the target market. In general, the cost per contact is very high for personal selling, public relations, and sales promotions like sampling and demonstrations. On the other hand, given the large number of people reached by national advertising and social media, they have a very low cost per contact. Usually, there is a trade-off among the funds available, the number of people in the target market, the quality of communication needed, and the relative costs of the promotional elements. In most instances there are plenty of low-cost options available to companies that do not have a huge budget. Many of these include online strategies and public relations efforts in which the company relies on free publicity.

15-7f Push and Pull Strategies

The last factor that affects the promotional mix is whether a push or a pull promotional strategy will be used. Manufacturers may use aggressive personal selling and trade advertising to convince a wholesaler or a retailer to carry and sell their merchandise. This approach is known as a **push strategy** (see Exhibit 15.7). The wholesaler, in turn, must often push the merchandise forward by persuading the retailer to handle the goods. The retailer then uses advertising, displays, and other forms of promotion to convince the consumer to buy the "pushed" products. Walmart uses aggressive discounts to push products out

Lay's demonstrates its commitment to natural ingredients as a differential attribute to help customers make a routine buying decision—purchasing Lay's snack foods.

EXHIBIT 15.7   PUSH STRATEGY VERSUS PULL STRATEGY

Push strategy

Manufacturer promotes to wholesaler → Wholesaler promotes to retailer → Retailer promotes to consumer → Consumer buys from retailer

Orders to manufacturer

Pull strategy

Manufacturer promotes to consumer → Consumer demands product from retailer → Retailer demands product from wholesaler → Wholesaler demands product from manufacturer

Orders to manufacturer

of its stores. In fact, former First Lady Michelle Obama praised Walmart for using drastically reduced prices to push fresh meat, produce, and other healthy options to consumers in low-income areas. The move proved to be a win–win strategy. Fresh foods generated 70 percent of Walmart's sales growth in recent years, and customers have saved more than $2.3 billion on fresh fruits and vegetables by shopping at Walmart.[16] This strategy also works well with services.

At the other extreme is a **pull strategy**, which stimulates consumer demand for products to obtain better distribution. Rather than trying to sell to the wholesaler, the manufacturer using a pull strategy focuses its promotional efforts on end consumers or opinion leaders. Social media and content marketing are the most recent (and best) example of pull strategy. The idea is that social media content does not interrupt a consumer's experience with media (like a commercial interrupts your favorite television program). Instead, the content invites customers to experience it on social media or a website. Consumer demand pulls the product through the channel of distribution (see Exhibit 15.7). Heavy sampling, introductory consumer advertising, cents-off campaigns, and couponing are part of a pull strategy.

Rarely does a company use a pull or a push strategy exclusively. Instead, the promotional mix will emphasize a combination of these strategies. For example, pharmaceutical companies generally use a push strategy (personal selling and trade advertising) to promote their drugs and therapies to physicians. Sales presentations and advertisements in medical journals give physicians the detailed information they need to prescribe medication to their patients. Most pharmaceutical companies supplement this push promotional strategy with a pull strategy targeted directly to potential patients through advertisements in consumer magazines and on television.

pull strategy a marketing strategy that stimulates consumer demand to obtain product distribution

16 | Advertising, Public Relations, and Sales Promotion

LEARNING OUTCOMES

After studying this chapter, you will be able to…

16-1 Discuss the effects of advertising on market share and consumers

16-2 Identify the major types of advertising

16-3 Discuss the creative decisions in developing an advertising campaign

16-4 Describe media evaluation and selection techniques

16-5 Discuss the role of public relations in the promotional mix

16-6 Define and state the objectives of sales promotion and the tools used to achieve them

Eric Broder Van Dyke/Shutterstock.com

16-1 THE EFFECTS OF ADVERTISING

Advertising was defined in Chapter 15 as impersonal, mass communication about a product or organization that is paid for by a marketer. It is a popular form of promotion, especially for consumer packaged goods and services. Increasingly, as more and more marketers consolidate their operations, advertising is seen as an international endeavor. Promotion makes up a large part of most brands' budgets. Typically, promotional spending is divided into *measured* and *unmeasured media*. Measured media ad spending includes network and cable TV, newspapers, magazines, radio, outdoor, and Internet (though paid search and social media are not included).

Unmeasured media spending includes direct marketing, promotions, co-op, coupons, catalogs, product placement, and event marketing. Forecasts for 2019 predict a 2.5 percent increase in total media spending in the United States and 4.1 percent worldwide. The United States is by far the largest spender ($199.2 billion). China, Japan, the United Kingdom, and Germany round out the top five countries in terms of advertising spending.[1] The top 25 largest U.S. advertisers spent more than $62.28 billion in 2017. Comcast is the new largest U.S. advertiser by spending $5.7 billion. Procter & Gamble (P&G) spent almost $4.4 billion in the United States alone. Telecommunications companies like AT&T ($3.5 billion), online retailer Amazon ($3.4 billion), and automotive companies like General Motors ($3.2 billion) are also top spenders. Samsung Electronics is the largest global advertiser at $11.2 billion in 2017.[2]

Advertising and marketing services, agencies, and other firms that provide marketing and communications services employ millions of people across America. Just as the producers of goods and services need marketers to build awareness for their products, media outlets such as magazines and websites need marketing teams to coordinate with producers and transmit those messages to customers. The longer one thinks about the business of marketing, the more apparent become the unique positions within the industry.

One particular area that has continued to see rapid growth is the data side of marketing. Companies are collecting huge amounts of information and need skilled, creative, web-savvy people to interpret the data coming in from web, mobile, and other digital ad campaigns. For example, P&G launched an online personality test called HairCode that aims to match people with its hair products by hair type. The site was pushed out via Facebook and Instagram, and illustrated the need for large companies to move more quickly and be more agile. The site was brought to market in less than 8 weeks. Ninety-seven percent of companies that have invested in developing data analytics programs believe that such programs are of strategic importance to their organizations.[3] According to IDC program vice president Dan Vesset, "A lot of the ultimate potential is in the ability to discover potential connections and to predict potential outcomes in a way that wasn't really possible before. Before you only looked at these things in hindsight."[4]

16-1a Advertising and Market Share

The five most valuable U.S. brands for 2019 are Apple ($182.8 billion), Google ($132.1 billion), Microsoft ($104.9 billion), Facebook ($94 billion), and Amazon ($70.9 billion).[5] These were all top brands in 2018, but some shifted in rank. All of these are technology brands and many of these brands were built over many years by heavy advertising and by marketing investments made long ago. Google is the only brand that was not in the top five in 2018.[6] Advertising budgets for most successful consumer brands in the United States are spent on maintaining brand awareness and market share.

New brands with a small market share tend to spend proportionately more of their promotion budget for advertising and sales promotion than those with a large market share, generally for two reasons. First, beyond a certain level of spending for advertising and sales promotion, diminishing returns set in. That is, sales and market share improvements slow down and eventually decrease no matter how much is spent on advertising and sales promotion. This phenomenon is called the **advertising response function**. Understanding the advertising response function helps marketers use promotion budgets wisely. A market leader like Johnson & Johnson's Neutrogena typically spends proportionately less on advertising

> **advertising response function** a phenomenon in which spending for advertising and sales promotion increases sales or market share up to a certain level but then produces diminishing returns

than a newer line, such as Unilever's Vaseline Spray & Go brand. Neutrogena has already captured the attention of most of its target market. It only needs to remind customers that its product is available and where.

The second reason new brands tend to require higher spending for advertising and sales promotion is that a certain minimum level of exposure is needed to measurably affect purchase habits. If Vaseline advertised its Spray & Go moisturizers in only one or two publications and bought only one or two television spots, it would not achieve the exposure needed to penetrate consumers' perceptual defenses, create awareness, and affect purchase intentions.

16-1b The Effects of Advertising on Consumers

Advertising affects peoples' daily lives, informing them about products and services and influencing their attitudes, beliefs, and ultimately their purchases. Advertising affects the television programs people watch, the content of the newspapers they read, the politicians they elect, the medicines they take, and the toys their children play with. Consequently, the influence of advertising on the U.S. socioeconomic system has been the subject of extensive debate in nearly all corners of society.

Interestingly, despite a proliferation of new digital options, consumers still spend a lot of time consuming traditional media (where much of advertising exists). The average person, for example, spends more than 250 minutes a day watching television and 329 minutes a day using digital media devices like desktops, laptops, and tablets.[7] Americans report an average of 5.2 leisure hours a day, and most of it is spent watching TV. As a result, American consumers are exposed to thousands of advertising messages each year.[8]

Though advertising cannot change consumers' deeply rooted values and attitudes, advertising may succeed in transforming a person's negative attitude toward a product into a positive one. For instance, serious or dramatic advertisements are more effective at changing consumers' negative attitudes. Humorous ads, on the other hand, have been shown to be more effective at shaping attitudes when consumers already have a positive image of an advertised brand.

Advertising also reinforces positive attitudes toward brands. A brand with a distinct personality is more likely to have a larger base of loyal customers and market share. The more consistent a brand's personality, the more likely a customer will build a relationship with that brand over his or her lifetime. Consider Apple, for example. Sixty percent of iPhone users report they would switch to Apple's latest iPhone without considering any other options, admitting to "blind loyalty."[9] This is why market leaders spend billions of dollars annually to reinforce and remind their loyal customers about the benefits of their products.

Advertising can also affect the way consumers rank a brand's attributes. In years past, car ads emphasized such brand attributes as roominess, speed, and low maintenance. Today, however, car marketers have added technology, safety, versatility, customization, and fuel efficiency to the list.

16-2 MAJOR TYPES OF ADVERTISING

A firm's promotional objectives determine the type of advertising it uses. If the goal of the promotion plan is to improve the image of the company or the industry, **institutional advertising** may be used. In contrast, if the advertiser wants to enhance the sales of a specific good or service, **product advertising** should be used.

16-2a Institutional Advertising

Historically, advertising in the United States has been product and service oriented. Today, however, companies market multiple products and need a different type of advertising. Institutional, or corporate, advertising is designed to establish, change, or promote the corporation's identity as a whole. Institutional advertising is also important for hiring and recruitment. It usually does not ask the audience to do anything but maintain a favorable attitude toward the advertiser and its goods or services. A beer company running a series of television spots advocating the use of a designated driver is an example of institutional advertising.

A form of institutional advertising called **advocacy advertising** is typically used to safeguard against negative consumer attitudes and to enhance the company's credibility among consumers who already favor its position. Corporations often use advocacy advertising to express their views on controversial issues. Nike made headlines during its 30 year anniversary of the "Just Do It" slogan. "Believe in something, even if it means sacrificing everything" was the Tweet sent out to

institutional advertising a form of advertising designed to enhance a company's image rather than promote a particular product

product advertising a form of advertising that touts the benefits of a specific good or service

advocacy advertising a form of advertising in which an organization expresses its views on controversial issues or responds to media attacks kick off Colin Kaepernick's video that would soon change the conversation around race and the NFL. Kaepernick has been an endorser since 2011, even though he has not played football since 2016, when he started to kneel during the national anthem, setting off a controversy between players, the NFL, and fans. While the campaign was risky and did have its detractors (mainly Baby Boomers, some Gen Xers, and conservatives), the message resonated with younger urban audiences at a time when Nike has been losing market share to Adidas and Under Armour. Revenue increased 10 percent over the prior year, digital sales soared 31 percent, brand engagement reached record levels, and the stock price increased as well. But more importantly for Nike, it reestablished the brand as one that stands for something bigger, in this case racial equity. "We have a long history of supporting those whose voices are not always heard. For the 30th anniversary for 'Just Do It,' we wanted to energize its meaning and introduce it to a new generation of athletes," said KeJuan Wilkins, Nike's VP of North America communications.

In another example, in response to heated political events and rhetoric, many companies aired advertisements promoting diversity and acceptance during Super Bowl LI. For example, Coca-Cola re-aired a previous commercial in which individuals from diverse backgrounds sang "America the Beautiful" in different languages. Airbnb aired a new commercial centered on the hashtag #WeAccept, that featured the text, "We believe no matter who you are, where you're from, who you love, or who you worship, we all belong. The world is more beautiful the more you accept." Following the Super Bowl, Airbnb's ad garnered more than 4.5 million views on YouTube and 342,000 likes on Facebook. During the original airing, Airbnb cofounder and executive chief Brian Chesky sent a tweet stating that the company aimed to "provide short-term housing over the next five years for 100,000 people in need." Some commenters did not agree with Airbnb's message, frustrated that they "can't even watch a football game without being lectured to," but others praised the company's efforts. One such viewer responded, "I applaud you for taking this step to helping the most vulnerable people."[11]

Alternatively, an advocacy campaign might also refute criticism or blame, or ward off increases in regulation, damaging legislation, or the unfavorable outcome of a lawsuit.

16-2b Product Advertising

Unlike institutional advertising, product advertising promotes the benefits of a specific good or service. The product's stage in its life cycle often determines which type of product advertising is used: pioneering advertising, competitive advertising, or comparative advertising.

PIONEERING ADVERTISING Pioneering advertising is intended to stimulate primary demand for a new product or product category. Heavily used during the introductory stage of the product life cycle, pioneering advertising offers consumers in-depth information about the benefits of the product class. Pioneering advertising also seeks to create interest, and can be quite innovative in its own right. For example, Amazon recently released the Echo smart speaker to broad critical and public acclaim. The Echo is the first device connected to a place (such as a particular room of your house) rather than a person. After launching the Echo, Amazon released a pioneering campaign showing different ways to use the device to assist with everyday tasks. The goal of the campaign was to get consumers to trust the technology prior to bringing it into their homes. The campaign has also made voice search as an element of the promotional mix even more important.[12]

COMPETITIVE ADVERTISING Firms use competitive or brand advertising when a product enters the growth phase of the product life cycle and as other companies begin to enter the marketplace with similar products. Instead of building demand for the product category, the goal of competitive advertising is to influence demand for a specific brand. In the growth phase, promotion often focuses less on being informative and appeals more to emotions. Generally, this phase is where an emphasis on branding begins. Advertisements focus on showing subtle differences between competitive brands, building recall of a brand name, and creating a favorable attitude toward the brand. GEICO uses competitive advertising that discusses the attributes of the brand, how little time it takes to get a quote, how much customers can save, and the ease of submitting a claim. All of its campaigns use humor to promote the brand above others in the industry but without actively comparing GEICO with other insurance companies.

COMPARATIVE ADVERTISING Comparative advertising directly or indirectly compares two or more competing brands

pioneering advertising a form of advertising designed to stimulate primary demand for a new product or product category

competitive advertising a form of advertising designed to influence demand for a specific brand

comparative advertising a form of advertising that compares two or more specifically named or shown competing brands on one or more specific attributes

Dunkin' ✔
@dunkindonuts

Follow ⌄

Let's take a break from our Fast Feud today... @McDonalds. Happy VDay!

Source: Twitter, Inc

7:45 AM - 14 Feb 2019

23 Retweets **188** Likes

What type of advertising is Dunkin Donuts using in this advertisement — institutional or product?

on one or more specific attributes. Some advertisers even use comparative advertising with their own brands. Products experiencing slow growth or those entering the marketplace against strong competitors are more likely to employ comparative claims in their advertising. In Taco Bell's "Get With the Times" advertisement, a narrator states, "I've been eating Egg McMuffins since 1984. When I saw Taco Bell made a waffle taco, I figured I would get with the times." The commercial then shows the man making various improvements to his life, such as upgrading to a smartphone and buying new clothes. The commercial closes with the narration, "Move on from your old McDonald's breakfast with Taco Bell's exciting new breakfast menu." In the ad, Taco Bell specifically compared itself to one of its main competitors in the fast-food industry by suggesting that it was a more modern, innovative brand.[13]

> **advertising campaign** a series of related advertisements focusing on a common theme, slogan, and set of advertising appeals

Before the 1970s, comparative advertising was allowed only if the competing brand was veiled and unidentified. In 1971, however, the Federal Trade Commission (FTC) fostered the growth of comparative advertising by saying that the advertising provided information to the customer and that advertisers were more skillful than the government in communicating this information. Federal rulings prohibit advertisers from falsely describing competitors' products and allow competitors to sue if ads show their products or mention their brand names in an incorrect, misleading, or false manner. FTC rules also apply to advertisers making false claims about their own products.

16-3 CREATIVE DECISIONS IN ADVERTISING

Advertising strategies are typically organized around an advertising campaign. An **advertising campaign** is a series of related advertisements focusing

These billboard were recently displayed outside the Los Angeles Convention Center during the Electronic Entertainment Expo. All of the ads focus on a video game, but each ad uses a different advertising appeal. The Call of Duty billboard at the far left promises an individual soldier's story; the Marvel vs. Capcom billboard in the center shows a diverse cast of well-known characters; and the LawBreakers billboard on the right displays chaotic, fast-paced action.

Troy Harvey/Bloomberg/Getty Images

EXHIBIT 16.1 COMMON ADVERTISING APPEALS

Appeal	Goal
Profit	Lets consumers know whether the product will save them money, make them money, or keep them from losing money.
Health	Appeals to those who are body conscious or who want to be healthy; love or romance is used often in selling cosmetics and perfumes.
Fear	Can center around social embarrassment, growing old, or losing one's health; because of its power, requires advertiser to exercise care in execution.
Admiration	Frequently highlights celebrity spokespeople.
Convenience	Is often used for fast-food restaurants and microwavable foods.
Fun and Pleasure	Are the keys to advertising vacations, beer, amusement parks, and more.
Vanity and Egotism	Are used most often for expensive or conspicuous items such as cars and clothing.
Environmental Consciousness	Centers around protecting the environment and being considerate of others in the community.

on a common theme, slogan, and set of advertising appeals. It is a specific advertising effort for a particular product that extends for a defined period of time.

Before creative work can begin on an advertising campaign, it is important to determine what goals or objectives the advertising should achieve. An **advertising objective** identifies the specific communication task a campaign should accomplish for a specified target audience during a specified period. The objectives of a specific advertising campaign often depend on the overall corporate objectives and the product being advertised.

The DAGMAR approach (defining advertising goals for measured advertising results) is one method of setting objectives. According to this method, all advertising objectives should precisely define the target audience, the desired percentage change in some specified measure of effectiveness, and the time frame in which that change is to occur.

Once objectives are defined, creative work can begin on the advertising campaign. Advertising campaigns often follow the AIDA model, which was discussed in Chapter 15. Depending on where consumers are in the AIDA process, the creative development of an advertising campaign might focus on creating attention, arousing interest, stimulating desire, and ultimately leading to the action of buying the product. Specifically, creative decisions include identifying product benefits, developing and evaluating advertising appeals, executing the message, and evaluating the effectiveness of the campaign.

16-3a Identifying Product Benefits

A well-known rule of thumb in the advertising industry is "Sell the sizzle, not the steak"—that is, in advertising, the goal is to sell the benefits of the product, not its attributes. Customers buy benefits, not attributes. An attribute is simply a feature of the product such as its easy-open package, special formulation, or new lower price. A benefit is what consumers will receive or achieve by using the product, such as convenience or ease of use. A benefit should answer the consumer's question, "What's in it for me?" Benefits might be such things as convenience, pleasure, improved health, savings, or relief. A quick test to determine whether you are offering attributes or benefits in your advertising is to ask "So?" Consider this example:

- **Attribute:** "Kind Bars are healthy snack bars made with various nuts and fruits. They also have additional healthy ingredients such as added antioxidants and protein." "So . . . ?"

- **Benefit:** "So . . . Kind Bars are healthy, but they also hit a sweet spot. You don't have to feel as bad about eating them because they are better for you than many other granola or candy bars."[14]

advertising objective
a specific communication task that a campaign should accomplish for a specified target audience during a specified period

EXHIBIT 16.2   TEN COMMON EXECUTIONAL STYLES FOR ADVERTISING

Executional Style	Description
Slice-of-Life	Depicts people in normal settings, such as at the dinner table or in their car. McDonald's often uses slice-of-life styles showing youngsters munching on french fries from Happy Meals on family outings.
Lifestyle	Shows how well the product will fit in with the consumer's lifestyle. As his Volkswagen Jetta moves through the streets of the French Quarter, a Gen X driver inserts a techno music CD and marvels at how the rhythms of the world mimic the ambient vibe inside his vehicle. Apple's "Welcome Home" ad shows how music can change a woman's entire apartment in NYC.
Spokesperson/ Testimonial	Can feature a celebrity, company official, or typical consumer making a testimonial or endorsing a product. Sheryl Crow represented Revlon's Colorist hair coloring, while Beyoncé Knowles was named the new face of American Express. Dell Inc. founder Michael Dell touts his vision of the customer experience via Dell in television ads. Amazon's "Alexa loses her voice" highlighted the use of several celebrities including Cardi B, Gordon Ramsey, Rebel Wilson, and Sir Anthony Hopkins auditioning to be the new voice of Alexa. Testimonials also include the growing area of social media influencers.
Fantasy	Creates a fantasy for the viewer built around use of the product. Carmakers often use this style to let viewers fantasize about how they would feel speeding around tight corners or down long country roads in their cars.
Humor	Often used by advertisers in their ads, such as Snickers' "Not Going Anywhere for a While" campaign featuring hundreds of souls waiting, sometimes impatiently, to get into heaven.
Real/Animated Product Symbols	Creates a character that represents the product in advertisements, such as the Energizer Bunny or Starkist's Charlie the Tuna. GEICO's suave gecko has become a cult classic for the insurance company.
Mood or Image	Builds a mood or image around the product, such as peace, love, or beauty. De Beers ads depicting shadowy silhouettes wearing diamond engagement rings and diamond necklaces portrayed passion and intimacy while extolling that "a diamond is forever."
Demonstration	Shows consumers the expected benefit. Many consumer products use this technique. Laundry detergent spots are famous for demonstrating how their product will clean clothes whiter and brighter. Fort James Corporation demonstrated in television commercials how its Dixie Rinse & ReUse disposable stoneware product line can stand up to the heat of a blowtorch and survive a cycle in a clothes washer.
Musical	Conveys the message of the advertisement through song. For example, Nike's ads depicted a marathoner's tortured feet and a surfer's thigh scarred by a shark attack while strains of Joe Cocker's "You Are So Beautiful" could be heard in the background.
Scientific	Uses research or scientific evidence to give a brand superiority over competitors. Pain relievers like Advil, Bayer, and Excedrin use scientific evidence in their ads.

16-3b Developing and Evaluating Advertising Appeals

An **advertising appeal** identifies a reason for a person to buy a product. The challenging task of developing advertising appeals is typically the responsibility of the creative team (e.g., art directors and copywriters) in the advertising agency. Advertising appeals are based on findings from data analytics and typically play off consumers' emotions or address some need or want consumers have.

Advertising campaigns focus on one or more advertising appeals. Often the appeals are quite general, thus enabling the firm to develop a number of subthemes or minicampaigns using advertising, sales promotion, and social media. Several possible advertising appeals are listed in Exhibit 16.1.

Choosing the best appeal usually requires market research and data analytics. Criteria for evaluation include desirability, exclusiveness, and believability. The appeal first must make a positive impression on and be desirable to the target market. It must also be exclusive or unique. Consumers must be able to distinguish the advertiser's message from competitors' messages. Most importantly, the appeal should be believable. An appeal that makes extravagant claims not only wastes promotional dollars but also creates ill will for the advertiser.

The advertising appeal selected for the campaign becomes what advertisers call its **unique selling proposition**. The unique selling proposition often becomes all or part of the campaign's slogan. The Snickers candy bar is known for its ability to stop hunger. To emphasize this attribute, the company recently changed the logo on its packaging to words associated with hunger, such as "snippy" and "grouchy." This move helped the brand stand out in a crowded snack market.[15]

advertising appeal a reason for a person to buy a product

unique selling proposition a desirable, exclusive, and believable advertising appeal selected as the theme for a campaign

Source: Mars, Incorporated

Snickers recently changed the logo on its packaging to words associated with hunger, such as "snippy" and "grouchy." This move helped the brand stand out in a crowded snack market.

16-3c Executing the Message

Message execution is the way an advertisement portrays its information. In general, the AIDA plan (see Chapter 15) is a good blueprint for executing an advertising message. Any ad should immediately draw the attention of the reader, viewer, or listener. The advertiser must then use the message to hold interest, create desire for the good or service, and ultimately motivate a purchase.

The style in which the message is executed is one of the most creative elements of an advertisement. Exhibit 16.2 lists some examples of executional styles used by advertisers. Executional styles often dictate what type of media is to be employed to convey the message. For example, scientific executional styles lend themselves well to print advertising, where more information can be conveyed. Testimonials by athletes are one of the more popular executional styles. This is particularly true for social media influencers whose following and influence is built on their testimonials for products and services.

Injecting humor into an advertisement is a popular and effective executional style. Humorous executional styles are more often used in radio and television advertising than in print or digital advertising, where humor is less easily communicated. Recall that humorous ads are typically used for lower-risk, low-involvement, routine purchases such as candy, cigarettes, and casual jeans, than for higher-risk purchases or for products that are expensive, durable, or flamboyant.[16]

16-3d Postcampaign Evaluation

Evaluating an advertising campaign can be the most demanding task facing advertisers. How can an advertiser determine whether the campaign led to an increase in sales or market share or elevated awareness of the product? For traditional media, this is sometimes difficult. However, digital advertising and social media generate more data that enable marketers to better understand how well campaigns work. For example, Wayfair sells affordable furniture online, and a large proportion of its audience is on Instagram. Instagram has enhanced its shopping features making it easier to drive consumers from Instagram posts to purchases on the website. Brands tag specific items in the post and these tags lead directly to the landing page. This allows Wayfair to test different options and use marketing analytics to measure how well its Instagram marketing is working.[17] Marketers spend considerable time studying advertising effectiveness and its probable impact on sales, market share, or awareness.

Testing ad effectiveness can be done before and/or after the campaign. Before a campaign is released, marketing managers use pretests to determine the best advertising appeal, layout, and media vehicle. After advertisers implement a campaign, they use several monitoring techniques to determine whether the campaign has met its original goals. Even if a campaign has been highly successful, advertisers still typically do a postcampaign analysis to identify how the campaign might have been more efficient and what factors contributed to its success.

16-4 MEDIA DECISIONS IN ADVERTISING

A major decision for advertisers is the choice of medium—the channel used to convey a message to a target market. Media planning, therefore, is the series of decisions advertisers make regarding the selection and use of media, enabling the marketer to optimally and cost-effectively communicate the message to the target audience. Specifically, advertisers use marketing analytics to determine which types of media will best communicate the benefits of their product or service

medium the channel used to convey a message to a target market

media planning the series of decisions advertisers make regarding the selection and use of media, allowing the marketer to optimally and cost-effectively communicate the message to the target audience

EXHIBIT 16.3 ADVANTAGES AND DISADVANTAGES OF MAJOR ADVERTISING MEDIA

Medium	Advantages	Disadvantages
Newspapers	Geographic selectivity and flexibility; short-term advertiser commitments; news value and immediacy; year-round readership; high individual market coverage; co-op and local tie-in availability; short lead time	Little demographic selectivity; limited color capabilities; low pass-along rate; may be expensive
Magazines	Good reproduction, especially for color; demographic selectivity; regional selectivity; local market selectivity; relatively long advertising life; high pass-along rate	Long-term advertiser commitments; slow audience buildup; limited demonstration capabilities; lack of urgency; long lead time
Radio	Low cost; immediacy of message; can be scheduled on short notice; relatively no seasonal change in audience; highly portable; short-term advertiser commitments; entertainment carryover	No visual treatment; short advertising life of message; high frequency required to generate comprehension and retention; distractions from background sound; commercial clutter
Television	Ability to reach a wide, diverse audience; low cost per thousand; creative opportunities for demonstration; immediacy of messages; entertainment carryover; demographic selectivity with cable stations	Short life of message; some consumer skepticism about claims; high campaign cost; little demographic selectivity with network stations; long-term advertiser commitments; long lead times required for production; commercial clutter
Internet	Fastest-growing medium; ability to reach a narrow target audience; relatively short lead time required for creating web-based advertising; moderate cost; ability to measure ad effectiveness; ability to engage consumers through search engine marketing, social media, display advertising, and mobile marketing	Most ad exposure relies on "click-through" from display ads; measurement for social media needs much improvement; not all consumers have access to the Internet, and many consumers are not using social media
Outdoor Media	Repetition; moderate cost; flexibility; geographic selectivity	Short message; lack of demographic selectivity; high "noise" level distracting audience

to the target audience and when and for how long the advertisement will run.

Promotional objectives and the appeal and executional style of the advertising strongly affect the selection of media. Both creative and media decisions are made at the same time: creative work cannot be completed without knowing which medium will be used to convey the message to the target market. In many cases, the advertising objectives dictate the medium and the creative approach to be used. For example, if the objective is to demonstrate how fast a product operates, a television commercial that shows this action may be the best choice.

In 2019, U.S. advertisers are expected to spend $210 billion on paid media: newspapers, magazines, radio, television, Internet, and outdoor/cinema.[18] This represents a 2.9 percent increase over paid media spending in 2018.[19] The remainder was spent on unmonitored media such as direct mail, trade exhibits, cooperative advertising, brochures, coupons, catalogs, and special events. More than 33.3 percent of every media dollar goes toward television ads (cable, syndicated, spot, and network), but this proportion is likely to decrease through 2021. At the same time, the current 40 percent of media dollars spent on Internet ads is expected to increase to

Digital advertising is growing rapidly, including video ads, display ads, search ads, and banner ads.

iStock.com/golibo

more than 48 percent by 2021; 10 percent are likely to be newspapers ads, 9 percent magazine ads, 12 percent radio ads, and 5 percent outdoor/cinema ads.[20] In short, traditional mass-market media are declining in usage as more targeted digital media are emerging. Future growth lies primarily in the digital realm, both in paid media (display ads, video ads, and search ads) and earned media (social media). The largest increase in spending is on mobile advertising, which is expected to account for 75 percent of digital spending by 2021.

16-4a Media Types

Advertising media are channels that advertisers use in mass communication. The six major advertising media are newspapers, magazines, radio, television, the Internet, and outdoor media. Exhibit 16.3 summarizes the advantages and disadvantages of some of these major channels. But in recent years alternative media channels have emerged that offer advertisers innovative ways to reach their target audience and reduce advertising clutter.

NEWSPAPERS Newspapers are one of the oldest forms of media. The advantages of newspaper advertising include geographic flexibility and timeliness. Although there has been a decline in circulation as well as in the number of newspapers, nationally, there are still several major newspapers including the *Wall Street Journal*, *USA Today*, the *New York Times*, the *Los Angeles Times*, and the *Washington Post*. Most newspapers, however, are local. Because newspapers are generally a mass-market medium, they may not be the best vehicle for marketers trying to reach a narrow market. Newspaper advertising also encounters distractions from competing ads and news stories. Therefore, one company's newspaper ad may not be particularly visible.

The main sources of newspaper ad revenue are local retailers, classified ads, and cooperative advertising. In **cooperative advertising**, the manufacturer and the retailer split the costs of advertising the manufacturer's brand. For example, Estée Lauder may split the cost of an advertisement with Macy's department store, provided that the ad focuses on Estée Lauder's products. One reason manufacturers use cooperative advertising is the impracticality of listing all their dealers in national advertising. Also, cooperative advertising encourages retailers to devote more effort to the manufacturer's lines.

MAGAZINES Magazines are another traditional medium that continues to be successful. Some of the top magazines according to circulation include *AARP*, *Game Informer Magazine*, *Better Homes and Gardens*, *Reader's Digest*, and *Good Housekeeping*. But the cost per contact in magazine advertising is usually high as compared with the cost of advertising in other media. The cost per potential customer may be much lower, however, because magazines are often targeted to specialized audiences and thus reach more potential customers.

RADIO Radio has several strengths as an advertising medium: selectivity and audience segmentation, a large out-of-home audience, low unit and production costs, timeliness, and geographic flexibility. Local advertisers are the most frequent users of radio advertising, contributing over 75 percent of all radio ad revenue. As with newspapers, radio also lends itself well to cooperative advertising.

TELEVISION Television broadcasting media include network television, independent stations, cable television, and direct broadcast satellite television. Network television reaches a wide and diverse market, and cable television and direct broadcast satellite systems, such as DIRECTV and DISH Network, broadcast a multitude of channels devoted to highly segmented markets. Because of its targeted channels, cable television is often characterized as "narrowcasting" by media buyers. DIRECTV is testing the ability to show ads based on household data (as opposed to demographic and geographic data). To stay relevant amid new technologies, DIRECTV and other television-focused companies are beginning to recognize the need for better audience targeting. In addition, an increasing number of adults 18 or over (about 12 percent have become "cord cutters" and do not subscribe to traditional legacy cable or satellite TV; instead they watch TV online.

Advertising time on television can be very expensive, especially for network and popular cable channels. Special events and first-run prime-time shows for top-ranked television programs command the highest rates for a typical commercial. For example, running a 30-second spot during CBS sitcom *The Big Bang Theory* costs $285,934, NBC's *This is Us* costs $433,866, and one spot during *NFL Sunday Football* costs $655,677. Programs such as *NFL Thursday Night Football* and *Empire* command similarly hefty price tags.[21] A 30-second spot during the Super Bowl costs approximately $5 million, which equates to $166,667 per second of advertising.[22] Despite its high cost, many brands feel that a Super Bowl ad is a good investment, given the earned media leading up to, during, and after the game.[23] An alternative to a commercial spot is the **infomercial**, a 30-minute or longer advertisement, which is relatively inexpensive to produce and air. Advertisers say that infomercials are an ideal way to present complicated information to potential customers, which other

cooperative advertising an arrangement in which the manufacturer and the retailer split the costs of advertising the manufacturer's brand

infomercial a 30-minute or longer advertisement that looks more like a television talk show than a sales pitch advertising vehicles typically do not allow time to do. Beachbody's P90X and Insanity exercise systems are advertised through infomercials.

One of the most significant worrisome trends in terms of television advertising is the rise in popularity of on-demand viewing. For every hour of television programming, an average of 20 minutes is dedicated to nonprogram material (ads, public service announcements, and network promotions), so the popularity of DVRs among ad-weary viewers is hardly surprising. Additionally, streaming services like Netflix and Hulu have allowed consumers to bypass cable TV altogether (along with much of the advertising). This is shaping the way TV ads will be created and distributed in the future.[24]

THE INTERNET Note that global online advertising spending reached $214.4 billion in 2018, eclipsing television's $200.8 billion.[25] Online advertising includes search engine marketing (e.g., pay-per-click ads like Google AdWords), display advertising (e.g., banner ads, video ads), social media advertising (e.g., Facebook ads), email marketing, and mobile marketing (including mobile advertising and SMS). Some online channels, like Google, offer the ability to *audience buy* (whereby advertisers can purchase ad space targeted to a highly specific group), but others, such as Turner, Digital, and FunnyorDie, believe the complex cookie-based strategy poses too many risks.[26]

Programmatic advertising uses technology to match audiences and websites with marketers seeking to purchase advertising. It is a rapidly growing and evolving field that started with the auction model used by Google. Programmatic advertising has also been used to purchase display and social media advertising and is beginning to be used with more traditional media purchases. The rise of programmatic ad buying means advertisers can purchase ad space targeting specific groups in real time, using audience insights and marketing analytics and thus maximizing reach and return on investment (ROI). But some brands have elected to follow "brand safety" guidelines, whereby marketers determine a list of websites acceptable for media placement instead of relying completely on marketing analytics to determine programmatic advertising. This strategy is a result of ads showing up on websites with questionable content.

Popular Internet sites and search engines generally sell advertising space to marketers to promote their goods and services. Internet surfers click on these ads to be linked to more

Ad blocking browser plugins enable users to disable online advertising, which lowers revenues for websites that rely on ads to survive. Google, Apple, and other companies are making an intrusive ad blocker app available to their browser users.

Pinone Pantone/Shutterstock.com

information about the advertised product or service. Both leading advertisers and companies whose ad budgets are not as large have become big Internet advertisers. Because of the relative low cost and high targetability, search engines generate nearly half of all Internet ad revenue. The fastest-growing platform for Internet advertising is the mobile space. In fact, mobile advertising will account for three-fourths of total ad spending in the United States by 2021, making it one of the fastest-growing platforms overall.[27]

More than 90 percent of Americans have mobile phones, 77 percent of which are smartphones. One in 10 American adults are "smartphone-only" Internet users, meaning they do not have a traditional home broadband service.[28] U.S. mobile advertising has reached a tipping point, with a projected $284 billion in sales by 2020. Mobile ads account for nearly all growth in digital advertising. The primary reason for this incredible growth is that people are spending more of their time (almost 20 percent) on mobile devices rather than on desktops and laptops.[29] And this trend is not just in the United States. Globally, mobile advertising has substantial upside potential, given the more than 6 billion mobile phone users in the world, an increasing number of whom have smartphones or tablets with Internet access. As advanced mobile devices continue to grow in popularity around the world, so too will mobile ad spending.

Another popular Internet advertising format is **advergaming**, whereby companies put ad messages in web-based, mobile, console, or handheld video games to advertise or promote a product, service, organization, or

advergaming placing advertising messages in web-based, mobile, console, or handheld video games to advertise or promote a product, service, organization, or issue

Audi set up dozens of free Wi-Fi hot spots at the New York Auto Show. Each of the hot spots featured a reason why the Audi A4 outclassed the BMW 328i. Creative alternative media campaigns like this are designed to generate publicity for the companies.

issue. *Gamification*, the process of using game mechanics and a gaming mind-set to engage an audience, is increasingly important for marketers to know about and utilize. Challenges, rewards, incentives, and competition are all important aspects in social media games like *Fortnite*, *Angry Birds*, *Exploding Kittens*, *Candy Crush Saga*, and *Clash of Clans*.[30] Some games amount to virtual commercials. Other games encourage players to buy in-game items and power-ups to advance, while still others allow advertisers to sponsor games or buy ad space for product placements. Many of these are social games, played on Facebook or mobile networks, where players can interact with one another, locally or globally. Social gaming has a huge audience—according to Facebook CEO Mark Zuckerberg, every month 375 million people play social games on Facebook. The Facebook gaming market is projected to more than double in the next three years, attracting 554 million people and generating $5.6 billion.[31]

OUT-OF-HOME MEDIA (OOH) Out-of-home advertising (OOH) or outdoor advertising is a flexible, low-cost medium that may take a variety of forms. Examples include billboards, skywriting, giant inflatables, mini billboards in malls and on bus stop shelters, signs in sports arenas, and lighted moving signs in bus terminals and airports, as well as ads painted on cars, trucks, buses, water towers, manhole covers, drinking glass coasters, and even people, called "living advertising." The plywood scaffolding surrounding downtown construction sites often holds ads, which in places like Manhattan's Times Square, can reach over a million viewers a day.

OOH advertising reaches a broad and diverse market and is therefore ideal for promoting convenience products and services as well as for directing consumers to local businesses. One of the main advantages of OHH advertising over other media is that its exposure frequency is very high, yet the amount of clutter from competing ads is very low. Outdoor advertising also can be customized to local marketing needs, which is why local businesses are the leading outdoor advertisers in any given region. At the same time, OOH advertising is seeing a lot of innovation by linking these ads to mobile phones and social media. Review the examples in Chapter 15 about Spotify's creative use of outdoor media and social media.

ALTERNATIVE MEDIA To cut through the clutter of traditional advertising media, advertisers are developing new media vehicles, like shopping carts in grocery stores, computer screen savers, interactive kiosks in department stores, advertisements run before movies at the cinema, posters on bathroom stalls, and *advertainments*—mini movies that promote a product and are shown online.

Marketers are looking for additional innovative ways to reach captive and often bored commuters. For instance, subway systems are now showing ads via lighted boxes installed along tunnel walls. Other advertisers seek consumers at home. Some marketers have begun replacing hold music on customer service lines with advertisements and movie trailers. This strategy generates revenue for the company being called and catches undistracted consumers for advertisers. The trick is to amuse and interest this captive audience without annoying them during their 10- to 15-minute wait.

16-4b Media Selection Considerations

An important element in any advertising campaign is the **media mix**, the combination of media to be used. Media mix decisions are typically based on several factors: cost per contact, cost per click, reach, frequency, target audience considerations, flexibility of the medium, noise level, and the life span of the medium.

Cost per contact, also referred to as **cost per thousand (CPM)**, is the cost of reaching one member of the target market. Naturally, as the size of the audience increases, so does the total cost. Cost per contact enables an advertiser to compare the relative costs of specific media vehicles (such as television versus radio or magazine versus newspaper), or more specifically, within a media category (such as *Wall Street Journal*

media mix the combination of media to be used for a promotional campaign

cost per contact (cost per thousand [CPM]) the cost of reaching one member of the target market versus *New York Times*). Thus, an advertiser debating whether to spend local advertising dollars for television spots or radio spots could consider the cost per contact of each. Alternatively, if the question is which magazine to advertise in, the advertiser might choose the one with the greater reach. In either case, the advertiser can pick the vehicle with the lowest cost per contact to maximize advertising punch for the money spent. **Cost per click** is the cost associated with a consumer clicking on a display or banner ad. Although there are several variations, this option enables the marketer to pay only for "engaged" consumers—those who opted to click on an ad.

Reach is the number of target customers who are exposed to a commercial at least once during a specific period, usually four weeks. Media plans for product introductions and attempts at increasing brand awareness usually emphasize reach. For example, an advertiser might try to reach 70 percent of the target audience during the first three months of the campaign. Reach is related to a medium's ratings, generally referred to in the industry as *gross ratings points*, or *GRP*. A television program with a higher GRP means that more people are tuning in to the show and the reach is higher. Accordingly, as GRP increases for a particular medium, so does cost per contact.

Because the typical ad is short-lived, and often only a small portion of an ad may be perceived at one time, advertisers repeat their ads so that potential customers will remember the message. **Frequency** is the number of times an individual is exposed to a given message during a specific period. Advertisers use average frequency to measure the intensity of a specific medium's coverage. Research suggests that the optimal number of exposure varies by medium, product category, and type of ad. Research from Facebook suggests that the ideal frequency is 1 to 2 impressions weekly over a 10-week campaign. Research on other media options suggests that a frequency of 3 to 5 is good for mobile ads, while 12 to 15 is needed for cable TV. Peloton, for example, would likely want an exposure frequency of 5 to 7 for its television ads, meaning that each of the television viewers saw the ad a minimum of 5 times and possibly as many as 7.[32]

Media selection is also a matter of matching the advertising medium with the product's target market. If marketers are trying to reach teenage females, they might select *Teen*

New media like virtual reality, augmented reality, and holographic displays are alternative ways for companies to create awareness and stimulate interest with their target markets.

Vogue or *Seventeen* magazine. A medium's ability to reach a precisely defined market is its **audience selectivity**. Some media vehicles, like general newspapers and network television, appeal to a wide cross section of the population. Others—such as *The Knot*, *Popular Mechanics*, *Architectural Digest*, *In Style*, MTV, ESPN, and Christian radio stations— appeal to very specific groups.

The *flexibility* of a medium can be extremely important to an advertiser. For example, because of layouts and design, the lead time for magazine advertising is considerably longer than for other media types, so it is a less flexible medium. By contrast, radio and Internet advertising provide maximum flexibility. If necessary, an advertiser can change a radio ad on the day it is aired.

Noise level is the amount of distraction experienced by the target audience in a medium. Noise can be created by competing ads, as when a street is lined with billboards or when a television program is cluttered with competing ads. While newspapers and magazines have a high noise level, direct mail is a private medium with a low noise level. Typically, no other advertising media or news stories compete for the attention of direct mail's readers.

Media have either a short or a long *life span*, which means that messages can either quickly fade or persist as tangible copy to be carefully studied. A radio commercial may last less than a minute, but advertisers can overcome this short life span by repeating radio ads often. In contrast, a magazine has a relatively long life span, which is further increased by a high pass-along rate.

Media planners have traditionally relied on the above factors in selecting an effective media mix, with reach, frequency, and cost often the overriding criteria.

cost per click the cost associated with a consumer clicking on a display or banner ad

reach the number of target consumers exposed to a commercial at least once during a specific period, usually four weeks

frequency the number of times an individual is exposed to a given message during a specific period

audience selectivity the ability of an advertising medium to reach a precisely defined market

But the ability to measure impact is increasingly important. Well-established brands with familiar messages generally need fewer exposures to be effective, while newer or unfamiliar brands likely need more exposures to create awareness and be effective. In addition, today's media planners have more media options than ever before. For example, there are over 1,600 television networks across the country, whereas 40 years ago there were only three.

The proliferation of media channels is causing *media fragmentation* and forcing media planners to pay as much attention to where they place their advertising as to how often the advertisement is repeated. That is, marketers should evaluate reach *and* frequency in assessing the effectiveness of advertising. In certain situations, it may be important to reach potential consumers through as many media vehicles as possible. When this approach is considered, however, the budget must be large enough to achieve sufficient levels of frequency in all media vehicles to have an impact. In evaluating reach versus frequency, therefore, the media planner ultimately must select an approach that is most likely to result in the ad being understood and remembered when a purchase decision is being made.

Advertisers also evaluate the qualitative factors involved in media selection. These include such things as attention to the commercial and the program, involvement, program liking, lack of distractions, and other audience behaviors that affect the likelihood of a commercial message being seen and, hopefully, processed to long-term memory. While advertisers can advertise their product in as many media as possible and repeat the ad as many times as they like, the ad still may not be effective if the audience is not paying attention. In general, research confirms the benefits of cross-media advertising campaigns.[33]

16-4c Media Scheduling

After choosing the media for the advertising campaign, advertisers must schedule the ads. A **media schedule** designates the medium or media to be used (such as magazines, television, or digital), the specific vehicles (such as *People* magazine, the show *This is Us* on television, or Rush Limbaugh's national radio program), and the insertion dates of the advertising.

There are four basic types of media schedules:

- A **continuous media schedule** is designed so that the ad runs steadily throughout the advertising period. Examples include Ivory soap and Charmin toilet tissue, which may have an ad in the newspaper

Positive publicity stimulates brand engagement and creates customer loyalty. Companies are increasingly choosing digital media alternatives, such as YouTube, to communicate with current and potential customers and enhance their brand equity.

melissamn/Shutterstock.com

every Sunday and a television commercial on NBC every night during the week at 7:30 p.m. over a three-month time period. Products in the later stages of the product life cycle, which are advertised on a reminder basis, often use a continuous media schedule.

- With a **flighted media schedule**, the advertiser may schedule the ads heavily every other month or every two weeks to achieve a greater impact with an increased frequency and reach at those times. Similarly, movie studios might schedule television advertising on Wednesday and Thursday nights, when moviegoers are deciding which films to see that weekend.

- A **pulsing media schedule** combines continuous scheduling with flighted scheduling; it is continuous advertising that is more frequent during the best sale periods. A retail department store may advertise on a year-round basis but place more advertising during

media schedule designation of the media, the specific publications or programs, and the insertion dates of advertising

continuous media schedule a media scheduling strategy in which advertising is run steadily throughout the advertising period; used for products in the later stages of the product life cycle

flighted media schedule a media scheduling strategy in which ads are run heavily every other month or every two weeks to achieve a greater impact with an increased frequency and reach at those times

pulsing media schedule a media scheduling strategy that uses continuous scheduling throughout the year coupled with a flighted schedule during the best sales periods certain sale periods, such as Thanksgiving, Christmas, and back to school. Or beer may be advertised more heavily during the summer months and football season, given the higher consumption levels at those times.

- Certain times of the year call for a **seasonal media schedule**. Products like Nyquil cold medicine and Coppertone sunscreen, which are used more during certain times of the year, tend to follow a seasonal strategy.

Research comparing continuous media schedules and flighted ones suggests that continuous schedules are more effective than are flighted ones at driving sales through television advertisements. Research also suggests that it is likely more important to reach a potential customer as close as possible to the time at which a purchase is being considered. Therefore, the advertiser should maintain a continuous schedule over as long a period of time as possible. Often called *recency planning*, this theory of scheduling is now commonly used for scheduling television advertising for frequently purchased products such as Coca-Cola and Tide detergent. Recency planning's main premise is that advertising works by influencing the brand choice of people who are ready to buy. Mobile advertising is one of the most promising tactics for contacting consumers when they are thinking about a specific product. For example, a GPS-enabled mobile phone can get text messages for area restaurants around lunchtime to advertise specials to professionals working in a big city.

16-5 PUBLIC RELATIONS

Public relations is the element in the promotional mix that evaluates public attitudes, identifies issues that may elicit public concern, and executes programs to gain public understanding and acceptance. Public relations is a vital link in a forward-thinking company's marketing communication mix. Marketing managers plan solid public relations campaigns that fit into overall marketing plans and focus on target audiences. These campaigns strive to maintain a positive image of the company in the eyes of the public. The campaigns should capitalize, therefore, on factors that enhance the firm's image and minimize the factors that could generate a negative image. The concept of earned media is based on public relations and publicity.

Publicity is the effort to capture media attention—for example, through articles or editorials in publications or through human-interest stories on radio or television programs. Companies usually initiate publicity through press releases that further their public relations plans. A company about to introduce a new product or open a new store may send press releases to the media in the hope that the story will be published or broadcast. Savvy publicity can often create overnight sensations or build up a reserve of goodwill with consumers. Corporate donations and sponsorships can also create favorable publicity.

16-5a Major Public Relations Tools

Public relations professionals commonly use several tools, many of which require an active role on the part of the public relations professional, such as writing press releases and engaging in proactive media relations. Sometimes, however, these techniques create their own publicity.

NEW-PRODUCT PUBLICITY Publicity is instrumental in introducing new products and services. Publicity can help advertisers explain what's different about their new product by prompting free news stories or positive word of mouth about it. During the introductory period, an especially innovative new product often needs more exposure than provided by conventional, paid advertising. Public relations professionals write press releases or develop videos in an effort to generate news about their new products. They also jockey for exposure of their product or service at major events, on popular television and news shows, or in the hands of influential people. Social media and the use of celebrities are important for new product publicity. For example, Kanye West's Yeezy brand skyrocketed due to West's social media strategy. West releases products in limited numbers. The Boost 350 sneakers—at $200 a pair—sold out in one hour. West's use of social media influencers (including his wife Kim Kardashian) led to a 45 percent spike in search for the Yeezy brand.[34]

PRODUCT PLACEMENT Marketers are increasingly using product placement to reinforce brand awareness and create favorable attitudes. **Product placement** is a strategy that involves getting one's product, service,

seasonal media schedule a media scheduling strategy that runs advertising only during times of the year when the product is most likely to be used

public relations the element in the promotional mix that evaluates public attitudes, identifies issues that may elicit public concern, and executes programs to gain public understanding and acceptance

publicity an effort to capture media attention, often initiated through press releases that further a corporation's public relations plans

product placement a public relations strategy that involves getting a product, service, or company name to appear in a movie, television show, radio program, magazine, newspaper, video game, video or audio clip, book, or commercial for another product, on the Internet, or at special events

The Snapbot vending machine is the only way to get a pair of Snapchat Spectacles—smart glasses that can take pictures and connect directly with the Snapchat app on your phone.

or name to appear in a movie, television show, radio program, magazine, newspaper, video game, video or audio clip, book, commercial for another product, on the Internet, or at special events. Including an actual product, such as a can of Pepsi, adds a sense of realism to a movie, television show, video game, book, or similar vehicle that cannot be created by a can simply marked "soda." Product placements are arranged through barter (trade of product for placement), through paid placements, or at no charge when the product is viewed as enhancing the vehicle it is placed in.[35]

Global product placement expenditures total about $10.5 billion annually, with the United States, Mexico, and Brazil accounting for more than three-quarters of that spending combined. (The United States alone accounts for $6 billion of the global total.[34]) More than two-thirds of product placements are in movies and television shows, but placements in alternative media are growing, particularly on the Internet and in video games. Digital technology now enables companies to "virtually" place their products in any audio or video production. Virtual placement not only reduces the cost of product placement for new productions but also enables companies to place their products in previously produced programs, such as reruns of television shows. Overall, companies obtain valuable product exposure, brand reinforcement, and increased sales through product placement.

CONSUMER EDUCATION Some major firms believe that educated consumers are more loyal customers. Financial planning firms often sponsor free educational seminars on money management, retirement planning, and investing

in the hope that the seminar participants will choose the sponsoring organization for their future financial needs.

SPONSORSHIP Sponsorships are increasing both in number and as a proportion of companies' marketing budgets. U.S. sponsorship spending is likewise increasing and is currently about $38 billion annually.[36] Probably the biggest reason for the increasing use of sponsorships is the difficulty of reaching audiences and differentiating a product from competing brands through the mass media.

With **sponsorship**, a company spends money to support an issue, cause, or event that is consistent with corporate objectives, such as improving brand awareness or enhancing corporate image. The biggest category of sponsorships is sporting events; this category accounts for almost 70 percent of spending in sponsorships and has grown steadily in recent years.[37] Nonsports categories include entertainment tours and attractions, causes, arts, festivals, fairs and annual events, and association and membership organizations.

Although the most popular sponsorship events are still those involving sports, music, or the arts, companies have recently been turning to more specialized events such as tie-ins with schools, charities, and other community service organizations. Marketers sometimes even create their own events tied to their products. For example, energy drink manufacturer Red Bull hosted Stratos, a multimillion-dollar event where Austrian Felix Baumgartner skydived from the edge of space—nearly 24 miles above Earth's surface. Baumgartner became the first human to break the sound barrier in free fall, reaching 834 miles per hour before touching down safely in New Mexico. A major marketing victory for Red Bull, Stratos set its own record as the most-watched YouTube livestream of all time—more than 8 million viewers tuned in to the event.[38]

Corporations sponsor issues as well as events. Sponsorship issues are quite diverse, but the three most popular are education, health care, and social programs. Firms often donate a percentage of sales or profits to a worthy cause favored by their target market.

EXPERIENTIAL MARKETING While the Internet enables consumers to connect with their favorite brands in a virtual environment, there is often nothing like experiencing the real thing live and in person. Experiential marketing involves engaging with consumers in a way that enables them to feel the brand—not just read about it. Experiential and event marketing have increased

sponsorship a public relations strategy in which a company spends money to support an issue, cause, or event that is consistent with corporate objectives, such as improving brand awareness or enhancing corporate image in recent years, with most of the growth coming from the world's largest brands. One example of experiential marketing is Snapbot vending machines, which travel to various locations around the United States. The Snapbot vending machine is the only way to get a pair of Snapchat Spectacles—smart glasses that can take pictures and connect directly with the Snapchat app on your phone. This exclusive product generates buzz in every city in which the vending machine appears. Another example was Budweiser's 4-D Immersive Reality Budweiser Brewery Tour, which let South by Southwest attendees see, hear, smell, and taste how Budweiser is made.[39]

COMPANY WEBSITES Companies are increasingly using the Internet in their public relations strategies. Company websites are used to introduce new products; provide information to the media, including social media news releases; promote existing products; obtain consumer feedback; communicate legislative and regulatory information; showcase upcoming events; provide links to related sites (including corporate and noncorporate blogs, Facebook, Twitter, and Instagram); release financial information; interact with customers and potential customers; and perform many more marketing activities. In addition, social media are playing a larger role in how companies interact with customers online, particularly through sites like Facebook, Yelp, and Twitter. Indeed, online reviews (good and bad) from opinion leaders and other consumers help marketers sway purchasing decisions in their favor.

16-5b Managing Unfavorable Publicity

Although marketers try to avoid unpleasant situations, crises do happen. In our free-press environment, publicity is not easily controlled, especially in a crisis. **Crisis management** is the coordinated effort to handle the effects of unfavorable publicity, ensuring fast and accurate communication in times of emergency.

When the Villa Fresh Italian Kitchen ran "Dub the Dew," an online contest to name a green apple–flavored variety of Mountain Dew exclusive to the restaurant, it was not long before Internet trolls descended. These digital pranksters submitted absurd and offensive names (such as "diabeetus," "gushing granny," and "Hitler did nothing wrong"), and then voted their submissions to the top of the contest leaderboard en masse. The contest's website was quickly taken offline, and Mountain Dew tweeted that the contest "lost to the internet." In an attempt to manage the crisis, the Villa Fresh Italian Kitchen issued an apologetic statement: "'Dub the Dew,' a local market promotional campaign that was created by one of our customers—not Mountain Dew—was compromised. We are working diligently with our customer's team to remove all offensive content that was posted and putting measures in place to ensure this doesn't happen again."[40]

16-6 SALES PROMOTION

In addition to using advertising and public relations, marketing managers can use sales promotion **to increase the effectiveness of their promotional efforts.** Sales promotion consists of marketing communication activities other than advertising, personal selling, and public relations, in which a short-term incentive motivates consumers or members of the distribution channel to purchase a good or service immediately, either by lowering the price or by adding value.

Sales promotion is usually less expensive than advertising and easier to measure. A major national television advertising campaign often costs $10 million or more to create, produce, and place. In contrast, promotional campaigns using the Internet or direct marketing methods can cost less than half that amount. It is also very difficult to determine how many people buy a product or service as a result of radio or television ads. With sales promotion, marketers know the precise number of coupons redeemed or the number of contest entries received.

Sales promotion usually has more effect on behavior than on attitudes. Giving the consumer an incentive to make an immediate purchase is the goal of sales promotion, regardless of the form it takes. Sales promotion is usually targeted toward either of two distinctly different markets. Trade sales promotion is directed to members of the marketing channel, such as wholesalers and retailers. Consumer sales promotion is targeted to the ultimate consumer market. The objectives of a promotion depend on the general behavior of targeted customers (Exhibit 16.4). For example, marketers who are targeting loyal users of their product need to reinforce existing behavior or increase product usage. An effective tool for strengthening brand loyalty is the *frequent-buyer*

crisis management a coordinated effort to handle all the effects of unfavorable publicity or another unexpected unfavorable event

sales promotion marketing communication activities other than advertising, personal selling, and public relations, in which a short-term incentive motivates consumers or members of the distribution channel to purchase a good or service immediately, either by lowering the price or by adding value

trade sales promotion promotion activities directed to members of the marketing channel, such as wholesalers and retailers

consumer sales promotion promotion activities targeted to the ultimate consumer market

EXHIBIT 16.4 TYPES OF CONSUMERS AND SALES PROMOTION GOALS

Type of Buyer	Desired Results	Sales Promotion Examples
Loyal customers People who buy your product most or all of the time	Reinforce behavior, increase consumption, change purchase timing	• Loyalty marketing programs, such as frequent-buyer cards or frequent-shopper clubs • Bonus packs that give loyal consumers an incentive to stock up or premiums offered in return for proofs of purchase
Competitor's customers People who buy a competitor's product most or all of the time	Break loyalty, persuade to switch to your brand	• Sampling to introduce your product's superior qualities compared to their brand • Sweepstakes, contests, or premiums that create interest in the product
Brand switchers People who buy a variety of products in the category	Persuade to buy your brand more often	• Any promotion that lowers the price of the product, such as coupons, price-off packages, and bonus packs • Trade deals that help make the product more readily available than competing products
Price buyers People who consistently buy the least expensive brand	Appeal with low prices or supply added value that makes price less important	• Coupons, price-off packages, refunds, or trade deals that reduce the price of the brand to match that of the brand that would have been purchased

From *Sales Promotion Essentials*, 2nd ed., by Don E. Schultz, William A. Robinson, and Lisa A. Petrison, published by McGraw-Hill Education.

program, which rewards consumers for repeat purchases. Other types of promotions are more effective with customers who are prone to brand switching or with those who are loyal to a competitor's product. A cents-off coupon, free sample, or eye-catching display in a store will often entice shoppers to try a different brand.

Once marketers understand the dynamics occurring within their product category and determine the particular customers and behaviors they want to influence, they can then go about selecting promotional tools to achieve these goals.

16-6a Tools for Trade Sales Promotion

As we'll discuss in Section 16-6b, consumer promotions pull a product through the channel by creating demand. However, trade promotions *push* a product through the distribution channel (see Chapter 13). When selling to members of the distribution channel, manufacturers use many of the same sales promotion tools used in consumer promotions, such as sales contests, premiums, and point-of-purchase displays. Several tools, however, are unique to manufacturers and channel intermediaries:

• **Trade allowances:** A trade allowance is a price reduction offered by manufacturers to intermediaries such as wholesalers and retailers. The price reduction or rebate is given in exchange for doing something specific, such as allocating space for a new product or buying something during special periods. For example, a local Best Buy outlet could receive a special discount for running its own promotion on Sony surround sound systems.

• **Push money:** Intermediaries receive push money as a bonus for pushing the manufacturer's brand through the distribution channel. Often the push money is directed toward a retailer's salespeople. LinoColor, the leading high-end scanner company, produces a Picture Perfect Rewards catalog filled with merchandise retailers can purchase with points accrued for every LinoColor scanner they sell.

• **Training:** Sometimes a manufacturer will train an intermediary's personnel if the product is rather complex—as frequently occurs in the computer and telecommunications industries. For example, representatives of major pharmaceutical companies receive extensive training because they need to provide accurate information to doctors and nurses.

• **Free merchandise:** Often a manufacturer offers retailers free merchandise in lieu of quantity discounts. Occasionally, free merchandise is used as payment for trade allowances normally provided through other sales promotions. Instead of giving a retailer a price reduction for buying a certain quantity of merchandise, the manufacturer may throw in extra merchandise "free" (i.e., at a cost that would equal the price reduction).

• **Store demonstrations:** Manufacturers can also arrange with retailers to perform in-store demonstrations. Food manufacturers often send rep-

trade allowance a price reduction offered by manufacturers to intermediaries such as wholesalers and retailers

push money money offered to channel intermediaries to encourage them to "push" products—that is, to encourage other members of the channel to sell the products

American Express is experimenting with Twitter to offer cardholders great deals at participating businesses.

resentatives to grocery stores and supermarkets to let customers sample a product while shopping.

- **Business meetings, conventions, and trade shows:** Trade association meetings, conferences, and conventions are an important aspect of sales promotion and a growing, multibillion-dollar market. At these shows, manufacturers, distributors, and other vendors have the chance to display their goods or describe their services to potential customers. Companies participate in trade shows to attract and identify new prospects, serve current customers, introduce new products, enhance corporate image, test the market response to new products, enhance corporate morale, and gather information on competing products.

Trade promotions are popular among manufacturers for many reasons. Trade sales promotion tools help manufacturers gain new distributors for their products, obtain wholesaler and retailer support for consumer sales promotions, build or reduce dealer inventories, and improve trade relations. Car manufacturers annually sponsor dozens of auto shows for consumers. The shows attract millions of consumers, providing dealers with increased store traffic as well as good leads.

16-6b Tools for Consumer Sales Promotion

Marketing managers must decide which consumer sales promotion devices to use in a specific campaign. The methods chosen must suit the objectives to ensure success of the overall promotion plan. The popular tools for consumer sales promotion, discussed in the following pages, have also been easily transferred to online versions to entice Internet users to visit sites, purchase products, or use services on the Web.

COUPONS AND REBATES A **coupon** is a certificate that entitles a consumer to an immediate price reduction when the product is purchased. Coupons are a particularly good way to encourage product trial and repurchase. They are also likely to increase the amount of a product bought.

coupon a certificate that entitles a consumer to an immediate price reduction when the product is purchased.

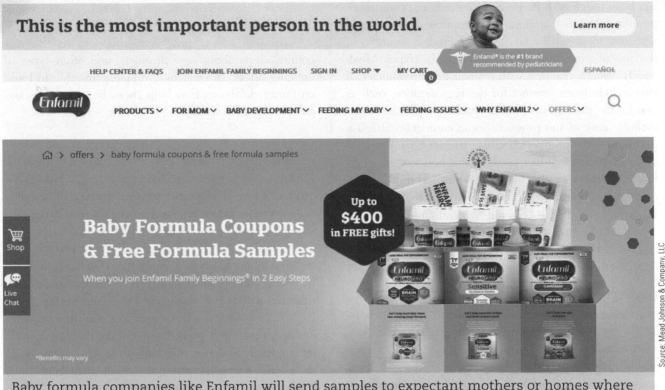

Source: Mead Johnson & Company, LLC

Baby formula companies like Enfamil will send samples to expectant mothers or homes where babies were recently born.

Coupons can be distributed in stores as instant coupons on packaging, on shelf displays with pull-off coupon dispensers, and at cash registers, printed based on what the customer purchased; through freestanding inserts (FSIs); and through various Internet daily deal sites.

FSIs, the promotional coupons inserts found in newspapers, are the traditional way of circulating printed coupons. FSIs are used to distribute approximately 89 percent of coupons. Such traditional types of coupon distribution, which also include direct mail and magazines, have been declining for several years, as consumers use fewer coupons. About 2.5 billion coupons are redeemed annually.

The Internet is changing how coupons are distributed and redeemed. In addition to Internet coupon sites such as Valpak.com and Coolsavings.com, and social coupon sites such as Groupon and LivingSocial, there are also deal sites like DealSurf.com that aggregate offers from different sites for convenience. While daily deal sites have been quite popular with consumers, sites like Groupon and LivingSocial are coming under some fire as many small businesses claim they lose money or drown under the flood of coupon redemptions. Apple is using ApplePay to provide customers with incentives, and American Express is using Twitter to drive card use. After syncing their credit cards to their Twitter accounts, American Express customers can send tweets using an approved hashtag (or "cashtag")

to pay for items purchased through third-party retailers. Cardholders can also receive automatic discounts from partner businesses on Twitter when they make purchases with their American Express cards.[41]

A **rebate** is similar to a coupon in that it offers the purchaser a price reduction. But because the purchaser must mail in a rebate form and usually some proof of purchase, the reward is not immediate. Manufacturers prefer rebates for several reasons. Rebates allow manufacturers to offer price cuts directly to consumers. Manufacturers have more control over rebate promotions because they can be rolled out and shut off quickly. Further, because buyers must fill out forms with their names, addresses, and other data, manufacturers use rebate programs to build customer databases. Perhaps the best reason to offer rebates is that although rebates are particularly good at enticing purchase, most consumers never bother to redeem them—only about 40 percent of consumers eligible for rebates collect them.[42]

PREMIUMS A **premium** is an extra item offered to the consumer, usually in exchange for some proof that the promoted product

> **rebate** a cash refund given for the purchase of a product during a specific period
>
> **premium** an extra item offered to the consumer, usually in exchange for some proof of purchase of the promoted product

has been purchased. Premiums reinforce the consumer's purchase decision, increase consumption, and persuade nonusers to switch brands. A long-standing example of the use of premiums is the McDonald's Happy Meal, which rewards children with a small toy. Premiums can also include more product for the regular price, such as two-for-the-price-of-one bonus packs or packages that include more of the product. Some companies attach a premium to the product's package, such as a small sample of a complementary hair product attached to a shampoo bottle. Premium models like FabFitFun and Birchbox are new subscription approaches in which customers pay a fee for delivery of a box of both full-size and sample products on a monthly or quarterly basis. These are great deals for marketers who want to get their beauty and home products into the hands of affluent customers.

LOYALTY MARKETING PROGRAMS A loyalty marketing program builds long-term, mutually beneficial relationships between a company and its key customers. One of the most popular types of loyalty programs, the **frequent-buyer program**, rewards loyal consumers for making multiple purchases. The objective of loyalty marketing programs is to build long-term, mutually beneficial relationships between a company and its key customers.

There are almost 3 billion loyalty programs in the United States, and 80 percent of American adults belong to some type of loyalty program.[43] Popularized by the airline industry through frequent-flyer programs, loyalty marketing enables companies to strategically invest sales promotion dollars in activities designed to capture greater profits from customers already loyal to the product or company. Co-branded credit cards are an increasingly popular loyalty marketing tool. Most department stores offer loyalty programs only if a customer opens their branded credit card. But high-end chain Bloomingdales recently changed its rewards program to include anyone who signs up. Members of the new Loyalist program receive one point for each dollar they spend and a $25 gift card after earning 5,000 points. While Bloomingdale's credit card holders receive more points per dollar spent, the company is hoping to monitor a greater number of its shoppers' spending habits by enabling noncardholders to join Loyalist.[44]

Through loyalty programs, shoppers receive discounts, alerts about new products, and other types of enticing offers. In exchange, retailers are able to build customer databases that help them better understand customer preferences.

CONTESTS AND SWEEPSTAKES Contests and sweepstakes are generally designed to create interest in a good or service, often to encourage brand switching. *Contests* are promotions in which participants use some skill or ability to compete for prizes. A consumer contest usually requires entrants to answer questions, complete sentences, or write a paragraph about the product and submit proof of purchase. Winning a *sweepstakes*, on the other hand, depends on chance, and participation is free. Sweepstakes usually draw about 10 times more entries than contests do.

While contests and sweepstakes may draw considerable interest and publicity, generally they are not effective tools for generating long-term sales. To increase their effectiveness, sales promotion managers must make certain the award will appeal to the target market. Offering several smaller prizes to many winners instead of one huge prize to just one person often will increase the effectiveness of the promotion, but there is no denying the attractiveness of a jackpot-type prize.

SAMPLING Sampling allows the customer to try a product risk-free. In one study, in-store sampling proved to be the most successful promotional tactic when a new dairy product was introduced to grocery stores. In-store sampling events increased sales 116 percent, outperforming aisle displays (70 percent), ad circulars (63 percent), and temporary price reductions (48 percent).[45]

Samples can be directly mailed to the customer, delivered door to door, packaged with another product, or demonstrated or distributed at a retail store or service outlet. Sampling at special events is a popular, effective, and high-profile distribution method that permits marketers to piggyback onto fun-based consumer activities—including sporting events, college fests, fairs and festivals, beach events, and chili cook-offs. Distributing samples to specific location types, such as health clubs, churches, or doctors' offices, is also one of the most efficient methods of sampling. Online sampling is catching up in popularity, however, with the growth of social media. Branded products not only run contests through Facebook, but also connect with fans, show commercials, and offer samples of new products in exchange for "liking" the brand.

loyalty marketing program a promotional program designed to build long-term, mutually beneficial relationships between a company and its key customers

frequent-buyer program a loyalty program in which loyal consumers are rewarded for making multiple purchases of a particular good or service

sampling a promotional program that allows the consumer the opportunity to try a product or service for free

POINT-OF-PURCHASE PROMOTION A point-of-purchase (POP) display includes any promotional display set up at the retailer's location to build traffic, advertise the product, or induce impulse buying. POP displays include shelf "talkers" (signs attached to store shelves), shelf extenders (attachments that extend shelves so products stand out), ads on grocery carts and bags, end-aisle and floor-stand displays, television monitors at supermarket checkout counters, in-store audio messages, and audiovisual displays. One big advantage of the POP display is that it offers manufacturers a captive audience in retail stores. According to POPAI's Shopper Engagement Study, approximately 82 percent of all retail purchase decisions are made in-store. Sixty-two percent of shoppers buy more than they anticipated once in the store, so POP displays can be very effective.[46] Other strategies to increase sales include adding cards to the tops of displays, changing messages on signs on the sides or bottoms of displays, adding inflatable or mobile displays, and using signs that advertise the brand's sports, movie, or charity tie-in.

16-6c Trends in Sales Promotion

The biggest trend in sales promotion on both the trade and consumer sides has been the increased use of the Internet. Promotions based on social media, email, and websites have expanded dramatically in recent years. Marketers are now spending billions of dollars annually on such promotions. Sales promotions online have proved both effective and cost-efficient—generating response rates three to five times higher than off-line promotions. The most effective types of online sales promotions are free merchandise, sweepstakes, free shipping with purchases, and coupons. One major goal of retailers is to add potential customers to their databases and expand marketing touch points.

Marketers have discovered that online coupon distribution provides another vehicle for promoting their products. Coupon redemption rates have seen a slight decline, while the users who *do* redeem coupons are increasingly inclined to make use of digital offers. These customers want more effective delivery models for coupons and discounts, making the shopping experience as simple as possible.[47] Online coupons can help marketers lure new customers, and with the speed of online feedback, marketers can track the success of a coupon in real time and adjust it based on changing market conditions.[48]

Online versions of loyalty programs are also popping up, and although many types of companies have these programs, the most successful are those run by hotel and airline companies. A final major trend in sales promotion is the utilization of sales promotions on social media and at the point of purchase. Google's Zero Moment of Truth (ZMOT) insights illustrate how important consumer feedback is to consumer purchases, highlighting the importance of behavioral data and marketing analytics when executing a targeted sales promotion.[49]

point of purchase (POP) display a promotional display set up at the retailer's location to build traffic, advertise the product, or induce impulse buying

17 | Personal Selling and Sales Management

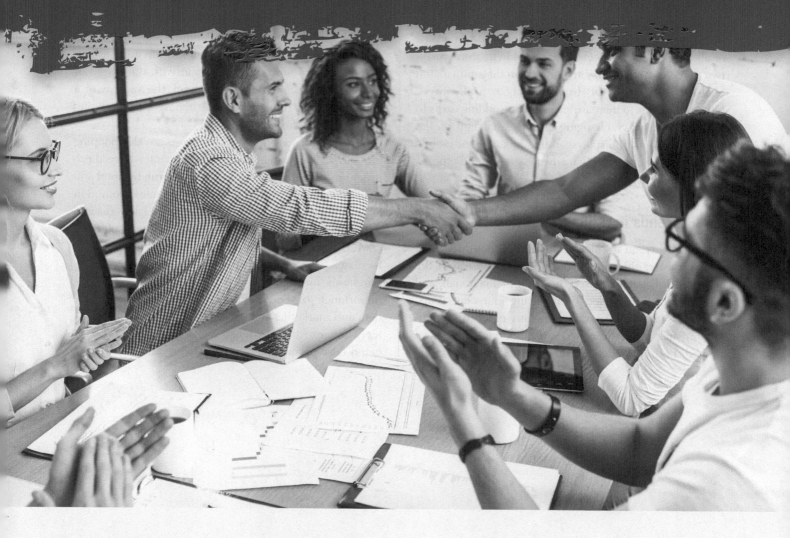

LEARNING OUTCOMES

After studying this chapter, you will be able to…

17-1 Understand the sales environment

17-2 Describe personal selling

17-3 Discuss technology's impact, including social media, on the sales environment

17-4 Discuss the key differences between relationship selling and transactional selling

17-5 List and explain the steps in the selling process

17-6 Understand the functions and roles of sales management

17-7 Describe the use of customer relationship management in the selling process

VGstockstudio/Shutterstock.com

17-1 THE SALES ENVIRONMENT

Many people around the world work in some form of selling. Traditionally, salespeople engage in direct face-to-face contact with customers. This can take place either at the salesperson's place of business or at a secondary location (such as when a salesperson travels door to door or meets a customer at her office or home). Salespeople can be consumer-focused (as in the case of retail) or business-focused (selling to other firms).

In many cases, consumer-focused salespeople require customers to come directly to a retail store, shortening the sales process time. Even though many retailers use multiple customer relationship management processes (including information kiosks, websites, and self-checkouts), one-to-one interactions are often key to retail success. Most major retailers use trained salespeople—not just order takers—to enhance the customer experience. Nordstrom's, for example, offers a retail management internship that provides both hands-on selling experience and classroom learning for students looking for careers in retail management and sales.[1] By having knowledgeable salespeople, retailers can help their customers select the products or services that are best for them.

As previously indicated, some consumer-focused salespeople travel to their customers' locations. For example, many home improvement and maintenance salespeople meet potential customers at their homes for purchases such as pools, fencing, or kitchen remodeling. Similarly, cosmetics, small appliances, and magazine subscriptions may be sold directly to customers at their homes. These salespeople are considered direct salespeople. Companies such as Cutco Cutlery, Avon, and Mary Kay Cosmetics have been very successful in direct selling.

Business-focused salespeople call on other companies to sell their products. These business-to-business salespeople often spend a great deal of time traveling to customer locations to make sales calls, and the sales process generally takes a longer period of time than consumer-focused selling. Often, business-to-business salespeople have more extensive sales training, are required to travel more, and in turn, receive a higher level of compensation.

The sales environment changes constantly as new competitors enter the market and old competitors leave. The ways customers interact with salespeople and learn about products and suppliers are changing as a result of the rapid increase in new sales technologies, including increased use of social media. Most salespeople are receptive to using social media, given that it has been shown to increase performance.[2] In order for companies to successfully sell products or services using a sales force, they must be very effective at personal selling, social media, technology, sales management, and customer relationship management—all of which play critical roles in building strong long-term relationships with customers.

17-2 PERSONAL SELLING

As mentioned in Chapter 15, *personal selling* is a purchase situation involving a personal, paid-for communication between two people in an attempt to influence each other. In a sense, all businesspeople are salespeople. An individual may become a plant manager, a chemist, an engineer, or a member of any profession, and yet still have to sell. For example, during a job search, applicants must "sell" themselves to prospective employers in an interview. Personal selling offers several advantages over other forms of promotion:

- Personal selling provides a detailed explanation or demonstration of the product. This capability is especially needed for complex or new goods and services.

- The sales message can be varied according to the motivations and interests of each prospective customer. Moreover, when the prospect has questions or raises objections, the salesperson is there to provide explanations and guidance. By contrast, advertising and sales promotion can respond only to the questions and objections the copywriter *thinks* are important to customers.

- Personal selling should be directed only toward qualified prospects. Other forms of promotion include some unavoidable waste because many people in the audience are not prospective customers.

- Costs can be controlled by adjusting the size of the sales force (and resulting expenses) in one-person increments. On the other hand, advertising and sales promotion must often be purchased in fairly large amounts.

- Perhaps the most important advantage is that personal selling is considerably more effective than other forms of promotion in obtaining a sale and gaining a satisfied customer.

Personal selling also has limitations when compared to other forms of promotion:

- Cost per contact is much greater than for mass forms of communication, leading companies to be highly selective about where and when they use salespeople.

- If the sales force is not properly trained, the message provided can be inconsistent and inaccurate. Continual sales force management and training are necessary.

- Salespeople may convince customers to buy unneeded products or services. This can lead to increased levels of cognitive dissonance among buyers if a salesperson is being pushed to meet certain quotas.

Personal selling often works better than other forms of promotion, given certain customer and product characteristics. Generally speaking, personal selling becomes more important when the number of potential customers decreases, as the complexity of the product increases, and as the value of the product grows (see Exhibit 17.1). For highly complex goods, such as business jets and private communication systems, a salesperson is needed to determine the prospective customer's needs and wants, explain the product's benefits and advantages, and propose the exact features and accessories that will best meet the client's needs. Many upscale clothing retailers offer free personal shopping, whereby consultants select and suggest designer clothing they believe will fit the customer's style and specified need. Bloomingdales' personal shoppers help customers select gifts for others, provide guidance tailored to the individual's personal tastes, coordinate gift wrapping and alterations, help

EXHIBIT 17.1	COMPARISON OF PERSONAL SELLING AND ADVERTISING/ SALES PROMOTION	
Personal selling is more important if . . .	Advertising and sales promotion are more important if . . .
The product has a high value.	The product has a low value.
It is a custom-made product.	It is a standardized product.
There are few customers.	There are many customers.
The product is technically complex.	The product is easy to understand.
Customers are concentrated.	Customers are geographically dispersed.
Examples: Insurance policies, custom windows, airplane engines	**Examples:** Soap, magazine subscriptions, cotton T-shirts

navigate the entire store from clothing to home goods, and even schedule reminders for special occasions.[3]

TECHNOLOGY'S IMPACT ON SELLING

Technology, including social media, plays an increasingly important role in personal selling. Instead of being handed traditional sales pamphlets and brochures, consumers are now able to easily learn about products and services by searching the Internet before entering a store. In fact, many consumers compare product features, prices, and quality online before even deciding which store to visit, and they are often influenced by social media.

Firms that succeed in having a consumer enter their story often find the consumer evaluates the products or services firsthand and then uses mobile technology to compare products for a potential purchase across a number of competing channels and companies—a process called showrooming (see Chapter 6).[4] In addition to their own research, consumers are being bombarded with in-store messages, coupons, and sale information using beacon technology, like Apple's iBeacon. Suffice it to say, consumers are more educated about products and services today than they have ever been before. If salespeople do not stay well informed about the products they are selling, consumers may enter the store knowing more than the salespeople do. This reduces the ability of the salesperson to build trust and confidence.

Like consumers, salespeople are increasingly using social media. For social media to be successful in this capacity, however, customers and organizations alike must understand and be comfortable with the technology.[5] LinkedIn, Facebook, blogs, and Twitter are not only a place to make sales; they can also help establish a salesperson's expertise within a field. With more than 500 million members, LinkedIn positions itself as the world's largest professional network.[6] In addition to its networking function, LinkedIn offers sales solutions to help salespeople find prospects, qualify leads, and make product recommendations to decision makers.[7] LinkedIn also provides advice on how to effectively sell using social media. For example, one featured article discusses the pillars of social selling, while another describes how to measure social selling success.[8] LinkedIn has even published an eBook on getting started with social selling, making the social network a great resource for salespeople looking to harness the power of social selling themselves.[9]

Transactional Selling Relationship Selling

Sales Techniques Often canned, nonflexible presentations that are repetitive from one presentation to the next. Flexible presentations that are customized for each buyer and are focused on identifying customer's needs and wants to reach the best solution(s).

Length of the Sales Cycle Short term—focused on closing the sale as quickly as possible and moving to the next potential customer/sale. It has limited to no focus on customer development. Long term—focused on maintaining the relationship over an extended period of time with the generation of higher-quality new customers who can be further developed over the long term.

Importance of Relationships between the Parties Low expectation and importance of the relationship between the two parties beyond the immediate transaction. It is important for the relationship to develop between buyers and sellers.

Levels of Trust Low-to-limited levels of trust are required beyond the actual transaction. High levels of trust are required to develop and maintain the relationship over an extended period of time.

Outcomes Win–lose—each party is trying to get the most benefit without considering the other party. Win–win—each party is trying to create additional value for both parties.

Performance Assessment Mainly output/sales-based and focused on the amount sold and/or profit per sale. While amount sold and profit per sale are important, customer satisfaction and support activities are also important and assessed.

Pros Lower levels of employee training are required.

Easy assessment of performance. Highly customer-centric.

More value-creation focused.

Less price-focused.

Higher levels of customer satisfaction.

In many instances, firms do not control the content on social media sites. It is important for salespeople to be aware and to understand what is being posted about the firm, products, competitors, and even the sales force itself. At the same time, the ability to share experiences quickly with a large number of people increases the impact of word of mouth, both positively and negatively. For example, prospective customers evaluating several different swimming pool companies can review what recent pool purchasers have posted about different companies through sites such as Houzz, which is a platform that provides customer reviews for home renovation and design services.[10] Social media also allows firms to listen to what customers, potential customers, or noncustomers are saying about the company, and it provides a sophisticated method of measuring how marketers meet and interact with consumers. Finally, social media enables firms to have more direct and meaningful conversations with customers.

 17-4 **RELATIONSHIP SELLING**

Historically, marketing theory and practice concerning personal selling have focused almost entirely on planned presentations to prospective customers for the sole purpose of making sales. Marketers were mostly concerned with making one-time sales and then moving on to the next prospect. Transactional selling methods attempt to persuade the buyer to either accept a point of view or take a particular action. Frequently, the objectives of the salesperson were at the expense of the buyer, creating a win–lose outcome. Although this type of sales approach has not disappeared entirely, it is being used less and less often by professional salespeople.

By contrast, modern views of personal selling emphasize the relationship that develops between a salesperson and a buyer. **Relationship selling**, or **consultative selling**, is a multistage process that emphasizes personalization, win–win outcomes, and empathy as key ingredients in identifying prospects and developing them as long-term, satisfied customers. The focus, therefore, is on building mutual trust between the buyer and seller through the delivery of long-term, value-added benefits that are anticipated by the buyer.

Relationship or consultative salespeople, therefore, become consultants, partners, and problem solvers for their customers. They

relationship selling (consultative selling) a sales practice that involves building, maintaining, and enhancing interactions with customers in order to develop long-term satisfaction through mutually beneficial partnerships strive to build long-term relationships with key accounts by developing trust over time. The emphasis shifts from a one-time sale to a long-term relationship in which the salesperson works with the customer to develop solutions for enhancing the customer's bottom line. The end result of relationship selling tends to be loyal customers who purchase from the company time after time, often with an increased share of purchase. A relationship selling strategy focused on retaining customers is often less expensive to a company than having to constantly prospect for and sell to new customers. Relationship selling provides many advantages over traditional selling in the consumer goods market. Still, relationship selling is more often used in selling situations for industrial-type goods, such as heavy machinery and computer systems, and services, such as airlines and insurance, than in selling situations for consumer goods. Exhibit 17.2 lists the key differences between transactional selling and relationship, or consultative, selling.

17-5 STEPS IN THE SELLING PROCESS

Completing a sale requires multiple steps. The **sales process**, or **sales cycle**, is the set of steps a salesperson goes through in order to sell a particular product or service. The sales process can be unique for each product or service offered. The actual sales process depends on the features of the product or service, characteristics of customer segments, and internal processes in place within the firm (such as how leads are gathered).

Some sales take only a few minutes to complete, but others may take much longer. Sales of technical products (like a Boeing or Airbus airplane) and customized goods and services typically take many months, perhaps even years, to complete. On the other end of the spectrum, sales of less technical products (like stationery) are generally more routine and often take less than a day to complete. Whether a salesperson spends a few minutes or a few years on a sale, there are seven basic steps in the personal selling process:

1. Generating leads
2. Qualifying leads
3. Approaching the customer and probing needs
4. Developing and proposing solutions
5. Handling objections

sales process (sales cycle) the set of steps a salesperson goes through in a particular organization to sell a particular product or service

lead generation (prospecting) identification of the firms and people most likely to buy the seller's offerings

6. Closing the sale
7. Following up

Like other forms of promotion, the steps of selling follow the AIDA concept discussed in Chapter 15. Once a salesperson has located and qualified a prospect with the authority to buy, he or she tries to get the prospect's attention. A thorough needs assessment turned into an effective sales proposal and presentation should generate interest. After developing the customer's initial desire (preferably during the presentation of the sales proposal), the salesperson seeks action in the close by trying to get an agreement to buy. Follow-up after the sale, the final step in the selling process, not only lowers cognitive dissonance (refer to Chapter 6) but also may open up opportunities for repeat business, sales of related products and services, and new-customer referrals.

Transactional selling and relationship selling follow the same basic steps. They differ, however, in the relative importance they place on certain key steps in the process. Transactional selling is transaction oriented—focusing on generating as many leads as possible, making as many presentations as possible, and closing as many sales as possible. Minimal effort is placed on asking questions to identify customer needs and wants, much less matching these needs and wants to the specific benefits of the good or service. Often, transactional selling allows little time for following up and ensuring that customers are satisfied. Perhaps not surprisingly, these types of sales usually result in lower levels of customer satisfaction, less repeat business, more price-based competition, and more win–lose transactions for salespeople.

By contrast, salespeople practicing relationship selling emphasize a long-term investment in the time and effort needed to uncover each customer's specific needs and wants and meet them with the product or service offering. By doing their homework up front, salespeople often create the conditions necessary for a relatively straightforward close. In general, customers are more satisfied, engage in more repeat business, and provide higher shares of purchase over longer periods of time with relationship salespeople. In the following sections, we examine each step of the personal selling process.

17-5a Step 1: Generating Leads

Initial groundwork must precede communication between the potential buyer and the salesperson. **Lead generation**, or **prospecting**, is the identification of firms and people most likely to buy the seller's offerings. These firms or people become "sales leads" or "prospects."

Sales leads can be obtained in many different ways, most notably through advertising, trade shows and conventions, social media, webinars, or direct mail and telemarketing programs. Favorable publicity also helps to create leads. Company records of past purchases by clients are another excellent source of leads. Many sales professionals are also securing valuable leads from their firm's website, including questions posted by leads about a product or service.

A basic unsophisticated method of lead generation is done through cold calling—a form of lead generation in which the salesperson approaches potential buyers without any prior knowledge of the prospects' needs or financial status. Although cold calling is still used in generating leads, many sales managers have realized the inefficiencies of having their top salespeople use their valuable selling time searching for the proverbial "needle in a haystack." Passing the job of cold calling to a lower-cost employee, typically an internal sales support person, allows salespeople to spend more time and use their relationship-building skills on prospects who have already been identified.

Another way to gather a lead is through a referral—a recommendation from a customer or business associate. The advantages of referrals over other forms of prospecting are highly qualified leads, higher closing rates, larger initial transactions, and shorter sales cycles. Referrals are often as much as 10 times more productive in generating sales than are cold calls. Unfortunately, although many clients are willing to give referrals, most salespeople do not ask for them. Effective sales training can help to overcome this reluctance to ask for referrals. To increase the number of referrals, some companies even pay or send small gifts to customers or suppliers that provide referrals. Generating referrals is one area that social media and technology can usually make much more efficient.

Salespeople should build strong networks to help generate leads. Networking is using friends, business contacts, coworkers, acquaintances, and fellow members in professional and civic organizations to identify potential clients. Indeed, a number of national networking clubs have been started for the sole purpose of generating leads and providing valuable business advice. Increasingly, sales professionals are also using online networking sites, like LinkedIn, to connect with targeted leads and clients around the world—24 hours a day, 7 days a week.

17-5b Step 2: Qualifying Leads

When a prospect shows interest in learning more about a product, the salesperson has the opportunity to follow up, or qualify, the lead. Typically, unqualified prospects give vague or incomplete answers to a salesperson's specific questions, try to evade questions on budgets, and request changes in standard procedures like prices and terms of sale. In contrast, qualified leads are real prospects who answer questions, value the salesperson's time, and are realistic about money and when they are prepared to buy.

Lead qualification involves determining whether the prospect has three things:

1. **A recognized need:** The most basic criterion for determining whether someone is a prospect for a product is a need that is not being satisfied. The salesperson should first consider prospects who are aware of a need, but should not disregard prospects who have not yet recognized that they have one. With a little more information about the product, they may decide they do have a need for it. Preliminary questioning can often provide the salesperson with enough information to determine whether there is a need.

2. **Buying power:** Buying power involves both authority to make the purchase decision and access to funds to pay for it. To avoid wasting time and money, the salesperson needs to identify the buyer's purchasing authority and ability to pay before making a presentation. Organizational charts and information about a firm's credit standing can provide valuable clues.

3. **Receptivity and accessibility:** The prospect must be willing to see and to be accessible to the salesperson. Some prospects simply refuse to see salespeople. Others, because of their stature in their organization, will see only a salesperson or sales manager with similar stature.

Often the task of lead qualification is handled by a telemarketing group or a sales support person who prequalifies the lead for the salesperson. Prequalification systems free sales representatives from the time-consuming task of following up on leads to determine need, buying power, and receptiveness. Prequalification systems may even set up initial appointments with the prospect for the salesperson. The result is more time for the sales force to spend in front of interested customers.

Companies are increasingly using their

cold calling a form of lead generation in which the salesperson approaches potential buyers without any prior knowledge of the prospects' needs or financial status

referral a recommendation to a salesperson from a customer or business associate

networking a process of finding out about potential clients from friends, business contacts, coworkers, acquaintances, and fellow members in professional and civic organizations

lead qualification determination of a sales prospect's (1) recognized need, (2) buying power, and (3) receptivity and accessibility websites and other software to qualify leads. When qualifying leads online, companies want visitors to register, indicate the products and services they are interested in, and provide information on their time frames and resources. Leads from the Internet can then be prioritized (those indicating short time frames, for instance, are given a higher priority) and then transferred to salespeople. Enticing visitors to register also enables companies to customize future electronic interactions.

Personally visiting unqualified prospects wastes valuable salesperson time and company resources. Many leads often go unanswered because salespeople are given no indication as to how qualified the leads are in terms of interest and ability to purchase. Inside salespeople and sales support staff assess leads to maximize successful meetings, while CRM systems provide resources to increase lead follow-up rates. Still, salespeople follow up on only 10 to 15 percent of leads.

17-5c Step 3: Approaching the Customer and Probing Needs

Before approaching customers, the salesperson should learn as much as possible about the prospect's organization and its buyers. This process, called the **preapproach**, describes the "homework" that must be done by the salesperson before contacting the prospect. This may include visiting the company's website; consulting standard reference sources, such as Moody's, Standard & Poor's, or Dun & Bradstreet; or contacting acquaintances or others who may have information about the prospect. Reading the prospect's social media sites (following the company's Twitter feed and reading its Facebook page, for example) is a great way to get to know the company culture, become acquainted with customer needs, and learn more about daily activities.[11] Another preapproach task is to determine whether the actual approach should be a personal visit, a phone call, a letter, or some other form of communication. Note that the preapproach applies to most business-to-business sales and outside consumer sales, but it is usually not possible when consumers approach salespeople in the retail store environment.

During the sales approach, the salesperson either talks to the prospect or secures an appointment to question the prospect further about his or her needs. Experts on relationship selling suggest that salespeople should begin developing mutual trust with their prospect during the approach. Salespeople must sell themselves before they can sell their firm's products. Small talk that projects sincerity and some suggestion of friendship is encouraged to build rapport with the prospect, but remarks that could be construed as insincere should be avoided.

The salesperson's ultimate goal during the approach is to conduct a **needs assessment** to find out as much as possible about the prospect's situation. The salesperson should determine how to maximize the fit between what he or she can offer and what the prospective customer wants. As part of the needs assessment, the consultative salesperson must know everything there is to know about the following:

- **The product or service:** Product knowledge is the cornerstone for conducting a successful needs analysis. The consultative salesperson must be an expert on his or her product or service, including technical specifications, features and benefits, pricing and billing procedures, warranty and service support, performance comparisons with the competition, other customers' experiences with the product, and current advertising and promotional campaign messages. For example, a salesperson who is attempting to sell a Canon copier to a doctor's office should be very knowledgeable about Canon's selection of copiers, their attributes, capabilities, technological specifications, and postpurchase servicing.

- **Customers and their needs:** The salesperson should know more about customers than he knows about himself. That's the secret to relationship and consultative selling, where the salesperson acts not only as a supplier

Financial planning, real estate, and other specialized service industries require a deep understanding of customer needs.

preapproach a process that describes the "homework" that must be done by a salesperson before he or she contacts a prospect

needs assessment a determination of the customer's specific needs and wants and the range of options they have for satisfying them of products and services, but also as a trusted consultant and adviser. The professional salesperson brings business-building ideas and solutions to problems to each client. For example, if the Canon salesperson is asking the "right" questions, then he or she should be able to identify copy-related areas where the doctor's office is losing or wasting money. Rather than just selling a copier, the Canon salesperson can act as a consultant on how the doctor's office can save money and time.

- **The competition:** The salesperson must know as much about the competitor's company and products as he or she knows about his or her own company. Competitive intelligence includes many factors: who the competitors are and what is known about them, whether or not their products are comparable (and to what extent), advantages and disadvantages, and strengths and weaknesses. For example, if the competitor's Xerox copy machine is less expensive than the Canon copier, the doctor's office may be leaning toward purchasing the Xerox. But if the Canon salesperson can point out that the cost of long-term maintenance and toner cartridges is lower for the Canon copier, offsetting its higher initial cost, the salesperson may be able to persuade the doctor's office to purchase the Canon copier.

- **The industry:** Knowing the industry requires active research by the salesperson. This means attending industry and trade association meetings, reading articles published in industry and trade journals, keeping track of legislation and regulations that affect the industry, being aware of product alternatives and innovations from domestic and foreign competition, understanding what is being said online and through social media sites, and having a feel for economic and financial conditions that may affect the industry. It is also important to be aware of economic downturns, as businesses may be looking for less expensive financing options.

Creating a *customer profile* during the approach helps salespeople optimize their time and resources. This profile is then used to help develop an intelligent analysis of the prospect's needs in preparation for the next step, developing and proposing solutions. Customer profile information is typically stored and managed using sales force automation software packages designed for use on laptop computers, smartphones, or tablets. Sales force automation software provides sales reps with a computerized and efficient method of collecting customer information for use during the entire sales process. Further, customer and sales data stored in a computer database can be easily shared among sales team members. The information can also be appended with industry statistics, sales or meeting notes, billing data, and other information that may be pertinent to the prospect or the prospect's company. The more salespeople know about their prospects, the better they can meet their needs.

A salesperson should wrap up the sales approach and need-probing mission by summarizing the prospect's need, problem, and interest. The salesperson should also get a commitment from the customer to some kind of action, whether it is reading promotional material or agreeing to a demonstration. This commitment helps to qualify the prospect further and justify additional time invested by the salesperson. When doing so, however, the salesperson should take care not to be too pushy or overbearing—a good salesperson will read a customer's social cues. The salesperson should reiterate the action he or she promises to take, such as sending information or calling back to provide answers to questions. The date and time of the next call should be set at the conclusion of the sales approach as well as an agenda for the next call in terms of what the salesperson hopes to accomplish, such as providing a demonstration or presenting a solution.

17-5d Step 4: Developing and Proposing Solutions

Once the salesperson has gathered the appropriate information about the client's needs and wants, the next step is to determine whether her company's products or services match the needs of the prospective customer. The salesperson then develops a solution, or possibly several solutions, in which the salesperson's product or service solves the client's problems or meets a specific need.

Salespeople often present their sales proposals to potential customers. Presentations are particularly important in explaining sales solutions and overcoming objections.

These solutions are typically presented to the client in the form of a sales proposal presented at a sales presentation. A **sales proposal** is a written document or professional presentation that outlines how the company's product or service will meet or exceed the client's needs. The **sales presentation** is the formal meeting in which the salesperson has the opportunity to present the sales proposal. The presentation should be explicitly tied to the prospect's expressed needs. Further, the prospect should be involved in the presentation by being encouraged to participate in demonstrations or by exposure to computer exercises, slides, video or audio, flip charts, photographs, and the like. Technology has become an important part of presenting solutions for many salespeople. In the past, salespeople took laptops with them to make presentations. Today, salespeople increasingly carry iPads or other tablets because they are lighter, more flexible, and can easily access information stored in the cloud.

Because the salesperson often has only one opportunity to present solutions, the quality of both the sales proposal and the presentation can make or break the sale. Salespeople must be able to present the proposal and handle any customer objections confidently and professionally. For a powerful presentation, salespeople must be well prepared, use direct eye contact, ask open-ended questions, be poised, use hand gestures and voice inflection, and focus on the customer's needs. Incorporating visual elements that impart valuable information, knowing how to operate the audio/visual or computer equipment being used for the presentation, and making sure the equipment works will make the presentation flow more smoothly. Nothing loses customers faster than a boring or ill-prepared presenter, and equipment mishaps can consume valuable (often limited) time for both the salesperson and customer. Often, customers are more likely to remember how salespeople present themselves than what they actually say.

17-5e Step 5: Handling Objections

Rarely does a prospect say "I'll buy it" right after a presentation. Instead, the prospect often raises objections or asks questions about the proposal and the product. The potential buyer may insist that the price is too high or that the good or service will not satisfy the present need.

One of the first lessons every salesperson learns is that objections to the product should not be taken personally as confrontations

sales proposal a formal written document or professional presentation that outlines how the salesperson's product or service will meet or exceed the prospect's needs

sales presentation a meeting in which the salesperson presents a sales proposal to a prospective buyer

or insults. A good salesperson considers objections a legitimate part of the purchase decision. To handle objections effectively, the salesperson should anticipate specific objections (such as concerns about price); fully investigate the objection with the customer; be aware of what the competition is offering; and, above all, stay calm.

Often salespeople can use objections to close the sale. The customer may try to pit suppliers against each other to drive down the price, so the salesperson should be prepared to point out weaknesses in the competitor's offer and stand by the quality and value of his or her own proposal.

17-5f Step 6: Closing the Sale

At the end of the presentation, the salesperson should ask the customer how they would like to proceed. If the customer exhibits behavior or actions indicating they are ready to purchase, all questions have been answered, and objections have been met, then the salesperson can try to close the sale. Customers often give signals during or after the presentation that they are ready to buy or are not interested. Examples include changes in facial expressions, gestures, and questions asked. The salesperson should look for these signals and respond appropriately.

Closing requires courage and skill. A salesperson should be prepared for either a positive or a negative outcome, and should keep an open mind in the event of the latter.[12] Often, a salesperson will be told "no" flat out. In such a case, the salesperson must be resilient and must be able to handle this type of rejection gracefully and effectively. The typical salesperson makes hundreds—potentially even thousands—of sales calls every year. Many of these are repeat calls to the same group of clients in an attempt to make a single sale.

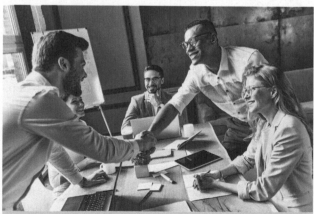

Negotiating and closing the sale require courage and skills. A team effort is often required for companies to complete a deal.

Building and developing a good relationship with the customer is very important. Often, if the salesperson has developed a strong relationship with the customer, only minimal efforts are needed to close a sale (increasing the salesperson's closure rate).

Negotiation often plays a key role in the closing of the sale. **Negotiation** is the process during which both the salesperson and the prospect offer special concessions in an attempt to arrive at a sales agreement. For example, the salesperson may offer a price cut, free installation, or a trial order. Effective negotiators, however, avoid using price as a negotiation tool and are able to show the greater value in their products or services. Because companies spend millions on advertising and product development to create value, when salespeople give in to price negotiations too quickly, it decreases the value of the product. Salespeople should also be prepared to ask for trade-offs and try to avoid giving unilateral concessions. Moreover, if the customer asks for a 5 percent discount, the salesperson should ask for something in return, such as higher volume or more flexibility in delivery schedules.

More and more U.S. companies are expanding their marketing and selling efforts into global markets. Salespeople selling in foreign markets should tailor their presentations and closing styles to each market. Personalities and skills that are successful in some countries will be absolute failures in others. For instance, if a salesperson is an excellent closer and always focuses on the next sale, doing business in Latin America might be difficult because customers there prefer to take a long time building a personal relationship with their suppliers. Similarly, personal space and physical contact are treated differently in various cultures. In many European and South American cultures, it is customary to kiss a business associate on both cheeks instead of shaking hands.[13]

17-5g Step 7: Following Up

A salesperson's responsibilities do not end with making the sale and placing the order. One of the most important aspects of the job is **follow-up**—the final step in the selling process, in which the salesperson must ensure delivery schedules are met, goods or services perform as promised, and buyers' employees are properly trained to use the products.

In the traditional sales approach, follow-up with the customer is generally limited to successful product delivery and performance. A basic goal of relationship selling is to motivate customers to come back again and again by developing and nurturing long-term relationships.

Most businesses depend on repeat sales, and repeat sales depend on thorough and continued follow-up by the salesperson. When customers feel abandoned, cognitive dissonance arises and repeat sales decline. Today, this issue is more pertinent than ever because customers are far less loyal to brands and vendors. Buyers are more inclined to look for the best deal, especially when they experience poor postsale follow-up. Automated email follow-up marketing—a combination of sales automation and Internet technology—is one tool that some marketers are using in an effort to enhance customer satisfaction and bring in more business. After the initial contact with a prospect, a software program automatically sends a series of personalized email messages over a period of time. Another approach is to use contact software like Skype, which facilitates live face-to-face exchanges via videoconferencing and direct access to cloud-based data centers. Mobile phones allow immediate visual contact through apps like FaceTime and Google Duo.[14]

17-5h Social Media and the Sales Process

Social media has specifically impacted the sales process through what is referred to as "social selling." Social selling focuses on using social network sites (SNS), such as LinkedIn, Twitter, and Facebook, to help with the sales process. Salespeople engage in social selling activities such as research, prospecting, networking, and relationship building.[16] Salespeople share and/or develop relevant content to answer questions posed by current and potential users. Relationships are built between salespeople providing the content and potential future customers. While the process may not generate immediate sales, foundations for relationships are already established when a prospect decides to move forward with the buying process. When that happens, the salesperson holds at least an initial advantage over the competition.

The modern sales presentation, using social media, can address likely concerns before they are raised. Success stories can be shared via Facebook. YouTube can be used to provide additional information and show individuals actually using the product.[17] Using swimming pools as an example, different options can be demonstrated for several different pools that were built by the salesperson's company.

negotiation the process during which both the salesperson and the prospect offer special concessions in an attempt to arrive at a sales agreement

follow-up the final step of the selling process, in which the salesperson ensures delivery schedules are met, goods or services perform as promised, and the buyers' employees are properly trained to use the products

For example, differences in decking around the pool can be highlighted or different finishes within the pool can be demonstrated. With social media tools, updates and changes can be easily adjusted from one presentation to the next, unlike the use of a printed sales packet that requires more effort, time, and money to change.

As with the initial selling process and presentation stage, social selling is critical in the feedback stage. Many firms are asking customers not only to provide them feedback in person, they are also requesting that customers complete reviews using social media platforms. Often, companies offer a free service call or discounts for future business if a customer completes an online review.

While using social media tools might be more effective in certain stages of the sales process, research suggests that salespeople's use of social media tools often occurs early in the sales process (generating leads to developing and proposing solutions) and then again at the end of the sales process (follow-up).[18] This leaves handling objections and closing the sale better served by face-to-face interactions between the salesperson and buyer. If customers feel objections can be handled in a non–face-to-face context, however, then companies potentially would be better off with an inside sales force or possibly use of artificial intelligence, instead of the costly outside sales force.

17-6 SALES MANAGEMENT

There is an old adage in business that nothing happens until a sale is made. Without sales, there is no need for accountants, production workers, or even a company president. Sales provide the fuel that keeps the company engines humming. Companies such as Cisco Systems, International Paper, Johnson Controls, and thousands of other manufacturers would cease to exist without successful salespeople. Even companies such as Procter & Gamble (P&G) and Kraft Foods, which mainly sell consumer goods and use extensive advertising campaigns, still rely on salespeople to move products through the channel of distribution. Thus, sales management must be one of every firm's most critical specialties. Effective sales management stems from a success-oriented sales force that accomplishes its mission economically and efficiently. Poor sales management can lead to unmet sales and profit objectives or even to the downfall of the corporation.

quota a statement of the salesperson's sales goals, usually based on sales volume

Just as selling is a personal relationship, so is sales management. Although the sales manager's basic job is to maximize sales at a reasonable cost while also maximizing profits, he or she also has many other important responsibilities and decisions:

1. Defining sales goals and the sales process
2. Determining the sales force structure
3. Recruiting and training the sales force
4. Compensating and motivating the sales force
5. Evaluating the sales force

17-6a Defining Sales Goals and the Sales Process

Effective sales management begins with a determination of sales goals. Without goals to achieve, salesperson performance would be mediocre at best, and the company would likely fail. Like any marketing objective, sales goals should be stated in clear, precise, and measurable terms and should always specify a time frame for their completion. Overall sales force goals are usually stated in terms of desired dollar sales volume, market share, and/or profit level. For example, a life insurance company may have a goal to sell $50 million in life insurance policies annually, to attain a 12 percent market share, and/or to achieve $4 million in profits. Individual salespeople are also assigned goals in the form of quotas. A **quota** is a statement of the salesperson's sales goals, usually based on sales volume alone, but sometimes including other focuses, such as key accounts (those with greatest potential), new account generation, volume of repeat sales, profit margin, and specific product mixes sold.

17-6b Determining the Sales Force Structure

Because personal selling is so costly, no sales department can afford to be disorganized. Proper design helps the sales manager organize and delegate sales duties and provide direction for salespeople. Sales departments are most often organized by geographic regions, product lines, marketing functions performed (such as account development or account maintenance), markets, industries, individual clients, or accounts. For example, the sales force for Hewlett-Packard (HP) could be organized into sales territories covering New England, the Midwest, the South, and the West Coast or into distinct groups selling different product lines. HP salespeople might also be assigned to specific industries or markets (such as the telecommunications industry), or to key clients (such as AT&T, Sprint, and Verizon).

Market or industry-based structures and key account structures are gaining popularity in today's competitive

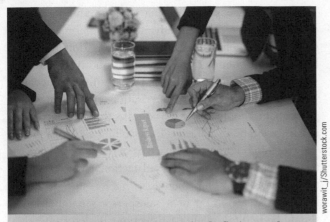

Part of sales management is defining sales goals for the sales force.

worawit_j/Shutterstock.com

selling environment, especially with the emphasis on relationship selling. Being familiar with one industry or market allows sales reps to become experts in their fields, and thereby, offer better solutions and service. Further, by organizing the sales force around specific customers, many companies hope to improve customer service, encourage collaboration with other arms of the company, and unite salespeople in customer-focused sales teams.

17-6c Recruiting and Training the Sales Force

Sales force recruitment should be based on an accurate, detailed description of the sales task as defined by the sales manager. For example, GE uses its website to provide prospective salespeople with explanations of different career entry paths and video accounts of what it is like to have a career at GE. Aside from the usual characteristics, such as level of experience or education, what traits should sales managers look for in applicants?

- **Ego strength:** Great salespeople should have a strong, healthy self-esteem and the ability to quickly bounce back from rejection.

- **Sense of urgency and competitiveness:** These traits push their sales to completion, as well as help salespeople to persuade customers.

- **Assertiveness:** Effective salespeople have the ability to be firm in one-to-one negotiations, to lead the sales process, and to get their point across confidently, without being overbearing or aggressive.

- **Sociable:** Wanting to interact with others is a necessary trait for great salespeople.

- **Risk takers:** Great salespeople are willing to put themselves in less-than-assured situations, and in doing so, often are able to close unlikely sales.

- **Capable of understanding complex concepts and ideas:** Quick thinking and comprehension allow salespeople to quickly grasp and sell new products or enter new sales areas.

- **Creativity:** Great salespeople develop client solutions in creative ways.

- **Empathetic:** Empathy—the ability to place oneself in someone else's shoes—enables salespeople to understand the client.

In addition to these traits, almost all successful salespeople say their sales style is relationship oriented rather than transaction oriented.[19]

Social media has emerged as an ideal tool for recruiters searching for qualified salespeople. LinkedIn is one of the most important sites for recruiters to find information about potential sales recruits. This includes searching by industry, company, job title, and even geographic area. For potential recruits, understanding how to develop a complete profile that highlights skills and talents viewed as desirable by prospective employers is key. Further, in the event recruiters examine a person's social media profile, it is critical that negative information (e.g., photos of questionable behavior) from other sites, including Facebook, does not appear.

After the sales recruit has been hired and given a brief orientation, initial training begins. A new salesperson generally receives instruction in company policies and practices, selling techniques, product knowledge, industry and customer characteristics, and nonselling duties, such as filling out sales and market information reports and using a sales automation computer program. Many companies provide new salespeople with sales coaches, who provide individualized one-on-one feedback in an experiential-based learning environment. This way, the new hire can acquire additional and more nuanced skills for long-term success.[20] Continuous training then keeps salespeople up to date on changes in products and services, technology, the competitive landscape, and sales techniques, among other issues. Continuous training can occur during sales meetings, annual meetings, or during the course of everyday business. Individuals seeking sales positions also need training in the basics of social selling and company policies on the use of sales media platforms. This is especially true for salespeople who did not grow up with social media technologies. Another consideration, however, is younger salespeople seem more reluctant to seek face-to-face

EXHIBIT 17.3 COMPARING INSIDE AND OUTSIDE SALES

Outside Salespeople	Inside Salespeople
Self-starters	Must be articulate and have effective communication skills
Manage their own schedules	More control over schedule
More frequent travel expectations	Often surrounded by others in an office environment
Ongoing workplace schedules	Office politics often an issue
Personality easily adapts to new environments and people	Rely heavily on cold calls
High importance placed on appearance	Cannot physically show the product
Less direct supervision	More direct supervision

Adapted from: Ron Coxsom, "Inside or Outside Sales?" Monster, https://www.monster.com/career-advice/article/Inside-Sales-or-Outside-Sales, accessed March 2019.

contacts, given they have grown up with social media and may be more comfortable communicating through social media versus in person.[21] Thus, they may need to be encouraged and actually trained on how to successfully complete face-to-face selling.

Training can take place in a classroom environment, in the field, or using online modules. Given the growth in learning technologies, sales training has transformed from relying solely on traditional methods (such as live sales calls, inside sales, and role playing) to eLearning methods, including the use of webinars and online tutorials. While mixed reviews are provided about eLearning, firms can realize both convenience and cost savings from the use of these tools.[22] When conducting job training in the field using a live sales call, the trainer should be a more experienced salesperson or sales manager. This type of training provides real-world experience for the trainee, but it may reduce the effectiveness of the call because it often entails reduced selling time. Another form of training involves the trainee working in inside sales, primarily phone-based sales, for an extended period of time before being given an outside territory to cover. This enables the trainee to develop selling skills with less important and/or less established accounts before facing the challenges of outside sales. Exhibit 17.3 provides key differences between inside and outside sales.

17-6d Compensating and Motivating the Sales Force

Compensation planning is one of the sales manager's toughest jobs. Only good planning will ensure that compensation attracts, motivates, and retains good salespeople. Generally, companies and industries with lower levels of compensation suffer higher turnover rates.

This increases costs (including training and recruiting costs), decreases sales effectiveness, and harms relationship management. Therefore, compensation needs to be competitive enough to attract and motivate the best salespeople. Firms sometimes take profit into account when developing their compensation plans. Instead of paying salespeople on overall volume, they pay according to the profitability achieved from selling each product.

Still other companies tie a part of the salesperson's total compensation to customer satisfaction. As the emphasis on relationship selling increases, many sales managers believe that a portion of a salesperson's compensation should be tied to a client's satisfaction. To determine this, sales managers can use surveys to question clients about a salesperson's ability to create realistic expectations and also their responsiveness to customer needs.

Although a compensation-based plan motivates a salesperson to sell, sometimes it is not enough to produce the volume of sales or the profit margin required by sales management. Sales managers, therefore, often offer rewards or incentives, such as recognition at ceremonies, plaques, and/or monetary-based rewards, such as vacations, merchandise, pay raises, and cash bonuses. Cash awards are the most popular sales incentive and are used by virtually all companies. Mary Kay Cosmetics offers a unique type of incentive, whereby salespeople can earn the use of different types of vehicles—from a lowly Ford Fiesta all the way up to the coveted pink Mary Kay Cadillac. To qualify for these vehicles, salespeople must reach certain sales quotas, and social media tools can facilitate achievement of these goals.[23]

Recognition and rewards may help increase overall sales volume, add new accounts, improve morale and goodwill, move slow items, and bolster slow sales. They can also be used to achieve short- and long-term objectives, such as reducing overstocked inventory and meeting a monthly or quarterly sales goal. In motivating their sales force, however, sales managers must be careful not to encourage unethical behavior.

17-6e Evaluating the Sales Force

The final task of sales managers is evaluating the effectiveness and performance of the sales force. To evaluate the sales force, the sales manager needs feedback—that is, regular information from salespeople. Typical performance measures include sales volume, contribution to profit, calls per order, sales or profits per call, customer satisfaction, or percentage of calls that achieve specific goals, such as sales of products that the firm is heavily promoting.

Performance information helps the sales manager monitor a salesperson's progress through the sales cycle and pinpoint where breakdowns might be occurring. For example, by learning the number of prospects an individual salesperson has in each step of the sales cycle process and determining where prospects are falling out of the cycle, a manager can determine how effective a salesperson might be at lead generation, needs assessment, proposal generation, presenting, closing, and follow-up stages. This information can then tell a manager which sales skills might need to be reassessed or retrained. For example, if a sales manager notices that a sales rep seems to be letting too many prospects slip away after presenting proposals, it might mean he or she needs help with developing proposals, handling objections, or closing sales.

Social media sites can also help assess the performance of salespeople. Using customer reviews, sales managers can better determine what salespeople are doing well and not so well. Further, negative reviews can tell sales managers where salespeople may be falling short. In our pool example, reviews might be posted about a company indicating the salesperson never showed up to an appointment, failed to follow up with a price quote, or was not as knowledgeable as competitors' salespeople. This information can help a sales manager determine areas for improvement for an individual salesperson.

17-7 CUSTOMER RELATIONSHIP MANAGEMENT AND THE SALES PROCESS

As we have discussed throughout the text, customer relationship management (CRM) is the ultimate goal of a new trend in marketing that focuses on understanding customers as individuals instead of as part of a group. To do this, marketers are making their communications more customer-specific using the CRM cycle, covered in Chapter 8, and by developing relationships with their customers through touch points and data mining. CRM was initially popularized as one-to-one marketing. But CRM is a much broader approach to understanding and serving customer needs than is one-to-one marketing.

Throughout the text, our discussion of a CRM system has assumed two key points. First, customers take center stage in any organization. Second, the business must manage the customer relationship across all points of customer contact throughout the entire organization. By identifying customer relationships, understanding the customer base, and capturing customer data, marketers and salespeople can leverage the information not only to

develop deeper relationships but also to close more sales with loyal customers in a more efficient manner.

17-7a Identify Customer Relationships

Companies that have CRM systems follow a customer-centric focus or model. **Customer-centric** is an internal management philosophy similar to the marketing concept discussed in Chapter 1. Under this philosophy, the company customizes its product and service offering based on data generated through interactions between the customer and the company. This philosophy transcends all functional areas of the business, producing an internal system in which all of the company's decisions and actions are a direct result of customer information.

Each unit of a business typically has its own way of recording what it learns, and perhaps, even has its own customer information system. The departments' different interests make it difficult to pull all of the customer information together in one place using a common format. To overcome this problem, companies using CRM rely on knowledge management. **Knowledge management** is a process through which customer information is centralized and shared in order to enhance the relationship between customers and the organization. Information collected includes experiential observations, comments, customer actions, and facts about the customer.

As Chapter 1 explained, *empowerment* involves delegating authority to solve customers' problems. Usually, organizational representatives, for example salespeople, are able to make changes during interactions with customers through phone, fax, email, social media, or face-to-face interactions.

An **interaction** occurs when a customer and a company representative exchange information and develop learning relationships. With CRM, the customer—not the organization—defines the terms of the interaction, often by stating his or her preferences. The organization responds by designing products and services around customers' desired experiences.

The success of CRM— building lasting and profitable relationships—can be directly measured by the effectiveness of the

customer-centric a philosophy under which the company customizes its product and service offerings based on data generated through interactions between the customer and the company

knowledge management the process by which customer information is centralized and shared in order to enhance the relationship between customers and the organization

interaction the point at which a customer and a company representative exchange information and develop learning relationships interaction between the customer and the organization. In fact, what further differentiates CRM from other strategic initiatives is the organization's ability to establish and manage interactions with its current customer base. The more latitude (empowerment) a company gives its representatives, the more likely the interaction will conclude in a way that satisfies the customer.

17-7b Understand Interactions of the Current Customer Base

The interaction between the customer and the organization is the foundation on which a CRM system is built. Only through effective interactions can organizations learn about the expectations of their customers, generate and manage knowledge about them, negotiate mutually satisfying commitments, and build long-term relationships.

Exhibit 17.4 illustrates the customer-centric approach for managing customer interactions. Following a customer-centric approach, an interaction can occur through different communication channels, such as a phone, the Internet, or a salesperson. Any activity or touch point a customer has with an organization, either directly or indirectly, constitutes an interaction.

Companies that effectively manage customer interactions recognize that data provided by customers affect a wide variety of **touch points**. In a CRM system, touch points are all areas of a business where customers have contact with the company and from which data might be gathered. Touch points might include a customer registering for a particular service; a customer communicating with customer service for product information; a customer completing and returning the warranty information card for a product; or a customer talking with salespeople, delivery personnel, and product installers. Data gathered at these touch points, once interpreted, provide information that affects touch points inside the company. Interpreted information may be redirected to marketing research to develop profiles of extended warranty purchasers, to production to analyze recurring problems and repair components, to accounting to establish cost-control models for repair service calls, and to sales for better customer profiling and segmentation.

WEB-BASED INTERACTIONS Web-based interactions are an increasingly popular touch point for customers to communicate with companies on their own terms. Web users can evaluate and purchase products,

> **touch points** areas of a business where customers have contact with the company and from which data might be gathered

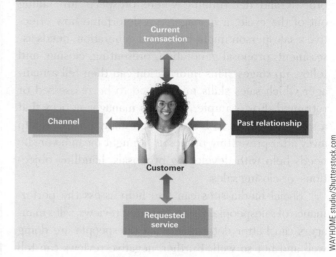

EXHIBIT 17.4 CUSTOMER-CENTRIC APPROACH FOR MANAGING CUSTOMER INTERACTIONS

WAYHOME studio/Shutterstock.com

make reservations, input preferential data, and provide customer feedback on services and products. Data from these web-based interactions are then captured, compiled, and used to segment customers, refine marketing efforts, develop new products, and deliver a degree of individual customization to improve customer relationships.

SOCIAL CRM As social media have become more popular many companies have begun to use these media for "social CRM." ZDNet journalist Paul Greenberg recently named Salesforce.com, Ernst & Young Advisory, and Microsoft as Watchlist Elite companies to watch in the field of social CRM.[24] Essentially, social CRM takes the most successful aspects of traditional CRM, such as behavioral targeting, and expands them to include ways to engage customers through social media. This new paradigm includes a new customer recommendation value, called the *net promoter score*. The net promoter score measures how much a customer influences the behavior of other customers through recommendations on social media. Its ultimate purpose is to gather all consumer interactions into a single database so that they can be analyzed and used to improve communication. Social CRM also enables marketers to focus more on the relationship aspect of CRM. For example, REI empowers customers to "carve your own adventure" through its YouTube channel. JetBlue uses Facebook and Twitter to provide advice and updates to travelers. To use social CRM effectively, companies must understand which sites customers use, whether they post opinions, and who the major influencers in the category are. They

Domino's Pizza stimulates customer engagement with its Chatbot ordering system.

can then marry this information with behavioral data like purchases and purchase frequency.

POINT-OF-SALE INTERACTIONS Another touch point is through **point-of-sale interactions** in stores or at information kiosks. Many point-of-sale software programs enable customers to easily provide information about themselves without feeling violated. The information is then used for marketing and merchandising activities and to accurately identify the store's best customers and the types of products they buy. Data collected at point-of-sale interactions are also used to increase customer satisfaction through the development of in-store services and customer recognition promotions.

17-7c Capture Customer Data

Vast amounts of data can be obtained from the interactions between an organization and its customers. Therefore, in a CRM system, the issue is not how much data can be obtained, but rather what types of data should be acquired and how the data can be used effectively for relationship enhancement.

The traditional approach for acquiring data from customers is through channel interactions. Channel interactions include store visits, conversations with salespeople, interactions via the Web, traditional phone conversations, and wireless communications. In a CRM system, channel interactions are viewed as prime information sources based on the channel selected to initiate the interaction, rather than on the data acquired. In some cases, companies use online chat to answer customer questions about products they are looking for. For example, 24 Hour Fitness has an online chat window that opens when a potential customer begins to review the website. If the visitor remains on the site, the online chat window asks if he or she needs help finding something specific.

Interactions between the company and the customer facilitate the collection of large amounts of data. Companies can obtain not only simple contact information (name, address, phone number) but also data pertaining to the customer's current relationship with the organization—past purchase history, quantity and frequency of purchases, average amount spent on purchases, sensitivity to promotional activities, and so forth.

In this manner, a large amount of information can be captured from one individual customer across several touch points. Multiply this by the thousands of customers across all of the touch points within an organization, and the volume of data can rapidly become unmanageable for company personnel. The large volume of data resulting from a CRM initiative can be managed effectively only through technology. Once customer data are collected, the

point-of-sale interactions a touch point in stores or information kiosks that uses software to enable customers to easily provide information about themselves without feeling violated question of who owns those data becomes extremely salient. In its privacy statement, Toysmart.com declared that it would never sell information registered at its website—including children's names and birth dates—to a third party. When the company filed for bankruptcy protection, it said that the information it collected constituted a company asset that needed to be sold off to pay creditors. Despite the outrage at this announcement, many dot-coms closing their doors found they had little in the way of assets and followed Toysmart's lead.

17-7d Leverage Customer Information

Data mining can be used to identify the most profitable customers and prospects. Managers can then design tailored marketing strategies to best appeal to the identified segments. In CRM, this is commonly referred to as leveraging customer information to facilitate enhanced relationships with customers. Exhibit 17.5 shows some common CRM marketing database applications.

CAMPAIGN MANAGEMENT Through campaign management, all areas of the company participate in the development of programs targeted to customers. **Campaign management** involves monitoring and leveraging customer interactions to sell a company's products and to increase customer service. Campaigns are based directly on data obtained from customers through various interactions. Campaign management includes monitoring the success of the communications based on customer reactions through sales, orders, callbacks to the company, and so on. If a campaign appears unsuccessful, it is evaluated and changed to better achieve the company's desired objective.

Campaign management involves developing customized product and service offerings for the appropriate customer segment, pricing these offerings attractively, and communicating these offers in a manner that enhances customer relationships. Customizing product and service offerings requires managing multiple interactions with customers, as well as giving priority to the products and services that are viewed as most desirable for a specifically designated customer. Even within a highly defined market segment, individual customer differences will emerge. Therefore, interactions among customers must focus on individual experiences, expectations, and desires.

RETAINING LOYAL CUSTOMERS If a company

campaign management
developing product or service offerings customized for the appropriate customer segment and then pricing and communicating these offerings for the purpose of enhancing customer relationships

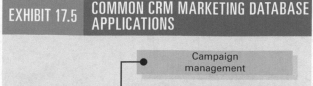

EXHIBIT 17.5 COMMON CRM MARKETING DATABASE APPLICATIONS

CRM Marketing Database
- Campaign management
- Retaining loyal customers
- Cross-selling other products or services
- Designing targeted marketing communications
- Reinforcing customer purchase decisions
- Inducing product trial by new customers
- Increasing effectiveness of distribution channel marketing
- Improving customer service

has identified its best customers, then it should make every effort to maintain and increase their loyalty. When a company retains an additional 5 percent of its customers each year, profits will increase by as much as 125 percent. What's more, improving customer retention by a mere 2 percent can decrease costs by as much as 10 percent. Loyalty programs reward loyal customers for making multiple purchases. The objective is to build long-term, mutually beneficial relationships between a company and its key customers.

CROSS-SELLING OTHER PRODUCTS AND SERVICES CRM provides many opportunities to cross-sell related products. Marketers can use the database to match product profiles and consumer profiles so that they can cross-sell products to customers that match their demographic, lifestyle, or behavioral characteristics. The financial services industry uses cross-selling better than most other industries do. Cross-selling is a key part of Wells Fargo's strategy, for example, and is a large contributor to the company's success in the industry. After engaging with customers to determine their financial needs and aspirations, Wells Fargo reps work to determine how the company's wide range of products can synergize to meet or exceed those financial goals.[25]

Internet companies use product and customer profiling to reveal cross-selling opportunities while customers surf their sites. Past purchases, tracking programs, and the site a surfer is referred from give online marketers clues about the surfer's interests and what items to cross-sell. Amazon, for example, has used profiling to better meet customer needs for years. The company systematically compares individuals' shopping habits and online activities to those of other Amazon customers in order to make better tailored recommendations. Customers are also able to proactively rate products, review products, add products to wishlists, recommend products, and save products for a later purchase—all of which make for a more customized experience.[26]

DESIGNING TARGETED MARKETING COMMUNICATIONS Using transaction and purchase data, a database allows marketers to track customers' relationships to the company's products and services and modify the marketing message accordingly.

Customers can also be segmented into infrequent users, moderate users, and heavy users. A segmented communications strategy can then be developed based on which group the customer falls into. Communications to infrequent users might encourage repeat purchases through a direct incentive, such as a limited-time price discount for ordering again. Communications to moderate users may use fewer incentives and more reinforcement of past purchase decisions. Communications to heavy users would be designed around loyalty and reinforcement of the purchase, rather than around price promotions.

18 | Social Media and Marketing

LEARNING OUTCOMES

After studying this chapter, you will be able to…

18-1 Describe social media, how they are used, and their relations to integrated marketing communications

18-2 Explain how to create a social media campaign

18-3 Evaluate the various methods of measurement for social media

18-4 Explain consumer behavior on social media

18-5 Describe the social media tools in a marketer's toolbox and how they are useful

18-6 Describe the impact of mobile technology on social media

18-7 Understand the aspects of developing a social media plan

18-1 WHAT ARE SOCIAL MEDIA?

The most exciting thing to happen to marketing and promotion in recent years is the increasing use of digital platforms to promote brands, particularly using social media. Social media have changed the way marketers can communicate messages with their brands—from mass messages to intimate conversations. As marketing moves into social media, marketers must remember that for most people, social media are meant to be a social experience, not a marketing experience. In fact, the term *social media* means different things to different people, though most people think it refers to specific digital platforms like Facebook, Twitter, or Instagram. **Social media** is any tool or service that uses the Internet to facilitate conversations.[1] But social media can also be defined relative to traditional advertising like television and magazines: whereas traditional marketing media offer a mass media method of interacting with consumers, social media offer more one-to-one ways to meet consumers. However, social media should be an integral part of any promotional campaign, regardless of what other methods are used.

Several key usage numbers include:

- There are 2.46 billion social media users worldwide, with a steady increase forecasted through 2021;
- Eighty-one percent of Internet users in the United States are social media users;
- While North America currently has the largest number of social media users, the largest growth is expected in China and India;
- Facebook is the largest social media platform, with over 2 billion active users. YouTube, Instagram and Qzone round out the list of the top platforms.[2]

Social media implies several things for marketers and the ways they interact with their customers. First, marketers must realize that they often do not control the content on social media sites. Consumers are sharing their thoughts, wishes, and experiences about brands with the world through social media. Because of this level of visibility and discussion, marketers must understand that having a great campaign is not enough—the product or service must be great, too.

Second, the ability to share experiences quickly and with such large numbers of people amplifies the impact of word of mouth in ways that can affect a company's bottom line. Celebrities have taken advantage of their ability to reach audiences through social media. Typically, celebrities will choose a platform like Instagram (Christiano Ronaldo, Kylie Jenner, Selena Gomez) or Twitter (Katy Perry, Justin Bieber) to reach their fans, and then use these platforms to influence their purchasing behaviors. Companies have also

> "Interaction and engagement [on social media] is something that you don't necessarily see in traditional media. That's why we [at Ford] continue to accelerate our digital advertising investment to more than 25% of our media dollars."
>
> —JIM FARLEY, FORD GLOBAL SALES AND MARKETING VICE PRESIDENT

Katy Perry's 110 million Twitter followers and 78 million Instagram followers give her a very large reach on social media.

Tinseltown/Shutterstock.com

and interact with consumers than traditional advertising. Social media include tools and platforms like social networks, blogs, microblogs, and media sharing sites that can be accessed through a growing number of devices, including smartphones, wearables, e-readers, digital assistants, televisions, tablets, smart watches, and video game consoles. This technology changes almost daily, offering consumers new ways to experience social media platforms. Therefore, social media must constantly innovate with new measurement tools to keep up with consumer demands and the ability to measure their impact.

Finally, social media enables marketers to have much more direct and meaningful conversations with customers. Social media offer a form of relationship building that brings customers and brands closer. Indeed, the culture of *participation* that social media fosters may well prove to be a fifth "P" for marketing. For example, sports brand Adidas recently initiated a long-form video project following the Tango Squad FC. The project is geared toward the influencer communities for Adidas's Tango Squads. The Tango Squad consists of eight soccer players in the UK and Europe. During each video, the team trains with players from clubs like AC Milan and Manchester United. The video series builds on the existing popularity of the Tango Squads and a network of football fans living in 15 cities worldwide who communicate with the brand via messaging apps like Facebook Messenger and WhatsApp. The Tango Squads are also given exclusive access to Adidas football content, new product information, and opportunities to work with the sponsored clubs and players.[7]

At the most basic level, consumers of social media want to exchange information, collaborate with others, and have conversations. Social media are designed for people to socialize with each other and have changed how and where conversations take place, even globalizing human interaction through rapidly evolving technology. Some technology enables companies to connect directly with consumers. Facebook Messenger Bots and Facebook Live, for example, enable customers to interact with companies in real time. BuzzFeed hosted one Facebook Live event that attracted more than 800,000 viewers.[8] Clearly, conversations are happening online. It is up to marketers to decide whether engaging in those conversations will be profitable and to find the most effective method of entering the conversation.

Companies are beginning to understand the implications of their employees' activities on social media. In fact, there have been several examples of employees

used social media to connect with customers. For example, fashion brands like Chanel and Louis Vuitton use Instagram as a way to promote their products and luxury lifestyle.[3] The total reach of these brands is difficult to quantify, but it is unquestionably massive.[4]

Third, social media have enabled marketers to listen more effectively. Dell, L.L.Bean, and Gatorade have taken social media monitoring to a whole new level, as they literally put social media at the center of their marketing efforts.[5] Without social media, it would have been much more difficult for Uber to learn that its customers were upset by their response to a national travel ban. Uber monitored social media, saw the responses, and urged customers not to delete the Uber app from their mobile devices.[6]

social media any tool or service that uses the Internet to facilitate conversations

Fourth, social media provide more sophisticated methods of measuring how marketers meet

Musical.ly cofounder and co-CEO Alex Zhu speaks at TechCrunch. The Musical.ly app, popular with teens and tweens, enables users to post short music videos of themselves lip-syncing.

being fired for airing their personal feelings on social media platforms. To combat this, many companies have begun developing social media policies on what can be posted and what is inappropriate. Some companies have rules concerning corporate blogs, Facebook, Twitter, LinkedIn, and even online comments. Adidas has a concise and less formal social media policy. The Associated Press, conversely, has a comprehensive policy with great examples. It tells employees to be careful who they follow, what they share, and any opinions they post. Similarly, Best Buy has a set of social media guidelines that make it clear any negative posts regarding religion, race, or ethnicity will not be tolerated.[9] Having a social media policy can certainly help mitigate risk, but there is no guarantee employees will not occasionally slip up.

Marketers are interested in online communication because it is wildly popular: brands, companies, individuals, and celebrities all promote their messages online.[10] Some companies go so far as to require Facebook and Twitter training for high-profile employees. Employees at Zappos receive Twitter training and are encouraged both to post on social media about their experiences at work and to share resources that consumers might find useful. Zappos also has a leaderboard to show who among its employees has the most followers.[11]

18-1a How Consumers Use Social Media

Before beginning to understand how to leverage social media for brand building, it is important to understand which social media consumers are using and how they are using them. It is safe to assume that many customers are active on Instagram and Facebook. But targeting can also be accomplished by using less ubiquitous platforms. Tencent QQ, WeChat, and Sina Weibo, for example, are the largest social media platforms in China. Bumble, OkCupid, and Tinder are great platforms to reach young adult singles. Teens tend to use platforms like Snapchat, Instagram, YouTube and TikTok. While Facebook is used widely by adults, its popularity among younger consumers is decreasing. Dedicated messaging apps have become more popular in terms of social media. These include WhatsApp, Groupme, Viber, WeChat, and Facebook Messenger.[12]

Videos are another of the most popular tools marketers can use to reach consumers, and YouTube is by far the largest online video repository—it has more content than any major television network. TikTok is an app where users can post short music videos of themselves lip-syncing. Similarly, Facebook Live, which enables live streaming of events, is becoming ever-more popular with consumers and brands alike.[13] The bottom line, according to Universal McCann's Comparative Study on Social Media Trends, is "if you are online, you are using social media."[14]

Increased usage of alternative platforms like smartphones, tablets and other mobile devices, has further contributed to the proliferation of social media usage. In the United States, 96 percent of adults own a mobile phone, and 77 percent of these own a smartphone. These numbers jump to 100 percent and 92 percent for adults ages 18 to 29.[15] Tablet usage has hit critical mass among mobile surfers—177 million U.S. adults own some sort of tablet. According to Mark Donovan, senior vice president of mobile at ComScore, "Tablets are one of the most rapidly adopted consumer technologies in history and are poised to fundamentally disrupt the way people engage with the digital world both on-the-go and perhaps most notably, in the home."[16] The overall impact of tablet computing on social media (and thus on the discipline of marketing) has yet to be recognized, but given the incredible impact the smartphone has had in its short life, tablets could indeed prove to be game changing.

SOCIAL COMMERCE An area of growth in social media is social commerce, which combines social media with the basics of e-commerce. **Social commerce** is a

> **social commerce** a subset of e-commerce that involves the interaction and user contribution aspects of social online media to assist online buying and selling of products and services

Social commerce sites like Yelp help consumers make more informed decisions on product and service purchases.

IB Photography/Shutterstock.com

subset of e-commerce that involves the interaction and user contribution aspects of social online media to assist online buying and selling of products and services.[17] Basically, social commerce relies on user-generated content on a website to assist consumers with purchases. Pinterest lets users collect ideas and products from all over the Web and "pin" favorite items to individually curated pinboards. Other users browse boards by theme, keyword, or product; click on what they like; and either visit the originating sites or re-pin the items on their own pinboards. Companies like Rewards Style use influencers who post photos of clothes and accessories on Instagram, and encourage customer to purchase straight from the liketoknowit site. Social commerce sites often include ratings and recommendations (as Amazon.com does) and social shopping tools (as Groupon does). In general, social commerce sites are designed to help consumers make more informed decisions about which products and services to purchase.

Social commerce has generated millions in revenue, with nearly half of all online sales coming through social media sites.[18] There are seven types of social commerce:

- Peer-to-peer sales platforms (like eBay and Etsy)
- Social networking websites driven by sales (like Pinterest and Twitter)
- Group buying platforms (like Groupon)
- Peer recommendation sites (like Yelp and JustBoughtIt)
- User-curated shopping sites (like The Fancy and Lyst)
- Participatory commerce platforms (like Kickstarter and Threadless)

- Social shopping sites (like Motilo and GoTryItOn).[19]
- Shoppable videos (from retailers like Burberry and Diesel).

As companies migrate to social commerce sites such as Pinterest, consumer interactions across the sites may change. One way companies are leveraging Pinterest's user base is by running promotions. For example, Favorite Family Recipes offered two iPads as prizes for users who followed and pinned the logos of 13 associated Pinterest boards. This type of promotion can undermine the authenticity that many consumers rely on when using social commerce sites. But some companies hope to cultivate authentic relationships by staying away from promotions. Whole Foods pins items that relate to the company's values but are not promotional or linked back to the Whole Foods site. Customers have built relationships with Whole Foods based on upcycled products and recipes, rather than on free products.[20]

18-1b Social Media and Integrated Marketing Communications

While marketers typically employ a social media strategy alongside traditional channels like print and broadcast, many budget pendulums are swinging toward social media. In the United States, digital marketing spending will grow from $83 billion in 2017 to almost $120 billion in 2021. Paid search, display advertising, social media advertising, online video advertising, and email marketing will account for almost 50 percent of all advertising by 2021.[21]

A unique consequence of social media is the widespread shift from one-to-many communication to many-to-many communication. Instead of simply putting a brand advertisement on television with no means for feedback, marketers can use social media to have conversations with consumers, forge deeper relationships, and build brand loyalty. Social media also allow consumers to connect with each other, share opinions, and collaborate on new ideas according to their interests.

With social media, the audience is often in control of the message, the medium, the response, or all three. This distribution of control is often difficult for companies to adjust to, but the focus of social marketing is unavoidably on the audience, and the brand must adapt to succeed. The interaction between producer and consumer becomes less about entertaining and more about listening, influencing, and engaging.

Using consumers to develop and market products is called **crowdsourcing**. Crowdsourcing describes how the input of many people can be leveraged to make decisions that used to be based on the input of only a few people.[22] Companies get feedback on marketing campaigns, new product ideas, and other marketing decisions by asking customers to share their thoughts. One company, called Talenthouse, is offering up the crowd to help musicians fulfill all sorts of needs—for example, someone to design album art or sew a dress for a lead singer. Talenthouse has users submit work to be voted on by Facebook and Twitter peers. The winner gets the job (though the musician has the final say in who wins). Some musicians see Talenthouse as a way to gain publicity or to help aspiring artists. English singer–songwriter Ellie Goulding set up a contest for Talenthouse competitors to submit a photograph that showed people connecting with music at a concert or festival. The winner received £1,000 (about $1,500), a new laptop, special promotion, and a job as the official photographer for an Ellie Goulding concert.[23] Crowdsourcing offers a way for companies to engage heavy users of a brand and receive input, which in turn increases those users' brand advocacy and lessens the likelihood that a change will be disliked enough to drive away loyal customers.

18-2 CREATING AND LEVERAGING A SOCIAL MEDIA CAMPAIGN

Social media is an exciting new field, and its potential for expanding a brand's impact is enormous. Because the costs are often low and the learning curve is relatively quick, some organizations are tempted to dive headfirst into social media. As with any marketing campaign, however, it is always important to start with a strategy. For most organizations, this means starting with a marketing or communications plan. Important areas such as situation analysis, objectives, and evaluation are still essential. It is important to link communication objectives (e.g., improving customer service) to the most effective social media tools (e.g., Twitter) and to be able to measure the results to determine whether the objectives were met. It is also important to understand the various types of media involved.

The new communication paradigm created by a shift to social media marketing raises questions about categorization. In light of the convergence of traditional and digital media, researchers have explored different ways that interactive marketers can categorize media types, namely owned, earned, and paid media (recall these concepts from Chapter 15). The purpose of owned media is to develop deeper relationships with customers. A brand's presence on Facebook, YouTube, Twitter, Pinterest, and other social platforms constitute owned media. Additional content such as videos, webinars, recommendations, ratings, and blog posts are also considered owned media, since they are sharable on social media platforms. This can be referred to as "content marketing" with the goal of organizing a brand's content across all platforms and expanding the message using paid media and influencer marketing. Basically, brand marketers want to drive customers to a digital destination like a website to complete some type of conversation or to generate earned media.

In digital marketing, attention is *earned* through word of mouth or online buzz about something the brand is doing. Earned media include viral videos, retweets, comments on blogs, and other forms of customer feedback resulting from a social media presence. An example of earned media is consumers passing along brand information in the form of retweets, blog comments, or ratings and recommendations. In other words, the word of mouth is spread online rather than face to face. Paid media are similar to marketing efforts that utilize traditional media, like newspaper, magazine, and television advertisements.

Most of the time marketers must put some money behind a campaign and cannot simply rely on earned media or a message going "viral." So marketers turn to paid media. In digital marketing, paid media include display advertising, paid search words, and other types of direct online advertising.[24] Ads purchased on Facebook, for example, are considered paid media, since the brand is paying for the text-based or visual ad that shows up on the right-hand side of Facebook profiles.

In some cases, social media can be thought of as an additional "layer" that many brands decide to develop. Some layers are quite deep—Doritos, Old Spice, and Nike can be said to have deeper layers of social media, since these are brands people talk about a lot. Other brands, for example, many B-to-B brands, may have a more shallow social media layer and provide access on only one or two social media platforms. At the end of the day, it really depends on the type of product being sold and the customer's propensity to participate in social media. Regardless, marketers are including in their campaigns more social media that is owned, paid, and earned.

crowdsourcing using consumers to develop and market products

To leverage all three types of media, marketers must follow a few key guidelines. First, they must maximize owned media by reaching out beyond their existing websites to create portfolios of digital touch points. This is especially true for brands with tight budgets, since the organization may not be able to afford much paid media. Second, marketers must recognize that public and media relations no longer translate into earned media. Instead, marketers must learn how to listen and respond to stakeholders. This will stimulate word of mouth. Finally, marketers must understand that paid media must serve as a catalyst to drive customer engagement and expand into emerging channels.[25] If balanced correctly, all three types of media can be powerful tools for interactive marketers.

18-2a The Listening System

The first action a marketing team should take when initiating a social media campaign is simple—it should just listen. Customers are on social media, and it is reasonable to assume the brand is there as well. Similarly, customers expect, and in some instances demand, a new level of engagement with brands. Developing an effective listening system is necessary to both understanding and engaging an online audience. Marketers must not only hear what is being said about the brand, the industry, the competition, and the customer, they must also pay attention to who is saying what and to act on that information. The specific ways that customers and noncustomers rate, rank, critique, praise, deride, recommend, snub, and generally discuss brands are all important. Thus, social media have created a new method of market research: customers telling marketers what they want and need (and do not want and do not need).

Once a company starts listening, it typically wants to develop a more formalized approach. **Social media monitoring** is the process of identifying and assessing what is being said about a company, individual, product, or brand. It can involve sentiment analysis and *text mining* specific key words on social networking websites, blogs, discussion forums, and other social media. Negative comments and complaints are particularly important, because they can illuminate unknown brand flaws, and also because negative comments and complaints are more likely to go viral. Listening is important because if consumers believe a brand is insincere based on whether negative comments go unanswered, consumers will take their business elsewhere.

social media monitoring
the process of identifying and assessing what is being said about a company, individual, product, or brand

Failure to respond to criticism typically leads to a larger crisis. Online tools such as Google Alerts, Social Mention, HootSuite, TweetReach, and Klout are extremely helpful in monitoring social media. Larger companies typically use an enterprise system such as Salesforce.com's Radian6 CRM software to monitor social media. Southwest Airlines has wall monitors that show media interactions in real time, and they are watched around the clock. As interactions appear on the screen, the system recognizes whether the comment is positive or negative so the team can respond to it as quickly as possible to ensure customers have an overall positive experience with the company.[26]

18-2b Social Media Objectives

After establishing a listening platform, the organization should develop a list of objectives for its social media team to accomplish. These objectives must be developed with a clear understanding of how social media change the communication dynamic with and for customers. Remember, attempting to reach a mass audience with a static message will never be as successful as influencing people through conversation. Marketing managers must set objectives that reflect this reality. The following are some practical ideas marketing managers should consider when setting social media objectives:

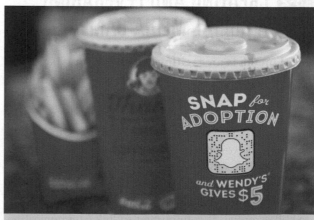

Fast-food chain Wendy's partnered with Snapchat to launch "Snap for Awareness," a campaign that was designed to create awareness about the needs of children in foster care. The campaign featured Wendy's cups with unique Snapcodes that could be scanned to unlock a Snapchat filter. When a filter was used, Wendy's donated $5 to the nonprofit Dave Thomas Foundation for Adoption.

- **Listen and learn:** Monitor what is being said about the brand and competitors, and glean insights about audiences. Use online tools and do research to implement the best social media practices. Though an established a listening strategy, this objective should already have been accomplished.

- **Build relationships and awareness:** Open dialogues with stakeholders by giving them compelling content across a variety of media. Engage in conversations, and answer customers' questions candidly. This will both increase web traffic and boost your search engine ranking. This is where crowdsourcing can be useful for product development and communication campaign feedback.

- **Promote products and services:** The clearest path to increasing the bottom line using social media is to get customers talking about products and services, which ultimately translates into sales.

- **Manage your reputation:** Develop and improve the brand's reputation by responding to comments and criticisms that appear on blogs and forums. In addition, organizations can position themselves as helpful and benevolent by participating in other forums and discussions. Social media make it much easier to establish and communicate expertise.

- **Improve customer service:** Customer comments about products and services will not always be positive. Use social media to search out dissatisfied customers and engage them directly in order to solve their product or service issues.

18-3 EVALUATION AND MEASUREMENT OF SOCIAL MEDIA

Social media have the potential to revolutionize the way organizations communicate with stakeholders. Given the relative ease and efficiency with which organizations can use social media, a positive return on investment (ROI) is likely for many—if not most—organizations. A Forrester Research report found that 95 percent of marketers planned to increase or maintain their investments in social media. However, while they understand it is a worthwhile investment, most marketers have not been able to figure out how to measure the benefits of social media.

As with traditional advertising, marketers lack hard evidence as to the relative effectiveness of these tools. Some marketers accept this unknown variable

and focus on the fact that social media are less about ROI than about deepening relationships with customers. Others work tirelessly to better understand the measurement of social media's effectiveness. A recent Ragan/NASDAQ OMX Corporate Solutions survey found that 40 percent of marketers are unsure of what evaluative tools to use, and about 70 percent are only "somewhat satisfied" or "not satisfied at all" with how their companies measure social media. "I'm not sure what to measure or how," said one survey participant. "I know it's important, but I can't show my boss how many retweets a post received and expect him to care." In fact, one CMO survey cited that only 15 percent of marketers could quantitatively prove the impact social media had on their business.[27]

While the use of social media continues to increase (by both marketers and consumers), social media are difficult to measure, because there is no common denominator to measure ROI. Some ways to measure ROI include followers or fans, purchases from social media referrals, retweets, and shares. In truth, there are countless measures. Regardless of the measure, there are five steps to help gauge the effectiveness of a social media effort:

1. Identify your *key performance indicators (KPIs)*.
2. Align your social media goals with your business objectives.
3. Set up Google Analytics (or a similar program) to track conversions.
4. Assign values to your KPIs (such as lifetime value or average sales).
5. Benchmark against your competitors.[28]

18-4 SOCIAL BEHAVIOR OF CONSUMERS

Social media have changed the way that people interact in their everyday lives. Some say that social media have made people smarter by giving them (especially children) access to so much information and interactivity. Social media enable people to stay in touch in ways never before experienced. Social media have also reinvented civic engagement. Consider that #BlackLivesMatter and #MeToo all started on social media. Social media have drastically changed the advertising business from an industry based on mass-media models (such as television) to an industry based on relationships and conversations. For example, social media played a huge part in the most recent presidential election by engaging voters and making politics more accessible as a whole. It also has played a role in connecting millions of women after the elections to participate in rallies and other events, including the Women's March. More recently it helped to elect women in the midterm elections and created awareness for many new candidates in the 2020 presidential election. Clearly, these developments have implications for how consumers use social media and the purposes for which they use those media.[29]

Once objectives have been determined and measurement tools have been implemented, it is important to identify which consumers the marketer is trying to reach. Who is using social media, and how often? What types of social media do they use? How do they use it? Are they just reading content, or do they actually create it? Does Instagram attract younger users? How are people using Facebook? Do Twitter users retweet viral videos? These types of questions must be considered because they determine not only which tools will be most effective but also, more importantly, whether launching a social media campaign even makes sense for a particular organization.

Understanding an audience necessitates understanding how that audience uses social media. Charlene Li and Josh Bernoff of Forrester Research identify the following types of social media users:

1. **Creators:** Those who produce and share online content like blogs, websites, articles, and videos. This is the fastest-growing sector of the audience.

2. **Conversationalist:** This group is also creating content, but only to facilitate communication. They want to express themselves through status updates.

3. **Critics:** Those who post comments, ratings, and reviews of products and services on blogs and forums. They respond to status updates and are crucial to the other types of users.

4. **Collectors:** Those who use RSS feeds to collect information and vote for websites online.

5. **Joiners:** Those who maintain a social networking profile and visit other sites.

6. **Spectators:** Those who read blogs, listen to podcasts, watch videos, and generally consume media. This is the largest category.

7. **Inactives: This is the smallest group and makes up** those who do none of the above.[30]

Despite the apparent slowdown, research also shows that more social networking "rookies" are classified as joiners. Another bright spot is a new category, "conversationalists," or people who post status updates on social networking sites and microblogging services such as Twitter. Conversationalists represent about 35 percent of users. This type of classification gives marketers a general idea of who is using social media and how to engage them. It is similar to any type of market segmentation—especially the 80/20 rule. Those who are creating content and are active on social media could be those consumers most likely to actively engage with a brand as well as actively post negative comments on social media. The critics and collectors make up most of this group. However, it is important not to miss the joiners and spectators, because they are eager to follow and act on the comments of their fellow customers.

Another aspect of how consumers use social media is through their attention to social media influencers and how some people even become influencers themselves. There are several types of social media influencers.[31] At the top of the hierarchy, **social media celebrities** are actors, singers, artists, or athletes who have millions of followers on social media platforms, typically Instagram and Twitter. Some of these celebrities have used their platforms as a voice for causes they care about while others have used social media to promote products. Some celebrities (like Kanye West and Kylie Jenner) have launched businesses based on their influence with their followers. These celebrities get paid thousands of dollars per post to promote a brand.

Social media stars are also people who have become popular because of their social media influence, as opposed to something outside of social media. Typically, they are popular in a specific arena—gaming, makeup, fashion, food, and so forth. Some you may not have heard of unless you are interested in a specific area. For example, Kayla Itsines is a fitness trainer with millions of followers on Instagram, including the wildly popular BBG (bikini body guides) and the Sweat app. James Charles is a makeup artist who became CoverGirl's first male makeup model. PewDiePie, who plays video games and comments on them, has a huge YouTube following. These social media stars also get paid thousands of dollars to promote brands. For example, Dan TDM has more than 18 million YouTube subscribers, and made $16 million last year playing Minecraft on YouTube.

social media celebrities actors, singers, artists, or athletes who have millions of followers on social media platforms, typically Instagram and Twitter

social media stars people who have become popular because of their social media influence in a specific arena—gaming, makeup, fashion, food, and so forth

In addition to regular influencers, there are **micro-influencers** that have a smaller number of followers on Instagram or Twitter, but are still influential in specific areas. Fitness company Peloton has instructors who have amassed hundreds of thousands of followers on Instagram. They promote the brand but promote other related fitness brands as well. This trend has provided an opportunity for ordinary people who have a unique voice and the ability to gain followers to connect with brands. Micro-influencers are also useful for more-local campaigns, since many times their influence is location-based.

18-5 SOCIAL MEDIA TOOLS: CONSUMER- AND CORPORATE-GENERATED CONTENT

Given that it is important for marketers to engage with customers on social media for many reasons, there are a number of tools and platforms that can be employed as part of an organization's social media strategy. Blogs, microblogs, social networks, media creation and sharing sites, social news sites, location-based social networking sites, review sites, virtual reality/artificial intelligence and online gaming all have their place in a company's social marketing plan. These are all tools in a marketing manager's toolbox, available when applicable to the marketing plan but not necessarily to be used all at once. Because of the breakneck pace at which technology changes, this list of resources will surely look markedly different five years from now. More tools emerge every day, and branding strategies must keep up with the ever-changing world of technology. For now, the resources highlighted in this section remain a marketer's strongest set of platforms for communicating and strengthening relationships with customers.

18-5a Blogs

Blogs are staples in many social media strategies. A **blog** is a publicly accessible web page that functions as an interactive journal, where readers can post comments on the author's entries. Some experts believe that every company should have a blog that speaks to current and potential customers, not as consumers, but as people.[32] Blogs enable marketers to create content in the form of posts, which ideally build customer trust and a sense of authenticity about the posts. Once posts are made, audience members can provide feedback through comments. Because it opens a dialogue and gives customers a voice, the comments section of a blog post is one of the most important avenues of conversation between brands and consumers. Blogs also allow companies to develop long-term relationships with their customers. Posting content yields dividends over time, serving as a lasting resource for a brand's current and future customer base. Blogs are particularly important to B-2-B companies, since they provide thought leadership and recommendations to customers, and brands are increasingly using other blog formats like Medium which has a built-in following.

Blogs can be divided into two broad categories: corporate and professional blogs, and noncorporate blogs such as personal blogs. **Corporate blogs** are sponsored by a company or one of its brands and are maintained by one or more of the company's employees. They disseminate marketing-controlled information and are effective platforms for developing thought leadership, fostering better relationships with stakeholders, maximizing search engine optimization, attracting new customers, creating favorable impressions of the organization using anecdotes and stories about brands, and providing an active forum for testing new ideas. Many companies have moved away from corporate blogs, and are replacing the in-depth writing and comment monitoring that are part of blog maintenance with the quick, easy, and more social Facebook, Twitter, or Tumblr. Coca-Cola, Walmart, Nike, and AllState operate some of the best big company corporate blogs. All are known for their creative and engaging content and the authenticity of their tone.[33]

On the other hand, **noncorporate blogs** are independent and not associated with the marketing efforts of any particular company or brand. Because these blogs contain information not controlled by marketers, they are perceived to be more authentic than corporate blogs. Mommy bloggers, women who review children's products and discuss family-related topics on their personal blogs, are one example of noncorporate blogs. The goal

micro-influencers people who have a smaller number of followers on Instagram or Twitter but are still influential in specific areas

blog a publicly accessible web page that functions as an interactive journal, where readers can post comments on the author's entries

corporate blogs blogs that are sponsored by a company or one of its brands and maintained by one or more of the company's employees

noncorporate blogs independent blogs that are not associated with the marketing efforts of any particular company or brand of mommy blogs is to share parenting tips and experiences and become part of a community. Food blogs are especially popular, particularly those posting restaurant reviews, diet and exercise tips, and recipes.

Because of the popularity of these and other types of blogs, many bloggers receive products and/or money from companies in exchange for a review. Many bloggers disclose where they received the product or if they were paid, but an affiliation is not always clear. Because of this, bloggers must disclose any financial relationship with a company per Federal Trade Commission rules. Marketing managers need to understand the rules behind offering complimentary products to bloggers before using them as a way to capitalize on the high potential for social buzz. For example, four out of five noncorporate bloggers post brand or product reviews. Even if a company does not have a formal social media strategy, chances are the brand is still out in the blogosphere, whether or not a marketing manager approached a blogger.

18-5b Microblogs

Microblogs are blogs that have shorter posts than traditional blogs. Twitter, the most popular microblogging platform, requires that posts be no more than 280 characters in length. There are several other platforms, including Tumblr, Apsense, and of course, Facebook's status updates. Unlike Twitter, these platforms allow users to post longer pieces of text, videos, images, and links. While some microblogs (such as Tumblr) do not have text length limits, their multimedia-based cultures discourage traditional blog-length text posts. The content posted on microblogs ranges from five-paragraph news stories to photos of sandwiches with the ingredients as captions (scanwiches.com). Twitter, originally designed as a short messaging system used for internal communication, is the most popular and is used as a communication and research tool by individuals and brands around the world. Twitter is effective for disseminating breaking news, promoting longer blog posts and campaigns, sharing links, announcing events, and promoting sales. By following, retweeting, responding to potential customers' tweets, and tweeting content that inspires customers to engage the brand, corporate Twitter users can lay a foundation for meaningful two-way conversation quickly and effectively. Celebrities also flock to Twitter to interact with fans, discuss tour dates, and efficiently promote themselves directly to fans. Research has found that when operated correctly, corporate Twitter accounts are well respected and well received. Twitter can be used to build communities, aid in customer service, gain prospects, increase awareness, and in the case of nonprofit organizations, raise funds.

After Yahoo acquired Tumblr, some companies decided to forgo using the platform. BuzzFeed, conversely, dedicated even more time and effort to the platform. This investment has paid off in terms of BuzzFeed's following on the site. The company has about a dozen Tumblr pages dedicated to various topics, including food spin-off Tasty. BuzzFeed has found that using Tumblr is a "great way to foster community engagement," as it "provides access to a lot of underrepresented audiences."[34]

18-5c Social Networks

Social networking sites enable individuals to connect—or network—with friends, peers, and business associates. Connections may be made around shared interests, shared environments, and personal relationships. Depending on the site, connected individuals may be able to send each other messages, track each other's activity, see each other's personal information, share multimedia, comment on each other's blog and microblog posts, or do all of these things. Depending on a marketing team's goals, several social networks might be engaged as part of a social media strategy: Facebook is the largest social network; Instagram and Snapchat are popular among younger audiences; LinkedIn is geared toward professionals and businesses who use it to recruit employees; and niche networks like BakeSpace (bakers), Dogster (dog lovers), Black Twitter, and ChristianMingle.com cater to specialized markets. There is a niche social network for just about every demographic and interest. Beyond those already established, an organization may decide to develop a brand-specific social network or community. Although each social networking site is different, some marketing goals can be accomplished on any such site. Given the right strategy, increasing awareness, targeting audiences, promoting products, forging relationships, highlighting expertise and leadership, attracting event participants, performing research, and generating new business are attainable marketing goals on any social network.

FACEBOOK Facebook originated as a community for college students; it opened to the general public as its popularity grew. At over 2 billion users per month, it is

microblogs blogs with strict post length limits

social networking sites websites that allow individuals to connect—or network—with friends, peers, and business associates

EXHIBIT 18.1   FACEBOOK LINGO

Nonindividual (Usually Corporate)	Individual
Page	Profile
Fan of a page, tells fan's friends that the user is a fan, creates mini-viral campaign	Friend a person, send private messages, write on the wall, see friend-only content
Public, searchable	Privacy options, not searchable unless user-enabled

the largest social networking site by far. Growth in new profiles is highest among Baby Boomers using Facebook as a way to connect with old friends and keep up with family. Facebook is popular not only with individuals but also with groups and companies. How an individual uses Facebook differs from the way a group or company uses Facebook, as you can see in Exhibit 18.1. Individual Facebook users create profiles, while brands, organizations, and nonprofit causes operate as pages. In contrast to individual profiles, all pages are public and are thus subject to search engine indexing.

By maintaining a popular Facebook page, a brand not only increases its social media presence but also helps to optimize search engine results. Pages often include photo and video albums, brand information, and links to external sites. One of the most useful page features is the Timeline. The Timeline enables a brand to communicate directly with fans via status updates, which enables marketers to build databases of interested stakeholders. When an individual becomes a fan of your organization or posts on your Timeline, that information is shared with the individual's friends, creating a mini-viral marketing campaign. Other Facebook marketing tools include groups, applications, and ads, as well as the recently launched Facebook Live and Facebook Stories. Whichever tools they use, Facebook is an extremely important platform for social marketers.

Facebook has proved to be fertile ground for new marketing ideas and campaigns. For example, St. Jude Children's Research Hospital has engaging posts and videos on its Facebook page, highlighting its status as a volunteer- and donation-driven organization. You can even donate to St. Jude and find out about volunteer opportunities without leaving Facebook. Threadless hosts T-shirt design contests that users can submit to and vote on through its Facebook page. The company even uses T-shirt designs submitted by users as its cover photo and always gives credit to the artists. While it provides many marketing opportunities, Facebook

is not a perfect platform. The company has faced numerous privacy and security concerns, and was at the center of a fake news controversy during the recent presidential election.[35]

LINKEDIN LinkedIn is used primarily by professionals who wish to build their personal brands online and businesses that are recruiting employees and freelancers. LinkedIn features many of the same services as Facebook (profiles, status updates, private messages, company pages, and groups), but is oriented around business and professional connections—it is designed to be information-rich rather than multimedia-rich. LinkedIn serves as a virtual Rolodex, providing recruiters and job seekers alike a network to connect and conduct business. LinkedIn's question-and-answer forum, endorsement system, job classifieds platform, and acquisition of presentation-hosting website SlideShare set it apart from Facebook as a truly business-oriented space. Additional features such as LinkedIn Pulse, Company Pages, InMail, Groups, and Get Introduced truly set LinkedIn apart as the optimal professional social media platform.[36] LinkedIn is the most effective social media platform for B2B marketing, as many use it for lead generation. Some companies use LinkedIn for recruiting, and others use it for thought leadership. Indeed, company pages on LinkedIn can serve as an effective hub for products and services, promotional videos, and company news.

18-5d Media Sharing Sites

Media sharing sites enable users to upload and distribute multimedia content like videos and photos. YouTube, Flickr, Pinterest, Instagram, and Snapchat are particularly useful to brands' social marketing strategies because they add a vibrant interactive channel on which to disseminate content. Suffice it to say, the distribution of user-generated content has changed markedly over the past few years. Today, organizations can tell compelling brand stories through videos, photos, and audio.

Photo-sharing sites enable users to archive and share photos. Flickr, Dropbox, Twitpic, Google Photos, Facebook, and Imgur all offer free photo-hosting services that can be utilized by individuals and businesses alike. Instagram is often used by brands to engage younger audience members. Instagram Stories is a wildly popular tool for

media sharing sites websites that allow users to upload and distribute multimedia content like videos and photos visual storytelling for both individuals and brands. Snapchat is also useful, but since photos and videos are only visible for a few seconds, complex marketing messages cannot easily be conveyed. To get around this, Snapchat developed Snapchat Discover, a storytelling feature that lets brands engage consumers more effectively.

Video creation and distribution have also gained popularity among marketers because of video's rich ability to tell stories. YouTube, the highest-trafficked video-based website and the second highest-trafficked site overall, allows users to upload and stream their videos to an enthusiastic and active community.[37] YouTube is not only large (in terms of visitors), but also attracts a diverse base of users: age and gender demographics are remarkably balanced.

Many entertainment companies and movie marketers have used YouTube as a showcase for new products, specials, and movie trailers. User-generated content can also be a powerful tool for brands that can use it effectively. While YouTube is still the champ, Vine is quickly becoming another popular platform for corporate promotion.

A podcast, another type of user-generated media, is a digital audio or video file that is distributed serially for other people to listen to or watch. Podcasts can be streamed online, played on a computer, uploaded to a portable media player, or downloaded onto a smartphone or other mobile devices. Podcasts are like radio shows that are distributed through various means and not linked to a scheduled time slot. Podcasts have amassed a steadily growing number of loyal devotees. For example, Etsy, an online marketplace for handmade and vintage wares, offers a podcast series introducing favorite craftspeople to the world—driving business for those individuals.

18-5e Social News Sites

Social news sites enable users to decide which content is promoted on a given website by voting that content up or down. Users post news stories and multimedia on crowdsourced sites such as Reddit for the community to vote on. The more interest from readers, the higher the story or video is ranked. Marketers have found that these sites are useful for promoting campaigns, creating conversations around related issues, and building website traffic.

If marketing content posted to a crowdsourced site is voted up, discussed, and shared enough to be listed among the most popular topics of the day, it can go viral across other sites, and eventually the entire web. Social bookmarking sites such as Reddit and Pinterest are similar to social news sites, but the objective of their users is to collect, save, and share interesting and valuable links. On these sites, users categorize links with short, descriptive tags. Users can search the site's database of links by specific tags or can add their own tags to others' links. In this way, tags serve as the foundation for information gathering and sharing on social bookmarking sites.[38]

18-5f Location-Based Social Networking Sites

Considered by many to be the next big development in social marketing, location sites like Foursquare and Loopt should be on every marketer's radar. Essentially, location-based social networking sites combine the fun of social networking with the utility of location-based global positioning system (GPS) technology. Foursquare, one of the most popular location sites, treats location-based micronetworking as a game: users earn badges and special statuses based on their number of visits to particular locations. Users can write and read short reviews and tips about businesses, organize meet-ups, and see which Foursquare-using friends are nearby. Foursquare updates can also be posted to linked Twitter and Facebook accounts for followers and friends to see.

Location sites such as Foursquare are particularly useful social marketing tools for local businesses, especially when combined with sales promotions like coupons, special offers, contests, and events. Location sites can be harnessed to forge lasting relationships and deeply ingrained loyalty among customers.[39] For example, a local restaurant can encourage customers to check in on Foursquare using their smartphones and receive coupons for that day's purchases. Facebook added Places to capitalize on location-based technology, making it possible for people to "check in" and share their location with their online friends. Newer location sites and apps combine some of the popular features of other social media platforms. Bivid, a newly released app, enables "users to share photos and videos from their daily lives, and discover content posted by other users near their location, or around the world."[40] Posts on Bivid disappear after 24 hours to keep content relevant. Posts are not

social news sites websites that allow users to decide which content is promoted on a given website by voting that content up or down

location-based social networking sites websites that combine the fun of social networking with the utility of location-based GPS technology

Live video streaming apps like Facebook Live and Periscope are changing the way we consume and share media. Comedians like Jim Gaffigan (pictured), Kevin Hart, Chris Hardwick, and Annie Lederman have embraced these new streaming apps as a way to connect with fans and increase awareness.

anonymous to ensure a safe and healthy environment for users. It will be interesting to see how the use of this technology grows over time.

18-5g Review Sites

Individuals tend to trust other people's opinions when it comes to purchasing. According to Nielsen Media Research, more than 70 percent of consumers seek opinions before buying, and over 80 percent of Millennials do. Online reviews are important for marketers hoping to influence consumers in the early stages of the purchase cycle who don't yet have an established plan for what and how to purchase. The percentage of individuals trusting other people's online opinions is much higher than that of consumers who

trust traditional advertising. Based on the early work of Amazon.com and eBay to integrate user opinions into product and seller pages, countless websites allowing users to voice their opinions have sprung up across every segment of the Internet market.

Review sites enable consumers to post, read, rate, and comment on opinions regarding all kinds of products and services. For example, Yelp, the most active local review directory on the Web, combines customer critiques of local businesses with business information and elements of social networking to create an engaging, informative experience. On Yelp, users scrutinize local restaurants, fitness centers, tattoo parlors, and other businesses, each of which has a detailed profile page. Business owners and representatives can edit their organizations' pages and respond to Yelp reviews both privately and publicly. Yelp even rewards its most popular (and prolific) reviewers with Elite status. Businesses like Pies & Pints in Worthington, Ohio, will throw Elite-only parties to enable these esteemed Yelpers to try out their restaurant, hoping to receive a favorable review. A Tiki Beach Party for Yelp Elites at Montreal, Canada's Le Lab garnered 13 reviews averaging five out of five stars.[41] By giving marketers the opportunity to respond to their customers directly and put their businesses in a positive light, review sites certainly serve as useful tools for local and national businesses.

18-5h Virtual Worlds and Online Gaming

Online gaming presents additional opportunities for marketers to engage with consumers. These include massive multiplayer online (MMO) games such as *World of Warcraft, Destiny, Minecraft,* and *EVE Online* and most recently the popular *Fortnite* game. Other possibilities include competitive online games such as *League of Legends, Overwatch, Street Fighter V,* and online communities (or virtual worlds) such as *Second Life, Poptropica,* and *Habbo Hotel.* Although these virtual worlds are unfamiliar to and even intimidating for many traditional marketers, they are becoming an important, viable, and growing consideration. Almost 200 million North American citizens play video games. The United States is the second largest gaming market in terms of revenue, with revenues forecasted to grow to more than $120 billion by 2021, with the largest increase in mobile media.[42]

review sites websites that allow consumers to post, read, rate, and comment on opinions regarding all kinds of products and services

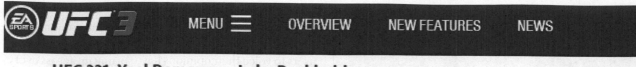
UFC 221: Yoel Romero vs. Luke Rockhold

Source: Electronic Arts Inc

Electronic Arts UFC 3 has in-game advertisements to increase the authenticity of the experience.

One particular area of growth is social gaming. The number of people playing games on Facebook like *Words with Friends, FarmVille,* and *Trivia Crack* recently increased almost 50 percent in a single year.[43] Facebook games have decreased in popularity more recently, but the company still views gaming as an important way to reach consumers. Social gaming has gained popularity in the past few years, but consumers are changing the way they play. Many users are playing games on their smartphones, which has pulled them away from the extremely popular games offered on Facebook, and in turn away from Facebook's advertisers. To recapture gamers, Facebook is developing a stand-alone gaming platform that will likely offer the same marketing benefits as traditional social gaming, and is also releasing instant games on its Messenger application. Snapchat is also introducing gaming in its app, with advertisers sponsoring simple augmented-reality games.[44]

The average player of social games is a 35-year-old male (users who play on mobile devices tend to be younger), but women make up nearly 48 percent of social gamers. Facebook is by far the largest social network for gaming, though up-and-comer hi5 is hoping to win over more users with its large variety of games. The top five games on Facebook are Candy Crush Saga, Clash of Clans, Candy Crush Soda Saga, Farm Heroes Saga, and 8 Ball Pool, which together entice more than 50 million users every day.[45] These games are attractive because they can be played in just five minutes.

Many mobile games use advertising to generate revenue for the game developers and publishers. As long as the ads are not overly intrusive, most users opt to play free versions of games with ads over paid versions that do not have ads. Another popular strategy is to give an ad-free game away for free and then charge small sums of money for in-game items and power-ups. These microtransactions account for about 80 percent of app revenue in the United States and almost 95 percent of app revenue in China and Japan. Microtransactions have become a popular source of revenue in non-mobile games as well. *League of Legends*, the most popular eSports game in the world, is generating more than $1.6 billion from in-game microtransactions alone.[46]

MMOs tend to draw a different group of consumers—18- to 34-year-old males. In MMO environments, thousands of people play simultaneously. Regardless of the type of experience, brands must be creative in how they integrate ads into games. Social and realistic titles are the most appropriate for marketing and advertising (as opposed to fantasy games). Promotions typically include special events, competitions, and sweepstakes, and for some games, having ads actually increases the authenticity. For example, Nike offers shoes in life simulator *The Sims Online* that enable players to run faster, while replays in football franchise *Madden* are sponsored by real-life companies.

18-6 SOCIAL MEDIA AND MOBILE TECHNOLOGY

While much of the excitement in social media has been based on website and new technology uses, much of the growth lies in new platforms. These platforms include the multitude of smartphones and wearables as well as iPads and other tablets. The major implication of this development is that consumers now can access popular websites like Facebook, Mashable, Instagram, Reddit, and BuzzFeed from all their various platforms.

18-6a Mobile Marketing

Worldwide, there are more than 6 billion mobile phones in use, about 20 percent of which are smartphones.[47] It is no surprise, then, that the mobile platform is such an effective marketing tool—especially when targeting a younger audience. Smartphones up the ante by allowing individuals to do nearly everything they can do with a computer—from anywhere. With a smartphone in hand, reading a blog, writing an email, scheduling a meeting, posting to Facebook, playing a multiplayer game, watching a video, taking a picture, using GPS, conducting banking transactions, and surfing the Internet might all occur during one 10-minute bus ride. Smartphone technology, often considered the crowning achievement in digital convergence and social media integration, has opened the door to modern mobile advertising as a viable marketing strategy.

Mobile advertising is driving digital advertising spending annually in the United States to more than $70 billion. There are several reasons for the recent popularity of mobile marketing. First, an effort to

Vuk Pavlovic, project manager for consumer research firm True Impact, demonstrates a headset that tracks eye movement and neural stimulation. As mobile marketing grows, these advanced marketing tools will become much more commonplace.

Chris So/Toronto Star/Getty Images

standardize mobile platforms has resulted in a low barrier to entry. Second, especially given mobile marketing's younger audiences, there are more consumers than ever acclimating to once-worrisome privacy and pricing policies. Third, because most people carry their smartphones with them at all times, mobile marketing is uniquely effective at garnering customer attention in real time. Fourth, mobile marketing is measurable: metrics and usage statistics make it an effective tool for gaining insight into consumer behavior. Fifth, in-store notification technology such as Apple's iBeacon can send promotional messages and in-store product locations based on real-time interactions with customers. Finally, mobile marketing's response rate is higher than that of traditional media types like print and broadcast advertisement. Video and banner advertising are the two most popular types of mobile advertising. Native advertising is also becoming more popular as a result of its the ability to customize. Some common mobile marketing tools include:

- **SMS (short message service):** 160-character text messages sent to and from cell phones. SMS is typically integrated with other tools.

- **MMS (multimedia messaging service):** Similar to SMS but allows the attachment of images, videos, ringtones, and other multimedia to text messages.

- **Mobile website (MOBI and WAP website):** Website designed specifically for viewing and navigation on mobile devices.

- **Mobile ads:** Visual advertisements integrated into text messages, applications, and mobile website. Mobile ads are often sold on a cost-per-click basis.

- **Bluetooth marketing:** A signal is sent to Bluetooth-enabled devices, allowing marketers to send targeted messages to users based on their geographic locations.

- **Smartphone applications (apps):** Software designed specifically for mobile and tablet devices.

A recent trend in mobile technology has been the advent of smartwatches and other wearables. These devices look like traditional watches, but they connect to your mobile phone or directly to the Internet. Smartwatches are an easy way for advertisers to gain the attention of consumers, but advertising on smartwatches is starting slowly. As smartwatch advertising develops, it will likely focus more on branded notifications and alerts than on the traditional forms of advertising seen on mobile phones and PCs. The watch is the starting point, but connected wearables open up a whole new avenue for advertisers.[48]

18-6b Apps and Widgets

Given the widespread adoption of Apple's iPhone, Android-based phones, and other mobile devices, it is no surprise that millions of apps have been developed for the mobile market. Dozens of new and unique apps that harness mobile technology are added to mobile marketplaces every day. While many apps perform platform-specific tasks, others convert existing content into a mobile-ready format. Whether offering new or existing content, when an app is well branded and integrated into a company's overall marketing strategy, it can create buzz and generate customer engagement.

Web widgets, also known as gadgets and badges, are software applications that run entirely within existing online platforms. Essentially, a web widget allows a developer to embed a simple application such as a weather forecast, horoscope, or stock market ticker into a website, even if the developer did not write (or does not understand) the application's source code. From a marketing perspective, widgets enable customers to display company information (such as current promotions, coupons, or news) on their own websites or smartphone home screens. Widgets are often cheaper to develop than apps, can extend an organization's reach beyond existing platforms, will broaden the listening system, and can make an organization easier to find.[49]

18-7 THE SOCIAL MEDIA PLAN

To effectively use the tools in the social media toolbox, it is important to have a clearly outlined social media plan. The social media plan is linked to larger plans such as a promotional plan or marketing plan and should fit appropriately into the objectives and steps in those plans (for more information, review Chapters 2 and 16). It is important to research throughout the development of the social media plan to keep abreast of the rapidly changing social media world. There are six stages involved in creating an effective social media plan:

1. **Listen to customers:** This is covered in more detail in Section 18-2a.

2. **Set social media objectives:** Set objectives that can be specifically accomplished through social media, with special attention to how to measure the results. Numerous metrics are available, some of which are mentioned throughout the chapter.

3. **Define strategies:** This includes examining trends and best practices in the industry. This includes designing the messaging that will appear across the campaign.

4. **Identify the target audience:** This should line up with the target market defined in the marketing plan, but in the social media plan, pay special attention to how that audience participates and behaves online.

5. **Select the tools and platforms:** Based on the result of Step 4, choose the social media tools and platforms that will be most relevant. These choices are based on the knowledge of where the target audience participates on social media.

6. **Implement and monitor the strategy:** Social media campaigns can be fluid, so it is important to keep a close eye on what is successful and what is not. Then, based on the observations, make changes as needed. It also becomes important, therefore, to go back to the listening stage to interpret how consumers are perceiving the social media campaign.

Listening to customers and market trends as well as continually revising the social media plan to meet the needs of the changing social media market are keys to successful social media marketing. Numerous industry leaders are sharing their best practices, and sources such as *Fast Company* and the *Wall Street Journal* report regularly on how large and small companies are successfully using social media to enhance engagement, gain market share and increase sales. A good example

EXHIBIT 18.2　SOCIAL MEDIA TRENDS

Trend	Change	Where Is It Now?
Fake news	The rise of intentionally misleading content	
Microsoft Office 365, Google Drive	Integrated file hosting	
Stories	Series of photos and videos that are only viewable for 24 hours	
Virtual reality and augmented reality	New mediums for content creation and sharing	
The Internet of Things	Integration into wearables, appliances, apparel, and more	
Apple Pay, Google Wallet, Bitcoin, and NFC-enabled payment options	Replacing credit cards with various forms of digital payment	
FitFabFun, Trunk Club, and NatureBox	Online and subscription-based personal shopping	
Facebook Live, Instagram Live	Live video streaming for everybody	
Chatbots	Companies using artificial intelligence to improve customer service	

of using social media strategies is HubSpot, a company that practices what it preaches. HubSpot advocates the benefits of building valuable content online and then using social media to pull customers to its website. Social engine profiles have increased HubSpot's website traffic, which has made its lead-generation program much more effective.

18-7a　The Changing World of Social Media

Some of the trends noted in this chapter may already seem ancient to you. The rate of change in social media is astounding—usage statistics change daily for sites like Facebook, Instagram, Pinterest, and Twitter. Some things in the rumor mill as we write this may have exploded in popularity, while others may have fizzled out without even appearing on your radar. In Exhibit 18.2, we have listed some of the items that seem to be on the brink of exploding on to the social media scene. Take a moment to fill in the current state of each in the third column. Have you heard of it? Has it come and gone? Maybe it is still rumored, or maybe it has petered out. This exercise highlights not only the speed with which social media change but also the importance of keeping tabs on rumors. Doing so may give you a competitive advantage by being able to understand and invest in the next big social media site.

19 | Pricing Concepts

Monkey Business Images/Shutterstock.com

LEARNING OUTCOMES

After studying this chapter, you will be able to . . .

19-1 Discuss the importance of pricing decisions to the economy and to the individual firm

19-2 List and explain a variety of pricing objectives

19-3 Explain the role of demand in price determination

19-4 Understand the concepts of dynamic pricing and yield management systems

19-5 Describe cost-oriented pricing strategies

19-6 Demonstrate how the product life cycle, competition, distribution and promotion strategies, customer demands, the Internet and extranets, and perceptions of quality can affect price

19-7 Describe the procedure for setting the right price

19-8 Explain how discounts, geographic pricing, and other pricing tactics can be used to fine-tune a base price

19-9 Identify the legal constraints on pricing decisions

19-1 THE IMPORTANCE OF PRICE

Price means one thing to the consumer and something else to the seller. To the consumer, it is the cost of something. To the seller, price is revenue—the primary source of profits. In the broadest sense, price allocates resources in a free-market economy. Marketing managers are frequently challenged by the task of price setting, but they know that meeting the challenge of setting the right price can have a significant impact on the firm's bottom line. Organizations that successfully manage prices do so by creating a pricing infrastructure within the company. This means defining pricing goals, searching for ways to create greater customer value, assigning authority and responsibility for pricing decisions, and creating tools and systems to continually improve pricing decisions. The importance of creating the right pricing strategy cannot be overstated.

19-1a What Is Price?

Price is that which is given up in an exchange to acquire a good or service. Price also plays two roles in the evaluation of product alternatives: as a measure of sacrifice and as an information cue. To some degree, these two effects are opposing.

THE SACRIFICE EFFECT OF PRICE Price is, again, "that which is given up," which means what is sacrificed to get a good or service. In the United States, the sacrifice is usually money, but it can be other things as well. It may also be time lost while waiting to acquire the good or service. Price might also include lost dignity for individuals who lose their jobs and must rely on charity. For a college student, paying tuition might mean skipping a vacation, buying a less luxurious car, or waiting longer to buy a first house.

THE INFORMATION EFFECT OF PRICE Consumers do not always choose the lowest-priced product in a category, such as shoes, cars, or wine, even when the products are otherwise similar. One explanation of this behavior, based on research, is that we infer quality information from price—that is, higher quality equals higher price. The information effect of price may also extend to favorable price perceptions by others because higher prices can convey the prominence and status of the purchaser to other people. Thus, both a Swatch and a Rolex can tell time accurately, but they convey different meanings. The price–quality relationship will be discussed later in the chapter.

VALUE IS BASED ON PERCEIVED SATISFACTION Consumers are interested in obtaining a "reasonable price." "Reasonable price" really means "perceived

> ### "Trying to set the right price is one of the most stressful and pressure-filled tasks of the marketing manager."

reasonable value" at the time of the transaction. One of your authors purchased a new juice machine for around $60 so he could quickly prepare fresh-squeezed orange juice in the morning. The machine worked just fine for about a year and a half, but one morning, it made a strange noise and that was the last of the fresh orange juice. The warranty was only good for a year, so the author had to buy a new machine. He did not receive the expected perceived reasonable value from the original juice machine.

19-1b The Importance of Price to Marketing Managers

As noted in the chapter introduction, prices are the key to revenues, which in turn are the key to profits for an organization. **Revenue** is the price charged to customers multiplied by the number of units sold. Revenue is what pays for every activity of the company: production, finance, sales, distribution, and so on. What is

price that which is given up in an exchange to acquire a good or service

revenue the price charged to customers multiplied by the number of units sold left over (if anything) is **profit**. Managers usually strive to charge a price that will earn a fair profit.

$$\text{Price} \times \text{Units} = \text{Revenue}$$

To earn a profit, managers must choose a price that is not too high or too low—a price that equals the perceived value to target consumers. If, in consumers' minds, a price is set too high, the perceived value will be less than the cost, and sale opportunities will be lost.

19-2 PRICING OBJECTIVES

To survive in today's highly competitive marketplace, companies need pricing objectives that are specific, attainable, and measurable. Realistic pricing goals, then, require continual monitoring to determine the effectiveness of the company's strategy. For convenience, pricing objectives can be divided into three categories: profit oriented, sales oriented, and status quo.

19-2a Profit-Oriented Pricing Objectives

Profit-oriented pricing objectives include profit maximization, satisfactory profits, and target return on investment.

PROFIT MAXIMIZATION *Profit maximization* means setting prices so that total revenue is as large as possible relative to total costs. Profit maximization does not always signify unreasonably high prices, however. Both price and profits depend on the type of competitive environment a firm faces, such as whether it is in a monopoly position (being the only seller) or in a much more competitive situation. Also, remember that a firm cannot charge a price higher than the product's perceived value. Sometimes managers say that their company is trying to maximize profits—in other words, trying to make as much money as possible. Although this goal may sound impressive to stockholders, it is not good enough for planning.

In attempting to maximize profits, managers can try to expand revenue by increasing customer satisfaction, or they can attempt to reduce costs by operating more efficiently. A third possibility is to attempt to do both. Some companies may focus too much on cost reduction at the expense of the customer. Lowe's lost market share when it cut costs by reducing the number of associates on the floor. Customer service declined—and so

did revenue. When firms rely too heavily on customer service, however, costs tend to rise to unacceptable levels. U.S. airlines used to serve full meals on two-hour flights and offered pillows and blankets to tired customers. This proved to be unsustainable. A company can maintain or slightly cut costs while increasing customer loyalty through customer service initiatives, loyalty programs, customer relationship management programs, and allocating resources to programs that are designed to improve efficiency and reduce costs.

SATISFACTORY PROFITS Satisfactory profits are a reasonable level of profits. Rather than maximizing profits, many organizations strive for profits that are satisfactory to the stockholders and management—in other words, a level of profits consistent with the level of risk an organization faces. In a risky industry, a satisfactory profit may be 35 percent. In a low-risk industry, it might be 7 percent.

TARGET RETURN ON INVESTMENT The most common profit objective is a target **return on investment (ROI)**, sometimes called the firm's return on total assets. ROI measures management's overall effectiveness in generating profits with the available assets. The higher the firm's ROI, the better off the firm is. Many companies use a target ROI as their main pricing goal. In summary, ROI is a percentage that puts a firm's profits into perspective by showing profits relative to investment.

Return on investment is calculated as follows:

$$\text{Return on investment} = \frac{\text{Net profits after taxes}}{\text{Total assets}}$$

Assume that in 2019 Orset Systems had assets of $4.5 million, net profits of $550,000, and a target ROI of 10 percent. This was the actual ROI:

$$\text{ROI} = \frac{\$550,000}{\$4,500,000}$$

As you can see, the ROI for Orset Systems exceeded its target, which indicates that the company prospered in 2019.

Comparing the 12.2 percent ROI with the industry average provides a more meaningful picture, however. Any ROI needs to be evaluated in terms of the competitive environment, risks in the industry, and economic conditions. Generally speaking, firms seek ROIs in the 10 to 30 percent range. In some industries, such as the grocery industry, however, a return of under 5 percent is common and acceptable.

profit revenue minus expenses

return on investment (ROI) net profit after taxes divided by total assets

A company with a target ROI can predetermine its desired level of profitability. The marketing manager can use the standard, such as 10 percent ROI, to determine whether a particular price and marketing mix are feasible.

In addition, however, the manager must weigh the risk of a given strategy even if the return is in the acceptable range.

19-2b Sales-Oriented Pricing Objectives

Sales-oriented pricing objectives are based on market share as reported in dollar or unit sales. Firms strive either for market share or to maximize sales.

MARKET SHARE Market share is a company's product sales as a percentage of total sales for that industry. Sales can be reported in dollars or in units of product. It is very important to know whether market share is expressed in revenue or units because the results may be different. Consider four companies competing in an industry with 2,000 total unit sales and total industry revenue of $4,000 (see Exhibit 19.1). Company A has the largest unit market share at 50 percent, but it has only 25 percent of the revenue market share. In contrast, Company D has only a 15 percent unit share but the largest revenue share: 30 percent. Usually, market share is expressed in terms of revenue and not units.

Many companies believe that maintaining or increasing market share is an indicator of the effectiveness of their marketing mix. Larger market shares have indeed often meant higher profits, thanks to greater economies of scale, market power, and ability to compensate top-quality management. Conventional wisdom also says that market share and ROI are strongly related. For the most part they are; however, many companies with low market share survive and even prosper. To succeed with a low market share, companies often need to compete in industries with slow growth and few product changes—for instance, industrial supplies. Otherwise, they must vie in an industry that makes frequently bought items, such as consumer convenience goods.

The conventional wisdom about market share and profitability is not always reliable, however. Because of extreme competition in some industries, many market share leaders either do not reach their target ROI or actually lose money. Procter & Gamble switched from market share to ROI objectives after realizing that profits do not automatically follow from a large market share.

SALES MAXIMIZATION Rather than strive for market share, sometimes companies try to maximize sales. A firm with the objective of maximizing sales ignores profits, competition, and the marketing environment as long as sales are rising.

If a company is strapped for funds or faces an uncertain future, it may try to generate a maximum amount of cash in the short run. Management's task when using this objective is to calculate which price–quantity relationship generates the greatest cash revenue. Sales maximization can also be effectively used on a temporary basis to sell off excess inventory. It is not uncommon to find Christmas cards, ornaments, and other seasonal items discounted at 50 to 70 percent off retail prices after the holiday season has ended.

Maximization of cash should never be a long-run objective because cash maximization may mean little or no profitability.

19-2c Status Quo Pricing Objectives

Status quo pricing seeks to maintain existing prices or to meet the competition's prices. This third category of pricing objectives has the major advantage of requiring little planning. It is essentially a passive policy.

Often, firms competing in an industry with an established price leader simply meet the competition's prices. These industries typically have fewer price wars than those with direct price competition. In other cases, managers regularly shop competitors' stores to ensure that their prices are comparable.

Status quo pricing often leads to suboptimal pricing. This occurs because the strategy ignores customers' perceived value of both the firm's goods or services and those offered by its competitors. Status quo pricing also ignores demand and costs. Although the policy is simple to implement, it can lead to a pricing disaster.

Company	Units Sold	Unit Price	Total Revenue	Unit Market Share	Revenue Market Share
A	1,000	$1.00	$1,000	50	25
B	200	4.00	800	10	20
C	500	2.00	1,000	25	25
D	300	4.00	1,200	15	30
Total	2,000		$4,000		

EXHIBIT 19.1 TWO WAYS TO MEASURE MARKET SHARE (UNITS AND REVENUE)

market share a company's product sales as a percentage of total sales for that industry

status quo pricing a pricing objective that maintains existing prices or meets the competition's prices

It is not uncommon to find Christmas cards, ornaments, and other seasonal items discounted at 50 to 70 percent off retail prices after the holiday season has ended.

19-3 THE DEMAND DETERMINANT OF PRICE

demand the quantity of a product that will be sold in the market at various prices for a specified period

supply the quantity of a product that will be offered to the market by a supplier at various prices for a specified period

elasticity of demand consumers' responsiveness or sensitivity to changes in price

elastic demand a situation in which consumer demand is sensitive to changes in price

inelastic demand a situation in which an increase or a decrease in price will not significantly affect demand for the product

After marketing managers establish pricing goals, they must set specific prices to reach those goals. The price they set for each product depends mostly on two factors: the demand for the good or service and the cost to the seller for that good or service. When pricing goals are mainly sales oriented, demand considerations usually dominate. Other factors, such as distribution and promotion strategies, perceived quality, needs of large customers,

the Internet, and the stage of the product life cycle, can also influence price.

19-3a The Nature of Demand

Demand is the quantity of a product that will be sold in the market at various prices for a specified period. The quantity of a product that people will buy depends on its price. The higher the price, the fewer goods or services consumers will demand. Conversely, the lower the price, the more goods or services they will demand.

Supply is the quantity of a product that will be offered to the market by a supplier or suppliers at various prices for a specified period. At higher prices, manufacturers earn more capital and can produce more products.

19-3b Elasticity of Demand

To appreciate the concept of demand, you should understand elasticity. **Elasticity of demand** refers to consumers' responsiveness or sensitivity to changes in price. **Elastic demand** is a situation in which consumer demand is sensitive to price changes. Conversely, **inelastic demand** means that an increase or a decrease in price will not significantly affect demand for the product.

FACTORS THAT AFFECT ELASTICITY Several factors affect elasticity of demand, including the following:

- **Availability of substitutes:** When many substitute products are available, the consumer can easily switch from one product to another, making demand more elastic. The same is true in reverse: A person with complete renal failure will pay whatever is charged for a kidney transplantation because there is no substitute.

- **Price relative to purchasing power:** If a price is so low that it is an inconsequential part of an individual's budget, demand will be inelastic. If the price of pepper doubles, for example, people won't stop putting pepper on their eggs or buying more when they run out.

- **Product durability:** Consumers often have the option of repairing durable products (like cars and washing machines) rather than replacing them, thus prolonging their useful life. In other words, people are sensitive to the price increase, and demand is more elastic.

- **A product's other uses:** The greater the number of different uses for a product, the more elastic demand tends to be. If a product has only one use, as may be true of a new medicine, the quantity purchased probably will not vary as price varies. A person will consume only the prescribed quantity, regardless of price. On the other hand, a product like steel has many possible applications. As its price falls, steel becomes more economically feasible in a wider variety of applications, thereby making demand relatively elastic.

- **The consumer mind-set—local or global:** Researchers have found that consumers with a local identity are less sensitive to price increases (inelastic demand) than persons with a global identify. *Local identity* refers to a consumer's mind-set that pertains to their respect for local traditions and cultures while also identifying with people in their local communities. These individuals patronize local stores and buy local (or regional) products. They tend to be less price sensitive to price increases, which leads to more inelastic demand.[1] *Global mind-set* refers to interest in global culture and identification with people around the world. These individuals are often less influenced by "buy local" promotions, resulting in demand being more elastic.

  Walmart, of course, procures merchandise from around the globe. However, when it announced price increases on some items, Walmart claimed that this would enable it to hire more local workers. The strategy, using a different twist on the local–global mind-set, focused not on products but on support for local causes. The firm increased revenue by 14.5%.[2]

- **Customer satisfaction:** Researchers have found a strong relationship between overall customer satisfaction and willingness to tolerate a price increase (inelastic demand).[3] Specifically, they showed that a 1 percent increase in consumer satisfaction should be associated with a 0.06 percent decrease in price

People who identify strongly with local traditions and local communities tend to be less price sensitive when shopping in local or region stores.

Makistock/Shutterstock.com

sensitivity.[4] Porsche owners tend to be very satisfied with their vehicles and willingly pay for new vehicles despite price increases. Singapore Airlines can slightly increase prices because it is the perennial winner of the "world's best airline" award.[5]

DYNAMIC PRICING AND THE GROWING USE OF ARTIFICIAL INTELLIGENCE IN SETTING PRICES

When competitive pressures are high, a company must know when it should raise or lower prices to maximize its revenues. More and more companies are turning to **dynamic pricing** to help adjust prices. Although dynamic pricing originated with airlines, which are limited by fixed capacity, the new thinking is that dynamic pricing can be used in any industry in which demand or supply fluctuates. Uber, for example, uses dynamic pricing by raising fares when more people need rides and vice versa. This is referred to as **surge pricing**. Dynamic pricing is the ability to adjust prices very quickly, often in real time using software programs. This technology has come to the aid of brick-and-mortar retailers, enabling them to compete more effectively with online alternatives.

Down a shot of tequila at The Blind Burro, and the second round may cost you more. Or less. It all depends on what everyone else is drinking. Tequila prices at the San Diego bar and restaurant change every five minutes, based on demand. If more people order one tequila brand, the price of another might drop. Software created by Los Angeles–based The Drink Exchange tracks what drinkers buy and flashes the changing prices of more than two dozen tequila brands on TV screens hung on the bar's walls. On a recent night, a shot of Espolon Blanco tequila dropped from $7.75 one minute to $7.25 the next. At the same time, another brand rose from $11 to $12 per shot.[6]

The Freshplum pricing program can predict which customers will leave a website without buying anything with over 99 percent accuracy. When integrated into an e-commerce platform, the program can automatically offer this group of customers a steeper discount than normal to entice them to purchase before leaving. Visitors to sites with active Freshplum promotions are 36 percent more likely to buy.[7]

> **dynamic pricing** the ability to change prices very quickly, often in real time using software programs
>
> **surge pricing** occurs in a fluid market, where demand changes rapidly, often hourly. When demand increases, so do prices and vice versa

19-4a The Addition of Artificial Intelligence (AI) to Dynamic Pricing

Freshplum is using newer software that moves beyond traditional dynamic pricing models that often used simple rules. Examples of old rules might include always increase the price of economy tickets "X" percent when "Y" number of seats have been sold on the 10:30 flight from Chicago to San Francisco; Charge "X" percent more for full-size rental cars between 7:00 am and 10:30 am because this is when business customers typically pick up their cars. The new systems incorporate huge amounts of historical and real-time data, both traditional structured data sources of information, for example, purchased item, price, financing, and newer nonstructured or semi-structured data sources such as videos, emails, photos, and blogs, social media posts, and audio files.

The new AI pricing software constantly updates the algorithms. The updates are based upon what the AI software has learned. Updates are created to more efficiently reach a preestablished objective such as an overall average gross profit of 28 percent. Staples, the office supply chain, uses AI-enabled software to change prices on 30,000 products a day on its website.[8] Some AI pricing software will even raise prices on an item when it learns, from a competitor's website, that the competitor has run out of stock on a similar item.

The more AI learns about you, including your interests, hobbies, lifestyle, and past behavior, the more effective it can be about targeting you with "the right price." For example, structured online data regarding your purchasing behavior will include:

1. What types of goods and services you perused online.

2. How long you were on each web page.

3. The items you put in your shopping cart.

4. The goods and services you actually bought.

Unstructured data might include:

1. The brands you wear or use in your photos.

2. What your lifestyle reveals about your pricing sensitivity.

3. What people who have the same psychographic and behavioral profile as yours pay for items.

4. What brands you discuss on social media and whether your comments are positive or negative.

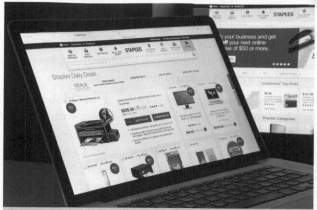

Staples uses AI to change prices each day on up to 30,000 items for sale on its website.

These are but a few of the data sources that AI pricing software can use to learn about you.

19-5 THE COST DETERMINANT OF PRICE

Sometimes companies minimize or ignore the importance of demand and decide to price their products largely or solely on the basis of the company's costs. Prices determined strictly on the basis of costs may be too high for the target market, thereby reducing or eliminating sales. On the other hand, cost-based prices may be too low, causing the firm to earn a lower return than it should. An entrepreneur might say, "I know what it costs to make this item, so I'll just add 40 percent to the cost, sell it for $70, and feel good about it." But what if the product creates $1,000 worth of value for the buyer? In that case, the seller created a lot of value but failed to capture it. Nevertheless, costs should generally be part of any price determination, if only as a floor below which a good or service must not be priced in the long run.

The idea of cost may seem simple, but it is actually a multifaceted concept, especially for producers of goods and services. A **variable cost** is a cost that varies with changes in the level of output; an example of a variable cost is the cost of materials. In contrast, a **fixed cost** does not change as output is increased or decreased. Examples include rent and executives' salaries. Costs can be used to set prices in a variety of ways. While markup pricing is relatively simple, break-even pricing uses more complicated concepts of cost.

19-5a Markup Pricing

Markup pricing, a method used by some wholesalers and retailers to establish a selling price, does not directly analyze the costs of production. Instead, **markup pricing**

variable cost a cost that varies with changes in the level of output

fixed cost a cost that does not change as output is increased or decreased

markup pricing the cost of buying the product from the producer, plus amounts for profit and for expenses not otherwise accounted for uses the cost of buying the product from the producer, plus amounts for profit and for expenses not otherwise accounted for. The total determines the selling price.

A retailer, for example, may add a certain percentage to the cost of the merchandise received to arrive at the retail price. An item that costs the retailer $1.80 and is sold for $2.20 carries a markup of 40 cents, which is a markup of 22 percent of the cost ($0.40 ÷ $1.80). Retailers tend to discuss markup in terms of its percentage of the retail price—in this example, 18 percent ($0.40 ÷ $2.20). The difference between the retailer's cost and the selling price (40 cents) is the gross margin.

The formula for calculating the retail price given a certain desired markup is as follows:

$$\text{Retail price} = \frac{\text{Cost}}{1 - \text{Desired return on sales}}$$

$$\frac{\$1.80}{1.00 - 0.18} = \$2.20$$

If the retailer wants a 30 percent return, then:

$$\text{Retail price} = \frac{\$1.80}{1.00 - 0.30}$$

$$= \$2.57$$

The reason that retailers and others speak of markups on selling price is that many important figures in financial reports, such as gross sales and revenues, are sales figures, not cost figures.

To use markup based on cost or selling price effectively, the marketing manager must calculate an adequate gross margin—the amount added to cost to determine price. The margin must ultimately provide adequate funds to cover selling expenses and profit. Once an appropriate margin has been determined, the markup technique has the major advantage of being easy to employ.

Markups are often based on experience. For example, many small retailers markup merchandise 100 percent over cost. (In other words, they double the cost.) This tactic is called **keystoning**. Some other factors that influence markups are the merchandise's appeal to customers, past response to the markup (an implicit demand consideration), the item's promotional value, the seasonality of the good, the fashion appeal of the good, the product's traditional selling price, and competition. Most retailers avoid any set markup because of such considerations as promotional value and seasonality.

19-5b Break-Even Pricing

Now, let's take a closer look at the relationship between sales and cost. **Break-even analysis** determines what

sales volume must be reached before the company breaks even (its total costs equal total revenue) and no profits are earned.

The typical break-even model assumes a given fixed cost and a constant average variable cost (total cost divided by quantity of output). Suppose that Amy's Cookies, a hypothetical firm, has fixed costs of $2,000 and that the cost of labor and materials for each unit produced is 50 cents. Assume that it can sell up to 6,000 units of its product at $1 without having to lower its price.

Exhibit 19-2a illustrates the break-even point for Amy's Cookies. As Exhibit 19.2b indicates, Amy's Cookies' total variable costs increase by 50 cents every time a new unit is produced, and total fixed costs remain constant at $2,000 regardless of the level of output. Therefore, for 4,000 units of output, Amy's Cookies has $2,000 in fixed costs and $2,000 in total variable costs (4,000 units × $0.50), or $4,000 in total costs.

The advantage of break-even analysis is that it provides a quick estimate of how much the firm must sell to break even and how much profit can be earned if a higher sales volume is obtained. If a firm is operating close to the break-even point, it may want to see what can be done to reduce costs or increase sales.

Break-even analysis is not without several important limitations. Sometimes it is hard to know whether a cost is fixed or variable. If labor wins a tough guaranteed-employment contract, are the resulting expenses a fixed cost? More important than cost determination is the fact that simple break-even analysis ignores demand. How does Amy's Cookies know it can sell 4,000 units at $1? Could it sell the same 4,000 units at $2 or even $5?

19-6 OTHER DETERMINANTS OF PRICE

Other factors besides demand and costs can influence price. For example, the stages in the product life cycle, the competition, the product distribution strategy, the Internet and extranets, the promotion strategy, price transparency, customer loyalty, appearance of being informed, demands of large customers, and the perceived quality can all affect pricing.

19-6a Stages in the Product Life Cycle

As a product moves through its life cycle (see

keystoning the practice of marking up prices by 100 percent, or doubling the cost

break-even analysis a method of determining what sales volume must be reached before total revenue equals total costs

EXHIBIT 19.2   COSTS, REVENUES, AND BREAK-EVEN POINT FOR AMY'S COOKIES

(a) Break-even point

(b) Costs and revenues

Output	Total fixed costs	Average variable costs	Total variable costs	Average total costs	Average revenue (price)	Total revenue	Total costs	Profit or loss
500	$2,000	$0.50	$250	$4.50	$1.00	$500	$2,250	($1,750)
1,000	2,000	0.50	500	2.50	1.00	1,000	2,500	(1,500)
1,500	2,000	0.50	750	1.83	1.00	1,500	2,750	(1,250)
2,000	2,000	0.50	1,000	1.50	1.00	2,000	3,000	(1,000)
2,500	2,000	0.50	1,250	1.30	1.00	2,500	3,250	(750)
3,000	2,000	0.50	1,500	1.17	1.00	3,000	3,500	(500)
3,500	2,000	0.50	1,750	1.07	1.00	3,500	3,750	(250)
4,000*	2,000	0.50	2,000	1.00	1.00	4,000	4,000	0
4,500	2,000	0.50	2,250	0.94	1.00	4,500	4,250	250
5,000	2,000	0.50	2,500	0.90	1.00	5,000	4,500	500
5,500	2,000	0.50	2,750	0.86	1.00	5,500	4,750	750
6,000	2,000	0.50	3,000	0.83	1.00	6,000	5,000	1,000

*Break-even point

Chapter 11), the demand for the product and the competitive conditions tend to change:

- **Introductory stage:** When not using pricing software, management often sets prices high during the introductory stage. One reason is that it hopes to recover its development costs quickly. In addition, demand originates in the core of the market (the customers whose needs ideally match the product's attributes) and thus is often relatively inelastic. On the other hand, if the target market is highly price sensitive, management often finds it better to price the product at market level or lower. When companies introduce highly innovative products such as

consumer electronics, medical devices, and pharmaceuticals, they must properly estimate the elasticity or demand for those products. This is particularly true today, when some life cycles are measured in months, not years.

- **Growth stage:** As the product enters the growth stage, prices generally begin to stabilize for several reasons. First, competitors have entered the market, increasing the available supply. Second, the product has begun to appeal to a broader market. Finally, economies of scale are lowering costs, and the savings can be passed on to the consumer in the form of lower prices.

- **Maturity stage:** Maturity usually brings further price decreases as competition increases and inefficient, high-cost firms are eliminated. Logistics become a significant cost factor, however, because of the need to offer wide product lines for highly segmented markets, extensive service requirements, and the sheer number of dealers necessary to absorb high-volume production. The manufacturers that remain in the market toward the end of the maturity stage typically offer similar prices. At this stage, price increases are usually cost initiated, not demand initiated. Nor do price reductions in the late phase of maturity stimulate much demand. Because demand is limited and producers have similar cost structures, the remaining competitors will probably match price reductions.

- **Decline stage:** The final stage of the life cycle may see further price decreases as the few remaining competitors try to salvage the last vestiges of demand. When only one firm is left in the market, prices begin to stabilize. In fact, prices may eventually rise dramatically if the product survives and moves into the specialty goods category, as horse-drawn carriages and vinyl records have.

19-6b Competition, Price Matching, and Customer Loyalty

Competition varies during the product life cycle, of course, and so at times it may strongly affect pricing decisions. Although a firm may not have any competition at first, the high prices it charges may eventually induce another firm to enter the market.

Fast-food giants McDonald's, Burger King, and Wendy's have been going head-to-head for years in their efforts to attract cost-conscious customers. A recent McDonald's promotion, McPick2, offered two items for $2. One way to counter a competitor's prices is price matching. The four biggest British supermarket chains all offer price-matching guarantees, ensuring that customers cannot save money by shopping elsewhere. When a shopper pays more for an item than it would cost at another store, he or she receives a voucher saying, "Your shopping would have been cheaper elsewhere, so here is a voucher for the difference."[9] Best Buy has been able to reverse its sales decline, caused primarily by online retailers, by offering price matching.

On the face of it, it seems that fierce competition is driving down prices. And this is often the case. However, economists warn that price matching may actually result in higher prices. A car dealership worried about losing clients to a lower-priced rival may offer a price-matching

Best Buy recently partnered with startup Lumoid to launch a try-before-you-buy program for customers wary of buying higher-priced electronics. Customers participating in the program can rent cameras, audio equipment, and other products for a small fee. If they decide to purchase those items, the fee is applied to their final bills.

guarantee. The hope is that the guarantee will persuade customers not to shop around; they will always pay the lowest price available by sticking with the usually higher-priced dealership. As a result, cutting prices no longer wins the competitor new business. Instead, it means lower profits on existing sales. Thus, the competitor will likely conclude that prices and profit margins are better left high.

Recall the British supermarket chains that give vouchers as a way to meet their price-matching guarantees. In order for a voucher to have value, the customer must return to the same supermarket chain. In this way, price matching can be a tool for building customer loyalty. And the more return customers the store gains over time, the greater the sales volume. Companies attempt to build customer loyalty in many ways. One approach is to offer discounts to regular patrons. This can lead to a loyalty-discount cycle, whereby loyal customers receive deeper discounts that in turn further increase their customer loyalty—resulting in downward pressure on the issuing firm's long-term pricing strategy.[10] Discounts can be an excellent tool to build customer loyalty, but care must be taken not to compromise profit goals. There are many other creative and industry-specific ways to reward loyalty. For example, airlines use unfilled seats to award free travel and upgrades to loyal customers. Some companies give branded gifts to drive customer loyalty. Hotel chains build databases on their most loyal customers so they can automatically service the room and amenity preferences of frequent customers.

19-6c Distribution Strategy

An effective distribution network can sometimes overcome other minor flaws in the marketing mix. For example, although consumers may perceive a price as being slightly higher than normal, they may buy the product anyway if it is being sold at a convenient retail outlet.

Adequate distribution for a new product can often be attained by offering a larger-than-usual profit margin to distributors. A variation on this strategy is to give dealers a large trade allowance to help offset the costs of promotion and further stimulate demand at the retail level.

19-6d The Impact of the Internet and Extranets

The Internet, **extranets** (private electronic networks), and wireless setups are linking people, machines, and companies around the globe—and connecting sellers and buyers as never before. These links are enabling buyers to quickly and easily compare products and prices, putting them in a better bargaining position. At the same time, the technology allows sellers to collect detailed data about customers' buying habits, preferences, and even spending limits so that sellers can tailor their products and prices.

USING SHOPPING BOTS A shopping bot is a program that searches the Web for the best price for a particular item that you wish to purchase. "Bot" is short for robot. Shopping bots theoretically give pricing power to the consumer. The more information that the shopper has, the more efficient his or her purchase decision will be.

There are two general types of shopping bots. The first is the broad-based type that searches (trawls) a wide range of product categories such as Google Shopping, Nextag, and PriceGrabber. These sites operate using a Yellow Pages type of model in that they list every retailer they can find. The second is the niche-oriented type that searches for prices for only one type of product such as consumer electronics (CNET), event tickets (SeatGeek), or travel-related services (Kayak).

Shopping bots have been around for quite some time, and security protocols have been developed by some Internet retailers to limit bot trawls. Still, shopping bots remain a powerful and impactful marketing tool to this day.

extranet a private electronic network that links a company with its suppliers and customers

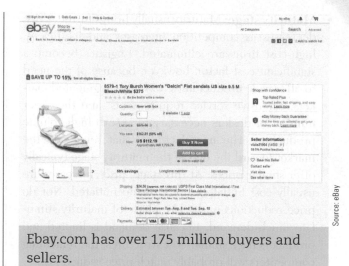

Source: eBay

Ebay.com has over 175 million buyers and sellers.

INTERNET AUCTIONS The Internet auction business is huge. Among the most popular consumer auction sites are:

- **www.onlineauction.com:** Charges a small monthly fee rather than listing and final value fees.

- **www.ebay.com:** The most popular auction site, with more than 175 million buyers and sellers.

- **www.ebid.com:** The second largest Internet auction site; fees are less than those for eBay.

Even though consumers are spending billions on Internet auctions, business-to-business auctions are likely to be the dominant form in the future. In a reverse auction, the buyer, rather than the seller, specifies the item or service that he or she is looking for. Sellers then compete to offer the lowest price to win the bid. A private company called FedBid has used reverse auctions to position itself between the federal government and private businesses. FedBid uses reverse auctions to put lucrative government contracts up for bid. In theory, since the lowest bid wins, the process can save taxpayers money by encouraging businesses to offer the best possible prices. Critics suggest that awarding government contracts based solely on price means that the government risks ending up with inferior products and services. For example, should the federal government award the next contract for a Navy aircraft carrier solely on the basis of price? Supporters contend that many items that the government purchases (such as automobiles, tools, painting services, and groundskeeping services) are entirely suitable for a reverse auction.

19-6e Promotion Strategy

Price is often used as a promotional tool to increase consumer interest. In many cases, consumer perceptions of a store's prices are more impactful than the actual prices themselves. For example, Nordstrom is perceived as a pricier alternative to Macy's even though it has similar prices in many categories and lower prices in other categories. Clearly, price promotion alone does not always create a low price image. Upscale ambience, expensive specialty offerings, premier locations, a high level of service, and a lack of price matching contribute to a high price image as well.

Often, the amount saved is the most important information when promoting a discount. For example, starting with a retail price of $80, a 40 percent discount creates a savings of $32, for a net sale price of $48. Of these four numbers—80, 40, 32, and 48—the most effective one to promote is the absolute savings of $32.[11]

19-6f Price Transparency

The worldwide proliferation of the Internet has resulted in a huge increase in price transparency. Researchers analyzing the Italian highway system found that when prices of gasoline were posted for a number of service stations on a single sign, the average price of gas decreased by 1 euro per liter.[12] This doesn't sound like much, but it represented about 20 percent of the stations' profit margins. So when drivers are better informed about gasoline prices, stations must compete by lowering prices. Now imagine how the Internet has enabled consumers to compare prices in real time online. In the health care industry, a website that tracks drug and procedure prices across various providers and insurance agencies could result in lower consumer health care costs across the board. For example, going to a dentist for a root canal can cost you anywhere from $400 to $3,000 depending on where you live—lower prices tend to be in the Midwest and higher prices tend to be in larger cities. But if you saw on the Internet that you could drive 10 miles outside your city to save thousands of dollars on a routine procedure—and did so—the industry would surely take notice.

19-6g The Appearance of Being Well-Informed or Not

Have you ever wondered if you paid too much for something because you had little knowledge of the product or service? Researchers have created an experiment using the auto repair shop business. Callers, using a script created by the researchers, requested a price quote for a radiator replacement on a Toyota Camry. The Auto MD database claimed that the price in that region should be around $365. A total of 2,778 independent repair shops were contacted. Three telephone scripts were used. The first script had callers disavow any knowledge about price (the uninformed consumer). The second script had callers claim that they had learned that the requested repair should cost about $365 (the informed consumer). In the third case, the caller stated that they understood the repair should cost around $510 (the misinformed consumer). Repair shop price quotes were not significantly different for the informed and uninformed callers. However, the shops quoted significantly higher prices to the misinformed callers. Women who didn't quote a benchmark price (uninformed scenario) were given a higher price (an average of $20) than uninformed men. Gender differences disappeared for both informed and misinformed callers.[13] The bottom line for consumers—go to the Internet or other source and try to get pricing information when purchasing moderately priced or expensive items.

19-6h Demands of Large Customers

Manufacturers find that their large customers, such as department stores often make specific pricing demands that the suppliers must agree to. Department stores are making greater-than-ever demands on their suppliers to cover the heavy discounts and markdowns on their own selling floors. They want suppliers to guarantee their stores' profit margins, and they insist on cash rebates if the guarantee is not met. They are also exacting fines for violations of ticketing, packing, and shipping rules. Cumulatively, the demands are nearly wiping out profits for all but the very biggest suppliers, according to fashion designers and garment makers.

Walmart is the largest retailer in the world, and the company uses that size to encourage companies to meet its needs. When Walmart decided that its grocery department needed to have everyday low prices instead of periodic rollbacks, it talked to its major suppliers, such as ConAgra, Quaker Oats, and McCormick & Co., to discuss the possibility of offering a consistently lower price to drive business. Some companies, like ConAgra, are struggling to lower costs while grain and other ingredients are steadily increasing in price. Other companies, like Kraft, have been steadily lowering costs and are having an easier time meeting Walmart's demands. Walmart's demands are not all about keeping prices low, however. The company has instituted a policy requiring suppliers to

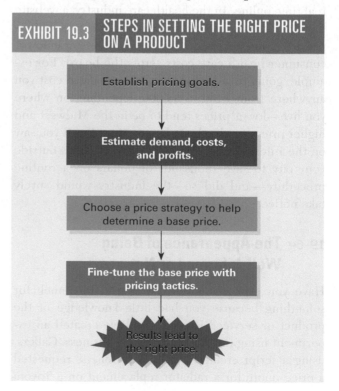

Walmart has dropped "Always Low Prices." Its new slogan is "Save Money. Live Better."

evaluate and disclose the full environmental costs of their products. The risk of not working with Walmart? Either your product is important enough to drive traffic so that Walmart keeps the item, or you lose the world's biggest sales outlet.

19-6i The Relationship of Price to Quality

As mentioned at the beginning of the chapter, when a purchase decision involves uncertainty, consumers tend to rely on a high price as a predictor of good quality. Reliance on price as an indicator of quality seems to occur for all products, but it reveals itself more strongly for some items than for others. Among the products that benefit from this phenomenon are coffee, aspirin, shampoo, clothing, furniture, whiskey, education, and many services. In the absence of other information, people typically assume that prices are higher because the products contain better materials, because they are made more carefully, or, in the case of professional services, because the provider has more expertise.

Researchers have found that price promotions of higher-priced, higher-quality brands tend to attract more business than do similar promotions of lower priced and lower quality brands. Higher prices increase expectation and set a reference point against which people can evaluate their consumption experiences. Passengers on expensive full-service airlines like Delta, United, and American complain about service failures much more often than do customers of low-cost airlines like Spirit, Southwest, and Easy Jet. A bad experience with a higher-priced product or service tends to increase the level of disappointment. Finally, products that generate strong emotions, such as perfumes and fine watches, tend to get more "bang for the buck" in price promotions.[14]

19-7 HOW TO SET A PRICE ON A PRODUCT

Setting the right price on a product is a four-step process, as illustrated in Exhibit 19.3 and discussed throughout this chapter:

1. Establish pricing goals.
2. Estimate demand, costs, and profits.
3. Choose a price strategy to help determine a base price.
4. Fine-tune the base price with pricing tactics.

19-7a Establish Pricing Goals

The first step in setting the right price is to establish pricing goals. Recall that pricing objectives fall into three categories: profit oriented, sales oriented, and status quo. These goals are derived from the firm's overall objectives. A good understanding of the marketplace and of the consumer can sometimes tell a manager very quickly whether a goal is realistic.

All pricing objectives have trade-offs that managers must weigh. A profit-maximization objective may require a bigger initial investment than the firm can commit to or wants to commit to. Reaching the desired market share often means sacrificing short-term profit, because without careful management, long-term profit goals may not be met. Meeting the competition is the

EXHIBIT 19.3 STEPS IN SETTING THE RIGHT PRICE ON A PRODUCT

Establish pricing goals.

↓

Estimate demand, costs, and profits.

↓

Choose a price strategy to help determine a base price.

↓

Fine-tune the base price with pricing tactics.

↓

Results lead to the right price.

easiest pricing goal to implement. But can managers really afford to ignore demand and costs, the life-cycle stage, and other considerations? When creating pricing objectives, managers must consider these trade-offs in light of the target customer, the environment, and the company's overall objectives. Pricing goals are a necessary input for pricing-AI software.

19-7b Estimate Demand, Costs, and Profits

Recall that total revenue is a function of price and quantity demanded and that quantity demanded depends on elasticity. Elasticity is a function of the perceived value to the buyer relative to the price. Often, pricing-AI software can answer this question. Some questions for pricing-AI software on demand and elasticity are:

- What price is so low that consumers would question the product's quality?

- What is the highest price at which the product would still be perceived as a bargain?

- What is the price at which the product is starting to be perceived as expensive?

- What is the price at which the product becomes too expensive for the target market?

After establishing pricing goals, managers should estimate total revenue at a variety of prices. This may require marketing research. Next, they should determine corresponding costs for each price. They are then ready to estimate how much profit, if any, and how much market share can be earned at each possible price. Managers can study the options in light of revenues, costs, and profits. In turn, this information can help determine which price base can best meet the firm's pricing goals.

19-7c Choose a Price Strategy

The basic, long-term pricing framework for a good or service should be a logical extension of the pricing objectives. The marketing manager's chosen **price strategy** defines the initial price and gives direction for price movements over the product's life cycle.

The price strategy, an integral part of pricing-AI software, sets a competitive price in a specific market segment based on a well-defined positioning strategy. Changing a price level from premium to super premium may require a change in the product itself, the target customers served, the promotional strategy, or the distribution channels.

A company's freedom in pricing a new product and devising a price strategy depends on the market conditions and the other elements of the marketing mix. If a firm launches a new item resembling several others already on the market, its pricing freedom will be restricted. To succeed, the company will probably have to charge a price close to the average market price. In contrast, a firm that introduces a totally new product with no close substitutes will have considerable pricing freedom.

The conventional wisdom is that store brands such as Target's Archer Farms and Kroger's Simple Truth should be priced lower than manufacturer's national brands. In fact, private label products are priced an average of 29 percent less than their national-brand counterparts.[15] However, savvy retailers doing pricing strategy research have found that store brands do not necessarily have to be cheap. When store brands are positioned as gourmet or specialty items, consumers will even pay more for them than for gourmet national brands.

Companies that do serious planning when creating a price strategy and/or use pricing-AI software usually select from three basic approaches: price skimming, penetration pricing, and status quo pricing.

PRICE SKIMMING Price skimming is sometimes called a "market-plus" approach to pricing because it denotes a high price relative to the prices of competing products. The term *price skimming* is derived from the phrase "skimming the cream off the top." Companies often use this strategy for new products when the product is perceived by the target market as having unique advantages. Often companies will use skimming and then lower prices over time. This is called "sliding down the demand curve." Manufacturers sometimes maintain skimming prices throughout a product's life cycle. A manager of the factory that produces Chanel purses (retailing for over $2,000 each) told one of your authors that it takes back unsold inventory and destroys it rather than selling it at a discount.

Price skimming works best when there is strong demand for a good or service. Apple, for example, uses skimming when it brings out a new iPhone or Watch. As new models are unveiled, prices on older versions are normally lowered. Firms can also effectively use price skimming when a product is well protected legally, when it represents a technological breakthrough, or when it has in some other way blocked the entry of competitors. Managers may follow a skimming strategy when production cannot be expanded rapidly because of technological

> **price strategy** a basic, long-term pricing framework that establishes the initial price for a product and the intended direction for price movements over the product's life cycle
>
> **price skimming** a pricing policy whereby a firm charges a high introductory price, often coupled with heavy promotion

difficulties, shortages, or constraints imposed by the skill and time required to produce a product (such as fine china, for example).

A successful skimming strategy enables management to recover its product development costs quickly. If the market perceives an introductory price as too high, managers can lower the price. Firms often believe that it is better to test the market at a high price and then lower the price if sales are too slow. Successful skimming strategies are not limited to products. Well-known athletes, lawyers, and celebrity hairstylists are experts at price skimming. Naturally, a skimming strategy will encourage competitors to enter the market.

PENETRATION PRICING Penetration pricing is at the opposite end of the spectrum from skimming. Penetration pricing means charging a relatively low price for a product when it is first rolled out as a way to reach the mass market. The low price is designed to capture a large share of a substantial market, resulting in lower production costs. If a marketing manager has made obtaining a large market share the firm's pricing objective, penetration pricing is a logical choice.

Penetration pricing does mean lower profit per unit, however. Therefore, to reach the break-even point, it requires a higher volume of sales than would a skimming policy. The recovery of product development costs may be slow. As you might expect, penetration pricing tends to discourage competition.

A penetration strategy tends to be effective in a price-sensitive market. Price should decline more rapidly when demand is elastic because the market can be expanded through a lower price. The ultra-low-cost airline Spirit is now a very profitable U.S. airline. Its cut-rate fares include little more than a seat—nearly everything else is sold à la carte. The only complimentary item in the cabin is ice. If you want water with your ice, it costs $3.00. Yet this airline maintains the highest load numbers in the industry and it continues its rapid growth. Clearly, price matters.[16]

If a firm has a low fixed-cost structure and each sale provides a large contribution to those fixed costs, penetration pricing can boost sales and provide large increases in profits—but only if the market size grows or if competitors choose not to respond. Low prices can attract additional buyers to the market. The increased sales can justify production expansion or the adoption of new technologies, both of which can reduce costs. And, if firms have excess capacity, even low-priced

Jay-Z has used both skimming and penetration pricing for his concerts in hopes of reducing ticket scalping.

business can provide incremental dollars toward fixed costs.

Penetration pricing can also be effective if an experience curve will cause costs per unit to drop significantly. The experience curve proposes that per-unit costs will go down as a firm's production experience increases. Manufacturers that fail to take advantage of these effects will find themselves at a competitive cost disadvantage relative to others that are further along the curve.

The big advantage of penetration pricing is that it typically discourages or blocks competition from entering a market. The disadvantage is that penetration means gearing up for mass production to sell a large volume at a low price. If the volume fails to materialize, the company will face huge losses from building or converting a factory to produce the failed product.

Jay-Z recently used a combination skimming and penetration strategy on his concert tour for his album *4:44*. He uses a skimming strategy for the very best seats, such as front row or with VIP experiences are ultra-high prices. For all other seats, a penetration strategy is used, with some seats going for as low as $6! This price leaves little room for sellers on the second-hand market to make a profit. It also reduces ticket-scalping, which is a notorious problem in the concert industry. Jay-Z's new pricing strategy is paying off. His revenue is up 21 percent over his previous tour.[17]

STATUS QUO PRICING The third basic price strategy a firm may choose is status quo pricing. Recall that this pricing strategy means charging a price identical to or very close to the competition's price. Although status quo pricing has the advantage of simplicity, its disadvantage is that the strategy may ignore demand or cost or both. If the firm is comparatively small, however,

penetration pricing a pricing policy whereby a firm charges a relatively low price for a product when it is first rolled out as a way to reach the mass market meeting the competition's price may be the safest route to long-term survival.

19-8 TACTICS FOR FINE-TUNING THE BASE PRICE

After managers understand both the legal and the marketing consequences of price strategies, they should set a base price—the general price level at which the company expects to sell the good or service. The general price level is correlated with the pricing policy: above the market (price skimming), at the market (status quo pricing), or below the market (penetration pricing). The final step, then, is to fine-tune the base price often using pricing-AI software.

Fine-tuning techniques are approaches that do not change the general price level. They do, however, result in changes within a general price level. These pricing tactics allow the firm to adjust for competition in certain markets, meet ever-changing government regulations, take advantage of unique demand situations, and meet promotional and positioning goals. Fine-tuning pricing tactics include various sorts of discounts, geographic pricing, and other pricing strategies.

19-8a Discounts, Allowances, Rebates, and Value-Based Pricing

A base price can be lowered through the use of discounts and the related tactics of allowances, rebates, low or zero percent financing, and value-based pricing. Managers use the various forms of discounts to encourage customers to do what they would not ordinarily do, such as paying cash rather than using credit, taking delivery out of season, or performing certain functions within a distribution channel. The following are the most common tactics:

- **Quantity discounts:** When buyers get a lower price for buying in multiple units or above a specified dollar amount, they are receiving a **quantity discount**. A **cumulative quantity discount** is a deduction from list price that applies to the buyer's total purchases made during a specific period; it is intended to encourage customer loyalty. In contrast, a **noncumulative quantity discount** is a deduction from list price that applies to a single order rather than to the total volume of orders placed during a certain period. It is intended to encourage orders in large quantities.

- **Cash discounts:** A **cash discount** is a price reduction offered to a consumer, an industrial user, or a marketing intermediary in return for prompt payment of a bill. Prompt payment saves the seller carrying charges and billing expenses and allows the seller to avoid bad debt.

- **Functional discounts:** When distribution channel intermediaries, such as wholesalers or retailers, perform a service or function for the manufacturer, they must be compensated. This compensation, typically a percentage discount from the base price, is called a **functional discount** (or **trade discount**). Functional discounts vary greatly from channel to channel, depending on the tasks performed by the intermediary.

- **Seasonal discounts:** A **seasonal discount** is a price reduction for buying merchandise out of season. It shifts the storage function to the purchaser. Seasonal discounts also enable manufacturers to maintain a steady production schedule year-round.

- **Gambled price discounts:** The customer receives a discount based on the outcome of a probabilistic gamble (and which is therefore uncertain). Discounts involving uncertainty have been growing in popularity recently. The Sears Super Scratch event involved customers receiving a scratch-and-save card that granted savings up to $500. After paying, the cashier scratched the card to reveal the discount. This is similar to a *roll-the-dice discount*, which involves paying for the item and then rolling dice to determine the discount. Several apparel chains (such as Jack Jones and Mustang Jeans) and restaurants (such as Hooters) have conducted roll-the-dice campaigns. Research shows that regular price discounts can create expectations of lower prices. This can have a negative impact on profitability. Gambled

base price the general price level at which the company expects to sell the good or service

quantity discount a price reduction offered to buyers buying in multiple units or above a specified dollar amount

cumulative quantity discount a deduction from list price that applies to the buyer's total purchases made during a specific period

noncumulative quantity discount a deduction from list price that applies to a single order rather than to the total volume of orders placed during a certain period

cash discount a price reduction offered to a consumer, an industrial user, or a marketing intermediary in return for prompt payment of a bill

functional discount (trade discount) a discount to wholesalers and retailers for performing channel functions

seasonal discount a price reduction for buying merchandise out of season price discounts, however, tend not to create long-run expectations of lower prices.

- **New Customer Discounts:** Many firms offer an initial discount to new customers. The objective is to create a long-term relationship with the new client and therefore a long-term revenue stream. Researchers have found that this is often an effective strategy. It was noted that a discount of approximately 15 to 20 percent was recommended to maximize customer lifetime revenues. An initial discount of 40 to 60 percent was not recommended, as it was too costly and also creates expectations of receiving large discounts in the future.[19]

- **Reframing discount and markdown math:** As Greg Revelle, Chief Marketing Officer of Kohl's, notes: "You shouldn't need a PhD in math to figure out our prices."[20] During the holidays, it has become quite common for large retail chains and other retailers to layer discounts one on top of the other. In some cases, this layering has confused shoppers, resulting in consumers both overestimating and underestimating the final price. Both Kohl's and JCPenney are making price reductions easier to understand. Both chains have started showing online shoppers the final price after all discounts on the product page and increasingly have been advertising sales with final dollar amounts, rather than percentage discounts. Kohl's also is testing a "Your Price" feature that shows the final cost after all discounts. For example, a Disney Princess Palace, regularly priced at $79.99, was on sale on the Kohl's website for $54.99 and eligible for an extra 25 percent off. The "Your Price" was $41.24.[21]

Researchers have approached the "clarifying of discount math for consumers" a bit differently. In an experiment, using "was X% higher," the researchers determined that this simple technique can often increase consumers' purchase intentions. This technique was found to be more successful if the retailers served either older, less-educated, or lower-income consumers.[22] The technique had a minimal impact on all consumers if the actual discount was small.

Other researchers examined the concept of "double mental discounting." For example, a promotion might advertise: "Spend $200 now and receive a $50 gift card to spend in the future!" Double mental discounting occurs when a potential buyer mentally deducts the $50 from $200 thinking "this product only cost me $150." Later on, when they receive the $50 gift card, the consumer may purchase an item for $75 but thinks "this only cost me $25 because I have a $50 gift card." The double mental discount perception is that their cost for the two items was lower than they actually were. This perception may trigger higher expenditures. The researchers found that consumers double mental discounts promotion credits (e.g., $50 gift card) are perceived as a greater discount over other types (e.g., mail-in rebates, percent off and cash-back offers).[23]

- **Promotional allowances:** A **promotional allowance** (also known as a **trade allowance**) is a payment to a dealer for promoting the manufacturer's products. It is both a pricing tool and a promotional device. As a pricing tool, a promotional allowance is like a functional discount. If, for example, a retailer runs an ad for a manufacturer's product, the manufacturer may pay half the cost.

- **Rebates:** A **rebate** is a cash refund given for the purchase of a product during a specific period. The advantage of a rebate over a simple price reduction for stimulating demand is that a rebate is a temporary inducement that can be taken away without altering the basic price structure. A manufacturer that uses a simple price reduction for a short time may meet resistance when trying to restore the price to its original, higher level.

- **Coupons:** A coupon is a discount offered via paper, a card, a printable web page, or an electronic code. U.S. marketers issue more than 293 billion coupons each year. Most coupons are still printed and distributed through newspaper inserts and mail. However, the use of digital coupons is increasing rapidly and printed coupons are declining around 10 percent a year. Consumers saved over $3.1 billion in 2017 by using coupons. Over 55 percent of consumers use both digital and print coupons. In 2018, 37 percent of shoppers received coupon offers via social media.[24] Insurance companies often raise copays on expensive drugs to get consumers to switch to low-cost alternatives. However, drug manufacturers have begun advertising "no copay" coupons for certain high-price drugs, leaving the insurance companies to pay the balance. The pharmaceutical industry now spends about $7 billion a year on copay coupons and discount cards.[25] When patients have a copay of $50, they are four times less likely to fill a prescription.[26] Drug companies say that they are just making their drugs more affordable for consumers, but are not offering similar discounts to insurance providers. Some pharmacy benefit managers, such as Express Scripts and CVS Health, have begun banning drugs from their programs because of high

promotional allowance (trade allowance) a payment to a dealer for promoting the manufacturer's products

rebate a cash refund given for the purchase of a product during a specific period

Zappos uses free shipping and returns to build customer loyalty and to gain new customers.

costs and coupon copays. United Health Group, the nation's largest health insurer, now bans 35 specialty drugs including growth hormones and medicines for pulmonary hypertension and infertility.[27]

- **Zero percent financing:** To get consumers into automobile showrooms, manufacturers sometimes offer zero percent financing, which enables purchasers to borrow money to pay for new cars with no interest charge. This tactic creates a huge increase in sales, but is not without its costs. A five-year interest-free car loan typically represents a loss of more than $3,000 for the car's manufacturer.

- **Free shipping:** Free shipping is another method of lowering the price for purchasers. Zappos, Nordstrom, and L.L.Bean offer free shipping with no minimum order amount. However, since shipping is an expense to the seller, it must be built into the cost of the product. It is estimated that American consumers will spend around $630 billion online in 2020. By then, there will be over 224 million digital shoppers in the United States. Free shipping is a prime motivation for shopping online. A study has found that 28 percent of online shoppers will abandon their shopping cart if the shipping costs are too high.[28] Today, over half of all orders from 30 of the biggest e-commerce merchants are shipped free of charge.[29]

VALUE-BASED PRICING *Value-based pricing*, also called *value pricing*, is a pricing strategy that has grown out of the quality movement. Value-based pricing starts with the customer, considers the competition and associated costs, and then determines the appropriate price. The basic assumption is that the firm is customer driven, seeking to understand the attributes customers want in the goods and services they buy and the value of that bundle of attributes to customers. Because very few firms operate in a pure monopoly, however, a marketer using value-based pricing must also determine the value of competitive offerings to customers. Customers determine the value of a product (not just its price) relative to the value of alternatives. In value-based pricing, therefore, the price of the product is set at a level that seems to the customer to be a good price compared with the prices of other options.

19-8b Geographic Pricing

Because many sellers ship their wares to a nationwide or even a worldwide market, the cost of freight can greatly affect the total cost of a product. Sellers may use several different geographic pricing tactics to moderate the impact of freight costs on distant customers. The following methods of geographic pricing are the most common:

- **FOB origin pricing:** *FOB origin pricing*, also called "FOB factory" or "FOB shipping point," is a price tactic that requires the buyer to absorb the freight costs from the shipping point ("free on board"). The farther buyers are from sellers, the more they pay, because transportation costs generally increase with the distance merchandise is shipped.

- **Uniform delivered pricing:** If the marketing manager wants total costs, including freight, to be equal for all purchasers of identical products, the firm will adopt uniform delivered pricing, or "postage stamp" pricing. With *uniform delivered pricing*, the seller pays the actual freight charges and bills every purchaser an identical, flat freight charge. This is sometimes called *postage stamp pricing* because a person can send a letter across the street or across the country for the same price.

- **Zone pricing:** A marketing manager who wants to equalize total costs among buyers within large geographic areas—but not necessarily all of the seller's market area—may modify the base price with a zone-pricing tactic. *Zone pricing* is a modification of uniform delivered pricing.

value-based pricing setting the price at a level that seems to the customer to be a good price compared to the prices of other options

FOB origin pricing a price tactic that requires the buyer to absorb the freight costs from the shipping point ("free on board")

uniform delivered pricing a price tactic in which the seller pays the actual freight charges and bills every purchaser an identical, flat freight charge

zone pricing a modification of uniform delivered pricing that divides the United States (or the total market) into segments or zones and charges a flat freight rate to all customers in a given zone

Rather than using a uniform freight rate for the entire United States (or its total market), the firm divides it into segments or zones and charges a flat freight rate to all customers in a given zone.

- **Freight absorption pricing:** In **freight absorption pricing**, the seller pays all or part of the actual freight charges and does not pass them on to the buyer. The manager may use this tactic in intensely competitive areas or as a way to break into new market areas, or increase sales (see "Free shipping").

- **Basing-point pricing:** With **basing-point pricing**, the seller designates a location as a basing point and charges all buyers the freight cost from that point, regardless of the city from which the goods are shipped. Thanks to several adverse court rulings, basing-point pricing has waned in popularity. Freight fees charged when none were actually incurred, called *phantom freight*, have been declared illegal.

19-8c Other Pricing Tactics

Unlike geographic pricing, other pricing tactics are unique and defy neat categorization. Managers use these tactics for various reasons—for example, to stimulate demand for specific products, to increase store patronage, and to offer a wider variety of merchandise at a specific price point. Such pricing tactics include a single-price tactic, flexible pricing, professional services pricing, price lining, leader pricing, bait pricing, odd–even pricing, price bundling, and two-part pricing.

SINGLE-PRICE TACTIC A merchant using a **single-price tactic** offers all goods and services at the same price (or perhaps two or three prices). Dollar Tree and Dollar Bill chains sell everything for $1 or less. Such a strategy can be quite successful.

FLEXIBLE PRICING **Flexible pricing** (or **variable pricing**) means that different customers pay different prices for essentially the same merchandise bought in equal quantities. This tactic is often found in the sale of shopping goods, specialty merchandise, and most industrial goods except supply items. Car dealers and many appliance retailers commonly follow the practice. It allows the seller to adjust for competition by meeting another seller's price. Thus, a marketing manager with a status quo pricing objective might readily adopt the tactic. Flexible pricing also enables the seller to close a sale with a price-conscious consumer.

The obvious disadvantages of flexible pricing are the lack of consistent profit margins, the potential ill will of high-paying purchasers, the tendency for salespeople to automatically lower the price to make a sale, and the possibility of a price war among sellers.

PROFESSIONAL SERVICES PRICING Professional services pricing is used by people with lengthy experience, training, and often certification by a licensing board—for example, lawyers, physicians, and family counselors. Professionals sometimes charge customers at an hourly rate, but sometimes fees are based on the solution of a problem or performance of an act (such as an eye examination) rather than on the actual time involved.

Those who use professional pricing have an ethical responsibility not to overcharge a customer. Because demand is sometimes highly inelastic, such as when a person requires heart surgery to survive, there may be a temptation to charge "all the traffic will bear."

PRICE LINING When a seller establishes a series of prices for a type of merchandise, it creates a price line. **Price lining** is the practice of offering a product line with several items at specific price points. For example, in 2018, Porsche cars were priced as follows:

Price lines are not limited to inexpensive consumer goods. Porche uses a price line for its very expensive vehicles.

blaskor/Shutterstock.com

---

freight absorption pricing a price tactic in which the seller pays all or part of the actual freight charges and does not pass them on to the buyer

basing-point pricing a price tactic that charges freight from a given (basing) point, regardless of the city from which the goods are shipped

single-price tactic a price tactic that offers all goods and services at the same price (or perhaps two or three prices)

flexible pricing (variable pricing) a price tactic in which different customers pay different prices for essentially the same merchandise bought in equal quantities

price lining the practice of offering a product line with several items at specific price points

Macan, \$47,800+; 718 Cayman, \$55,300+; 718 Boxster, \$57,400; Cayenne, \$60,600; Panamera, \$85,000+; and the 911, \$91,100+. In contrast, men's Gold Toe dress socks have a price line starting at \$7.00 a pair, then \$8.00, \$9.00, \$17,00, \$18.00, \$19.00, \$21,00, and \$24.00.[30]

Price lining reduces confusion for both the salesperson and the consumer. The buyer may be offered a wider variety of merchandise at each established price. Price lines may also enable a seller to reach several market segments. For buyers, the question of price may be quite simple: all they have to do is find a suitable product at the predetermined price. Moreover, price lining is a valuable tactic for the marketing manager, because the firm may be able to carry a smaller total inventory than it could without price lines. The results may include fewer markdowns, simplified purchasing, and lower inventory carrying charges.

Price lines also present drawbacks, especially if costs are continually rising. Sellers can offset rising costs in three ways. First, they can begin stocking lower-quality merchandise at each price point. Second, sellers can change the prices, although frequent price-line changes confuse buyers. Third, sellers can accept lower profit margins and hold quality and prices constant. This third alternative has short-run benefits, but its long-run handicaps may drive sellers out of business.

LEADER PRICING Leader pricing (or loss-leader pricing) is an attempt by the marketing manager to attract customers by selling a product near or even below cost in the hope that shoppers will buy other items once they are in the store. This type of pricing appears weekly in the newspaper advertising of supermarkets, drug stores, and other retailers. Leader pricing is normally used on well-known items that consumers can easily recognize as bargains.

A new condo in a prime location may be listed for \$1,000,000 and not \$999,999. The even price implies quality and prestige.

Leader pricing is not limited to products. Health clubs offer a one-month free trial as a loss leader.

BAIT PRICING In contrast to leader pricing, which is a genuine attempt to give the consumer a reduced price, bait pricing is deceptive. Bait pricing tries to get consumers into a store through false or misleading price advertising and then uses high-pressure selling to persuade them to buy more expensive merchandise. You may have seen an ad such as this:

> REPOSSESSED . . . Singer slant-needle sewing machine . . . take over 5 payments of \$20.00 per month . . . ABC Sewing Center.

This is bait. When a customer goes in to see the machine, a salesperson says that it has just been sold or else shows the prospective buyer a piece of junk. Then the salesperson says, "But I've got a really good deal on this fine new model." This is the switch that may cause a susceptible consumer to walk out with a \$400 machine. The Federal Trade Commission considers bait pricing a deceptive act and has banned its use in interstate commerce. Most states also ban bait pricing, but sometimes enforcement is lax.

ODD–EVEN PRICING Odd–even pricing (or psychological pricing) means pricing at odd-numbered prices to connote a bargain and pricing at even-numbered prices to imply quality. For years, many retailers have priced their products in odd numbers— for example, \$99.95—to make consumers feel they are paying a lower price for the product. Even-numbered pricing is often used for "prestige" items, such as a fine perfume at \$100 a bottle or a good watch at \$1,000. The demand curve for such items would also be saw-toothed, except that the outside edges would represent even-numbered prices and, therefore, elastic demand.

PRICE BUNDLING Price bundling is marketing two or more products in a single package for a special

leader pricing (loss-leader pricing) a price tactic in which a product is sold near or even below cost in the hope that shoppers will buy other items once they are in the store

bait pricing a price tactic that tries to get consumers into a store through false or misleading price advertising and then uses high-pressure selling to persuade consumers to buy more expensive merchandise

odd–even pricing (psychological pricing) a price tactic that uses odd-numbered prices to connote bargains and even-numbered prices to imply quality

price bundling marketing two or more products in a single package for a special price

price. For example, Microsoft offers "suites" of software that bundle spreadsheets, word processing, graphics, email, Internet access, and groupware for networks of microcomputers. Price bundling can stimulate demand for the bundled items if the target market perceives the price as a good value. Consumers expect to pay less for a bundle than they do for each item sold individually.[31]

Services like hotels and airlines sell a perishable commodity (hotel rooms and airline seats) with relatively fixed costs. Bundling can be an important income stream for these businesses because the variable costs tend to be low—for instance, the cost of cleaning a hotel room. To account for this variability, hotels sometimes charge a resort fee that covers things like use of the gym, pool, and wi-fi.

Bundling is also widely used in the telecommunications industry. Companies offer local service, long distance, Internet service, wireless, and even cable television in various bundled configurations. Telecom companies use bundling as a way to protect their market share and fight off competition by locking customers into a group of services. For consumers, comparison shopping may be difficult since they may not be able to determine how much they are really paying for each component of the bundle.

You inevitably encounter bundling when you go to a fast food restaurant. McDonald's Happy Meals and Value Meals are bundles, and customers can trade up these bundles by super sizing them. Super sizing provides a greater value to the customer and creates more profits for the fast food chain.

TWO-PART PRICING Two-part pricing means establishing two separate charges to consume a single good or service. Consumers sometimes prefer two-part pricing because they are uncertain about the number and the types of activities they might use at places like an amusement park. Also, the people who use a service most often pay a higher total price. Two-part pricing can increase a seller's revenue by attracting consumers who would not pay a high fee even for unlimited use. For example, a health club might be able to sell only 100 memberships at $700 annually with unlimited use of facilities, for a total revenue of $70,000. However, it could sell 900 memberships at $200 with a guarantee of using the racquetball courts 10 times a month. Every use over 10 would require the member to pay a $5 fee. Thus, membership revenue would provide a base of $180,000, with some additional usage fees throughout the year.

PAY WHAT YOU WANT To many people, paying what you want or what you think something is worth is a very risky tactic. Obviously, it would not work for expensive durables like automobiles. Imagine someone paying $1 for a new BMW! Yet this model has worked in varying degrees in digital media marketplaces, restaurants, and other service businesses. One of the authors of this text has patronized a restaurant close to campus that asks diners to pay what they think their meals are worth. After several years, the restaurant is still in business. The owner says that the average donation is around $12 for lunch. Social pressures can come into play in a "pay what you want" environment because an individual does not want to appear poor or cheap to his or her peers.

PACKAGE CONTENT REDUCTION Manufacturers can keep the price and package size the same while reducing the amount of content, thereby increasing the price per ounce or pound.

19-8d Consumer Penalties

More and more businesses are adopting consumer penalties—extra fees paid by consumers for violating the terms of a purchase agreement. Airlines often charge a fee for changing a return date on a ticket. Businesses impose consumer penalties because they will allegedly suffer an irrevocable revenue loss and/or incur significant additional transaction costs should customers be unable or unwilling to complete their purchase obligations. For the company, these customer payments are part of doing business in a highly competitive marketplace. With profit margins in many companies increasingly coming under pressure, organizations are looking to stem losses resulting from customers not meeting their obligations. Some medical professionals charge a penalty fee if you don't show up for an appointment. However, the perceived unfairness of a penalty may affect some consumers' willingness to patronize a business in the future.

19-9 THE LEGALITY OF PRICE STRATEGY

As mentioned in Chapter 4, some pricing decisions are subject to government regulation. Among the issues that fall into this category are unfair trade practices, price fixing, price discrimination, and predatory pricing.

two-part pricing a price tactic that charges two separate amounts to consume a single good or service

consumer penalty an extra fee paid by the consumer for violating the terms of the purchase agreement

19-9a Unfair Trade Practices

In half of the United States, **unfair trade practice acts** put a floor under wholesale and retail prices. Selling below cost in these states is illegal. Wholesalers and retailers must usually take a certain minimum percentage markup on their combined merchandise cost and transportation cost. The most common markup figures are 6 percent at the retail level and 2 percent at the wholesale level. If a specific wholesaler or retailer can provide conclusive proof that operating costs are lower than the minimum required figure, lower prices may be allowed.

The intent of unfair trade practice acts is to protect small local firms from giants like Walmart, which operates very efficiently on razor-thin profit margins. State enforcement of unfair trade practice laws has generally been lax, however, partly because low prices benefit local consumers.

However, enforcement has not been lax in all states. Meijer is a superstore that sells everything from groceries to electronics to pharmaceuticals. In 2015, when it opened its first two stores in Wisconsin, the greeting Meijer received wasn't pleasant. Rivals filed complaints accusing it of pricing 37 items—including bananas, dog food, ice cream, and Cheerios—below cost. Meijer, which runs 200 stores in five states, says this was the first time it had ever been accused of hurting consumers by charging too little. Nonetheless, the Wisconsin Department of Agriculture, Trade and Consumer Protection sent the superstore a letter explaining the requirements of the state's Unfair Sales Act.

Minimum markups do hurt consumers, since they act as a hidden tax that disproportionately harms poor and middle-income households. Wisconsin's markup law increases the price of back-to-school supplies, such as books, markers, and crayons, by 12 to 146 percent as compared with neighboring states, according to a study by the MacIver Institute.[32]

19-9b Price Fixing

Price fixing is an agreement between two or more firms on the price they will charge for a product. Suppose two or more executives from competing firms meet to decide how much to charge for a product or to decide which of them will submit the lowest bid on a certain contract. Such practices are illegal under the Sherman Act and the Federal Trade Commission Act. Offenders have received fines and sometimes prison terms. Price fixing is one area where the law is quite clear, and the U.S. Justice Department's enforcement is vigorous.

19-9c Price Discrimination

The Robinson–Patman Act of 1936 prohibits any firm from selling to two or more different buyers, within a reasonably short time, commodities (not services) of like grade and quality at different prices where the result would be to substantially lessen competition. The act also makes it illegal for a seller to offer two buyers different supplementary services and for buyers to use their purchasing power to force sellers into granting discriminatory prices or services.

The Robinson–Patman Act provides three defenses for sellers charged with price discrimination (in each case the burden is on the sellers to defend themselves):

- **Cost:** A firm can charge different prices to different customers if the prices represent manufacturing or quantity discount savings.

- **Market conditions:** Price variations are justified if designed to meet fluid product or market conditions. Examples include the deterioration of perishable goods, the obsolescence of seasonal products, a distress sale under court order, and a legitimate going-out-of-business sale.

- **Competition:** A reduction in price may be necessary to stay even with the competition. Specifically, if a competitor undercuts the price quoted by a seller to a buyer, the law authorizes the seller to lower the price charged to the buyer for the product in question.

19-9d Predatory Pricing

Predatory pricing is the practice of charging a very low price for a product with the intent of driving competitors out of business or out of a market. Once competitors have been driven out, the firm raises its prices. This practice is illegal under the Sherman Act and the Federal Trade Commission Act. To prove predatory pricing, the Justice Department must show that the predator—the destructive company—explicitly tried to ruin a competitor and that the predatory price was below the predator's average variable cost.

Prosecutions for predatory pricing suffered a major setback when a federal judge threw out a predatory pricing suit filed by the Department of Justice against American

unfair trade practice acts laws that prohibit wholesalers and retailers from selling below cost

price fixing an agreement between two or more firms on the price they will charge for a product

predatory pricing the practice of charging a very low price for a product with the intent of driving competitors out of business or out of a market

Airlines. The Department of Justice argued that the definition should be updated and that the test should be whether there was any business justification, other than driving away competitors, for American's aggressive pricing. Under that definition, the Department of Justice attorneys thought they had a great case. Whenever a fledgling airline tried to get a toehold in the Dallas market, American would meet its fares and add flights. As soon as the rival retreated, American would jack its fares back up.

Under the average variable cost, however, the case would have been almost impossible to win because, like a high-tech industry, the airline industry has high fixed costs and low marginal costs. Once a flight is scheduled, the marginal cost of providing a seat for an additional passenger is almost zero. Thus, it is very difficult to prove that an airline is pricing below its average variable cost. The judge was not impressed by the Department of Justice's argument, however, and kept to the average variable cost definition of predatory pricing.

APPENDIX

LEARNING OBJECTIVES

A-1 Understand the importance of marketing analytics

A-2 Define and explain marketing analytics

A-3 Describe data management

A-4 Explain how companies bridge the gap between data and business needs

A-5 Identify and describe examples of advanced analytics

A-6 Explain why marketing metrics are important

MARKETING ANALYTICS

Has the cost of a product, an interaction with customer service, or the environment of a store ever influenced how satisfied you were as a customer? Have you ever responded to a digital marketing campaign by searching for more information about a product or making a purchase? Do you frequently purchase more than one product at the same time, such as purchasing milk, cereal, and bread during a single visit to the grocery store? Are your purchase habits influenced by the weather, time of day, or day of the week? Do your social media interactions affect your purchase decisions? These are behaviors that marketers, such as those for Walmart, Target, and Home Depot, explore among the millions of customers each week using their marketing analytics programs. In this appendix we introduce you to the new and exciting world of marketing analytics and explain its tremendous popularity and endless possibilities.

 ## A-1 THE GROWING IMPORTANCE OF MARKETING ANALYTICS

Throughout the text, you have learned that marketing consists of processes that provide value and benefits to customers through products and services, communications, distribution, and pricing strategies. As pointed out in Chapter 1, it is the marketers' responsibility to assess the wants and satisfactions of present and potential customers, design and manage product offerings, determine prices and pricing policies, develop distribution strategies, communicate with present and potential customers, and maintain long-term customer relationships. The survival of companies is dependent on these marketing capabilities, since more customers typically translates into higher profitability. So how do marketers make critical decisions that facilitate these capabilities? They use insights that can be accurately understood only through marketing research and analytics.

Marketing analytics applies quantitative techniques that enable companies to identify hidden customer shopping patterns and produce actionable insights. The value of marketing analytics, however, is dependent on the data that companies possess. Companies collect an abundance of data from different exchange relationships with channel partners and customers. But they also collect external data such as economic, competitor, and weather events. The large amount of data now available through traditional and digital sources—such as in-store sales, e-commerce sites, social media, digital connectivity, and other technologies—provides marketers with a unique resource to improve and expand their businesses. Considering the use of "always connected" smartphones, wearables such as the iWatch or FitBit, and intelligent personal assistants such as the Amazon Echo, it is evident that technology has drastically changed the way customers search for information, interact with companies, and purchase products.

When was the last time you searched online for product information, or jumped on social media to explore your friend's latest updates? These technologies impact not only the customer's journey, they also produce data to enhance a company's ability to understand and respond to customers. Can you imagine the amount of data generated from millions of customers each day? Although having so much data seems like an asset, the large amount of data can sometimes produce significant challenges. As a result, marketers rely on information systems to capture and manage these data collections.

Marketers often access much of the information they need from **customer relationship management (CRM)** systems or marketing information systems (MIS). Recall that CRM is a company-wide business strategy designed to optimize profitability, revenue, and customer satisfaction by focusing on highly defined and precise customer groups. A marketing information system is a **management information system (MIS)** designed to support marketing decision making. These systems store data about customers, supply chain partners, and other data internal and external to the company, such as weather patterns, locations, and competitor decisions. For example, a CRM system might store multichannel customer data from mobile apps, online websites, in-store locations, social media sites, and call centers that indicate how and where customers are engaging with the company. Whether you call customer service, purchase a product in a store, browse a company website or place an order online, the data you generate is stored in a CRM system. Information from each touchpoint is captured to enhance the potential that companies can meet the needs and wants of customers. You can easily recognize the value as marketers leverage information from these databases to optimize profitability, determine marketing strategy, differentiate themselves from competitors, personalize experiences, and identify their best customers. Regardless of the specific strategy, data are used in marketing analytics to identify patterns and get to know customers on a personal level. Marketing analytics converts data into actionable information. Consequently, the information can then be used to improve customer satisfaction, drive innovative ideas, assess performance, and develop more effective marketing strategies.

Home Depot, like many other major retailers, has lots of data. The company analyzes more than 1.7 trillion data points each week to make decisions. Investing almost $6 billion through 2020, the company has high expectations for the potential of **data analytics**, with the goal of engaging with customers seamlessly whether they purchase in the store or on the website. Using marketing analytics insights, Home Depot has launched advertisements triggered by weather conditions, targeted customers with digital advertising, and used mobile location data to learn about customer traffic patterns.[1] Similarly, Stitch Fix, an online subscription shopping service, has grown rapidly in the personalized retail industry by using data and marketing analytics. When customers initially open an account, Stitch Fix gathers personal style information and preferences. The company then integrates preferences with prior customer selections and runs analytics assessments to determine what products will best satisfy the customer. As new data become available through purchase behavior and customer feedback, marketing analytics software updates the information to improve performance.[2] Other retailers such as Amazon and Target have successfully implemented similar recommender systems online that suggest products for customers based upon search history and items placed in the basket.

As described in the above examples, company data can be used to understand behavioral patterns and to optimize customer engagement and experiences. Walmart, for example, is building an advanced analytics lab driven by artificial intelligence (AI) inside one of its existing stores. **Artificial intelligence** is the development of computer systems that can perform tasks that normally requires a person such as visual perception, decision making and speech recognition. The big-box retailer is examining the use of video camera systems to detect inventory-control management issues and to identify customers that might need assistance to prevent them from leaving the store when they cannot find what they want.[3] The benefit of developing marketing strategies based on these metrics is that increasing customer retention rates by 5 percent can increase profits by as much as 125 percent. Thus, there is a clear financial benefit for proactively sensing and responding to customers who might decide to make purchases elsewhere. Depending on the business strategy, companies investigate data in a distinct manner to achieve different goals. These examples demonstrate why more and more companies are embracing a culture focused on collecting and analyzing data to make better and more timely decisions.

Companies often have more data than they realize. But the data are valuable only if companies use it to improve decision making. Unfortunately, some companies do not realize the value of data early enough. JCPenney collected behavioral data on customer attitudes for many years. But until recently, the company relied on intuition rather than on marketing analytics and customer trends. The company was surprised to discover through its marketing analytics program that customers were more receptive to discounts and coupons than to everyday low pricing. While the strategic move toward analytics occurred several years ago, JCPenney still faces challenges in identifying core customers. On the other hand, retailers such as Amazon, Target, Kohl's, and Macy's chose to use marketing analytics to examine patterns in their data and improve strategic decision making, expand sales, and increase customer satisfaction. Clearly, marketers can leverage data using analytics to create a competitive advantage and provide a more personalized experience to customers.

A-1a Data Types

What types of data do companies collect? They collect all types of data, including both structured and unstructured data.

Structured data consist of numeric fields. For example, ZIP Codes, sales figures, and numerical or categorical survey results are all structured data. This type of data provides an efficient way to run statistical analyses to identify purchasing patterns, but it sometimes limit potential insights. Let's consider that a company wants to know the amount of purchases occurring online from different geographic areas. The company can extract cities, states, or ZIP Codes from CRM systems to obtain this information. But what type of data can be used when a company is interested in understanding why customers are purchasing products or how customers feel about the products? In this situation, companies can use **unstructured data** (data that are not organized in a predefined manner) from social media posts, online communications, customer service call records, or emails with the company. This type of data consists of images, videos, audio files, and text—such as reviews or social media posts—and makes up about 80 percent of the existing data today. Social media and digital marketing environments are contributing to the growing availability of unstructured data. Combining structured with unstructured data enables companies to capture a broader view of the customer.

 ## A-2 DATA SOURCES AND COLLECTION

Data sources involve both primary data and secondary data. Recall from Chapter 9 that **primary data** are collected for the first time to solve a specific problem or answer specific questions. Results from surveys, interviews, and experiments are examples of primary data—the research is conducted to achieve a specific purpose. For instance, companies that develop surveys

and collect responses often do so to accomplish a specific objective. Perhaps the company initiates a survey to understand recent shopping experiences at a particular store, or they might inquire specifically about customer perceptions regarding a new product. Eye-tracking technology is also increasingly being used by retail stores to determine what a customer might look at first when approaching a product display or when viewing packaging designs. P&G has adopted this approach and conducts experiments at their headquarters inside artificial environments that look like the aisles of a supermarket.[4] The information is then used to determine different packaging designs, advertisements, or the appropriate product shelf placement that is more likely to catch the attention of a consumer. These examples illustrate how companies design methods of data collection for which there is a specific purpose in mind. Primary data has a significant advantage in that this type of data can answer specific questions. But it can also be costly and require a lot of time to collect. In contrast, *secondary data* are data that have been previously collected for another reason. Secondary data might not be capable of answering a specific question but is usually available immediately and might provide an initial starting point to assist in further development of a research study. It is also much less expensive to gather than primary data.

Examples of secondary data include those from various digital channels such as computers, smartphones, tablets, and video game consoles. People are often willing to share ideas with others via social media. The best conversations are often organically derived, with customers offering advice and feedback about product quality and use. The Clorox Company, owner of Hidden Valley Ranch brands, recognized this as a source of secondary data. Using social media chatter, researchers discovered that customers were creating their own flavors of Hidden Valley Ranch dressing with other condiments.[5] These insights played a pivotal role in inspiring the company to create a sriracha-flavored Hidden Valley ranch dressing. Through interacting with others, searching for information, purchasing products, and playing video games, people generate a variety of data from these digital channels. Companies capture conversations on social media websites such as Pinterest or Facebook, but they also collect data from customer purchases on websites, location data from mobile phones, and other sources.

There are many sources of secondary data, such as the following:

- **Government:** Companies can access data such as Census or North American Industry Classification System (NAICS) details through government websites. Census data can be integrated with internal customer data to improve understanding of other drivers of purchasing behavior. For example, do specific demographics in an area have an impact on sales of particular products or brands? Business-to-business salespeople might also explore NAICS codes, a format that provides a classification of industries, in an effort to develop an understanding of a particular industry or type of customer.

- **Channel partners:** There are often many partners in a channel—suppliers, manufacturers, wholesalers, distributors, and retailers—that can provide important data. Each channel partner collects data of value to them. Manufacturers or retailers might share sales data or customer preferences with each other to benefit production or inventory control. As an example, Ford Motor Company maintains a Smart Inventory Management System that integrates many sources of data to make inventory recommendations to the dealer network. As a result of sharing this information, dealers acquire the inventory with models, styles, and features that customers in their market want to purchase.

- **Commercial entities:** Data brokers collect and sell data. Retailers might be interested in credit card purchasing history to investigate whether customers are also purchasing from a competitor. Similarly, to identify high-risk patients, hospitals have purchased data so that they can examine lifestyles to determine whether patients might be more likely to experience specific medical issues.[6] Hospitals use the data to target specific types of patients in their market area and in general to improve medical decision making.

- **Corporate:** Companies collect data that are stored internally in a variety of databases. Data can be integrated across the organization from accounting, finance, sales, customer service, and marketing to gain a better understanding of sales and customer satisfaction.

- **Mobile and social media**: Companies can obtain valuable feedback about products and brands from online sources such as Facebook, Twitter, and Instagram. For example, Ford Motor Company collected consumer opinions by exploring social media posts. Using marketing analytics, the company discovered that potential customers preferred an easy-to-operate power liftgate. This liftgate was subsequently included on the Ford Escape. This finding helped reduce the cost of manufacturing vehicles that might be difficult to sell and led to more satisfied customers.

- **Online websites:** Existing websites are sources of secondary data. Some companies use weather data to predict consumer behavior.[7] Weather patterns can predict emotions or result in different habits in consumer behavior, such as the desire to attend a movie, plan a spa day, or remain inside. A rainy day might cause consumers to rent a movie rather than venture out to shop. Retailers can also use weather data in combination with demographic and sales data to personalize communications or sales in specific geographic areas.

A-3 DATA MANAGEMENT

Walmart processes huge amounts of internal and external data every hour, 24/7. The company not only collects transactional data from its approximately 140 million customers per week, it also includes data from 200 other sources.[8] Walmart might collect weather data or data pertaining to local area events to promote certain products or they might use the data to determine strategic pricing for different geographic regions. They also rely upon economic data and social media data to help design solutions to other problems. Walmart's massive amount of data is considered big data, which was introduced in Chapter 9. Big data requires special tools to manage, process, and analyze the huge amounts of data. In the case of Walmart, the company has created a data management system that helps them to improve marketing decisions. The proper management of data creates an efficient method for employees throughout the company to access the data and efficiently solve business problems.

To create value from big data, an integration process that combines three stages is executed: extract data, transform data, and load data. The process, referred to as _ETL_, _extracts_ data from the original source, _transforms_ the data into a usable format, and _loads_ the data into a system designated for storing data. Multichannel retailers rely on this process to integrate customer data from multiple channels, sort records, and provide a more complete profile of customers. ETL enables data that are complex and dynamic to be collected and integrated from various sources. Integrating data from these different sources improves the measurement of market potential, and marketing analytics software uses data to develop new insights, identify business trends, and discover opportunities.

A-3a Databases and Data Warehousing

With technology enhancements and collaboration between the marketing and information technology departments, the same guidance is now applied to understand

EXHIBIT A.1 RELATIONAL DATABASE EXAMPLE

Record Number	Customer ID	Purchase Amount	Products Purchased	Name
1	4	55	2	Shirley
2	1	78	5	Tim
3	2	17	1	Katrina
4	3	104	6	Frank

databases and data warehousing. Although marketers may not be responsible for maintaining these systems, they should have an understanding of the terminology and processes.

A **database** is a collection of data that is organized for efficient retrieval and analysis by people throughout a company. These systems store, manage, and track current business information. Recent customer relationship management (CRM) transactions, such as customer names and recent purchase information, are commonly stored in **relational databases** (Exhibit A-1). These types of databases are organized into structured tables that contain neatly separated rows and columns.

A-3b Data Warehouse

Although companies often use databases to store current data such as customer transactions that occurred in a particular week and to monitor events in real time, data that represents previous points in time and multiple sources are often contained in a data warehouse. A **data warehouse** is a centralized storage area that includes historical data from multiple databases used by different departments throughout the company. The data warehouse stores a combination of data relating to areas such as customers, sales, human resources, and financial data. Data warehouses are structured for simplicity, yet offer powerful, high-speed querying performance for historical data analysis.

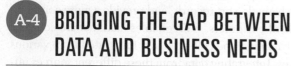

A-4 BRIDGING THE GAP BETWEEN DATA AND BUSINESS NEEDS

Similar to the marketing research process introduced in Chapter 9, there is an established method that is commonly used when engaging in marketing analytics initiatives.

It is a sequence of six stages to guide data analysis:

1. Business understanding
2. Data understanding
3. Data preparation
4. Data modeling
5. Evaluation of results
6. Deployment of a plan

It is important for marketers to first understand the business situation when applying this method, since data analysis is dependent on the type of questions that need to be answered. Researchers cannot use customer age, for example, to answer questions pertaining to weather patterns and purchase history.

A-4a Marketing Analytics Tools and Techniques: Application in Marketing

Once there is a complete understanding of the business and available data, the information can be used with the correct analytics technique to answer marketing questions. It might seem unlikely that you will need to understand marketing analytics techniques. But if you pursue a marketing career, it is highly likely you will be expected to know something about analytics techniques. Marketing analytics is increasingly being used by companies to make decisions and improve their operations. For example, Nokia trains all employees on the basics of their marketing analytics techniques.

Analytics techniques vary in complexity and are often classified as producing results that are descriptive, predictive or prescriptive. *Descriptive analytics* are explanatory and provide results such as how many products are sold each day or how often customers visit a website. *Predictive analytics* assists companies in forecasting what is likely to occur in the future, such as how customers will respond to certain products or whether a customer might decide to purchase from a competitor. Companies also use *prescriptive analytics* to identify optimal business outcomes, such as knowing what pricing approaches to use to achieve increase sales or reduce costs.

A-4b Marketing Analytics

Marketing analytics includes a variety of statistical techniques that can be categorized into supervised or unsupervised learning. *Supervised learning* is when an output has been determined for the analysis. Let's say you are interested in why customers remain loyal to a particular company. Why would customers decide to continue purchasing from the company or possibly seek a competitor's alternative? When you use marketing analytics, you specify an input for supervised learning, such as whether customers have remained loyal to your business or have started buying from a competitor. The objective is to determine whether the customer's decision to stay or leave is based on their perceptions of the quality of products, product pricing, loyalty toward the brand, or something else. On the other hand, *unsupervised learning* is when there is not a designated outcome. A company might want to understand how customer markets are segmented. What similarities do customers share and how are they clustered together by needs and wants? When we discuss advanced analytics, we are referring a broad concept used to describe quantitative analysis techniques that use high-speed technology and processing. We now describe a few examples of advanced analytics and how marketers can use insights to make better decisions.

Market Basket Analysis

Are certain products most frequently purchased together? For example, when a customer purchases milk, do they also purchase bread? Market basket analysis determines, for example, the strength of association between the likelihood that milk and bread will be purchased at the same time. Market basket techniques use association rules to detect products that are commonly purchased together.

Understanding that the purchase of one item might lead to the purchase of another item is helpful to marketers. Market basket analysis might also take into consideration seasonal baskets of behavior as a response to anticipated weather-related events, such as snow or hurricanes. This information can be used by retailers to maintain levels of inventory that ensure that items are always on the shelf, to determine product placement on store shelves or websites, and to identify how a customer might respond to a coupon.

Social Media Network Analytics

Who are the influencers of the social media group? Do subgroups exist in the social networks? Are messages being viewed or shared? What is the number of unique or return visitors? What is the length of follower comments? Social media is used to generate brand awareness, brand engagement, and word of mouth. Social networks or people participating in social media have the potential to provide immediate return by rapidly increasing conversations about the brand. In general, social media network analytics help discover basic performance metrics such as how many likes a post possesses or how frequently a person responds to posts. However, measures such as centrality can identify more complex relationships such as trends and clusters of people that are connected.

Web Analytics

What factors are attracting visitors to the website? Are email campaigns highlighting seasonal sales and driving people to the site? How are visitors navigating through the website? How long are visitors spending on the website before converting to a sale or leaving? Companies dedicate substantial budgets to driving traffic to their websites, where a significant number of people visit each day. Web analytics offers companies an understanding of basic visitor behavior through click stream and customer browsing behavior.

Results from web analytics provide insights into whether companies should refocus efforts on driving visitors to its website or which webpage designs result in more online purchases. Attracting customers to a website is one way to expose them to more information about products and services. Whether customers visit websites to investigate products or to actually make purchases, understanding their behavior is valuable as the company plans future digital initiatives. Tools such as Google Analytics, Adobe Analytics, and Adobe Target have been developed to comprehensively analyze website performance.

A-4c Marketing Metrics

Acquiring and retaining customers is necessary to achieve financial success. Resources are used to attract new customers and retain loyal customers. Measuring *customer acquisition costs (CAC)* helps companies determine whether resources associated with gaining customers results in a return on investment. If you watch *Shark Tank*, you are familiar with the sharks frequently asking about what types of marketing the companies use and the customer acquisition costs. How much are they really spending to gain a single customer? Understanding customer acquisition costs can help companies determine whether they are spending too much to acquire customers or too little. Marketing spending that is not acquiring customers should be eliminated or allocated to other marketing opportunities.

When the company has acquired good customers, it should focus on managing those relationships to increase satisfaction and achieve loyalty. The greater the satisfaction and loyalty, the more likely a customer is to remain with the company. *Customer retention rate* and *churn ratios* provide an understanding of the company's ability to retain customers; they also identify customers at risk of leaving. The *customer retention rate*, or the percent of customers that have been retained within a certain time frame, is calculated as the [(number of customers at the end of a specified period – the number of new customers acquired during the period) / the number of customers at the start of the period] × 100. *Customer churn* is when a customer ceases to make purchases. Although companies might include other variables, a simple measure of customer churn within a given time period (month) can be measured as (the number of customers lost last month / the total customers at the beginning of that month) × 100. Companies that increase acquisition and reduce churn improve the value over the lifetime that a customer remains a customer.

The measure of *customer lifetime value (CLV)* is focused on the long-term, future relationship with a customer. Profits generated by a customer over their lifetime can be useful to companies in assessing the value of the relationship. Is the cost of acquiring and maintaining the relationship worth the investment? Although it might be surprising, companies sometimes stop pursuing relationships when discovering that they are no longer valuable. As the customer lifetime value decreases, so does the company's financial performance. Thus, CLV also provides companies information on forecasting future financial performance. The CLV relies on several values. First, companies should know the gross margin of a customer—the sales revenue minus the cost of the service to the company. Next, companies should have an idea of the acquisition cost of each customer and how many customers are being retained. Finally, companies understand the time value of money. That is, the value of money today is worth more than it will be next year. Therefore, companies determine a discount rate to reflect this difference in value.

DISCUSSION QUESTIONS

1. Define marketing analytics. How do marketing analytics facilitate marketing decision making?

2. Explain the difference between a relational database and a nonrelational database.

3. What are some sources of secondary data? How can companies use secondary data as the sole source or to complement existing data when conducting marketing analytics?

4. What is the difference between structured and unstructured data?

5. What are some applications of marketing analytics?

Assignment 1: Understanding the Data

1. Ask students to search for and download a dataset on www.Kaggle.com related to a marketing situation.

2. Ask students to explain the data fields included in the data set. What are three questions that can be answered by the data?

3. Determine what additional types of data would be helpful to obtain more comprehensive insights.

Assignment 2: How Valuable Is a Customer?

A local cable company is expanding its business-to-business services. The company has been signing up business customers that represent two different segments: the premium service customers and the tier 1 service customers. The marketing team is interested in understanding the value of these two segments.

The revenue of each segment is considered stable since the business customers are in contractual agreements and the subscription price is set for life. Although consumer customers pay on a monthly basis, the business segments pay in full each year during the month of January.

Segment 1, the premium service customers, subscribes to the package that consists of cable with the extra HD and HBO channels, high-speed Internet, and telephone service. The gross margin is $4,500. These customers initially require a high level of effort and the acquisition costs of this segment are $300. Segment 2, tier 1 service, subscribes to only the minimum business telephone service. This segment generates $3,000 in gross margin each year. Acquisition costs for this segment are only $50.

Since each segment operates on a contractual agreement, accounts remain stable and both segments maintain a 90 percent (0.90) retention rate. The cable company uses a discount rate of 10 percent (0.10). The company is trying to understand the value of each customer segment during its lifetime. Although CLV can be calculated in various ways, a simple example is introduced.

1. Using the basic formula, calculate the CLV for each customer segment. (Use the decimal number for the discount rate and retention rate.)

   [gross margin a customer generates in year* (1 + the interest rate used for discounting) / (1 – the retention rate + the interest rate used for discounting)] – the acquisition cost

2. How does CLV for the premium service customers change if the retention rate drops to 80 percent (0.8)? Does changing the retention rate impact the CLV substantially?

3. What is revealed from each segment's CLV value? Based on the CLV results of each segment, what

should marketing consider in the acquisition of new customers? Should the cable company focus marketing efforts on obtaining and retaining one segment over another?

CLASS ACTIVITY

Scenario

Discuss companies that are currently underperforming. Ask student groups to locate an article in the media about a struggling company and research reasons for its problems.

Step 1: Identify a potential business problem the company is facing. Develop two research questions that might provide an understanding of the situation or address the business problem.

Step 2: Determine what type of primary and secondary data could be used to answer these questions. Require students to select several sources of data that might be helpful to generate deeper insights.

Step 3: Based on the questions and types of data that will be needed to answer the questions developed in step 1, what analytic techniques could you use? For example, a company wants to explore their social media sites to better understand how they might engage customers.

ENDNOTES

1

1. "Definition of Marketing," American Marketing Association, www.marketingpower.com/AboutAMA/Pages/DefinitionofMarketing.aspx (accessed October 3, 2018).

2. Maggie McGrath, with Lauren Gensler and Samantha Sharf, "Competition is the New Union," *Forbes*, December 26, 2017, pp. 56–58.

3. Michael E. Bush and Sarah Lewis-Kulin, "100 Best Companies to Work for 2018," *Fortune.com*, March 1, 2018, pp. 53–93.

4. Philip Kotler and Kevin Lane Keller, *A Framework for Marketing Management*, 6th ed. (Upper Saddle River, NJ: Prentice Hall, 2016).

5. Zach Lazzari, "Examples of a Sales-Oriented Business," https://yourbusiness.azcentral.com/examples-salesoriented-business-11277.html, May 7, 2018.

6. Charles Fleming, "Harley's New Hogs, Ready for the 21st Century," http://www.latimes.com/business/autos/la-fi-hy-harley-softail-review-20170825-story.html, August 25, 2017.

7. "Service Satisfaction Key to Increasing Brand Advocacy, J.D. Power Finds" https://www.jdpower.com/business/press-releases/jd-power-2018-us-customer-service-index-study (accessed October 20, 2018).

8. Douglas A. McIntyre, "10 Brands That Will Disappear in 2016," *Huffington Post*, http://www.huffingtonpost.com/entry/10-brands-disappear-in-2016_us_56379cdee4b0c66bae5d23fc (accessed October 21, 2018).

9. Susan McPherson, "6 CSR Trends to Watch in 2017," *Forbes*, January 19, 2017, http://www.forbes.com/sites/susanmcpherson/2017/01/19/6-csr-trends-to-watch-in-2017/#11d328b04ece (accessed October 21, 2018).

10. "Fortune Recognizes CVS Health on 2018 List of 'World's Most Admired Companies,'" https://cvshealth.com/newsroom/press-releases/fortune-recognizes-cvs-health-2018-list-worlds-most-admired-companies, January 19, 2018.

11. A. G. Laffey and Ron Charon, cited in George S. Day and Christine Moorman, *Strategy from the Outside In: Profiting from Customer Value* (New York, NY: McGraw-Hill, 2010), 235.

12. George Day and Christine Moorman, *Strategy from the Outside In* (New York, NY: McGraw-Hill, 2010).

13. Werner Huttenrauch, "The Customer Is Not an Interruption in Our Work; He Is the Purpose of It," https://www.linkedin.com/pulse/customer-most-important-visitor-our-premises-werner-hüttenrauch, July 28, 2017 (accessed October 25, 2018).

14. George Day and Christine Moorman, *Strategy from the Outside In* (New York, NY: McGraw-Hill, 2010).

15. *Ibid.*

16. Rob Brunner, "America Shacks Up," *FastCompany*, July/August 2015, 77–95.

17. Samuel Stebbins, Michael B. Sauter, and Evan Comen, "Customer Service Hall of Shame," https://247wallst.com/special-report/2017/08/24/customer-service-hall-of-shame-6/2/, August 24, 2017 (accessed October 25, 2018).

18. Eric Almquist, John Senior, and Nicolas Bloch, "Elements of Value," *Harvard Business Review*, September 2016, pp. 47–53.

19. David Vanamburg, "National Banks Improve Customer Experience," ACSI Matters, December 29, 2016, https://acsimatters.com/2016/12/29/national-banks-improve-the-customer-experience/ (accessed October 25, 2018).

20. "4 Examples of Businesses Leveraging CRM to Improve Productivity and Efficiency," Salesforce.com, February 8, 2017, https://www.salesforce.com/crm/examples/ (accessed October 25, 2018).

21. Neal Gabler, "The Magic in the Warehouse," *Fortune*, December 15, 2016, 182–189.

22. "Creating a Culture of Innovation and Care," *Fortune*, March 2018, ad section.

23. David Kirkalday, "12 Service Values Ritz Carlton Uses (And You Can Too)," David Kirkaldy, www.davidkirkaldy.com/12-service-values-ritz-carlton-uses-and-you-can-too (accessed October 25, 2018).

24. Paul J. Zak, "The Neuroscience of Trust," *Harvard Business Review*, January–February 2017, pp. 85–90.

25. Lawrence Gregory, "Microsoft's Mission and Vision Statement (An Analysis)," http://panmore.com/microsoft-corporation-vision-statement-mission-statement-analysis, August 30, 2018.

26. Lindsay Kolowich, "17 Truly Inspiring Vision and Mission Statement Examples," https://blog.hubspot.com/marketing/inspiring-company-mission-statements, July 9, 2018.

27. Adrainne Pasquarelli, "How a Millennial Mindset Is Helping This 116-Year-Old Retailer," Advertising Age, January 30, 2017, http://adage.com/article/cmo-strategy/a-millennial-mindset-helping-116-year-retailer/307734/ (accessed October 26, 2018).

28. Julie Jargon, "Restaurants See Value in Big Data," *The Wall Street Journal*, October 3, 2018, p. R5.29.

29. U.S. Census Bureau, "U.S. & World Population Clocks," October 26, 2018, www.census.gov/main/www/popclock.html.

30. C Wanamaker, "How Much Food Do Americans Eat?" https://caloriebee.com/misc/Food-Consumption-by-The-Numbers, April 6, 2018.

2

1. Suzanne Kapner, "West Elm to Launch Its Own Boutique Hotels," *Wall Street Journal*, September 25, 2016, https://www.wsj.com/articles/west-elm-to-launch-its-own-boutique-hotels-1474844931 (accessed November 6, 2018).

2. Shirley Brady, "Ford Pivots from Passenger Cars in Massive Transformation of Business," https://www.brandchannel.com/2018/04/25/ford_exits_passenger_cars_transformation_042518/, April 25, 2018.

3. George Anderson, "What Does Giving Up Alcohol Say about Starbucks?" *RetailWire*, January 11, 2017, https://www.retailwire.com/discussion/what-does-giving-up-alcohol-say-about-starbucks/ (accessed February 9, 2019).

4. Shelly Banjo, "Amazon's Path to Profitability," *Bloomberg Gadfly,* January 28, 2016, https://www.bloomberg.com/gadfly/articles/2016-01-28/amazon-holiday-earnings-a-glimpse-at-retail-s-future (accessed November 7, 2018).

5. Eric Schwartzberg, "How 3 Major Retailers are Reinventing to Keep Customers," https://www.journal-news.com/news/how-major-retailers-are-reinventing-keep-customers/FKeueY1Q9M0udMVNXuLFFJ/, June 19, 2018.

6. Dale Buss, "Danone Makes a Bigger Push Into Vegan and Non-Dairy Products," https://www.journal-news.com/news/how-major-retailers-are-reinventing-keep-customers/FKeueY1Q9M0udMVNXuLFFJ/, July 2, 2018.

7. Saabira Chaudhuri, "Lego Clicks with China's Tencent to Develop Online Games," https://www.wsj.com/articles/lego-clicks-with-chinas-tencent-to-develop-online-games-1516029387, January 15, 2018.

8. Dale Buss, "Blue Apron Is Heading to Stores as Meal Kit Competition Heats Up," https://www.brandchannel.com/2018/03/15/blue-apron-meal-kit-competition/ March 15, 2018.

9. Rueben Yonaton, "The Biggest Cash Cows of the Largest Companies," https://getvoip.com/blog/2018/05/29/cash-cows/, May 29, 2018.

10. Douglas Imaralu, "Can Africa Save Blackberry?" *Ventures*, May 30, 2014, www.ventures-africa.com/2014/05/can-africa-save-blackberry/ (accessed November 7, 2018).

11. Zach Brooke, "10 Brands That Came Back from the Dead," American Marketing Association, August 8, 2016, https://www.ama.org/publications/eNewsletters/Marketing-News-Weekly/Pages/10-brands-that-came-back-from-the-dead.aspx (accessed November 7, 2018).

12. Peter Burrows and Jim Aley, "Why the iPad's Success May Spell the End of the Computer Industry as We Know It," *Bloomberg Businessweek*, March 26–April 1, 2012, 4–5, http://magsreview.com/bloomberg-businessweek/bloomberg-businessweek-march-26-2012/3264-nice-try.html (accessed November 7, 2018).

13. Anshul, "BCG Matrix of Samsung/BCG Matrix Analysis of Samsung," http://heartofcodes.com/bcg-matrix-of-samsung/, July 25, 2018.

14. Matthew Stern, "Starbucks Dumps Tea Bar Concept, Keeps Tea," *RetailWire*, January 27, 2016, http://retailwire.com/discussion/18809/starbucks-dumps-tea-bar-concept-keeps-tea (accessed November 7, 2018).

15. "A Strong Performance in 2016 Positions Airbus Commercial Aircraft for the Future," *Airbus*, January 11, 2017, http://www.aircraft.airbus.com/newsevents/news-events-single/detail/a-strong-performance-in-2016-positions-airbus-commercial-aircraft-for-the-future/ (accessed November 7, 2018).

16. "Writing a Plan Does Increase Odds of Success," *Harvard Business Review,* November–December 2017, 26.

17. "Ben & Jerry's Ice Cream—Ben & Jerry's Mission Statement," www.benjerry.com/activism/mission-statement (accessed November 7, 2018).

18. Lia Sestric, "How Your Favorite Brands Reinvented Themselves and Made Big Money," *Go Banking Rates,* September 5, 2016, https://www.gobankingrates.com/personal-finance/favorite-brands-reinvented-themselves-made-big-money/ (accessed November 7, 2018).

19. "Kodak: Failing to Maintain Relevancy," *StealingShare,* December 14, 2016, http://www.stealingshare.com/pages/kodak-failing-to-maintain-relevancy/ (accessed November 7, 2018).

20. J. L. Johnson, "Opinion: Nine Reasons Why I Think Southwest Is the Best," *AirlineReporter,* May 11, 2016, http://www.airlinereporter.com/2016/05/opinion-nine-reasons-southwest-best/ (accessed November 7, 2018).

21. Andrew Nusco, "Google: In Search of Consumer Electronics and Software with Soul," *Fortune,* January 1, 2018, p. 60.

22. "Blue Bell History," Bluebell Creameries, www.bluebell.com/the_little_creamery/our_history.html (accessed November 7, 2018).

23. "About the Farm," The Chef's Garden, www.chefs-garden.com/about-the-farm (accessed February 20, 2018).

24. Erika Fry, "Tesla: Redefining an Industry," *Fortune,* January 1, 2018, 68–69.

25. Chitra Reddy, "14 Reasons Why Google Is the Best Place to Work," March 5, 2016, https://content.wisestep.com/reasons-google-best-place-work/ (accessed November 8, 2018).

3

1. "Social Control: From Hunter-Gatherer Bands to the United Nations," *Anthropology Now,* April 17, 2014, http://anthropologynow.wordpress.com/tag/social-control (accessed January 16, 2015).

2. Eric Cardella, "Slapping a 'Natural' Label on Everything," *Bloomberg Businessweek,* November 5, 2015, 62.

3. "In the Maple-Rich Areas of New England and the Upper Midwest Producers Don't Approve of Fakers," *U.S. News & World Report,* February 16, 2016, http://www.usnews.com/news/business/articles/2016-02-16/maple-syrup-producers-question-foods-labeled-maple (accessed February 3, 2017); also see Tamara Manelly, "Guess What? You're Buying Fake Maple Syrup," Oh Lardy, https://ohlardy.com/guess-what-youre-eating-fake-maple-syrup/ (September 29, 2018).

4. "California Bans Restaurants from Automatically Giving Out Plastic Straws," https://www.eater.com/2018/9/21/17886256/california-straw-ban-plastic (accessed September 29, 2018).

5. "FTC Imposes Largest COPPA Civil Penalties to Date—Children's Online Privacy a Growing Concern," https://corporate.findlaw.com/law-library/ftc-imposes-largest-coppa-civil-penalties-to-date-children-s.html (accessed October 3, 2018).

6. "Spark Learning with G Suite for Education," https://edu.google.com/products/gsuite-for-education/?modal=none (accessed February 19, 2019).

7. "Consumers Say Corporate Ethics Matter," *Quirk's Marketing Research Review,* January 2016, 17.

8. *Ibid.*

9. Catherine Rainbow, "Descriptions of Ethical Theories and Principles," Davidson College, http://www.bio.davidson.edu/people/kabernd/indep/carainbow/Theories.htm (accessed January 10, 2015).

10. "WalMart Stuck in Probe Limbo," *Wall Street Journal,* January 28–29, 2017, B1–B2. Also see: "Walmart Six Years Later," April 19, 2018, fcpaprofessor.com/Walmart-six-years-later (accessed October 3, 2018).

11. Amna Kirmani, Rebecca W. Hamilton, Debora V. Thompson, and Shannon Lantzy, "Doing Well versus Doing Good: The Differential Effect of Underdog Positioning on Moral and Competent Service Providers," *Journal of Marketing,* January 2017, 103–117.

12. Anusorn Singhapakdi, Scott Vitell, and Kenneth Kraft, "Moral Intensity and Ethical Decision Making of Marketing Professionals," *Journal of Business Research,* 36, no. 3 (1996): 245–255; Ishmael Akaah and Edward Riordan, "Judgments of Marketing Professionals about Ethical Issues in Marketing Research: A Replication and Extension," *Journal of Marketing Research,* 26, no. 1 (1989): 112–120; see also Shelby Hunt, Lawrence Chonko, and James Wilcox, "Ethical Problems of Marketing Researchers," *Journal of Marketing Research,* 21, no. 3 (1984): 309–324; Kenneth Andrews, "Ethics in Practice," *Harvard Business Review,* September 1989, 99–104; Thomas Dunfee, Craig Smith, and William T. Ross Jr., "Social Contracts and Marketing Ethics," *Journal of Marketing,* 63, no. 3 (1999): 14–32; Jay Handelman and Stephen Arnold, "The Role of Marketing Actions with a Social Dimension: Appeals to the Institutional Environment," *Journal of Marketing,* 63, no. 3 (1999): 33–48; David Turnipseed, "Are Good Soldiers Good? Exploring the Link between Organizational Citizenship Behavior and Personal Ethics," *Journal of Business Research,* 55, no. 1 (2002): 1–15; and O. C. Ferrell, John Fraedrich, and Linda Ferrell, *Business Ethics: Ethical Decision Making and Cases,* 10th ed. (Stamford, CT: Cengage Learning, 2015), 128–137.

13. "Workplace Ethics in Transition," Ethics.org, http://www.ethics.org/resource/webcasts (accessed January 12, 2015).

14. *Ibid.*

15. "Message from Larry Merlo, President and CEO," CVS Health, February 5, 2014, http://cvshealth.com/newsroom/message-larry-merlo (accessed April 15, 2016).

16. "Pharma's Newest Poster Boy," *Business Week,* December 28, 2015–January 10, 2016, 10–11.

17. *Ibid.*

18. *Ibid.*

19. "Pharma-Bro Martin Shkreli Moved to Low-Security Federal Prison in New Jersey," https://www.theguardian.com/us-news/2018/Apr/19/pharma-bro-martin-shkreli-moved-to-low-security-federal-prison-in-new-jersey (accessed October 3, 2018).

20. "How to Keep Compliance and Ethics on Target," *Journal of Accountancy,* January 1, 2017, http://www.journalofaccountancy.com/issues/2017/jan/keep-compliance-and-ethics-on-target.html (accessed February 6, 2017).

21. "State of Ethics in Large Companies," Ethics and Compliance Initiative, https://www.ethics.org/knowledge-center/state-of-ethics-in-large-companies (accessed April 15, 2016).

22. "Teaching Ethics to AI," *Marketing News,* September 2018, 18–20.

23. *Ibid.*

24. "Xi Jinping's Anti-Corruption Campaign," August 24, 2018, https://www.scmp.com/topics/xi-jinpings-anti-corruption-campaign (accessed October 4, 2018).

25. "Prolonged Exposure to Heat Is Making Takata Airbags Explode during a Crash, Prompting Recall," August 30, 2018, Fortune.com/2018/08/29/takata-airbags-recall-exploding-extreme-heat/ (accessed October 5, 2018).

26. Madeleine Stone, "Facebook Made Billionaires of These 8 People—Here's What They're Doing Now," *Business Insider,* July 7, 2015, https://www.businessinsider.com/where-are-they-now-facebook-billionaires-2015-7 (accessed February 1, 2017).

27. Saurabh Mishra and Sachin B. Modi, "Corporate Social Responsibility and Shareholder Wealth: The Role of Marketing Capability," *Journal of Marketing,* January 2016, 26–46.

28. "Free Exchange-Believing Is Seeing," *The Economist,* August 27, 2016, 58.

29. Christian Homburg, Marcel Stierl, and Torsten Bornemann, "Corporate Social Responsibility in Business-to-Business Markets: How Organizational Customers Account for Supplier Corporate Social Responsibility Engagement," *Journal of Marketing,* November 2013, 53–72; Daniel Korschun, C. B. Bhattacharya, and Scott Swain, "Corporate Social Responsibility, Customer Orientation, and the Job Performance of Frontline Employees," *Journal of Marketing,* May 2014, 20–37; Farnoosh Khodakarami, J. Andrew Petersen, and Rajkumar Venkatesan, "Developing Donor Relationships: The Role of the Breadth of Giving," *Journal of Marketing,* July 2015, 77–93; Charles Kang, Frank Germann, Rajdeep Grewal, "Washing Away Your Sins? Corporate Responsibility, Corporate Social Irresponsibility, and Firm Performance," *Journal of Marketing,* March 2016, 59–79 and "Good Behavior, Heavenly Returns," *Fortune,* September 1, 2018, 45–48.

30. David Aaker, "5 Reasons Brands Need a Higher Purpose," *Marketing News,* July 2017, 22–23

31. "The Halo Effect," *The Economist,* June 27, 2015, 56.

32. "Change the World," *Fortune,* September 21, 2016, 59–60.

33. https://www.gsk.com/media/4629/fy-2017-results-announcement.pdf (accessed October 5, 2018).

34. "Change the World."

35. "Study: 81% of Consumers Say They Will Make Personal Sacrifices to Address Social, Environmental Issues," Sustainable Brands, May 27, 2015, http://www.sustainablebrands.com/read/stakeholder-trends-and-insights/sustainablebrands/study-81-of-consumers-say-they-will-make-personal-sacrifices-to-address-social-environmental-issues (accessed February 19, 2019).

36. "The Future of Corporate Responsibility," June 18, 2018, https://www.forbes.com/sites/georgkell/2018/06/18/the-future-of-corporate-responsibility/#2180255e6105 (accessed February 10, 2019).

37. https://bcorporation.net (accessed October 7, 2018).

38. https://bimpactassessment.net/case-studies/elissa-loughman (accessed October 7, 2018).

39. Katrijn Gielens, Inge Geyskens, Barbara Deleersnyder, and Max Nohe, "The New Regulator in Town: The Effect of Walmart's Sustainability Mandate on Supplier Shareholder Value," *Journal of Marketing,* March 2018, 124–141.

40. "Detergent Makers Clean Up Their Act," *Businessweek,* December 18, 2017, 17.

41. "Marketing to the Green Consumer—US—March 2014," Mintel, http://www.mintel.com/marketing-to-the-green-consumer-us-March-2014

(accessed February 4, 2017). To better understand the notion of "greenness," see Andrew Gershoff and Judy Frels, "What Makes It Green? The Role of Centrality of Green Attributes in Evaluations of the Greenness of Products," *Journal of Marketing*, January 2015, 97–110.

42. Jeonggyu-Lee, Siddharth Bhatt, and Rajneesh Suri, "When Consumers Penalize Not So Green Products," *Psychology & Marketing*, December 13, 2017, https://onlinelibrary.wiley.com/doi/full /10.1002/mar.21069 (accessed October 7, 2018).

43. *Ibid.*

44. "The Green Guidelines," Federal Trade Commission, https://www.consumer.ftc.gov /features/feature-0013-going-green (accessed February 18, 2019).

45. Jessica Lyons Hardcastle, "FTC Fines Major Retailers $1.3 Million for Misleading Environmental Claims," Environmental Leader, January 6, 2016, https://www.environmentalleader. com/2016/01/ftc-fines-major-retailers-1.3-million -for-misleading-environmental-claims/ (accessed February 9, 2017).

46. *Ibid.*

47. "The Activist Company," Patagonia, https:// www.patagonia.com/the-activist-company.html (accessed February 9, 2017).

48. "The Tao of Rose," *Fortune*, September 15, 2015, 155–161.

49. "The Parable of St. Paul," *The Economist*, September 2, 2017, 58.

50. "The Fresh Scent of Success," Businessweek, September 4, 2017, 46–51.

51. "Social Impact Statistics You Should Know," https://engageforgood.com/guides/statistics-every -cause-marketer-should-know/ (accessed February 18, 2019).

52. *Ibid.*

53. "10 Amazing (and Spectacular!) Cause Marketing Campaign Examples," https://www .doublethedonation.com/tips/blog/2017/04/cause -marketing-examples/ (accessed October 9, 2018).

4

1. Mike Berinato, "Standing Out from the Pile," *Quirks Marketing Research Review*, July 2018, 24–27.

2. *Ibid.*

3. *Ibid.*

4. V. Kumar, "Transformative Marketing," *Journal of Marketing*, July 2018, 1–12.

5. *Ibid.*

6. https://wearesocial.com/us/blog/2018/01/global -digital-report-2018 (accessed October 21, 2018).

7. *Ibid.*

8. "Never Unplugged," *Fortune*, July 1, 2018, 13.

9. https://zephoria.com/top-15-valuable-facebook -statistics/ (accessed October 21, 2018).

10. https://statista.com/statistics/248074/most -popular-us-social-networking-apps-ranked-by -audience (accessed October 21, 2018).

11. "Express Yourself—Just a Bit," *Quirks Marketing Research Review*, February 18, 2018, 14.

12. Christine Moorman, "The Social Media Multiplier Effect," *Marketing News*, February 2017, 26–27.

13. *Ibid.*

14. *Ibid.*

15. Zoe Dowling, "Seeing Is Believing," *Quirks Marketing Research Review*, February 2018, 32–35.

16. *Ibid.*

17. *Ibid.*

18. "The Warm Fuzzy," https://www.wyzowl .com/video-social-media-2019/ (accessed February 18, 2019).

19. https://buypeel.com/blogs/peel-stories (accessed February 18, 2019).

20. https://wipster.io/blog/top-5-brand-videos -of-2017-that-will-inspire-you-in-2018 (accessed October 24, 2018).

21. www.worldpopulationreview.com (accessed October 27, 2018).

22. https://www.newsweek.com/fastest-growing -cities-where-are-americans-flocking-1084740 (accessed October 27, 2018).

23. *Ibid.*

24. "Cheap Sex and the Decline of Marriage," *Wall Street Journal*, September 30–October 1, 2017, C3.

25. "Bearing the Burden Alone," *Quirk's Marketing Research Review,* January 2018, 16.

26. "Millennials Spending Power to Increase by 2017." *Retail Leader*, https://retailleader. com/millennials-spending-power-increase-2017 (accessed February 27, 2017); also see: "Who Are the Millennial Shoppers? And What Do They Really Want?" https://www.accenture.com/us-en /insight-outlook-who-are-millennial-shoppers-what -do-they-really-want (accessed February 27, 2017).

27. "My (Kid's) Generation: 5 Ways Today's Tweens Are Changing Retail," http://www.forbes. com/sites/bryanpearson/2016/04/14/my-kids -generation-5-ways-todays-tweens-are-changing -retail/#4269fd6442ef (accessed October 28, 2018).

28. *Ibid.*

29. www.pewinternet.org/2018/05/31/teens-social -media-technology-2018/ (accessed October 28, 2018).

30. Ibid.

31. *Ibid.*

32. "Your New Workers Are Gen Z—Get Ready," *Wall Street Journal*, September 7, 2018.

33. *Ibid.*

34. "Engaging Generation Z: Marketing to a New Brand of Consumer," https://www.adweek.com /digital/josh-perlstein-response-media-guest-post -generation-Z/ (accessed October 28, 2018).

35. "Taking Stock with Teens," https://www .piperjaffray.com/3col.aspx?id=4986 (accessed October 29, 2018).

36. "Understanding Shopping Habits of Gen Z," https://gocommandoapp.com/blog/understanding -shopping-habits-gen-z/ (accessed October 29, 2018).

37. *Ibid.*

38. "Gallup Analysis: Millennials, Marriage and Family," *Gallup*, http://www.gallup.com /poll/191462/gallup-analysis-millennials-marriage -family.aspx (accessed February 27, 2017).

39. *Ibid.*

40. https://www.buxtonco.com/blog/10-facts-about -millenials-that-every-retailer-should-know (accessed October 29, 2018).

41. Joseph Rydhold, "Money Can't Buy Happiness for Millennials, or Can It?" *Quirks Marketing Research Review,* January 2018, 10.

42. *Ibid.*

43. *Ibid.*

44. "Best Places to Live in America," *Money*, October 2018, 46.

45. "The Shopper Retailers Want Is 26 Years Old," *Wall Street Journal*, October 10, 2017, A1, A14.

46. *Ibid.*

47. *Ibid.*

48. Robin Hafitz, "Finding the Right Routes," *Quirks Marketing Research Review*, February 2018, 24-26.

49. *Ibid.*

50. "Perspectives on Retirement: Baby Boomers, Generation X, and Millennials," https://www .transamericacenter.org/docs/default-source /retirement-survey-of-workers/tcrs2016_sr _perspectives_on_retirement_baby_boomers_genx _millennials.pdf (accessed February 27, 2017).

51. "Here's What Gen Xers Have Saved for Retirement," https://www.fool.com/retirement /2018/02/07/heres-what-gen-xers-have-saved -for-retirement.aspx (accessed October 29, 2018).

52. "Buying Habits of Baby Boomers," https://www.alexisabramson.com/buying-habits-of- baby-boomers (accessed October 29, 2018).

53. "Social Media Matters for Baby Boomers," https://www.forbes.com/sites/ forbestechcouncil/2018/03/06/social-media-matters- for-baby-boomers/ (accessed October 29, 2018).

54. *Ibid.*

55. https://www.brookings.edu/blog/the- avenue/2018/03/14/the-us-will-become-minority- white-in-2045-census-projects/ (accessed October 29, 2018).

56. www.pewresearch.org/fact-tank/2018/09/13/ key-facts-about-young-latinos/ (accessed October 29, 2018).

57. *Ibid.*

58. "Hispanic Shoppers' New Product Purchasing Habits," https://cstoredecisions. com/2018/06/25/hispanic-shoppers-new-product- purchasing-habits/ (accessed October 30, 2018).

59. "Hispanic Consumers: A Rising Market," https://abasto.com/en/news/hispanic-consumers-a- rising-market (accessed February 28, 2017).

60. "Hispanics Love Social Media—Especially Video," https://www.pm360online.com/Hispanics- love-social-media-especially-video/ (accessed October 30, 2018).

61. "Hispanic Fact Pack: What You Need to Know about This Market," https://adage .com/article/hispanic-marketing/hispanic-fact -pack-2018/314518 (accessed October 30, 2018).

62. "3 U.S. Hispanic Ad Campaigns That We Just Love," http://info.moravia.com/blog/3-us -hispanic-ad-campaigns-that-we-just-love (accessed March 1, 2017).

63. https://www.nytimes.com/ interactive/2017/10/12/business/media/toyota- camry-ads-different-ethnicities.html (accessed February 18, 2019).

64. "United States Population," worldpopulationreview.com/countries/united-states -population (accessed October 30, 2018).

65. "U.S. Census Bureau Facts for Features— National African American History Month: February 2017," http://www.prnewswire.com/ news-releases /us-census-bureau-facts-for- features—national-african-american-history-month- february-2017-300388921.html/ (accessed March 1, 2017).

66. https://www.brookings.edu/blog/brookings -now/2018/02/23/charts-of-the-week -african-americans-economy/ (accessed October 30, 2018).

67. "Church Central to the Lives of Many Black Americans," *Quirks Marketing Research Review*, April 2018, 12–14.

68. "Nielsen Examines the Digital Habits and Impact of Black Consumers," https://www.nielsen.com/us/en/press-room/2018/nielsen-examines-the-digital-habits-and-impact-of-black-consumers.html (accessed October 30, 2018).

69. "Agents of Courage: Initiative Advances the Narrative and Economic Status of Black Men," https://www.fordbetterworld.org/content/agents-courage (accessed October 30, 2018).

70. "Asian Americans Make Up Most of the New U.S. Immigrant Population," https://www.nationalgeographic.com/culture-exploration/2018/09/asian-immigrants-latin-americans-united-states-study-news/ (accessed October 26, 2018).

71. Joseph Rydholm, "Asian-Americans Deserving of More Marketer Interest," *Quirk's Marketing Research Review*, June 2018, 10.

72. *Ibid.*

73. "Asian American Buying Power to Hit $1 Trillion by 2018," http://asianjournal.com/news/asian-american-buying-power-to-hit-1-trillion-by-2018 (accessed March 2, 2017).

74. www.pewresearch.org/fact-tank/2018/04/05/a-record-64-million-americans-live-in-multigenerational-households/ (accessed October 28, 2018).

75. Rydholm, "Asian-Americans ..."

76. "Median Household Income Rose 1.8% in 2017," *Wall Street Journal*, September 13, 2018, A1.

77. *Ibid.*

78. *Ibid.*

79. "Firms Choose Bonuses over Raises," *Wall Street Journal*, September 19, 2018, A1, A2.

80. "Incomes Rise, Poverty Falls Again," *Wall Street Journal*, September 13, 2018, A3.

81. "Fast Facts: Income of Young Adults," *Institute of Education Sciences*, http://nces.ed.gov/fastfacts/display.asp?id=77 (accessed March 3, 2017); also see: "Wages Gain, Payrolls Rise as Expansion Rolls Ahead," *Wall Street Journal*, September 8–9, 2018, A1, A2.

82. "The Average Income in Every State—And What It's Really Worth," *Money*, May 2018, 67-69.

83. https://usinflationcalculator.com/inflation/current-inflation-rates (accessed October 31, 2018).

84. "IMF Projects Venezuela Inflation Will Hit 1,000,000 Percent in 2018," https://www.reuters.com/article/us-venezuela-economy/img-projects-venezuela-inflation-will-hit-1000000-percent-in-2018-idUSKBN1KD2L9 (accessed October 31, 2018).

85. Chris Bradley and Clayton O'Toole, "An Incumbent's Guide to Digital Disruption," https://www.mckinsey.com/business-functions/strategy-and-corporate-finance/our-insights/an-incumbents-guide-to-digital-disruption (accessed October 31, 2018).

86. *Ibid.*

87. "Best Buy Is Back," *Business Week*, July 23, 2018, 44–49.

88. https://www.mckinsey.com/business-functions/mckinsey-analytics/our-insights/where-is-technology-taking-the-economy (accessed October 31, 2018).

89. John F. Sargent Jr. "U.S. Research and Development Funding and Performance: Fact Sheet," https://fas.org/sgp/crs/misc/R44307.pdf (accessed October 31, 2018).

90. "Trump, Congress Approve Largest U.S. Research Spending Increase in a Decade," https://www.sciencemag.org/news/2018/03/updated-us-spending-deal-contains-largest-research-spending-increase-decade (accessed October 31, 2018).

91. "Closing America's Idea Gap," *Fortune*, December 15, 2017, 152–157.

92. *Ibid.*

93. https://www.washingtonpost.com/national/health-science/trump-administration-rewrites-aca-insurance-rules-to-give-more-power-to-states/2018/04/09/94b738fa-3c0f-11e8-a7d1-e4efec6389f0_story.html?noredirect=on&utm_term=.3ddd3426472d (accessed November 2, 2018).

94. "Bureau of Consumer Financial Protection Announces Settlement With Wells Fargo for Auto-Loan Administration and Mortgage Practices," https://www.consumerfinance.gov/about-us/newsroom/bureau-consumer-financial-protection-announces-settlement-wells-fargo-auto-loan-administration-and-mortgage-practices/ (accessed November 2, 2018).

95. https://www.fortune.com/2018/04/20/wells-fargo-fined-1-billion-loans/(accessed February 18, 2019).

96. https://www.emarketer.com/content/emarketer-total-ad-media-spending-worldwide-will-rise-7-4-in-2018 (accessed November 2, 2018).

97. "Google Hid Data Breach for Months," *Wall Street Journal*, October 9, 2018, A1, A2.

98. "Butt Out, Alexa," *Quirks Marketing Research Review*, January 2018, 8.

99. "Europe Gets a Grip on Data," *Businessweek*, March 26, 2018, 42–43.

100. "Bed, Bath & Beyond Is Missing Out on the Retail Rally," *Wall Street Journal*, October 5, 2018, B3.

101. *Ibid.*

102. http://www.mckinsey.com/business-functions/marketing-and-sales/our-insights/the-new-battleground-for-marketing-led-growth (accessed November 3, 2018).

5

1. https://www.americangeosciences.org/critical-issues/faq/which-mineral-commodities-used-united-states-need-be-imported (accessed November 8, 2018).

2. "A Fractured World," *Wall Street Journal*, January 23, 2018, R1–R2.

3. https://data.worldbank.org/indicator/NE.TRD.GNFS.ZS (accessed November 8, 2018).

4. https://www.exim.gov/about (accessed November 8, 2018).

5. https://sba.gov/about-sba (accessed November 8, 2018).

6. https://www.wsj.com/articles/big-u-s-companies-reveal-how-much-they-rely-on-overseas-workers-1523448000 (accessed November 8, 2018).

7. "Will Global Trade Survive 2018?" https://foreignpolicy.com/2018/01/05/will-global-trade-survive-2018 (accessed November 8, 2018)

8. Author's estimate.

9. https://247wallst.com/special-report/2018/06/27/manufacturers-bringing-the-most-jobs-back-to-america/ (accessed November 9, 2018).

10. "Which Manufacturers Are Bring the Most Jobs Back to America?" https://www.usatoday.com/story/money/business/2018/06/28/manufacturers-bringing-most-jobs-back-to-america/36438051/ (accessed November 9, 2018).

11. Theodore Levitt, "The Globalization of Markets," *Harvard Business Review*, May 1983, 92–100.

12. https//www.data.worldbank.org/indicator/ny.gnp/pcap.cd (accessed November 9, 2018).

13. *Ibid.*

14. "The 18 Most Expensive Cities to Live in the World in 2018," https://www.businessinsider.com/most-expensive-cities-to-live-in-the-world-2018-6#6-luanda-angola-13 (accessed November 9, 2018).

15. "US Trade Deficit and How It Hurts the Economy," https://www.thebalance.com/trade-deficit-by-country-3306276 (accessed November 7, 2018).

16. https://wwww.thebalance.com/u-s-trade-deficit-causes-effects-trade-partners-3306264 (accessed November 7, 2018).

17. https://qz.com/135696/why-is-the-us-dollar-so-strong/ (accessed November 8, 2018).

18. "Trump Is Right About China Trade," *Wall Street Journal*, October 3, 2018, A15.

19. "Tackling China's Protectionism." *Wall Street Journal*, March 21, 2018, A16.

20. https://en.portal.santandertrade.com/establish-overseas/india/foreign-investment (accessed November 7, 2018).

21. www.doingbusiness.org/en/rankings (accessed February 21, 2019).

22. "Mercosur: South America's Fractious Trade Bloc," https://www.cfr.org/backgrounder/mercosur-south-americas-fractious-trade-bloc (accessed November 7, 2018).

23. *Ibid.*

24. "*New U.S.* Tariffs Hit China; Beijing Vows to Strike Back," *Wall Street Journal*, September 18, 2018, A1, A10.

25. "Tariffs on China Take Their Toll on U.S. Factories," *Wall Street Journal*, October 15, 2018, B1, N2.

26. "Trade Fight Spurs Tariff Dodges, with 18,927 Options," *Wall Street Journal*, October 9, 2018, A1, A10.

27. *Ibid.*

28. "New Tariffs Pose Broad Economic Risks Amid Escalating Threat," *Wall Street Journal*, June 4, 2018, A6.g

29. "Peace Offering," *The Economist*, December 22, 2018–January 4, 2019, 91–93.

30. "USMCA, the New Trade Deal between the US, Canada, and Mexico, Explained," https://www.vox.com/2018/10/2/17923638/usmca-trump-nafta-trade-agreement (accessed October 5, 2018).

31. "NEWFTA," *The Economist*, October 6, 2018, 31–32.

32. "Foreign Car Makers Sweat Details," *Wall Street Journal*, October 2, 2018, A9.

33. "Trump Forges New Model on Trade," *Wall Street Journal*, October 5, 2018, A1, A9.

34. "'Unprecedented Challenges' Confront Appellate Body, Chair Warns, https://www.wto.org/english/news_e/news18_e/ab_22jun18_e.htm (accessed October 6, 2018).

35. "Understanding the WTO," World Trade Organization, https://www.wto.org/english/thewto_e/whatis_e/tif_e/tif_e.htm (accessed February 21, 2019).

36. "How to Make Trade Peace with China," *Wall Street Journal*, April 5, 2018, A17.

37. "Tit for Tat," *The Economist*, September 22, 2018, 66.

38. "TPP Points Way toward Other Deals," *Wall Street Journal*, May 15, 2017, A2.

39. Louise Yaxley, "TPP Resurrected: Here's What's in the Latest Trans-Pacific Partnership Trade Deal and What It Means for You," https://www.abc.net.au/news/2018-01-24/what-is-the-new-tpp-and-what-does-it-mean-for-australia/9357020 (accessed November 5, 2018).

40. Jason Marczak, "Latin America's Future Begins with the Pacific Alliance," http://www.atlanticcouncil.org/blogs/new-atlanticist/latin-america-s-future-begins-with-the-pacific-alliance (accessed November 5, 2018).

41. https://countryeconomy.com/countries/groups/pacific-alliance (accessed November 5, 2018).

42. Kimberly Amadeo, "CAFTA Explained, with Its Pros and Cons," https://www.thebalance.com/what-is-cafta-3305580 (accessed November 4, 2018).

43. "Trade," European Union, http://ec.europa.eu/trade/policy/countries-and-regions/countries /united-states/ (accessed November 4, 2018).

44. "EU Says Trade with U.S. Is Fair," *Wall Street Journal*, March 21, 2018, A8.

45. *Ibid*.

46. *Ibid*.

47. "Qualcomm Takes Hit in EU," *Wall Street Journal*, January 25, 2018, B3.

48. "The Wrong Way on Data," *Businessweek*, May 14, 2018, 12.

49. "Google, EU in Online Border War," *Wall Street Journal*, September 10, 2018, B1–B4.

50. *Ibid*.

51. Liz Alderman, "Europe Says Greece Is a Comeback Story. The I.M.F. Isn't Convinced," https://nytimes.com/2018/07/31/business/greece-imf-bailout.html (accessed November 8, 2018).

52. "G-20 Split over U.S. Trade Plan Deepens," *Wall Street Journal*, March 21, 2018, A9.

53. Mark Leon Goldberg, "These Are the Latest Trends in World Population," https://www.undispatch.com/these-are-the-latest-trends-in-world-population/ (accessed November 16, 2018).

54. "Decline of Global Extreme Poverty Continues but Has Slowed: World Bank," https://www.worldbank.org/en/news/press-release/2018/09/19/decline-of-global-extreme-poverty-continues-but-has-slowed-world-bank (accessed November 16, 2018).

55. Andy Kiersz, "Here's What the Typical American Worker Earns at Every Age," https://www.businessinsider.com/typical-salary-americans-at-every-age-2018-6 (accessed November 16, 2018).

56. https://www.theladders.com/career-advice/if-you-graduate-this-year-youre-likely-to-make-more-than-50K-in-your-first-job (accessed November 16, 2018).

57. https://www.fool.com/investing/2018/07/14/americas-oil-gas-industry-is-on-pace-to-be-a-recor.aspx (accessed November 16, 2018).

58. *Ibid*.

59. www.unwater.org/water-facts/scarcity (accessed November 18, 2018).

60. https://www.trade.gov/mas/ian/employment/index.asp (accessed November 20, 2018).

61. Chris Isidore, "These Are the Top US Exports," https://money.cnn.com/2018/03/07/news/economy/top-us-exports/index.html (accessed November 20, 2018).

62. https://www.trade.gov/cs/ (accessed November 10, 2018).

63. https://www.franchisedirect.com/top100globalfranchises/rankings (accessed November 20 2018).

64. Julie Jargon, "Yum Looks to Be Leaner after China Spinoff," https://www.wsj.com/articles/yum-looks-to-be-leaner-after-china-spinoff-1476185810 (accessed November 20, 2018).

65. https://joynbio.com (accessed November 21, 2018).

66. https://www.statista.com/statistics/188571/united-states-direct-investments-abroad-since-2000/ (accessed November 21, 2018).

67. https://ofii.org/report/foreign-direct-investment-in-the-united-states-2018 (accessed November 21, 2018).

68. "These Eight Countries Account for Three-Quarters of FDI in the USA," https://ofii.org/blog/these-eight-countries-account-for-three-quarters-of-fdi-in-the-usa (accessed November 21, 2018).

69. https://appleinsider.com/articles/18/07/14/here-are-all-of-the-apple-stores/openings-moves-and-remodels-2018 (accessed November 21, 2018).

70. Shannon Liao, "After a Single Day, Facebook Is Pushed Out of China Again," https://www.theverge.com/2018/7/25/17612162/facebook/technology-subsidiary-blocked-china-censor (accessed November 21, 2018).

71. "Tesla Makes a U-Turn in China," *Fortune*, June 15, 2017, 129–136.

72. Yue Wang, "Tesla Will Be Challenged Like Never Before in China—Here's Why," https://www.forbes.com/sites/ywang/2018/08/27/tesla-will-be-challenged-like-never-before-in-china-heres-why/#7da4101be1 (accessed November 23, 2018).

73. "How Japanese Kit Kats Got So Hot," *Fortune*, April 2, 2018.

74. "Trying to Speak India's Language(s)," *Businessweek*, November 13, 2017 19.

75. Rajeev Batra, Y. Charles Zhang, Nilufer Aydinoglu, and Fred Feinberg, "Positioning Multi-Country Brands: The Impact of Variation in Cultural Values and Competitive Set," *Journal of Marketing Research*, December 2017, 914–931.

76. Roger Aliaga-Diaz, "What's Behind the Latest Surge in the Dollar?" https://vanguardblog.com/2018/09/04/whats-behind-the-latest-surge-in-the-dollar/ (accessed November 24, 2018).

77. https://www.economist.com/news/2018/07/the-big-mac-index (accessed November 24, 2018).

78. https://www.usitc.gov/trade_remedy/731_ad_701_cvd/investigations.htm (accessed November 24, 2018).

6

1. Tonya Williams Bradford, "Beyond Fungible: Transforming Money into Moral and Social Resources," *Journal of Marketing*, March 2015, 79–97; "Budget Allocation Signals Consumers' Need States, Research Finds," *Marketing News*, April 2015, 7.

2. Masroor Ahmed, "Is Social Media the Biggest Influencer of Buying Decisions?" *Social Media Today*, May 31, 2015, http://www.socialmediatoday.com/marketing/masroor/2015-05-28/social-media-biggest-influencer-buying-decisions (accessed April 15, 2016); also see, "How Social Media Influences Shopping Behavior," eMarketer, March 17, 2016, https://www.emarketer.com/Article/How-Social-Media-Influences-Shopping-Behavior/1013718 (accessed January 24, 2017)

3. Dhruv Grewal, Carl-Phillip Ahlbom, Laure Beitelspacher, Stephanie Noble, and Jens Nordfalt, "In-Store Mobile Phone Use and Consumer Shopping Behavior: Evidence from the Field," *Journal of Marketing*, July 2018, 102–126.

4. Ashish Kumar, Ram Bezawada, Rishika Rishika, Ramkumar Janakiraman, and P.K. Kannan, "From Social to Sale: The Effects of Firm-Generated Content in Social Media on Customer Behavior," *Journal of Marketing*, January 2016, 7–25.

5. Uma Karmarkar, Baba Shiv, and Brian Kuntson, "Cost Conscious? The Neural and Behavioral Impact of Price Primacy on Decision Making," *Journal of Marketing Research*, August 2015, 467–481.

6. "Read the Story to Learn How Behavioral Economics Can Improve Marketing," *Marketing News*, January 2018, 32–41.

7. *Ibid*.

8. *Ibid*

9. Evert deHaan, P.K. Kannan, Peter Verhoef, and Thorsten Wiesel, "Device Switching in Online Purchasing: Examining the Strategic Contingencies," *Journal of Marketing*, September 2018, 1–19.

10. "9 Out of 10 Shoppers Make Impulse Purchases," http://www.newmediaandmarketing.com/9-out-of-10-shoppers-make-impulse-purchases/ (accessed January 22, 2017).

11. Iiro Jussila, Anssi Tarkiainen, Marko Sarstedt, and Joe Hair, "Individual Psychological Ownership: Concepts, Evidence and Implications for Research in Marketing," *Journal of Marketing Theory and Practice*, March 2015, 121–139; Bernadette Kamleitner and Silva Feuchtl, "'As If It Were Mine': Imaginary Works by Inducing Psychological Ownership," *Journal of Marketing Theory and Practice*, March 2015, 208–223.

12. Suzanne Shu and Joann Peck, "Psychological Ownership and Affective Reaction: Emotional Attachment Process Variables and the Endowment Effect," *Journal of Consumer Psychology*, March 2011, 439–452; Colleen Patricia Kirk, Bernard McSherry and Scott Swain, "Investing the Self: The Effect of Nonconscious Goals on Investor Psychological Ownership and Word-of-Mouth Intentions," *Journal of Behavioral and Experimental Economics*, January 2015, 186–194.

13. Colleen Patricia Kirk, Scott Swain, and James Gaskin, "I'm Proud of It: Consumer Technology Appropriation and Psychological Ownership," *Journal of Marketing Theory and Practice*, February 2015, 166–184.

14. Aaron Garvey, "The 'Jilting' Effect: How Dashing Consumers' Hopes Isn't Always a Bad Thing," *Marketing News*, February 2018, 18–20.

15. "11 of the Largest Data Breaches of All Time," https://www.opswat.com/blog (accessed September 29, 2018).

16. *Ibid*.

17. Ramkumar Janakiraman, Joon Ho Lim, and Rishika Rishika, "The Effect of a Data Breach Announcement on Consumer Behavior: Evidence from a Multichannel Retailer," *Journal of Marketing*, March 2018, 85–105.

18. "Forget 'Omni.' Just Help Me," *Quirk's Marketing Research Review*, October 2015, 44–49.

19. *Ibid.*

20. David Edelman, "Branding in the Digital Age: You're Spending Your Money in All the Wrong Places," *Harvard Business Review*, December 2010, https://hbr.org/2010/12/branding-in-the-digital-age-youre-spending-your-money-in-all-the-wrong-places (accessed April 15, 2016).

21. David Edelman and Marc Singer, "The New Consumer Decision Journey," McKinsey & Company, October 2015, https://www.mckinsey.com/marketing-and-sales/our-insights/the-new-consumer-decision-journey (accessed February 23, 2019). Also see: "Customer Journey Mapping in 3 Steps," *Marketing News*, September 2018, 4–5.

22. David Edelman and Marc Singer, "Competing on Customer Journeys," *Harvard Business Review*, November 2015, https://hbr.org/2015/11/competing-on-customer-journeys (accessed September 26, 2018).

23. "Putting the Right Price on Customer Interactions," https://www.mckinsey.com/industries/health-care-systems-and-services/our-insights/putting-the-right-price-on-customer-interactions, November 2017 (accessed September 27, 2018).

24. *Ibid.*

25. David Aaker and Andrew Marcum, "The Satisfied vs Committed Brand Loyalist and What Drives Them," *Marketing News*, January 2017, pp. 24–25.

26. *Ibid.*

27. V. Kumar, Agata Leszkiewicz, and Angeliki Herbst, "Are You Back for Good or Still Shopping Around? Investigating Customers' Repeat Churn Behavior," *Journal of Marketing Research*, April 2018, 208–225.

28. "Top 10 Most Expensive Cars in the World—2019," www.beautifullife.info/automotive-design/top-10-most-expensive-cars-in-the-world/ (accessed (accessed February 23, 2019).

29. https://www.healthcare.gov/glossary/federal-poverty-level-fpl/ (accessed September 29, 2018).

30. "NFL Record? With $90 Million over 12 months, Aaron Rodgers Will Be Near No. 1 across All Sports," https://www.forbes.com/sites/Kurtbadenhausen/2018/08/29/aaron-rodgers-mega-payday-90-million-over-the-next-12-months/#185448091d9c (accessed February 23, 2019).

31. "Gender's Role in Purchases: I Don't Mean to Sound Sexist, But . . .," https://stevensoncompany.com/genders-role-in-purchases-i-don't-mean-to-sound-sexist-but/ (accessed February 22, 2019).

32. Gretchen Livingston, "About One-Third of U.S. Children Are Living with an Unmarried Parent," www.pewresearch.org./fact-tank/2018/04/27/about-one-third-of-u-s-children-are-living-with-an-unmarried-parent (accessed September 29, 2018).

33. https://www.forbes.com/sites/forbesagencycouncil/2017/08/25/finding-brand-success-in-the-digital-world/#4d8dd44526e (accessed February 22, 2019).

34. Girish Mallapragada, Sandeep R. Chandukala, and Qing Liu, "Exploring the Effects of 'What' (Product) and 'Where' (Website) Characteristics on Online Shopping Behavior," *Journal of Marketing*, March 2016, 21–38.

7

1. Michael D. Hutt and Thomas W. Speh, *Mindtap Marketing for Business Marketing Management B2B*, 12th ed. (Boston, MA: Cengage, 2017).

2. Lisa Murton Beets and Ann Handley, "B2B Content Marketing: 2018 Benchmarks, Budgets, and Trends – North America," *Content Marketing Institute*, https://contentmarketinginstitute.com/wp-content/uploads/2017/09/2018-b2b-research-final.pdf (accessed November 26, 2018).

3. "Online Measurement," Nielsen, https://www.nielsen.com/us/en/solutions/measurement/online.html (accessed November 26, 2018).

4. *Ibid.*

5. Meghan Keaney Anderson, "The Best of B2B Marketing Content: 10 Examples," Hubspot, March 18, 2018, https://blog.hubspot.com/marketing/b2b-content-marketing-examples (accessed November 26, 2018).

6. AJ Agrawal, "3 Ways B2B Companies Must Market Themselves in 2016," *Forbes*, January 5, 2016, https://www.forbes.com/sites/ajagrawal/2016/01/05/3-ways-b2b-companies-must-market-themselves-in-2016/#25a22535b821 (accessed November 26, 2018).

7. Tonya Riley, "The Apple Watch Has a Secret Weapon That Helps It Dominate the Market," CNBC, May 4, 2018, https://www.cnbc.com/2018/05/03/apple-watch-has-a-secret-weapon-that-helps-it-dominate-the-market.html (accessed November 26, 2018).

8. "Nestlé Pays Starbucks $7.15B to Form Global Coffee Alliance," *Brandchannel*, May 6 , 2018, https://www.brandchannel.com/2018/05/06/nestle_starbucks_coffee_alliance_050618/ (accessed November 26, 2018).

9. Sheila Shayon, "Sustainable Alliances: 5 Questions with Caterpillar Sr. Tech Pro Mark Kelly," Brandchannel, March 16, 2016, https://www.brandchannel.com/2016/03/16/5-questions-caterpillar-031616/ (accessed November 26, 2018).

10. Robert M. Morgan and Shelby D. Hunt, "The Commitment-Trust Theory of Relationship Marketing," *Journal of Marketing*, 58, no. 3 (1994), 23.

11. *Ibid.*

12. Winnie Sun, "What the New Costco Visa Card Means for Consumers and Millennials," *Forbes*, March 31, 2016, http://www.forbes.com/sites/winniesun/2016/03/31/costco-visa-amex/#95f7dcb717d9 (accessed November 26, 2018).

13. "Microsoft and 21Vianet Reinforce Long-term Cooperation on Cloud Services in China," Microsoft Azure, March 14, 2018, https://azure.microsoft.com/en-us/blog/microsoft-and-21vianet-reinforce-long-term-cooperation-on-cloud-services-in-china/ (accessed November 26, 2018).

14. Kimberly Amadeo, "FY 2017 Federal Budget Compared to Trump's Spending," *The Balance*, November 26, 2018, https://www.thebalance.com/how-trump-amended-obama-budget-4128986 (accessed November 26, 2018).

15. *Ibid.*

16. *Ibid.*

17. *Ibid.*

18. David Millward, "Urgent Repairs Ordered on Boeing 787 Dreamliner Engines," *Telegraph*, April 24, 2016, https://www.telegraph.co.uk/news/2016/04/24/urgent-repairs-repairs-ordered-on-boeing-787-dreamliner-engines/ (accessed November 26, 2018).

19. Jim Melvin, "S.C. Forestry Industry Has Plenty of Room for Growth," *Times and Democrat*, February 21, 2016, http://thetandd.com/business /agriculture/s-c-forestry-industry-has-plenty-of -room-for-growth/article_e7659d8d-6adf-5024-abee-3300df0a2220.html (accessed November 26, 2018).

20. Mary Wisniewski, "CTA Board Approves Contract to Replace Half of Rail Cars," *Chicago Tribune*, March 10, 2016, http://www.chicagotribune.com/news/local/breaking/ct-cta-board-rail-cars-0310-20160309-story.html (accessed November 26, 2018).

21. Michael D. Hutt and Thomas W. Speh, *Mindtap Marketing for Business Marketing Management B2B*, 12th ed. (Boston, MA: Cengage, 2017).

22. "What Is Alibaba? An Introduction," Billboard, May 27, 2016, https://www.billboard.com/articles/business/7385970/what-is-alibaba-introduction (accessed November 26, 2018).

23. William Boston, "BMW Slows Some Production Due to Parts Shortage from Supplier Bosch," *Fox Business*, May 29, 2017, https://www.foxbusiness.com/features/bmw-slows-some-production-due-to-parts-shortage-from-supplier-bosch (accessed November 26, 2018).

24. Kellie Ell, "Secondary Issues from Trade Tensions Could Impact International Paper: CEO," *CNBC*, July 26, 2018, https://www.cnbc.com/2018/07/26/secondary-issues-from-trade-tensions-could-impact-international-paper.html (accessed November 27, 2018).

25. Michael D. Hutt and Thomas W. Speh, *Mindtap Marketing for Business Marketing Management B2B*, 12th ed. (Boston, MA: Cengage, 2017).

26. *Ibid.*

27. Athony Sills, "5 Keys for Selling to the C-Suite," HireVue's Coach Blog, April 16, 2015, http://www.hirevue.com/build-blog/5-keys-for-selling-to-the-c-suite (accessed November 26, 2018).

28. *Ibid.*

29. Michael D. Hutt and Thomas W. Speh, *Mindtap Marketing for Business Marketing Management B2B*, 12th ed. (Boston, MA: Cengage, 2017).

30. *Ibid.*

8

1. Joris Zwegers and Dmitri Seredenko, "What's Wrong with Segmentation?" https://www.ama.org/partners/content/Pages/whats-wrong-with-segmentation.aspx (accessed December 2, 2018).

2. Katherine Schwab, "How Ikea Quietly Tweaks Its Designs Around the World," https://www.fastcompany.com/90215773/how-ikea-quietly-tweaks-its-design-around-the-world, August 18, 2018.

3. Dale Buss, "I'll Shrink Manhattan: Target Opens Flexible Format Store in NYC's Tribeca," *Brandchannel*, October 5, 2016, http://www.brandchannel.com/2016/10/05/target-100516/ (accessed December 2, 2018).

4. "Amazon Nurtures Young Readers with Prime Book Box Service," https://www.brandchannel.com/2018/05/01/amazon_prime_book_box/, May 1, 2018 (accessed February 16, 2018).

5. Katie Richards, "What Brands Need to Know about Gen Z to Reach the New Generation of

Consumer," *Adweek*, January 25, 2017, http://www.adweek.com/brand-marketing/what-brands-need-know-about-gen-z-reach-new-generation-consumers-175745/ (accessed December 3, 2018).

6. Daphne Howland, "Target Gets Creative Help from Gen Z in New Apparel Line," *RetailWire*, http://www.retailwire.com/discussion/target-gets-creative-help-from-gen-z-in-new-apparel-line/ (accessed December 3, 2018).

7. Ray A. Smith, "The 9-Year-Old with a Nike Deal," *Wall Street Journal*, October 8, 2018, p. A13.

8. Mark J. Miller, "Innovation Watch: Marriott Tests Generation Z Ideas in Charlotte, NC," *Brandchannel*, August 2, 2016, http://www.brandchannel.com/2016/08/02/marriott-generation-z-080216/ (accessed December 3, 2018).

9. Richard Fry, "Millennials Projected to Overtake Baby Boomers as America's Largest Generation," *Pew Research*, March 1, 2018, http://www.pewresearch.org/fact-tank/2016/04/25/millennials-overtake-baby-boomers/ (accessed December 3, 2018).

10. Ray A. Smith, "Retailers Stalk the Elusive Millennial Shopper," https://www.wsj.com/articles/retailers-stalk-the-elusive-millennial-shopper-1527692005, *Wall Street Journal*, May 30, 2018.

11. Denise Leathers, "Why Do Millennials Love Private Label Groceries So Much," https://www.retailwire.com/discussion/why-do-millennials-love-private-label-groceries-so-much/, *RetailWire*, November 12, 2018.

12. William F. Schroer, "Generations X, Y, Z and the Others," *Social Librarian*, http://www.socialmarketing.org/newsletter/features/generation3.htm (accessed December 3, 2018).

13. Dale Buss, "The 'Unstoppable' Ford Explorer and Gen X: 5 Questions with Omar Odeh," *Brandchannel*, August 10, 2016, http://brandchannel.com/2016/08/10/5-questions-ford-081016/ (accessed December 3, 2018).

14. David Wright, "50+ Facts and Fiction: Size, Wealth and Spending of 50+ Consumers," *Immersion Active*, March 9, 2015, https://www.immersionactive.com/resources/size-wealth-spending-50-consumers/ (accessed December 3, 2018).

15. "Hey, Big Spenders," *Scribd*, October 24, 2016, https://www.scribd.com/article/328329061/Hey-Big-Spenders (accessed December 3, 2018).

16. Gina Binole, "Senior Market Isn't Sexy, but It's Served Consumer Cellular Well," *Crains*, December 2, 2016, http://www.crains.com/article/news/senior-market-isn't-sexy-it's-served-consumer-cellular-well (accessed December 3, 2018).

17. Alexis Abramson, "The Silent Generation Characteristics You Need to Know," https://www.alexisabramson.com/the-silent-generation-characteristics-and-facts-you-need-to-know/, July 3, 2018.

18. Stephen M. Golant, "Aging in the American Suburbs: A Changing Population," *Aging Well*, http://www.agingwellmag.com/news/ex_06309_01.shtml (accessed December 3, 2018).

19. "Women Make Up 85% of All Consumer Purchases," *Bloomberg*, February 17, 2017, https://www.bloomberg.com/news/videos/b/9e28517f-8de1-4e59-bcda-ce536aa50bd6 (accessed December 3, 2018).

20. Anne Marie Chaker, "Supermarkets Lure in Male Shoppers," *Wall Street Journal*, July 10, 2018, p. A9.

21. Robert Williams, "Moisturize This!," *Bloomberg Businessweek*, March 12, 2018, pp. 18, 19.

22. Alexandra Bruell, "ESPN's New Pitch to Advertisers: 'We Reach Women,'" https://www.wsj.com/articles/espns-new-pitch-to-advertisers-we-reach-women-1515409200, *Wall Street Journal*, January 8, 2018.

23. Sheila Savon, "Harrys Launches Flamingo Shaving Brand for Women," https://www.wsj.com/articles/espns-new-pitch-to-advertisers-we-reach-women-1515409200, October 17, 2018.

24. "Making Affordable Products for Low-Income Shoppers," The Clorox Company, July 15, 2016, https://www.thecloroxcompany.com/blog/making-affordable-products-for-low-income-shoppers/ (accessed December 4, 2018).

25. Lauren Zumbach, "Bargain Chains Lead List of Fastest Growing Retailers," *Chicago Tribune*, September 22, 2016, http://www.chicagotribune.com/business/ct-fastest-growing-retailers-0923-biz-20160922-story.html (accessed December 4, 2018).

26. Vincent Bastien, "Marketing to a High-End Consumer, Using the Luxury Strategy," *Entrepreneur*, September 20, 2015, http://entrepreneur.com/article/250745 (accessed December 4, 2018).

27. Abe Sauer, "Targeting Millennials, Stouffer's Shines a Light on Families and Inclusivity," *Brandchannel*, February 7, 2017, http://brandchannel.com/2017/02/07/stouffers-families-020717/ (accessed December 4, 2018).

28. Taylor Bryant, "How the Beauty Industry Has Failed Black Women," *Refinery 29*, February 27, 2016, http://www.refinery29.com/2016/02/103964/black-hair-care-makeup-business (accessed December 4, 2018).

29. "60 Minutes/Vanity Fair Poll: Marriage," CBS, January 5, 2017, http://www.cbsnews.com/news/60-minutes-vanity-fair-poll-marriage/ (accessed December 4, 2018).

30. "US Singles Statistics," *UPCI Single Adult Ministry*, http://www.upcisam.com/about/singles-statistics/ (accessed December 4, 2018); Adam Desanctis, "First-Time Buyers, Single Women Gain Traction in NAR's 2016 Buyer and Seller Survey," *NAR*, October 31, 2016, https://www.nar.realtor/news-releases/2016/10/first-time-buyers-single-women-gain-traction-in-nar-s-2016-buyer-and-seller-survey (accessed December 4, 2018).

31. Lanie Woods, "The Coolest College Brand Ambassador Programs," *Lala*, January 15, 2017, http://thelala.com/coolest-college-brand-ambassador-programs-2017/; Carrie Robinson, "Campus Representative: A Rewarding Experience," *The Odyssey Online*, July 28, 2014, https://www.theodysseyonline.com/campus-representative-rewarding-experience (accessed December 4, 2018).

32. "New Research from DuPont Nutrition & Health Identifies Six Health and Wellness Consumer Segments," *Danisco*, March 15, 2016, http://www.danisco.com/about-dupont/news/news-archive/2016/new-research-identifies-six-health-and-wellness-consumer-segments/ (accessed December 4, 2018).

33. Gene Marks, "What's the Rush? A Grocery Chain Starts a Check-out Line for People Who Want to Take It Slow," *Washington Post*, February 23, 2017, https://www.washingtonpost.com/news/on-small-business/wp/2017/02/23/whats-the-rush-a-grocery-chain-starts-a-check-out-line-for-people-who-want-to-take-it-slow/ (accessed December 4, 2018).

34. Richard Kestenbaum, "Who's Shopping in Department Stores Now?" *Forbes*, December 6, 2016, https://www.forbes.com/sites/richardkestenbaum/2016/12/06/whos-shopping-in-department-stores-now/ (accessed December 4, 2018).

35. "Amazon Webstore," Amazon, http://webstore.amazon.com/ (accessed December 5, 2018).

36. Matthew Stern, "Segmentation Is Central to Nike's Success," https://www.retailwire.com/discussion/segmentation-is-central-to-nikes-success/, March 22, 2018.

37. "Campus Solutions," *Zipcar*, http://zipcar.com /universities/solutions (accessed December 5, 2018).

38. James Hetherington, "Apple and Samsung Smartphones May Struggle in 2018, and It's Their Own Fault," https://www.newsweek.com/apple-samsung-and-google-smartphones-may-struggle-2018-and-its-their-own-fault-845923, March 15, 2018.

39. Joseph Pigato, "How 9 Successful Companies Keep Their Customers," *Entrepreneur*, April 3, 2015, https://www.entrepreneur.com/article/243764 (accessed December 5, 2018).

40. "All Brands," Coca-Cola, http://www.thecocacolacompany.com/brands/brandlist.html (accessed December 5, 2018).

41. Dale Buss, "A Return to Salad Days? 5 Questions with Ruby Tuesday CMO Dave Skena," *Brandchannel*, March 9, 2016, http://www.brandchannel.com/2016/03/09/5-questions-ruby-Tuesday (accessed December 5, 2018).

42. Dale Buss, "Super Bowl Watch: 5 Questions with Wendy's VP Brandon Rhoten," *Brandchannel*, February 1, 2017, http://www.brandchannel.com/2017/02/01/super-bowl-questions-wendys-020117/ (accessed December 5, 2018).

43. "Our Brands," *Gap Inc.*, http://www.gapinc.com/content/gapinc/html/aboutus/ourbrands.html (accessed December 5, 2018).

44. Alan Zorfus and Daniel Leemon, "An Emotional Connection Matters More Than Customer Satisfaction," August 29, 2016, *Harvard Business Review*, https://hbr.org/2016/08/an-emotional-connection-matters-more-than-customer-satisfaction (accessed December 5, 2018).

45. Matthew Stern, "New Store Concept Is Next Step in Dunkin' Rebranding," *RetailWire*, https://www.retailwire.com/discussion/new-store-concept-is-next-step-in-dunkin-rebranding/, January 24, 2018.

9

1. "Ranks of Avid Campers Still Growing," *Quirks Marketing Research Review*, July 2018, 12–14.

2. *Ibid.*

3. "In Store Shoppers Happy to Go It Alone," *Quirks Marketing Research Review*, July 2018, 14–15.

4. "Connected Devices Gaining in Popularity," *Quirks Marketing Research Review*, March 2015, 16–17; and Aaron Pressman, "Spending on Internet of Things May More Than Double to Over Half a Trillion Dollars," *Fortune*, August 8, 2018, www.fortune.com/2018/08/08/internet-of-things-iot-trillion-dollars-bain/ (accessed November 4, 2018).

5. "Decoding the Product Page," Quirks Marketing Research Review, July 2018, 32–35.

6. https://www.statista.com/statistics/346167/facebook-global-dau/ (accessed November 4, 2018).

7. Jasmine Garsd, "Does Facebook Really Work? People Question Effectiveness of Ads," September 12, 2018, https://www.npr.org/2018/09/12/647040758/advertising-on-facebook-is-it-worth-it (accessed November 5, 2018).

8. "Mighty Neighborly," *Quirks Marketing Research Review*, January 2018, 12–14.

9. "Shopability: The Science of Shopping," https://kelley.iu.edu/cerr/about/spotlights/page29034.html (accessed February 23, 2019).

10. https://marketingplatform.google.com/about/surveys/how-it-works/ (accessed February 23, 2019).

11. Carl McDaniel and Roger Gates, *Marketing Research*, 11th ed. (Hoboken: Wiley, 2018), 147.

12. "Taking Our Seat at the Table," *Quirks Marketing Research Review*, January 2018, 26–27.

13. "Mobile Is the Fastest Growing Technology for Marketing Research," Mobile Market Research Association, http://www.MMRA-global.org (November 6, 2018); also see: "At the Breaking Point," *Quirks Marketing Research Review*, June 2018, 32–37.

14. *Ibid.*

15. Carl McDaniel ... *Marketing Research*, 148.

10

1. Marl J. Miller, "CES 2016: Under Armour Goes All in on Fitness Tech with Healthbox," *Brandchannel*, January 5, 2016, http://www.brandchannel.com/2016/01/05/under-armour-healthbox-010516/ (accessed December 14, 2018).

2. "Cat's Pride Introduces New Fresh & Light Ultimate Care," Cat's Pride, March 7, 2016, http://catspride.com/cat-matters/in-the-news/ (accessed December 15, 2018).

3. Dale Buss, "SeaWorld CEO Joel Manby Details Rebrand to Orca Conservation," *Brandchannel*, March 24, 2016, http://brandchannel.com/2016/03/24/seaworld-joel-manby-032416/ (accessed December 15, 2018).

4. Nathan Bomey, "Weight Watchers Rebrands as WW, Eliminates Artificial Ingredients in Focus on Wellness," https://www.usatoday.com/story/money/2018/09/24/weight-watchers-international-ww/1408238002/, September 24, 2018.

5. Dale Buss, "Chobani Keeps Growth Momentum Going with Flips, Yogurt Drinks," *Brandchannel*, http://brandchannel.com/2017/01/17/chobani-growth-011717/ (accessed December 15, 2018).

6. Dale Buss, "Toyota Axes Scion Brand, Rolls Models into Toyota Lineup," *Brandchannel*, February 4, 2016, http://brandchannel.com/2016/02/04 /toyota-axes-scion-020416/ (accessed December 15, 2018).

7. Susan Reiter, "Activating Brave: Interbrand's Best Global Brands 2018," https://www.brandchannel.com/2018/10/04/interbrand-best-global-brands-2018/, October 4, 2018.

8. Lisa Goller, "Private Labels Emerge as Unstoppable Brands," https://www.rangeme.com/blog/private-labels/, July 25, 2018.

9. Nathaniel Meyersohn, "Who Needs Brand Names? Now Amazon Makes the Stuff It Sells," https://www.cnn.com/2018/10/08/business/amazon-private-label-brands/index.html, October 8, 2018.

10. Rebekah Marcarelli, "Praise for Private Label," January 31, 2017, https://www.winsightgrocerybusiness.com/praise-private-label (accessed December 15, 2018).

11. Keith Nunes, "Sales Growth Continuing for Kroger's Simple Truth Line," *Food Business News*, March 22, 2016, http://www.foodbusiness news.net/articles/news_home/Food-Service-Retail/2016/03/Sales_growth_continuing_for_Kr.aspx (accessed December 15, 2018).

12. Lindsay Kolowich, "Examples of Successful Co-Branding Partnerships (and Why They're So Great)," *HubSpot*, March 8, 2016, https://blog.hubspot.com/marketing/best-cobranding-partnerships (accessed December 15, 2018).

13. "Bruegger's Bagels and Jamba Juice Launch Co-Branded Concept," *Bruegger's*, February 25, 2016, https://www.brueggers.com/news/brueggers-jamba-juice-cobranded-concept-melrose/ (accessed December 16, 2018).

14. Abe Sauer, "Louis Vuitton × Supreme Collaboration Combines Luxury with Street Cred," *Brandchannel*, January 25, 2017, http://www.brandchannel.com/2017/01/25/louis-vuitton-x-supreme-012517/ (accessed December 16, 2018).

15. "Trademark Applications—Intent-to-Use (ITU) Basis," https://www.uspto.gov/trademarks-application-process/filing-online/intent-use-itu-applications (accessed December 17, 2018).

16. Murray Hunter, "DMCA Abuse: How Corporations Are Using US Copyright Law to Harass and Silence Individuals," NSNBC, September 24, 2016, http://foreignpolicynews.org/2016/09/25/dmca-abuse-corporations-using-us-copyright-law-harass-silence-individuals/ (accessed December 17, 2018).

17. Dominic Patten, "'Empire' & Fox Win Trademark Suit in Time for Season 2 Spring Return," *Deadline*, February 3, 2016, http://deadline.com/2016/02/empire-fox-trademark-infringement-lawsuit-order-lee-daniels-1201695714 (accessed December 17, 2018).

18. Matt Scyoc, "Tiffany & Co. Successfully Asserts Trademark Infringement Claims against Costco," *IP Watchdog*, January 6, 2017, http://www.ipwatchdog.com/2017/01/06/tiffany-trademark-infringement-claims-against-costco/id=76383/ (accessed December 17, 2018).

19. The Fashion Law, "Louis Vuitton, Prada Targeted by Fake Stores in Chinese Cities," http://www.thefashionlaw.com/home/louis-vuitton-prada-targeted-by-fake-stores-in-chinese-cities, September 6, 2018.

20. U.S. Food and Drug Administration, "Changes to the Nutrition Facts Label," https://www.fda.gov/Food/GuidanceRegulation/GuidanceDocumentsRegulatoryInformation/LabelingNutrition/ucm385663.htm (accessed December 18, 2018).

21. Government of Canada, "Consultation on Front-of-Package Labeling," https://www.canada.ca/en/health-canada/programs/front-of-package-nutrition-labelling.html, February 13, 2018.

22. Jay Moye, "A Bottle Diet Coke Fans Can Call Their Own," https://www.coca-colacompany.com/stories/diet-coke-its-mine, January 7, 2016 (accessed December 18).

23. Wendy Knowler, "Why No Cure for Wrap Rage?" *Times Live*, January 23, 2017, http://www.timeslive.co.za/consumerlive/2017/01/23/Why-no-cure-for-wrap-rage1 (accessed December 18, 2018); Nathan Rao, "'Wrap Rage' Soars over Packaging We Can't Open," *Express*, January 28, 2014, http://www.express.co.uk/news/uk/456493/Wrap-Rage-soars-over-packaging-we-can-t-open (accessed December 18, 2018).

24. Lisa McTigue Pierce, "5 Top Packaging Developments in May 2018," *Packaging Digest*, https://www.packagingdigest.com/packaging-design/5-top-packaging-developments-in-may-2018-2018-06-08/page/0/4, June 8, 2018.

25. Anne Marie Mohan, "Six Packaging Trends for 2016," *Packaging World*, February 15, 2016, http://www.packworld.com/trends-and-issues/global/six-packaging-trends-2016 (accessed December 18, 2018).

26. "Top Packaging Trends for 2017," *Brand Packaging*, January 11, 2017, http://www.brandpackaging.com/articles/85690-top-packaging-trends-for-2017 (December 18, 2018).

27. "Food Safety Innovation: Smart Packaging," *Mobile Future*, October 7, 2015, http://mobilefuture.org/food-safety-innovation-smart-packaging (accessed December 18, 2018).

28. "About Green Seal," Green Seal, April 12, 2016, http://www.greenseal.org/AboutGreenSeal.aspx (accessed December 18, 2018).

29. "One Brand, One Disc, One Look: Coca-Cola Unveils Global Packaging," *Brandchannel*, April 18, 2016, http://www.brandchannel.com/2016/04/18/coca-cola-one-brand-packaging-041816/ (accessed December 18, 2018).

11

1. "The Most Innovative Companies of 2018," *Fast Company*, http://www.fastcompany.com/most-innovative-companies/2018 (accessed December 31, 2018).

2. "What Are Clinical Trials: Phases of Development," *Pfizer*, http://www.pfizer.com/research/clinical_trials/phases_of_development (accessed December 31, 2018).

3. Barry Jaruzelski, Robert Chwalik, and Brad Goehle "What the Top Innovators Get Right (study report)," *strategy+business*, October 30, 2018, https://www.strategy-business.com/feature/What-the-Top-Innovators-Get-Right?gko=e7cf9 (accessed December 31, 2018).

4. Nick Statt, "Apple Announced New MacBook Air with Retina Display Starting at $1,199," *The Verge*, October 30, 2018, https://www.theverge.com/2018/10/30/17832426/new-apple-macbook-air-retina-display-2018-laptop-price-release-date-specs (accessed December 31, 2018).

5. Mike Esterl, "Gatorade Sets Its Sights on Digital Fitness," *Wall Street Journal*, March 10, 2016, http://www.wsj.com/articles/gatorade-sets-its-sights-on-digital-fitness-1457640150 (accessed December 31, 2018).

6. "Moleskine World," *Moleskine*, https://us.moleskine.com/company (accessed December 31, 2018).

7. Jeanine Poggi, "Inside Taco Bell's Not-So-Secret Super Bowl Product Launch," *Ad Age*, February 7, 2016, http://adage.com/article/special-report-super-bowl/inside-taco-bell-s-secret-super-bowl-product-launch/302553/ (accessed December 31, 2018).

8. Dave Smoth, "Apple's Big September event Was One of the Most Disappointing iPhone Launches in Recent Memory," *Business Insider*, September 13, 2018, https://www.businessinsider.com/apple-iphone-xs-september-event-disappointing-2018-9 (accessed December 31, 2018).

9. Adrienne LaFrance, "How to Play Like a Girl," *The Atlantic*, May 25, 2016, http://www.theatlantic.com/entertainment/archive/2016/05/legos/484115/ (accessed December 31, 2018).

10. Adam Robinson, "Want to Boost Your Bottom Line? Encourage Your Employees to Work on Side Projects," *Inc.*, March 12, 2018, https://www.inc.com/adam-robinson/

google-employees-dedicate-20-percent-of-their-time-to-side-projects-heres-how-it-works.html (accessed December 31, 2018).

11. Laurie Brookins, "Hollywood's Go-To Clutch Brand, Edie Parker, Arrives on Madison Avenue," *The Hollywood Reporter*, March 7, 2017, https://www.hollywoodreporter.com/news/hollywoods-go-clutch-brand-edie-parker-arrives-madison-ave-984294 (accessed December 31, 2018).

12. Ron Johnson, "Why Google Rewards Its Employees for Failing,'" *LinkedIn*, December 15, 2017, https://www.linkedin.com/pulse/why-google-rewards-its-employees-failing-ron-johnson/ (accessed December 31, 2018).

13. "Fuld & Company Is the World's Preeminent Research and Consulting Firm in the Field of Competitive Intelligence," *Fuld & Company*, http://www.fuld.com (accessed December 31, 2018).

14. "Winterstick Snowboards Opens R&D Site Near Sugarloaf," *Mainebiz*, March 9, 2017, http://www.mainebiz.biz/article/20170309/NEWS0101/170309942/winterstick-snowboards-opens-r&d-site-near-sugarloaf (accessed December 31, 2018).

15. Paul Davidson, "Why China is Beating the U.S. at Innovation," *USA Today*, April 18, 2017, https://www.usatoday.com/story/money/2017/04/17/why-china-beating-us-innovation/100016138/ (accessed December 31, 2018).

16. "Company Profile," *Continuum*, http://continuuminnovation.com/about/company-profile (accessed December 31, 2018).

17. Michael Wolf, "With New Contest, Tupperware Looks to Discover the Future of Food Containers," *the spoon*, December 7, 2018, https://thespoon.tech/with-new-contest-tupperware-looks-to-discover-the-future-of-food-containers/ (accessed December 30, 2018).

18. Michael McWhertor, "Marvel Games' New Mandate Is 'Make Epic Games,' and Spider-Man Is Just the Beginning," *Polygon*, June 14, 2016, http://www.polygon.com/e3/2016/6/14/11937012/marvel-games-aaa-spider-man-insomniac-games-jay-ong (accessed December 30, 2018).

19. Michael D. Hutt and Thomas W. Speh, *Mindtap Marketing for Business Marketing Management B2B*, 12th ed. (Boston: Cengage, 2017).

20. Dennis Beers, "Dewalt and Its Customer-Driven Innovation," *Consumer Value Creation*, March 4, 2017, https://consumervaluecreation.com/2017/03/04/dewalt-and-its-customer-driven-innovation/ (accessed December 30, 2018).

21. Richard Bowie, "Wendy's Vegan-Friendly Burger a Hit in Test Markets," *Veg News*, April 26, 2016, http://vegnews.com/articles/page.do?pageId=7758&catId=1 (accessed December 30, 2018).

22. Will Racke and Coral Garnick, "Starbucks Is Testing Ice Cream in Coffee," *Pacific Business News*, February 15, 2017, http://www.bizjournals.com/pacific/news/2017/02/15/starbucks-is-testing-ice-cream-in-coffee.html (accessed December 30, 2018).

23. "P&G Everyday," *Procter & Gamble*, http://www.pgeveryday.com/offers (accessed December 30, 2018).

24. Copernicus Marketing Consulting and Research, "Top 10 Reasons for New Product Failure," *Green-Book*, June 13, 2010, http://www.greenbook.org/marketing-research.cfm/top-10-reasons-for-new-product-failure (accessed December 30, 2018).

25. "When Corporate Innovation Goes Bad—The 141 Biggest Product Failures of All Time," *CB Insights*, December 19, 2018, http://www.cbinsights.com/blog/corporate-innovation-product-fails/ (accessed February 18, 2019).

26. Megan Mosley, "Why Is Word of Mouth Marketing So Incredibly Important?" *Business to Community*, February, 23, 2018, https://www.business2community.com/marketing/word-mouth-marketing-incredibly-important-02017025 (accessed December 30, 2018).

27. *Nathan Resnick*, "Backed by Psychology, Reviews Are Big for Your Business—Here's Why," *The Next Web*, July 19, 2018, https://thenextweb.com/contributors/2018/07/19/backed-by-psychology-reviews-are-big-for-your-business-heres-why/ (accessed December 30, 2018).

28. Kerry Windle, "Share a Coke and a Word: How Coca-Cola Captured Millennials through Word of Mouth Marketing," *Medium*, May 19, 2016, https://medium.com/@kwindle/share-a-coke-and-a-word-how-coca-cola-captured-millennials-through-word-of-mouth-marketing-44896573d21c (accessed December 30, 2018).

29. *Ibid*.

30. Aaron Smith and Monica Anderson, "Online Reviews," *Pew Research Center*, December 19, 2016, http://www.pewinternet.org/2016/12/19/online-reviews/ (accessed December 30, 2018).

31. Lionel Menchaca, "Effective Employee Advocacy Opens the Door for Influencer Engagement," *Dynamic Signal*, May 26, 2016, http://dynamicsignal.com/2016/05/26/effective-employee-advocacy-opens-the-door-for-influencer-engagement/ (accessed December 30, 2018).

32. Vivian Giang, "100 Fastest-Growing Companies," *Fortune*, http://fortune.com/100-fastest-growing-companies/ (accessed December 30, 2018).

33. "Why Nearly 46 Percent of Households Still Have Landlines," *New York Post*, May 4, 2017, https://nypost.com/2017/05/04/why-nearly-46-percent-of-household-still-have-landlines/ (accessed December 30, 2018).

12

1. "Distribution of the Workforce across Economic Sectors in the United States from 2007 to 2017," https://www.statista.com/statistics/270072/distribution-of-the-workforce-across-economic-sectors-in-the-united-states/ (accessed December 23, 2018).

2. Dinah Eng and Isadore Sharp, "Building Great Service at the Four Seasons," *Fortune*, April 1, 2016, https://www.researchgate.net/publication/301583992_Building_Great_Service_at_the_Four_Seasons (accessed December 23, 2018).

3. Ed Tittel and Kim Lindros, "Best Big Data Certifications," https://www.businessnewsdaily.com/10754-best-big-data-certifications.html, May 23, 2018.

4. Samuel Stebbins, "Companies with the Best and Worst Reputations," https://247wallst.com/special-report/2018/04/20/companies-with-the-best-and-worst-reputations-6/5/, *24/7 Wall St*, April 20,2018; Michael B. Sauter, Evan Comen, and Samuel Stibbins, "Companies with the Best (and Worst) Reputations," *24/7 Wall St*, March 3, 2017, http://247wallst.com/special-report/2017/03/03/companies-with-the-best-and-worst-reputations-5/5/ (accessed December 27, 2018); Kevin McCoy, "Wells Fargo Revamps Pay Plan after Fake-Accounts Scandal," *USA Today*, January 11, 2017, http://www.usatoday.com/story/money/2017/01/11/wells-fargo-revamps-pay-plan-after-fake-accounts-scandal/96441730/ (accessed December 27, 2018).

5. Darren Hudson, "How I Did It . . . Priceline's CEO on Creating an In-House Multilingual Customer Service Operation," *Harvard Business Review*, April 2016, 37–40.

6. "Revolutionizing Customer Service," *Harvard Business Review*, April 2016, 26–27.

7. Valarie Zeithaml, Mary Jo Bitner, and Dwayne Gremler, *Services Marketing: Integrating Customer Service Across the Firm*, 7th ed. (New York: McGraw-Hill, 2018).

8. *Ibid*.

9. Pam Goodfellow, "L.L. Bean, Amazon and Nordstrom Are Customer Service Champions, According to Customers," *Forbes*, March 29, 2016, http://www.forbes.com/sites/forbesinsights/2016/03/29/l-l-bean-amazon-and-nordstrom-are-customer-service-champions-according-to-consumers/#4170693d7bc2 (accessed December 23, 2018).

10. "Best Mobile Banking Apps in 2018," https://www.mobileappdaily.com/2018/07/16/mobile-banking-apps-2018 (accessed December 23, 2018).

11. Samuel Stebbins, Michael B. Sauter, and Evan Comen, "24/7 Wall St.'s Customer Service Hall of Fame," https://247wallst.com/special-report/2017/08/24/customer-service-hall-of-fame-5/4/, August 24, 2017 (accessed December 23, 2018).

12. Much of the material in this section is based on Jochen Wirtz and Christopher H. Lovelock, *Services Marketing: People, Technology and Strategy*, 8th ed. (Upper Saddle River, NJ: Prentice Hall, 2016).

13. Asit Sharma, "How Consumer and Retail Companies Are Embracing Mass Customization," https://www.fool.com/investing/2016/10/09/how-consumer-and-retail-companies-are-embracing-ma.aspx, October 9, 2016 (accessed December 23, 2018).

14. Mara Leighton, "6 Brands Bringing the Convenience of Online Shopping to Your Home with 'Try Before You Buy' Policies," https://www.businessinsider.com/try-before-you-buy-clothing-brands-stitch-fix-warby-parker-amazon-prime-fashion, January 29, 2018.

15. April Glaser, "Domino's Is Going to Use Sidewalk Robots in Germany to Deliver Pizza," *Recode*, March 29, 2017, https://www.recode.net/2017/3/29/15100748/dominos-deliver-pizza-robots-germany-starship (accessed December 23, 2018).

16. Jochen Wirtz and Christopher H. Lovelock, *Services Marketing: People, Technology and Strategy*, 8th ed. (Upper Saddle River, NJ: Prentice Hall, 2016).

17. Iris Kuo, "How to Keep Them Coming Back," *Inc.*, April 2016, 80–81.

18. *Ibid*.

19. Much of the material in this section is based on Valarie Zeithaml, Mary Jo Bitner, and Dwayne Gremler, *Services Marketing: Integrating Customer Service Across the Firm*, 7th ed. (New York: McGraw-Hill, 2018).

20. Jean Carmela, "5 Luxury Travel Trends for 2017," *World Travel Market*, February 22, 2017, http://news.wtm.com/5-luxury-travel-trends-for-2017/ (accessed December 23, 2018).

21. "100 Best Companies to Work for 2018," http://fortune.com/best-companies/ (accessed December 23, 2018).

22. Heidi Mitchell, "Why Cities Need to Create Their Own Global Brands," *Wall Street Journal*, April 16, 2017, https://www.wsj.com/articles/why-cities-need-to-create-their-own-global-brands-1492394882 (accessed December 26, 2018).

23. "Glasses USA Partners with Alex's Lemonade Stand Foundation to Help Fight Childhood Cancer, One Pair at a Time," https://engageforgood.com/glassesusa-com-partners-with-alexs-lemonade-stand-foundation-alsf-to-help-fight-childhood-cancer-one-pair-at-a-time/, December 18, 2018.

24. Minda Smiley, "This Comically Savage Election PSA Should Scare Every Millennial into Voting," https://www.adweek.com/creativity/this-comically-savage-election-psa-should-scare-every-millennial-into-voting-in-the-next-election/, September 28, 2018.

25. "Pizza Hut International," Pizza Hut, https://www.pizzahut.co.uk/aboutus/international (accessed December 26, 2018).

13

1. "Fresh Gab Press Releases," *Fresh Gab*, https://www.instagram.com/freshgab_(accessed March 18, 2018).

2. Alan Chan, Karen Moon, and Eric Ngai, "The Effects of Strategic Manufacturing Flexibilities and Supply Chain Agility on Firm Performance in the Fashion Industry," *European Journal of Operational Research*, 259, no. 2, 486–499; and "Collapsing the Supply Chain—The Secret behind Zara's Success," *QuantIQ*, June 4, 2018, https://www.quantiq.com/news-success/collapsing-the-supply-chain/

3. Kenco, http://www.kencogroup.com (accessed February 4, 2017).

4. Clara Lu, "Walmart's Successful Supply Chain Management," *TradeGecko*, October 4, 2018,

5. Jessica Lyons Hardcastle, "How Hewlett-Packard, General Motors, Other Major Purchasers Helped Suppliers Save $12.4 Billion by Reducing Emissions," *Environmental Leader*, January 24, 2017, https://www.environmentalleader.com/2017/01/how-hewlett-packard-general-motors-other-major-purchasers-helped-suppliers-save-12-4-billion-by-reducing-emissions/ (accessed December 2018).

6. "Production," Airbus, http://www.airbus.com/company/aircraft-manufacture/how-is-an-aircraft-built/production/ (accessed November 2018).

7. Mark A. Moon, *Demand and Supply Integration: The Key to World-Class Demand Forecasting* (New York: Financial Times Press, 2013).

8. Much of this section is based on material adapted from Donald J. Bowersox, David J. Closs, and Theodore P. Stank, *21st Century Logistics: Making Supply Chain Integration a Reality* (Oak Brook, IL: Council of Logistics Management, 1999); Barbara Flynn, Michiya Morita, and Jose Machuca, *Managing Global Supply Chain Relationships: Operations, Strategies and Practices* (Hershey, Pennsylvania: Business Science, 2010); and David Sims, "Integrated Supply Chains Maximize Efficiencies and Savings," *ThomasNet*, July 23, 2013, http://news.thomasnet.com/imt/2013/07/23/integrated-supply-chains-maximize-efficiencies-and-savings (accessed March 2019).

9. "Häagen-Dazs and General Mills to Help Smallholder Vanilla Farmers Increase Yields and Improve Sustainability Practices in Madagascar," *CSRwire*, February 20, 2013, http://www.csrwire.com/press_releases/35228-H-agen-Dazs-and-General-Mills-to-Help-Smallholder-Vanilla-Farmers-Increase-Yields-and-Improve-Sustainability-Practices-in-Madagascar (accessed March 2019).

10. Much of this and the following sections are based on material adapted from Douglas M. Lambert, ed., *Supply Chain Management: Processes, Partnerships and Performance* (Sarasota, FL: Supply Chain Management Institute, 2004); "The Supply Chain Management Processes," *Supply Chain Management Institute*, https://www.emeraldinsight.com/doi/pdfplus/10.1108/IJLM-12-2015-0242 (accessed March 18, 2019).

11. Customer Communications Group, Inc. "Retail CRM Strategies That Go beyond Loyalty Programs," *Retail Marketing Blog*, https://www.salesforce.com/form/industries/comms-unify-journey-demo/?d=7010M000000NvNL&nc=7010M000000O4ve&DCMP=KNC-Bing&DCMP=KNC-Bing&s_kwcid=AL!4604!10!81226456537541!81226489413497&ef_id=W2ao2QAAAEPlA1dn:20190318164928:s (accessed March 18, 2019).

12. "Four Examples of Businesses Leveraging CRM to Improve Productivity and Efficiency." www.salesforce.com/crm/examples (accessed November 2018).

13. Steve Banker, "An American Steel Company Transforms Their Supply Chain into a Competitive Weapon," *Logistics Viewpoints*, February 6, 2017, https://logisticsviewpoints.com/2017/02/06/an-american-steel-company-transforms-their-supply-chain-into-a-competitive-weapon/ (accessed March 14, 2018).

14. "Top 20 Order Fulfillment Services and Companies of 2018," *Finances Online: Reviews for Business*, https://financesonline.com/top-20-order-fulfillment-services/ (accessed March 18, 2019).

15. Tony Hines, *Supply Chain Strategies: Demand Driven and Customer Focused*, 2nd ed. (New York: Routledge, 2013).

16. "Boeing CEO Dennis Muilenberg's Moonshot," *ChiefExecutive*, January 2018, https://chiefexecutive.net/boeing-ceo-dennis-muilenbergs-moonshot/2/

17. "AT&T Completes Acquisition of Time Warner Inc." *AT&T*, June 15, 2018, https://newswire.telecomramblings.com/2018/06/att-completes-acquisition-time-warner-inc/ (accessed March 18, 2019).

18. Kenneth J. Petersen, Robert Handfield, and Gary Ragatz, "Supplier Integration into New Product Development: Coordinating Product, Process, and Supply Chain Design," *Journal of Operations Management*, 23, no. 3–4, (2005): 371–388; Stephen Trimble, "Analysis: US South Rises on Airbus, Boeing Expansion," *Flight Global*, http://www.flightglobal.com (accessed November 2018).

19. Mary Hanbury, "These stores have the best return policies in retail." *Business Insider*, 24 September 2018, https://www.businessinsider.com/costco-trader-joes-ikea-best-return-policy-2018-3.

20. Lauren Levy, "Sustainable Pallets, Packages & More," *Food Logistics*, May 17, 2013, http://www.foodlogistics.com/article/10944473/sustainable-pallets-packages-more (accessed November 2018).

21. UPS, "Logistics of Sustainability," *Compass*, Spring 2012, 10, https://sustainability.ups.com/committed-to-more/fuels-and-fleets/ (accessed December 2018).

22. Steve Szilagyi, keynote address, Warehousing Education and Research Council Annual Conference, Atlanta, GA, May 2012; and Judy Owen, "Lowe's Ramps Up Disability Inclusion," *Forbes*, April 2013.

23. "Global CSR Risk and Performance Index 2018," Index.ecovadis.com (accessed November 2018).

24. Amit Regev, "Drone Deliveries Are No Longer Pie in the Sky," *Forbes*, April 10, 2018; Jeffery Lin and P. W. Singer, "Meet China's Growing Fleet of Automated Delivery Drones," *Popular Science*, July 3, 2018.

25. "Ford and Walmart Collaborate to Design Automated Vehicle Delivery," www.CNBC.com (accessed December 2018).

26. Gene Marks, "Are Robots Coming for Your Lawyer?" *The Guardian*, September 13, 2018, https://www.theguardian.com/business/2018/sep/13/ai-firm-atrium-legal-law-attorneys

27. Barbara Thau, "Make It Yourself; Lowe's Tests Profit Potential of 3D Printed, Personalized Products," *Forbes*, September 8, 2016.

28. Brian Lord, "Reebok's 3D Printed Shoe Line Dashes into Production." *3D Printing Industry: The Authority on 3D Printing*, August 3, 2018, https://3dprintingindustry.com/news/reeboks-3d-printed-shoe-line-dashes-into-production-137497/.

29. "Additive manufacturing can reduce industry's environmental impact." *The Engineer*, November 14, 2018.

30. Adrian Clarke, "What Supply Chain Executives Need to Know about Blockchain," *Supply and Demand Chain Executive*, November 14, 2018.

31. Andreas Fürst, Martin Leimbach, and Jana-Kristin Prigge, "Organizational Multichannel Differentiation: An Analysis of Its Impact on Channel Relationships and Company Sales Success," *Journal of Marketing*, 81, no. 1 (2017): 59–82.

32. Eric Savitz, "Apple Screens for iPad3 in Short Supply," *Forbes*, March 1, 2012, 9.

33. Bernazzani, Sophia. "13 Examples of Successful Co-Branding Partnerships (And Why They're So Great)." *HubSpot*, August 6, 2018.

34. "Intel® NUC, Intel® Compute Stick, and Intel® Compute Card US Recycling Program." Intel, November 18, 2018, https://www.intel.com/content/www/us/en/nuc/nuc-compute-stick-recycling-program.html; Cortina, Hernando. "These Five Companies Are Leading the Charge on Recycling." *Forbes*, April 20, 2018, https://www.forbes.com/sites/justcapital/2018/04/20/these-5-companies-are-leading-the-charge-on-recycling/#68ed7dfb23ec.

35. "Transaction Value of Global M-Commerce Sales from 2014 to 2019 (in billion U.S. dollars)." *Statista: The Statistics Portal*, 2018, https://www.statista.com/statistics/557951/mobile-commerce-transaction-value-worldwide/.

36. Alex Hamilton, "M-Commerce Causing Sales Figures to Explode," *TechRadar*, https://www.techradar.com/news/phone-and-communications/mobile-phones/m-commerce-casuing-sales-figures-to-explode-1207089 (accessed March 18, 2019).

37. McPherson, Doug. "Retail Sales on the Rise; E-Commerce, Mobile Will Enjoy Surge." *Response: The Magazine for Media, Technology & Commerce*, February 14, 2018, https://www.bing.com/search?q=37.%09McPherson%2C+Doug.+%E2%80%9C Retail+Sales+on+the+Rise%3B+E-Commerce%2 C+Mobile+Will+Enjoy+Surge.%E2%80%9D+Re sponse%3A+The+Magazine+for+Media%2C+Te chnology+%26+Commerce%2C+14+February+2 018%2C+++&form=PRLNC1&pc=LCTE&mkt= en-us&httpsmsn=1&refig=6143ef56a0d94fb0a1d3 017fb7821e5a&sp=-1&pq=http%3A%2F%2Fwww. techradar.com%2Fnews%2Fphone-and-communications%2Fmobile-phones%2Fm-commerce-causing-sales-

figures-to-explode-1207089+&sc=0-121&qs=n&sk=&cvid=6143ef56a0d94-fb0a1d3017fb7821e5a (accessed March 18, 2019); "Percentage of Retail m-Commerce Sales via Tablet in the United States from 2017 to 2021." *Statista: The Statistics Portal*, 2018, https://www.statista.com/statistics/534123/e-commerce-share-of-retail-sales-worldwide/ (accessed March 18, 2019).

38. "Mobile Fact Sheet." *Pew Research Center*, 5 February 2018, http://www.pewinternet.org/fact-sheet/mobile/; "U.S. and World Population Clock." *United States Census Bureau*, November 21, 2018, https://www.census.gov/popclock/

39. Ksenia Dobreva, "Global E-Commerce Trends and Statistics [2017-2018]." *Amasty Blog*, https://amasty.com/blog/global-e-commerce-trends-and-statistics-2017-2018/#MOBILE_MAJORITY (accessed January 29, 2018); "America's Household Enthusiast." *RetailMeNot Inc.*, https://research.retailmenot.com/p/1 (accessed March 2018).

40. Jack Uldrich, "The Future of Retail Isn't So Foreign," *Jump the Curve*, January 30, 2013, http://jumpthecurve.net/retail-marketing/the-future-of-retail-isnt-so-foreign/ (accessed December 2018).

41. McCue, TJ. "Social Media Is Increasing Brand Engagement and Sales." *Forbes*, June 26, 2018, https://www.forbes.com/sites/tjmccue/2018/06/26/social-media-is-increasing-brand-engagement-and-sales/#70ce50d27cb3 ; "30 Social Media Marketing Statistics That Will Change the Way You Think About Social Media." *Lyfe Marketing*, March 5, 2018, https://www.lyfemarketing.com/blog/social-media-marketing-statistics/.

42. J.J. Wang, X. Zhao, and J.J. Li. "Group Buying: A Strategic Form of Consumer Collective," *Journal of Retailing*, 89, no. 3, (2013), 338–351.

43. Granados, Dr. Nelson, Mooney, Dr. John. "Popcorn or Snack? Empirical Analysis of Movie Release Windows." *Pepperdine Business School*, November 2018, https://digitalcommons.pepperdine.edu/cgi/viewcontent.cgi?article=1005&context=graziadiowps

44. Taurn Kushwaha and Venkatesh Shankar, "Are Multichannel Customers Really More Valuable? The Moderating Role of Product Category Characteristics," *Journal of Marketing*, 77, no. 4, 67–85; Jennifer Lonoff Schiff, "Eight Ways to Create a Successful Multichannel Customer Experience," CIO, https://www.cio.com/article/2887285 /e-commerce/8-ways-to-create-a-successful -multichannel-customer-experience.html (accessed December 2018).

14

1. Kimberley Amadeo, "The Retail Industry and Its Impact on the Economy," *The Balance*, November 7, 2018 (updated December 18, 2018), https://www.thebalance.com/what-is-retailing-why-it-s-important-to-the-economy-3305718 (accessed February 21, 2019); Akrur Barua and Daniel Bachman, "Retail Sales: Trends in Revenue and Employment," *Deloitte Insights*, January 23, 2018, https://www2.deloitte.com/insights/us/en/economy/behind-the-numbers/changes-in-retail-sales-economic-impact.html (accessed November 30, 2018).

2. "State of Retail," *National Retail Federation (NRF)*, November 9, 2018, https://nrf.com/insights/economy/state-retail (accessed November 30, 2018); "Table B-1. Employees on Nonfarm Payrolls by Industry Sector and Selected Industry Detail," *Bureau of Labor Statistics*, October 2018, https://www.bls.gov/news.release/empsit.t17.htm (accessed November 30, 2018); "Retail's Impact: California,"
National Retail Federation (NRF), November 9, 2018, https://nrf.com/retails-impact/california (accessed November 30, 2018); "Retail's Impact: New York," *National Retail Federation (NRF)*, November 9, 2018, https://nrf.com/retails-impact/new-york (accessed November 30, 2018).

3. "State of Play: Global Employee Engagement Trends," *Qualtrics*, November 2018, https://www.qualtrics.com/employee-experience/employee-engagement-research/#section1 (accessed March 18, 2019); "How Americans View Their Jobs," *Pew Research Center*, October 6, 2016, http://www.pewsocialtrends.org/2016/10/06/3-how-americans-view-their-jobs/ (accessed December 12, 2018); "2018 Small Business Profile: United States," *U.S. Small Business Administration Office of Advocacy*, 2018, https://www.sba.gov/sites/default/files/advocacy/2018-Small-Business-Profiles-US.pdf (accessed December 12, 2018); "Company Facts," *Walmart*, 2018, https://corporate.walmart.com/newsroom/company-facts (accessed December 1, 2018); "Countries in the World by Population (2018)," *Worldometers*, 2018, http://www.worldometers.info/world-population/population-by-country/ (accessed December 1, 2018).

4. "2019 Top 500 Franchises from Entrepreneur's 500 List," *Entrepreneur*, https://www.entrepreneur.com/franchise500 (accessed November 15, 2018).

5. John Nicolopoulos, "Top 5 Trends for Food and Beverage Industry Businesses in 2018 (video)," *Boston Business Journal*, January 29, 2018, https://www.bizjournals.com/boston/news/2018/01/29/top-5-trends-for-food-and-beverage-industry.html (accessed December 5, 2018).

6. Kyuseop Kwak, Sri D. Duvvuri, and Gary J. Russell, "An Analysis of Assortment Choice in Grocery Retailing," *Journal of Retailing*, 91, no. 1 (2015): 19–33.

7. Susan Johnston, "Beware These Online Retail Pricing Strategies," *US News and World Report*, June 24, 2013.

8. "Flexible Figures," *Economist*, January 28, 2016, http://www.economist.com/news/business/21689541-growing-number-companies-are-using-dynamic-pricing-flexible-figures (accessed January 30, 2017); David Streitfeld, "It's Discontinued, but Is It a Deal? How List Prices Lost Their Meaning," *New York Times*, March 6, 2016, http://www.nytimes.com/2016/03/06/technology/its-discounted-but-is-it-a-deal-how-list-prices-lost-their-meaning.html?_r=0 (accessed December 21, 2018).

9. Nat Levy, "Walmart Employees Can Now Complete Online Orders for In-Store Customers Seeking Sold Items," *GeekWire*, December 4, 2018, https://www.geekwire.com/2018/walmart-employees-can-now-complete-online-orders-store-customers-seeking-sold-items/ (accessed December 5, 2018).

10. April Berthene, "Target Launches a Rewards Program in the Cartwheel App," *International Retailer*, https://www.digitalcommerce360.com/2016/09/12/target-launches-rewards-program-cartwheel-app/ (accessed March 18, 2019).

11. Stephanie Maida, "This Williamsburg Hotel Now Has a Luxury Jewelry Vending Machine," *Guest of a Guest*, July 25, 2018, https://guestofaguest.com/new-york/fashion/williamsburg-hotel-now-has-a-luxury-jewelry-vending-machine (accessed December 5, 2018).

12. "Bank of America Adds Human Touch to New ATMs," *Bank of America*, April 4, 2013, https://www.businesswire.com/news/home/20130404005586/en/Bank-America-Adds-Human-Touch-New-ATMs (accessed March 18, 2019).

13. "A New Career, A New Life: What Is a Wine Guide?" *Traveling Vineyard*, 2018, https://www.travelingvineyard.com/guide/wine/home-based-business/ (accessed December 5, 2018).

14. "2018 B2B Marketing Mix Report," *Sagefrog Marketing Group*, 2018, https://cdn2.hubspot.net/hubfs/455263/Marketing_Mix_2018_Report%20v3.pdf?t=1513614524815 (accessed December 5, 2018).

15. Tianyi Jiang and Alexander Tuzhilin, "Dynamic Microtargeting: Fitness-Based Approach to Predicting Individual Preferences," *Knowledge and Information Systems*, 19, no. 3 (2009): 337–360.

16. "Direct Mail Industry Findings: Our Review of The DMA Statistical Fact Book," *The Feed*, August 14, 2018, https://www.modernpostcard.com/blog/DMA-40th-Edition-Stats (accessed December 5, 2018).

17. "Online-Shopping and E-Commerce Worldwide: Statistics & Facts," *Statista*, 2017, https://www.statista.com/topics/871/online-shopping/ (accessed December 5, 2018); "amazon.com," *ecommerceDB*, https://ecommercedb.com/en/store/amazon.com#general-information (accessed December 5, 2018); "How Many Products Does Amazon Sell Worldwide—January 2018," *ScrapeHero*, January 15, 2018, https://www.scrapehero.com/how-many-products-amazon-sell-worldwide-january-2018/ (accessed December 5, 2018).

18. Evert de Haan, Peter K. Kannan, Peter C. Verhoef, and Thorsten Wiesel. "Device Switching in Online Purchasing: Examining the Strategic Contingencies," *Journal of Marketing*, 82, no. 5, (2018) 1–19.

19. Yunhui Huang and Charles Zhang, "The Out-of-Stock (OOS) Effect on Choice Shares of Available Options," *Journal of Retailing*, 92, no. 1 (2015): 13–24.

20. Ashley Lutz, "Zara's Genius Business Model Could Destroy JCPenney and Sears," *Business Insider*, March 4, 2013, http://www.businessinsider.com/zaras-genius-business-model-2013-3 (accessed December 10, 2018).

21. Andrew Asch, "Nordstrom Local, the Americana at Brand Popping in Holiday Pop-up Shops," November 18, 2018, https://www.apparelnews.net/news/2018/nov/08/nordstrom-local-americana-brand-popping-holiday-po/

22. "Delivery Platform for Retail Logistics," *Bringg*, https://www.bringg.com/industries/retailers/ (accessed December 6, 2018); "Capitalizing on Its Tremendous Market Momentum, Bringg Appoints Guy Bloch as Its New Chief Executive Officer," *Cision*, September 26, 2018, https://www.prnewswire.com/news-releases/capitalizing-on-its-tremendous-market-momentum-bringg-appoints-guy-bloch-as-its-new-chief-executive-officer-860818369.html (accessed December 6, 2018).

23. Jonathan Crowl, "How Amazon Spun Its Whole Foods Acquisition into a Marketing Opportunity," *ContentStandard*, October 18, 2017, https://www.skyword.com/contentstandard/marketing/amazon-spun-whole-foods-acquisition-marketing-opportunity/ (accessed December 6, 2018).

24. Taryn Luna, "Retailer T.J. Maxx Quietly Relaunches Online Store," *Boston Globe*, September 18, 2013, http://www.bostonglobe.com/business/2013/09/17/without-advance-notice-maxx-launches-its-online-store/8HKY5v2OjjV9NK9ofO3DGN/story.html (accessed December 6, 2018).

25. "J.C. Penney Partners with 'Project Runway' for Exclusive Merchandise, TV Appearance,"

Revenue Analytics, https://www.revenueanalytics.com/news/j-c-penney-partners-project-runway-exclusive-merchandise-tv-appearance (accessed December 6, 2018).

26. Shari Waters, "Choosing a Retail Store Location," *The Balance,* September 6, 2018, https://www.thebalancesmb.com/choosing-a-retail-store-location-2890245 (accessed December 6, 2018).

27. Pamela N. Danziger, "4 Models of the Shopping Mall of the Future," *Forbes,* April 7, 2018, https://www.forbes.com/sites/pamdanziger/2018/04/07/4-models-of-the-shopping-mall-of-the-future/#6587a77b5c3b (accessed December 6, 2018).

28. Barbara Thau, "Retail's Dirty Open Secret: Store Traffic Declines Are Shaking Up the Shopping Experience," *Forbes,* June 24, 2016, http://www.forbes.com/sites/barbarathau/2016/06/24/retails-dirty-open-secret-store-traffic-declines-are-shaking-up-the-shopping-experience/#1ebae6746697 (accessed December 15, 2018).

29. Carl L. Esmark, Stephanie M. Noble, and Michael J. Breazeale, "I'll be Watching You: Shoppers' Reactions to Perceptions of Being Watched By Employees," *Journal of Retailing,* 93, no. 3, 336–349.

30. Adrian C. North, Lorraine P. Sheridan, and Charles S. Areni, "Music Congruity Effects on Product Memory, Perception, and Choice," *Journal of Retailing,* 92, no. 1 (2015): 82–95.

31. Klemens M. Knoeferle, Vilhelm C. Paus, and Alexander Vossen, "An Upbeat Crowd: Fast In-store Music Alleviates Negative Effects of High Social Density on Consumers' Spending," *Journal of Retailing,* 93, no. 4, 541–549.

32. Adriena V. Madzharov, Lauren G. Block, and Maureen Morrin, "The Cool Scent of Power: Effects of Ambient Scent on Consumer Preferences and Choice Behavior," *Journal of Marketing,* 79, no. 1 (2015): 83–96.

33. Adam Blair, "The Drive to Localize," *RIS News,* May 7, 2011, http://risnews.edgl.com/retail-news/The-Drive-to-Localize72436 (accessed November 30, 2018).

34. Haithem Zourrig, Jean-Charles Chebat, and Roy Toffoli, "Consumer Revenge Behavior: A Cross-Cultural Perspective," *Journal of Business Research,* 62, no. 10 (2009): 995–1001.

35. Christopher Ratcliff, "iBeacons: The Hunt for Stats," *Econsultancy.com,* August 26, 2014; Rachel Abrams, "Psst! It's Me, the Mannequin," *New York Times,* 2015, A8.

36. Brian Laney, "5 Things Retailers Need to Know about RFID Technology," *Alert Tech,* June 16, 2015, http://alerttech.net/retail-rfid-technology/ (accessed December 15, 2018).

37. Richard Ventura, "Taking a Look at NRF16: Trends in Retail Industrial Technology," *Digital Signage Today,* February 18, 2016, http://www.digitalsignagetoday.com/articles/taking-a-look-at-nrf16-trends-in-retail-industry-technology/ (accessed November 30, 2018).

38. Scott Clarke, "How Voice-Assisted Commerce Is Speaking Up in Retail," *ITProPortal,* March 6, 2018, https://www.itproportal.com/features/how-voice-assisted-commerce-is-speaking-up-in-retail/ (accessed December 6, 2018).

39. Ben Kersey, "Wal-Mart Tries a Blended Channel Approach to Survive in a Digital World," *Verge,* November 23, 2012, http://www.theverge.com/2012/11/23/3681694/walmart-hybrid-model (accessed December 6, 2018).

40. Stuart Miller, "Customers Have High Expectations for Click and Collect," Real Business,

November 28, 2013, http://realbusiness.co.uk/article/24866-customers-have-high-expectations-for-click-and-collect (accessed December 6, 2018).

41. "10 Examples of Augmented Reality in Retail," *Creative Guerrilla Marketing,* March 17, 2014, http://www.creativeguerrillamarketing.com/augmented-reality/10-examples-augmented-reality-retail/ (accessed December 12, 2018).

15

1. Alexandra Jardine, "'Thanks 2016, It's Been Weird,' Says Spotify in Biggest-Ever Global Campaign," *Creativity Online,* November 28, 2016, http://creativity-online.com/work/spotify-thanks-2016/50063 (accessed March 30, 2017); Tim Nudd, "How Spotify Makes Its Data Driven Outdoor Ads and Why They Work So Well," *Adweek,* December 1, 2017, https://www.adweek.com/creativity/how-spotify-makes-its-data-driven-outdoor-ads-and-why-they-work-so-well/ (accessed January 2019).

2. "Our Epic Battle #likeagirl," Always, https://always.com/en-us/about-us/our-epic-battle-like-a-girl (accessed January 2019).

3. *Ibid.*

4. *Ibid.*

5. "Case Study: Always #Likeagirl," D & Ad, https://www.dandad.org/en/d-ad-always-like-a-girl-campaign-case-study-insights/ (accessed January 2019).

6. "Apple Watch—Introducing Series 2," YouTube, https://www.youtube.com/results?search_query=%E2%80%9CApple+Watch%E2%80%94Introducing+Apple+Watch+2%2C%E2%80%9D (accessed January 2019).

7. Alex Fitzpatrick, "Dr. Watch Will See You Now," *Time,* December 17, 2018, 76–80.

8. Adriane Pasquarelli, "True Blue" *Advertising Age,* November 5, 2018, 12–16.

9. Ben Tobin, "IHOP: Fake Name Change to IHOb to Boost Burger Business Was Risk Worth Taking," *USA Today,* July 19, 2018, https://www.usatoday.com/story/money/2018/07/19/ihop-chose-fish-where-fish-find-non-breakfast-footing/796897002/ (accessed January 2019).

10. Katie Richards, "Adidas Created Personalized Videos for 30,000 Boston Marathon Runners in 24 Hours" *Adweek,* April 19, 2018, https://www.adweek.com/brand-marketing/adidas-created-personalized-videos-for-30000-boston-marathon-runners-in-24-hours/ (accessed January 2019).

11. Adrianne Pasquarelli, "Macy's Parade Marches on" *Advertising Age,* November 19, 2018, 10

12. Keith Loria, "How Whole Foods Leverages Data Analysis," *Grocery Dive,* February 27, 2018, www.grocerydive.com/news/grocery-how-whole-foods-leverages-data-analysis/535407/ (accessed January 2019).

13. The AIDA concept is based on the classic research of E. K. Strong Jr. as theorized in *The Psychology of Selling and Advertising* (New York: McGraw-Hill, 1925); "Theories of Selling," *Journal of Applied Psychology* 9, no. 1 (1925): 75–86.

14. "iPad User in the United States 2013–2020," *Statista,* https://www.statista.com/statistics/208039/ipad-users-forecast-in-the-us/ (accessed January 2019).

15. Thomas E. Barry and Daniel J. Howard, "A Review and Critique of the Hierarchy of Effects in Advertising," *International Journal of Advertising* 9, no. 2 (1990): 121–135.

16. Diana Reese, "Why Is Michelle Obama Praising Walmart in Springfield, MO?" *Washington Post,* March 1, 2013, https://www.washingtonpost.com/blogs/she-the-people/wp/2013/03/01/why-is-michelle-obama-praising-walmart-in-springfield-mo/?noredirect=on&utm_term=.200f6e0ea4bb (accessed January 2019).

16

1. "Marketing Fact Pack—2019 Edition," *Advertising Age,* http://adage.com/d/resources/resources/whitepaper/marketing-fact-pack-2019 (accessed March 2019).

2. *Ibid.*

3. Jack Neff, "P&G Plays Matchmaker" *Advertising Age* December 3, 2018, p. 8.

4. Darryl K. Taft, "IBM's Not-So-Secret Weapon: Big Data," *eWeek,* February 26, 2013, https://www.eweek.com/database/ibm-s-not-so-secret-weapon-big-data-marketing (accessed January 2019).

5. "BrandFinance Global 500 (100)| 2019," https://www.rankingthebrands.com/The-Brand-Rankings.aspx?rankingID=30 (accessed January 2019).

6. Kurt Badenhausen, "The World's Most Valuable Brands," *Forbes,* http://www.forbes.com/powerful-brands/ (accessed January 2019).

7. "How Americans Use Leisure Time," Advertising Age 2018 Edition Marketing Fact Pack, 30, *Advertising Age,* http://gaia.adage.com/images/bin/pdf/20151211marketingfactpackweb.pdf (accessed March 2019).

8. "Time Spent Using Media," Advertising Age 2018 Edition Marketing Fact Pack, 21, *Advertising Age,* https://adage.com/trend-reports/report.php?id=130 (accessed March 2019).

9. Matthew Sparkes, "iPhone Owners Admit Having 'Blind Loyalty' to Apple," *Telegraph,* February 12, 2014, http://www.telegraph.co.uk/technology/apple/10632787/iPhone-owners-admit-having-blind-loyalty-to-Apple.html (accessed January 2019).

10. "Marketing Fact Pack–2018 Edition," *Advertising Age,* https://adage.com/trend-reports/report.php?id=130 (accessed March 2019).

11. Adrianne Pasquarelli and E.J. Schultz, "Marketer A List 2018: Nike Marketer of the Year," *Advertising Age,* December 3, 2018, pp. 16–17; Sapna Maheshwari, "Super Bowl Commercials Feature Political Undertones and Celebrity Cameos," *New York Times,* February 5, 2017, https://andrewgoodman.org/news-list/seven-super-bowl-commercials-aim-increase-awareness-not-sales-2017/?gclid=Cj0KCQiAvqDiBRDAARIsADWh5TdE1Q8Sn2gatuuspYjKxJz_62hoquc0b5T6xbcmwFDwS6lMIDNw6gwaAgKlEALw_wcB (accessed March 2019); "Airbnb—Home," Facebook, http://www.facebook.com/airbnb/ (accessed January 2019).

12. Patrick Kulp, "Amazon Gives You New, Everyday Ways to Use Its Echo Home Assistant," *Mashable,* October 3, 2016, http://mashable.com/2016/10/03/amazon-echo-ad-campaign/ (accessed January 2019); Anil Dash, "Amazon Echo and Alexa Really Matter," *Business Insider,* June 22, 2016, https://www.businessinsider.com/amazon-echo-and-alexa-really-matter-2016-6 (accessed January 2019).

13. Jenn Harris, "In New Ad, Taco Bell Wants You to Ditch Your Old McDonald's Breakfast," *Los Angeles Times,* April 8, 2014, http://www.latimes.com/food/dailydish/

la-dd-taco-bell-mcdonalds-breakfast-20140407-story.html (accessed January 2019).

14. "The Fastest-Growing Energy Bar, Bar None," *CBS Sunday Morning*, April 12, 2015, https://www.cbsnews.com/news/the-fastest-growing-energy-bar-bar-none/ (accessed January 2019).

15. Tim Nudd, "Snickers Swaps Out Its Brand Name for Hunger Symptoms on Painfully Honest Packaging," *Adweek*, September 21, 2015, https://www.adweek.com/creativity/snickers-swaps-out-its-brand-name-hunger-symptoms-painfully-honest-packaging-167061/ (accessed January 2019).

16. Lauren Cleave, "Using Humour to Cope, Is It Healthy?" https://talklaurentalk.wordpress.com/2018/08/16/using-humour-to-cope-is-it-healthy/ (accessed March 2019).

17. Jackson, Dominique "8 Social Media Marketing Examples from 2018," https://sproutsocial.com/insights/social-media-marketing-examples/ (accessed January 2019).

18. Marketing Fact Back—2018 Edition, *Advertising Age,* http://prcouncil.net/wp-content/uploads/2018/01/Marketing-Fact-Pack-2018.pdf (accessed March 2019).

19. *Ibid*

20. *Ibid*.

21. *Ibid*

22. Bradley Johnson, "Super Bowl, Supersized: $4.9 Billion in Ad Spending Over 51 Years," *Advertising Age*, January 10, 2017, https://adage.com/article/special-report-super-bowl/super-bowl-supersized-4-9-billion-ad-spending-51-years/307361/ (accessed January 2019).

23. "Cost for a 30-Second Television Spot," *Advertising Age* 2018 Edition Marketing Fact Pack, *Advertising Age*, http://prcouncil.net/wp-content/uploads/2018/01/Marketing-Fact-Pack-2018.pdf (accessed March 2019).

24. Jeanine Poggi, "The Future of TV? No More Commercials, Says Netflix Chief Product Officer," *Advertising Age*, http://adage.com/article/media/future-tv-commercials-netflix-exec/293275/ (accessed January 2019).

25. Jeanine Poggi, "Global Digital Ad Sales Will Top TV in 2017, Magna Forecast Predicts," *Advertising Age*, December 5, 2016, https://adage.com/article/agency-news/magna-digital-ad-sales-top-tv-2017/306997/ (accessed May 2, 2017).

26. David Kaplan, "For Turner Digital, Audience Buying Risk Outweighs Reward," AdExchanger, October 9, 2012, https://adexchanger.com/online-advertising/for-turner-digital-audience-buying-risk-outweighs-reward/ (accessed January 2019).

27. Marketing Fact Book 2018, *Advertising Age,* http://prcouncil.net/wp-content/uploads/2018/01/Marketing-Fact-Pack-2018.pdf (accessed March 2019).

28. "Mobile Fact Sheet," Pew Research Center, http://www.pewinternet.org/fact-sheet/mobile (accessed January 2019).

29. *Ibid*.

30. "Most Popular Facebook Games in February 2016," Statista, http://www.statista.com/statistics/267003/most-popular-social-games-on-facebook-based-on-daily-active-users/ (accessed January 2019).

31. "Facebook vs. Non-Facebook Social Network Gaming Ecosystem and Market Analysis 2013–2018," *MarketWatch*, February 4, 2014, http://www.marketwatch.com/story/facebook-vs-non-facebook-social-network-gaming-ecosystem-and-market-analysis-2013-2018-2014-02-04 (accessed January 2019).

32. Jeff Neff, "What's the Frequency, Pritchard?" *Advertising Age*, November 5, 2018, 7.

33. John Moulding, "ABC Proves the Value of the Unified TV/Digital Ad Buy," Videonet, October 23, 2013, http://www.v-net.tv/abc-proves-the-value-of-the-unified-tvdigital-ad-buy/ (accessed January 2019).

34. Mary Hanbury, "Kanye West's Secret to Building a Footwear Empire to Compete with Nike" *Business Insider*, April 26, 2018, https://www.businessinsider.com/how-kanye-west-made-yeezy-brand-a-success-2018-4 (accessed January 2019).

35. "PQ Media: Double-Digit Surge in Product Placement Spend in 2014 Fuels Higher Global Branded Entertainment Growth as Media Integrations & Consumer Events Combo for $73.3B," *Cision PR Web*, March 13, 2015 (accessed February 23, 2019); Jon Lafayette, "Product Placement Revenue Climbing 13.2% This Year," Broadcasting & Cable, June 15, 2015, https://www.broadcastingcable.com/news/product-placement-revenue-climbing-132-year-141746 (accessed January 2019).

36. "US Ad Spending Forecast from Zenith Optimedia," Advertising Age 2017 Edition Marketing Fact Pack, 14, *Advertising Age*, https://www.zenithmedia.com/wp-content/uploads/2017/03/Adspend-forecasts-June-2017-executive-summary.pdf (accessed March 2019).

37. *Ibid*.

38. Jennifer Wang, "10 Marketing Masterworks," *Entrepreneur*, February 18, 2013, http://www.entrepreneur.com/article/225462 (accessed January 2019).

39. Kristina Monllos, "5 Experiential Marketing Activations from SXSW That You Need to See," *Adweek*, March 16, 2016, https://www.adweek.com/brand-marketing/5-experiential-marketing-activations-sxsw-you-need-see-170242/ (accessed January 2019).

40. Philip Caulfield, "Web Pranksters Hijack Restaurant's Mountain Dew Naming Contest," *New York Daily News*, August 15, 2012, https://www.nydailynews.com/news/national/web-pranksters-hijack-mountain-dew-online-crowdsourced-naming-effort-new-green-apple-flavored-soda-article-1.1136204 (accessed January 2019).

41. Caitlin McGarry, "Pay by Hashtag: Twitter Wants to Get Inside Your Wallet," *TechHive*, January 24, 2014, http://www.techhive.com/article/2090822/pay-by-hashtag-twitter-wants-to-get-inside-your-wallet.html (accessed January 2019); Andrew R. Johnson, "@AmericanExpress Tries #Deals via Twitter," *Wall Street Journal*, March 7, 2012, http://www.wsj.com/articles/SB10001424052970204781804577267402969728444 (accessed January 2019).

42. Donna L. Montaldo, "How to Avoid the Rebate Rip-off," howtodothings.com, http://www.howtodothings.com/finance-real-estate/how-to-avoid-the-rebate-rip-off (accessed January 2019).

43. "Much Love for Loyalty Programs," Reuters, https://www.reuters.com/brandfeatures/synchrony/inside-retail/much-love-for-loyalty-programs (accessed January 2019).

44. Elizabeth Holmes, "At Bloomies, Loyalty for All," *Wall Street Journal*, February 24, 2012, B5.

45. Kelly Short, "Study Shows In-Store Sampling Events Outperform Other Top In-Store Marketing Tactics," *Interactions*, February 28, 2013, http://www.interactionsmarketing.com/news/?p=352 (accessed January 2019).

46. Jim Tierney, "Study Shows Most Customers Make Purchase Decisions in the Store,"

Loyalty360, November 11, 2013, https://loyalty360.org/content-gallery/daily-news/study-shows-most-customers-make-purchase-decisions-in-the-store (accessed January 2019).

47. Don Davis, "Consumers Redeem 141% More Digital Coupons in 2013," *Internet Retailer*, January 16, 2014, https://www.digitalcommerce360.com/2014/01/16/consumers-redeem-141-more-digital-coupons-2013/ (accessed January 2019).

48. Rachel King, "Google Trying Out Real-Time, Targeted Digital Coupons with Zavers," *ZDNet*, January 11, 2013, http://www.zdnet.com/google-trying-out-real-time-targeted-digital-coupons-with-zavers-7000009722/ (accessed January 2019).

49. "Zero Moment of Truth (ZMOT)," Google, http://www.thinkwithgoogle.com/collections/zero-moment-truth.html (accessed January 2019).

17

1. "Nordstrom Careers," Nordstrom, https://careers.nordstrom.com/#/student-center/retail (accessed March 2019).

2. Michael Rodriquez, Haya Ajjan, and Robert M. Peterson, "Social Media in Large Sales Forces: An Empirical Study of the Impact of Sales Process Capability and Relationship Performance," *Journal of Marketing Theory and Practice*, 24, no. 3 (2016), 365–379.

3. "Personal Shoppers," Bloomingdales, http://fashion.bloomingdales.com/about-us/shopping/personal-shopper-complimentary-service/ (accessed December 22, 2018).

4. Adam Rapp, Thomas L. Baker, Daniel G. Bachrach, Jessica Ogilvie, and Lauren Skinner Beitelspacher (2015), "Perceived Customer Showrooming Behavior and the Effect on Retail Salesperson Self-Efficacy and Performance," *Journal of Retailing*, 91, 358–369.

5. Rodrigo Guesalaga, "The Use of Social Media in Sales: Individual and Organizational Antecedents, and the Role of Customer Engagement in Social Media," *Industrial Marketing Management*, 54 (2015), 71–79.

6. "About LinkedIn?," LinkedIn, https://about.linkedin.com/ (accessed December 22, 2018).

7. "Sales Navigator Product Datasheet," LinkedIn, https://business.linkedin.com/sales-solutions/site-forms/sales-navigator-datasheet (accessed December 22, 2018).

8. "What Is Social Selling," LinkedIn, https://business.linkedin.com/sales-solutions/social-selling/what-is-social-selling (accessed December 22, 2018).

9. "Getting Started with Social Selling on LinkedIn," LinkedIn, https://business.linkedin.com/sales-solutions/social-selling/getting-started-with-social-selling-on-linkedIn-ebook (accessed December 22, 2018).

10. "Welcome to Houzz," Houzz, https://www.houzz.com/aboutUs (accessed December 22, 2018).

11. Kim Garst, "Find Prospects on Social Media and Turn Them into Customers," *Huffington Post*, February 18, 2014, http://www.huffingtonpost.com/kim-garst/find-prospects-on-social-_b_4785711.html (accessed December 22, 2018).

12. Jeff S. Johnson, Scott B. Friend, Brian N. Rutherford, and G. Alexander Hamwi, "Absolute versus Relative Sales Failure," *Journal of Business Research*, 69 (2015), 596–603.

13. Linda Ray, "Examples of Cultural Differences in Business," *Demand Media*, http://smallbusiness.

chron.com/examples-cultural-differences-business-21958.html (accessed December 22, 2018).

14. "Use FaceTime with your iPhone, iPad, or iPod touch," Apple, https://support.apple.com/en-us/HT204380 (accessed March 8, 2017).

15. "Leadership Program," General Electric, https://www.ge.com/careers/culture/university-students/commercial-leadership-program/global (accessed December 22, 2018).

16. Laurence Minsky and Keith A. Quesenberry (2016), "How B2B Sales Can Benefit from Social Selling," *Harvard Business Review*, https://hbr.org/2016/11/84-of-b2b-sales-start-with-a-referral-not-a-salesperson (accessed March 2019).

17. James "Mick" Andzulis, Nikolaos G. Panagopoulos, and Adam Rapp, "A Review of Social Media and Implications for the Sales Process," *Journal of Personal Selling and Sales Management*, 32, no. 3 (2012), 305–316.

18. Jesse N. Moore, Mary Anne Raymond, and Christopher D. Hopkins, "Social Selling: A Comparison of Social Media Usage Across Process State, Markets, and Sales Job Functions," *Journal of Marketing Theory and Practice*, 23, no. 1 (2015), 1–20.

19. Castleberry, Steven, and Jeff Tanner, *Selling*, 10th ed. New York: McGraw-Hill, 2016.

20. Zahed Subhan, Roger Brooksbank, Scott Rader, Duncan Steel, and Kimberley Mackey, "Running an Effective Induction Program for New Sales Recruits: Lessons from the Financial Services Industry," *Journal of Selling*, 14, no. 1 (2014), 20–32.

21. William C. Moncrief, "Are Sales as We Know It Dying . . . or Merely Transforming?" *Journal of Personal Selling and Sales Management*, 37, no. 4 (2017), 271–279.

22. Michael Rodriquez and Stefanie L. Boyer, "An Exploratory Study of Sales Managers' and Sales Professionals' Perceptions of eLearning and Job Performance," *Journal of Selling*, 16, no. 1 (2016), 5–17.

23. Peter Criscione, "Mary Kay's Top Salespeople are Pretty in Pink," *Brampton Guardian*, February 25, 2014, http://www.bramptonguardian.com/news-story/4384280-mary-kay-s-top-salespeople-are-pretty-in-pink/ (accessed December 22, 2018).

24. Paul Greenberg, "CRM Watchlist 2019: And the Winners Are….," *ZDNet*, https://www.zdnet.com/article/crm-watchlist-2019-and-the-winners-are/(accessed March 2019).

25. Saul Perez, "Why Cross-Selling Is Part of Wells Fargo's Strategy," *Market Realist*, October 10, 2014, http://finance.yahoo.com/news/why-cross-selling-part-wells-130018022.html (accessed March 2019).

26. "About Recommendations," Amazon, https://www.bing.com/search?q=%E2%80%9CAbout+Recommendations%2C%E2%80%9D+Amazon%2C+&form=PRLNC1&pc=LCTE&mkt=en-us&httpsmsn=1&refig=86d690fd738e493c89b32209990149b1&sp=-1&pq=%E2%80%9Cabout+recommendations%2C%E2%80%9D+amazon%2C+&sc=0-33&qs=n&sk=&cvid=86d690fd738e493c89b32209990149b1 (accessed March 2019).

18

1. Larry Bodine, "Building a Law Practice with Social Media," American Bar Association, November 8, 2018, https://abaforlawstudents.com/2018/11/08/building-a-law-practice-with-social-media/ (accessed January 2019).

2. "Number of Social Media Users Worldwide from 2010 to 2021 (in Billions)" https://www.statista.com/statistics/278414/number-of-worldwide-social-network-users/ (accessed January 2019); "Top 15 Most Popular Social Networking Sites and Apps" https://www.dreamgrow.com/top-15-most-popular-social-networking-sites/ (accessed January 2019).

3. "Twitter: Most Followers," *FriendOrFollow*, http://friendorfollow.com/twitter/most-followers/ (accessed January 2019).

4. "Facebook Statistics—Brands," *Socialbakers*, http://www.socialbakers.com/statistics/facebook/pages/total/brands/ (accessed January 2019).

5. "7 Ways a Social Media Command Center will Empower Your Brand," https://www.talkwalker.com/blog/social-media-command-center-for-your-brand (accessed January 2019).

6. Aimee Rawlins, "Uber Pushes Back on Trump's Order after #DeleteUber Starts Trending," CNN, January 29, 2017, http://money.cnn.com/2017/01/29/technology/uber-lyft-trump-muslim-ban/ (accessed January 2019).

7. Charlotte Rogers, "Adidas on the Power of Using Microinfluencers in Long-Form Video," *Marketing Week*, March 22, 2018, https://www.marketingweek.com/2018/03/22/adidas-micro-influencer-long-form-video/ (accessed January 2019).

8. Aaron Agius, "5 Brands Using Facebook Messenger Bots to Level Up Their Social Media Strategies," *Social Media Today*, February 7, 2017, http://www.socialmediatoday.com/marketing/5-brands-using-facebook-messenger-bots-level-their-social-media-strategies (accessed January 2019); Jayson DeMers, "5 Awesome Examples of Brands Using Live Video for Marketing," *Forbes*, November 23, 2016, http://www.forbes.com/sites/jaysondemers/2016/11/23/5-awesome-examples-of-brands-using-live-video-for-marketing (accessed January 2019).

9. "5 Terrific Examples of Company Social Media Policies," *Hire Rabbit*, http://blog.hirerabbit.com/5-terrific-examples-of-company-social-media-policies/ (accessed January 2019).

10. Tessa Stuart, "Secrets of a Celebrity Twitter Coach," *BuzzFeed*, February 19, 2013, http://www.buzzfeed.com/tessastuart/secrets-of-a-celebrity-twitter-coach#.wiM2vVjgE (accessed January 2019).

11. Ryan Holmes, "How to Turn Your Entire Staff into a Social Media Army," *Fast Company*, November 6, 2015, http://www.fastcompany.com/3053233/how-to-turn-your-entire-staff-into-a-social-media-army (accessed January 2019); Liz Azyan, "How to Turn Employees into Social Media Advocates: Case Examples," *Social Media Examiner*, April 28, 2015, http://www.socialmediaexaminer.com/turn-employees-into-social-media-advocates/ (accessed January 2019).

12. Dave Chaffey, "Global Social Media Research Summary 2016," *Smart Insights*, https://www.smartinsights.com/social-media-marketing/ (accessed January 2019).

13. *Ibid.*

14. *Ibid*

15. Paul Hitlin, "Internet, Social Media Use and Device Ownership in U.S. Have Plateaued after Years of Growth," Pew Research Center, http://www.pewresearch.org/fact-tank/2018/09/28/internet-social-media-use-and-device-ownership-in-u-s-have-plateaued-after-years-of-growth/ (accessed January 2019).

16. Steven Musil, "U.S. Tablet Usage Hits 'Critical Mass' ComScore Reports," CNet, June 10, 2012, https://www.cnet.com/news/u-s-tablet-usage-hits-critical-mass-comscore-reports (accessed January 2019).

17. Sid Gandotra, "Why Social Commerce Matters," *Social Media Today*, November 6, 2012, https://www.socialmediatoday.com/content/why-social-commerce-matters (accessed January 2019).

18. Michael Lazar, "E-commerce Statistics & Technology Trendsetters for 2017," IBM, March 3, 2017, https://www.ibm.com/developerworks/community/blogs/d27b1c65-986e-4a4f-a491-5e8eb23980be/entry/Ecommerce_Statistics_Technology_Trendsetters_for_2017?lang=en (accessed January 2019).

19. Lauren Indvik, "The 7 Species of Social Commerce," *Mashable*, May 10, 2013, https://mashable.com/2013/05/10/social-commerce-definition/#.rE01zeVDEqB (accessed January 2019).

20. "Giveaway!!! Pin It to Win It! An iPad Mini for Two Lucky Winners!!!" Favorite Family Recipes, March 10, 2013, https://www.pinterest.com/pin/119626933824603590/ (accessed January 2019).

21. Christopher Heine, "12 Really Intriguing Digital Marketing Stats from This Week," *Adweek*, January 26, 2017, https://www.adweek.com/digital/12-interesting-and-fun-digital-marketing-stats-last-week-164801/ (accessed January 2019); "US Digital Ad Spending to Surpass TV This Year," *eMarketer*, September 13, 2016, https://www.emarketer.com/Article/US-Digital-Ad-Spending-Surpass-TV-this-Year/1014469 (accessed January 2019).

22. Eric Mosley, "Crowdsource your Performance Reviews," *Harvard Business Review*, June 15, 2013, http://blogs.hbr.org/cs/2012/06/crowdsource_your_performance_r.html (accessed January 2019).

23. "Photograph for Ellie Goulding with HP Connected Music," *Talenthouse*, http://www.talenthouse.com/photograph-for-ellie-goulding-and-hp-connected-music#description (accessed January 2019).

24. "Paid Media Marketing," *Greenlight*, https://www.semrush.com/lp/ppc-2/en/?httpss%3A%2F%2Fwww.semrush.com%2Flp%2Fppc-2%2Fen%2F%3Fkw=paid_media_marketing&cmp=US_SRCH_New_PPC_Tool_BING&label=PPC_Tool&Network=o&Device=c&msclkid=25349f737a1211ab95c2c3de71eb6571&utm_source=bing&utm_medium=cpc&utm_campaign=US_SRCH_PPC_Tool_BING&utm_term=%2Bpaid%20%2Bmedia%20%2Bmarketing&utm_content=paid%20media%20marketing (accessed January 2019).

25. *Ibid.*

26. Kevin Cokely, "Inside Southwest Airlines' Social Media 'Listening Center,'" NBC, http://www.nbcdfw.com/news/local/Inside-Southwest-Airlines-Social-Medias-Listening-Center-379991601.html (accessed January 2019).

27. Russell Working, "Most Unhappy with Social Media Measurement, Survey Says," Ragan Communications, http://www.ragan.com/Main/Articles/Most_unhappy_with_social_media_measurement_survey_45919.aspx (accessed January 2019).

28. Graham Gullans, "Five Steps to Measuring Your Social Media ROI," *Advertising Age*, April 27, 2016, http://adage.com/article/digitalnext/steps-measuring-social-media-roi/303730/ (accessed January 2019); Andy Williams, "How Social Media Has Changed the Way we Complain," *Koozai*, February 25, 2013, http://www.koozai.com/blog/branding/reputation-management/how-social-media-has-changed-the-way-we-complain (accessed

January 2019); Dan Jeffers, "How Social Media Has Changed Politics: It's Not Just Tactics," *The Social Media Monthly,* January 18, 2013, http://thesocialmediamonthly.com/how-social-media-has-changed-politics-its-not-just-tactics (accessed January 2019); "How Social Media Has Changed the Way We Communicate," *Information Gateway,* January 24, 2013, http://dastornews.com/2018/02/how-social-media-has-changed-the-way-we-communicate/ (accessed January 2019).

29. Social Technographics Ladder, https://keepingitsocialsite.wordpress.com/2016/02/02/social-technographics-ladder/ (accessed January 2019); Gina Sverdlov, "Global Social Technographics Update: US and EU Mature, Emerging Markets Show Lots of Activity," *Forrester,* January 4, 2012, https://go.forrester.com/blogs/12-01-04-global_social_technographics_update_2011_us_and_eu_mature_emerging_markets_show_lots_of_activity/ (accessed April 2019).

30. Charlene Li and Josh Bernoff, *Groundswell: Winning in a World Transformed by Social Technologies,* revised ed. (Boston, MA: Harvard Business Press, 2011); What Are Types of Social Media Influencers? https://www.bing.com/news/search?q=30.+What+Are+Types+Of+Social+Media+Influencers%3f&qpvt=30.%09What+Are+Types+of+Social+Media+Influencers%3f+&FORM=EWRE (accessed April 2019).

31. Social Media Use Continues to Rise in Developing Countries but Plateaus Across Developed Ones, https://www.pewglobal.org/2018/06/19/social-media-use-continues-to-rise-in-developing-countries-but-plateaus-across-developed-ones/ (accessed April 2019).

32. Shanna Mallon, "Should Every Company Have a Blog?" *The Media Revolution,* January 30, 2014, http://www.blogworld.com/2014/01/30/should-every-company-have-a-blog/ (accessed January 2019).

33. Mark Schaefer, "The 10 Best Big Company Blogs in the World," *Businesses Grow,* January 12, 2015, http://www.businessesgrow.com/2015/01/12/best-company-blogs/ (accessed January 2019).

34. Lucia Moses, "BuzzFeed Didn't Give Up on Tumblr, and It's Reaping the Benefits," *Digiday,* June 20, 2016, http://digiday.com/media/buzzfeed-didnt-give-tumblr-reaping-benefits/ (accessed January 2019).

35. Lindsay Kolowich, "Top 10 Facebook Pages and Instagram Accounts In 2018," https://www.forbes.com/sites/ninaangelovska/2019/01/07/top-10-facebook-fan-pages-and-instagram-accounts-in-2018-cristiano-ronaldo-takes-the-lead/#4ba331ea58bb; 20 Facebook Pages That Will Make You Even Smarter, https://www.themuse.com/advice/20-facebook-pages-that-will-make-you-even-smarter (accessed January 2019).

36. Josh Bersin, "Facebook Vs. LinkedIn—What's the Difference?" *Forbes,* May 21, 2012, http://www.forbes.com/sites/joshbersin/2012/05/21/facebook-vs-linkedin-whats-the-difference (accessed January 2019).

37. "Top Sites," Alexa, http://www.alexa.com/topsites (accessed January 2019).

38. "How Relevant Is Social Bookmarking for SEO Today?", https://moz.com/community/q/how-relevant-is-social-bookmarking-for-seo-today (accessed April 2019).

39. Brandy Shaul, "Bivid Location-Based Social Networking App Launches on iOS," *Adweek,* January 25, 2016, http://www.adweek.com/digital/bivid-location-based-social-networking-app-launches-on-ios/ (accessed January 2019).

40. *Ibid*

41. "Yelp Elite Event: Tiki Beach Party at Le Lab," Yelp, http://www.yelp.com/biz/yelp-elite-event-tiki-beach-party-at-le-lab-montreal (accessed January 2019).

42. "2016 Global Games Market Report," *New Zoo,* June 2016, http://resources.newzoo.com/hubfs/Reports/Newzoo_Free_2016_Global_Games_Market_Report.pdf (accessed January 2019).

43. Emanuel Maiberg, "Top 25 Facebook Games of May 2013," *Inside Social Games,* May 1, 2013, http://www.bbgsite.com/socialgames/content/2013-05-05/the-top-25-facebook-games-of-may-2013.shtml (accessed April 2019).

44. Jillian D'Onfro, "Facebook Just Made a Surprising Move That Could Save Its One Shrinking Business," *Business Insider,* August 20, 2016, http://www.businessinsider.com/facebook-pc-gaming-could-reverse-payments-revenue-decline-2016-8 (accessed January 2019); Justin Choi, "What Publishers Can Learn from the Rise and Fall of Social Gaming on Facebook," *Advertising Age,* June 30, 2016, http://adage.com/article/digitalnext/publishers-learn-social-gaming-facebook/304758/ (accessed January 2019); Ben Gilbert, "Facebook Is Taking on an Entirely New Frontier: Video Games," *Business Insider,* August 18, 2016, http://www.businessinsider.com/facebook-is-creating-a-competitor-to-steam-2016-8 (accessed January 2019).

45. "Most Popular Facebook Games as of February 2016, Based on Number of Daily Active Users (in Millions)," Statista, http://www.statista.com/statistics/267003/most-popular-social-games-on-facebook-based-on-daily-active-users/ (accessed January 2019).

46. John Gaudiosi, "This Company Is Hosting the First Ever eSports Event at Madison Square Garden," *Fortune,* June 9, 2015, http://fortune.com/2015/06/09/riot-games-esports/ (accessed January 2019).

47. "Global Mobile Statistics 2014 Part A: Mobile Subscribers; Handset Market Share; Mobile Operators," *mobiThinking,* March 2013, https://mobiforge.com/research-analysis/global-mobile-statistics-2014-part-a-mobile-subscribers-handset-market-share-mobile-operators (accessed April 2019); John Koetsier "Mobile Advertising Will Drive 75% of Digital Advertising Spend in 2018," February 22, 2018, https://www.forbes.com/sites/johnkoetsier/2018/02/23/mobile-advertising-will-drive-75-of-all-digital-ad-spend-in-2018-heres-whats-changing/#5603b9b2758b (accessed January 2019); Ingrid Lunden, "Digital Ads Will Be 22% of All U.S. Ad Spend in 2013, Mobile Ads 3.7%; Total Global Ad Spend in 2013 $503B," https://finance.yahoo.com/news/digital-ads-22-u-ad-094110553.html (accessed January 2019).

48. Olga Kharif, "Coming Soon to Your Smartwatch: Ads Targeting Captive Eyeballs," *Bloomberg,* May 12, 2015, http://www.bloomberg.com/news/articles/2015-05-12/coming-soon-to-your-smartwatch-ads-targeting-captive-eyeballs (accessed January 2019).

49. Ben Dickson, "Unlocking the Potential of Eye Tracking Technology," *TechCrunch,* February 19, 2017, https://techcrunch.com/2017/02/19/unlocking-the-potential-of-eye-tracking-technology/ (accessed January 2019); Daniel Howley, "The Best iPhone Widgets You're Not Using," Yahoo, January 24, 2015, https://www.yahoo.com/tech/the-best-iphone-widgets-youre-not-using-108954809304.html (accessed January 2019).

19

1. Huachao Gao, Yinlong Zhang, and Vikas Mittal, "How Does Local-Global Identify Affect Price Sensitivity," *Journal of Marketing,* May 2017, 62–70.

2. *Ibid.*

3. Vikas Mittal, "Customer-Based Strategy for Raising Prices," *Marketing News,* November/December 2016, 20–22.

4. *Ibid.*

5. "The World's Best Awards–Transportation," *Travel and Leisure,* August 2018, 42.

6. "How Much for That Tequila? It All Depends on Demand," *The Island Packet-The Beaufort Gazette,* May 12, 2016, 8B.

7. "How Much Did You Pay for That Lipstick?" *Forbes,* April 14, 2015, 46–49.

8. "To Set Prices, Stores Turn to Algorithms," *Wall Street Journal,* May 9, 2017, A1, A10.

9. "Guaranteed Profits," *Economist,* February 14, 2016, 68.

10. "The Effect of Customer Loyalty on Retail Pricing," *Marketing News,* January 2016, 3.

11. Keith Coulter and Anne Roggeveen, "Price Number Relationships and Deal Processing Fluency: The Effects of Approximation Sequence and Number Multiples," *Journal of Marketing Research,* February 2014, 69–82.

12. Federico Rossi and Pradeep K. Chintagunta, "Price Transparency and Retail Price: Evidence from Fuel Price Signs in the Italian Highway System," *Journal of Marketing Research,* June 2016, 407–423.

13. Meghan Busse, Ayelet Israeli, and Florian Zettelmeyer, "Repairing the Damage: The Effect of Price Knowledge and Gender on Auto Repair Price Quotes," *Journal of Marketing Research,* February 2017, 75–95.

14. Aylin Aydinli, Marco Bertini, and Anja Lambrecht, "Price Promotion for Emotional Impact," *Journal of Marketing,* 78, no. 4 (July 2014): 80–96.

15. "Future of Private Labels Looks Bright," *McLoone,* January 31, 2014.

16. "Spirit Airlines: The Power of a Clear Strategy," Strongbrands, February 23, 2015, http://timcalkins.com/branding-insights/spirit-airlines-power-clear-strategy/ (accessed February 28, 2015).

17. Amy X. Wang, "Jay-Z Has Figured Out How to Make Concerts Cheap—By Selling Crazy Expensive Tickets," November 6, 2017, https://qz.com/1121269/jay-z-concert-ticket-prices-are-a-brilliant-strategy (accessed September 7, 2018).

18. "These Prices Are a Steal—And In Some States, That's Illegal," *Wall Street Journal,* January 27–28, 2018, A11.

19. M.J. del Rio Olivares, Kristina Wittkowski, Jaakko Aspara Tomas Falk, and Pekka Mattila, "Relational Price Discounts: Consumers' Metacognitions and Nonlinear Effects of Initial Discounts on Customer Retention," *Journal of Marketing,* January 2018, 115–131.

20. "Retailers Simplify Prices by Doing Markdown Math," *Wall Street Journal,* December 12, 2017, B2.

21. Ibid.

22. Abhijit Guha, Abhijit Biswas, Dhruv Grewal, Swati Verma, Somak Banerjee, and Jens Nordfalt, "Reframing the Discount as a Comparison Against the Sales Price: Does It Make the Discount More Attractive?" *Journal of Marketing Research,* June 2018, 339–351.

23. Andong Cheng and Cynthia Cryder, "Double Mental Discounting: When a Single Price Promotion Feels Twice As Nice," *Journal of Marketing Research*, April 2018, 226–238.

24. "Coupon Statistics: The Ultimate Collection," https://blog.accessdevelopment.com/ultimate-collection-coupon-statistics (accessed September 24, 2018).

25. Cynthia Koons and Robert Langreth, "That Drug Coupon Isn't Really Clipping Costs," *Businessweek*, December 28, 2015, 21–22.

26. *Ibid.*

27. *Ibid.*

28. "35 Amazing Online Shopping and Ecommerce Statistics," https://founderu.selzcom/40-online-shopping-ecommerce-statistics-know/ (accessed September 14, 2018).

29. Laura Stevens, "Free Shipping Crowds Out Small Retailers," *Wall Street Journal*, April 27, 2016, http://www.wsj.com/articles/for-online-shoppers-free-shipping-reigns-supreme-1461789381 (accessed January 21, 2017).

30. *https://goldtoe.com/shop/mens/socks/dress (accessed September 18, 2018).*

31. Franklin Shaddy and Ayelet Fishbach, "Seller Beware: How Bundling Affects Valuation," *Journal of Marketing Research*, October 2017, 737–751.

Appendix

1. Matthew Cochrane, "How Home Depot Is Using Big Data to Gain a Big Advantage," https://www.fool.com/investing/2018/01/15/how-home-depot-is-using-big-data-to-gain-a-big-adv.aspx (accessed January 2, 2019); Jamie Grill-Goodman, "Home Depot's Massive Investment Makes Use of 1.7 Trillion Data Points," https://risnews.com/home-depots-massive-investment-makes-use-17-trillion-data-points (accessed January 2019); Greg Petro, "Opportunity Meets Preparation: How Home Depot Became 'Amazon-Proof,'" https://www.forbes.com/sites/gregpetro/2016/10/13/opportunity-meets-preparation-how-the-home-depot-became-amazon-proof-using-data-and-analytics/#60daada41fef (accessed January 3, 2019); Renee Changnon, "How Home Depot Analyzes and Uses Customer Data," http://www.hardwareretailing.com/how-home-depot-analyzes-uses-customer-data/ (accessed January 2019); James Melton, "Home Depot Plans to Spend $5.4 Billion to Sharpen Its Omnichannel Strategy," https://www.digitalcommerce360.com/2017/12/08/home-depot-spend-5-4-billion-sharpen-omnichannel-strategy/ (accessed February 2019); Stephanie Pandolph, "Home Depot Ups Omnichannel Strategy," https://www.businessinsider.com/home-depot-ups-omnichannel-strategy-2017-12 (accessed February 2019).

2. Bernard Marr, "Stitch Fix: The Amazing Use Case Of Using Artificial Intelligence In Fashion Retail," https://www.forbes.com/sites/bernardmarr/2018/05/25/stitch-fix-the-amazing-use-case-of-using-artificial-intelligence-in-fashion-retail/#472e17e13292 (accessed January 2019); Natalie Gagliordi, "How Stitch Fix Uses Machine Learning to Master the Science of Styling," https://www.zdnet.com/article/how-stitch-fix-uses-machine-learning-to-master-the-science-of-styling/ (accessed January 3, 2019); Katrina Lake, "Stitch Fix's CEO on Selling Personal Style to the Mass Market," https://hbr.org/2018/05/stitch-fixs-ceo-on-selling-personal-style-to-the-mass-market (accessed January 2019).

3. Jefferson Graham, "Walmart Wants to Monitor Shoppers' Facial Expressions," https://www.usatoday.com/story/money/2017/08/08/walmart-wants-monitor-shoppers-facial-expressions/550671001/ (accessed January 2019); Leticia Miranda, "Thousands Of Stores Will Soon Use Facial Recognition, and They Won't Need Your Consent," https://www.buzzfeednews.com/article/leticiamiranda/retail-companies-are-testing-out-facial-recognition-at (accessed January 2019); George Anderson, "Walmart's Facial Recognition Tech Would Overstep Boundaries," https://www.forbes.com/sites/retailwire/2017/07/27/walmarts-facial-recognition-tech-would-overstep-boundaries/#56a7b1d145f8 (accessed January 2019).

4. Christopher Heine, "P&G Slashes Wasteful Display Ad Budgets Using Eye-Tracking," https://www.adweek.com/digital/pg-says-eye-tracking-saving-it-big-cash-display-ads-149883/ (accessed January 2019).

5. Sharon Terlep, "Focus Groups Fall Out of Favor," https://www.wsj.com/articles/focus-groups-fall-out-of-favor-1474250702?ns=prod/accounts-wsj (accessed January 2019); Russ Carpenter, "Focus Groups: Marketing's Oldest Technique Adapts to the Digital Age," https://www.digitalcurrent.com/digital-marketing/focus-groups-in-digital-age/ (accessed January 2019).

6. Jordan Valinsky, "Hospitals Are Using Credit Card Data to Predict People's Health," https://gizmodo.com/hospitals-are-using-credit-card-data-to-predict-peoples-1600594944 (accessed January 2019); Shannon Pettypiece and Jordan Robertson, "Hospitals Are Mining Patients' Credit Card Data to Predict Who Will Get Sick," https://www.bloomberg.com/news/articles/2014-07-03/hospitals-are-mining-patients-credit-card-data-to-predict-who-will-get-sick (accessed January 2019); Mohana Ravindranath, "Does Your Doctor Need to Know What You Buy on Amazon?" https://www.politico.com/story/2018/10/30/the-doctor-will-see-through-you-now-893437 (accessed January 2019); Katie Jennings, "How Your Doctor and Insurer Will Know Your Secrets—Even If You Never Tell Them," https://www.businessinsider.com/hospitals-and-health-insurers-using-data-brokers-2014-7 (accessed January 2019).

7. Zach Brooke, "Marketers Are Using the Weather to Predict Buyer Behavior," https://www.ama.org/publications/MarketingNews/Pages/how-marketers-are-using-the-weather-to-predict-buyer-behavior.aspx (accessed January 2019); James Kobielus, "Weather Data Analytics: Helping Retailers Predict and Meet Customer Demand," https://www.ibmbigdatahub.com/blog/weather-data-analytics-helping-retailers-predict-and-meet-customer-demand (accessed January 2019); Jeffrey F. Rayport. "Use Big Data to Predict Your Customers' Behaviors," https://hbr.org/2012/09/use-big-data-to-predict-your-c (accessed January 2019); Cindy Elliott, "Combining AI and Location Intelligence to Predict Market Demand," https://www.forbes.com/sites/esri/2018/05/30/combining-ai-and-location-intelligence-to-predict-market-demand/#1d93971838bf (accessed January 2019).

8. Bernard Marr, "Really Big Data at Walmart: Real-Time Insights From Their 40+ Petabyte Data Cloud," https://www.forbes.com/sites/bernardmarr/2017/01/23/really-big-data-at-walmart-real-time-insights-from-their-40-petabyte-data-cloud/#67d633836c10 (accessed January 2019); Joe McKendrick, "Walmart's Gigantic Private Cloud for Real-Time Inventory Control," https://www.rtinsights.com/walmart-cloud-inventory-management-real-time-data/ (accessed January 2019); "How Big Data Analysis Helped Increase Walmarts Sales Turnover?" https://www.dezyre.com/article/how-big-data-analysis-helped-increase-walmarts-sales-turnover/109 (accessed January 2019).

INDEX

Ethnic markets, 57–60
  African Americans, 59
  Hispanic Americans, 58–59
Ethnic segmentation, 145
Ethnographic research, 166–167
ETL, 372
E*TRADE, 67, 236
Etsy, 43, 152, 332, 340
European Commission, 83, 84, 86
European Union (EU), 83–84
  Brexit, 83–84
  governance, 84
  United States and, 83
Evaluation, of marketing plan, 30
Evaluators, 136
Evoked set, 101
Exchange, conditions for, 3–4
Exchange control, 78–79
Exchange rate, 93
  effect of on pricing strategies, 93–94
Exchange utility, 238
Exclusive distribution, 247
Executional styles of advertising, 294
Executive interviews, 164
E4X Inc., 95
Expedia, 99
Experience curves, 25
Experience quality, 211
Experiential learning, 122
Experiential marketing, 303–304
Experiments, 167–168
Export agents, 88
Export broker, 88
Export-Import Bank, 72–73
Exporting, 87
Exports
  of good and services, 72–73
  risk level for entering global
    marketplace, 87
  small and medium-sized businesses,
    72, 87–88
Express Scripts, 110
Express warranty, 193
Extensive decision making, 106
External information search, 99
External marketing environment
  competitive factors, 68–69
  demographic factors, 53–57
  economic factors, 60–62
  global marketers, 75–86
  growing ethnic markets, 57–60
  political and legal factors, 63–68
  social factors, 51–53
  technological factors, 62–63
  understanding, 49–51
External stimuli, 98
Extranets, impact on pricing, 356
Eye-tracking technology, 343, 372

F

Facebook, 274, 329, 338
  in China, 90
  ideal frequency, 300
  importance of data from, 160–161
  Live, 330, 331, 341
  Messenger Bots, 330
  as microblogging platform, 338
  photo sharing, 339
  Places, 340

popularity of, 338–339
social gaming, 342
usage
  for B-to-B marketing, 127
  by consumers, 331
  by Gen Z, 55
  for marketing, 52, 338–339
  by salespeople, 312
  statistics change, 345
user, 52
value of, 289
Facebook Messenger, 52
Factory outlet, 254
Family, influence on consumer buying
  decisions, 116–117
Family brand, individual brand vs., 186
Family Dollar Stores, 144, 162
Family Educational Rights and Privacy Act
  (FERPA), 34
Family life-cycle segmentation, 145, 146
The Fancy, 332
Farbman, Seth, 271
Farley, Jim, 329
Fast Company, innovative company
  rankings, 195
FedBid, 356
FedBizOpps, 130
Federal Food and Drug Act of 1906, 65
Federal government, marketing to, 130
Federal Hazardous Substances Act of 1960, 65
Federal legislation, 63–64
Federal Trade Commission (FTC), 66
  bait pricing, 365
  comparative advertising, 292
  consumer privacy, 66
  green marketing, 45
  greenwashing, 190–191
  Magnuson-Moss Warranty-Federal
    Trade Commission Improvement
    Act, 1975, 193
Federal Trade Commission Act of 1914,
  64, 367
FedEx
  customer service, 139
  order fulfillment process, 230
  strategy for reaching c-level executives
    at, 137
Feedback, 274
Femvertising, 272
Fertility rates, 86
Fidget spinner, 203
Field service firm, 170
Final goods and services, 72
Financial relationship marketing, 218–219
First stage multinational corporations, 74
Fitbit, 9
Fixed cost, 352
Flexibility of media, 300
Flexible pricing, 364
Flickr, 339
Flighted media schedule, 301
Floating exchange rates, effect on pricing
  strategies, 94
Floor stock, 258
Fluctuating demand, 132–133
FOB origin pricing, 363
Focus groups, 164
Follow-up, 29–31, 319
Food and Drug Administration (FDA),
  65–66, 189, 190

Food stamp program, 36
Ford, 67, 74, 235
  consumer involvement and marketing,
    107–108
  demographic segmentation, 144
  exchange control, 78
  marketing strategies of, 59
  robotics, 25
  Smart Inventory Management System, 373
  social media presence of, 329
  strategic planning of, 17
  undifferentiated marketing strategy of
    Model T, 150
Foreign Corrupt Practices Act (FCPA), 36,
  39–40, 64
Foreign direct investment, 89
Formal groups, 33–34
Form utility, 238
Forrester Research, 8
Fortune's "100 Best Companies to Work
  For," 3, 4
Foursquare, 340
Fourth stage multinational corporations, 74
Frame error, 169
France, 78
  fine to Google in, 84
Franchise, 251
Franchisee, 252
Franchising, global marketing and, 88–89
Franchisor, 252
Frank, Barney, 66
Free merchandise, 305
Free shipping, 363
Freestanding inserts (FSIs), 307
Free trade, 72. See also Globalization
Freight absorption pricing, 364
Fremont-Smith, Tom, 198
Frequency, 300, 301
Frequent-buyer program, 304–305, 308
Fresh Del Monte Produce, 73
Fresh Gab, 225
Freshplum, use of dynamic pricing by,
  351–352
Fresh water, 86
Freyre, Michelle, 145
Frito-Lay, 24
Frost, Scott, 276
FTC Act of 1938, 64
Fuld & Company, 198
Fulfillment times, 259
Full-line discount stores, 254
Functional discounts, 361
Functional modification, 182–183
FunnyOrDie.com, 298

G

G-20, 85
Gaffigan, Jim, 341
Gambled price discounts, 361–362
Gamification, 299
Gander Mountain, 157
Gap Inc., product user positioning, 154
Gap model, of service quality, 213–215
Gatekeepers, 136
Gatorade
  discontinuous innovation of, 195
  social media monitoring, 330
GEICO, use of competitive advertising
  by, 291

1-1 **Define the term *marketing*.** Marketing is the activity, set of institutions, and processes for creating, communicating, delivering, and exchanging offerings that have value for customers, clients, partners, and society at large. Marketing also requires all facets of a company to work together to pool ideas and resources. One major goal of marketing is to create an exchange. An exchange has five conditions, as listed below. Even if all five conditions are met, however, an exchange might not occur. People engage in marketing whether or not an exchange happens.

Five conditions of exchange

1. There must be at least two parties.

2. Each party has something that might be of value to the other party.

3. Each party is capable of communication and delivery.

4. Each party is free to accept or reject the exchange offer.

5. Each party believes it is appropriate or desirable to deal with the other party.

Salesforce was selected number 1 in Fortune's "100 Best Companies to Work\For" in 2018, partly based on it's unique company culture.

Bjorn Bakstad/Shutterstock.com

marketing the activity, set of institutions, and processes for creating, communicating, delivering, and exchanging offerings that have value for customers, clients, partners, and society at large (p. 3)

exchange people giving up something in order to receive something else they would rather have (p. 3)

1-2 **Describe four marketing management philosophies.** The role of marketing and the character of marketing activities within an organization are strongly influenced by the organization's marketing philosophy and orientation. A production-oriented organization focuses on the internal capabilities of the firm rather than on the desires and needs of the marketplace. A sales orientation is based on the beliefs that people will buy more products and services if aggressive sales techniques are used and that high sales volumes produce high profits. A market-oriented organization focuses on satisfying customer wants and needs while meeting organizational objectives. A societal marketing orientation goes beyond a market orientation to include the preservation or enhancement of individuals' and society's long-term best interests.

production orientation a philosophy that focuses on the internal capabilities of the firm rather than on the desires and needs of the marketplace (p. 4)

sales orientation the belief that people will buy more goods and services if aggressive sales techniques are used and that high sales result in high profits (p. 4)

marketing concept the idea that the social and economic justification for an organization's existence is the satisfaction of customer wants and needs while meeting organizational objectives (p. 5)

market orientation a philosophy that assumes that a sale does not depend on an aggressive sales force but rather on a customer's decision to purchase a product; it is synonymous with the marketing concept (p. 6)

societal marketing orientation the idea that an organization exists not only to satisfy customer wants and needs and to meet organizational objectives but also to preserve or enhance individuals' and society's long-term best interests (p. 6)

1-3 **Discuss the differences between sales and market orientations.** First, sales-oriented firms focus on their own needs; market-oriented firms focus on customers' needs and preferences. Second, sales-oriented companies consider themselves to be deliverers of goods and services, whereas market-oriented companies view themselves as satisfiers of customers. Third, sales-oriented firms direct their products to everyone; market-oriented firms aim at specific segments of the population. Fourth, sales-oriented organizations place a higher premium on making a sale, while market-oriented businesses seek a long-term relationship with the customer. Finally, sales-oriented businesses pursue maximum sales volume through intensive promotion, whereas market-oriented businesses pursue customer satisfaction through coordinated activities.

Thanks to Costco's high pay, generous benefits, and trust in its employees, the company's retention rate is 94 percent—significantly higher than that of its competitors.

Tim Boyle/Getty Images News/Getty Images

CHAPTER **REVIEW**

CHAPTER 1 LEARNING OUTCOMES / KEY TERMS

customer value the relationship between benefits and the sacrifice necessary to obtain those benefits (p. 8)

customer satisfaction customers' evaluation of a good or service in terms of whether it has met their needs and expectations (p. 8)

relationship marketing a strategy that focuses on keeping and improving relationships with current customers (p. 8)

empowerment delegation of authority to solve customers' problems quickly—usually by the first person the customer notifies regarding a problem (p. 10)

teamwork collaborative efforts of people to accomplish common objectives (p. 10)

customer relationship management (CRM) a company-wide business strategy designed to optimize profitability, revenue, and customer satisfaction by

focusing on highly defined and precise customer groups (p. 12)

Big Data the discovery, interpretation, and communication of meaningful patterns in data (p. 12)

on-demand marketing delivering relevant experiences, integrated across both physical and virtual environments, throughout the consumer's decision and buying process (p. 12)

1-4 **Describe several reasons for studying marketing.** First, marketing affects the allocation of goods and services that influence a nation's economy and standard of living. Second, an understanding of marketing is crucial to understanding most businesses. Third, career opportunities in marketing are diverse, profitable, and expected to increase significantly during the coming decade. Fourth, understanding marketing makes consumers more informed.

CHAPTER 2 LEARNING OUTCOMES / KEY TERMS

2-1 Understand the importance of strategic planning. Strategic planning is the basis for all marketing strategies and decisions. These decisions affect the allocation of resources and ultimately the financial success of the company.

strategic planning the managerial process of creating and maintaining a fit between the organization's objectives and resources and the evolving market opportunities (p. 17)

2-2 Define strategic business units (SBUs). An SBU should have these characteristics: a distinct mission and a specific target market, control over its resources, its own competitors, a single business, and plans independent from other SBUs in the organization. Each SBU has its own rate of return on investment, growth potential, and associated risks, and requires its own strategies and funding.

strategic business unit (SBU) a subgroup of a single business or collection of related businesses within the larger organization (p. 17)

2-3 Identify strategic alternatives and know a basic outline for a marketing plan. Ansoff's opportunity matrix presents four options to help management develop strategic alternatives: market penetration, market development, product development, and diversification. A marketing plan should define the business mission, perform a situation analysis, define objectives, delineate a target market, and establish components of the marketing mix.

market penetration a marketing strategy that tries to increase market share among existing customers (p. 18)

market development a marketing strategy that entails attracting new customers to existing products (p. 18)

product development a marketing strategy that entails the creation of new products for present markets (p. 18)

diversification a strategy of increasing sales by introducing new products into new markets (p. 18)

portfolio matrix a tool for allocating resources among products or strategic business units on the basis of relative market share and market growth rate (p. 20)

star in the portfolio matrix, a business unit that is a fast-growing market leader (p. 20)

cash cow in the portfolio matrix, a business unit that generates more cash than it needs to maintain its market share (p. 20)

problem child (question mark) in the portfolio matrix, a business unit that shows rapid growth but poor profit margins (p. 20)

dog in the portfolio matrix, a business unit that has low growth potential and a small market share (p. 20)

planning the process of anticipating future events and determining strategies to achieve organizational objectives in the future (p. 22)

marketing planning designing activities relating to marketing objectives and the changing marketing environment (p. 22)

marketing plan a written document that acts as a guidebook of marketing activities for the marketing manager (p. 22)

2-4 Develop an appropriate business mission statement. The firm's mission statement establishes boundaries for all subsequent decisions, objectives, and strategies. A mission statement should focus on the market(s) the organization is attempting to serve rather than on the good or service offered.

mission statement a statement of the firm's business based on a careful analysis of benefits sought by present and potential customers and an analysis of existing and anticipated environmental conditions (p. 23)

marketing myopia defining a business in terms of goods and services rather than in terms of the benefits customers seek (p. 23)

2-5 Describe the components of a situation analysis. In the situation (or SWOT) analysis, the firm should identify its internal strengths (S) and weaknesses (W) and also examine external opportunities (O) and threats (T). When examining external opportunities and threats, marketing managers must analyze aspects of the marketing environment in a process called environmental scanning.

SWOT analysis identifying internal strengths (S) and weaknesses (W) and also examining external opportunities (O) and threats (T) (p. 24)

environmental scanning collection and interpretation of information about forces, events, and relationships in the external environment that may affect the future of the organization or the implementation of the marketing plan (p. 24)

2-6 Identify sources of competitive advantage. There are three types of competitive advantage: cost, product/service differentiation, and niche. Sources of cost competitive advantage include experience curves, efficient labor, no-frills goods and services, government subsidies, product design, reengineering, production innovations, and new methods of service delivery. A product/service differentiation competitive advantage exists when a firm provides something unique that is valuable to buyers beyond just low price. Niche competitive advantages come from targeting unique segments with specific needs and wants.

competitive advantage a set of unique features of a company and its products that are perceived by the target market as significant and superior to those of the competition (p. 25)

cost competitive advantage being the low-cost competitor in an industry while maintaining satisfactory profit margins (p. 25)

experience curves curves that show costs declining at a predictable rate as experience with a product increases (p. 25)

product/service differentiation competitive advantage the provision of something that is unique and valuable to buyers beyond simply offering a lower price than that of the competition (p. 26)

niche competitive advantage the advantage achieved when a firm seeks to target and effectively serve a small segment of the market (p. 26)

sustainable competitive advantage an advantage that cannot be copied by the competition (p. 26)

2-7 **Explain the criteria for stating good marketing objectives.** Objectives should be realistic, measurable, time specific, and compared to a benchmark. They must also be consistent and indicate the priorities of the organization. Good

marketing objectives communicate marketing management philosophies, provide management direction, motivate employees, force executives to think clearly, and form a basis for control.

marketing objective a statement of what is to be accomplished through marketing activities (p. 27)

2-8 **Discuss target market strategies.** Targeting markets begins with a market opportunity analysis (MOA), which describes and estimates the size and sales potential of market segments that are

of interest to the firm. In addition, an assessment of key competitors in these market segments is performed. After the market segments are described, one or more may be targeted by the firm.

marketing strategy the activities of selecting and describing one or more target markets and developing and maintaining a marketing mix that will produce

mutually satisfying exchanges with target markets (p. 27)

market opportunity analysis (MOA) the description and estimation of the size

and sales potential of market segments that are of interest to the firm and the assessment of key competitors in these market segments (p. 28)

2-9 **Describe the elements of the marketing mix.** The marketing mix is a blend of product, place, promotion, and pricing strategies (the four Ps) designed to produce mutually satisfying exchanges with a target market. The starting point of the marketing mix is the product offering. Place (distribution) strategies are concerned with

making products available when and where customers want them. Promotion includes advertising, public relations, sales promotion, and personal selling. Price is what a buyer must give up in order to obtain a product.

marketing mix (four Ps) a unique blend of product, place (distribution), promotion, and pricing strategies designed

to produce mutually satisfying exchanges with a target market (p. 28)

2-10 **Explain why implementation, evaluation, and control of the marketing plan are necessary.** Before a marketing plan can work, it must be implemented—that is, people must perform the actions in the plan. The plan should also be evaluated to see if it has achieved its objectives. Poor implementation can be

a major factor in a plan's failure, but working to gain acceptance can be accomplished with task forces. Once implemented, one major aspect of control is conducting and following through on a marketing audit.

implementation the process that turns a marketing plan into action assignments and ensures that these assignments are executed in a way that accomplishes the plan's objectives (p. 30)

evaluation gauging the extent to which the marketing objectives have

been achieved during the specified time period (p. 30)

control provides the mechanisms for evaluating marketing results in light of the plan's objectives and for correcting actions that do not help the organization

reach those objectives within budget guidelines (p. 30)

marketing audit a thorough, systematic, periodic evaluation of the objectives, strategies, structure, and performance of the marketing organization (p. 31)

2-11 **Identify several techniques that help make strategic planning effective.** First, management must realize that strategic planning is an ongoing process and not a once-a-year exer-

cise. Second, good strategic planning involves a high level of creativity. The last requirement is top management's support and participation.

CHAPTER 3 LEARNING OUTCOMES / KEY TERMS

3-1 **Explain the determinants of a civil society.** Societal order is created through the six modes of social control. Ethics are the moral principles or values that generally govern the conduct of an individual or a group. Laws come into being when ethical rules and guidelines are codified into law. Formal and informal groups have codes of conduct that prescribe acceptable and desired behaviors of their members. Self-regulation involves the voluntary acceptance of standards established by nongovernmental entities. The media play a key role in informing the public about the actions of individuals and organizations—both good and bad. An informed and engaged society can help mold individual and corporate behavior.

social control any means used to maintain behavioral norms and regulate conflict (p. 33)

behavioral norms standards of proper or acceptable behavior. Several modes of social control are important to marketing (p. 33)

ethics the moral principles or values that generally govern the conduct of an individual or a group (p. 33)

3-2 **Explain the concept of ethical behavior.** Ethics are the standards of behavior by which conduct is judged. Standards that are legal may not always be ethical. An ethics violation offends a person's sense of justice or fairness. Ethics basically constitute the unwritten rules developed to guide interactions. Many ethical questions arise from balancing a business's need to produce profit for shareholders against its desire to operate honestly and with concern for environmental and social issues.

Several ethical theories apply to marketing. Deontological theory states that people should adhere to their obligations and duties when analyzing an ethical dilemma. Utilitarian ethical theory says that the choice that yields the greatest benefit to the most people is the choice that is ethically correct. The casuist ethical theory compares a current ethical dilemma with examples of similar ethical dilemmas and their outcomes. Moral relativists believe in time-and-place ethics; that is, ethical truths depend on the individuals and groups holding them. Virtue ethics suggests that individuals become able to solve ethical dilemmas when they develop and nurture a set of virtues.

deontological theory ethical theory that states that people should adhere to their obligations and duties when analyzing an ethical dilemma (p. 35)

utilitarian ethical theory ethical theory that is founded on the ability to predict the consequences of an action (p. 35)

casuist ethical theory ethical theory that compares a current ethical dilemma with examples of similar ethical dilemmas and their outcomes (p. 35)

moral relativism a theory of time-and-place ethics; that is, the belief that ethical truths depend on the individuals and groups holding them (p. 35)

virtue a character trait valued as being good (p. 36)

3-3 **Describe ethical behavior in business.** Business ethics may be viewed as a subset of the values of society as a whole, with a foundation based on the cultural values and norms that constitute a culture's morals. The ethical conduct of businesspeople is shaped by societal elements, including family, education, and religious institutions. Morals are the rules people develop as a result of cultural values and norms. As members of society, businesspeople are morally obligated to consider the ethical implications of their decisions. Ethical decision making can be grouped into three basic approaches. The first approach examines the consequences of decisions. The second approach relies on rules and laws to guide decision making. The third approach is based on a theory of moral development that places individuals or groups in one of three developmental stages: preconventional morality, conventional morality, or postconventional morality.

In addition to personal influences, there are many business influences on ethical decision making. Some of the most influential include the extent of ethical problems within the organization, top management's actions on ethics, potential magnitude of the consequences, social consensus, probability of a harmful outcome, length of time between the decision and the onset of consequences, and the number of people affected.

Many companies develop a code of ethics to help their employees make ethical decisions. A code of ethics can help employees identify acceptable business practices, be an effective internal control on behavior, help employees avoid confusion when determining whether decisions are ethical, and facilitate discussion about what is right and wrong.

Studies show that ethical beliefs vary little from country to country. However, there are enough cultural differences, such as the practice of bribery or gift giving, that laws such as the Foreign Corrupt Practices Act (FCPA) have been put in place to discourage and attempt to modify the current acceptance of such practices.

morals the rules people develop as a result of cultural values and norms (p. 36)

code of ethics a guideline to help marketing managers and other employees make better decisions (p. 38)

Foreign Corrupt Practices Act (FCPA) a law that prohibits U.S. corporations from making illegal payments to public officials of foreign governments to obtain business rights or to enhance their business dealings in those countries (p. 39)

3-4 **Discuss corporate social responsibility.** Corporate social responsibility (CSR) is a business's concern for society's welfare. Responsibility in business refers to a firm's concern for the way its decisions affect society. Stakeholder theory says that social responsibility means paying attention to the interest of every affected stakeholder in every aspect of a firm's operation, including employees, management, customers, the local community, suppliers, and owners. According to the pyramid of corporate social responsibility, CSR has four components: economic, legal, ethical, and philanthropic. These are intertwined, yet the most fundamental is earning a profit. If a firm does not earn a profit, the other three responsibilities are moot.

EXHIBIT 3.3 | **THE PYRAMID OF CORPORATE SOCIAL RESPONSIBILITY**

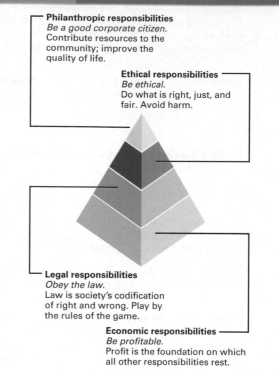

Philanthropic responsibilities
Be a good corporate citizen.
Contribute resources to the community; improve the quality of life.

Ethical responsibilities
Be ethical.
Do what is right, just, and fair. Avoid harm.

Legal responsibilities
Obey the law.
Law is society's codification of right and wrong. Play by the rules of the game.

Economic responsibilities
Be profitable.
Profit is the foundation on which all other responsibilities rest.

corporate social responsibility (CSR) a business's concern for society's welfare (p. 40)

stakeholder theory ethical theory stating that social responsibility is paying

attention to the interest of every affected stakeholder in every aspect of a firm's operation (p. 40)

pyramid of corporate social responsibility a model that suggests

corporate social responsibility is composed of economic, legal, ethical, and philanthropic responsibilities and that a firm's economic performance supports the entire structure (p. 41)

3-5 **Describe the arguments for and against society responsibility.** Most businesspeople believe they should do more than pursue profits. Although a company must consider its economic needs first, it must also operate within the law, do what is ethical and fair, and be a good corporate citizen. Sustainability is the concept that socially responsible companies will outperform their peers by focusing on the world's social problems and viewing

them as an opportunity to earn profits and help the world at the same time. Social responsibility is growing, but it can be costly and the benefits are not always immediate. In addition, some surveys report that consumer desire to purchase responsible products does not always translate to actually purchasing those products. One branch of social responsibility is green marketing, which aids the environment and often the bottom line of a business.

sustainability the idea that socially responsible companies will outperform their peers by focusing on the world's social problems and viewing

opportunities to build profits and help the world at the same time (p. 44)

green marketing the development and marketing of products designed to minimize

negative effects on the physical environment or to improve the environment (p. 44)

greenwashing Adding a minimal number of green product attributes in order to promote it as green (p. 44)

3-6 **Explain cause-related marketing.** Cause-related marketing is the cooperative effort between a for-profit firm and a nonprofit organization. It is different from philanthropy, which is a specific, tax-deductible donation. Cause-related marketing is very popular

because it can enhance the reputation of the corporation and also make additional profit for the company. However, consumers sometimes come to believe that every company is tied to a cause, resulting in consumer cause fatigue.

cause-related marketing the cooperative marketing efforts between a for-profit

firm and a nonprofit organization (p. 46)

4-1 **Discuss the external environment of marketing and explain how it affects a firm.** The external marketing environment consists of social, demographic, economic, technological, political and legal, and competitive variables. Marketers generally cannot control the elements of the external environment. Instead, they must understand how the external environment is changing and the impact of that change on the target market. Then marketing managers can create a marketing mix to effectively meet the needs of target customers.

target market a group of people or organizations for which an organization designs, implements, and maintains a marketing mix intended to meet the needs of that group, resulting in mutually satisfying exchanges (p. 49)

4-2 **Describe the social factors that affect marketing.** Within the external environment, social factors are perhaps the most difficult for marketers to anticipate. Several major social trends are currently shaping marketing strategies. First, people of all ages have a broader range of interests, defying traditional consumer profiles. Second, social media, web-based, and mobile technology change how people and marketers interact by allowing one-to-one, one-to-many, and many-to-many communications. Because Facebook is about human-to-human interaction, companies are turning to it and other forms of social media with ever-increasing speed.

component lifestyles the practice of choosing goods and services that meet one's diverse needs and interests rather than conforming to a single, traditional lifestyle (p. 51)

4-3 **Explain the importance to marketing managers of current demographic trends.** There are more than 7.5 billion people alive today. China has the largest population with 1.38 billion people; India is second with 1.27 billion. Census data puts the U.S. population at more than 323 million, with metropolitan areas growing and rural areas shrinking in population. Marketers are faced with increasingly experienced consumers among the younger generations such as tweens and teens. Because the population is also growing older, marketers are offering more products that appeal to middle-aged and older consumers.

demography the study of people's vital statistics, such as age, race and ethnicity, and location (p. 53)

Generation Z people born between 1997 and 2012 (p. 55)

Millennials people born between 1981 and 1996 (p. 55)

Generation X people born between 1965 and 1980 (p. 57)

baby boomers people born between 1946 and 1964 (p. 57)

4-4 **Explain the importance to marketing managers of growing ethnic markets.** The minority population today is about 118 million. By 2050, around one in three U.S. residents will be Hispanic. The United States will flip completely to a majority-minority makeup in 2035. Many companies are creating departments and product lines to target multicultural market segments effectively. Companies have quickly found that ethnic markets are not homogeneous.

4-5 **Identify consumer and marketer reactions to the state of the economy.** The annual median household income in the United States in 2015 was approximately $56,516, though the median household income varies widely from state to state. During a time of inflation, marketers generally attempt to maintain level pricing to avoid losing customer brand loyalty. During times of recession, many marketers maintain or reduce prices to counter the effects of decreased demand; they also concentrate on increasing production efficiency and improving customer service. The Great Recession was the largest economic downturn since the Great Depression. While the causes of recession are very complex, this one began with the collapse of inflated housing prices.

purchasing power a comparison of income versus the relative cost of a standard set of goods and services in different geographic areas (p. 61)

inflation a measure of the decrease in the value of money, expressed as the percentage reduction in value since the previous year (p. 61)

recession a period of economic activity characterized by negative growth, which reduces demand for goods and services (p. 61)

4-6 **Identify the impact of technology on a firm.** Technological success is based upon innovation, and innovation requires imagination and risk taking. Monitoring new technology and encouraging research and development (R&D) of new technology are essential to keeping up with competitors in today's marketing environment. Innovation through R&D needs to be stimulated by upper management and fostered in creative environments. Although developing new technology internally is a key to creating and maintaining a long-term competitive advantage, external technology is also important to managers.

basic research pure research that aims to confirm an existing theory or to learn more about a concept or phenomenon (p. 62)

applied research research that attempts to develop new or improved products (p. 63)

4-7 **Discuss the political and legal environment of marketing.** All marketing activities are subject to state and federal laws and the rulings of regulatory agencies. Marketers are responsible for remaining aware of and abiding by such regulations. Some key federal agencies that affect marketing are the Consumer Product Safety Commission, the Food and Drug Administration, and the Federal Trade Commission. Many laws, including privacy laws, have been passed to protect the consumer as well. In 2012, the FTC called for online data collectors to adopt better privacy policies and asked Congress to pass comprehensive privacy legislation. Despite federal efforts, online tracking has become widespread and pervasive.

Consumer Product Safety Commission (CPSC) a federal agency established to protect the health and safety of consumers in and around their homes (p. 65)

Food and Drug Administration (FDA) a federal agency charged with enforcing regulations against selling and distributing adulterated, misbranded, or hazardous food and drug products (p. 65)

Federal Trade Commission (FTC) a federal agency empowered to prevent persons or corporations from using unfair methods of competition in commerce (p. 66)

EXHIBIT 4.2 PRIMARY U.S. LAWS PROTECTING CONSUMERS

Legislation	Impact on Marketing
Federal Food and Drug Act of 1906	Prohibits adulteration and misbranding of foods and drugs involved in interstate commerce; strengthened by the Food, Drug, and Cosmetic Act (1938) and the Kefauver-Harris Drug Amendment (1962).
Federal Hazardous Substances Act of 1960	Requires warning labels on hazardous household chemicals.
Kefauver-Harris Drug Amendment of 1962	Requires that manufacturers conduct tests to prove drug effectiveness and safety.
Consumer Credit Protection Act of 1968	Requires that lenders fully disclose true interest rates and all other charges to credit customers for loans and installment purchases.
Child Protection and Toy Safety Act of 1969	Prevents marketing of products so dangerous that adequate safety warnings cannot be given.
Public Health Smoking Act of 1970	Prohibits cigarette advertising on television and radio and revises the health hazard warning on cigarette packages.
Poison Prevention Labeling Act of 1970	Requires safety packaging for products that may be harmful to children.
National Environmental Policy Act of 1970	Established the Environmental Protection Agency to deal with various types of pollution and organizations that create pollution.
Public Health Cigarette Smoking Act of 1971	Prohibits tobacco advertising on radio and television.
Consumer Product Safety Act of 1972	Created the Consumer Product Safety Commission, which has authority to specify safety standards for most products.
Child Protection Act of 1990	Regulates the number of minutes of advertising on children's television.
Children's Online Privacy Protection Act of 1998	Empowers the FTC to set rules regarding how and when marketers must obtain parental permission before asking children marketing research questions.
Aviation Security Act of 2001	Requires airlines to take extra security measures to protect passengers, including the installation of stronger cockpit doors, improved baggage screening, and increased security training for airport personnel.
Homeland Security Act of 2002	Protects consumers against terrorist acts; created the Department of Homeland Security.
Do Not Call Law of 2003	Protects consumers against unwanted telemarketing calls.
CAN-SPAM Act of 2003	Protects consumers against unwanted email, or spam.
Credit Card Act of 2009	Provides many credit card protections.
Restoring American Financial Stability Act of 2010	Created the Consumer Financial Protection Bureau to protect consumers against unfair, abusive, and deceptive financial practices.
Patient Protection and Affordable Care Act	Overhauled the U.S. healthcare system; mandated and subsidized health insurance for individuals.

4-8 **Explain the basics of foreign and domestic competition.** The competitive environment encompasses the number of competitors a firm must face, the relative size of the competitors, and the degree of interdependence within the industry. Declining population growth, rising costs, and shortages of resources have heightened domestic competition.

5-1 Discuss the importance of global marketing.

Businesspeople who adopt a global vision are better able to identify global marketing opportunities, understand the nature of global networks, create effective global marketing strategies, and compete against foreign competition in domestic markets. Large corporations have traditionally been the major global competitors, but more and more small businesses are entering the global marketplace. Despite fears of job losses to other countries with cheaper labor, there are many benefits to globalization, including the reduction of poverty and increased standards of living.

global marketing marketing that targets markets throughout the world (p. 71)

global vision recognizing and reacting to international marketing opportunities, using effective global marketing strategies, and being aware of threats from foreign competitors in all markets (p. 71)

absolute advantage when a country can produce a product or service at a lower cost than any other country or when it is the only country that can provide the product or service (p. 71)

principle of comparative advantage each country should specialize in the products or services that it can produce most readily and cheaply and trade those products or services for goods and services that foreign countries can produce most readily and cheaply (p. 72)

free trade policy of permitting individuals and businesses in a country to buy and sell in other countries without restrictions (p. 72)

protectionism where a nation protects its home industries from foreign competitors by establishing artificial barriers, such as tariffs and quotas (p. 72)

gross domestic product (GDP) the total market value of all final goods and services produced in a country for a given time period (p. 72)

outsourcing sending U.S. jobs abroad (p. 73)

inshoring returning production jobs to the United States (p. 73)

5-2 Discuss the impact of multinational firms on the world economy.

Multinational corporations are international traders that regularly operate across national borders. Because of their vast size and financial, technological, and material resources, multinational corporations have great influence on the world economy. They have the ability to overcome trade problems, save on labor costs, and tap new technology. There are critics and supporters of multinational corporations, and the critics question the actual benefits of bringing capital-intensive technology to impoverished nations. Many countries block foreign investment in factories, land, and companies to protect their economies.

Some companies presume that markets throughout the world are more and more similar, so some global products can be standardized across global markets.

multinational corporation a company that is heavily engaged in international trade, beyond exporting and importing (p. 74)

capital intensive using more capital than labor in the production process (p. 74)

global marketing standardization production of uniform products that can be sold the same way all over the world (p. 75)

multidomestic strategy when multinational firms enable individual subsidiaries to compete independently in domestic markets (p. 75)

5-3 Describe the external environment facing global marketers.

Global marketers face the same environmental factors as they do domestically: culture, economic and technological development, the global economy, political structure and actions, demography, and natural resources. Cultural considerations include societal values, attitudes and beliefs, language, and customary business practices. A country's economic and technological status depends on its stage of industrial development, which, in turn, affects average family incomes. A global marketer today must be fully aware of the intertwined nature of the global economy. The political structure is shaped by political ideology and such policies as tariffs, quotas, boycotts, exchange controls, trade agreements, and market groupings. Demographic variables include the size of a population and its age and geographic distribution. A shortage of natural resources also affects the external environment by dictating what is available and at what price.

EXHIBIT 5.3	MEMBERS OF THE G-20		
Argentina	European Union	Italy	South Africa
Australia	France	Japan	Republic of Korea
Brazil	Germany	Mexico	Turkey
Canada	India	Russia	United Kingdom
China	Indonesia	Saudi Arabia	United States

balance of trade the difference between the value of a country's exports and the value of its imports over a given period (p. 77)

balance of payments the difference between a country's total payments to other countries and its total receipts from other countries (p. 77)

Mercosur the largest Latin American trade agreement; full members include Argentina, Brazil, Paraguay, Uruguay. Associate members are French Guiana, Suriname, Guyana, Chile, Colombia, Ecuador, Peru, and Bolivia (p. 79)

World Trade Organization (WTO) a trade organization that replaced the old General Agreement on Tariffs and Trade (GATT) (p. 81)

Uruguay Round a trade agreement to dramatically lower trade barriers worldwide; created the World Trade Organization (p. 81)

foreign direct investment a business investment in a foreign country, either by establishing business operations or by acquiring business assets in that country (p. 82)

Dominican Republic-Central America Free Trade Agreement (CAFTA-DR) a trade agreement instituted in 2005 that includes Costa Rica,

the Dominican Republic, El Salvador, Guatemala, Honduras, Nicaragua, and the United States (p. 82)

European Union (EU) a free trade zone encompassing 28 European countries (p. 83)

World Bank an international bank that offers low-interest loans, advice, and information to developing nations (p. 84)

International Monetary Fund (IMF) an international organization that acts

as a lender of last resort, providing loans to troubled nations, and also works to promote trade through financial cooperation (p. 85)

Group of Twenty (G-20) a forum for international economic development that promotes discussion between industrial and emerging-market countries on key issues related to global economic stability (p. 85)

5-4 **Identify the various ways of entering the global marketplace.** Firms use the following strategies to enter global markets, in descending order of risk and profit: direct investment, joint venture, contract manufacturing, licensing and franchising, and exporting.

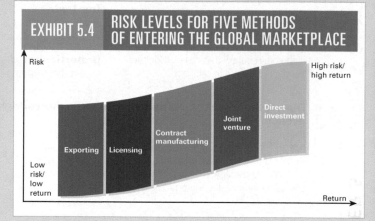

EXHIBIT 5.4 **RISK LEVELS FOR FIVE METHODS OF ENTERING THE GLOBAL MARKETPLACE**

exporting selling domestically produced products to buyers in other countries (p. 87)

buyer for export an intermediary in the global market that assumes all ownership risks and sells globally for its own account (p. 88)

export broker an intermediary who plays the traditional broker's role by bringing buyer and seller together (p. 88)

export agent an intermediary who acts like a manufacturer's agent for the exporter; the export agent lives in the foreign market (p. 88)

licensing the legal process whereby a licensor allows another firm to use its manufacturing process, trademarks, patents, trade secrets, or other proprietary knowledge (p. 88)

contract manufacturing private-label manufacturing by a foreign company (p. 89)

joint venture when a domestic firm buys part of a foreign company or joins with a foreign company to create a new entity (p. 89)

5-5 **List the basic elements involved in developing a global marketing mix.** A firm's major consideration is how much it will adjust the four Ps—product, promotion, place (distribution), and price—within each country. One strategy is to use one product and one promotion message worldwide. A

second strategy is to create new products for global markets. A third strategy is to keep the product basically the same but alter the promotional message. A fourth strategy is to slightly alter the product to meet local conditions.

exchange rate the price of one country's currency in terms of another country's currency (p. 93)

floating exchange rates a system in which prices of different currencies move up and down based on the demand for and the supply of each currency (p. 94)

dumping the sale of an exported product at a price lower than that charged for the same or a like product in the "home" market of the exporter (p. 94)

countervailing duty a tax on imported goods to offset a subsidy or other financial assistance given to a foreign exporter by

its government that enables the foreign exporter to sell at an artificially low price in the global marketplace (p. 95)

countertrade a form of trade in which all or part of the payment for goods or services is in the form of other goods or services (p. 95)

5-6 **Discover how the Internet is affecting global marketing.** Simply opening an e-commerce site can open the door for international sales. International carriers, such as UPS, can help solve logistics problems. Language translation software can help

an e-commerce business become multilingual. Yet cultural differences and old-line rules, regulations, and taxes hinder rapid development of e-commerce in many countries.

6-1 **Explain why marketing managers should understand consumer behavior.** An understanding of consumer behavior reduces marketing managers' uncertainty when they are defining a target market and designing a marketing mix.

consumer behavior processes a consumer uses to make purchase decisions, as well as to use and dispose of purchased goods or services; also includes factors that influence purchase decisions and product use (p. 99)

consumer behavior processes a consumer uses to make purchase decisions, as well as to use and dispose of purchased

goods or services; also includes factors that influence purchase decisions and product use (p. 97)

value a personal assessment of the net worth one obtains from making a purchase, or the enduring belief that a specific mode of conduct is personally or socially preferable to another mode of conduct (p. 97)

perceived value the value a consumer *expects* to obtain from a purchase (p. 97)

utilitarian value a value derived from a product or service that helps the consumer solve problems and accomplish tasks (p. 97)

hedonic value a value that acts as an end in itself rather than as a means to an end (p. 97)

6-2 **Analyze the components of the consumer decision-making process.** The consumer decision-making process begins with need recognition, when stimuli trigger awareness of an unfulfilled want. If additional information is required to make a purchase decision, the consumer may engage in an internal or external information search. The consumer then evaluates the alternatives using the additional information and establishes purchase guidelines. Finally, a purchase decision is made.

consumer decision-making process a five-step process used by consumers when buying goods or services (p. 98)

need recognition result of an imbalance between actual and desired states (p. 98)

want recognition of an unfulfilled need and a product that will satisfy it (p. 98)

stimulus any unit of input affecting one or more of the five senses: sight, smell, taste, touch, hearing (p. 98)

internal information search the process of recalling information stored in the memory (p. 99)

external information search the process of seeking information in the outside environment (p. 99)

non-marketing-controlled information source a product information source that is not associated with advertising or promotion (p. 99)

marketing-controlled information source a product information source that originates with marketers promoting the product (p. 100)

evoked set (consideration set) a group of brands resulting from an information search from which a buyer can choose (p. 101)

nudge a small intervention that can change a person's behavior (p. 102)

6-3 **Explain the consumer's postpurchase evaluation process.** Consumer postpurchase evaluation is influenced by prepurchase expectations, the prepurchase information search, and the consumer's general level of self-confidence. When a purchase creates cognitive dissonance, consumers tend to react by seeking positive reinforcement for the purchase decision, avoiding negative information about the purchase decision, or revoking the purchase decision by returning the product.

jilting effect anticipation of receiving a highly desirable option only to have it become inaccessible (p. 103)

cognitive dissonance inner tension that a consumer experiences after recognizing an inconsistency between behavior and values or opinions (p. 104)

6-4 **Identify the types of consumer buying decisions and discuss the significance of consumer involvement.** Consumer decision making falls into three broad categories: routine response behavior, limited decision making, and extensive decision making. High-involvement decisions usually include an extensive information search and a thorough evaluation of alternatives. By contrast, low-involvement decisions are characterized by brand loyalty and a lack of personal identification with the product.

involvement the amount of time and effort a buyer invests in the search, evaluation, and decision processes of consumer behavior (p. 105)

routine response behavior the type of decision making exhibited by consumers buying frequently purchased, low-cost goods and services; requires little search and decision time (p. 105)

limited decision making the type of decision making that requires a moderate amount of time for gathering information and deliberating about an unfamiliar brand in a familiar product category (p. 105)

extensive decision making the most complex type of consumer decision making, used when buying an unfamiliar, expensive product or an infrequently

bought item; requires use of several criteria for evaluating options and much time for seeking information (p. 106)

showrooming the practice of examining merchandise in a physical retail location without purchasing it, and then shopping online for a better deal on the same item (p. 107)

6-5 **Describe how some marketers are reconceptualizing the consumer decision making process.** The balance of power has shifted largely from the marketer to the consumer. The consumer decision journey begins when a stimulus causes a consumer to research a number of products, continues through to purchase, and ends with a feedback loop of ratings, rankings, and referrals. In order to minimize the "consider and evaluate" phases of the consumer journey, a company must have four distinct but interconnected capabilities: automation, proactive personalization, contextual interaction, and journey innovation.

churning when a significant number of customers are switching brands (p. 110)

6-6 Identify and understand the cultural factors that affect consumer buying decisions. Cultural influences on consumer buying decisions include one's subcultures and social class, as well as the values, language, myths, customs, rituals, laws, and artifacts transmitted from one generation to the next.

culture the set of values, norms, attitudes, and other meaningful symbols that shape human behavior and the artifacts, or products, of that behavior as they are transmitted from one generation to the next (p. 111)

subculture a homogeneous group of people who share elements of the overall culture as well as unique elements of their own group (p. 112)

social class a group of people in a society who are considered nearly equal in status or community esteem, who regularly socialize among themselves both formally and informally, and who share behavioral norms (p. 112)

6-7 Identify and understand the social factors that affect consumer buying decisions. Consumers seek out others' opinions for guidance on products with image-related attributes or because attribute information is lacking. Consumers may use products to identify with a reference group or to follow an opinion leader. Family members also influence purchase decisions.

reference group all of the formal and informal groups in society that influence an individual's purchasing behavior (p. 114)

primary membership group a reference group with which people interact regularly in an informal, face-to-face manner, such as family, friends, and coworkers (p. 114)

secondary membership group a reference group with which people associate less consistently and more formally than

a primary membership group, such as a club, professional group, or religious group (p. 114)

aspirational reference group a group that someone would like to join (p. 115)

norm a value or attitude deemed acceptable by a group (p. 115)

nonaspirational reference group a group with which an individual does not want to associate (p. 115)

opinion leader an individual who influences the opinions of others (p. 116)

socialization process how cultural values and norms are passed down to children (p. 116)

separated self-schema a perspective whereby a consumer sees himself or herself as distinct and separate from others (p. 117)

connected self-schema a perspective whereby a consumer sees himself or herself as an integral part of a group (p. 117)

6-8 Identify and understand the individual factors that affect consumer buying decisions. Men and women differ in their social and economic roles, and that affects consumer buying decisions. A consumer's age generally indicates what products he or she may be interested in purchasing. Marketers often define their target markets in terms of life cycle stage, following changes in consumers' attitudes and behavioral tendencies as they mature. Finally, certain products reflect consumers' personality, self-concept, and lifestyle.

personality a way of organizing and grouping the consistencies of an individual's reactions to situations (p. 119)

self-concept how consumers perceive themselves in terms of attitudes, perceptions, beliefs, and self-evaluations (p. 119)

ideal self-image the way an individual would like to be perceived (p. 119)

real self-image the way an individual actually perceives himself or herself (p. 119)

6-9 Identify and understand the psychological factors that affect consumer buying decisions. Perception allows consumers to recognize their consumption problems. Motivation is what drives consumers to take action to satisfy specific consumption needs. Almost all consumer behavior results from learning, which is the process that creates changes in behavior through experience.

perception the process by which people select, organize, and interpret stimuli into a meaningful and coherent picture (p. 120)

selective exposure a process whereby a consumer notices certain stimuli and ignores others (p. 120)

selective distortion a process whereby a consumer changes or distorts information that conflicts with his or her feelings or beliefs (p. 120)

selective retention a process whereby a consumer remembers only that information that supports his or her personal beliefs (p. 120)

motive a driving force that causes a person to take action to satisfy specific needs (p. 121)

Maslow's hierarchy of needs a method of classifying human needs and motivations into five categories in ascending order of importance: physiological, safety, social, esteem, and self-actualization (p. 121)

learning a process that creates changes in behavior, immediate or expected, through experience and practice (p. 122)

stimulus generalization a form of learning that occurs when one response is extended to a second stimulus similar to the first (p. 123)

stimulus discrimination a learned ability to differentiate among similar products (p. 123)

7-1 Describe business marketing. Business marketing provides goods and services that are bought for use in business rather than for personal consumption. Intended use, not physical characteristics, distinguishes a business product from a consumer product.

business marketing (industrial, business-to-business, B-to-B, or B2B marketing) the marketing of goods and services to individuals and organizations for purposes other than personal consumption (p. 125)

business product (industrial product) a product used to manufacture other goods or services, to facilitate an organization's operations, or to resell to other customers (p. 125)

consumer product a product bought to satisfy an individual's personal wants or needs (p. 125)

7-2 Describe trends in B-to-B Internet marketing. B-to-B companies use the Internet in three major ways. First, they use their websites to facilitate communication and orders. Second, they use digital marketing to increase brand awareness. Third, they use digital marketing—primarily in the form of content marketing—to position their businesses as thought leaders and therefore generate sales leads. Content marketing, a strategic marketing approach focused on creating and distributing valuable, relevant, and consistent content, has played an important role for B-to-B marketers. As they build reputations in their business areas, many B-to-B marketers use social media to share content, increase awareness, and build relationships and community. Some metrics that are particularly useful for increasing the success of a social media campaign are awareness, engagement, and conversion.

Content marketing a strategic marketing approach that focuses on creating and distributing content that is valuable, relevant, and consistent (p. 126)

7-3 Discuss the role of relationship marketing and strategic alliances in business marketing. Relationship marketing entails seeking and establishing long-term alliances or partnerships with customers. A strategic alliance is a cooperative agreement between business firms. Firms form alliances to leverage what they do well by partnering with others that have complementary skills. Although the concepts of relationship marketing and strategic alliances are relatively new to American marketers, these ideas have long been used by marketers in other cultures.

strategic alliance (strategic partnership) a cooperative agreement between business firms (p. 128)

relationship commitment a firm's belief that an ongoing relationship with another firm is so important that the relationship warrants maximum efforts at maintaining it indefinitely (p. 128)

trust the condition that exists when one party has confidence in an exchange partner's reliability and integrity (p. 128)

keiretsu a network of interlocking corporate affiliates (p. 129)

7-4 Identify the four major categories of business market customers. Producer markets consist of for-profit individuals and organizations that buy products to use in producing other products, as components of other products, or in facilitating business operations. Reseller markets consist of wholesalers and retailers that buy finished products to resell for profit. Government markets include federal, state, county, and city governments that buy goods and services to support their own operations and serve the needs of citizens. Institutional markets consist of very diverse nonbusiness institutions whose main goals do not include profit.

original equipment manufacturers (OEMs) individuals and organizations that buy business goods and incorporate them into the products they produce for eventual sale to other producers or to consumers (p. 129)

7-5 Explain the North American Industry Classification System. The North American Industry Classification System (NAICS) provides a way to identify, analyze, segment, and target business and government markets. Organizations can be identified and compared by a numeric code indicating business sector, subsector, industry group, industry, and industry subdivision. NAICS is a valuable tool for analyzing, segmenting, and targeting business markets.

EXHIBIT 7.1 HOW NAICS WORKS

The more digits in the NAICS code, the more homogeneous the groups at that level.

NAICS Level	NAICS Code	Description
Sector	51	Information
Subsector	513	Broadcasting and telecommunications
Industry group	5133	Telecommunications
Industry	51332	Wireless telecommunications carriers, except satellite
Industry subdivision	513321	Paging

North American Industry Classification System (NAICS) a detailed numbering system developed by the United States, Canada, and Mexico to classify North American business establishments by their main production processes (p. 131)

7-6 Explain the major differences between business and consumer markets.

In business markets, demand is derived, inelastic, joint, and fluctuating. Purchase volume is much larger than in consumer markets, customers are fewer and more geographically concentrated, and distribution channels are more direct. Buying is approached more formally using professional purchasing agents, more people are involved in the buying process, negotiation is more complex, and reciprocity and leasing are more common. And, finally, selling strategy in business markets normally focuses on personal contact rather than on advertising.

derived demand the demand for business products (p. 131)

joint demand the demand for two or more items used together in a final product (p. 132)

multiplier effect (accelerator principle) phenomenon in which a small increase or decrease in consumer demand can produce a much larger change in demand for the facilities and equipment needed to make the consumer product (p. 132)

business-to-business online exchange an electronic trading floor that provides companies with integrated links to their customers and suppliers (p. 133)

reciprocity a practice whereby business purchasers choose to buy from their own customers (p. 134)

7-7 Describe the seven types of business goods and services.

Major equipment includes capital goods such as heavy machinery. Accessory equipment is typically less expensive and shorter lived than major equipment. Raw materials are extractive or agricultural products that have not been processed. Component parts are finished or near-finished items to be used as parts of other products. Processed materials are used to manufacture other products. Supplies are consumable and not used as part of a final product. Business services are intangible products that many companies use in their operations.

major equipment (installations) capital goods such as large or expensive machines, mainframe computers, blast furnaces, generators, airplanes, and buildings (p. 134)

accessory equipment goods, such as portable tools and office equipment, that are less expensive and shorter-lived than major equipment (p. 134)

raw materials unprocessed extractive or agricultural products, such as mineral ore, lumber, wheat, corn, fruits, vegetables, and fish (p. 135)

component parts either finished items ready for assembly or products that need very little processing before becoming part of some other product (p. 135)

processed materials products used directly in manufacturing other products (p. 135)

supplies consumable items that do not become part of the final product (p. 135)

business services expense items that do not become part of a final product (p. 136)

7-8 Discuss the unique aspects of business buying behavior.

Business buying behavior is distinguished by five fundamental characteristics. First, buying is normally undertaken by a buying center consisting of many people who range widely in authority level. Second, business buyers typically evaluate alternative products and suppliers based on quality, service, and price—in that order. Third, business buying falls into three general categories: new buys, modified rebuys, and straight rebuys. Fourth, the ethics of business buyers and sellers are often scrutinized. Fifth, customer service before, during, and after the sale plays a big role in business purchase decisions.

EXHIBIT 7.2 BUYING CENTER ROLES FOR COMPUTER PURCHASES

Role	Illustration
Initiator	Division general manager proposes replacing the company's computer network.
Influencers/ evaluators	Corporate controller's office and vice president of information services have an important say in which system and vendor the company will deal with.
Gatekeepers	Corporate departments for purchasing and information services analyze the company's needs and recommend likely matches with potential vendors.
Decider	Vice president of administration, with advice from others, selects the vendor the company will deal with and the system it will buy.
Purchaser	Purchasing agent negotiates the terms of sale.
Users	All division employees use the computers.

buying center all the people in an organization who become involved in the purchase decision (p. 136)

new buy a situation requiring the purchase of a product for the first time (p. 138)

modified rebuy a situation in which the purchaser wants some change in the original good or service (p. 138)

straight rebuy a situation in which the purchaser reorders the same goods or services without looking for new information or investigating other suppliers (p. 138)

8-1 **Describe the characteristics of markets and market segments.** A market is composed of individuals or organizations with the ability and willingness to make purchases to fulfill their needs or wants. A market segment is a group of individuals or organizations with similar product needs as a result of one or more common characteristics.

market people or organizations with needs or wants and the ability and willingness to buy (p. 141)

market segment a subgroup of people or organizations sharing one or more characteristics that cause them to have similar product needs (p. 141)

market segmentation the process of dividing a market into meaningful, relatively similar, and identifiable segments or groups (p. 141)

8-2 **Explain the importance of market segmentation.** Before the 1960s, few businesses targeted specific market segments. Today, segmentation is a crucial marketing strategy for nearly all successful organizations. Market segmentation enables marketers to tailor marketing mixes to meet the needs of particular population segments. Segmentation helps marketers identify consumer needs and preferences, areas of declining demand, and new marketing opportunities.

8-3 **Discuss the criteria for successful market segmentation.** Successful market segmentation depends on four basic criteria: (1) a market segment must be substantial and have enough potential customers to be viable; (2) a market segment must be identifiable and measurable; (3) members of a market segment must be accessible to marketing efforts; and (4) a market segment must respond to particular marketing efforts in a way that distinguishes it from other segments.

8-4 **Describe the bases commonly used to segment consumer markets.** Five bases are commonly used for segmenting consumer markets. Geographic segmentation is based on region, size, density, and climate characteristics. Demographic segmentation is based on age, gender, income level, ethnicity, and family life cycle characteristics. Psychographic segmentation includes personality, motives, and lifestyle characteristics. Benefits sought is a type of segmentation that identifies customers according to the benefits they seek in a product. Finally, usage segmentation divides a market by the amount of product purchased or consumed.

segmentation bases (variables) characteristics of individuals, groups, or organizations (p. 142)

geographic segmentation segmenting markets by region of a country or the world, market size, market density, or climate (p. 142)

demographic segmentation segmenting markets by age, gender, income, ethnic background, and family life cycle (p. 143)

family life cycle (FLC) a series of stages determined by a combination of age, marital status, and the presence or absence of children (p. 145)

psychographic segmentation segmenting markets on the basis of personality, motives, lifestyles, and geodemographics (p. 146)

geodemographic segmentation segmenting potential customers into neighborhood lifestyle categories (p. 147)

benefit segmentation the process of grouping customers into market segments according to the benefits they seek from the product (p. 147)

usage-rate segmentation dividing a market by the amount of product bought or consumed (p. 147)

80/20 principle a principle holding that 20 percent of all customers generate 80 percent of the demand (p. 147)

8-5 **Describe the bases for segmenting business markets.** Business markets can be segmented on two general bases. First, businesses may segment markets based on company characteristics, such as customers' geographic location, type of company, company size, and product use. Second, companies may segment customers based on the buying processes those customers use.

satisficers business customers who place an order with the first familiar supplier to satisfy product and delivery requirements (p. 148)

optimizers business customers who consider numerous suppliers (both familiar and unfamiliar), solicit bids, and study all proposals carefully before selecting one (p. 148)

8-6 **List the steps involved in segmenting markets.** Six steps are involved when segmenting markets: (1) selecting a market or product category for study; (2) choosing a basis or bases for segmenting the market; (3) selecting segmentation descriptors; (4) profiling and evaluating segments; (5) selecting target markets; and (6) designing, implementing, and maintaining appropriate marketing mixes.

8-7 **Discuss alternative strategies for selecting target markets.** Marketers select target markets using three different strategies: undifferentiated targeting, concentrated targeting, and multisegment targeting. An undifferentiated targeting strategy assumes that all members of a market have similar needs that can be met with a single marketing mix. A concentrated targeting strategy focuses all marketing efforts on a single market segment. Multisegment targeting is a strategy that uses two or more marketing mixes to target two or more market segments.

target market a group of people or organizations for which an organization designs, implements, and maintains a marketing mix intended to meet the needs of that group, resulting in mutually satisfying exchanges (p. 150)

undifferentiated targeting strategy a marketing approach that views the market as one big market with no individual segments and thus uses a single marketing mix (p. 150)

concentrated targeting strategy a strategy used to select one segment of a market for targeting marketing efforts (p. 150)

niche one segment of a market (p. 150)

multisegment targeting strategy a strategy that chooses two or more well-defined market segments and develops a distinct marketing mix for each (p. 151)

cannibalization a situation that occurs when sales of a new product cut into sales of a firm's existing products (p. 152)

8-8 **Explain how CRM can be used as a targeting tool.** Companies that successfully implement CRM tend to customize the goods and services offered to their customers based on data generated through interactions between carefully defined groups of customers and the company. CRM relies on four things to be successful: personalization, time savings, loyalty, and technology. Although mass marketing will probably continue to be used, the advantages of CRM cannot be ignored.

8-9 **Explain how and why firms implement positioning strategies and how product differentiation plays a role.** Positioning is used to influence consumer perceptions of a particular brand, product line, or organization in relation to competitors. The term position refers to the place that the offering occupies in consumers' minds. To establish a unique position, many firms use product differentiation, emphasizing the real or perceived differences between competing offerings. Products may be differentiated on the basis of attribute, price and quality, use or application, product user, product class, competitor, or emotion. Some firms, instead of using product differentiation, position their products as being similar to competing products or brands. Sometimes products or companies are repositioned in order to sustain growth in slow markets or to correct positioning mistakes.

positioning developing a specific marketing mix to influence potential customers' overall perception of a brand, product line, or organization in general (p. 153)

position the place a product, brand, or group of products occupies in consumers' minds relative to competing offerings (p. 153)

product differentiation a positioning strategy that some firms use to distinguish their products from those of competitors (p. 153)

perceptual mapping a means of displaying or graphing, in two or more dimensions, the location of products, brands, or groups of products in customers' minds (p. 153)

repositioning changing consumers' perceptions of a brand in relation to competing brands (p. 155)

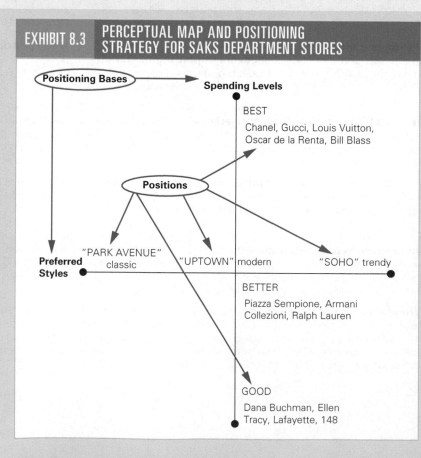

EXHIBIT 8.3 **PERCEPTUAL MAP AND POSITIONING STRATEGY FOR SAKS DEPARTMENT STORES**

9-1 **Define marketing research and explain its importance to marketing decision making.** Marketing research is a process of collecting and analyzing data for the purpose of solving specific marketing problems. Practically speaking, marketers use marketing research to improve the decision-making process, trace problems, serve customers, gauge the value of goods and services, understand the marketplace, and measure customer service efforts.

marketing research the process of planning, collecting, and analyzing data relevant to a marketing decision (p. 157)

9-2 **Describe the steps involved in conducting a marketing research project.** The marketing research process involves several basic steps. First, the researcher and the decision maker must agree on a problem statement or set of research objectives. Social media and big data may be helpful in this pursuit. The researcher then creates an overall research design to specify how primary data will be gathered and analyzed. Before collecting data, the researcher decides whether the group to be interviewed will be a probability or nonprobability sample. Field service firms are often hired to carry out data collection. Once data have been collected, the researcher analyzes them using statistical analysis. The researcher then prepares and presents oral and written reports, with conclusions and recommendations, to management. As a final step, the researcher determines whether the recommendations were implemented and what could have been done to make the project more successful.

marketing research problem determining what information is needed and how that information can be obtained efficiently and effectively (p. 159)

marketing research objective the specific information needed to solve a marketing research problem; the objective should be to provide insightful decision-making information (p. 159)

management decision problem a broad-based problem that uses marketing research in order for managers to take proper actions (p. 160)

secondary data data previously collected for any purpose other than the one at hand (p. 160)

big data the exponential growth in the volume, variety, and velocity of information and the development of complex, new tools to analyze and create meaning from such data (p. 161)

research design specifies which research questions must be answered, how and when the data will be gathered, and how the data will be analyzed (p. 161)

primary data information that is collected for the first time; used for solving the particular problem under investigation (p. 162)

survey research the most popular technique for gathering primary data, in which a researcher interacts with people to obtain facts, opinions, and attitudes (p. 162)

mall intercept interview a survey research method that involves interviewing people in the common areas of shopping malls (p. 162)

computer-assisted personal interviewing an interviewing method in which the interviewer reads questions from a computer screen and enters the respondent's data directly into the computer (p. 163)

computer-assisted self-interviewing an interviewing method in which a mall interviewer intercepts; each respondent reads questions off the screen and directly keys his or her answers into the device (p. 163)

central-location telephone (CLT) facility a specially designed phone room used to conduct telephone interviewing (p. 163)

executive interview a type of survey that usually involves interviewing business people at their offices concerning industrial products or services (p. 164)

focus group 7 to 10 people who participate in a group discussion led by a moderator (p. 164)

open-ended question an interview question that encourages an answer phrased in the respondent's own words (p. 164)

closed-ended question an interview question that asks the respondent to make a selection from a limited list of responses (p. 164)

scaled-response question a closed-ended question designed to measure the intensity of a respondent's answer (p. 165)

observation research a research method that relies on four types of observation: people watching people, people watching an activity, machines watching people, and machines watching an activity (p. 166)

mystery shoppers researchers posing as customers togather observational data about a store (p. 166)

behavioral targeting (BT) a form of observation marketing research that combines a consumer's online activity with psychographic and demographic profiles compiled in databases (p. 166)

social media monitoring the use of automated tools to monitor online buzz, chatter, and conversations (p. 166)

ethnographic research the study of human behavior in its natural context; involves observation of behavior and physical setting (p. 166)

experiment a method of gathering primary data in which the researcher alters one or more variables while observing the effects of those alterations on another variable (p. 167)

sample a subset from a larger population (p. 168)

universe the population from which a sample will be drawn (p. 168)

probability sample a sample in which every element in the population has a known statistical likelihood of being selected (p. 168)

random sample a sample arranged in such a way that every element of the population has an equal chance of being selected as part of the sample (p. 168)

nonprobability sample any sample in which little or no attempt is made to get a representative cross section of the population (p. 168)

convenience sample a form of nonprobability sample using respondents who are convenient or readily accessible to the researcher—for example, employees, friends, or relatives (p. 168)

measurement error an error that occurs when there is a difference between the information desired by the researcher and the information provided by the measurement process (p. 169)

sampling error an error that occurs when a sample somehow does not represent the target population (p. 169)

frame error an error that occurs when a sample drawn from a population differs from the target population (p. 169)

random error an error that occurs when the selected sample is an imperfect representation of the overall population (p. 169)

field service firm a firm that specializes in interviewing respondents on a subcontracted basis (p. 170)

cross-tabulation a method of analyzing data that lets the analyst look at the responses to one question in relation to the responses to one or more other questions (p. 170)

9-3 **Discuss the profound impact of the Internet on marketing research.** The Internet has simplified the secondary data search process. Internet survey research is surging in popularity. Internet surveys can be created rapidly, are reported in real time, are relatively inexpensive, and are easily personalized.

Often, researchers use the Internet to contact respondents who are difficult to reach by other means. The Internet can also be used to conduct focus groups, to distribute research proposals and reports, and to facilitate collaboration between the client and the research supplier.

9-4 **Describe the growing importance of mobile research.** Mobile survey traffic now accounts for approximately 30 percent of interview responses. Mobile surveys are designed to fit into the brief cracks of time that open up when a person waits for a plane, is early for an appointment, commutes to work on a train, or stands in a line. Marketers strive to engage respondents in the

moment because mobile research provides immediate feedback when a consumer makes a decision to purchase, consumes a product, or experiences some form of promotion. Mobile research has also expanded into qualitative research. Using an app, respondents can participate in bulletin board and research community discussions.

9-5 **Discuss the growing importance of scanner-based research.** A scanner-based research system enables marketers to monitor a market panel's exposure and reaction to such variables as advertising, coupons, store displays, packaging, and price. By

analyzing these variables in relation to the panel's subsequent buying behavior, marketers gain useful insight into sales and marketing strategies.

scanner-based research a system for gathering information from a single group of respondents by continuously monitoring the advertising, promotion, and pricing they are exposed to and the things they buy (p. 174)

InfoScan a scanner-based sales-tracking service for the consumer packaged-goods industry (p. 175)

neuromarketing a field of marketing that studies the body's responses to marketing stimuli (p. 175)

9-6 **Explain when marketing research should be conducted.** Because acquiring marketing information can be time-consuming and costly, deciding to acquire additional decision-making information depends on managers' perceptions of its quality, price, and timing. Research, therefore, should be

undertaken only when the expected value of the information is greater than the cost of obtaining it. A customer relationship management system is integral to analyzing, transforming, and leveraging customer data.

9-7 **Explain the concept of competitive intelligence.** Intelligence is analyzed information, and it becomes decision-making intelligence when it has implications for the organization. By helping managers assess their competition and vendors,

competitive intelligence (CI) leads to fewer surprises. CI is part of a sound marketing strategy, helps companies respond to competitive threats, and helps reduce unnecessary costs.

competitive intelligence (CI) an intelligence system that helps managers assess their competition and vendors in order

to become more efficient and effective competitors (p. 176)

10-1

Define the term *product*. A product is anything, desired or not, that a person or organization receives in an exchange. The basic goal of purchasing decisions is to receive the tangible and intangible benefits associated with a product. Tangible aspects include packaging, style, color, size, and features. Intangible qualities include service, the retailer's image, the manufacturer's reputation, and the social status associated with a product. An organization's product offering is the crucial element in any marketing mix.

product everything, both favorable and unfavorable, that a person receives in an exchange (p. 179)

10-2

Classify consumer products. Consumer products are classified into four categories: convenience products, shopping products, specialty products, and unsought products. Convenience products are relatively inexpensive and require limited shopping effort. Shopping products are of two types: homogeneous and heterogeneous. Because of the similarity of homogeneous products, they are differentiated mainly by price and features. In contrast, heterogeneous products appeal to consumers because of their distinct characteristics. Specialty products possess unique benefits that are highly desirable to certain customers. Finally, unsought products are either new products or products that require aggressive selling because they are generally avoided or overlooked by consumers.

convenience product a relatively inexpensive item that merits little shopping effort (p. 179)

shopping product a product that requires comparison shopping because it is usually more expensive than a convenience product and is found in fewer stores (p. 180)

specialty product a particular item for which consumers search extensively and are very reluctant to accept substitutes (p. 180)

unsought product a product unknown to the potential buyer or a known product that the buyer does not actively seek (p. 180)

10-3

Define the terms *product item*, *product line*, and *product mix*. A product item is a specific version of a product that can be designated as a distinct offering among an organization's products. A product line is a group of closely related products offered by an organization. An organization's product mix includes all the products it sells. Product mix width refers to the number of product lines an organization offers. Product line depth is the number of product items in a product line. Firms modify existing products by changing their quality, functional characteristics, or style. Product line extension occurs when a firm adds new products to existing product lines.

EXHIBIT 10.1

COCA-COLA COMPANY'S PRODUCT LINES AND PRODUCT MIX

	Width of the Product Mix				
	Soft Drinks	**Juice**	**Water**	**Sports Drinks**	**Tea**
	Coca Cola	Minute Maid	Aquarius	Powerade	Fuze
	Coca Cola Vanilla	Orange Juice			
DEPTH	Sprite	Simply Orange	Dasani	Powerade Zero	Gold Peak sweetened
	Barq's Root Beer	Odwalla Smoothie	Dasani Sparkling		Gold Peak unsweetened
	Fresca	Honest Kids	Smartwater		Honest Tea Lemon
	Fanta		Vitamin Water		Honest Tea Raspberry

Somchai Som/Shutterstock.com

product item a specific version of a product that can be designated as a distinct offering among an organization's products (p. 180)

product line a group of closely related product items (p. 180)

product mix all products that an organization sells (p. 181)

product mix width the number of product lines an organization offers (p. 181)

product line depth the number of product items in a product line (p. 181)

product modification changing one or more of a product's characteristics (p. 182)

planned obsolescence the practice of modifying products so those that have already been sold become obsolete before they actually need replacement (p. 183)

product line extension adding additional products to an existing product line in order to compete more broadly in the industry (p. 183)

10-4

Describe marketing uses of branding. A brand is a name, term, or symbol that identifies and differentiates a firm's products. Established brands encourage customer loyalty and help new products succeed. Branding strategies require decisions about individual, family, manufacturers', and private brands.

EXHIBIT 10.3

COMPARISON OF MANUFACTURER'S AND PRIVATE BRANDS FROM THE RESELLER'S PERSPECTIVE

Key Advantages of Carrying Manufacturers' Brands	Key Advantages of Carrying Private Brands
• Heavy advertising to the consumer by manufacturers such as Procter & Gamble helps develop strong consumer loyalties.	• A wholesaler or retailer can usually earn higher profits on its own brand. In addition, because the private brand is exclusive, there is less pressure to mark down the price to meet competition.
• Well-known manufacturers' brands, such as Kodak and Fisher-Price, can attract new customers and enhance the dealer's (wholesaler's or retailer's) prestige.	• A manufacturer can decide to drop a brand or a reseller at any time or even become a direct competitor to its dealers.
• Many manufacturers offer rapid delivery, enabling the dealer to carry less inventory.	• A private brand ties the customer to the wholesaler or retailer. A person who wants a DieHard battery must go to Sears.
• If a dealer happens to sell a manufacturer's brand of poor quality, the customer may simply switch brands and remain loyal to the dealer.	• Wholesalers and retailers have no control over the intensity of distribution of manufacturers' brands. Walmart store managers don't have to worry about competing with other sellers of Sam's American Choice products or Ol' Roy dog food. They know that these brands are sold only in Walmart and Sam's Club stores.

brand a name, term, symbol, design, or combination thereof that identifies a seller's products and differentiates them from competitors' products (p. 184)

brand name that part of a brand that can be spoken, including letters, words, and numbers (p. 184)

brand mark the elements of a brand that cannot be spoken (p. 184)

brand equity the value of a company or brand name (p. 184)

global brand a brand that obtains at least a one-third of its earnings from outside its home country, is recognizable outside its home base of customers, and has publicly available marketing and financial data (p. 185)

brand loyalty consistent preference for one brand over all others (p. 185)

manufacturer's brand the brand name of a manufacturer (p. 185)

private brand a brand name owned by a wholesaler or a retailer (p. 185)

captive brand a brand manufactured by a third party for an exclusive retailer, without evidence of that retailer's affiliation (p. 186)

individual branding using different brand names for different products (p. 186)

family branding marketing several different products under the same brand name (p. 186)

co-branding placing two or more brand names on a product or its package (p. 186)

trademark the exclusive right to use a brand or part of a brand (p. 187)

service mark a trademark for a service (p. 187)

generic product name identifies a product by class or type and cannot be trademarked (p. 188)

10-5 Describe marketing uses of packaging and labeling. Packaging has four functions: containing and protecting products; promoting products; facilitating product storage, use, and convenience; and facilitating recycling and reducing environmental damage. As a tool for promotion, packaging identifies the brand and its features. It also serves the critical function of differentiating a product from competing products and linking it with related products from the same manufacturer. The label is an integral part of the package, with persuasive and informational functions. In essence, the package is the marketer's last chance to influence buyers before they make a purchase decision.

persuasive labeling a type of package labeling that focuses on a promotional theme or logo; and consumer information is secondary (p. 190)

informational labeling a type of package labeling designed to help consumers make proper product selections and lower their cognitive dissonance after the purchase (p. 190)

universal product codes (UPCs) a series of thick and thin vertical lines (bar codes) readable by computerized optical scanners that represent numbers used to track products (p. 191)

10-6 Discuss global issues in branding and packaging. In addition to brand piracy, international marketers must address a variety of concerns regarding branding and packaging, including choosing a brand name policy, translating labels and meeting host-country labeling requirements, making packages aesthetically compatible with host-country cultures, and offering the sizes of packages preferred in host countries.

Global Branding Considerations

One name

Modify or adapt one name

Different names in different markets

Global Packaging Considerations

Labeling

Aesthetics

Climate

10-7 Describe how and why product warranties are important marketing tools. Just as a package is designed to protect the product, a warranty protects the buyer and gives essential information about the product. A warranty confirms the quality or performance of a good or service. An express warranty is a written guarantee. Express warranties range from simple statements—such as "100 percent cotton" (a guarantee of quality) and "complete satisfaction guaranteed" (a statement of performance)—to extensive documents written in technical language. In contrast, an implied warranty is an unwritten guarantee that the good or service is fit for the purpose for which it was sold. All sales have an implied warranty under the Uniform Commercial Code.

Express warranty = written guarantee

Implied warranty = unwritten guarantee

warranty a confirmation of the quality or performance of a good or service (p. 193)

express warranty a written guarantee (p. 193)

implied warranty an unwritten guarantee that the good or service is fit for the purpose for which it was sold (p. 193)

11-1 **Explain the importance of developing new products and describe the six categories of new products.** New products are important to sustain growth and profits and to replace obsolete items. New products can be classified as new-to-the-world products (discontinuous innovations), new product lines, additions to existing product lines, improvements or revisions of existing products, repositioned products, or lower-priced products. To sustain or increase profits, a firm must innovate.

new product a product new to the world, the market, the producer, the seller, or some combination of these (p. 195)

11-2 **Explain the steps in the new-product development process.** First, a firm forms a new-product strategy by outlining the characteristics and roles of future products. Then new-product ideas are generated by customers, employees, distributors, competitors, vendors, and internal research and development personnel. Once a product idea has survived initial screening by an appointed screening group, it undergoes business analysis to determine its potential profitability. If a product concept seems viable, it progresses into the development phase, in which the technical and economic feasibility of the manufacturing process is evaluated. The development phase also includes laboratory and use testing of a product for performance and safety. Following initial testing and refinement, most products are introduced in a test market to evaluate consumer response and marketing strategies. Finally, test market successes are propelled into full commercialization. The commercialization process involves starting up production, building inventories, shipping to distributors, training a sales force, announcing the product to the trade, and advertising to consumers.

EXHIBIT 11.1 NEW-PRODUCT DEVELOPMENT PROCESS

1 New-product strategy
2 Idea generation
3 Idea screening
4 Business analysis
5 Development
6 Test marketing
7 Commercialization

New product

new-product strategy a plan that links the new-product development process with the objectives of the marketing department, the business unit, and the corporation (p. 196)

product development a marketing strategy that entails the creation of marketable new products; the process of converting applications for new technologies into marketable products (p. 198)

brainstorming the process of getting a group to think of unlimited ways to vary a product or solve a problem (p. 198)

screening the first filter in the product development process, which eliminates ideas that are inconsistent with the organization's new-product strategy or are obviously inappropriate for some other reason (p. 199)

concept test a test to evaluate a new-product idea, usually before any prototype has been created (p. 199)

business analysis the second stage of the screening process, where preliminary figures for demand, cost, sales, and profitability are calculated (p. 199)

development the stage in the product development process in which a prototype is developed and a marketing strategy is outlined (p. 199)

simultaneous product development a team-oriented approach to new-product development (p. 200)

test marketing the limited introduction of a product and a marketing program to determine the reactions of potential customers in a market situation (p. 201)

simulated (laboratory) market testing the presentation of advertising and other promotional materials for several products, including a test product, to members of the product's target market (p. 202)

commercialization the decision to market a product (p. 202)

11-3 **Understand why some products succeed and others fail.** Despite the amount of time and money spent on developing and testing new products, a large proportion of new-product introductions fail. Products fail for a number of reasons. Failure can be a matter of degree—absolute failure occurs when a company cannot recoup its development, marketing, and production costs, while relative product failure occurs when the product returns a profit but fails to achieve sales, profit, or market share goals.

11-4 **Discuss global issues in new-product development.** A marketer with global vision seeks to develop products that can easily be adapted to suit local needs. The goal is not simply to develop a standard product that can be sold worldwide. Smart global marketers also look for good product ideas worldwide.

11-5 **Explain the diffusion process through which new products are adopted.** The diffusion process is the spread of a new product from its producer to ultimate adopters. Adopters in the diffusion process belong to five categories: innovators, early adopters, the early majority, the late majority, and laggards. Product characteristics that affect the rate of adoption include product complexity, compatibility with existing social values, relative advantage over existing substitutes, visibility, and "trialability." The diffusion process is facilitated by word-of-mouth communication and communication from marketers to consumers.

innovation a product perceived as new by a potential adopter (p. 203)

diffusion the process by which the adoption of an innovation spreads (p. 203)

11-6 **Explain the concept of product life cycles.** All brands and product categories undergo a life cycle with four stages: introduction, growth, maturity, and decline. The rate at which products move through these stages varies dramatically.

Marketing managers use the product life cycle concept as an analytical tool to forecast a product's future and devise effective marketing strategies.

product life cycle (PLC) a concept that provides a way to trace the stages of a product's acceptance, from its introduction (birth) to its decline (death) (p. 205)

product category all brands that satisfy a particular type of need (p. 206)

introductory stage the full-scale launch of a new product into the marketplace (p. 206)

growth stage the second stage of the product life cycle, when sales typically grow at an increasing rate; many competitors enter the market; large companies may start to acquire small pioneering firms; and profits are healthy (p. 207)

maturity stage a period during which sales increase at a slower rate (p. 207)

decline stage a long-run drop in sales (p. 208)

EXHIBIT 11.2   FOUR STAGES OF THE PRODUCT LIFE CYCLE

CHAPTER 12 LEARNING OUTCOMES / KEY TERMS

12-1 **Discuss the importance of services to the economy.** The service sector plays a crucial role in the U.S. economy, accounting for approximately 80 percent of U.S. economic output.

Services have unique characteristics that distinguish them from goods, and marketing strategies need to be adjusted for these characteristics.

service the result of applying human or mechanical efforts to people or objects (p. 211)

12-2 **Discuss the differences between services and goods.** Services are distinguished by four characteristics. Services are intangible performances in that they lack clearly identifiable physical characteristics, making it difficult for marketers to communicate their specific benefits to potential customers. The production and consumption of services occurs simultaneously.

Services are heterogeneous because their quality depends on such elements as the service provider, individual consumer, location, and the like. Finally, services are perishable in the sense that they cannot be stored or saved. As a result, synchronizing supply with demand is particularly challenging in the service industry.

intangibility the inability of services to be touched, seen, tasted, heard, or felt in the same manner that goods can be sensed (p. 211)

search quality a characteristic that can be easily assessed before purchase (p. 211)

experience quality a characteristic that can be assessed only after use (p. 211)

credence quality a characteristic that consumers may have difficulty assessing even after purchase because they do not have the necessary knowledge or experience (p. 211)

inseparability the inability of the production and consumption of a service to be separated; consumers must be present during the production (p. 212)

heterogeneity the variability of the inputs and outputs of services, which causes services to tend to be less standardized and uniform than goods (p. 212)

perishability the inability of services to be stored, warehoused, or inventoried (p. 212)

12-3 **Describe the components of service quality and the gap model of service quality.** Service quality has five components: reliability (ability to perform the service dependably, accurately, and consistently), responsiveness (providing prompt service), assurance (knowledge and courtesy of employees and

their ability to convey trust), empathy (caring, individualized attention), and tangibles (physical evidence of the service).

The gap model identifies five key discrepancies that can influence customer evaluations of service quality. When the gaps are

EXHIBIT 12.1 **GAP MODEL OF SERVICE QUALITY**

The gap analysts model measures consumer perceptions of service quality. Managers use the model to analyze sources of quality problems and to understand how service quality can be improved.

Source: Based on Valarie A. Zeithaml, Mary Jo Bitner, and Dwayne Gremler, *Services Marketing*, 4/e, © 2006 (New York: McGraw-Hill, 2006).

large, service quality is low. As the gaps shrink, service quality improves. Gap 1 is found between customers' expectations and management's perceptions of those expectations. Gap 2 is found between management's perception of what the customer wants and specifications for service quality. Gap 3 is found between service quality specifications and delivery of the service. Gap 4 is found between service delivery and what the company promises to the customer through external communication. Gap 5 is found between customers' service expectations and their perceptions of service performance.

reliability the ability to perform a service dependably, accurately, and consistently (p. 212)

responsiveness the ability to provide prompt service (p. 212)

assurance the knowledge and courtesy of employees and their ability to convey trust (p. 213)

empathy caring, individualized attention to customers (p. 213)

tangibles the physical evidence of a service, including the physical facilities, tools, and equipment used to provide the service (p. 213)

gap model a model identifying five gaps that can cause problems in service delivery and influence customer evaluations of service quality (p. 213)

12-4 **Develop marketing mixes for services.** "Product" (service) strategy issues include what is being processed (people, possessions, mental stimulus, information), core and supplementary services, customization versus standardization, and the service mix. Distribution (place) decisions involve convenience, number of outlets, direct versus indirect distribution, and scheduling. Stressing tangible cues, using personal sources of information, creating strong organizational images, and engaging in postpurchase communication are effective promotion strategies. Pricing objectives for services can be revenue oriented, operations oriented, patronage oriented, or any combination of the three.

core service the most basic benefit the consumer is buying (p. 215)

supplementary services a group of services that support or enhance the core service (p. 215)

mass customization a strategy that uses technology to deliver customized services on a mass basis (p. 216)

12-5 **Discuss relationship marketing in services.** Relationship marketing in services involves attracting, developing, and retaining customer relationships. There are four levels of relationship marketing: level 1 focuses on pricing incentives; level 2 uses pricing incentives and social bonds with customers; level 3 focuses on customization; and level 4 uses pricing, social bonds, and structural bonds to build long-term relationships.

12-6 **Explain internal marketing in services.** Internal marketing means treating employees as customers and developing systems and benefits that satisfy their needs. Employees who like their jobs and are happy with the firm they work for are more likely to deliver good service.

internal marketing treating employees as customers and developing systems and benefits that satisfy their needs (p. 219)

12-7 **Describe nonprofit organization marketing.** Nonprofit organizations pursue goals other than profit, market share, and return on investment. Nonprofit organization marketing facilitates mutually satisfying exchanges between nonprofit organizations and their target markets. Several unique characteristics distinguish nonbusiness marketing strategy, including a concern with services and social behaviors rather than manufactured goods and profit; a difficult, undifferentiated, and in some ways marginal target market; a complex product that may have only indirect benefits and elicit very low involvement; distribution that may or may not require special facilities depending on the service provided; a relative lack of resources for promotion; and prices only indirectly related to the exchange between the producer and the consumer of services.

nonprofit organization an organization that exists to achieve some goal other than the usual business goals of profit, market share, or return on investment (p. 219)

nonprofit organization marketing the effort by nonprofit organizations to bring about mutually satisfying exchanges with target markets (p. 220)

public service advertisement (PSA) an announcement that promotes a program of a federal, state, or local government or of a nonprofit organization (p. 222)

12-8 **Discuss global issues in services marketing.** The United States has become the world's largest exporter of services. Although competition is keen, the United States has a competitive advantage because of its vast experience in many service industries. To be successful globally, service firms must adjust their marketing mix for the environment of each target country.

13-1 Define the terms *supply chain* and *supply chain management*, and discuss the benefits of supply chain management. Management coordinates and integrates all of the activities performed by supply chain members into a seamless process from the source to the point of consumption. The benefits of supply chain management include reduced inventory, transportation, warehousing, and packaging costs; greater supply chain flexibility; improved customer service; and higher revenues.

supply chain the connected chain of all of the business entities, both internal and external to the company, that perform or support the logistics function (p. 225)

supply chain management a management system that coordinates and integrates all of the activities performed by supply chain members into a seamless process, from the source to the point of consumption, resulting in enhanced customer and economic value (p. 225)

supply chain agility an operational strategy focused on creating inventory velocity and operational flexibility simultaneously in the supply chain (p. 225)

outsourcing (contract logistics) a manufacturer's or supplier's use of an independent third party to manage an entire function of the logistics system, such as transportation, warehousing, or order processing (p. 226)

third-party logistics company (3PL) a firm that provides functional logistics services to others (p. 226)

reshoring the reinstitutionalization of a business process from an outsource location/country back to the original location for the purpose of gaining economic advantage (p. 226)

nearshoring the transfer of an outsourced activity from a distant to a nearby country (p. 226)

RFID radio-frequency identification; a device that uses radio waves as a means of locating a piece of inventory within a confined geographic space (p. 227)

13-2 Discuss the concepts of internal and external supply chain integration and explain why each of these types of integration is important. In the modern supply chain, integration can be either internal or external. Internally, the very best companies develop a managerial orientation toward demand-supply integration. Externally, five types of integration are sought by firms interested in providing top-level service to customers: relationship integration, measurement integration, technology and planning integration, material and service supplier integration, and customer integration.

supply chain orientation a system of management practices that are consistent with a "systems thinking" approach (p. 227)

supply chain integration when multiple firms or business functions in a supply chain coordinate, their activities and processes so that they are seamlessly linked to one another in an effort to satisfy the customer (p. 227)

demand-supply integration (DSI) a supply chain operational philosophy focused on integrating the supply-management and demand-generating functions of an organization (p. 227)

13-3 Identify the eight key processes of excellent supply chain management, and discuss how each of these processes affects the end customer. The key processes that leading supply chain companies focus on are (1) customer relationship management, (2) customer service management, (3) demand management, (4) order fulfillment, (5) manufacturing flow management, (6) supplier relationship management, (7) product development and commercialization, and (8) returns management.

business processes bundles of interconnected activities that stretch across firms in the supply chain (p. 229)

customer relationship management (CRM) process allows companies to prioritize their marketing focus on different customer groups according to each group's long-term value to the company or supply chain (p. 229)

customer service management process presents a multicompany, unified response system to the customer whenever complaints, concerns, questions, or comments are voiced (p. 229)

demand management process seeks to align supply and demand throughout the supply chain by anticipating customer requirements at each level and creating demand-related plans of action prior to actual customer purchases (p. 230)

sales and operations planning (S&OP) a method companies use to align production with demand by merging tactical and strategic planning methods across functional areas of the business (p. 230)

order fulfillment process a highly integrated process, often requiring persons from multiple companies and multiple functions to come together and coordinate to create customer satisfaction at a given place and time (p. 230)

order cycle time the time delay between the placement of a customer's order and the customer's receipt of that order (p. 230)

manufacturing flow management process concerned with ensuring that firms in the supply chain have the needed resources to manufacture with flexibility and to move products through a multi-stage production process (p. 231)

modular a standardized form of component parts manufacturing designed so the parts are easily replaced or interchanged (p. 231)

supplier relationship management process supports manufacturing flow by identifying and maintaining relationships with highly valued suppliers (p. 231)

product development and commercialization process includes the group of activities that facilitates the joint development and marketing of new offerings among a group of supply chain partner firms (p. 231)

returns management process enables firms to manage volumes of returned product efficiently while minimizing returns-related costs and maximizing the value of the returned assets to the firms in the supply chain (p. 232)

13-4 **Understand the importance of sustainable supply chain management to modern business operations.** Sustainable supply chain management involves the integration and balancing of environmental, social, and economic thinking into all phases of the supply chain management process.

sustainable supply chain management a supply chain management philosophy that embraces the need for optimizing social and environmental costs in addition to financial costs (p. 232)

triple bottom line the financial, social, and environmental effects of a firm's policies and actions that determine its viability as a sustainable organization (p. 233)

greenwashing when a firm publicly feigns support for environmental or social sustainability but fails to live up to these standards in practice (p. 233)

13-5 **Discuss how new technology and emerging trends are impacting the practice of supply chain management.** Some of the business trends affecting supply chain management include outsourcing logistics, public-private partnerships, electronic distribution, maintaining a secure supply chain, and new analytics tools. While these changes exert pressure on managers to change the way their supply chains function, they also help make supply chain management more integrated and easier to track.

digitalization the use of digital technologies to change a business model and provide new revenue or value (p. 234)

Internet of Things (IoT) a system of interrelated computing devices, mechanical and digital machines, objects, animals, or people that are connected and able to transfer data over a network without overt human effort (p. 234)

big data the rapidly collected and difficult-to-process large-scale data sets that have recently emerged and push the limits of current analytical capability (p. 234)

supply chain analytics data analyses that support the improved design and management of the supply chain (p. 234)

artificial intelligence (AI) the computer science area focused on making machines that can simulate human intelligence processes (p. 235)

machine learning (ML) an application of artificial intelligence that provides systems the ability to automatically learn and improve from experience without being explicitly programmed (p. 235)

cloud computing the practice of using remote network servers to store, manage, and process data (p. 235)

advanced robotics devices that act largely or partially autonomously, that interact physically with people or their environment, and that are capable of modifying their behavior based on sensor data (p. 235)

automated vehicles cars, trucks, or other ground transportation modes for which human drivers are not required to take control to safely operate the vehicle (p. 235)

drones unmanned aerial vehicles that can be controlled remotely or can fly autonomously when executing a task (p. 235)

digital distribution includes any kind of product or service that can be distributed electronically, whether over traditional forms such as fiber-optic cable or through satellite transmission of electronic signals (p. 236)

three-dimensional printing (3DP) the creation of three-dimensional objects via an additive manufacturing (printing) technology that layers raw material into desired shapes (p. 236)

supply chain traceability the degree to which a business is able to track a product's development through stages beginning with a raw material state and ending with delivery to the final consumer (p. 237)

blockchain a digital ledger in which transactions are made and recorded chronologically and publicly (p. 237)

13-6 **Explain what marketing channels and channel intermediaries are, and describe their functions and activities.** A marketing channel is a business structure of interdependent organizations that reach from the point of production to the consumer. Intermediaries negotiate with one another, buy and sell products, and facilitate the change of ownership between buyer and seller. Retailers are those firms in the channel that sell directly to consumers.

marketing channel (channel of distribution) a set of interdependent organizations that eases the transfer of ownership as products move from producer to business user or consumer (p. 237)

channel members all parties in the marketing channel who negotiate with one another, buy and sell products, and facilitate the change of ownership between buyer and seller in the course of moving the product from the manufacturer into the hands of the final consumer (p. 237)

form utility the elements of the composition and appearance of a product that make it desirable (p. 238)

time utility the increase in customer satisfaction gained by making a good or service available at the appropriate time (p. 238)

place utility the usefulness of a good or service as a function of the location at which it is made available (p. 238)

exchange utility the increased value of a product that is created as its ownership is transferred (p. 238)

merchant wholesaler an institution that buys goods from manufacturers and resells them to businesses, government agencies, and other wholesalers or retailers and that receives and takes title to goods, stores them in its own warehouses, and later ships them (p. 238)

agents and brokers wholesaling intermediaries who do not take title to a product, but facilitate its sale from producer to end user by representing retailers, wholesalers, or manufacturers (p. 239)

retailer a channel intermediary that sells mainly to consumers (p. 239)

EXHIBIT 13.1 HOW MARKETING CHANNELS REDUCE THE NUMBER OF REQUIRED TRANSACTIONS

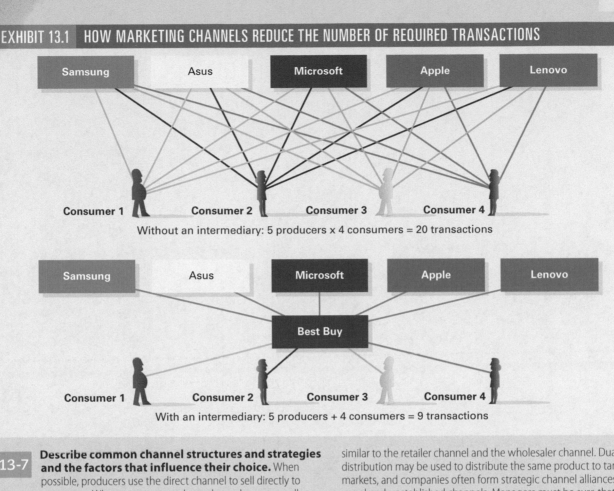

Without an intermediary: 5 producers x 4 consumers = 20 transactions

With an intermediary: 5 producers + 4 consumers = 9 transactions

13-7 **Describe common channel structures and strategies and the factors that influence their choice.** When possible, producers use the direct channel to sell directly to consumers. When one or more channel members are small companies, an agent/broker channel may be the best solution. Most consumer products are sold through distribution channels similar to the retailer channel and the wholesaler channel. Dual distribution may be used to distribute the same product to target markets, and companies often form strategic channel alliances to use already-established channels. Managers must be sure that the channel strategy chosen is consistent with market factors, product factors, and producer factors.

direct channel a distribution channel in which producers sell directly to consumers (p. 240)

dual or multiple distribution the use of two or more channels to distribute the same product to target markets (p. 242)

nontraditional channels nonphysical channels that facilitate the unique market access of products and services (p. 242)

strategic channel alliance a cooperative agreement between business firms to use the other's already established distribution channel (p. 242)

gray marketing channels secondary channels that are unintended to be used by the producer, and which often flow illegally obtained or counterfeit product toward customers (p. 243)

reverse channels channels that enable customers to return products or components for reuse or remanufacturing (p. 243)

drop and shop a system used by several retailers that allows customers to bring used products for return or donation at the entrance of the store (p. 243)

digital channels electronic pathways that allow products and related information to flow from producer to consumer (p. 243)

M-commerce the ability to conduct commerce using a mobile device for the purpose of buying or selling goods or services (p. 243)

intensive distribution a form of distribution aimed at having a product available in every outlet where target customers might want to buy it (p. 246)

selective distribution a form of distribution achieved by screening dealers to eliminate all but a few in any single area (p. 247)

exclusive distribution distribution to only one or a few dealers within a given area (p. 247)

13-8 **Discuss multichannel and omnichannel marketing in both B-to-B and B-to-C structures, and explain why these concepts are important.** In multichannel marketing strategies customers are offered information, goods, services, and/or support through one or more synchronized channels. While it can promote better consumer behavior, the multichannel design also creates redundancy and complexity in the firm's distribution system. Many companies are transitioning to omnichannel distribution operations that support their multichannel retail operations and unify their retail interfaces.

CHAPTER 14 LEARNING OUTCOMES / KEY TERMS

14-1 **Explain the importance of the retailer within the channel and the U.S. economy.** Retailing represents all the activities directly related to the sale of goods and services to the ultimate consumer for personal, nonbusiness use, and has enhanced the quality of our daily lives. When we shop for groceries, hair styling, clothes, books, and many other products and services, we are doing business with retailers. Retailing affects all people directly or indirectly. Trends and innovations relating to customer data, social media, and alternative forms of shopping are constantly developing, and retailers have no choice but to react.

retailing all the activities directly related to the sale of goods and services to the ultimate consumer for personal, nonbusiness use (p. 251)

retailer a channel intermediary that sells mainly to consumers (p. 251)

14-2 **List and understand the different types of retailers.** Retail establishments can be classified according to ownership, level of service, product assortment, and price. These variables can be combined in several ways to create various retail operating models. Retail ownership takes one of three forms: independent, part of a chain, or a franchise outlet. The service levels that retailers provide range from full-service to self-service. Retailers can also be categorized by the width and depth of their product lines. Price is the fourth way to position retail stores. Many stores fall into the basic types of retailers, but some companies have begun to experiment with alternative formats.

independent retailer a retailer owned by a single person or partnership and not operated as part of a larger retail institution (p. 251)

chain store a store that is part of a group of the same stores owned and operated by a single organization (p. 251)

franchise a relationship in which the business rights to operate and sell a product are granted by the franchisor to the franchisee (p. 251)

franchisor the originator of a trade name, product, methods of operation, and the like that grants operating rights to another party to sell its product (p. 252)

franchisee an individual or business that is granted the right to sell another party's product (p. 252)

gross margin the amount of money the retailer makes as a percentage of sales after the cost of goods sold is subtracted (p. 253)

department store a store housing several departments under one roof (p. 253)

specialty store a retail store specializing in a given type of merchandise (p. 253)

supermarket a large, departmentalized, self-service retailer that specializes in food and some nonfood items (p. 253)

drugstore a retail store that stocks pharmacy-related products and services as its main draw (p. 253)

convenience store a miniature supermarket, carrying only a limited line of high-turnover convenience goods (p. 254)

discount store a retailer that competes on the basis of low prices, high turnover, and high volume (p. 254)

full-line discount store a discount store that carries a vast depth and breadth of product within a single product category (p. 254)

supercenter a large retailer that stocks and sells a wide variety of merchandise including groceries, clothing, household goods, and other general merchandise (p. 254)

specialty discount store a retail store that offers a nearly complete selection of single-line merchandise and uses self-service, discount prices, high volume, and high turnover (p. 254)

category killer a large discount store that specializes in a single line of merchandise and becomes the dominant retailer in its category (p. 254)

warehouse club a large, no-frills retailer that sells bulk quantities of merchandise to customers at volume discount prices in exchange for a periodic membership fee (p. 254)

off-price retailer a retailer that sells at prices 25 percent or more below traditional department store prices because it pays cash for its stock and usually doesn't ask for return privileges (p. 254)

factory outlet an off-price retailer that is owned and operated by a manufacturer (p. 254)

used goods retailer a retailer whereby items purchased from one of the other types of retailers are resold to different customers (p. 254)

restaurant a retailer that provides both tangible products—food and drink—and valuable services—food preparation and presentation (p. 254)

14-3 **Explain why nonstore retailing is on the rise, and list the advantages of its different forms.** Nonstore retailing enables customers to shop without visiting a physical store location. It adds a level of convenience for customers who wish to shop from their current locations. Due to broader changes in culture and society, nonstore retailing is currently growing faster than in-store retailing.

nonstore retailing shopping without visiting a store (p. 254)

automatic vending the use of machines to offer goods for sale (p. 255)

self-service technologies (SST) technological interfaces that allow customers to provide themselves with products and/or services without the intervention of a service employee (p. 256)

direct retailing the selling of products by representatives who work door-to-door, office-to-office, or at home sales parties (p. 256)

direct marketing (DM) techniques used to get consumers to make a purchase from their home, office, or other nonretail setting (p. 256)

telemarketing the use of the telephone to sell directly to consumers (p. 256)

direct mail the delivery of advertising or marketing material to recipients of postal or electronic mail (p. 256)

microtargeting the use of direct marketing techniques that employ highly detailed data analytics in order to isolate potential customers with great precision (p. 256)

shop-at-home television network a specialized form of direct response marketing whereby television shows display merchandise, with the retail price, to home viewers (p. 257)

online retailing (e-tailing) a type of shopping available to consumers with personal computers and access to the Internet (p. 257)

sharing economy the way connected consumers exchange goods and services with each other through a digital marketplace (p. 257)

14-4 **Discuss the different retail operations models, and understand why they vary in strategy and format.** Retail formats are co-aligned with unique operating models that guide the decisions made by their managers. Each operating model can be summarized as a set of guiding principles. Today, most retail stores remain operationally and tactically similar to those that have been in business for hundreds of years; with one or more physical locations that the customer must visit in order to purchase a stocked product, and with strategies in place to attract customers to visit.

floor stock inventory displayed for sale to customers (p. 258)

back stock inventory held in reserve for potential future sale in a retailer's storeroom or stockroom (p. 258)

14-5 **Explain how retail marketing strategies are developed and executed.** Retail managers develop marketing strategies based on the goals established by stakeholders and the overall strategic plans developed by company leadership. Strategic retailing goals typically focus on increasing total sales, reducing costs of goods sold, and improving financial ratios such as return on assets or equity. The first and foremost task in developing a retail strategy is to define the target market. Then comes combining the elements of the retailing mix to come up with a single retailing method to attract that target market.

EXHIBIT 14.2   THE RETAILING MIX

Product — Width and depth of product assortment

Place (distribution) — Location and hours

Promotion — Advertising, publicity, and public relations

Price

Presentation — Layout and atmosphere

Personnel — Customer service and personal selling

Target market

CHAPTER 14 LEARNING OUTCOMES / KEY TERMS

retailing mix a combination of the six Ps—product, promotion, place, price, presentation, and personnel—to sell goods and services to the ultimate consumer (p. 260)

brand cannibalization the reduction of sales for one brand as the result of the introduction of a new product or promotion of a current product by another brand (p. 260)

destination store a store that consumers purposely plan to visit prior to shopping (p. 262)

atmosphere the overall impression conveyed by a store's physical layout, decor, and surroundings (p. 263)

layout the internal design and configuration of a store's fixtures and products (p. 264)

shopper marketing understanding how one's target consumers behave as shoppers, in different channels and formats, and leveraging this intelligence to generate sales or other positive outcomes (p. 264)

shopper analytics searching for and discovering meaningful patterns in shopper data for the purpose of fine-tuning, developing, or changing market offerings (p. 265)

14-6 Discuss how services retailing differs from goods retailing. The fastest-growing part of our economy is the service sector. Although distribution in the service sector is difficult to visualize, the same skills, techniques, and strategies used to manage inventory can also be used to manage service inventory, such as hospital beds, bank accounts, or airline seats. Because service industries are so customer oriented, service quality is a priority.

14-7 Understand how retailers address product/service failures and discuss the opportunities that service failures provide. No retailer can be everything to every customer, and by making strategic decisions related to targeting, segmentation, and the retailing mix, retailers implicitly decide which customers will be delighted and which will probably leave the store unsatisfied. The best retailers have plans in place not only to recover from inevitable lapses in service but also perhaps even to benefit from them.

14-8 Summarize current trends related to customer data, analytics, and technology. Retailers are constantly innovating. They are always looking for new products and services (or ways to offer them) that will attract new customers or inspire current ones to buy in greater quantities or more frequently. Big data analytics, shopper marketing, mobile technology, and social media are at the front of this innovation. Some retailers have turned to channel omnification, while others have embraced click-and-collect.

big data analytics the process of discovering patterns in large data sets for the purposes of extracting knowledge and understanding human behavior (p. 266)

beacon a device that sends out connecting signals to customers' smartphones and tablets in order to bring them into a retail store or improve their shopping experience (p. 266)

retail channel omnification the reduction of multiple retail channel systems into a single, unified system for the purpose of creating efficiencies or saving costs (p. 268)

click-and-collect the practice of buying something online and then traveling to a physical store location to take delivery of the merchandise (p. 269)

CHAPTER 15 LEARNING OUTCOMES / KEY TERMS

15-1 **Discuss the role of promotion in the marketing mix.**
Promotional strategy is the plan for using the elements of promotion—advertising, public relations, sales promotion, personal selling, and social media—to meet the firm's overall objectives and marketing goals. Based on these objectives, the elements of the promotional strategy become a coordinated promotion plan. The promotion plan then becomes an integral part of the total marketing strategy for reaching the target market along with product, distribution, and price. Promotional strategies have changed a great deal over the years as many target customer segments have become harder and harder to reach.

promotion communication by marketers that informs, persuades, and reminds potential buyers of a product in order to influence an opinion or elicit a response (p. 271)

promotional strategy a plan for the optimal use of the elements of promotion: advertising, public relations, personal selling, sales promotion, and social media (p. 271)

competitive advantage one or more unique aspects of an organization that cause target consumers to patronize that firm rather than competitors (p. 271)

15-2 **Describe the communication process.** The communication process has several steps. When an individual or organization has a message it wishes to convey to a target audience, it encodes that message using language and symbols familiar to the intended receiver and sends the message through a channel of communication. Noise in the transmission channel distorts the source's intended message. Reception occurs if the message falls within the receiver's frame of reference. The receiver decodes the message and usually provides feedback to the source. Normally, feedback is direct for interpersonal communication and indirect for mass communication. The Internet and social media have had an impact on the communication model in two major ways: consumers are now able to become senders, and marketers can personalize the feedback channel by initiating direct conversations with customers.

communication the process by which we exchange or share meaning through a common set of symbols (p. 272)

interpersonal communication direct, face-to-face communication between two or more people (p. 272)

mass communication the communication of a concept or message to large audiences (p. 272)

sender the originator of the message in the communication process (p. 272)

encoding the conversion of a sender's ideas and thoughts into a message, usually in the form of words or signs (p. 273)

channel a medium of communication—such as a voice, radio, or newspaper—for transmitting a message (p. 273)

noise anything that interferes with, distorts, or slows down the transmission of information (p. 273)

receiver the person who decodes a message (p. 274)

decoding interpretation of the language and symbols sent by the source through a channel (p. 274)

feedback the receiver's response to a message (p. 274)

EXHIBIT 15.2   COMMUNICATION PROCESS

15-3 **Explain the goals and tasks of promotion.** The fundamental goals of promotion are to induce, modify, or reinforce behavior by informing, persuading, reminding, and connecting. Informative promotion explains a good's or service's purpose and benefits. Promotion that informs the consumer is typically used to increase demand for a general product category or to introduce a new good or service. Persuasive promotion is designed to stimulate a purchase or an action. Promotion that persuades the consumer to buy is essential during the growth stage of the product life cycle, when competition becomes fierce. Reminder promotion is used to keep the product and brand name in the public's mind. Promotions that remind are generally used during the maturity stage of the product life cycle. Connection promotion is designed to form relationships with customers and potential customers using social media. Connecting encourages customers to become brand advocates and share their experiences via social media.

15-4 **Discuss the elements of the promotional mix.** The elements of the promotional mix include advertising, public relations, sales promotion, personal selling, and social media. Advertising is a form of impersonal, one-way mass communication paid for by the source. Public relations is the function of promotion concerned with a firm's public image. Sales promotion is typically used to back up other components of the promotional mix by stimulating immediate demand. Personal selling typically involves direct communication, in person or by telephone; the seller tries to initiate a purchase by informing and persuading one or more potential buyers. Finally, social media are promotion tools used to facilitate conversations among people online.

promotional mix the combination of promotional tools—including advertising, public relations, personal selling, sales promotion, and social media—used to reach the target market and fulfill the organization's overall goals (p. 277)

advertising impersonal, one-way mass communication about a product or organization that is paid for by a marketer (p. 277)

public relations the marketing function that evaluates public attitudes, identifies areas within the organization the public may be interested in, and executes a program of action to earn public understanding and acceptance (p. 277)

publicity public information about a company, product, service, or issue appearing in the mass media as a news item (p. 278)

sales promotion marketing activities—other than personal selling, advertising, and public relations—that stimulate consumer buying and dealer effectiveness (p. 278)

personal selling a purchase situation involving a personal, paid-for communication between two people in an attempt to influence each other (p. 278)

paid media a category of promotional tactic based on the traditional advertising model, whereby a brand pays for media space (p. 280)

earned media a category of promotional tactic based on a public relations or publicity model that gets customers talking about products or services (p. 280)

owned media a new category of promotional tactic based on brands becoming publishers of their own content in order to maximize the brands' value to customers (p. 280)

15-5 **Discuss the AIDA concept and its relationship to the promotional mix.** The AIDA model outlines the four basic stages in the purchase decision-making process, which are initiated and propelled by promotional activities: (1) attention, (2) interest, (3) desire, and (4) action. The components of the promotional mix have varying levels of influence at each stage of the AIDA model. Advertising is a good tool for increasing awareness and knowledge of a good or service. Sales promotion is effective when consumers are at the purchase stage of the decision-making process. Personal selling is most effective in developing customer interest and desire.

AIDA concept a model that outlines the process for achieving promotional goals in terms of stages of consumer involvement with the message; the acronym stands for attention, interest, desire, and action (p. 281)

15-6 **Discuss the concept of integrated marketing communications.** Integrated marketing communications is the careful coordination of all promotional messages for a product or service to ensure the consistency of messages at every contact point where a company meets the consumer—advertising, sales promotion, personal selling, public relations, and social media, as well as direct marketing, packaging, and other forms of communication. Marketing managers carefully coordinate all promotional activities to ensure that consumers see and hear one message. Integrated marketing communications has received more attention in recent years due to the proliferation of media choices, the fragmentation of mass markets into more segmented niches, and the decrease in advertising spending in favor of promotional techniques that generate an immediate sales response.

integrated marketing communications (IMC) the careful coordination of all promotional messages for a product or a service to ensure the consistency of messages at every point at which a company has contact with the consumer (p. 283)

CHAPTER 15 LEARNING OUTCOMES / KEY TERMS

15-7

Describe the factors that affect the promotional mix.
Promotion managers consider many factors when creating promotional mixes. These factors include the nature of the product, product life cycle stage, target market characteristics, the type of buying decision involved, availability of funds, and feasibility of push or pull strategies. As products move through different stages of the product life cycle, marketers will choose to use different promotional elements. Characteristics of the target market, such as geographic location of potential buyers and brand loyalty, influence the promotional mix, as does whether the buying decision is complex or routine. The amount of funds a firm has to allocate to promotion may also help determine the promotional mix. Last, if a firm uses a push strategy to promote the product or service, the marketing manager might choose to use aggressive advertising and personal selling to wholesalers and retailers. If a pull strategy is chosen, then the manager often relies on aggressive mass promotion, such as advertising and sales promotion, to stimulate consumer demand.

CHAPTER 16 LEARNING OUTCOMES / KEY TERMS

16-1 Discuss the effects of advertising on market share and consumers. Advertising helps marketers increase or maintain brand awareness and, subsequently, market share. Typically, more is spent to advertise new brands with a small market share than to advertise older brands. Brands with a large market share use advertising mainly to maintain their share of the market. Although advertising can seldom change strongly held consumer attitudes and values, it may transform a consumer's negative attitude toward a product into a positive one. By emphasizing different brand attributes, advertisers can change their appeal in response to consumers' changing needs or try to achieve an advantage over competing brands.

advertising response function a phenomenon in which spending for advertising and sales promotion increases sales or market share up to a certain level but then produces diminishing returns (p. 289)

16-2 Identify the major types of advertising. Advertising is any form of nonpersonal, paid communication in which the sponsor or company is identified. The two major types of advertising are institutional advertising and product advertising. Institutional advertising is not product oriented; rather, its purpose is to foster a positive company image among the general public, investment community, customers, and employees. Product advertising is designed mainly to promote goods and services, and it is classified into three main categories: pioneering, competitive, and comparative. A product's place in the product life cycle is a major determinant of the type of advertising used to promote it.

institutional advertising a form of advertising designed to enhance a company's image rather than promote a particular product (p. 290)

product advertising a form of advertising that touts the benefits of a specific good or service (p. 290)

advocacy advertising a form of advertising in which an organization expresses its views on controversial issues or responds to media attacks (p. 290)

pioneering advertising a form of advertising designed to stimulate primary demand for a new product or product category (p. 291)

competitive advertising a form of advertising designed to influence demand for a specific brand (p. 291)

comparative advertising a form of advertising that compares two or more specifically named or shown competing brands on one or more specific attributes (p. 291)

16-3 Discuss the creative decisions in developing an advertising campaign. Before any creative work can begin on an advertising campaign, it is important to determine what goals or objectives the advertising should achieve. The objectives of a specific advertising campaign often depend on the overall corporate objectives and the product being advertised and are often determined using the DAGMAR approach. Once objectives are defined, creative work can begin (e.g., identifying the product's benefits, developing possible advertising appeals, evaluating and selecting the advertising appeals, executing the advertising message, and evaluating the effectiveness of the campaign).

advertising campaign a series of related advertisements focusing on a common theme, slogan, and set of advertising appeals (p. 292)

advertising objective a specific communication task that a campaign should accomplish for a specified target audience during a specified period (p. 293)

advertising appeal a reason for a person to buy a product (p. 294)

unique selling proposition a desirable, exclusive, and believable advertising appeal selected as the theme for a campaign (p. 294)

EXHIBIT 16.1	COMMON ADVERTISING APPEALS
Appeal	**Goal**
Profit	Lets consumers know whether the product will save them money, make them money, or keep them from losing money.
Health	Appeals to those who are body conscious or who want to be healthy; love or romance is used often in selling cosmetics and perfumes.
Fear	Can center around social embarrassment, growing old, or losing one's health; because of its power, requires advertiser to exercise care in execution.
Admiration	Frequently highlights celebrity spokespeople.
Convenience	Is often used for fast-food restaurants and microwavable foods.
Fun and Pleasure	Are the keys to advertising vacations, beer, amusement parks, and more.
Vanity and Egotism	Are used most often for expensive or conspicuous items such as cars and clothing.
Environmental Consciousness	Centers around protecting the environment and being considerate of others in the community.

cost per contact (cost per thousand or [CPM]) the cost of reaching one member of the target market (p. 299)

cost per click the cost associated with a consumer clicking on a display or banner ad (p. 300)

reach the number of target consumers exposed to a commercial at least once during a specific period, usually four weeks (p. 300)

frequency the number of times an individual is exposed to a given message during a specific period (p. 300)

audience selectivity the ability of an advertising medium to reach a precisely defined market (p. 300)

media schedule designation of the media, the specific publications or programs, and the insertion dates of advertising (p. 301)

continuous media schedule a media scheduling strategy in which advertising is run steadily throughout the advertising period; used for products in the later stages of the product life cycle (p. 301)

flighted media schedule a media scheduling strategy in which ads are run

heavily every other month or every two weeks to achieve a greater impact with an increased frequency and reach at those times (p. 301)

pulsing media schedule a media scheduling strategy that uses continuous scheduling throughout the year coupled with a flighted schedule during the best sales periods (p. 301)

seasonal media schedule a media scheduling strategy that runs advertising only during times of the year when the product is most likely to be used (p. 302)

16-5 **Discuss the role of public relations in the promotional mix.** Public relations is a vital part of a firm's promotional mix. A company fosters good publicity to enhance its image and promote its products. Popular public relations tools include new-product publicity, product placement, consumer education, sponsorship, and company websites. An equally important aspect of public relations is managing unfavorable publicity in a way that is least damaging to a firm's image.

public relations the element in the promotional mix that evaluates public attitudes, identifies issues that may elicit public concern, and executes programs to gain public understanding and acceptance (p. 302)

publicity an effort to capture media attention, often initiated through press releases that further a corporation's public relations plans (p. 302)

product placement a public relations strategy that involves getting a product, service, or company name to appear in a movie, television show, radio program, magazine, newspaper, video game, video or audio clip, book, or commercial for another product, on the Internet, or at special events (p. 302)

sponsorship a public relations strategy in which a company spends money to

support an issue, cause, or event that is consistent with corporate objectives, such as improving brand awareness or enhancing corporate image (p. 303)

crisis management a coordinated effort to handle all the effects of unfavorable publicity or another unexpected unfavorable event (p. 304)

16-6 **Define and state the objectives of sales promotion and the tools used to achieve them.** Marketing managers can use sales promotion to increase the effectiveness of their promotional efforts. Sales promotion can target either trade or consumer markets. Trade promotions may push a product through the distribution channel using sales contests, premiums, POP displays, trade allowances, push money, training, free merchandise, store demonstrations, and business meetings. Consumer promotions may push a product through the distribution channel using coupons, rebates, premiums, loyalty marketing programs or frequent buyer programs, contests, sweepstakes, sampling, and POP displays.

sales promotion marketing communication activities other than advertising, personal selling, and public relations, in which a short-term incentive motivates consumers or members of the distribution channel to purchase a good or service immediately, either by lowering the price or by adding value (p. 304)

trade sales promotion promotion activities directed to members of the marketing channel, such as wholesalers and retailers (p. 304)

consumer sales promotion promotion activities targeted to the ultimate consumer market (p. 304)

trade allowance a price reduction offered by manufacturers to intermediaries such as wholesalers and retailers (p. 305)

push money money offered to channel intermediaries to encourage them to "push" products—that is, to encourage other members of the channel to sell the products (p. 305)

coupon a certificate that entitles a consumers to an immediate price reduction when the product is purchased. (p. 306)

rebate a cash refund given for the purchase of a product during a specific period (p. 307)

premium an extra item offered to the consumer, usually in exchange for some proof of purchase of the promoted product (p. 307)

loyalty marketing program a promotional program designed to build long-term, mutually beneficial relationships between a company and its key customers (p. 308)

frequent-buyer program a loyalty program in which loyal consumers are rewarded for making multiple purchases of a particular good or service (p. 308)

sampling a promotional program that allows the consumer the opportunity to try a product or service for free (p. 308)

point of purchase (POP) display a promotional display set up at the retailer's location to build traffic, advertise the product, or induce impulse buying (p. 309)

17-1 Understand the sales environment. Salespeople can be consumer-focused (as in the case of retail) or business-focused. The sales environment changes constantly as new competitors enter the market and old competitors leave. The ways that customers interact with salespeople and learn about products and suppliers are changing due to the rapid increase in new sales technologies. In order for companies to successfully sell products or services using a sales force, they must be very effective at personal selling, sales management, customer relationship management, and technology—all of which play critical roles in building strong long-term relationships with customers.

17-2 Describe personal selling. Personal selling is direct communication between a sales representative and one or more prospective buyers in an attempt to influence each other in a purchase situation. Broadly speaking, all business-people use personal selling to promote themselves and their ideas. Personal selling offers several advantages over other forms of promotion. Generally speaking, personal selling becomes more important as the number of potential customers decreases, as the complexity of the product increases, and as the value of the product grows. Technology plays an increasingly important role in personal selling. If salespeople do not stay well informed about the products they're selling, consumers may enter the store knowing even more than they do.

17-3 Discuss technology's impact, including social media, on the sales environment

EXHIBIT 17.1	COMPARISON OF PERSONAL SELLING AND ADVERTISING/ SALES PROMOTION
Personal selling is more important if . . .	**Advertising and sales promotion are more important if . . .**
The product has a high value.	The product has a low value.
It is a custom-made product.	It is a standardized product.
There are few customers.	There are many customers.
The product is technically complex.	The product is easy to understand.
Customers are concentrated.	Customers are geographically dispersed.
Examples: Insurance policies, custom windows, airplane engines	**Examples:** Soap, magazine subscriptions, cotton T-shirts

17-4 Discuss the key differences between relationship selling and transactional selling. Relationship selling is the practice of building, maintaining, and enhancing interactions with customers to develop long-term satisfaction through mutually beneficial partnerships. Traditional selling, on the other hand, is transaction focused. That is, the salesperson is most concerned with making a one-time sale and moving on to the next prospect. Salespeople practicing relationship selling spend more time understanding a prospect's needs and developing solutions to meet those needs.

relationship selling (consultative selling) a sales practice that involves building, maintaining, and enhancing interactions with customers in order to develop long-term satisfaction through mutually beneficial partnerships (p. 313)

17-5 List and explain the steps in the selling process. The selling process is composed of seven basic steps: (1) generating leads, (2) qualifying leads, (3) approaching the customer and probing needs, (4) developing and proposing solutions, (5) handling objections, (6) closing the sale, and (7) following up. The actual sales process depends on the features of the product or service, characteristics of customer segments, and internal processes in place within the firm (such as how leads are gathered). Some sales take only a few minutes to complete, but others may take much longer. Like other forms of promotion, the steps of selling follow the AIDA concept.

sales process (sales cycle) the set of steps a salesperson goes through in a particular organization to sell a particular product or service (p. 314)

lead generation (prospecting) identification of the firms and people most likely to buy the seller's offerings (p. 314)

cold calling a form of lead generation in which the salesperson approaches potential buyers without any prior knowledge of the prospects' needs or financial status (p. 315)

referral a recommendation to a salesperson from a customer or business associate (p. 315)

networking a process of finding out about potential clients from friends, business contacts, coworkers, acquaintances, and fellow members in professional and civic organizations (p. 315)

lead qualification determination of a sales prospect's (1) recognized need, (2) buying power, and (3) receptivity and accessibility (p. 315)

preapproach a process that describes the "homework" that must be done by a salesperson before he or she contacts a prospect (p. 316)

needs assessment a determination of the customer's specific needs and wants and the range of options they have for satisfying them (p. 316)

sales proposal a formal written document or professional presentation that outlines how the salesperson's product or service will meet or exceed the prospect's needs (p. 318)

sales presentation a meeting in which the salesperson presents a sales proposal to a prospective buyer (p. 318)

negotiation the process during which both the salesperson and the prospect offer special concessions in an attempt to arrive at a sales agreement (p. 319)

follow-up the final step of the selling process, in which the salesperson ensures delivery schedules are met, goods or services perform as promised, and the buyers' employees are properly trained to use the products (p. 319)

17-6 **Understand the functions and roles of sales management.** The sales manager's basic job is to maximize sales at a reasonable cost while also maximizing profits. The sales manager's responsibilities include (1) defining sales goals and the sales process, (2) determining the sales force structure, (3) recruiting and training the sales force, (4) compensating and motivating the sales force, and (5) evaluating the sales force.

quota a statement of the salesperson's sales goals, usually based on sales volume (p. 320)

17-7 **Describe the use of customer relationship management in the selling process.** Companies that have CRM systems follow a customer-centric focus or model. The interaction between the customer and the organization is the foundation on which a CRM system is built. Only through effective interactions can organizations learn about the expectations of their customers, generate and manage knowledge about them, negotiate mutually satisfying commitments, and build long-term relationships. If a company has identified its best customers, then it should make every effort to maintain and increase their loyalty.

customer-centric a philosophy under which the company customizes its product and service offerings based on data generated through interactions between the customer and the company (p. 323)

knowledge management the process by which customer information is centralized and shared in order to enhance the relationship between customers and the organization (p. 323)

interaction the point at which a customer and a company representative exchange information and develop learning relationships (p. 323)

touch points areas of a business where customers have contact with the company and from which data might be gathered (p. 324)

point-of-sale interactions a touch point in stores or information kiosks that uses software to enable customers to easily provide information about themselves without feeling violated (p. 325)

campaign management developing product or service offerings customized for the appropriate customer segment and then pricing and communicating these offerings for the purpose of enhancing customer relationships (p. 326)

18-1 Describe social media, how they are used, and their relation to integrated marketing communications. Social media, commonly thought of as digital technology, offer a way for marketers to communicate one-on-one with consumers and measure the effects of those interactions. Social media include social networks, microblogs, and media sharing sites, all of which are used by the majority of adults. Smartphones and tablet computers have given consumers greater freedom to access social media on the go, which is likely to increase usage of social media sites. Many advertising budgets are allotting more money to online marketing, including social media, mobile marketing, and search marketing.

social media any tool or service that uses the Internet to facilitate conversations (p. 330)

social commerce a subset of e-commerce that involves the interaction and user contribution aspects of social online media to assist online buying and selling of products and services (p. 331)

crowdsourcing using consumers to develop and market products (p. 333)

18-2 Explain how to create a social media campaign. A social media campaign should take advantage of owned media, earned media, and paid media. To use these types of media in a social media campaign, first implement an effective listening system. Marketers can interact with negative feedback, make changes, and effectively manage their online presence. Paying attention to the ways that competing brands attract and engage with their customers can be particularly enlightening for both small businesses and global brands. Second, develop a list of objectives that reflects how social media dynamically communicate with customers and build relationships.

social media monitoring the process of identifying and assessing what is being said about a company, individual, product, or brand (p. 334)

18-3 Evaluate the various methods of measurement for social media. Most marketers have not been able to figure out how to measure the benefits of social media. Hundreds of metrics have been developed to measure social media's value, but these metrics are meaningless unless they are tied to key performance indicators. Some social media metrics to consider include buzz, interest, participation, search engine rank and results, influence, sentiment analysis, and website metrics.

18-4 Explain consumer behavior on social media. To effectively leverage social media, marketers must understand who uses social media and how they use it. If a brand's target market does not use social media, a social media campaign might not be useful. There are six categories of social media users: creators, critics, collectors, joiners, spectators, and inactives. A new category is emerging called "conversationalists," who post status updates on social networking sites or microblogs.

social media celebrities actors, singers, artists, or athletes who have millions of followers on social media platforms, typically Instagram and Twitter (p. 336)

social media stars people who have become popular because of their social media influence in a specific arena— gaming, makeup, fashion, food, and so forth (p. 336)

micro-influencers people who have a smaller number of followers on Instagram or Twitter but are still influential in specific areas (p. 337)

18-5 Describe the social media tools in a marketer's toolbox and how they are useful. A marketer has many tools to implement a social media campaign. However, new tools emerge daily, so these resources will change rapidly. Some of the strongest social media platforms are blogs, microblogs, social networks, media creation and sharing sites, social news sites, location-based social networking sites, and virtual worlds and online gaming. Blogs allow marketers and consumers to create content in the form of posts, which ideally build trust and a sense of authenticity in customers. Microblogs allow brands to follow, repost, respond to potential customers, and post content that inspires customers to engage the brand, laying a foundation for meaningful two-way conversation. Social networks allow marketers to increase awareness, target audiences, promote products, forge relationships, attract event participants, perform research, and generate new business. Media sharing sites give brands an interactive channel to disseminate content. Social news sites are useful to marketers to promote campaigns, create conversations, and build website traffic. Location-based social networking sites can forge lasting relationships and loyalty in customers. Review sites allow marketers to respond to customer reviews and comments about their brand. Online and mobile gaming are fertile grounds for branded content and advertising.

EXHIBIT 18.1 FACEBOOK LINGO

Nonindividual (Usually Corporate)	Individual
Page	Profile
Fan of a page, tells fan's friends that the user is a fan, creates mini-viral campaign	Friend a person, send private messages, write on the wall, see friend-only content
Public, searchable	Privacy options, not searchable unless user-enabled

CHAPTER REVIEW

CHAPTER 18 LEARNING OUTCOMES / KEY TERMS

blog a publicly accessible web page that functions as an interactive journal, whereby readers can post comments on the author's entries (p. 337)

corporate blogs blogs that are sponsored by a company or one of its brands and maintained by one or more of the company's employees (p. 337)

noncorporate blogs independent blogs that are not associated with the marketing efforts of any particular company or brand (p. 337)

microblogs blogs with strict post length limits (p. 338)

social networking sites websites that allow individuals to connect—or network—with friends, peers, and business associates (p. 338)

media sharing sites websites that allow users to upload and distribute multimedia content like videos and photos (p. 339)

social news sites websites that allow users to decide which content is promoted on a given website by voting that content up or down (p. 340)

location-based social networking sites websites that combine the fun of social networking with the utility of location-based GPS technology (p. 340)

review sites websites that allow consumers to post, read, rate, and comment on opinions regarding all kinds of products and services (p. 341)

18-6 **Describe the impact of mobile technology on social media.** The mobile platform is such an effective marketing tool—especially when targeting a younger audience. There are six reasons for the popularity of mobile marketing: (1) mobile platforms are standardized, (2) fewer consumers are concerned about privacy and pricing policies, (3) advertising can be done in real time, (4) mobile marketing is measurable, (5) in-store notification technology such as Apple's iBeacon can send promotional messages based on real-time interactions with customers, and (6) there is a higher response rate than with traditional advertising. Because of the rapid growth of smartphones, well-branded, integrated apps allow marketers to create buzz and generate customer engagement. Widgets allow customers to post a company's information to its site, are less expensive than apps, and broaden that company's exposure.

18-7 **Understand the aspects of developing a social media plan.** The social media plan should fit into the overall marketing plan and help marketers meet the organization's larger goals. There are six stages in creating an effective social media plan; (1) listening, (2) setting social media objectives, (3) defining strategies, (4) identifying the target audience, (5) selecting the appropriate tools and platforms, and (6) implementing and monitoring the strategy. Listening and revising the social media plan to accommodate changing market trends and needs is key to an effective social media plan.

EXHIBIT 18.2 SOCIAL MEDIA TRENDS

Trend	Change	Where Is It Now?
Fake news	The rise of intentionally misleading content	
Microsoft Office 365, Google Drive	Integrated file hosting	
Stories	Series of photos and videos that are only viewable for 24 hours	
Virtual reality and augmented reality	New mediums for content creation and sharing	
The Internet of Things	Integration into wearables, appliances, apparel, and more	
Apple Pay, Google Wallet, Bitcoin, and NFC-enabled payment options	Replacing credit cards with various forms of digital payment	
FitFabFun, Trunk Club, and NatureBox	Online and subscription-based personal shopping	
Facebook Live, Instagram Live	Live video streaming for everybody	
Chatbots	Companies using artificial intelligence to improve customer service	

19-1 **Discuss the importance of pricing decisions to the economy and to the individual firm.** Pricing plays an integral role in the U.S. economy by allocating goods and services among consumers, governments, and businesses. Pricing is essential in business because it creates revenue, which is the basis of all business activity.

price that which is given up in an exchange to acquire a good or service (p. 347)

revenue the price charged to customers multiplied by the number of units sold (p. 347)

profit revenue minus expenses (p. 348)

19-2 **List and explain a variety of pricing objectives.** Profit-oriented pricing is based on profit maximization, a satisfactory level of profit, or a target return on investment (ROI). Sales-oriented pricing focuses on either maintaining a percentage share of the market or maximizing dollar or unit sales. Status quo pricing aims to maintain the status quo by matching competitors' prices.

EXHIBIT 19.1	TWO WAYS TO MEASURE MARKET SHARE (UNITS AND REVENUE)				
Company	Units Sold	Unit Price	Total Revenue	Unit Market Share	Revenue Market Share
A	1,000	$1.00	$1,000	50	25
B	200	4.00	800	10	20
C	500	2.00	1,000	25	25
D	300	4.00	1,200	15	30
Total	2,000		$4,000		

return on investment (ROI) net profit after taxes divided by total assets (p. 348)

market share a company's product sales as a percentage of total sales for that industry (p. 349)

status quo pricing a pricing objective that maintains existing prices or meets the competition's prices (p. 349)

19-3 **Explain the role of demand in price determination.** When establishing prices, a firm must first determine demand for its product. A typical demand schedule shows an inverse relationship between quantity demanded and price: when price is lowered, sales increase; when price is increased, the quantity demanded falls. Elasticity of demand is the degree to which the quantity demanded fluctuates with changes in price. If consumers are sensitive to changes in price, demand is elastic; if they are insensitive to price changes, demand is inelastic.

demand the quantity of a product that will be sold in the market at various prices for a specified period (p. 350)

elasticity of demand consumers' responsiveness or sensitivity to changes in price (p. 350)

inelastic demand a situation in which an increase or a decrease in price will not significantly affect demand for the product (p. 350)

supply the quantity of a product that will be offered to the market by a supplier at various prices for a specified period (p. 350)

elastic demand a situation in which consumer demand is sensitive to changes in price (p. 350)

19-4 **Understand the concepts and yield management systems of dynamic pricing** When competitive pressures are high, a company must know when it should raise or lower prices to maximize its revenues. Companies are increasingly turning to dynamic pricing to help adjust prices. Although dynamic pricing originated with airlines, which are limited by fixed capacity, the new thinking is that dynamic pricing can be used in any industry where demand or supply fluctuates. Dynamic pricing is the ability to adjust prices very quickly, often in real time.

dynamic pricing the ability to change prices very quickly, often in real time using software programs (p. 351)

surge pricing occurs in a fluid market, where demand changes rapidly, often hourly. When demand increases, so do prices and vice versa (p. 351)

19-5 **Describe cost-oriented pricing strategies.** Wholesalers and retailers commonly use markup pricing to cover expenses and turn a profit. With this strategy, they tack an extra amount on to the manufacturer's original price. With break-even pricing, a firm determines how much it must sell to break even; this amount in turn is used as a reference point for adjusting price.

variable cost a cost that varies with changes in the level of output (p. 352)

fixed cost a cost that does not change as output is increased or decreased (p. 352)

markup pricing the cost of buying the product from the producer, plus amounts

for profit and for expenses not otherwise accounted for (p. 352)

keystoning the practice of marking up prices by 100 percent, or doubling the cost (p. 353)

break-even analysis a method of determining what sales volume must be reached before total revenue equals total costs (p. 353)

19-6 **Demonstrate how the product life cycle, competition, distribution and promotion strategies, customer demands, the Internet and extranets, and perceptions of quality can affect price.** The price of a product normally changes as it moves through the life cycle and as demand for the product and competitive conditions change. Management often sets a high price at the introductory stage, and the high price tends to attract competition. The competition usually drives prices down because individual competitors lower prices to gain market share. Adequate distribution for a new product can sometimes be obtained by offering a larger-than-usual profit margin to wholesalers and retailers. The Internet enables consumers to compare products and prices quickly and efficiently. Perceptions of quality can also influence pricing strategies.

extranet a private electronic network that links a company with its suppliers and customers (p. 356)

19-7 **Describe the procedure for setting the right price.** The process of setting the right price on a product involves four major steps: (1) establishing pricing goals; (2) estimating demand, costs, and profits; (3) choosing a price policy to help determine a base price; and (4) fine-tuning the base price with pricing tactics. A price strategy establishes a long-term pricing framework for a good or service. The three main types of price policies are price skimming, penetration pricing, and status quo pricing.

price strategy a basic, long-term pricing framework that establishes the initial price for a product and the intended direction for price movements over the product life cycle (p. 359)

price skimming a pricing policy whereby a firm charges a high introductory price, often coupled with heavy promotion (p. 359)

penetration pricing a pricing policy whereby a firm charges a relatively low price for a product when it is first rolled out as a way to reach the mass market (p. 360)

19-8 **Explain how discounts, geographic pricing, and other pricing tactics can be used to fine-tune a base price.** Discounts, allowances, and rebates give lower prices to those who pay promptly, order a large quantity, or perform some function for the manufacturer. Geographic pricing tactics are used to moderate the impact of shipping costs on distant customers. A variety of other pricing tactics stimulate demand for certain products, increase store patronage, and offer more merchandise at specific prices.

base price the general price level at which the company expects to sell the good or service (p. 361)

quantity discount a price reduction offered to buyers buying in multiple units or above a specified dollar amount (p. 361)

cumulative quantity discount a deduction from list price that applies to the buyer's total purchases made during a specific period (p. 361)

noncumulative quantity discount a deduction from list price that applies to a single order rather than to the total volume of orders placed during a certain period (p. 361)

cash discount a price reduction offered to a consumer, an industrial user, or a marketing intermediary in return for prompt payment of a bill (p. 361)

functional discount (trade discount) a discount to wholesalers and retailers for performing channel functions (p. 361)

seasonal discount a price reduction for buying merchandise out of season (p. 361)

promotional allowance (trade allowance) a payment to a dealer for promoting the manufacturer's products (p. 362)

rebate a cash refund given for the purchase of a product during a specific period (p. 362)

value-based pricing setting the price at a level that seems to the customer to be a good price compared to the prices of other options (p. 363)

FOB origin pricing a price tactic that requires the buyer to absorb the freight costs from the shipping point ("free on board") (p. 363)

uniform delivered pricing a price tactic in which the seller pays the actual freight charges and bills every purchaser an identical, flat freight charge (p. 363)

zone pricing a modification of uniform delivered pricing that divides the United States (or the total market) into segments or zones and charges a flat freight rate to all customers in a given zone (p. 363)

freight absorption pricing a price tactic in which the seller pays all or part of the actual freight charges and does not pass them on to the buyer (p. 364)

basing-point pricing a price tactic that charges freight from a given (basing) point, regardless of the city from which the goods are shipped (p. 364)

single-price tactic a price tactic that offers all goods and services at the same price (or perhaps two or three prices) (p. 364)

flexible pricing (variable pricing) a price tactic in which different customers pay different prices for essentially the same merchandise bought in equal quantities (p. 364)

price lining the practice of offering a product line with several items at specific price points (p. 364)

leader pricing (loss-leader pricing) a price tactic in which a product is sold

CHAPTER 19 LEARNING OUTCOMES / KEY TERMS

near or even below cost in the hope that shoppers will buy other items once they are in the store (p. 365)

bait pricing a price tactic that tries to get consumers into a store through false or misleading price advertising and then uses high-pressure selling to persuade consumers to buy more expensive merchandise (p. 365)

odd-even pricing (psychological pricing) a price tactic that uses odd-numbered prices to connote bargains and even-numbered prices to imply quality (p. 365)

price bundling marketing two or more products in a single package for a special price (p. 365)

two-part pricing a price tactic that charges two separate amounts to consume a single good or service (p. 366)

consumer penalty an extra fee paid by the consumer for violating the terms of the purchase agreement (p. 366)

19-9 | **Identify the legal constraints on pricing decisions.**

Government regulation helps monitor four major areas of pricing: unfair trade practices, price fixing, price discrimination, and predatory pricing. Many states have enacted unfair trade practice acts that protect small businesses from large firms that operate on extremely thin profit margins. The Sherman Act and the Federal Trade Commission Act prohibit both price fixing and predatory pricing. The Robinson-Patman Act of 1936 makes it illegal for firms to discriminate between two or more buyers in terms of price. Predatory pricing is the practice of charging a very low price for a product with the intent of driving competitors out of business or out of a market.

unfair trade practice acts laws that prohibit wholesalers and retailers from selling below cost (p. 367)

price fixing an agreement between two or more firms on the price they will charge for a product (p. 367)

predatory pricing the practice of charging a very low price for a product with the intent of driving competitors out of business or out of a market (p. 367)